ROGER SESSIONS: A BIOGRAPHY

Recognized as the primary American symphonist of the twentieth century, Roger Sessions (1896–1985) is one of the leading representatives of high modernism. His stature among American composers rivals Charles Ives, Aaron Copland, and Elliott Carter. Influenced by both Stravinsky and Schoenberg, Sessions developed a unique style marked by rich orchestration, long melodic phrases, and dense polyphony. In addition, Sessions was among the most influential teachers of composition in the United States, teaching at Princeton, the University of California at Berkeley, and The Juilliard School. His students included John Harbison, David Diamond, Milton Babbitt, Frederic Rzewski, David Del Tredici, Conlon Nancarrow, Peter Maxwell Davies, George Tsontakis, Ellen Taaffe Zwilich, and many others.

Roger Sessions: A Biography brings together considerable previously unpublished archival material, such as letters, lectures, interviews, and articles, to shed light on the life and music of this major American composer. Andrea Olmstead, a teaching colleague of Sessions at Juilliard and the leading scholar on his music, has written a complete biography charting five touchstone areas through Sessions's eighty-eight years: music, religion, politics, money, and sexuality.

Andrea Olmstead, the author of *Juilliard: A History*, has published three books on Roger Sessions: *Roger Sessions and His Music*, *Conversations with Roger Sessions*, and *The Correspondence of Roger Sessions*. The author of numerous articles, reviews, program and liner notes, she is also a CD producer.

ROGER SESSIONS: A BIOGRAPHY

Andrea Olmstead

Routledge
Taylor & Francis Group

NEW YORK AND LONDON

First published 2008
by Routledge
270 Madison Ave, New York, NY 10016

Simultaneously published in the UK
by Routledge
2 Park Square, Milton Park, Abingdon, Oxon OX14 4RN

Routledge is an imprint of the Taylor & Francis Group, an informa business

© 2008 Andrea Olmstead

Typeset in Garamond 3 by
RefineCatch Limited, Bungay, Suffolk
Printed and bound in the United States of America on acid-free paper by
Sheridan Books, Inc. MI

Library of Congress Cataloging in Publication Data
A catalog record has been requested for this book

ISBN 10: 0–415–97713–4 (hb)
ISBN 10: 0–415–97714–2 (pb)
ISBN 10: 0–203–93147–5 (ebk)

ISBN 13: 978–0–415–97713–5 (hb)
ISBN 13: 978–0–415–97714–2 (pb)
ISBN 13: 978–0–203–93147–9 (ebk)

TO GORDON HARDY

Remember that all the great composers, even Brahms, were exceedingly great men, and that they have done a lot for the world. They are far greater than you or I. Remember also that great men have their faults and shortcomings—every one of them; but do not let their shortcomings blind you to their real greatness or their raison d'être.

Letter from Roger Sessions (age eighteen) to George Bartlett
September 28, 1915

CONTENTS

List of Figures x

Acknowledgments xii

Introduction xiv

CHAPTER 1
Family History 1

Forty Acres and Phelps House 3

Archibald Sessions 18

417 Washington Avenue 25

109 Elm Street 34

Cloyne, Kingsley, and Kent 40

Harvard 51

Harvard Musical Review 68

CHAPTER 2
Yale through the Cleveland Institute 79

Yale 81

World War I 99

Barbara Foster 116

George Bartlett 128

Ernest Bloch 137

Cleveland Institute of Music 143

The Black Maskers 153

Friends 164

CONTENTS

Summer of 1924   170

Stravinsky   184

CHAPTER 3
The European Period, 1925–1933   189

Father figures   191

Florence   200

Symphony No. 1   207

Boulanger and Copland   215

The American Academy in Rome   226

Berlin   234

CHAPTER 4
The Decade 1936–1946   241

Marriage and the Violin Concerto   243

David Diamond   256

Princeton   263

Symphony No. 2   273

CHAPTER 5
The Trial of Lucullus **through** *Montezuma*   281

Berkeley   283

The Trial of Lucullus   294

Schoenberg and Dallapiccola   302

Symphonies Nos 3 and 4   316

Montezuma   328

CHAPTER 6
The Last Two Decades   339

California and Juilliard   341

Religious music   348

The symphonies   354

CONTENTS

Death and posthumous reputation 368

Notes 374
Bibliography 412
Discography and Works List (online) 417
Index 419

FIGURES

1   Hilltop cabin at Forty Acres   4
2   Hannah Dane Sargent and Bishop Frederic Dan Huntington, 1895   6
3   Ruth Huntington   8
4   Forty Acres   11
5   Phelps House   12
6   Archibald Sessions at Harvard, 1883   19
7   Archibald Sessions, 1908   19
8   Roger's birthplace   27
9   Ruth, Roger, and John Sessions   32
10 109 Elm Street (Sessions House)   35
11 Roger at age eight   36
12 Huntington family, 1903   38
13 Kingsley School   44
14 Roger at age eleven   47
15 Roger Sessions, 1915 and 1940   62
16 George Hodges Bartlett   86
17 Frederik van den Arend   87
18 George Hodges Bartlett   100
19 Barbara Foster   117
20 Ruth Huntington, Catharine Huntington, Barbara Sessions, and
    Roger Sessions   125
21 Ernest Bloch, 1925   138
22 Cleveland Institute   144
23 Bloch and pupils   147
24 Program for *The Black Maskers*   157
25 Roger Sessions, 1924   171
26 Samuel Barber, Igor Stravinsky, Lukas Foss, Aaron Copland, Roger
    Sessions, 1959   186
27 Villino Corbignano in Settignano   201
28 Igor Stravinsky and Roger Sessions   209
29 Roger Sessions portrait   231
30 Sessions, Gian Francesco Malipiero, Alban Berg, Egon Wellesz, 1933   240
31 Lisl Sessions   244
32 Elizabeth and John Sessions   254
33 Roger and Lisl Sessions   255
34 Black Mountain Summer Music Institute faculty, 1944   271
35 70 Alexander Street, Princeton   291

36 Douglas Moore, Roger Sessions, Aaron Copland, Elliott Carter,
    Wallingford Riegger, William Schuman, and Walter Piston, ca. 1958   292
37 Music building at Berkeley   295
38 Luigi Dallapiccola   309
39 Symphonic Prelude compared with Symphony No. 3   318
40 The Opera Company of Boston 1976 production of *Montezuma*,
    Act I   329
41 Quetzalcoatl   335
42 Roger Sessions and Ellen Taaffe Zwilich in the early 1970s   345
43 Andrea Olmstead and Roger Sessions, 1976   345
44 63 Stanworth Lane, Princeton   346
45 Elizabeth Sessions Pease, Roger Pease, and Suzie, ca. 1981   358
46 Roger Sessions, 1982   359
47 Sessions's last signature   370
48 Sessions's grave marker   371

ACKNOWLEDGMENTS

I would like to acknowledge the following people for their generous assistance and credit those who provided permissions.

Elizabeth Sessions Pease, daughter of the composer, for her warm friendship and help over many years. And I would like to remember Bob Pease's kindness here. Wayne Shirley's expertise and editorial experience was of enormous help in reading the manuscript. Letters of support from John Harbison, Lewis Lockwood, David Diamond, Mark deVoto, and James Schmidt. Richard Carlin, former editor at Routledge, and editor Constance Ditzel. Composer Larry Bell, for insights into the music. The Handel & Haydn Society, for their 2005–2007 Christopher Hogwood Research Fellowship.

Numerous libraries and archives were useful. Bonnie J. Houser, reference librarian and archivist at the Cleveland Institute of Music went beyond the call of duty in her helpfulness. Andrea Goldstein and the staff at Harvard University Archives. Susan Lisk of the Porter-Phelps-Huntington House Foundation and Daria D'Arienzo from the Amherst College Archives and Special Collections. Kendall Crilly, Suzanne Lovejoy, and Richard Boursy at the Irving S. Gilmore Music Library of Yale University. Yale University's Beinecke Rare Book and Manuscript Library. Loris Schissel at the Library of Congress, Sessions Collection. Mike Vitale, archivist, and Christina Huemer, librarian, of the American Academy in Rome. Nancy Carroll and Wendy Kieron-Sanchez, Redwood Library and Athenaeum, Newport, Rhode Island. Bridget Carr, archivist of Boston Symphony Orchestra. Kristin Parker, archivist of the Isabella Stewart Gardner Museum. Autumn Mather at the Newberry Library in Chicago.

The Radcliffe College and Smith College archives. The New England Historic Genealogical Society and The Massachusetts Historical Society. The University of California at Berkeley Jean Hargrove Music Library librarians John Roberts, Manuel Erviti, and Matthew Weber. The University archives at the Bancroft Library at the University of California, Kathryn Neal. Also Jonathan Elkus for his memories of his father, Albert Elkus, and of Sessions and Berkeley. Princeton University Seeley Mudd Library librarian Tad Bennicoff, and Princeton Archives and Rare Books Library librarians Dan Skemer and AnnaLee Pauls. Carol S. Jacobs, archivist of the Cleveland Orchestra.

Gordon Tanselle at the Guggenheim Foundation. Marge Othrow of Brooklyn, New York. German musicologist Thorsten Preuss. Martin Brody, who provided a photograph of I Tatti villino. Georganne Mennin for a Sessions letter. The former Kent School publications director Barbara Humphreys. Alex Johnstone and Susan Oatzu at the American Composers Orchestra. Marie Parik of Historic Northampton.

For permissions, in addition to those mentioned above, I would like to thank:

Elizabeth Sessions Pease, for permissions to quote from her father, Roger Sessions, aunt Hannah Sessions, and her grandparents Ruth and Archibald Sessions. Also her permission to use material from letters, interviews, unpublished articles, as well as prose publications. Thanks are due, too, for several family photographs she generously let me reproduce.

George Bartlett, nephew of the eponymous Sessions friend, for permission to quote from his uncle's letters and for a photograph of him. Mary Marshall Clark for permission to quote from the Sessions interviews for Columbia University Oral History project. The late Laura Dallapiccola for permission to quote from her husband's letters. The Fondation International Nadia et Lili Boulanger, Dominique Merlet, President, for permission to quote from letters by Nadia Boulanger. Alexander Eliot for the use of Samuel Eliot Jr's letter to this author. Anne W. Gordon, daughter of Roy D. Welch, for use of a manuscript. James M. Kendrick, Secretary of the Aaron Copland Fund for Music, Inc., for permission to quote Copland's letters, which are "Reprinted by permission of The Aaron Copland Fund for Music, Inc."

William L. Porter for permission to quote from Quincy Porter's concert diary. Jean Toombs, of the Cleveland Institute of Music, for permission to quote from materials in their archives. Lynne W. Knox for permission to quote from Mina Kirstein Curtiss's letters. John MacMillan, editor of the *Smith Alumnae Quarterly*, to quote from the *Quarterly*.

The late Rosamond Sheldon, for permission to use her sister Barbara Sessions's letters. Megan Sniffin-Mrinoff, University Archivist, Harvard University, for materials in the Harvard University Archive. Anthony Smith, son of Suzanne Bloch, for permission to quote from her interview with this author. Charles Calmer for information on Philip Greeley Clapp. Ruth Voorhis, daughter of Tossy Spivakovsky, for a letter. Christopher Wagstaff for his Berkeley class notes of a course with Sessions.

For permissions for photographs I particularly wish to thank Elizabeth Pease, Larry Bell, Ulli Steltzer, Stan Fellerman, Don Hunstein, Lloyd Morgan of the Barbara Morgan Archive, Lynn Wayne, and Ellen Taaffe Zwilich. For permission to use her original drawings of 417 Washington Avenue and of Mexican art depicting Quelzalcoatl, I want to thank Maddy Rosenberg.

INTRODUCTION

When Metropolitan Opera artistic director James Levine first conducted the Boston Symphony Orchestra as its resident conductor, the opening piece he programmed was Roger Sessions's Piano Concerto. One concertgoer declared flatly, "I think Roger Sessions is the greatest American composer of the twentieth century." Such is Sessions's reputation among both top-notch musicians and serious audience members.

Recognized as the primary American symphonist of the twentieth century, Roger Sessions is also one of the leading representatives of high modernism. Sessions wrote nine symphonies and kept a long-standing musical superstition about the number nine (related to Beethoven's nine) by calling his tenth a Concerto for Orchestra. Leighton Kerner, critic of *The Village Voice*, said Sessions was the greatest symphonist since Mahler. *The New Grove Dictionary of Music and Musicians* article on the symphony states, "It may be that in the last resort the most interesting American symphonist is the subtle and introspective Roger Sessions."[1] Critics such as Kerner, Michael Steinberg, and Andrew Porter share the opinion of some scholars in Classical music. Sessions's music appeals not only to the intelligentsia, but also to audience members and critics who extend what he described as "a willing ear."

Sessions's stature among modernist American composers rivals Charles Ives, Aaron Copland, and Elliott Carter. While Sessions never met Ives, both Copland and Carter were friends who demonstrated their admiration for Sessions's music—Copland in print and Carter both in print and by a violin piece named "Remembering Roger." Copland, an early and strong supporter of Sessions's music, called the First Piano Sonata (1930) "a cornerstone upon which to base an American music."[2]

Major European composers recognized Sessions as well. Igor Stravinsky wrote in 1963: "Roger Sessions is one of the people I most admire and respect: as composer, scholar, teacher, intellect. But last and most, he is a dear friend."[3] Arnold Schoenberg expressed his admiration of Sessions to their mutual pupil Leon Kirchner, who showed him the score and played a tape of the Second Piano Sonata. Schoenberg told Kirchner, "Now I know how Schumann must have felt when he first heard the music of Brahms." Schoenberg continued in a letter to Sessions: "I was very pleased that I could follow your thoughts almost throughout the whole piece and it is that, why I said: 'This is a language.' I mean, it conveys a message and in this respect it seems to me one of the greatest achievements a composer could arrive at."[4]

Sessions's career spanned most of the twentieth century. He began as a Wagnerian, and later was influenced by Stravinsky and Neo-Classicism. Like the Russian master, he eventually found himself attracted to the techniques of Arnold Schoenberg, but did not use the twelve-tone technique in any consistent manner. Indeed, it would be inaccurate to call him a twelve-tone composer. What he learned from these composers only deepened his own personal style, which constituted in part, in John Harbison's view, "a fascination with long phrases and a love of elaborated transitions and dense accompanying polyphonies."[5] Colorful orchestration can also be added to this list of stylistic features. Sessions wrote in important genres such as symphonies, concertos, string quartets, piano sonatas, cantatas, and operas. Edward T. Cone pointed to the "fact that Sessions the man and Sessions the musician are indistinguishable. No composer of our day has stressed more cogently or exemplified more conscientiously the responsibilities that composers share with all other artists: 'responsibilities of craftsmanship, or singlemindedness . . . of vision and imagination.' "[6]

Only one measure of this stature is awards. These include two Pulitzer prizes, election to the American Academy of Arts and Letters, and winning the Brandeis Creative Arts Award, the Gold Medal of the American Academy of Arts and Letters, and a MacDowell Medal. In addition he was awarded 14 honorary doctorates.

Sessions was the most influential teacher of composition in the United States during most of the second half of the twentieth century, the period from Schoenberg's death (1951) to his own in 1985. He taught at Princeton University, the University of California at Berkeley, Princeton again, and lastly at The Juilliard School. Indeed, the so-called "Princeton school" centers around him. His pedagogical influence compares favorably with that of Schoenberg himself, Paul Hindemith, and the Parisian teacher Nadia Boulanger.

To demonstrate this one need only consider the music written by some of Sessions's students. These include Milton Babbitt, Larry Bell, Edward T. Cone, Peter Maxwell Davies, David Del Tredici, Mark DeVoto, David Diamond, John Eaton, Joel Feigen, Vivian Fine, Kenneth Frazelle, Miriam Gideon, John Harbison, Andrew Imbrie, Leon Kirchner, Tod Machover, Ursula Mamlock, Donald Martino, Conlon Nancarrow, Dika Newlin, Frederic Rzewski, Eric Salzman, George Tsontakis, Hugo Weisgall, Ellen Taaffe Zwilich, and many others. Many of these composers also taught or are still teaching; therefore at least two generations of Sessions's students continue his legacy. The number of significant female composers on this list is striking. Indeed, Sessions may well be the most important composition teacher of women composers in the twentieth century.

Sessions's skill as a writer paralleled his abilities as a composer. Indeed, he attended Harvard at the age of 14 as an intellectual prodigy. Sessions published four books, and his essays were collected in a fifth. These are his Norton lectures at Harvard, *Questions about Music* (W. W. Norton & Co., 1971); his frequently used harmony textbook, *Harmonic Practice* (Harcourt Brace, 1951); his 1949 Juilliard lectures, *The Musical Experience of Composer, Performer, Listener* (Princeton University Press, 1950); his Italian Fulbright lectures translated into English as *Reflections on the Music Life in the United States* (Merlin, 1956); and Princeton University Press's collection, *Roger Sessions on Music; Collected Essays* (1979), edited by Cone. His views on music, articulated in prose in his books and verbally to his students, have been read, taught, and widely assimilated.

This full-scale biography stresses five areas of Sessions's life: musical, religious, political, sexual, and financial. Most chapters contain detailed discussion of one or more major works. To understand both the left-leaning political views and the religious aspects of Sessions's development (he veered from non-belief to Roman Catholicism), as well as his frequent writing "blocks," I dwell at some length—more than other biographers of musicians might do—on family members. Both parents were politically active, and several relatives were priests. Sessions's political views were firmly expressed in both prose and music (his choices of texts indicate this) during his long lifetime. Internal family dynamics, however, were also responsible for acute self-criticism that took decades to overcome. I intend to "shake up" received wisdom about Sessions's life and music, reinforcing some familiar notions, but at the same time presenting, for example, a sexual ambiguity of which even his family was unaware. Finances, salaries, and debt are dwelt upon, with references to specific amounts of money. In addition, I shall present an entirely new view of Sessions's so-called twelve-tone techniques. Indeed, I assert that Sessions is not—in any meaningful sense—a twelve-tone composer at all. Finally, I argue that many of Sessions's major works, including both operas, *Lilacs*, and most of the symphonies, deal either directly or indirectly with death. The "knottiness" critics often hear in the music and do not recognize as such is that of a major musical talent grappling with the ultimate reality. As we shall see, there are important biographical reasons why he should do so.

The author got to know both Sessions and his music at The Juilliard School where he taught composition (1966–1983) and I taught music history (1972–1980). I worked with him—tape recording our interviews—for almost seven years and published three books: *Roger Sessions and His Music* (1985), *Conversations with Roger Sessions* (1987), and *The Correspondence of Roger Sessions* (1992), as well as the revised *New Grove* entry and numerous other articles. All three books on Sessions are now available to read or download for free at www.AndreaOlmstead.com. Additional material, such as a list of works with a discography, is also found on this site.

When the composer David Diamond, a former Sessions student and his long time friend, telephoned in 1992 to praise *The Correspondence of Roger Sessions* (that he had urged me to write), he then declared, "Now it's time to write the biography." I changed direction, however, to write *Juilliard: A History* (1999). Now I have returned to the subject to address Diamond's challenge. Diamond died in 2005, however, just before he received my letter telling him I had begun work on the book he had promoted.

This book builds on my previous Sessions work while concentrating on much unpublished material: letters, interviews, articles, lectures, recent doctoral dissertations, and further musical analysis. *Roger Sessions: A Biography* thoroughly documents his life and family background, musical training and development, career, range and extent of composition, influence as a teacher, critical reception, honors and recognition, general place in the musical world, his death and posthumous reputation, and significant cultural and literary events shaping his works. In addition the book deals with his family: his parents and their ancestors, both of his wives, his friends, his students, and his two children. Relations with close musical colleagues are discussed in detail: Bloch, Jean Binet, Copland, Stravinsky, Boulanger, Diamond, Schoenberg, and Dallapiccola.

I compiled detailed timetables of events for certain periods—sometimes down to the day. I then discovered that for pivotal events, for example Sessions's reaction to the entry of the United States into the Great War, knowing *when* something happened helped explain *why* it happened. Educated guesses are duly labeled with such words as "perhaps," or "possibly."

Sessions wrote to college friends and his fiancée using Greek and French; in Italian to his librettist Borgese, and to Dallapiccola, as well as delivering a set of Fulbright lectures in Italian; and to Stravinsky, Serge Koussevitzky, and Nicolas Slonimsky in Russian. Others friends, such as Thomas Mann, wrote to him in German, which Sessions had studied and spoke while living in Berlin. Sessions knew Latin and Greek well enough at one time to feel that he could teach them. His fluency in six languages surely helped cement his reputation as "brainy."

Evaluating sources, I gave primacy to newly discovered letters, interviews, and his prose written contemporaneously with events discussed. Second, Sessions gave several sets of interviews in his life. One set of five was from 1962 for the Columbia University Oral History Collection (COHC); another, during the 1970s with me (*Conversations*), and, finally, interviews in the 1980s with Frederik Prausnitz are quoted in his book.[7] Differences occur among these interviews from three separate decades. I shall assume Sessions's memory was sharpest in 1962; that he remembered only certain events in a rehashed sort of way in the 1970s; and that in the 1980s, he was too old to remember events clearly (for example, he forgot he had a sister-in-law). Worse, he let indiscretion trump his usual reserve and New England upbringing. He slipped and told Prausnitz stories he had asked me not to publish (and I had not). Unfortunately, Prausnitz was apt to count on Sessions's memory for some dates and events that could have been verified— and, as a result, should have been changed. After reading Prausnitz's book, which did not incorporate anything from my three books and omitted numerous other significant sources, I felt I should set the record straight.

When Sessions listened to the COHC tape recordings to correct the transcript, he observed, "You know, it's funny, when I hear voices over tape, and I very rarely hear any except my own, it seems a thousand times as slow as it does in actual speech."[8] Those who knew Sessions would laugh over this remark, because one of the defining character-istics of his speech throughout his life was its extreme slowness (no matter in which language).

In 1978 I observed about Sessions, "By far his favorite implement is a pipe, since continual attention is required to clean, fill, and light it. Comparatively little time is spent smoking the apparatus relative to the incessant handling it receives. This pre-occupation appears to be a nervous habit, replaced only by rolling up matchbooks or fidgeting with the nearest convenient object. The apparent contradiction between this uneasiness and the basic sturdiness of the man can only be guessed at. Since music constantly streams through his head, his feet kept the pulse, even polyrhythmically."[9] Having written this book, I now think I can more than "guess" at why Sessions still retained remnants of what had been, earlier in his life, considerable nervousness.

A biography of Sessions is not easy to write: Sessions was a complicated person. Milton Babbitt, noting this, asked perceptively, "Why shouldn't he be?" Suzanne Bloch was describing his music as well as the person when she said, "The man is so thick, so full of stuff." The introduction to *The Correspondence of Roger Sessions* concludes with my observation: "Ultimately, however, the artist never gives up all his secrets. To document is not to explain. And to explain is not necessarily to understand."[10] Former Princeton students remember Sessions's parting words, "Toujours l'audace!" Perhaps audaciously, I now attempt both to explain and to understand the complexity of the man and his music.

Chapter 1

FAMILY HISTORY

FORTY ACRES AND
PHELPS HOUSE

Roger Sessions liked to tell a story that began with the novelist's opening cliché: "It was a dark and stormy night." The subject of the anecdote was his ancestry, and both a letter to George Bartlett and a diary kept by two participants reveal why this particular night would be memorable. At 4:00 p.m. on August 9, 1917, during World War I, violinist Quincy Porter and pianist Bruce Simonds gave one of their series of concerts of French and Belgian music at Amherst College.[1] (Bartlett had arranged a similar concert in Webster, Massachusetts, on July 27.) These concerts were to raise money for the Red Cross; at a dollar a ticket they made $91.38 that August evening. Afterwards, 20-year-old Sessions and the two performers had a "wild time" at a dinner and musicale at Mme Bianchi's, Emily Dickinson's niece who lived in Austin Dickinson's home next to where the poet had lived. Around 11:00 p.m. they "tore [them]selves away" from Amherst to leave for Sessions's family home in Hadley. Sessions drove a horse-drawn cart powered by the family animal, Rex, with only one seat to accommodate "the three geniuses."[2] The skittish horse preferred to walk downhill and proceeded at a snail's pace.

Rex also disliked thunderstorms, which soon enveloped the quartet. "Drove by ghostly barns," Porter wrote, "illuminated by flashes of lightening. Strange flowing sound in the distance—nearer and nearer—covered up violin case by putting it in the bottom of the buggy and stretching feet over it."[3] They then "Drove furiously over the narrow road, boughs swishing past our faces; pitch blackness, except for the dim lantern on the buggy." Sessions, who could not see with water streaming over his glasses, "disappeared into the darkness with the violin" to leave it for the night at his maiden aunts'—Arria and Molly Huntington's—cabin, "lonely and surrounded by woods." Sessions's older sister Hannah answered the door. The aunts insisted on entertaining them—it was now midnight—so the trio tied up Rex and, soaked to the skin, the two performers "plunged through a tunnel of sopped bushes" (they were wearing summer concert attire and white pants) and reached the bungalow with no running water or electricity. The "storm raged outside in picturesque confusion, and we stood and dripped until dry enough to sit down."[4] All three signed the aunts' guestbook: Simonds gave the date with time (12m–1 a.m.), and wrote in the "remarks" column, "Macbeth Act I, Sc. I;" Porter wrote "Noah's Ark;" and Sessions inscribed "Après moi, le deluge."[5]

Hannah (known as Nan) got dressed and talked with them, but aunt Arria, in night-clothes, conversed "from behind a screen [which was only proper for a Victorian lady] on the subject of genealogy."[6] Arria was born in 1848 and Molly in 1862, and Arria had written a book about her family history.[7] The conversation between Quincy Porter and Sessions's "1848 aunt" concerned whether their common ancestor was Hezekiah Porter, six generations back, or Eleazar Porter, five generations back. They concluded that the relative was Eleazar, and therefore the two musicians were fifth cousins, rather than sixth cousins. "So I mean, this is a dangerous subject, that's all," Sessions remarked later.[8] "That kind of snobbish interest in family ancestors is oppressive, stifling, and dreadful. There's an awful lot of Huntington family pride in [the book *Forty Acres*], and that always bored me very much."[9]

The three decided to venture forth at 1:00 a.m. They led Rex through the mud, but a blinding flash sent them for cover in a nearby shed, where they stayed for 20 minutes. They started once again, Sessions "having discarded coat and necktie and clad in shirt, white flannels, best low shoes, and straw hat, leading the horse, Quincy similarly clad carrying the lantern, and Bruce sitting in the wagon, and all three of us singing at the top of our lungs like larks—of the genus *polonius bacchanalis*."[10] "Oceans of mud, and no cessation in the torrent. Steep down-hill," Porter recalled. They discovered one of the workhorses loose and seeking shelter from the rain by the barn door of Forty Acres, the Huntington house. "Sharp lightening and thunder, put in at a shed after flash which dazzled us for three seconds, giving us splendid after-images." They arrived at Sessions's family's home, Phelps House, about 1:40 a.m. "R[oger] bade B[ruce] go into the house and assure the family that we were alive, saying 'Hello' reassuringly as he opened the door: which B. did, but found the lower house deserted, and only after climbing the stairs, heard Mrs. S. say drowsily 'Roge, is that you?' Anticlimax. John appeared in pajamas. No one had worried, thought of us in Amherst."[11] Sessions's mother Ruth and younger brother John also wanted to hear their exploits, which were retold. The three Yale musicians finally got to bed around 3:00 a.m.

All of the *dramatis personae* in this story (except Rex) shall return in fuller guise in this book. Their first appearance here is, however, emblematic of their characteristics and situations. Sessions, for example, may perhaps surprise the reader with his unexpected

Figure 1 The hilltop cabin where Arria and Molly Huntington lived. It was struck by lightening and burned to the ground in 1948.

lustiness, his closeness to nature and animals, his ambivalence about his New England ancestry, and his sense of humor—even if revealed in jokes in Latin.

If this book were a mystery story rather than a biography (which, after all, tries to solve the mystery of a human being), we might ask some investigative questions. For example, who was Martha Bianchi (so different from her aunt, the reclusive poet Emily Dickinson)? Why were three student-age men working for the Red Cross instead of serving in Europe during World War I? Who was George Bartlett? Why was Nan staying with her aunts rather than with her mother and brother? Who were the Huntingtons, Porters, Phelpses, and Sessionses, and what role did they play in Sessions's life? Perhaps the biggest mystery is the dog that did not bark in the night, as Sherlock Holmes would have put it: Where was the composer's father, Archibald Sessions? In the coming pages the author shall strive to solve these puzzles.

Sessions said of his ancestral home across the street from Phelps House, "Forty Acres is haunted, you know. Very strange things have happened there. There's even a secret passage. I love it very much, and I feel like one of the trees there."[12] It is "a wonderful old place, a beautiful place, but these things can have various implications. I'm very attached to it myself, in a way, but I have a kind of horror of it, too."[13] Sessions described Forty Acres and his background:

> We have an old, old family house in Hadley, Massachusetts, right on the Con-
> necticut River. It's a wonderful old house. One of my ancestors was one of the
> founders of Hadley. In 1752 Moses Porter decided it was safe to build a house
> outside the town stockade. Sometimes it was subject to attack by the Indians,
> even by the French from Canada. Porter was a captain in the [colonial militia].
>
> I remember my grandfather. He died when I was seven years old. He became
> bishop of Central New York. First he was a Unitarian minister. He became a
> professor of Christian Knowledge [Morals] at Harvard. Then he got bored, so to
> speak, with the Unitarian church, and joined the Episcopal church and became
> a minister in Boston, and then became bishop of Central New York. . . .
>
> He married a wonderful lady from Boston. I always told people I had a
> grandmother complex. She was descended from a man who was a general in the
> revolutionary war.[14]

Sessions has been pegged by critics as a Puritan New Englander. "I've run across that in my career, because my music was supposed to be very New England and so forth and austere. Of course, it's just the opposite. I don't think anybody who has ever known me has thought I was conspicuously austere."[15] Nevertheless, religion played an important role in his family.

Moses Porter, the builder of Forty Acres, had been, like all of the Bishop's ancestors, a Puritan. A succession of five Elizabeths, mothers and daughters, grew up in Hadley at Forty Acres. Elizabeth Phelps, the third Elizabeth, married—on the first day of the nineteenth century, January 1, 1801—Dan Huntington from Connecticut. They had eleven children, of whom Elizabeth Huntington was second oldest and Frederic Dan the youngest.[16] The father, Dan Huntington was a retired clergyman. Elizabeth Phelps Huntington had been influenced by William Ellery Channing, whose books persuaded her to believe no longer in devils and hell or the Trinity, but rather to believe in human goodness and the power of reason. Church pastors in Hadley warned her not to rely on Channing's Unitarianism; she would be expelled from the Calvinist church if she did not give it up.

Indeed, a delegation in two buggies appeared at Forty Acres to belabor the heretic. After repeated stern visits, they cut both Huntington parents from the communion with the Hadley Calvinist congregation. The couple became Unitarians. Their youngest son, Frederic Dan, who was graduated from Amherst in 1839 and from Harvard Divinity School in 1842, became a popular Unitarian minister. Because of this faith, his education, and ability to preach, he was made Preacher to the University and Plummer Professor of Christian Morals at Harvard College in 1855. He was Sessions's maternal grandfather.

It turned out, however, that Frederic Dan Huntington had a great deal in common with his heretical mother. In 1861 he underwent a religious conversion: he felt closer to a Trinitarian theology and converted to Episcopalianism. Many ties were severed with the Harvard community when he, his wife Hannah Dane Sargent, and his oldest of five children George were confirmed in the Episcopal Church.[17] Frederic Dan Huntington accepted the rectorship of Emmanuel Church in Boston. Sons George and James were graduated from Harvard, and George attended divinity school. Their sisters were Arria, Ruth, and Molly.

Ruth Huntington was born in Cambridge in an old house on the corner of Quincy Street and Massachusetts Avenue overlooking Harvard Square. Her parents had seven children of whom five survived. They were: George Putnam (1844–1904); Arria Sargent (1848–1921); Charles Edward (born October 2, 1852; died October 17, 1852); James Otis Sargent (1854–July 1, 1935); William (born and died on the same day in July 1856); Ruth Gregson (November 3, 1859–December 2, 1946); and Mary Lincoln (known as Molly; 1862–1936).

Figure 2 Hannah Dane Sargent and Bishop Frederic Dan Huntington, 1895.

Like her husband, Ruth came from a family in which two siblings did not live long. Besides Ruth, only George married; he married Lilly St Agnam Barrett (1848–1926). They had eight children of whom six, five sons and a daughter, survived.[18] One son, Michael Paul, became an Episcopal priest like his father and grandfather. These six Huntingtons were Sessions's only first cousins on his mother's side.

Ruth grew up in the 1860s at 68 Bolyston Street facing the Boston Public Garden. The home boasted a square Chickering piano in the living room (the Chickering factory was several blocks west). Back Bay was still just that, a broad body of shallow water. Her father's church, Emmanuel Church, was nearby on Newbury Street. Entering it today one can see on the left a bas-relief portrait of its rector Frederic Dan Huntington.

The Huntington children felt they were at the center, the "hub," as Boston was famously described, of the universe. Ruth's grandmother lived in Roxbury; she was the daughter of Abner Lincoln, a son of General Lincoln, George Washington's aide-de-camp. Ruth's mother, Hannah Dane Sargent, was one of five children of Epes Sargent and Mary Lincoln. The Sargents lived in a huge Boston house.

Having a cook, maids, a dressmaker, and the respect of the upper crust of Boston society gave Ruth a sense of entitlement that never left her. All four of her siblings, however, responded to their situation quite differently from her—with self-abnegation: the two brothers became priests, and the two sisters, spinster aunts who worked for decades for social betterment. Although Ruth did some good works, including teaching Indians music in Syracuse, she never lost a desire for praise and admiration, for which the Bishop admonished her. "From all accounts R's visit [to Cornell] in Ithaca," the Bishop wrote, "was a very gay one. I have no doubt she enjoyed it, but with her weakness for admiration and pleasure, to which such experiences pander, I fear it may not have been a helpful influence."[19] Furious, Ruth argued the point with her mother, but the Bishop understood her perfectly.

The most important thing to know about Ruth Sessions is that she was born a Huntington. A direct ancestor, Samuel Huntington, was a signer of the Declaration of Independence. Like Scarlett O'Hara's attachment to the fictional Tara, Ruth's attachment to her father and to Forty Acres would trump all other considerations in her life. Sessions recalled, "I used to say all ladies were in love with their fathers at that time. And of course when the father was a *bishop*, he was the old man of the tribe."[20]

Ruth Sessions's granddaughter, Sarah Chapin, described her "complex personality— kind, sympathetic, generous, resourceful, treacherous and combative. Growing up in a family dominated by her father, with two older brothers and a sister solidly involved in the church, the Fourth Child (as she called herself) carried a heavy burden of responsibility to follow them into church work, but to everyone's distress she developed 'nerves.' . . . The attacks continued throughout her long life causing powerful repercussions for her and everyone around her. It is by no means clear, however, that her attacks were always calculated and deliberate; they only seemed that way to her hapless relatives."[21]

Ruth's autobiography, *Sixty-Odd; A Personal History*, published in 1936 but ending its narrative in 1920, is our major source about her. The eminently readable book reveals a writer of considerable skill in evoking time and place. She had plenty of previous writing experience, having published stories, essays, and children's books. Her life was certainly adventurous—she had met famous people, and her family was distinguished enough to merit an autobiography. Perhaps, too, her ego demanded it: those who write autobiographies generally consider themselves important. Sessions himself never devoted his time to an autobiography.

Figure 3 Ruth Huntington in 1885.

Whenever *Sixty-Odd* was mentioned, however, Sessions cautioned readers that its rosy scenario ought not to be taken too literally.

> It's a book about herself. Don't believe anything about me. . . . My mother was a very remarkable woman. I won't say disturbed, exactly; that's exaggerated, because the word "disturbed" carries a kind of psychiatric connotation; but she was, oh, very proud of being the daughter of a bishop and belonging to a very old New England family on the one hand, and very liberal on the other hand. But liberal in the sense of charity rather than real recognition of human equality. She was very kind to everybody. When I came home from school and spoke of "niggers" she hit the ceiling, so to speak. Of course, she explained to me why; after all, I was nine or ten. She treated people as equals in their presence, but in the privacy of the home she didn't. You could see that wasn't her attitude. . . .
>
> In the book I'm as she would have liked me to be. She was always afraid I was too serious about my music. She wanted me to entertain her guests by playing the piano, and I *hated* that. And I always wanted to play something that *I* liked, but she wanted me to play those darling little pieces that the guests liked. She herself knew much better, but she was living the social life of the world. *I was always thoroughly rebellious.* As far as the children were concerned, my older sister and my brother and I—they're all her rosy dreams in the book.[22]

Indeed, it is not the children who are represented as "rosy dreams" in the book; it is Ruth herself. *Sixty-Odd*, published when Sessions was 40, does not in fact devote much space to him and none at all to his accomplishments. Further, what Ruth did mention about Sessions's childhood he more or less confirmed by remembering the events himself. Some of her other stories that could be verified, however, turn out in reality not quite as they appear in her book. The omissions are more serious. And we shall find some discrepancies—even Freudian slips—in partnership with the expected inclination to write about one's own life by making oneself the heroine. In *Sixty-Odd* she removed her blemishes (to be fair, she removed others' blemishes as well) and cast her life decisions—especially one highly questionable decision—in the best possible light.

Ruth's autobiography is sketchy about her nervous condition. One event she related was the frequent cannon fire on the Boston Common during the Civil War. One cannon went off close to Ruth, who was "brought home in a nervous convulsion which alarmed the family seriously and left its traces in twitching muscles and agonized sensitiveness to loud sounds."[23] She remembered the end of the Civil War and the day her solemn parents told her bitterly that President Lincoln had been killed.

Ruth studied music, first from the introductions to the oblong-shaped Lowell Mason psalm books. She attended concerts by the Handel and Haydn Society in the old Music Hall (the Boston Symphony was not yet founded). She heard Italian operas in Boston, and her mother sang arias at home and also played the piano. Sunday church, however, was the busiest musical day of the week. Her parents, beginning to believe her "musical," sent her to a first-rate music school in Boston directed by the French Mademoiselle Gabrielle de la Motte. Ruth was thus able to distinguish herself from the family, "to learn piano-playing would be my own accomplishment, not just like those of my family; and to play as Mother did—to get beautiful sounds out of the big books and the white keys—to be able to sit in Grandmother's shady parlor as Aunt Kate [her grandmother's sister] could do, playing on and on with people listening—that was the sum of my ambition and desire."[24] Eight years old, she studied in a room with seven others at four square pianos. An assistant, Miss Jones, gave practice lessons reinforcing Mlle de la Motte's teaching. She "rap[ped] my fingers sharply with a wooden knitting-needle if I made mistakes."[25] Ruth played on a recital at Chickering Hall and felt study of music was beneficial: "It gave me a new world in which I could live alone, independent of my parents, my brothers, and sisters. In enjoying it, I had no obligation to anyone but myself."[26] The desire to escape into music and her obligation to self remained embedded in her.

On the day in 1868 that Huntington was consecrated as bishop, a great ceremony took place in Boston. Ruth, however, managed to upstage her father by sneaking away from Aunt Kate's and breaking her leg playing in a vacant lot. Her brother George had been ordained to the ministry the next day, but Ruth took delight in the attention given to her for being an invalid. "It really did make one a little bit important, apparently, to break one's leg."[27] In fact, she romanticized being a "cripple," a fantasy undone by healing perfectly normally. She learned that illness placed her at the center of attention, a lesson she employed.

The rector having been made a bishop meant a family move to Syracuse, New York, practically the brink of civilization for these New Englanders. Always aware of social distinctions, Ruth quickly summed up Syracuse society, the pinnacle of which was Judge Andrews, whose carriage was drawn by a pair of impressive bay horses. His son William also became a jurist. William's son Paul would enter the lives of the Sessionses later. Piano lessons were resumed with Ernest Held, a German teacher long known in Syracuse. Hannah had insisted to Held that Ruth be taught only the best music; he was both incredulous and delighted. She began with Beethoven's six variations on a duet by Paisiello, "Nel Cor Più non Mi Sento," and Mendelssohn's *Songs without Words*. Ruth developed as a sight-reader, playing four-hand arrangements of symphonies, overtures, and quartets. Theodore Thomas's orchestra came from New York to perform, and local choruses gave *Elijah, The Creation*, and *Messiah*. At twelve, Ruth took up the organ and played church services during Lent.

The year 1875, when Ruth was almost 16 years old, was pivotal for Ruth and also for the evolution of women's rights. The Women's Congress was held in October in Syracuse. Louisa May Alcott attended; her father Bronson held one of his "conversations" at the Huntington home. Mrs Mary A. Livermore, Miss Maria Hitchel, Elizabeth Cady Stanton, Catherine Beecher, and Julia Ward Howe were all present. Ruth soon became a convert for the Cause of Women. A second important event also took place in 1875, this one near Forty Acres—namely, the founding of Smith College. Sophia Smith, whose father owned the land abutting Forty Acres, had left her fortune to build a college for women. Perhaps Ruth had had too much excitement that year. Her "nervous system" was depleted; the doctor's course of treatment was "salt and tan," which meant a six-week trip to her cousins in Hingham, Massachusetts, on the ocean. There Ruth enjoyed herself: to have "nerves" brought such rewards.

Meanwhile her sister Arria, 12 years older, had started a school for women prisoners called The Shelter. Many of the inmates were first-time offenders for prostitution, and this work was—to put it mildly—novel for a society woman at the time. As a teenager, Ruth also did social work, but was more interested in attracting boys—a somewhat difficult task, since, unlike Arria, she was not notably attractive. By her own admission, she was an unsatisfactory student. Since the Bishop had slightly hurt his right hand and was no longer able to write legibly, she was useful in copying out the Bishop's many sermons, publications, and letters, which he dictated. He was a master of English and had received more honorary degrees than any other Episcopal church dignitary at that time. Doubtless Ruth, who did not attend college, learned and developed her own considerable writing skills by this work.

Like George, her brother James had also attended Harvard, as well as St Andrews Theological Seminary in Scotland. From 1878 to 1881 he assisted his father at Calvary Church in Syracuse and became a priest in 1880. Like his ancestors, James, too, was to depart from the orthodoxy of his family's religion. In 1884 he founded a monastic order, the Order of the Holy Cross, and did important work in labor reform in New York City. On November 25, 1884, he took vows of poverty, chastity, and obedience.

The Huntington family spent every summer at the ancestral home and farm, Forty Acres.[28] The Bishop had been born, married, and eventually died in the old house. Ruth and her family loved it beyond anything. In that small neighborhood, quite near Northampton, the Huntington family was viewed almost as "monarchs": the sense of the importance and history of their family were felt everywhere. One of Frederic Dan's older sisters, Bethia, lived at Forty Acres. Distinguished guests such as Harriet Beecher Stowe and Lavinia Dickinson (sister of the poet) arrived for visits.

Phelps House, which Ruth romantically called "The House of Mystery," was a quarter of a mile away from Forty Acres. It was built by Charles Porter Phelps, the Bishop's uncle. In 1816 Charles Phelps suddenly gave up his Boston legal practice and profitable importing business to take up farming Forty Acres. In 1817 his wife Sarah Parsons died after having had five children, and Charles later married her sister Charlotte; the two had five more children. The oldest daughter, also a Sarah, left Boston to come to Forty Acres and take care of her father and the new children. All ten children would come to Forty Acres, staying at Phelps House, at various times. "Cousin Sarah" took permanent care of three of the brothers who lived there year-round and were by any account "peculiar": Charles, completely silent; Theophilus, considered crazy with 17 cats who marched single-file behind him; and Billy, last of the "uncommon Phelps Brothers," handicapped both physically and mentally, who spoke his own language. The Bishop inherited Phelps House and bequeathed it to his daughter Ruth.

Although George had moved away and established himself as a minister, the lives of the four remaining unmarried children and their mother had circled around the Bishop and his work until James's break with the family in the early 1880s. Ruth's attachment to her father could not be duplicated to another man her own age: no one could live up to the Bishop's reputation, success, and genuine goodness toward others. Ruth was so deeply ensconced in this tight structure that it was nearly impossible to marry outside the family. Indeed, she would never leave the shadow of this family tree.

Her plain looks, her "less evenly balanced temperament," and general lack of popularity among the opposite sex might have signaled a life devoted to service such as all four of her siblings shared. She harbored romantic fantasies, however. These came to full fruition when at 19 she met her slightly younger second cousin in the Long Room at Forty Acres. She noted the date in her autobiography: August 15, 1879. Molly informed her that her cousin Lizzie's son, "a quiet one from Brooklyn," was there along with his

Figure 4 Forty Acres (drawing by Arria S. Huntington).

11

Figure 5 Phelps House owned by Ruth Huntington.

older sister Grace. Lizzie was the fifth of the five Elizabeths, the Bishop's older sister's daughter. Molly's first reaction about the Brooklyn boy was, "He's awfully good-looking but he doesn't say much."[29] Ruth had already formed the opinion that "he's his sisters' pet." True, Archibald Sessions, "the boy with a name like an English curate," had three older sisters who adored him. Ruth had heard his name before; his mother Lizzie had been a bridesmaid at Frederic Dan and Hannah Sargent's wedding. Once Ruth saw the "brown-eyed lad of nineteen," she agreed, "Yes, rather handsome."[30]

The name Sessions is fairly uncommon. A great uncle of Roger Sessions was a governor of Michigan. "The family tradition is that it's French," Sessions said, "comes from the south of France, and I suppose that means they were Huguenot. There is a tradition of French ancestry in several branches of the family."[31] The Sessions family could also trace its heritage directly to 1630, when Samuel Sessions arrived in America. Samuel begat Alexander, who begat Nathaniel, and so on through Amasa, another Amasa, down to John Sessions, Archibald's father and the composer's grandfather. John Sessions married Elizabeth Phelps Fisher Huntington ("Lizzie"). This Elizabeth's mother (also an Elizabeth) was the second child of Dan Huntington. Dan Huntington's eleventh child, Elizabeth's youngest brother, was Ruth's father, Bishop Frederic Dan Huntington.[32]

Elizabeth Sessions and her brothers had been educated in France. According to Ruth, "There was an element of cosmopolitan tolerance in their outlook and a breadth of view that counterbalanced the Puritan inheritance she shared with her generation."[33] Lawyer John Sessions, who came from a family of six lawyers and had attended Yale, and his wife Elizabeth had six children: Archibald was the fifth child of those six. They were: Elizabeth Huntington Sessions (1853–1860); Clara Fisher (Wheeler; September 16, 1854–February 19, 1893); Adeline B. Sessions (December 23, 1856–September 10,

1936; she never married); Grace Martin (Hooper, 1858–1932); Archibald Lowery Sessions (January 12, 1860–January 5, 1927); and John Sessions (November 1, 1866–1867). Archibald was born the year his oldest sibling, Elizabeth, the sixth in the line of Elizabeths, died at the age of seven. When Archibald himself was seven he witnessed the birth and death of his only brother.

Archibald had attended preparatory school at Adelphi Academy, Brooklyn, and was further educated by Arthur H. Cutler in New York. He entered Harvard as a freshman in 1878, but became so sick with an unidentified illness he had to drop out and begin his freshman year again in 1879. (He met Ruth that summer.) Therefore he was graduated with the class of 1883.

The Bishop got along well with Archibald, whom he invited to stay for a ten-day visit that summer of 1879. Ruth was smitten. The two spoke alone together about "mutual likings one of which was music. The boy had enjoyed fine concerts and had inherited his mother's lovely voice. The Damrosch and Sessions family were friends, and Theodore Thomas, the great conductor, had been intimates with them. Walter and Frank Damrosch were about our age and were planning to follow their father's [Leopold] profession."[34]

Another topic of discussion between the two was religion, one which Ruth herself had never really questioned. Episcopalianism was the faith of her family; how could there be any possible dispute? Archibald, however, was reading Newman's *Grammar of Assent*.[35] When Ruth asked him why, he responded, "When I went to college last year I was a comfortable Unitarian, but when I was sick, I began to think I wasn't satisfied. A man has to have some basis of faith if he is going to accomplish anything, and know what he believes and why. I made up my mind to watch other people's religion, so I came up here to do it."[36] Archibald knew the history of the family members' conversions and wanted to see these relatives. He also had a Catholic friend who lent him the *Grammar of Assent*. Ruth felt "It would be incongruous for one of our tribe to go over to Rome, after all the other departures!" Archibald was "not very religious myself, so far. But I'd like to be, I think." Ruth also learned that Archibald, who had spent a good deal of time by himself, hoped to study law, as his family, which had included six lawyers, thought best. He entered law because his lawyer father John wished it; indeed, he began his career in his father's law office. Archibald loved literature more, however.

When the time came for Archibald to leave Forty Acres, Ruth lent him a copy of *The Imitation of Christ*. She explained, "You see, I have absolutely no theology to fall back upon; I'm ashamed to say that I never seemed to need it, with such a large supply in the family. But Thomas à Kempis is different. He's helped me to *live* what I couldn't understand. I believe that's the thing to do; you may wait forever to be entirely settled, and meanwhile one gets a chance to see how faith works out. Anyway, when you feel you've got what you're looking for, just send this back some day. I'll know then that it proved to be what you wanted."[37]

The next summer, 1880, when Ruth saw Archibald again in the Berkshires, he was staying with his family. Neither family had any inkling of the affection between the two. The reader suspects the reason was because this affection was one-sided, entirely in Ruth's mind. Ruth returned to Syracuse "puzzled and slightly embittered."[38] Perhaps as a result of this disappointment, Ruth began to languish—with sallow skin, dark circles under the eyes, and the return of the nervous twitching habit. Her aunt Kate noticed her indolence and lack of initiative, what today we might see as signs of depression. Ruth's worried parents took a highly unusual step for their day.

Ruth was sent to a noted Polish female doctor, Marie Zakrzewska. She was not especially interested in the physical symptoms brought on by the Civil War cannons. Like a good psychiatrist, she wanted to know what was important to Ruth now. Ruth declared that music meant the most to her. When Dr Zakrzewska asked, "What does it mean?", Ruth faltered, disconcerted. She admitted that she was swayed by music but never accomplished anything with it. She also felt she had not succeeded in what she had expected to be her life work, church work.

Dr Zakrzewska arrived at a diagnosis and a prescription in that one meeting: "You've lived in a sort of fairy wood and obeyed your impulses and the call of beauty in many forms . . . everything has come to you easily, and you've been satisfied to let it come. But the great things are not achieved passively. Music, for instance, is not merely an escape, not just a means of forgetting what is sordid and disagreeable in our environment. Art is not; literature is not. They are elements of life and governed by the laws of life. . . . I want you to get out into a broader world. . . . I want you to go to Europe for three years and study there."[39]

Although her parents would do anything to help her, Ruth felt she was not as worthy as her siblings. Once assisted with money, they brought back tangible results in the fields of religion and social work. Ruth felt that she would only be indulging in a long vacation. Dr Zakrzewska had an answer: "You will study music to teach it; study it as an art, not an accomplishment. And you will study [German] . . . Will you promise me that if you go you will work to prepare yourself for paying back what you are taking from your parents by supporting yourself for three years—for as long a time as you will have spent in Europe? That should be the agreement."[40]

Because she was in Boston for this interview while Archibald was a student at Harvard, Ruth saw him the afternoon of the momentous prescription. This meant a six-year separation: three in Germany and three working off her debt. Archibald did not feel the same loss Ruth did. Their last evening together before her voyage to Europe in January 1881 was spent hearing *Carmen*. Indeed, she told him that he should feel free in the next three years to see other people. "But here I recoiled at my own daring. I was offering myself to him, instead of refusing him, when he had not even proposed."[41] A Victorian through and through when it came to romance, Ruth felt that if Archibald kissed her, it would constitute a pledge. And it probably would have; however, he did not kiss her. His letters did not communicate a great affection. She nevertheless remained determined that he was in love with her.

One could easily question Archibald's commitment to her over the next six years. We have no evidence from his side of this equation; nevertheless it did not appear that marriage was uppermost in his mind. Chapin wrote, "Ruth went abroad to study music in Leipzig. Although the primary intention was educational, there was an additional objective: to strengthen her emotional fiber. As things turned out she had a very good time but she did not obtain bona fide teaching certification, and, worse, her nervous afflictions persisted."[42]

Ruth attended the Leipzig Conservatory between the ages of 21 and 23. Sessions related, "As she told me once, 'Of course the teachers there weren't interested in just an American girl who wanted to study piano,' but she had a roaring good time."[43] She realized that she was not a serious student according to the standards at the Conservatory. Karl Muck, later conductor of the Boston Symphony, and Felix Weingartner were students there at the same time to provide a comparison.

Chapin gathered from Ruth's 75 letters from Germany that for some reason she was too ill to enter the Conservatory at Easter in 1881. Her condition also seemed to preclude a professional career as a pianist. Ruth's letters, like those of her son, contained almost no corrections and never misspellings. She did not, as she had told herself she would do for Archibald's sake, study theology. Herr Doktor Erb, her German doctor, prescribed plenty of walking and fresh air. Ruth had studied piano privately in Germany with Herr Coccius. Coccius, called "the Apostle of the fourth finger," started her on a Beethoven sonata, variations of Schubert, and some Bach. Practicing the piano was gloomy in comparison with the fun of learning German. At the Conservatory she studied harmony and counterpoint with Dr Rust, and listened to rehearsals of the Gewandhaus orchestra.

Ruth joined the choir of the English chapel in the old Bachschule in the Thomasplatz. She was introduced to Bach's own organ and allowed to play a chorale on its yellow keys. Ruth and her friends attended operas: *Fidelio* first, then Gluck's *Alceste, Barber of Seville*, and *Magic Flute*. She also heard Wagner: *Tristan und Isolde, Die Walküre*, and *Tannhäuser*. The musical highlight was probably the Lutheran celebration at the Thomaskirche of Good Friday and Easter Sunday. She also heard performers and conductors Sarasate, Moszkowski, Scharwenka, Rubinstein, and Hans von Bülow. She perceived that von Bülow, conductor of the Saxe-Meinigen Orchestra, was in a "nervous condition," perhaps because his wife, Cosima, left him for Wagner. The great composer himself died in February 1883. Every shop window displayed Wagner's picture; commemorative services, masses, and operas were given. The whole country was absorbed in honoring Wagner. Ruth provided the first direct link between German culture and Sessions, who was culturally and musically more German than either French or Italian.

An especially touching experience was Ruth's listening to Clara Schumann practice for a performance of Mendelssohn's G minor concerto, Beethoven's *Les Adieux* sonata, and Robert Schumann's quintet. Ruth and Nora Cabot, having made friends with the janitor, sneaked in. They saw a white-haired lady of 63 and her daughter. Schumann looked up from the piano and caught sight of the two young women and "she gave us a smile all for ourselves, which sent shivers of delight down our spines."[44] After the performance Ruth asked Schumann to sign a photograph of her; she eventually gave it to Sessions. In doing this she was braver than her son, who as a student was so shy he would never intrude on conductors or performers after a concert.

A trip to Italy took her to what she called the "country of saints." Ruth still had not given serious thought to theology, but was aware enough of Archibald's "weary struggle," a search for a fundamental truth underlying all faiths, to be embarrassed by both that fact and that she had not written to him for several months. The summer of 1882 in Italy was a "luxurious" vacation during which Ruth did not practice the piano, and she "dreaded the return to Leipzig and lessons" after it.[45]

One January day in 1883 Ruth received her copy of *The Imitation of Christ* that she had lent Archibald four years earlier. This meant to her that he had found the answer to his questions and was practicing the Way of Life that led to Christian faith. As recently as the previous year, he had let her know he was experiencing a resurgence of doubts. Ruth persuaded herself that a marked passage in the returned book, as opposed to the lack of mention of love in the accompanying letter, was proof of his affection. "It occurred to me that perhaps he was really the honest one, expressing gratitude but trying to make it clear that that was the limit of his feeling for me."[46] No, of course not, she rationalized; he was desperately in love with her. Dr Zakrzewska saw Ruth in Dresden. Ruth already wanted to be released from her pledge; she pleaded with the doctor to not have to stay the entire three years. She dissembled, using Archibald as an excuse and telling her about his supposed affection for her. Zakrzewska relented to the point of half a year. If Ruth left in May of 1883, it would have been two and a half years. She returned, however, on March 27.

Ruth then taught in Syracuse at a Young Ladies' Seminary. At first she gave instruction in German, but then also taught music and the piano. She did not attend Archibald's Harvard graduation in the spring of 1883, finding, implausibly, no excuse to go to Cambridge. (She chalked this up to cowardice in the face of her family.) Possibly she did not want to be in a position where she was not the center of attention, or she could not face the reality that he was not as interested in her as she wished.

Indeed, Archibald and Ruth would not have seen each other ever again were it not for a chance meeting at a concert in New York. In January 1885, six years since their first meeting and almost two years after her return from Europe, they were able to talk about their patchy relationship. Ruth felt confident enough to declare, "One thing; I've had enough, please note, of 'due, respective thrift.' I shall spend recklessly here-after."[47] She clearly wanted Archibald to take care of her in the style to which her family had accustomed her. The lesson Dr Zakrzewska had tried to teach about discipline and self-sufficiency had not taken. It appears that Ruth pursued Archibald, not the reverse.

Rather than Archibald approaching the Bishop for Ruth's hand, Ruth herself tried to gain permission to marry. The Bishop, not realizing there had been any romance at all to consider between the two family members, was "a trifle staggered" over how close a relative Archibald was.[48] He felt the two were being "percipitate." Ruth told him dis-ingenuously that the two had waited six years to be alone together; the Bishop reminded her that the Biblical Jacob had served *seven* years for Rachel. Clearly, the Bishop was not entirely pleased with this arrangement. He made Ruth promise secrecy from the family about the engagement—if he could not prevent it—until their prospects were more settled. (Secrecy about engagements would also be a theme in Sessions's life.) Huntington suggested they wait a conventional six months before announcing a betrothal. Ruth even asked permission of the Bishop to write to Archibald. He proposed that the two avoid extreme expressions of love while still not publicly engaged and wrote as much to Archibald, who, for his part, felt the two were being treated like children. Ruth still had a year to fulfill of her pledge to Dr Zakrzewska, nevertheless, there was no contradicting the Bishop: the two decided they could pretend to remain affectionate cousins for six more months. After that, when the engagement was announced, convention dictated that another year elapse before the wedding.

After the six months, in the early fall of 1885, when the Bishop thought the two had met his "test," he himself announced the engagement. The family, except suspicious Molly, kept in the dark, was duly amazed and surprised. Ruth throve on this kind of secrecy and drama. The documented (and actual, as opposed to imagined) romance between Archibald and Ruth began in 1885. In October a passive Archibald wrote to Ruth's brother, "Cousin George," describing Ruth's attachment to him (but, tellingly, not his toward her).

> If I had made more of my opportunities of seeing + getting acquainted with you while I was in Cambridge I'm afraid you would have been less willing to express your kind opinion of me; especially as my own family who think they know me pretty well refused to believe me when I broke the news to them + [my sister] Addie was frank enough to give as a reason for the incredulity that she didn't believe Ruth would have me!
>
> It is useless of course for me to try to express my appreciation of the blessing of Ruth's affection. You have known her all her life + know her character + can understand the rare good fortune of the man for whom she acknowledges an attachment. It is a subject of continual wonder to me that such happiness should

be meant for me for I can't see what I have done to deserve it. I can only accept it as a fact that I don't understand + I am selfish enough to be willing to leave it so.[49]

By this time Ruth had taught for two years at Mrs Piatt's Seminary at Utica, New York. The school was modeled somewhat on Mrs Porter's school in Farmington, Connecticut, where Mrs Piatt had been an assistant to the principal. Ruth's salary had gone from $400 to "the really dazzling sum" of $1,500 once she added music instruction to her duties as a teacher of German. Even as a working woman, Ruth was at a disadvantage about how money was earned, budgeted, and spent. Victorian New England society held the subject of money too vulgar to speak of. Only misty romantic and adventurous notions of marriage to a lawyer sustained her; she had no inkling that financial matters may be more difficult than they appear. By the time she wrote her autobiography, she realistically assessed how little prepared she was for the financial reality of marriage. In this regard, too, her son was exactly like her.

Ruth eventually taught for four years at Mrs Piatt's school, from fall 1883 to spring 1887. Because of a new opening for a lawyer, Archibald wrote that he could set the date. Two months before the wedding Archibald wrote to "My own precious Ruth" on September 13, 1887, a date that for two years had held special significance for the two (perhaps September 13, 1885, was the day they became engaged). In his letters Archibald wrote more openly about religious issues than did Ruth, the daughter of a bishop. He had received three letters from her that day and responded with one.

> We love each other Darling + have passed the point where it would be possible for us to go different ways as I believe many husbands and wives do, so that now our two lives are merged in one more truly + really than they ever were, complete as we have been pleased to think the union before. The consciousness of this has been growing on me by degrees + this summer I have come to see how utterly impossible it would be for us to live separately + by that I mean to include something more than the unhappiness of bodily separation. Our whole beings spiritual, intellectual + physical must follow one path, for they are so completely necessary to each other that separation is simply inconceivable.[50]

Like her parents and her composer son, Ruth married in mid-November, the 16th, 1887. If ever there were a time to become the center of attention, one's wedding—as the bride, anyway—was the occasion. To ensure she received plenty, Ruth mailed 1,500 wedding invitations. In no way could she have more distinctly differentiated herself from her brother, the Rev. James Huntington, who lived among the poor on Avenue C in New York. The wedding took place in Syracuse. The Bishop led Ruth up the aisle; Archibald accompanied Hannah Huntington; and brothers George and James performed the ceremony together along with six other vested clergy. The couple had memorized their vows rather than recite them. A choir sang. The two took a train eastward to their honeymoon location: Forty Acres. Ruth could never leave the family farm, although Archibald was most definitely a city dweller. The two made grandiose plans, but then doubted whether those could be accomplished. Archibald foretold the future, saying, "If we find we don't amount to much ourselves, let's make our contribution by having lots of worth-while children."[51]

ARCHIBALD SESSIONS

Archibald Sessions was graduated from Harvard in 1883 in the same class as Edward Everett Hale, Franklin Hooper, and Morris Loeb (the brother of James Loeb who donated the Music Building at Harvard). He left Harvard for New York City, and in May 1884 passed the New York bar examination. At some unknown point he went to Europe, possibly in 1884 or 1885, if not before he entered Harvard. Ruth, our only source, is vague on this point. The Sessions family was musical.

For 25 years (1866 to 1891) Theodore Thomas was sole conductor of the Brooklyn Philharmonic Society. In 1882 he gave the first of seven concerts in the Seventh Regiment Armory, with a chorus of 3,000 and 300-member orchestra before an audience of 8,000. In 1877 Thomas was elected conductor of the New York Philharmonic Orchestra, a position that lasted to 1891. Later he founded the Chicago Symphony Orchestra. More than any other American musician of his day, he was widely viewed to have popularized Classical music.

Archibald and his sisters Clara and Adeline were friendly with Theodore Thomas; all three sang in his chorus. Archibald was a baritone, and Clara and Adeline, sopranos. Adeline began as a soloist with the Thomas chorus, called the New York Chorus Society, but gave up her career because of stage fright. In the 1970s interviews Sessions said, "My aunt was a soloist. She couldn't stand it—she got so scared every time she sang that she couldn't endure it any more and gave it up."[1] Later he changed the story: "But my Aunt Addie *was* a concert singer. She did *not* give up her career because of stage fright."[2]

Records show Adeline as soloist and leader of the second women's chorus (which included her sister Clara) with Thomas's orchestra in the years between 1881 and 1887. She was one of six soloists, along with chorus and orchestra, for Schumann's *Gypsy Life*, opus 29, no. 3, performed April 23, 1881. In 1883 she was one of six soloists for Gounod's trilogy "The Redemption" with the Philharmonic Society of Brooklyn performing at the Academy of Music. She led the second women's chorus for several concerts in 1883 in memory of Richard Wagner (*Tannhäuser, Parsifal, Die Götterdämmerung*, and *Die Meistersinger von Nürnberg*). On an 1884 program she was listed as one of the soloists for Schumann's *Scenes from Goethe's "Faust"* and Beethoven's Ninth Symphony. Thomas gave Adeline the baton with which he had conducted the Wagner Festival; she gave it to Archibald, who gave it to Sessions, who treasured it; its whereabouts now is unknown. Adeline had many musical friends in New York whom Sessions met.

Archibald had brown eyes, was prematurely bald, and sported a handlebar mustache (characteristics his son shared, the mustache without the handlebar, however). Considered handsome, Archibald was dark skinned. Born in Brooklyn in 1860, he lived in New York most of his life. Sessions remembered him as "really a New Yorker—not really happy anywhere else."

Figure 6 Archibald Sessions at Harvard in 1883.

Figure 7 Archibald Sessions in 1908.

Two of Archibald's three surviving sisters married and had children, Roger's first cousins. Clara Fisher Sessions married Edwin W. Wheeler and had two children, Elizabeth Fisher Wheeler and Edwin Sessions Wheeler. Clara died in 1893, at the age of thirty-nine.[3] That death left Roger with two aunts, Grace and Adeline. Cousin Edwin Sessions

Wheeler, from Concord, married Mildred Hunting (no relation to the Huntingtons) on December 3, 1929, when he was 38. After the death of his wife he married Helen McCoy.[4]

Grace Martin Sessions married, only a month before Archibald's marriage, Franklin Hooper, a classmate of Archibald's at Harvard.[5] Grace and Franklin Hooper also had two children: Catherine Hooper, born the same year as Hannah Sessions and who attended Smith in the class of 1911, and Leverett Hooper, who attended Harvard in the class of 1915, Roger's class.[6] Both of Grace's children attended the same colleges at the same times as Hannah and Roger.

Everyone in this family married late, with the exception of Adeline who did not marry at all, giving Roger his third maiden aunt (in addition to Arria and Molly Huntington). Clara married at 31 and died eight years later. Grace married when she was 29, and Archibald, shortly afterwards, at 27. Given the much shorter life spans in the nineteenth century, these siblings' lengthy wait until marriage might indicate a slight aversion to the institution, or at least a hesitation to commit to a marriage. Perhaps their own parents' marriage was not ideal; there is some reason to believe that John Sessions was a difficult person.

Grace and Archibald appear to have been quite close, in living arrangements as well as emotionally, as siblings. The Hoopers lived at 158 Washington Avenue in Brooklyn, from 1888 to 1890, when they moved to 73 West 92nd Street. Their father, John Sessions, worked at 30 Pine Street and lived at two addresses (141 and 195 Amity Street, Brooklyn) until his death in 1899. His law firm at 30 and 32 Pine Street was at the corner of 35 Wall Street.

Archibald's work addresses change somewhat frequently: in 1886–1887 he worked with his father at 35 Wall Street. When Archibald married Ruth, she was 28 and he 27. After his marriage, he moved to a job at 120 Broadway; and in 1888–1889 to one at 140 Nassau Street.[7] (The couple then lived in Englewood, New Jersey.) During the winter of 1887–1888, just after their marriage, they lived on West 92nd Street three flights up, in a small flat with view of Central Park. They had $1,000 as a wedding gift and free use of an Englewood home for two years. Archibald's sister Grace Hooper also lived on West 92nd Street. Possibly, the newly wed couple moved in with or near to his sister and her husband. Ruth loved the glamour of New York. She enjoyed the hospitality of Old New York's Four Hundred and sometimes lived a life out of an Edith Wharton novel.

"My father hated Theodore Roosevelt, mainly because they had known each other at Harvard," Sessions said of Archibald. "In the 1884 presidential campaign the Republicans put up a crook [James G. Blaine]. Everybody knew he was a thoroughly dishonest man. And the Democrats put up Grover Cleveland, who was certainly a very honest man and an intelligent man, and a lot of the Republicans switched over. They were called the Mugwumps."[8] In 1888 Cleveland was defeated for re-election by Benjamin Harrison, seen as a blow to the reform movement. Sessions remembered his father as "tremendous supporter of Grover Cleveland all his life, whom he idolized. So I was brought up on the legend, so to speak, of Grover Cleveland. My father was violently against Theodore Roosevelt."[9]

New York's Young Men's Democratic Club took up the challenge. Ruth credited her husband with the idea of persuading Cleveland to run again; in any case David B. Hill, the Democratic Party Chair, and Frederick Hinrichs, President of the Young Men's Democratic Club of Brooklyn, put forward the idea. Because Cleveland won the Presidential election of 1892, Hinrichs gained the position of New York commissioner of tax arrears. Archibald became his deputy, a political appointment.

Sessions felt that Archibald became quite conservative at the end of his life. Indeed, Archibald eventually left the Democrats for the Republican Party. In 1920, for example, Archibald voted for Warren G. Harding. (Ruth, of course, could not vote until she was over 60 years old.)

Four months after their marriage an event occurred that, Ruth felt, affected his heath permanently. The New York City blizzard of 1888 began at midnight Monday, March 12, and lasted until midnight on Tuesday, March 13. The worst blizzard in New York since 1857, the total snow accumulation was 21 inches. Damages were estimated at between $20 and $25 million, and the city did not recover for two weeks. Electrical wiring, above ground on poles, was weighed down by snow and snapped, causing blackouts. One result of the storm was the mayoral decision that all overhead wires be placed underground, a situation that later included telephone wires and obtains today.[10] Archibald had walked without stopping through the freezing wind and heavy snow the more than one hundred blocks from Pine Street to the west Nineties. Spent, he did not go to the office for two days. Ruth felt that permanent harm had been done: "Thereafter he had always an abnormally slow pulse, and though he was told that this often went with longevity, we learned in time that his heart could not stand strain."[11] Although Archibald died almost four decades later, Ruth blamed this famous blizzard.

Despite her new house in New Jersey, during the spring and summer of 1888, the first of their marriage, and during the next few summers, Ruth moved either to Forty Acres or to Syracuse to be with her parents. During the summer of 1888 Ruth was pregnant. Archibald visited Forty Acres when he had time off from his law firm. Ruth simply could not sever the parental tie; she chose her immediate family over her husband. On February 16, 1889, Hannah (Nan) Sargent Sessions, named after Ruth's mother, was born in Englewood.

Hannah's parents fought over money and the lack of it. Ruth could not understand why some bills were overdue; she declined both to be reasoned with or to understand credit, so gentle Archibald made sure she never saw bills so as not to upset her. Of course, the two had a horse and carriage, a cook, and a helper named James. After Hannah was born, they also would have a live-in nurse. They were clearly living beyond their means, but Ruth insisted that all the bills be paid and not held over a month; that was how it was done in the Bishop's house. She worried more about what other people would think than about the financial situation itself.

Ruth felt these debts resulted in her "nervous breakdown," caused also by caring for the six-month-old "heavy" baby. "I had a sort of nervous breakdown; she was a heavy baby, and I had overdone a little in taking care of her."[12] They hired a full-time nurse, a woman named Melissa, for both bedridden Ruth and to take the nursing of Hannah "off my hands." This meant adding to the debt, "but it was a necessity." Here began a long and stormy relationship between mother and daughter; somehow Nan was blamed for her mother's breakdown, which might well have been post-partum depression. Possibly Ruth, who admitted that she knew nothing of mothering after the first nurse left (to take care of baby Hamilton Fish), found she was not up to the challenge of taking care of a child. From then on Archibald paid for live-in nurses for every new baby. There would be four altogether.

During the summer and until December of 1889 Ruth, Melissa, and Hannah removed to more comfortable quarters—with Ruth's parents in Syracuse. She returned to Brooklyn and Archibald's new apartment, but remembered the next two years as extremely unhappy. In the spring of 1890 the family moved to small apartment in Brooklyn

Heights. In the fall of 1891 the Sessionses had leased a small apartment "uptown
... on a broad and airy street." Their furniture from Englewood was set up there
and when Ruth, pregnant, arrived in September the apartment was ready. Waiting in the apartment was a maid named Edith, who remained a family friend for
40 years.

A second child, Mary Huntington, named after Ruth's sister (known as Molly) arrived
"in December [1891], a Christmas baby. . . . Her arrival was so quick and easy that it
hardly interrupted the natural order of events; she seemed perfectly healthy except for a
little darkness of the skin."[13]

When Dr Eliza Mosher arrived two days after Christmas, the baby "could not eat, was
breathing too rapidly, and lay back on my arm with eyes wide open, gazing into mine
with a strange depth of expression, quite unlike the look of so young a child." The
instant Dr Mosher saw the baby, she asked, "Has she been as dark as this from the first?
So blue? . . . Don't worry, child; I shall take off my things and stay right on here; we'll
fight for her life."[14]

A half an hour later Mosher diagnosed an infection of the bronchial tubes and a
problem with Mary's heart. Three-year-old Nan and Edith left, but Archibald remained
with his wife and they both prayed. In the middle of the afternoon the doctor thought
that Mary was breathing naturally and there was hope. But the nurse ran in to call her
back; the baby had stopped breathing. Mosher handed the body to Ruth saying, "But
think of the brightness that 'eye hath not seen nor ear heard, neither hath entered into
the heart of man.' "[15]

Ruth felt their mourning drew the couple closer together. She does not mention the
fact, but each of their own families had experienced two children's deaths: Ruth had not
been born when her parents lost two children, but Archibald was seven when his
younger brother died. "Neither of us felt for an instant that the littleness of our baby,
her short stay with us, or the suddenness of her passing would minimize that sorrow; it
was destined to last for many years, and to remind us at each birthday anniversary of
what she might have been if she had lived and grown. And for both [sic] of us it was the
first immediate experience of death."[16] Yet Archibald listed in his class reports two
different December dates for Mary's birth and two (including December 28) for her
death—none of these matching the cemetery records and gravestone—and Ruth wrote
the wrong year (1892) in her autobiography. Mary Huntington Sessions was born on
December 15 and died December 27, 1891. A white marble cross, identified only as
"Mary" and those dates, marks her grave in the Old Hadley Cemetery whose record
reads, "I am Alpha and Omega." Sessions remarked, "My mother romanticized Mary and
Mary's death a lot. My mother was a very strange woman."[17] A year and two months
later, Archibald's sister Clara died. This goes unmentioned in Ruth's autobiography, as
does any contribution of the Sessions family to her own.

Once again Ruth was unable even with help to cope with running the household, near
a noisy elevated rail line. By June 1892 she "began to wilt" while "another slump in
finances brought discouragement."[18] The Bishop took charge and wrote a letter basically
ordering Ruth and Nan to come to Forty Acres, where he had leased the old Phelps
house, closed for three years and now put in order for her. He told her which train to
take, that she would be met with a key to Phelps House, and that Archibald could come
later, on occasional weekends. All expenses were paid by the Bishop. Once there, Ruth
reveled in the ancestral atmosphere that permeated Phelps House; indeed, she could not
sleep the first night for excitement and walked in the garden in a "trance." Whenever
any aspect of life got tough for Ruth, the Bishop bailed her out. She simply laid aside

her husband's worries and enjoyed one of the most pleasant summers of her life. Archibald, struggling financially, had lost a daughter and would soon lose a sister; his wife was halfway out the door.

"On February 1, 1894," Archibald wrote of himself, "I was appointed Deputy Registrar of Arrears of the City of Brooklyn . . . In the same year I was a delegate from Brooklyn to the Conference of the National Municipal League at Philadelphia, and again at Cleveland in 1895. I am the author of no books, pamphlets or magazine articles, but have delivered a number of addresses, mostly on questions of municipal government, before various organizations of a political and semi-political character."[19] This position lasted until the election of 1896, when the Democratic Party lost seats at the mid-term elections and Archibald lost his appointment.

In 1896 Archibald was offered a law partnership with a former Harvard friend. No sooner had Ruth moved to 417 Washington Avenue in the spring of 1896 than she left again, this time pregnant with Roger; she spent her early pregnancy at Phelps House and Forty Acres. In October, with Ruth's parents back in Syracuse, Archibald came to Forty Acres, possibly to persuade her to return to Brooklyn with him.

On December 28, 1896, Ruth, back in Brooklyn, gave birth to Roger (see below). Six months later, Archibald's mother, Elizabeth, died. Two years after that, in 1899, Archibald's father also died, on February 1, 1899. In addition, his law partner died suddenly (according to Ruth, but this is unverifiable). Four months later, on May 21, 1899, his second son John (named after his father) was born. Released from his father's influence, Archibald decided to give up the law. During the summer of 1899, it hardly needs stating, his family went to Forty Acres again while he remained in New York.

In 1899 Archibald got a position with publisher of the *Encyclopedia Britannica*, for less salary than he had been making. He had gained a small inheritance from the death of his father. Ruth wrote that in the spring 1900 the *Encyclopedia Britannica* publisher closed down its New York office; they would continue in London. Moving abroad was not an option for the Sessions family. At least, this is Ruth's version of the story. Unmentioned is the fact that Archibald's brother-in-law, Franklin Hooper, was for 39 years the American editor of the *Encyclopedia Britannica*, whose offices moved to various midtown locations in Manhattan, but never closed in New York. Hooper oversaw the tenth to the fourteenth editions of the *Encyclopedia Britannica*, including the famous eleventh edition. Hooper began as the publisher in 1898 and spent almost half his time in London.[20] Shortly after 1900 Archibald became editor of *Ainslee's* Magazine, whose office was at 79 Seventh Avenue at Fifteenth Street. *Ainslee's* was a publication of Street & Smith, which another Harvard classmate, Ormand Gerald Smith, had founded in the year of their graduation, 1883.[21]

If Archibald had read William Dean Howells's two novels—*A Hazard of New Fortunes* (1890) or *The World of Chances* (1893), both classic novels of nineteenth-century New York literary ambition—he might have related to the protagonists. The heroes get to the mountain, New York, become dizzy looking up, wander in a daze and fall off the summit (or, conversely, arrive at the top unaware of the fact). Howells felt New York was devoted to commercial laws of chance. When chance ruled, Archibald was one of the unlucky ones. We do not know exactly why Archibald left the *Encyclopedia Britannica*. It hardly seems likely that his brother-in-law would fire him. Ruth's autobiography has omitted vital information and distorted the facts.

Sessions remembered Archibald's view of Ruth: " 'Roger,' said Archibald Sessions, 'if your mother were a man, she'd be Emperor of the United States.' 'You mean president, Daddy.' 'No, we wouldn't have presidents anymore, just an emperor.' "[22]

Our view of Archibald is heavily skewed by Ruth's version of history. She wrote an autobiography, while, despite a career in publishing, Archibald is not known to have published either fiction or nonfiction. Sessions's niece polled her family: "Everyone remembers Ruth as affectionate and good-humored with children; no one has a clear memory of Archie."[23]

417 WASHINGTON AVENUE

Both of Ruth's older brothers, George and James, became ministers. James decided in 1884 to found a monastic order; he lived in the German tenements in New York on Seventh Street and Avenue C and devoted his life after 1884 to poverty, celibacy, and labor among these people. One could interpret this as an act of rebellion against his family and father. It was the third successive religious conversion in as many generations. Father James Huntington became a historic figure through his promotion of social welfare. Huntington had dressed as a working man and sought—vainly—for a job in New York's factories. He startled his colleagues by joining the Knights of Labor and becoming an ardent supporter of Henry George in the 1886 New York mayoral campaign. Sessions remembered his uncle as "very intellectual and [possessing] a great deal of intellectual curiosity."[1]

In 1887 the Church Association for the Advancement of the Interest of Labor (CAIL) was founded by Huntington, Bishop Potter, and 38 other bishops who served as vice presidents. The first powerful Protestant group actively to defend labor's right to organize, CAIL also declared solidarity with the struggle against slums, sweatshops, and child labor. One author asserts "The Episcopalians' pleas for social solidarity constituted a dramatic break with the bleak tooth-and-claw approach to which other Protestants still adhered."[2]

Ruth Sessions came from a family highly placed in the progressive movement and, inevitably, she became involved in these causes. Ruth kept a copy of Henry George's *Progress and Poverty*, frequently lent to others, its main argument underlined lest somehow they miss it. Frustrated that she could not vote, she worked for the Social Reform Club. The Club established a legal aid association to which Archibald belonged. He helped the underprivileged by *pro bono* legal work and hastened delayed cases to a solution.

Father Huntington exhorted the middle class to "correct the social evil that permits their unfortunate sisters to be so frightfully overworked and badly paid."[3] Five hundred thousand wage earners toiled in the city; of those 200,000 were women, 75,000 of whom worked under dreadful conditions or for starvation wages. The city Consumers' League proposed boycotting department stores and retail shops that did not treat employees properly. They took a page from abolitionist women shoppers who had given up slave-made cotton and sugar; now women would decline to purchase any items identified by the League as made by exploited women. Shoppers could determine this by process of elimination: a White List of department stores that dealt fairly with their employees was printed and distributed to 4,000 names from the *Social Register*, placed in ladies' parlors in the largest hotels, published in the papers, and printed on postcards. If a store did *not* show up on this list, the buyer would know that a store treated their female employees badly. This was defined as: paying women less than men; firing women after five years of satisfactory work so that no raise had to be paid; harsh and arbitrary discipline (at Macy's, for example, women were forbidden to sit at any time during a 16-hour workday); fining lateness; dismissal for "unnecessary conversations;" and squalid facilities. The White List found it could include only eight of the large department stores.

Ruth continued to write, edit, and publish, the fervor of her father's sermons turning her preachy on occasion. She published a story in *Munsey's Magazine* that paid for a new coat.[4] By late 1896, while in her final trimester of her pregnancy with Roger, Ruth was editing a magazine, working at the Woman's Club and the Social Reform Club, and attending the meetings of the Consumers' League. According to Ruth's autobiography, when she visited the *Brooklyn Eagle* the week before Christmas in order to publish the White List on its editorial page, she was met with a certain reserve and embarrassment. The *Eagle's* editor explained that their biggest advertisers had threatened to withdraw from the newspaper, claiming discrimination, if the newspaper printed the names of White List firms and not theirs, and the *Eagle* felt it could not afford to alienate them. Ruth argued that the firms on the list were given the League's word that their names would appear in the next day's paper; the previous year there had been no trouble at all. The man suggested the White List firms pay to have their names put in as a regular advertisement. "No," Ruth answered. After consultation with his peers the editor had a suggestion (which he hoped would deter Ruth by its near impossibility): if she could get about twice as many names on her list, including other types of stores, they could print it. After four hours of calling corset-shops, tailor shops, and bookstores, as well as some businesses who had previously refused, she succeeded—much to the dismay of the *Eagle*, who said, all right this one time, but not next year.[5]

Exciting and plausible as this episode sounds, it proves difficult to verify by consulting the pages of the *Brooklyn Daily Eagle* for the month of December 1896. On December 4, a brief report appears under "Consumers' League Meets." The President, Mrs R. H. Sessions "stated that the object was not to boycott the Brooklyn shops, but to recommend those which complied with the regulations of the White List. . . . One prominent Fulton street proprietor replied . . . that the Consumers' League was a blot on the city. Mrs. Sessions also stated that two stores had been inspected—Liebmann's and Journeay & Burnham's—and that the arrangements for the welfare of the employees in both stores were found satisfactory. . . . Miss [Leonora] O'Reilly of New York spoke for the working women, referring particularly to the sweatshops and work in the tenement districts."[6] Alas, no White List was published by the *Eagle* that Christmas. Perhaps Ruth conflated the incident from other experiences.

After lengthy introspection and study, Archibald in his twenties had been baptized in the Episcopalian faith. Roger's sister and brother, Hannah and John, remained Episcopalians throughout their lives. Of his generation, only Roger was to give up the religion of his upbringing and refuse to be married in a church; he would eventually embrace a "proto Catholic[ism]." Always politically liberal, even a Socialist in college, Roger nevertheless rebelled in a second way: he did not work for the causes of the poor and underprivileged. Because those two areas, religion and social work, were the Huntington family's life work, Sessions's striking out in the unusual direction of the arts might have been seen as turning his back on the values of his mother's family: "I was always thoroughly rebellious." In addition, the arts bore the scent of self-indulgence, of one's not being serious about important things such as eradicating poverty. Musicians recognize this attitude: it amounts to "Do something useful; get a real job."

After Archibald's political position had ended when the other party got a majority at the mid-term elections in 1896, he had returned to practice law. A college friend had opened a law office and asked Archibald to be his partner. The unnamed friend had inherited money, according to Ruth. Since the financial rewards were good, the couple could consider moving from their third-story apartment on Washington Avenue to "a quaint little house [that they could see from their apartment] which had just enough antiquity for our idea of homeliness; a good back yard, a grand old peach-tree at one side, a sturdy maple between porch and sidewalk, and a roomy nursery in the ell with a step down into it and a fireplace."[7] The artist owners had restored the house on the inside while paying attention to its historical features, the low ceilings and broad-boarded floors. They rented it to the Sessionses for a price no higher than their apartment rent. Not financially savvy, however, the couple overlooked the many added expenses such a place entailed: lighting, heating, carpeting, and water rates. Against the warnings of both families, Archibald signed the lease for May 1, 1896.

In a part of Brooklyn now called Clinton Hills, 417 Washington Avenue is located generally between the Bedford-Stuyvesant and South Brooklyn neighborhoods. Washington Avenue runs north–south from the Naval Shipyard to Prospect Park. The Sessions birth house is today near the Pratt Institute.

The "Bird House," as neighbors in the mid-1890s called it, was a clapboard house built in 1832. In the 1870s a mansard roof replaced the third floor with its dormer windows. At the same time the semicircular porch with a balustrade hanging from its

Figure 8 Roger's birthplace as it would have looked in the 1890s (drawing by Maddy Rosenberg).

roof was added. The building, in a landmark neighborhood, had four working fireplaces, three floors, and a basement. The first floor had a front parlor and the kitchen in the rear; the second floor had bedrooms (the bedroom above the kitchen has a freestanding fireplace parallel with the back wall behind which a staircase leads to the kitchen), and the third floor was the children's rooms. A small yard surrounds the front porch; a narrow side yard runs along the right-hand side of the house; and the back yard is spacious—larger than the house itself. After a concert in the winter of 1960 Sessions returned to see the Washington Avenue house in which he was born. Slightly surprised to find it still standing, he considered it a nice-looking frame house.[8]

In 1964 two couples, again artists, bought 417 Washington Avenue intending to renovate it.[9] One of those artists, a cartoonist, still lives there. She became aware of its other significance in 1971, when her husband jumped up from reading his Sunday *New York Times* and said, "Our house is the birthplace of a composer named Roger Sessions! Our address is in the newspaper!"[10] She even bought a book about the composer.[11]

An ordinary middle-class neighborhood in the 1880s and 1890s, Clinton Hills was predominantly Irish and Italian, with a few Jewish families scattered among them. Six blocks south, Washington Avenue is intersected at a sharp angle by Dean Street. On the northwest corner of Washington Avenue and Dean Street (the opposite side of Washington Avenue from the Sessions house) was "H. M. Copland's Department Store," established in 1884 and moved to this location in 1890. It remained there until Harris Copland's retirement in 1922. Copland, who had rented 626 and 628 Washington Avenue, in 1897 had acquired numbers 630 and 632 and built a new expansion. In November 1900 Aaron Copland was born in the expanded building. By 1907 Harris acquired 771 and 772 Dean Street, and had a dozen employees, a horse and wagon, and a telephone!

The Coplands' house was above and on the side of the store. Similar in its floor plan to the Sessions "Bird House," it, too, had three floors and a private entryway. On the first floor was a kitchen, dining room, and maid's room. The second floor has the parlor and master bedroom; the children's rooms were on the third. "The glory of the household," an upright Steinway piano sat in the parlor. The Sessions house also had an upright piano in the parlor, where Ruth Sessions gave piano lessons. Perhaps Ruth walked to the Copland dry goods store, not only to buy shoes, toys, household items, and clothing, but also to visit Vollmuth's (the landlord's) bakery. Roger Sessions's mother might have met Aaron Copland's parents there before the turn of the century.

No sooner had Archibald and Ruth signed the 417 Washington Avenue lease than Ruth discovered she was pregnant. The child they "had longed for since our baby's death in 1892 [*sic*; 1891] was on its way." It was due on the fifth anniversary of Mary's death. Immediately Ruth, 36, spent more than six weeks in bed. "It was an ordeal, that. So much to be done, and yet such an impossible weakness and weariness." She left for Forty Acres in June for the summer. She distracted herself from morning sickness by listening carefully to nature at Forty Acres and reheard in her mind's ear concerts she had attended at the Leipzig Gewandhaus: Beethoven symphonies, Joachim and Sarasate performances, the Wagner operas, and Bach's Passion. Archibald visited and read aloud to her Dumas's *The Three Musketeers*. She stayed at Forty Acres during most of the pregnancy, until into October, when, as mentioned above, her husband persuaded her to move back to the Bird House. "Somehow it seemed to have been decided that the coming child was a boy, although we had no expert advice on the subject. He would love Forty Acres as we all loved it, and would fish and hunt and swim; perhaps would till the soil, and live as his forbears had lived, we said."[12] Here she was not merely indulging in a fantasy; she fervently wanted a son to continue the family tradition of living at Forty Acres and farming the land. Three of her siblings had no children and she had a daughter; it was up to her new son to stake a claim. Sessions would escape this fate, but his younger brother, John, did not.[13]

Back in Brooklyn in mid-October, Ruth took on several piano students and edited. There was also the Woman's Club, the Social Reform Club, and the meetings of the Consumers' League. "We expected our baby just after Christmas, and it became rather a problem to get time off for bringing him into the world; all sorts of civic activities and obligations piled up."[14] She worked on her White List, managed Christmas obligations, and "On the morning of the twenty-seventh [sic], just in time to be welcomed by daylight, our oldest son appeared; a funny little baby, all mouth, as the nurse observed, and with eyes as dark as the proverbial fruit of the blackthorn."[15] The Freudian slip of the date—27th instead of the correct 28th—appears to result from her fixation with the dead daughter, Mary Huntington, who had died on the 27th five years earlier.

According to his birth certificate, filed January 6, 1897, Roger was born at 7:00 a.m. on December 28th at 417 Washington Ave. Both parents' ages are given as 37. Ruth's age is correct; Archibald, however, was just shy of his thirty-seventh birthday, January 12, 1897. The other blanks filled out are: no. of child of mother, "3," and the printed words "White" or "Colored" have "Colored" crossed out, according to the instructions. The medical attendant was "BB Mosher," who lived at "202 Scher Ave." This was the same physician who had taken care of Archibald and Nan during an influenza epidemic and who had attended Mary, Dr Eliza Mosher. Ruth seemed to trust female doctors.

The birth certificate listed Roger's name as "Roger Pitkin Sessions." (Pitkin was the surname of Moses Porter's wife, Elizabeth.) Ruth's sister Arria and nephew Henry Barrett Huntington, however, had their own ideas about the new baby's middle name. His baptism took place on the third Sunday in Epiphany, January 24, 1897, at St Mary's Church in Brooklyn.[16] Father W. W. Bellinger officiated, and when he asked Arria to "name this child," she said clearly, "Roger Huntington." Ruth "had no chance to protest, and we promised with mutual stoutness that he should fight manfully against the world, the flesh and the devil, name or no name."[17] One wonders if Archibald supported this last-minute surprise. Huntington, after all, was Arria, Barrett, and Ruth's family name, and it was also the middle name of Roger's dead sister. Although for years he signed Huntington as his middle name, Sessions eventually dropped it. To obtain a passport in 1924, Sessions was made, because of his belief that his middle name was Huntington, to produce both the birth certificate and the baptismal certificate. Only then did he discover his legal middle name was Pitkin. He never formally changed it to Huntington. To confuse matters further, Reverend Bellinger recorded the wrong year for the birth date: December 28, 1897.

How are we to interpret the Freudian slips of incorrect dates given by both mother and father (in his Harvard class reports) regarding the birth and death of their daughter Mary and the birth of their son? Ruth had described Roger's pregnancy as both an "ordeal" and a "problem." Possibly her age, 37, unusually late for a woman in the nineteenth century to give birth, contributed to her physical difficulties. Her pregnancy with Roger mirrored exactly the seasonal time frame of Mary's pregnancy; she could hardly have helped but think often of her previous pregnancy. Possibly she invested all of her hopes for the dead child into the newborn. Roger was born within hours of the fifth anniversary of Mary's death and was given Mary's middle name. Those who die young can achieve a mythic status of perfection. An actual, breathing child such

29

as Roger could never live up to the idealized image his romanticizing mother had constructed for Mary.

One of Ruth's stories about the baby deserves repetition.

> He was a strong young fellow, very sleepy and hungry, but awakened suddenly one cold night when the tinny jangle of a hurdy-gurdy started up under our window, ground out by a forlorn man who appears to have been moved by desperation to attempt an out-of-season performance. I have never been able to remember the melody he produced, probably some rattling jig, for the baby claimed our attention. His eyes opened wide, his face grew pink, his hands moved excitedly. Evidently he was listening.
>
> "That child's going to be musical," cried the nurse. "Look at him; he's all stirred up."
>
> . . . We found our surmise was correct; the infant's diminutive ear was sensitive to tonal vibrations, and his whole nerve-system responded to them.[18]

In order to cure, or at least mollify, the "serious" baby of his terror of being carried down the steep, rounded-corner staircase by his father, Ruth played a gavotte from Bach's French Suite to suit the rhythm of Archibald's stepping. Soon the baby began to indicate he wanted to be carried again.

In the summer of 1897 Roger's Brooklyn grandmother Elizabeth Fisher Sessions died. She had taken care of her invalid husband, who died two years later. Elizabeth had often visited 417 Washington. Ruth saw in her a strong likeness to their grandmother Huntington; she also looked a little like Aunt Bethia and Elizabeth Phelps's pictures. Ruth had help with the new baby from the old family friend, Melissa.

Ruth reserved space in her biography for discussions of Roosevelt, Henry George (whose death in 1897 was keenly felt by many), and other non-relatives. While the death of Archibald's mother was briefly recorded, his father's death was not mentioned at all except to note a "small windfall came to us through inheritance."[19] She described John Sessions as "an old man with many ideals shattered; the necessary diplomacy and what he considered chicanery in legal procedure, the political rivalry and the legislative complications, had embittered his later years, and his attitude toward the profession [of law] was no longer one of such reverence and confidence as it had been when he had urged a legal career upon his son."[20] Of course, the death of the Bishop would merit considerable attention.

In March 1898 President McKinley took the oath of the Presidency, and on May Day Admiral Dewey triumphed over the Spanish fleet in Manila. In July Roosevelt and his Rough Riders charged up San Juan Hill. When Dewey returned, Ruth and Archibald "took the children up to a roof on Brooklyn Heights to see the victorious ships steam up the harbor. I can remember the thrill of it, and the reflection that we had done our duty by Nan and Roger in giving them this great event to remember."[21] Remember it he did, but whether it lived in his mind as a genuine memory, or as a story his mother often referred to, is hard to determine. The couple were not as patriotic about Roosevelt and his Rough Riders as they had been about Dewey. Roger, aware of neither politics nor the war at such a young age, nevertheless was "much stirred" by the bands and the navy's brass buttons.

"He could not yet talk, beyond a queer jargon which served to acquaint the family with his desires. But he sang, from morning till night, in his bath, his baby-carriage, and his bed, reproducing all the popular melodies and war choruses, with isolated syllables for words—usually *wa*, a contraction of *Hurrah*—but perfectly correct and recognizable in time and tune. People used to stop and demand the name of the 'singing baby,' and asked for *Marching through Georgia* or *My Country 'Tis of Thee*, which were delivered with entire indifference to the beholder."[22] After a while Roger stopped singing and began putting words together, but he was a late talker, a trait more common in boys than in girls.

In the 1899–1900 season Ruth had a Metropolitan Opera box seat ticket. She recalled:

> Walter Damrosch was then conducting a series of young people's matinees, one of the most important moves in the history of American music. I took Roger to one of those; he was three now, and more musical than ever, always wanting to be at the piano, where he touched one note at a time, prolonging it and listening to its last vibration, and then perhaps playing a chord, stretching his small fingers apart and striking the keys almost timidly with a smile to himself. He never attempted tunes.
>
> I was a little doubtful about giving him the excitement of hearing an orchestra, but still longed to try its effect on him, and decided to let him come with me. We sat in a proscenium box, the second tier, and the concert began with the *Pilgrims' Chorus* from *Tannhäuser*. Listening so intently that I had forgotten the small figure beside my knee, in white kilts which made him look particularly infantile, I happened to turn my head toward the audience once, and noticed that people were looking toward the box and smiling. Roger was standing there with one hand in the air, following Damrosch's baton with absolute fidelity, beat by beat, a broad grin on his countenance. He kept it up unconsciously until the very last notes of the overture, for I hated to interrupt him; then he climbed up in my lap, still smiling but saying not a word.[23]

Unfortunately, Roger also drew attention by coughing before the next piece was over. As he developed a long siege of whooping cough, this concert was his last musical entertainment for months. It may, however, have been significant that the first orchestral music the future composer heard was Wagner and the *Pilgrims' Chorus*.

As had been the case for most of their married life, by the turn of the century the Sessionses were yet again finding it difficult to make ends meet. Their last child, John, was born on May 21, 1899, at the "Bird House." That house grew more costly every year, and they felt they had to move. The unrealistic and idealistic notion of living out their political convictions was given lip service; they could live in a tenement, as did James, or live as wage earners, such as those they championed politically. Ruth's leaving the home to work was considered impossible because of the three children. They also took into account the distress their relatives—particularly the Bishop—would feel. Neither would live with the other's relatives. When Archibald, in 1900, left his *Encyclopedia Britannica* job, the die seemed cast. The two were 40 years old and possibly felt like failures.

Ruth had been frequently bailed out by her parents, who welcomed, encouraged, and on one occasion even ordered, her to stay at Forty Acres for possibly all 13 summers during her marriage, pregnant or not. She had family resources, even if Archibald had to earn his way. Her housing solution represented the opposite of her political beliefs about the working class. She would move back to Northampton, while Archie pursued a literary career in New York. She rationalized this questionable decision as giving him a chance to succeed without the necessity of taking care of the four of them.

In spite of all the preconceived, traditional views of the essence of matrimonial responsibility, all the ordinances of social life which made a wife a dependent under the law, it was an absolutely clear conviction in my mind growing with each year of marital experience that the mother's obligation for the support of her children was as great as the father's. Her share of the work for the household might with equal propriety consist in wage earning.[24]

Sessions recalled part of the reason was that his younger brother John was very ill "and my mother, I think in order to help him out, moved up to Massachusetts."[25] Ruth did not refer to any illness in her book. She fails to mention that Archibald regularly sent her checks.

The first action Ruth took was to write to the Bishop. The next day Rev. Huntington spoke to his friend, President Seelye of Smith College, saying he wanted his grandchildren to grow up in New England "in the spirit of their forefathers."[26] Seelye had no opening at that time for Archibald to teach (one wonders how strenuously the Bishop pushed for him), but the Bishop's daughter would be welcome to come to Northampton and open a house for students. Ruth's sense of status was nevertheless wounded. When first married, she and Archibald had dined with members of the Four Hundred, the epitome of Old New York society. "And now to go back to a quiet New England town to earn support for one's children and one's self through the commercialization of

Figure 9 Ruth, Roger, and John Sessions in 1901.

everyday comfort; to sell one's household labor, and count achievement in columns of red and blue lines, in dollar-marks and dots and ciphers; was that to be the sum of achievement?"[27] She thought of the Victorian phrase concerning women who "had come down to taking boarders."

In a gloomy mood Ruth oversaw the departure from the Bird House on May 1, 1900; saying goodbye to Annie, the African-American woman who had helped out for two years, and Annie's relatives; watching the van pack up their furniture; and a last-minute search for baby John, who had suddenly disappeared. Ruth left New York and Brooklyn for good.

Sessions's earliest memories include walking with the nurse, his brother in the "perambulator" (a baby carriage). The nurse declared, "It's the twentieth century today." That memory, combined with seeing Admiral Dewey, as well as the scary masks and costumes worn by children during Thanksgiving, constituted almost all of his conscious awareness of 417 Washington Avenue. He also remembered his "fatal passion" later for a girl named Sybil Bergman, with whom he was later not allowed to walk down the kindergarten stairs holding hands; he was "shattered by that." Asked by *The New York Times* in 1971 what he remembered of living in Brooklyn, he replied he had "the faintest memory of it—suburban streets and the man who came to light the carbon lamps."[28]

Roger, three years and four months old, could not have foreseen that he would never live with both his parents again. Divorce was out of the question for Ruth, in whose family nothing of that kind had *ever* occurred in three centuries. Sessions tried to reconcile the situation. "I was very devoted to my father. They didn't really separate, but he lived in New York and she lived in Northampton. He came up and visited us from time to time. I don't know what went on, it was always a puzzle; it didn't simplify life for the children. I have come to this conclusion: I'm sure my mother was passionately in love with my father. And when they left each other, it was very different from what it was after two or three years. I think they both enjoyed their independence."[29] Precisely what Archibald's life was like after 1900 is somewhat difficult to determine. Ruth's departure, however, "didn't simplify life for the children."

However Sessions justified Ruth's behavior to himself, it is hard to see her action as anything but self-serving. She retreated into the protective arms of her Huntington family, returning to what she considered "home," as opposed to Archibald's apartments and house. She would cease to be a small fish in the big ponds of New York and Brooklyn (after 1898 a borough of New York City) and resume her birthright as a big fish in the Northampton pond. Despite the fact that she had pursued him, was "passionately in love," and had held a huge wedding, she did not take seriously her commitment to her husband. She left Archibald when he was still reeling from the deaths of both his parents and his law partner, plus his job loss. Life had become difficult for him, but *she* had an escape hatch. Worst of all, she took their three children, 12-year-old Hannah, a three-year-old, and a one-year-old, permanently away from their father who adored them. The two boys, in particular, would grow up without a daily paternal presence. What recourse did Archibald have in the face of Ruth's willfulness and the Huntington clan's financial support of her? He pleaded for the last time for Ruth to stay with him. This did not matter to Ruth; as she had always done when life got tough, she sought escape, and, as they had always done, her family enabled her to escape.

109 ELM STREET

In May 1900 Ruth Sessions took the three children to Hadley, where a resigned Archibald helped paint the blinds at Phelps House. The children took long drives in a cart harnessed to Charlie, the family horse from Englewood. Ruth taught the children to listen to bird songs and learn the names of the wildflowers. Sessions knew bird songs so well that decades later they would appear in his music, especially *When Lilacs Last in the Dooryard Bloom'd*. In old age, he could mimic the sounds of various western Massachusetts birds.

In the fall of 1900 Ruth moved across the Connecticut River to Northampton. Archibald returned to help her settle into the house that Smith President Seelye had spoken of; it would board four freshman. The house, 32 Round Hill, had a view of the eastern hills, Mount Holyoke, and Mount Pomeroy. Ruth was never far from reminders of her relatives: just below, on Elm Street, was the house that her uncle (the Bishop's older brother) had built and long occupied. In addition, Forty Acres was just six miles away. "It seems to me that I had always lived in New England; and known its ways," Ruth wrote, "it was the place of all others where I could best rear my children, and fit them for a useful life."[1] She rapidly became one of the foremost citizens of Northampton.

Ruth was taken up by Northampton society and the Smith faculty; she even attended lectures; for example, by Mary August Jordan of the English faculty, by Julia Caverno of the Greek department, Elizabeth Hanscom's Shakespeare course, one on an unspecified subject taught by Jenette Lee (the wife of Gerald Stanley Lee) who had a reputation as a writer, and Dr Irving Woods's course on biblical literature. Her boarder-students also discussed their own courses with Ruth. Extremely intelligent and intellectually curious, Ruth had herself been denied a college education, since the Bishop had not much use for educated women except in religious matters. Ruth told herself that she had finally joined the wage-earner class for whom she had worked so hard in New York and Brooklyn. Organized labor, however, was taboo in Northampton, and its friends were considered dangerous radicals.

The three children fell in line with the regulations of campus housing, learned to go to sleep among commotion, and retreated to their big room at the back of the house. Girls and their friends ran in and out of the house constantly. The students and young faculty women were somewhat in awe of Roger, who that year, when three, had supposedly taught himself to read (Ruth wrote, "we never knew how"). They would ask him to recite bits from Shakespeare, putting him up on a table from which he could declaim, "Friends, Romans, Countrymen." He remembered, however, being a late talker.

One year at Round Hill taught Ruth that caring for only four students would not be profitable. An old mansion on the broad street that bordered the college grounds was for sale. The large elms in its yard gave the street its name: Elm Street. Judge Samuel

Figure 10 109 Elm Street (Sessions House) in Northampton.

Henshaw had once owned the house, known as Henshaw House ever since. The owner in 1901 was Sidney Bridgman.

Overnight Henshaw House became the oldest house on the Smith campus. Built in 1700 (so says a stone tablet set in one of the fireplaces) by Captain Jonathan Hunt, it was the first house in Northampton outside of the stockade. The staircase was originally designed as a secret passageway used to hide from the Indians. Supposedly, during the Civil War it was part of the underground railroad, although Ruth did not relate that story (which, as an abolitionist, she certainly would have had it been true). The most popular legend is that the staircase was the site of secret trysts between Lucy, Captain Hunt's granddaughter, and John ("Gentleman Johnny") Burgoyne, the surrendering British general held captive in the house during the Revolutionary War. Lucy and Johnny's ghosts are said still to rendezvous throughout the house in search of one another. It is still today an annual Halloween tradition, begun by Ruth, for new residents to hunt for the secret staircase.

The rooms were large, low-studded, built around a huge chimney that furnished two fireplaces on each floor. Another fireplace at the back of the house accomplished the same function. The front door had a stately knocker. Ruth made several structural changes, including cutting through a narrow hall beside the chimney to connect the front of the house with the back hall. The architect found an old verandah to run along the east side of the house (similar to the one at Forty Acres). An ample backyard provided the two boys with room to play and a doghouse for Nan's collie. The family also owned a cat. Roger would spend from age four to nine in this house.

Ruth's mother had purchased the house for her; Ruth considered it a loan, but it was never repaid and her mother died in 1910. This purchase so soon after Archibald's and Ruth's separation could only mean that Ruth's parents approved of her leaving Archibald and that the separation was not, as she told herself and the children at the time, temporary.

That summer (1901) Archibald returned to approve the alterations. Having been

Figure 11 Roger Sessions at age eight.

made editor of *Ainslee's Magazine*, he was glad to enter the field of publishing and editing. He spent only a few days at "109." The boys had been placed in one of the long second-floor rooms. Ruth hired a cook, Mary Brown, who, with helpers, not only ruled the kitchen but the children as well. Mary cooked a huge meal for the arriving 14 girls—freshmen and sophomores. Sessions was to record that his first musical studies were in October 1901.

Not only did Mary have authority over the children, but so did all 14 girls:

> I was to consider them my helpers in the up-bringing of the children, with full freedom to discipline the boys, since I was not the lioness type of mother. [!] The children were kept to a hard-and-fast rule that they should never enter any room on the second floor, save their own nursery, under any pretext whatever, nor accept so much as a cracker in the way of refreshment. . . . The two were brought up on alternate petting and snubbing, which made for unselfconsciousness.[2]

Whether this plural upbringing led to unselfconsciousness or the reverse, clearly Roger and John were reared in an entirely female environment. And while they had lost much contact with their father, they now had to share their mother with at least 14 others who all called Ruth "Mother Sessions."

The once White House Inn, next door, was converted in 1977 into a residence for women. Now both the main house and the annex operate as one house unit called Sessions House, housing 52 students, in 28 single rooms and 12 doubles. It was fully renovated during the summer of 1996, and in 2001 the annex was renovated.

Sarah Chapin's judgment of Ruth rings true: "She regulated her life according to principles more closely aligned to the Bishop's dictates than to her husband's. . . . It should come as no surprise that her devotion to her children was more like her father's intensely protective and narrowly self-serving domination than her mother's steadfast inspiration."[3] Chapin disagreed with Sessions's statement in *Conversations with Roger Sessions* that her father, John, was Ruth's favorite child. "I believe otherwise. Neither Hannah nor John was Ruth's intellectual peer as Roger was. Ruth's interferences with John's management of her farm, which she gave him in 1928, were meddlesome intrusions stemming from frustration, not gestures of affectionate cooperation."[4] Sessions had said, simply and devastatingly: "She was a very jealous woman, and my younger brother was her favorite, and that really wrecked his life."[5] On other occasions Sessions stressed that his mother "ruined" John's life.

Ruth's relations with her daughter Nan were often fraught with disagreements. Ruth may have been jealous of Nan, who was close to the Bishop. They fought frequently, and not infrequently Ruth struck Nan; this behavior continued even during Nan's adult years. Roger was not spared Ruth's violent mood swings, and he developed distancing strategies to cope with his powerful and erratic mother:

> My mother and I had our differences. I didn't know how to deal with her, except I did learn gradually. She would burst out at me. When I learned to take it absolutely quietly and not fight back at all, but just keep my own counsel, then she would be shattered with remorse. Eventually, toward the end of her life, I thought, "She wants to be treated like a woman," and we got along beautifully at the end of her life [1946].[6]

Sessions tried to employ disassociation as a youngster. Whether Ruth hit Roger and John, as she did Nan, cannot be directly determined from the available evidence. When Sessions said he did "not fight back at all," it did not occur to this interviewer, who at the time did not know of Nan's abuse, to ask if he meant it literally. The experiences of dealing with his unstable mother shaped his behavior his entire life: confrontation and conflict had to be avoided at all costs—even if it meant some duplicity or equivocation, peace must reign.

Bishop Huntington died in 1904. Roger and John had been taken a week before to say goodbye to him. "A bird had sung softly as they stood by his bed in the sunset light, and Roger, then eight [*sic*; seven and a half], always remembered that Grandfather opened his eyes and smiled, saying, 'Hear that? It is the robin's vesper song.' "[7] It was Roger's first direct experience with death. Nan had formed a particularly close relationship with the Bishop; note, for example, in the 1903 family portrait that she sits away from her family and holds the Bishop's hand. Ruth may well have felt competitive with her own daughter for the Bishop's attention.

On July 11 the Sessions family gathered at Forty Acres to face the inevitable. (James and George Huntington could not be there.) Reporters from the New York and Massachusetts newspapers hung about waiting for half-hour updates on the Bishop's condition from Archibald or Ruth. The two finally were able to tell the press the plans for the funeral. The next morning's Syracuse paper read "The Best-Loved Man in Syracuse" over his obituary. Working people struck a little button with Huntington's face and the words "We mourn Bishop Huntington." Thousands of telegraph boys, factory-hands, salesmen and women, and wage-earners all over the city wore the buttons. Telegrams arrived at Forty Acres in bundles.

Ruth had, however, to face a second tragic event. The next morning, after having written a long letter to her brother George, she handed it to Archibald to mail. He wavered and said he could not send it: word had come among the many telegrams that

Figure 12 Golden wedding anniversary photo on porch at Forty Acres, September 4, 1903. Back row standing: Archibald L. Sessions, James Lincoln Huntington, Mary Lincoln Huntington, James Otis Sargent Huntington, Henry Barrett Huntington, Paul St Agnan Huntington. Front row: John A. Sessions, Ruth H. Sessions, Roger Huntington Sessions, George Putnam Huntington, Lilly St Agnan, [unknown], Catharine Sargent Huntington, Constant Huntington, Hannah Dane Sargent, Bishop Frederick Dan Huntington, Hannah Sargent Sessions, Arria Sargent Huntington.

George had died suddenly of heart failure only three hours after his father's passing; George was unaware of the Bishop's death. At this news Ruth completely crumbled. George's body was brought to Forty Acres and lay in the Long Room next to his father. Newly arrived, James provided his customary spiritual strength. The widow could not face a church funeral; so the service was held at the house. The double burial was held in the Old Hadley Cemetery. Ruth and the boys spent the next two months at Forty Acres. She and James answered the 800 letters of condolence. This double dose of death remained embedded in the impressionable seven-year-old's mind.

In his own chronology prepared late in life, Sessions wrote under 1902, "First piano lessons Mr. Edwards, organist of the Episcopal church in Northampton; later with Mr. Chase, who succeeded him; later with my mother."[8] Roger started piano lessons at five. He played a great deal of four-hand music with his mother, then a principal method of learning the major works of the musical repertory. Around 1907 and 1908 Archibald sent music from New York, including pieces by contemporary composers Debussy and Strauss.

In the autumn of 1906 Roger was sent away to boarding school. Ruth wrote that during the previous five years "his capacity had carried him beyond the age of the children in our little private school."[9] This may have been Miss Elizabeth Clarke's School at 41 Henshaw Ave.[10] (By 1906 it was no longer in business.) Like most mothers, Ruth was ambitious for her children, whom she felt, again like most mothers, were unusually gifted. Sessions partially credited this school: "I went to a small private school in Northampton when I was a small child, and when I got to boarding school I found I was ahead of my class."[11] When asked whether he thought that this was because of the school, Sessions answered equivocally,

> Well, that's the simplest explanation. I don't know at all, but I would have been, I could have been ready for Harvard when I was 13, but I waited a year and went when I was 14. . . . Which I don't think was a good idea at all. Let me say I don't think it is a good idea at all. But it was quite the fashion in those days.[12]

The conviction that the Sessions children were exceptionally bright began with Nan. She had asked to spend her last year of college preparation in Northampton, and to avoid her mother took a room at a neighbor's house, coming to 109 only for meals. Nan had spent two years at Smith College, beginning at age 16, and, probably as a result of a fight with her mother, at the last minute in September 1907 transferred to Radcliffe to join the class of 1910. With the same logic Ruth was to apply to Roger later, she saw no reason to hold Nan back, since she had obtained high ratings on examinations.

During the winter of 1909–1910 Hannah S. Huntington died. Roger, then 13, had always said he had a "grandmother fixation:" she was the last of his four grandparents to die. Arria and Molly had cared for their mother. Forty Acres had been exclusively Hannah's property, and her death meant much had to be settled there. George's five sons inherited Forty Acres and Ruth got Phelps House. Ruth's two sisters then moved into the cabin built for them on the top of a hill on Huntington Road between Amherst and Forty Acres, where we met them in the first pages of this book. The two sisters also had a share of the land, while James added his portion of the property to Ruth's for her to be able to start farming. (His vow of poverty prevented him from benefiting from his mother's will.) Her quota of livestock was five cows and two calves, and with her share of the estate she built a small house for a manager, made over the old barn to hold a larger herd, and installed a married couple to take care of the place and supply 109 Elm with chickens, eggs, and milk. As 109 Elm could not accommodate the number of students applying for admission, it needed to have a substantial addition. In 1910 Ruth paid for 16 rooms and a number of bathrooms to be added at the back, as well as a recreation hall called the Hilarium. The idea of moving back to New York to live with her husband did not seem to have crossed her mind, although now she had considerable holdings in real estate and an inheritance.

Ruth occasionally did travel to New York, where Archibald, looking handsome, would dress in evening clothes and take her to the theater, concerts, and restaurants. They play-acted being a couple. She rationalized that he had at last found his destined work and absolved herself of any possible guilt. In the same paragraph, however, she admitted not all was entirely well with the two boys: in 1911 Ruth and Archibald attended Roger's graduation at Kent—"a satisfying experience and joy to the boy himself, for both brothers felt the lack of paternal companionship, and were thankful to have their father share in any achievement."[13]

CLOYNE, KINGLSEY, AND KENT

According to Ruth, Roger's "capacity had carried him beyond the age of the children in our little private school, and we felt he could advance better among boys and men."[1] In September 1906 nine-year-old Roger was sent to his first boarding school—the Episcopal Cloyne House School in Newport, Rhode Island. This school was a brief and unsatisfactory experience for Roger. Nan's son later attended St George's, also an Episcopal school. Cloyne House did not have quite the status of St George's—at the time Cloyne was "the other one."

Oliver Mayhew Whipple Huntington and Arthur Leslie Green, acting on the suggestion of Dr Peabody of Groton, founded Cloyne House in 1896. (It would regard itself as a preparatory school for Groton.) Huntington's mother had died when he was ten, and he was reared in Cambridge by his father's sister. This sister was Mary Huntington Cooke, Ruth's relative who had married Dr Josiah P. Cooke, a professor of chemistry at Harvard. Working with his uncle at Harvard, Oliver obtained his A.B. in 1881, and was appointed assistant in chemistry and instructor in mineralogy (his field was meteorites) at Harvard. In 1886 he received his Ph.D. and A.M. and was elected a Fellow of the American Academy of Arts and Sciences.

In 1894 Oliver Huntington resigned from the Harvard faculty and spent a year in Newport, Rhode Island. He and Green went to visit schools abroad. Green reviewed schools in Germany and France and Huntington examined those in England; he lived in London for a year. When he returned to the United States in the fall of 1896, he purchased the Hunter Dunn estate, just outside Newport and near the training school for the US Navy. The ship *Constellation* was anchored nearby. Cloyne Court today is on a lovely inlet and still abuts the Navy land. Huntington opened a not-for-profit boarding school, "Cloyne House," with Green in the year of Roger's birth. They selected Newport for its climate and its proximity to both Boston and New York. The grounds had a hospital, basketball court, and indoor baseball field, a theater, a chemistry lab, and two large boathouses, which were furnished by boats and canoes that the boys themselves built. Twenty acres on the shore were designated for playing sports. The school was named after Bishop Berkeley, Lord Bishop of Cloyne. Huntington's mission for the school was to develop in the boys "good habits and character."

He and Green were the headmasters; the two also taught there. They determined their school should be based on German educational principles. Huntington and his wife, Ellen Mary Balch, ran it for a limited number of carefully selected boys; the couple had no children. Sessions considered Oliver Huntington a "weak man" but Green something of a sadist.[2]

Cloyne's first term began September 22, 1896. The school grew rapidly: six boys in the first year, 12 in the second, 20 in the third.[3] Discipline was strict—rigid rules were enforced—and each boy was expected to fulfill a daily schedule on time. This schedule included periods for five subject areas: English, arithmetic, geography, science, and arts (including music). The school started its own magazine in 1900, a monthly written by the students.[4] Dormitories were color coded by age. Roger, at nine, would have been in the Red Dormitory, for students in the lower school, ages eight to ten.

In June 1912 the daily schedule was as follows: 7:00 a.m. rising bell; 7:30 breakfast; 8:00 prayers; 8:15 to 10:00 school sessions; 10:00 to 10:30 recess; 10:30 to 12:00 school sessions; 12:00 to 12:50 make-up of unsatisfactory lessons; 1:00 to 2:00 dinner; 2:00 to 2:30 make-up of unsatisfactory lessons; 2:30 to 4:45 athletics; 4:45 dress for supper; 5:00 to 6:00 school sessions; 6:00 to 6:30 free period; 6:30 supper; 7:00 prayers; 7:30 end of study period for Red Dormitory; 8:00 Bedtime for Red Dormitory; 8:30 end of study for Blue Dormitory; 8:45 bedtime for Blue Dormitory; 9:00 end of study of White Dormitory; 9:30 p.m. bedtime for White Dormitory.[5]

Roger's piano lessons were not continued at Cloyne; the school had no piano teacher. His mother did not in any case take his interest in music seriously. His short experience at Cloyne, however, was mixed and decidedly memorable.

He played football, although a contemporary remembered, "Roger Sessions on the football field is totally eclipsed by his shin guards, trousers, padded jersey, and head-gear."[6] A member of the Aquidnecks team (versus the Narragansetts), Roger later joined the Baby Giants in opposing the Butter Balls. The Baby Giants lost, but "Roger's successful attempts to put the opposing tackle, Donald, out of the plays were loudly cheered."[7] Later Roger, along with Saunders Jones, became quarterback of the Baby Giants. The team beat the Butter Balls.

Success on the football field was paralleled by success in the classroom. Roger had received several weekly red ribbons, which students wore as a high honor that indicated good grades. The November *Cloyne Magazine* reported that "Roger Sessions has gone by leaps and bounds from the foot to first place in the school. At this rate he bids fair to have his room covered with red ribbons before June."[8]

Sessions described it

> like a school out of Dickens . . . very very much modeled on what they felt was the English type of school. And I didn't get along there at all. . . . It was run by two headmasters, one of whom was another of these [Huntington] cousins who are always popping up. He was a rather weak character. The other man was a very strong character, and a very unbalanced man who later met his end by setting fire to his own house and burning in it.[9]

Sessions went on,

> But I think the key to all I saw of Cloyne was these two rather strange men who were headmasters. The one who went crazy—the one, let's say, who was the stronger character—it seems strange to say it, but he took a violent dislike to me. I was only nine years old, somewhat naive, as you may imagine, and I made what they considered mistakes there, and was made to suffer for them, that's all.[10]

Roger did well in his studies in Latin, French, math, and English, and he was among the first three or four in the school each week to receive red ribbons.

I was extremely self-conscious, that's that main thing. I wrote a letter home in which I used the name of a school hero. My father thought it was amusing, and inadvertently told the headmaster about it. The headmaster was absolutely livid with rage. My father was there, and before he left he could see that I was upset. The headmaster had already come and attacked me for having dared to use the name of this other boy—quite innocently, I assure you. . . . I argued, I finally told my father that I was sure the headmaster would make a spectacle of me before the whole school that evening. My father said, "That's absolutely impossible, he's a gentleman and gentlemen don't behave that way. You realize that a letter is a sacred thing." Well, of course, it happened. I wrote to my father, and I got a rather equivocal public apology later on . . . You see, the school hero was a hero because of his scholarship record, and his athletic record. My athletics weren't very good, but my scholarship was excellent. I had heard another boy being referred to as "perhaps a second ____"—(I won't mention the name because it's a rather well known name, which has nothing to do with the situation)—and I wrote to my family that I was very self conscious, this was the idea, at the thought of marching up and getting this prize. I wouldn't like to be called "a second _____." Of course, there was really no danger of it at all, but after all, there again, I don't think boys of nine should be treated that way. For about a week, I didn't hear the last of it.[11]

Green publicly sneered at Roger for having said such a thing. The other boys doubtless took Roger's confidential comparison—expressed only in a letter to his father and now made public by the headmaster—as evidence of his "big head." He may also have expressed his pride in his accomplishments a little too obviously.

In the next month's *Cloyne Magazine* an alphabet of students listed "R is for Roger who stands high, by my! / He brags and he brags 'till we all wist to fly."[12] And elsewhere in the same issue he was described thus: "Roger Sessions has had to write home for hats several sizes larger since he has been wearing the red ribbon. We are glad to see Roger doing well, but to make your success almost painful to your friends by continuing to thank Heaven that you are not as they are isn't the best way to retain an admiring audience."[13] Roger was the victim of Green, but also of his father's boasting and carelessness. (He could never criticize Archibald, though.) As an adult, Sessions never bragged or indicated superiority in any way; neither, however, was he self-deprecating.

Huntington and Green fostered such treatment. Sessions thought "the headmasters were snobs, and they were trying to ingratiate themselves with certain people."[14] Nevertheless, at the time Roger was filled with notions of loyalty to the school, which made it difficult for his parents to find out what was the matter.

A more wistful side of the nine-year-old Roger is shown in a paragraph he contributed, entitled "Queer Things I Used To Think," under the heading "Small Boys' Compositions" for the December *Magazine*:

I used to think that the earth was flat and didn't move at all, but that the sun was a light that somebody put out every night. I used to think that there were ghosts, especially when my sister put on sheets and acted like one. I used to, too, think that there were such things as mermaids. I used to play with them all the time. But I soon got tired of them. Then I used to think that all masks which people put on their faces, had the power of killing somebody, because they were so odd that it seemed that they must have something to do with killing people. I used to think, too, that every time a door creaked, that it was crying because it got hurt. I used to think that kindergarten was real, school. Then I used to think when I was four years old that my father was only four, too. I used to think that my birthday was on Christmas, and that the presents were late in coming. I used to think that my mother was once a little boy. Roger Sessions.[15]

Several elements of this paragraph are interesting: first, his fear of masks from Thanksgiving 1899 on Washington Avenue. We can foresee his first acknowledged and successful piece, *The Black Maskers*, a play in which creatures in black masks put out the light and represent death. That his father would seem to be his own age at four, but his mother "once a little boy" may elicit psychological analysis. The most poignant "Queer Thing" image is of the door crying.

Simultaneous with his successes Roger experienced humiliation. He was forced to wear a yellow ribbon for misbehaving, which meant that no one was allowed to talk with him. He was also made to memorize Longfellow's *Evangeline*, "rather awful doggerel," as a punishment for some other misbehavior. When Roger cried, headmaster Green shook his fist at the boy, reminding him of the school motto, "Prompt and silent obedience is the first duty of the soldier and the schoolboy," and admonished him not to cry.

Prausnitz tells of one Cloyne incident related by Sessions in his mid-eighties:

The final calamity began with a box of cookies from home. For once, to his delight, Roger found himself the instant center of his schoolmates' attention. That evening, after lights-out, he trudged happily across to a friend's bed to share his treasure with a boisterous gathering of munching little boys. The noise soon attracted the law, and at the first sound of approaching footsteps Roger's more experienced guests disappeared magically into their own beds. Terrified, Roger dived under his friends' blanket. He was caught, of course, and taken to the headmaster. Of the oration Roger had to endure he understood only that his had been "the worst offense a boy could commit."[16]

All his long life, Sessions felt bitter about his experience at Cloyne. Something there had deeply upset his sense of himself. At Christmas break his parents recognized problems: Roger had some evidence to back up his humiliation—the *Cloyne Magazine* quotations given here. Possibly he blamed his mother for sending him to a place in which he felt terrorized. Ruth and Archibald saw their error. Although some of his troubles at Cloyne may have arisen from homesickness and humiliation, Ruth related the situation to her own "nervous terrors:" "He came home at Christmas time a bundle of nervous terrors, and we felt we must find a new school at once, where a moderate, sympathetic headmaster would handle those fears by quietly carrying confidence with him."[17] Melodramatically, Ruth wrote that she wanted to ask her son's forgiveness, and that she could never adequately make reparation for this "great blunder."

Six years later a note about Sessions in the alumni news section of the Cloyne magazine, read: "Roger Sessions is fast distinguishing himself as a musician."[18] Sessions was finishing his first year at Harvard when someone sent news of him to Cloyne House School's magazine. In December 1912 Sessions wrote to his former headmaster Father Sill, "Did I tell you that Cloyne had been after me to join the Alumni Association. Of course I would not think of such a thing. I think I shall write them pretty soon about it."[19]

Sessions related his experience there:

I went to boarding school in Newport, Rhode Island, for three months and that was *not* a good experience at all, although I think in the long run it had a very good effect, which was different from the one they wanted to produce. They wanted to produce good little boys who were ready to take their place in the very straitlaced society of that day. It's appalling.[20]

The Cloyne School did not survive. It continued until 1917 when the US entered the war. Then, since it was near the War College, the government appropriated the school together with all its property. The navy used it as a cadet school, and it was returned to the Huntingtons in much damaged condition. Dr Huntington re-opened his school; by 1921 he was still head and owner, but not well. He became seriously ill in 1922, closed the school, and died in 1924.[21]

After the calamity of Cloyne, Archibald may have prevailed (for the only time) over his wife to enroll Roger in a school not associated with the Huntingtons. Instead, he was sent, again as a boarder, to Kingsley School. Kingsley School was located in Essex Fells, New Jersey, just west of Montclair and therefore New York City. (It was also near his hero, Grover Cleveland's, birthplace.) Archibald and his sisters Adeline and Grace had more frequent access to his son. Roger's thank-you letters included drawings and paintings.

Roger attended the long-defunct Kingsley School for a year and a half, from January 1907 to June 1908. He took first-year Latin, "studying Collar & Daniel," French, arithmetic, history, and geography. The headmaster, Mr Campbell, wrote to Ruth, "So far he seems to have been getting along very nicely in his contact with the boys and with the teachers. The younger boys think he is a very smart little chap, because he is in advance of most of his own age."[22] He liked that school "very much," although discipline was similar to Cloyne's. Indeed, Kingsley was a military academy whose students wore uniforms, paraded with guns, and lived in pseudo-military barracks. The headmaster was a former field officer in the Spanish–American War. Sessions had one specific memory of Kingsley regarding his father's visits there. Archibald, always considered exceptionally good looking, was dark-complexioned like his son. Roger's Kingsley classmates called him "the Spaniard," not a compliment given the recent war, and which Roger felt as an affront to his adored father.

Unlike the unconditional love Archibald and his sisters gave Roger, Ruth seemed to place prerequisites on her love, always expecting something from the boy that to her mind constituted a well-behaved ten year old. He had written to her in 1907 to complain about the teasing over his "Spaniard" father and mentioned his stamp collection. Judgmental Ruth chastised Roger for his enthusiasm over his stamp collection; it bored

Figure 13 Kingsley School.

others. Roger's next letter tried not to mention his father or his stamps. Still he could not win Ruth's approval. She awarded his letters number grades: "9 1/2 for that letter—no, 9, for it was not very tidy or very newsy."[23] She did not want to hear about what interested him, only what she herself found interesting. She issued an ultimatum, after declaring herself "ashamed of my son's letters," that

> If you don't write me a well written letter, I shall give up writing you at all, except on Sundays. You must begin now to think of giving your mother pleasure instead of just sending notes about stamps. Don't write about stamps *at all* this time . . . Your grandfather always wrote such beautiful letters that I want you to be like him.[24]

The Bishop wrote sermons professionally; Ruth wanted her ten year old to compare favorably with an accomplished, much older, and now deceased, man. Any personal concern he expressed, such as fearing he might not be a good dancer, would engender a maternal lecture. Ruth's desire for pleasure now became a demand. Prausnitz summed up the situation aptly: "If being a nag were the hallmark of fine teaching, Ruth Sessions would have ranked at the top of the profession. It is hardly surprising that Roger learned to avoid mentioning matters of real concern to him, a skill he would practice and perfect for all time."[25]

The year and a half Roger spent at Kingsley was long enough for Ruth to overcome her self-criticism for sending him to Cloyne. She now persuaded herself that another school founded by yet another relative would be the perfect place for her son. Sessions explained,

> Then I went from [Kingsley], not because they didn't like this school but because my family, as you may have gathered, was very, very Episcopalian. My mother's older brother was a monk, one of them, and he had founded Kent School. So I left Kinsgley School and went to Kent, and stayed at Kent for three years.[26]

The choice of Kent School represented a compromise between the parents. Near the western border of Connecticut, it lay approximately half-way between New York City, where Archibald lived, and Northampton, where Ruth lived. James Huntington, the superior of the Order of the Holy Cross, and Father Frederick Sill, one of the younger members, founded Kent School. Despite the fact the Order was monastic, Kent was not a monastic school. "It was where a good Episcopalian boy should go."[27] Ruth triumphed again. Roger was taken out of the school he liked and transferred to his third school in as many years. He began the Kent School in September 1908. Ruth had written to Father Sill:

> I am very anxious for [Roger] to have a training in the Faith and a strong enough spiritual influence to touch the deepest part of his nature. He has mental gifts which will make it possible, I think, for him to grow into a useful man, but which are also dangerous because of the possibility of dilettantism which always threatens a versatile nature. He is reasonable and truthful, very studious, but also very fond of open-air games: [inclined] however to be deeply absorbed in his own pursuits and interests and needing to be kept awake to the ideals of service for others. Religiously he is very responsive, and has known for the last two years

the comfort and strength of prayer. He was eleven years old in December. . . .
His great failing is untidiness—his strong characteristic perseverance in what he
cares for, whether study or amusement.[28]

The Reverend Frederick Herbert Sill, born in 1874 and admitted to the Order of the
Holy Cross on May 3, 1902, was Kent's founder. Father James Huntington of the Order
was a large presence in Father Sill's life. (Ruth was a member of the Companionship
of the Holy Cross.) Sill had been reared on the lower West Side of Manhattan where
his father was vicar of St Chrysostom's Chapel. Sill was graduated from Columbia
University; he was the editor of the school magazine. He was also graduated from the
General Theological Seminary, after which he performed pastoral service in Baltimore.
At that time many small towns and villages did not provide a high school. Sill wanted to
found a moderately priced boarding school, charging $250 for tuition rather than the
then-usual $800–$1,000.

In October 1904 Sill had conducted a mission at St Andrew's Church in Kent. In
April 1906 Sill brought Father Huntington to visit the small town. Huntington gave
the idea of a school his complete support. Sill found a beautiful tract of land with a run-
down large house overlooked by Algo Mountain. The parents of 17 boys between 8 and
17 signed up for the school, based solely on their faith in Sill. He needed $250,000 to
begin the school, but the amount he raised was merely $300. Sill told Huntington, "If
God wants me to start a school with $300, I'll do it."[29]

Three teachers—Mssrs Haley, Hobbie, and Holsapple—were drawn to the place in
September 1906 following nothing more than Sill's personal charisma and faith. By
opening day the altar was the only structure finished. There were mattresses, but no
beds; more important, no books or desks had arrived. A nearby landowner, Joel Pratt,
watched the first day's activities and made a bet, backed by a growing pig, that "the
little monk and them boys won't last the winter." He lost the bet, and gave the school
200 pounds of pork. On the first day, Sill cooked (the cook was sick), the boys themselves waited on tables (the waiter had quit immediately after slipping on the floor), and
the boys slept on the mattresses on the floor. The faculty and Sill made out a schedule of
physical labor for the boys and a review of writing and spelling. From sheer necessity,
Kent became distinguished by simplicity of life, directness of purpose, and self-reliance.
In fact, those three phrases became its motto.

One of the first 17 boys, Anson Gardner, described the 32-year-old Sill as short and
slight with a boyish face and "stringy, straw-colored hair plastered so flat against his
forehead that it looked almost painted on. His monastic habit resembled a billowing
white nightgown, topped with a broad shoulder cowl that flapped like a hen's wings
when he flailed his arms to emphasize a point." This "odd white apparition, [was] often
referred to later as 'The Great White Tent.' "[30] Sill, thereafter known to all the boys
as "Pater," was Kent School's active headmaster for 35 years, until 1941. In 1940
Sill suffered the first of several paralyzing strokes that forced him to retire to a wheel
chair. Nothing shook his faith. He remained headmaster emeritus until his death on
July 17, 1952.

In accordance with the stated vision of the motto—"Simplicity of Life, Directness of
Purpose, and Self-Reliance"—Sill conceived of the school as "democratic." Therefore all
students participated in a daily work program, which helped cut the costs. Sill also
committed the school to educating students from "all walks of life," which in effect
meant that the tuition was based on a sliding scale; parents paid what Sill felt they could
afford. He insisted on outdoor activity every day, despite weather conditions; during the

first 15 years he coached the hockey team and introduced a cup-winning crew team to the school. While penny-pinching concerning matchsticks and much else, Sill never employed frugality when it came to the boys' welfare. Knowing that boys could have a hard time adjusting to college, he told graduates, "Telephone me, *collect*, at any hour of the day or night when you're in trouble."[31] These phone calls ran into the thousands of dollars over the years, and, as we shall see, Roger frequently relied on Pater's generosity following his graduation. For over a decade Pater had to some extent replaced Archibald as a father figure.

Sill, who was very likely gay,

> was a complicated man, of course, but he was quite a remarkable man. A friend
> of mine, whom I knew at Kent [and] who actually lives at Princeton, were
> talking about him one day and he said: "It's amazing. Father Sill was, in a way,
> everything that a headmaster theoretically ought not to be. But he was a marvel-
> ous headmaster just the same." And I think this is true. He was a marvelous man
> in dealing with boys, there's no question about it.[32]

Today, awarding four million dollars annually in financial aid, Kent has a lovely 1,500-acre campus in the same location that borders both the Housatonic River and the Appalachian Trail. In 1959 it began admitting female students, kept on a separate facility, and by 1991 plans were being carried out to integrate the two campuses. Alumni include actor Ted Danson and Secretary of State Cyrus Vance. Although run by Episcopal ministers, at Kent students of all faiths are admitted and their beliefs encouraged.

Roger's piano lessons were continued after the hiatus of Cloyne and Kingsley. His piano teacher at Kent was Mr William H. Whittingham, who had arrived there in 1907, the school's second year. Whittingham was the son of a minister and nephew of the former bishop of Maryland. He received his early education at the Newberlin Academy in western New York State. Whittingham's first job was music instructor at St Stephen's College in Annandale, New York. He later became organist and choirmaster at St Paul's Church in Baltimore; later positions as organist included those at the Church of the Redeemer in Brooklyn, St Luke's in Baltimore, and Holy Trinity in Middletown, Connecticut. Whittingham also taught courses at Kent in English, history, and English literature. Roger was punished for a remark about Sill by being banned from the piano for a time. Nevertheless he liked Kent.

Figure 14 Roger at age eleven.

Arriving at Kent in only the third year of its existence, Roger had contact with the original faculty. The school had six forms, or levels: Roger entered at the fourth form. His teachers included two of Kent's original instructors. Mr Eben R. Haley was the first master to teach at Kent. A 1904 graduate of Bowdoin College, he took a post-graduate course in French at Johns Hopkins University and taught French at Kent. Mr Theodore Hobbie prepared for college at the Newark Academy and attended Princeton University. After two years at Princeton, Sill asked Hobbie to teach mathematics. Later teachers at Kent when Roger studied there included Mr Horace E. Schiedt, who had gone to preparatory school at Chestnut Hill Academy and entered Harvard in September 1905. He majored in history and languages, received an A.B., and came to Kent in January 1910 to teach history, Latin, and chemistry. Mr Arthur E. Monroe built up the "point" system at Kent. He had attended Harvard in 1904 and came to Kent in January 1909, where he prepared students for college entrance examinations in elementary and advanced Latin and German. He began immediately preparing Roger for Harvard that spring. Monroe also coached dramatics.

Roger typed a letter to his mother about his academic progress. There is no date, but grades and honors are spelled out. It said it included a copy of an essay (likely one of two essays on Wagner, see below), which, "Although it did not win the prize, I have the satisfaction of knowing that it came in second, and that the winner was a literary genius, who everybody knew would win before the contest began." As he would do at Harvard, he reported studying for exams he had yet to take (Latin, Greek, algebra, English, French, plane geometry). In addition he gave his previous examination marks: Cicero 78, Xenophon 85, Geometry 100, Alegbra 100, English (A) 70, English (B) 70, French 79. And "I won the prize for the head of the fifth form in scholarship, a beautiful copy of Lamb's Tales from Shakespeare." Roger asked Ruth to "tell Daddy that I need $8 for my journey home together with my debt to the school."[33]

Roger's classmates included Robert Hillyer, Frederik van den Arend (known as Van), Azel (known as Junior) Hatch, and Cuthbert Wright. Van entered in September 1909 and was active on the football team (captain twice), on the *Quarterly* Board, in dramatics, and served as secretary of the class of 1913 and class president in both 1912 and 1913. These four students would attend Harvard or Yale and thus reappear in Sessions's life.

Almost Roger's first experience at Kent was to have his appendix removed. Although his mother gave permission for Roger to return to the football field, Archibald had consulted with the doctor who said that much more time, ten or eleven weeks, was needed for the abdominal wall to become "reconstructed and until that process is completed there would always be danger of a permanent weakening which might bring on hernia."[34] Indeed, Roger felt unsteady about swimming for almost two years afterwards; only by July 31, 1910, when he wrote to Sill that he had "gotten back my confidence in the water, which I lost completely on account of my operation."[35]

Enclosing a check for Roger's train fare home at Christmas, Ruth wrote to Sill:

> [Roger] is a queer sort of child, apparently so unrealizing at times and so self-absorbed. I think it is partly because he doesn't know how to *give out*, + is naturally rather over-inquisitive, and it will be hard to balance those traits to make him understand how to use his gifts. They are those of one of his forerunners who led a selfish life, without faith or energy, and my prayer is that Roger may have the early training and principle to use his gifts instead of storing them away in a napkin of reserves and self-interest.[36]

Although we do not have a record of Roger's confirmation in the church, Ruth alluded to his preparation for the sacrament in a letter (February 20, 1910) to Sill about John's upcoming confirmation. We would assume it took place in any case: all members of the Huntington family would have been confirmed in the Episcopalian church.

Roger wrote two papers while at Kent that survive. One, "Wagner as a Composer," was three single-spaced pages; the other, "The Music of Wagner's 'The Nibelung's Ring,' " occupies six single-space pages with narrow margins. Such an interest in opera was understandable in one who was already composing one himself: *Lancelot and Elaine*. Roger began the *Ring* paper by placing the reader in Bayreuth for the performance and, in numbered paragraphs, took him act-by-act through the entire cycle. Describing the third act of *Siegfried*, the approximately 13-year-old Roger wrote,

> If Bellini had composed the music to the *Siegfried* poem, Erda would probably have declared the fall of the gods in a suave, placid, flowing aria, which, of course, would be utterly inconsistent with the idea of a music-drama. This scene, though, is perhaps only for musical epicures; the real beauty of the act finds itself in Bruennhilde's glorious greeting to the world, and to her lover, amid brilliant arpeggiation on the harps and violins. I always preferred the *Siegfried* love duo to that of *Tristan and Isolde:* the Tristan love music always seemed to me to border on sensuality; that is to say, it tends to excite rather than to inspire one, while we are truly inspired by the *Siegfried* duo. Take, besides the above example, the two motives which appear in the *Siegfried Idyll—Peace*, and *Siegfried, Treasure of the World*. Is there anything in the whole range of music more beautiful than these two in their calm, peaceful inspiration? They may be transported to the concert hall, and still contain that unsurpassable beauty which impregnates them in the music-drama. And what a wonderful climax of ecstasy is the very final scene, where Bruennhilde throws herself rapturously into the open arms of Siegfried, the music intensifying the action. Right here begins the decline of evil and the victory of love which, as we shall see later, is the essence of this marvelous tragedy. The gods heroically await their doom, with the remains of the world ash tree piled high around their royal abode.[37]

Writing on black-bordered paper because of the death of her mother, Ruth inquired of Sill about John's coming to Kent the following year and the possibility of his continuing his violin lessons there. Nevertheless, she said she wrote to Roger "not to stick so closely to the piano this Spring. I want him to be out as much as possible."[38] Shortly afterward, Sill's own father died, and Roger wrote a proper letter of condolence.[39] Roger's grades were disappointing; he did not pass French, which he would take again in 1910–1911.

Ruth viewed Roger's low marks as the result of his spending too much time on music. She wrote to Sill,

> He has promised to try + do better, and from what Mr. Haley told me, I fancy the masters realize how much extra brain-matter is expended on his music these days. I do not feel sure that that is going to be his eventual choice by any means, for a life work; but it must be put to the test of hard labor, I think, + then we shall know just how far it is likely to carry him.[40]

R. D. Perry (Kent class of 1910) recalled that Roger was "a peculiar little genius, but an expert piano player even at that young age."[41]

A few months later, after Roger had escaped an infectious disease going around Kent, Ruth wrote from Syracuse about "a very large and virulent abscess in [Roger's] ear, involving the martial cells, and threatening dire results of course: but to our great thanksgiving it has subsided healthily, and he is to sit up today, having had a temperature for thirty-six hours. He has been very patient under so much suffering, and amuses himself with his music now, and reading."[42] He would be delayed returning to school for the second semester because of this; in fact, he could not even be moved from Syracuse to Northampton. Any musician, however, would be alarmed at the medical treatment both given and proposed:

> The Dr thought it best for him to have his ear blown out again twice more this week . . . for his nose and throat are filled up and will have to be operated upon at Easter as they are apparently the cause of the abscess in the ear. He has promised me to be out of doors as much as possible, and is to *do no work on music* for the rest of the term. He is at a pretty nervous age, and we feel that he ought to spend what nerve-force he has into his School-work only.[43]

Both solutions—blowing out the ear, and staying away from music—seem particularly drastic.

Nevertheless, Ruth's prescription became even more dire once Roger returned to school. He faced the dreaded tonsillectomy at Easter break 1911: "If [before Easter] he should have any ear-ache, the orders are that the ear-drum should be pierced at once, without waiting for any further developments, and I should want to be sent for and to have the best specialist that could be found. . . . He is still decidedly 'off his nerve.' "[44]

Roger spent three years at Kent, although considering the appendectomy, the ear infection, and tonsillectomy, he missed a fair amount of school. Despite his writing skills, his grades were not such that would indicate a genius level of intellectual accomplishment. Nevertheless, perhaps because Nan had entered college early and had taken and passed the Harvard examinations to enter Radcliffe, Ruth surmised that Roger could do the same and enter at an even younger age than Hannah had in going to Smith—"not a good idea at all," Sessions later said. We have reason to believe that Archibald hesitated to send Roger to Harvard, his alma mater, at the age of 14. Indeed, Archibald already had reservations about Kent as the proper place for Roger to study music. He wrote of his "anxiety about instruction for him in his music" at the beginning of the 1910–1911 year. Ruth, the more dominant personality, would prevail.

Roger had been composing since the summer of 1909, but waited until the fall of 1910 to announce to his parents he wanted to be a composer. Asked when the first time he thought about being a composer, Sessions remembered a scene from Kent:

> It was some time when I was at Kent, because I remember coming off the football field one afternoon in November, to meet my parents, who'd come up to visit me over the weekend, and telling them that I was going to be a composer. I remember the scene. I think they sort of hesitated, but accepted the situation, because they always were very very nice about it.[45]

Not always. Archibald was proud that his son wanted to enter the creative world, but Ruth had serious reservations about Roger pursuing music professionally, and those reservations would persist.

HARVARD

The trouble with having a father, uncles, and grandfather who went to Harvard is that you were expected to go there, too. We have no evidence of any discussion of alternatives. The real debate between Archibald and Ruth was whether Roger had the makings of a composer (who should nevertheless go to Harvard). They also disagreed about *when* to send him to college.

When Roger announced to his parents that he wanted to be a composer, in the fall of 1910, his mother considered "the fact that I loved music . . . a picturesque, peculiar trait."[1] Archibald, on the other hand, took steps to determine whether such a career was feasible. That fall he asked the opinion of at least two composers about the prospects of his 13-year-old son; he brought some of the boy's music, *Lancelot and Elaine* included. Engelbert Humperdinck, in New York for the Metropolitan Opera premiere of his *Koenigskinder*, was consulted; he gave a positive response. Puccini was also asked: his *La Fanciulla del West* was being presented there. Much later, Luigi Dallapiccola told Sessions that Puccini had paced the floor all night over advice to some young composer and finally had decided he could not make a decision of that importance for someone else. He was probably referring to Sessions, since that was precisely what Puccini told Archibald. Nevertheless, Archibald consistently supported his son in his musical endeavors. Ruth hoped music was a passing stage—like his stamp collection—that he would outgrow.

Lancelot and Elaine's manuscript is in the Princeton Rare Books Library.[2] There two dates are given, 1909 and 1911; we can assume it took more than a year to compose around the time the composer was 13. At 129 pages, it is an ambitious opera in three acts and four scenes, fully orchestrated in ink for the first 75 pages; from then on written as a piano–vocal score, also in ink. The voice parts are completely established for the whole opera. The plot is drawn from Tennyson's *Idylls of the King*. Heavily influenced by Wagner's *Tannhäuser* prelude (which, according to Ruth, was the first orchestral work Roger ever heard), in *Lancelot and Elaine*, as in the Pilgrims' Chorus, one hears Wagner's trademark opening perfect fourth down followed by a repeated dotted-note figure. The sense of scale is Wagnerian. For a 13-year-old, a remarkable level of harmonic and contrapuntal technique is found here. Roger had apparently already taught himself chromatic harmony. He shows a firm grasp of leitmotivic transformation and large-scale continuity. The vocal lines are idiomatically composed and challenging to sing. The famous "long line" of Sessions, already present, can here be directly traced to Wagner's "endless melody." Only the occasional clumsiness and incompleteness of the orchestration reveal the composer's inexperience. The score shows Roger fully engaged in the most advanced folk-saga music dramas of his time, and with the technique to express his ideas at an unusually young age.

Sessions later recalled his first major piece from a more professional point of view.

> There were some rather nice little things in my *Lancelot and Elaine* which I wrote as a child and which I still remember with a certain, well, nostalgia, if you like. My mother, in her book, makes it much too complicated. The Guinevere melody has a resemblance to a motive in *Die Meistersinger*. And it wasn't well written, because I didn't know much about counterpoint. She doesn't sing the melody; it's in the accompaniment.[3]

The grandson of Bishop Huntington had no chance to pursue a purely professional conservatory path. The irony was that only twice during Sessions's long teaching career, both at conservatories, at the Cleveland Institute of Music and at The Juilliard School, did he truly feel comfortable in his milieu. He never considered academia—Smith, Princeton, the University of California—places where he really belonged. From Harvard he wrote to his mother, "[My fellow students] seem to regard [music] as merely a pastime, while the real emotion in it does not appeal to them."[4] He later said of the university, "We were taught to learn the 'rules.' We were not taught or made to feel that there was much more to it besides learning the rules—of course, you even learn the rules in order to disobey them effectively afterwards!"[5] Sessions noted the fact that none of his classmates at Harvard became professional musicians.

Despite the prevailing attitude that composers must study in Europe—or better still, be Europeans—music conservatories did exist in the United States that could have served a young composer's needs: the Oberlin Conservatory of Music (founded 1865); the Cincinnati Conservatory of Music and the New England Conservatory of Music in Boston (both founded 1867); and the Peabody Conservatory in Baltimore. Close to Archibald's home in New York were numerous conservatories. The elder Sessions, who had sung in Theodore Thomas's chorus, must have been aware of these music schools; indeed, he knew the Damrosches. The Institute of Musical Art (IMA), founded in 1905 by Frank Damrosch and James Loeb, was already attaining a high reputation. The IMA offered a thorough training in all subjects of music and languages, attracted some of the best teacher–performers of the day, and was structured in such a way, because of Loeb's generosity, that payment for lessons covered all courses as well. Among the faculty were the entire Kneisel Quartet, critic/authors Henry E. Krehbiel and William J. Henderson, numerous famous singers and pianists, and composition and theory teacher Percy Goetschius.

The American Goetschius had spent 17 years teaching in Germany. He came to the IMA in 1905 to head the theory department. Highly conservative, "Daddy" Goetschius was nevertheless a real influence on composition graduates before 1910, Leo Ornstein and Wallingford Riegger, as well as on later students such as Theodore Chanler and Richard Rodgers. Sessions would own a copy of Goetschius's book.[6] The IMA later became The Juilliard School.[7] There was, however, no hope of Roger attending it.

The year Roger went to Harvard, 1911, Stravinsky composed *Petrouchka* and Mahler died. In order to enter Harvard certain examinations, not at all similar to the IMA exams, had to be passed. Although President Lowell's New Plan began in 1911, Roger was one of 593 of his class of 739 who took the old point-system exams.[8] The required four exams, to be taken in either June or September, were: a) English, b) Latin, or French or German, c) Mathematics, Physics, or Chemistry, and d) any one of the following not duplicating one of the above: Greek, French, German, History, Mathematics, Physics, and Chemistry. A successful applicant must earn 26 points to enter.

Twelve-year-old Roger had begun a three-year process to prepare to attend in June 1909 when he took the Harvard entrance exams in Elementary Greek and Latin (he failed), French (passed with a B; 2 points), and History (D minus; 2 points). The next June, in 1910, he retook the Greek (D; 4 points) and Latin (B; 4 points), Elementary Algebra (B; 2 points), and Plane Geometry (C; 2 points). What remained in the spring of 1911 was to pass English (4 points), receive a C in Elementary Physics (2 points), and pass both Advanced Greek (2 points) and Advanced Latin (2 points). He failed Advanced French, however.

Before Roger went to Harvard, he had met Arnold Dolmetsch, the English music antiquarian. Dolmetsch advised the young composer not to bother with harmony but rather to study counterpoint. Harvard, however, had a harmony prerequisite for counterpoint, and Roger took the six-week harmony course with George C. Vieh, a pianist and pupil of Bruckner, in order to enter Harvard's counterpoint classes. He received a B in his Harmony exam (no points, but admitted to music). By June 1911 Roger had acquired the 26 points necessary—18 prescribed and 8 elective—to enter Harvard.

The percentage of those applying to those admitted was high: in 1910, 71.9 percent of applicants entered the College. The enrollment at Harvard College in 1911 was 2,262 students. Sessions was one of a freshman class of 739, of whom 173 had dropped out by the end of the year.[9] This class numbered 496 graduates in 1915. The department of music had similarly mushroomed in those years.

By 1910 most of the chief academic figures from the post-Civil War period had died or retired, and younger educators came to the fore. In 1909 Abbott Lawrence Lowell became the new President of Harvard. One history of Harvard calls the pre-War years "The Golden Years."[10] Those lively years included students' political involvement in progressive issues of the day, such as Henry George's Single Tax and women's suffrage.

According to a history of the music department written by one of Sessions's teachers, music at Harvard during its first 175 years had existed in the school "purely as an aspect of religion, and a religion of a type that laid less stress on music than any cult in history."[11] This changed with the advent of John Knowles Paine (1839–1906), who molded Harvard's music department. A professor of music from 1875 to 1903, he had persuaded the administration to make music a major course of study. The requirements, even the course numbers, were all Paine's doing, and those went into effect in 1908. They requirements fell under two large headings: first, five courses in music, which included harmony, counterpoint, canon and fugue, free composition, plus a music elective, in addition to three language courses–German, French, and Italian. This would total eight courses that had to be completed while also complying with Harvard College's own required three-course groupings. The second requirement for an A.B. was "one or more original compositions in large form." This requirement appears not to have been enforced. No record of a thesis piece by Sessions exists—nor are found compositions by such predecessors as: Frederick S. Converse (class of 1893), Edward Burlingame Hill (1894), Daniel Gregory Mason (1895), John Alden Carpenter (1897), Archibald Davison (1906), Edward Ballantine (1907), Philip Greeley Clapp (1911), and Chalmers Clifton (1912). There is evidence that Sessions began a symphonic work in 1911–1912 and abandoned it.[12]

By 1911 the music faculty had solidified into a group of three, who would remain as a triumvirate at the helm of the department for several decades. First was Edward Burlingame Hill (1872–1960), the son of Henry Hill, himself the son of former Harvard President Thomas Hill. A student of John Knowles Paine, George Chadwick and Charles-Marie Widor, Hill had joined the Harvard faculty in 1908 and would teach until 1940. After his death in 1960 the faculty wrote of him:

Ned Hill (as he was called by his friends) was a person of extraordinary modesty, even diffidence, although he was delightfully communicative in conversation and had a delectable wit and an unfailing personal charm. Courteous in the extreme to his friends and colleagues, he was extraordinarily courteous to students. To elect one of his course was to be instructed not only in music but also in deportment.[13]

Sessions wrote to "My darling mother" that "Mr Hill can't stand anything except modern music, and has practically said so in so many words that good music should be like ragtime, no piece living more than fifteen years at most."[14] Hill, Roger's teacher, would become Roger's staunchest supporter and a behavioral role model.

Walter Spalding (1865–1962, class of 1887) had graduated with a joint concentration in Greek, Latin, German, and Music, and received an A.M. The handsome, dark-haired, long-mustached Spalding began teaching at Harvard in 1895 and continued until 1932. He was responsible for persuading James Loeb (class of 1888) to donate money for the new music building. Spalding wrote the first history of the music department. In the same letter to his mother describing Hill, Roger wrote: "Mr Spalding can never say anything without trying to be funny." In 1915 Roger's friend George Bartlett wrote of Spalding, "He is so damned foolish in the classroom that it is hard to take him seriously."[15]

Third of the triumvirate was Archibald Davison (1883–1961; class of 1906), a younger, handsome, blond organist and choirmaster who became a member of the music department in 1910 where he continued until 1954. One of Davison's first acts was to abolish the boy's choir and establish a men's chorus, new to Harvard in 1911. A student-run Glee Club of about 40 singers sought Davison's advice. Davison replaced Hill as the advisor for the *Harvard Musical Review*. Roger took all of his music courses from Hill, Spalding, and Davison.

Other teachers on the faculty, such as William Allan Nielson, a professor of English, with his dark mustache and long goatee, were known to the music students. At Harvard, Roger could not escape his distant relatives. Eluard Vermilye Huntington, Ph.D., was an assistant professor of mathematics. Except for Kingsley, every school Roger had attended had a Huntington as headmaster, founder, or professor. In an era when three names were commonly used, life might have been a little easier if he had known about and retained his original middle name, Pitkin.

Ruth recollected, "Roger entered Harvard in the fall of 1911: at fourteen he was large and strong, with the appearance of a sixteen-year-old. But he was mortally afraid of being recognized for the youngster he really was, and had a nervous terror of publicity."[16] Roger had cause: he was between four and eight years younger than all the other undergraduates.

Roger, who had attended three boarding schools in the past five years, now entered a fourth, Harvard College. He lived for the first two years in Cambridge, first with his sister at the brand-new apartment house 41 Hawthorn Street run by Mrs Cady. One of four addresses at a multi-unit building, each contained nine modest apartments with bay windows on its three floors. "When I got there it wasn't quite finished and we stayed at the boarding house next door."[17] Nan and Roger had an elderly maid to look after them.

Not only was Roger's own housing being built, but also during his time at Harvard (1911–1915) the university itself was undergoing a construction spree. Numerous buildings all over the campus were being erected. The most important was Widener Library, dedicated the afternoon of June 24, 1915, the day Roger's graduating class received their degrees. During the building boom the 1913 Gore Hall was erected, and in 1914 the Music Building also rose. An anonymous gift from alumnus and IMA founder James Loeb, the Music Building reflected Loeb's generosity, which was initiated by his memory of his own music study at a Harvard (he was a cellist in the Pierian Sodality) without the benefit of a building of its own.[18] In the architectural design, space was allotted for the *Harvard Musical Review*. The concert hall upstairs was named after John Knowles Paine. (One idea had been to name the entire building after Paine.) Paine Hall's acoustician was Wallace Sabine, the acoustician for the 1900 Boston Symphony Orchestra hall. The music building was ready for use in the fall of 1914.

Indeed, Boston itself had undergone a recent binge of building concert halls and an opera house. In 1900 the Boston Symphony Orchestra moved into Symphony Hall, still considered one of the best halls acoustically in the US. In 1904 New England Conservatory built the marvelous Jordan Hall a block away, considered especially suitable for chamber music. And in 1909 Jordan's son, Eben D. Jordan Jr, built and supported the 2,700-seat Boston Opera Company at 349–53 Huntington Avenue. Edmund M. Wheelwright and Sabine designed the Boston Opera Company. The Company's first season was 1909, but its costly spring 1914 season resulted in bankruptcy.[19] All three halls were within a few blocks of each other on Huntington Avenue, named in 1868 after Ralph Huntington (a relative of Frederic Dan).

In addition, train tracks were laid so that in the summer of 1912 one could travel in eight minutes, via a tunnel under Beacon Hill, on the "Cambridge Main Line" (later called the Red Line) to Boston's "Park Street Under." Roger and his friends could catch the Huntington Avenue train at Park Street Under to the Symphony and the Opera House. The Boston lines are part of the oldest subway system in the US. The more direct route to the Boston Symphony from Cambridge, however, was taking the trolley along Massachusetts Avenue straight across the Charles River right to the Symphony. Roger subscribed to the Symphony and took the trolley to get there; he and his friends Frederik van den Arend and George Bartlett often walked home. Each year since its inception, the BSO had given nine concerts in Sanders Theater at Harvard. These were not free, but talented students were appointed as ushers, and part of the hall was reserved for Harvard students for 25 cents.

The conductor of the Boston Symphony was German-born Karl Muck, whom Ruth had seen in Leipzig. He had obtained a Ph.D. in classical philology, never having completed a course in conducting. In 1892 he became Kapellmeister in Berlin and in 1908 general music director there, under the Kaiser. He was especially known for his conducting of Wagner, including three decades of *Parsifal* at Bayreuth. In his day he was considered the greatest conductor of Wagner's works, and also unchallenged as a Bruckner conductor. His conducting traits included an unerring ear, enforcing strict orchestral training, and fidelity to the score. The Boston Symphony Orchestra rose to previously unachieved excellence under his baton. A leading critic of the time, Philip Hale, wrote in the *Boston Herald*:

> For the Boston Symphony Orchestra is not merely one that contains certain accomplished virtuosos; the orchestra is a virtuoso. It is an instrument that, having been brought to a state of perfect mechanism by Dr Muck, responds to his imaginative and poetic wishes. He stands there calm, undemonstrative, graceful, elegant, aristocratic; a man of singularly commanding and magnetic personality even in repose. The orchestra is his speech, the expression of the composer's music as it appeals to the conductor's brain, heart, and soul.[20]

Roger did not feel that music courses at Harvard were directed toward students who planned to become serious musicians. "Few people knew what a really good music education involved."[21] His musical education gained more from his regular attendance at Boston Symphony Orchestra concerts than from class work. Roger retained the sound of this orchestra as his model—its principal oboist, Georges Longy, produced the ideal oboe sound for Roger, who played oboe for a year in the Pierian Sodality. The Boston Symphony played almost every week—or every other week—starting in October two concerts at Symphony Hall, one on Friday at 2:30 p.m. and one on Saturday at 8:00 p.m. The BSO's frequent performances of Wagner, under Karl Muck, also influenced the young composer. On one set of concerts, May 3 and 4, 1912, Muck programmed Wagner's Prelude to *Tristan und Isolde*, the Funeral music from *Die Götterdämmerung*, the Prelude to *Lohengrin*, and the overture to *Tännhauser*. Roger had an extremely good musical memory; he learned music by heart very easily.

He heard Sibelius's Fourth Symphony there and was impressed.[22] A glance through the Boston Symphony's repertory during the period of Roger's attendance shows the young composer hearing such soloists as Rudolf Ganz, Harold Bauer, Epfrem Zimbalist, Alwin Schroeder, Josef Hofmann, and many others. It was not the soloists who interested him, however—he rarely mentioned them—it was the music itself. For example, he heard Hugo Wolf's Songs on February 16 and 17, 1912, "Der Freund," "Verborgenheit," "Er ists;" Strauss's *Sinfonia Domestica* on March 15 and 16, 1912; and the first performance of the dance from Strauss's *Salome* April 26 and 27, 1912 (those concerts included a performance of the Funeral March from Beethoven's Third Symphony "in Memoriam April 14, 1912," the sinking of the *Titanic*).

Sessions thought the Symphony "an absolutely fantastically wonderful orchestra . . . when I heard other orchestras, I never felt they could compare with it."[23] He attempted to describe how Muck conducted Wagner:

> It was much less neurotic than it is nowadays [in 1962]. I mean, he wasn't afraid of slow tempi. . . . When I speak of the slow tempi, I was thinking of the "Parsifal" prelude. It was slow, but it was alive, it was just quivering all the time. The [*Tristan*] "Liebestod" was very, very calm, but tremendous. Well, it was the kind of performance that is I think almost the highest achievement of a performing artist.[24]

He heard Muck play the first performance he had heard of Schönberg's Five Pieces for Orchestra, December 18 and 19, 1914.[25] Sessions already knew two works by Schönberg—the Three Piano Pieces, Opus 11, which he bought in 1912 and played himself, and the String Quartet Opus 7, which he also played at the piano. "A lot of it sounded still extremely strange, stranger than anything else has ever sounded since then."[26] Between 1907 and 1918 the BSO also performed Harvard graduates' work. Under Muck from 1906 and 1908 they played Paine and Converse twice. Under Max Fiedler (1908–1912) they played Philip G. Clapp, Arthur Foote, and Frederick Converse each twice. With Muck back at the helm from 1912 to 1918, the BSO played Eduard Ballantine twice, Clapp twice, Carpenter three times, Converse three times, Hill, and Davison. Too shy to go backstage to congratulate Karl Muck, Roger never met hid idol.

Roger occasionally traveled from Boston to hear the Metropolitan Opera in New York, but he heard *Tristan, Don Giovanni* (the Metropolitan did not do Mozart in those days), and *Die Meistersinger* for the first time in Boston at the Boston Opera Company. (His mother had taken him to *Meistersinger* before he went to Harvard, when Toscanini conducted.) The Boston Opera Company, originally under Felix Weingartner, also played *Pelléas, Don Pasquale, L'Elisir d'Amore, Lakmé*, Charpentier's *Louise*, Wolf-Ferrari's *Jewels of the Madonna*, Aubert's *Le Forêt Bleue*, Fevier's *Monna Vanna*, Montemezzi's *L'Amore dei Tre Re, Otello, Aïda*, and *Carmen*.

The allure of Boston's Symphony and Opera Company were too much of a draw for Roger, who would rather hear music live than go to classes. "I spent a lot of my father's money going to concerts and buying scores and all that sort of thing. I heard the Boston Symphony every week—sometimes two or three times a week—and I went to many other concerts."[27]

Roger wrote home to "My darling mother" often about the music he had heard and seen. He had bought some of Schönberg's piano music.

> It is very interesting and may be really worth something; it is, however, much easier to make music of perpetual dissonance than really euphonious—at least so it seems to me. His "music," however, is not without effect on the hearer—it has a distinctly depressing effect upon the hearer: it reminds me of a picture of a "portrait bust" I saw in the *Literary Digest*—a triangular affair with terribly large eyes. If art was ever decadent, it was here. I think that Schoenberg's system of harmony might however be employed sometimes, say, in the course of a long piece, with wonderful effect; but a perpetual discord seems to be too much of a good thing. . . . Can't you and I go over some modern music this summer. You see, you have not had the opportunity to become acquainted with the works of Debussy or Strauss as I have. And my mind has changed in regard to Schoenberg, too. I think that *perhaps* he has discovered a new medium of beauty, and that just as Debussy which seemed so complicated some years ago sounds as child's play today, Schoenberg may sound beautiful in a few years. Strauss, moreover, has in his opera, *Elektra*, made marvelous use of dissonance, yet the composer says that he never writes what to him sounds disagreeably dissonant or cacophonous. Although *Elektra* was denounced by the critics when produced in America, it is certainly one of the most inspiriting things written since Wagner; and the public showed their appreciation of it . . . I don't want to say, as I once did, that Schönberg is crazy, mad, etc. But his dissonances do not seem nearly so bad as Wagner's and Strauss's did when I first heard them. They certainly sounded no worse to the audience than Wagner first did to his audiences.[28]

When Roger entered Harvard, *Elektra* was Strauss's most recent work.

Having just heard the performance at the BSO of Schönberg's Five Pieces, op. 16, Roger sent his mother an example from the third movement, *Farben*:

> To me it suggested a gray, misty horizon on the ocean. It is founded on this chord [he wrote out the chord], which is modified with constantly changed in precise color [*sic*], but it always remains greyish in suggestion. But this does not give a complete impression. It must be heard. I will bring home the score, and show it to you.[29]

In the summer of 1915 Roger was reading Schönberg's *Harmonielehre* and considered writing an article for the *Harvard Musical Review* about it.[30]

At the end of their freshman year, students were presented with a Freshman Red Book, something like a year book with photographs of each of the teams and clubs. The

Red Book gives a fair example of the emphasis that Harvard placed on sports. Freshman teams were constituted for: football, baseball, track, cross-country, relay, crew, hockey, soccer, Lacrosse, tennis, golf, gun club, and swimming. There was a German club, a French club, and four musical clubs (glee, quartet, banjo, and mandolin). Roger belonged to none of these.

Finally, at the beginning of his sophomore year, Roger got badly needed glasses, and could see clearly. By December 1912, in his sophomore year, he had joined the Musical Club and was elected to the Pierian Sodality, the social organization that ran and played in the orchestra. He was nominated November 18, 1912, and elected at the December 2nd meeting, as an oboist in the orchestra. (Both references in the Sodality's minutes refer to him as class of 1916; perhaps he was trying to pass as slightly older.) The Sodality, the forerunner to the Harvard–Radcliffe Orchestra founded at the beginning of the nineteenth century, gave an annual concert at Sanders Theater and 8 to 12 other concerts per season. Annual dues were $10 and the initiation fee was $5.

One of the four questions the freshman debating team debated was, "Should Mrs Pankurst have been allowed to use a college hall?"[31] The Pankurst question was of immediate importance. Emmeline Pankurst, the British suffragette, made a short visit in 1911 to the United States between serving jail terms. She accepted an invitation from Harvard's Men's League for Women's Suffrage, of which Roger claimed membership in his senior class album, to speak in Sanders Theater. The University—that is, President Lowell—refused the use of the hall, and the Men's League hired Brattle Hall for her to speak. Samuel A. Eliot, Jr, a member of the Men's League and later director of *The Black Maskers*, wrote of their protest of Lowell's decision. The speaker was so ladylike, however, that the huge crowd was a trifle disappointed that she did not raise the rafters on the issue of the vote. Later in 1914 the Men's League marched in a suffrage parade in Boston. There is no way to know whether Roger participated in this parade, but it would have been likely, given his membership in the League and that both his mother and his sister were participating in similar parades in western Massachusetts. In 1919 Ruth would march up Beacon Hill in Boston to push for the Nineteenth Amendment's passage in the Senate. Ruth, "bred in the stronghold of suffrage [in Syracuse], and closely associated with its promulgators . . . had taken it as much for granted as [her] very religion."[32] Arria Huntington was an active campaigner, and Susan B. Anthony had visited the Huntington home. Hannah had already met Pankurst in 1910 in England.

The Progressive Era was at its height despite the Harvard administration, and some—but not many—agitated, both politically and socially, to include women and Radcliffe students at Harvard. John Reed, class of 1910, was perhaps the best-known leftist activist from Harvard of the time. In 1913 both the Sixteenth and the Seventeenth amendments to the Constitution were ratified.

Despite Roger's intellectual ability to pass the examinations and otherwise fulfill the requirements for entering Harvard, he must have felt somewhat strange in an environment where the thousands of fellow students were so much older than he. "So far I have succeeded in keeping my age fairly secret," he wrote Pater (Father Sill).[33] He remembered four "abnormally young students at Harvard at the time."[34] The youngest was William James Sidis, who had qualified to enter at nine, but had to wait until he was eleven, in 1910. Sidis was a mathematical genius, had a stratospheric IQ, and knew six languages. His father, a Harvard graduate, was an early psychotherapist. Sidis's career as an adult, as may be suspected, did not turn out well. He tried to avoid the press, and in 1924 a newspaper found him working a $23-a-week clerk job as a calculator operator. He wrote a book on collecting streetcar transfers, his hobby. Sessions remembered that

Sidis "broke down completely, later, and committed suicide finally [at 46]. You see, his father was a psychologist, and his father actually, so to speak, trained him to be precocious. Absolutely ghastly thing to do. I think that Norbert Weiner's father also [did the same]."[35] Sessions knew Weiner's father, head of the Slavic Language Club at Harvard and a "very very remarkable man." The younger Weiner, who received a Ph.D. in 1913, was the founder of cybernetics.[36] Roger did not know Adolph Berle personally, who became an economist and government advisor, but knew Berle was in the school. A fourth prodigy, Cedric Houghton, died while in college, possibly a suicide. "A friend of my father's has put Wiener on my track to form a club of young students, which of course, I have no idea of doing, as I do not want to be classified with the 'grinds' of the college," Roger wrote at the time.[37]

Three of Roger's contemporaries became famous as writers: E. E. Cummings (1915), Robert Hillyer (1917), and John dos Passos (1916). They published regularly in *The Harvard Monthly* to which Roger also contributed.

In the boarding house that Roger and Nan shared in 1911 (before 41 Hawthorn was completed) lived Mrs Wilmerding, whom Sessions remembered as the sister-in-law of Theodore Thomas. Mrs Wilmerding asked to speak seriously with Roger about his future. He brought his compositions, but she did not want to discuss the music at all, sure that he was talented because everyone had said so. She urged him "from the bottom of [her] heart to give up all thought of being a composer, because an American can't be a composer."[38] He should become a conductor. Roger concluded that she was not as sophisticated as the furs and feathers had first made her seem. She felt that only being born and reared in Europe could produce a composer—America could not. Sessions thought he may have reacted internally, "I'm jolly well going to be the first, then." She continued, "You'll go to Europe, you'll see it, and you will always realize that you don't really belong to it."[39] Her advice was to play the oboe or the trombone and get an orchestra job; the conductor would somehow notice that he knew a lot about music and one day would be ill and ask him to take the rehearsal over, and his future would be made possible in that way. (Perhaps that was Thomas's route to fame.) Her general attitude, unfortunately, was extremely common at that time. "I never seriously thought of not being [a composer]. It was absolutely what I had to be, and always, so far as I can remember, I took it for granted that I would be one."[40] Ernest Bloch, not much later, hooted at the idea that an American could not be a composer; so did many Europeans Sessions met.

Roger strove to receive a Degree with Distinction in Music or Honors in Music by following the course plan such a degree and honors required: "suitable courses in German, French, and Italian." He took these languages in addition to ones he had already studied, Greek and Latin. His transcript indicates that regarding grades, at least, Roger was an average student. He never earned an A in any subject for four years, his only B grades were in music, and for the remainder of the courses he received either C or D grades, or failed them. A glance at Harvard's grade statistics indicates that professors then graded on a bell curve. C was the most often awarded grade.

Roger wanted to compete for the Francis Boott Prize Chorus, begun in 1831 and still run today; $250 for the best composition in vocal music, from three to eight parts, lasting no more than ten minutes. "At last I have found a subject for my Boott Prize Chorus," he wrote Ruth. "I have already the germ of the music in mind. It is Dryden's 'Ode for St Cecilia's Day'—a poem to which, when we read it over, music instinctively shapes itself. If I can carry my ideas out, it will be the best thing, by far, that I have done so far."[41] He did not win, and very likely did not finish the piece. Quite possibly this competition represented the first documented instance of Sessions's expression of confidence about his musical ideas, his forecasting success before completion, and his inability to follow through, especially to meet a deadline.

Roger's attitude about college was not as serious as his parents would have liked:

> When I was in college, I spent most of my time reading and going to concerts. Every now and then I'd go to class. And sometimes, especially toward the exams, I'd do some studying. I read all sorts of things when I was in college. I read all the plays of Ibsen; didn't understand a word of them of course, but I thought they were wonderful. . . . I was always in the habit of undertaking much more [course work] than I could do. . . . I'm still not a very good planner of things.[42]

He studied orchestration with Hill, and liked this course so much he repeated it. Indeed, orchestration would later be considered Sessions's forte. In his junior year Roger felt close enough to Hill to confide in him his ambitions as a composer.

> [Hill] took me for a walk [on Brattle Street] and said to me, somewhat confidentially—or I assumed that it was: "I want to tell you that we are not in a position here to give you what you need. I won't go into the reasons why." And he urged me very strongly to go after I graduated to France to study with Ravel.
>   This was the spring of 1914, and so I didn't go to study with Ravel. Obviously [war was declared and] I couldn't have. And in some ways I don't regret it at all. In fact I'm sure it was much better that I didn't; because in the first place I was eighteen years old [when he graduated], and I didn't know anything about the musical world, except what I had gotten from going to concerts. I was quite shy—very shy, in fact—and I don't know at all how being precipitated into French musical life would have affected me.[43]

During Roger's last semester, Hill wrote a letter of recommendation for an unnamed job.

> I have found him exceedingly bright, he has shown an acquaintance with modern orchestral literature which I have rarely found exceeded in my course Music 6, which he took for *two* years, with independent work in the second year. As might be expected his mental habits are somewhat immature [at 18], and I should question whether it might not be wiser for him to postpone taking a position until he has had more experience. In his work on the *Harvard Musical Review*, he has shown unusual critical ability, and a good deal of journalistic ability.[44]

During his freshman year Roger took English A (and received a D grade), two German Bs (C in each), French I (C), and Music II (Counterpoint, with Spalding assisted by Archibald Davison, which "require[d] knowledge of Harmony" and which Sessions had passed on entrance exams; he received a B). In November, when he took his first hour exams in each of those courses, he had done better, getting an A in Music, C minus in German, C minus in English, and C in French.

All of Roger's good traits were being tested at Harvard, while his bad work habits were already evident and seem never to have been overcome during his entire lifetime. In a letter of December 4, 1911, he acknowledged there was no excuse for not writing to Father Sill earlier, and he apologized for not having told Pater his address at Harvard: Sill's letters had been misdirected to the Union, while Sessions lived at 41 Hawthorn Street and had only recently learned of their existence.

In the second semester, however, he wrote to Sill, and he was "studying especially hard now, so as to redeem to low marks I got at Mid-years and April, and replace them by good ones, if possible."[45] It was not possible, as he missed classes and received a D in English. This put him on probation as of April 30, 1912, removed on October 8 the next semester. He planned to learn the oboe during that summer in order to play for the Pierian Sodality orchestra. He probably could not play with the Sodality until the probation was lifted; indeed he joined it (as noted above) in December 1912. Ruth wrote to the dean a week later:

> I discovered during a visit to Cambridge three weeks ago that he was not preparing his lessons properly, and hoped he would retrieve himself before this: but I think the disgrace of a probation will probably stimulate him to do so now. He is perfectly capable of working well, even brilliantly, but it is a case of mania for one interest, and as this is music, he has neglected other things in order to do extra compositions, and has felt that he could not miss any concerts or other musical opportunities—a kind of intemperance which we hoped his college life would break up. I heartily hope that his determination to make good, before the finals, will bear fruit.[46]

In his sophomore year Roger received a C in English D2 (Composition), and Ds in History 1 (Medieval History) and in Physiology 1, and he failed German F1 (Conversation and Composition). In January 1913 he passed the required oral exam in a language; his was French. He received Bs in all three music courses. One was Music 6, Instrumentation, primarily a graduate course, taught by Hill. He also continued his summer study of oboe during this year.[47] He also took lessons on the organ; he hoped to get a job playing around Cambridge. He took Music 2a half (vocal composition, taught by Spalding), which included part writing, strict and free, together with analysis of choral repertoire. He wrote several pieces for this course.[48] Music 5 half (Canon and Fugue) was taught by Walter Spalding assisted by Davison; later Roger remembered Davison as the only teacher. For the fugue class Sessions wrote a "monstrous fugue with all sorts of modulations."[49] He wrote of it to his mother, "Mr Spalding's latest criticism of my fugue is that I modulate too much and that I have too many dissonances. I am going to keep quiet; but leave them as they are, as I don't want to get in the habit of giving in when it is merely a matter of taste. And besides, I had an inspiration for every measure."[50]

By his junior year older students whom he had known at Kent School were now joining him—at the regular college entrance age—as freshmen at Harvard. These included Frederik van den Arend and Robert Hillyer. That year Roger moved from 41 Hawthorn Street to 19 Matthews Hall on campus. He wrote to Pater Sill regularly, telling him which courses he took and his mid-term grades, but neglected to report the final grades or the probations.

Writing on *Harvard Musical Review* stationery to Father Sill sometime before March of 1914, Roger referred to having visited Kent to coach its music club. He enclosed a review of the most recent *Musical Review*. "I think that this review will please you, although it does just what I tried to attack in my article—it tries to classify me. Needless to say, I have no more desire to be a 'conservative radical,' a 'radical conservative,' or a 'radical conservative radical,' etc etc., than a plain ordinary radical or conservative."[51]

He received a C in Chemistry A (Elementary Chemistry); D's in Italian and in Psychology A2 (General Introduction to Psychology, taught by the bespeckled, bald, and mustachioed Professor Hugo Münsterberg); and he failed both German (again) and Philosophy 2 second half (Introduction to Philosophy through Problems of Conduct and Religion), Josiah Royce was the instructor in Philosophy 2; Sessions was in Mr Loewenberg's section.[52] He received a B in Music 6 (Instrumentation, Hill). He skipped the remaining elective music courses; Music 3 (History of Music from the Time of Palestrina to the Present Day, taught by Spalding); Music 4 (Appreciation); Music 4a half (Brahms, Tchaikovsky, and Franck, taught by the stern-looking Heilman); and Music 4b half (d'Indy, Fauré, Debussy, by Hill). Sessions appears not to have taken Music 7 half with Hill, primarily for graduates, "A Preliminary Course in Composition, devoted chiefly to the smaller forms."[53] He had exhausted all the required music courses, but considered inventing some of his own if he returned for an A.M. the following year.

His German teacher, A. H. Herrick, dealt with Roger for two years in an effort to make him pass German F. After he failed German (a grade of E) in the spring of 1913, Roger had told Herrick that he would "redeem his self respect" by applying himself to the course again the in the fall. Unfortunately, because Roger's "attendance [was] erratic," Herrick was forced to give him and two other students another E at the end of the fall semester.[54] Sessions had to take German 2a (Introduction to German Literature of the Eighteenth and Nineteenth Centuries, Professor von Jagemann and Dr Schoenemann) yet again in the fall of 1914 and finally earned a C.

Roger moved during his senior year to 27 Matthews Hall. Senior-year courses were English 2 (six plays of Shakespeare, a grade of D[55]); German 2a (Introduction to Goethe and Schiller, the German course taken for the third time: C); Greek 2 (Greek literature: Aristophanes [*Birds* and *Archanians*], Books 6 and 7 of Thuclydides, Aeschylus [*Prometheus Bound*], Sophocles [*Oedipus Tyrannus*], Professors Jackson and Post; Roger earned a C); Philosophy 1 (C, General Problems of Philosophy, Professor Hoernlé); Philosophy 2 (taken for second time, C); and an ill-fated Chemistry 3 half (Qualitative Analysis, Professor George Shannon Forbes and assistants; Roger failed it.) He had

Figure 15 Roger Sessions as a student in 1915 and in 1940, for his twenty-fifth class year report at Harvard.

begun Psychology 10, a laboratory course, but dropped it. He also went out for track, despite flat feet.

The failure in chemistry meant that Roger faced a second probation, issued on January 5, 1915, that lasted through May 4. He had already been "admonished for cutting" on December 8, 1914.[56] If he had not already left the Pierian Sodality that year, he would have had to resign because of this second probation. In any case, Roger played oboe with that orchestra for only one year.

Chemistry was one of a group of classes necessary to graduate.

> It was a course in qualitative analysis. We were told to clean out our little dishes with hydrochloric acid. I was in a hurry one day, and I thought I might help things along if I added some sulfuric acid too. The sulfuric acid absorbs all the water, so the clouds of hydrochloric acid and smoke kept coming along. And finally some students came and took me by the arms and rushed me to the window. And I was all right. And I was terribly tempted by the pot of cyanide of potassium. I wanted to smell it to see what it was really like, but luckily I didn't quite dare.[57]

His defense about failing was that he was taking six courses rather than the required four (although the previous two years he had taken seven courses), and that he was president of the *Harvard Musical Review*. The immediate result, however, was his suspension from the *Review*; his last signed article was December 1914, and the next time he would appear would be October 1915, after he graduated. Nevertheless, he published an pseudonymous article, and possibly an unsigned article, in the *Review* during his suspension[58] (see section "*Harvard Musical Review*").

In addition to taking on more than he could manage successfully, Roger was socializing more and undergoing a (temporary) strengthening of his religious views. He wrote to Pater,

> I feel that last year [junior year] was a failure for me in every respect and am doing my best to atone for it. I have gotten fully over my religious difficulties and feel the stronger for having fought it out myself; my own faith, I feel, is much stronger for what I have been thru. I am hoping this year to establish a permanent correspondence with my uncle [Rev. James Huntington], whose visit [to Forty Acres] I enjoyed more than ever last summer. The sermon he preached there I thought easily the finest I had ever heard.[59]

He also felt "monstrously remiss in doing my duty toward Kent, ever since I left." Now that he was a senior, his situation felt changed:

> You see, I am having to concentrate all my four years of college life into one, as I never took the part I should have before. But I think college has done more for me than it would have, if I had entered at the "right age." Associating with fellows older than myself has licked me into shape in a manner which is far more effective with me, than it could have been, had I come in at the age of eighteen and gone out for everything and had an easy time of it. But I have had opportunities (and not wasted them, by any means) of making as ass of myself in every one of the innumerable means, and have emerged as a Senior, wiser— though not, in the profoundest sense, sadder. And, as I am now a Senior and not

a Sophomore, the men in my class are beginning to have some respect for me, which was impossible formerly, and to treat me as one of themselves, and not condescendingly.[60]

A fascinating annotation on his heavily marked class record, found under his home address of 109 Elm Street, Northampton, reads "[Do not use this address; send as below]" to "father—#79 Seventh Ave., New York, N.Y," Archibald's business address at Street and Smith. Presumably this note was meant to protect Roger against Ruth's wrath over his bad grades. Despite this instruction, when news of Roger's probations was mailed, Ruth received the letters first and then sent them to her husband. Both parents wrote to the dean, Mr Byron Satterlee Hurlbert. First Ruth:

> Up to this year, Roger, who was only eighteen on Dec. 28th [1914], has been simply a precocious child, brilliant in some respects but most immature in others. His father and I have been puzzled to know what to do with him, and would never have sent him to college so young, but that it was manifestly a mistake to let him stay at a preparatory school after he had finished the required courses, to be doing special work and likely to be petted by the masters as an erratic but interesting pupil! . . . He is very lovable, steady, and with strong principles, but he has not learned efficiency in work, as is instanced by his undertaking to write an ordinary thesis last week, and then getting interested in it, asking for an extension of time, and staying up two entire nights to express his ideas. . . . I sincerely hope he will be able to pull himself together, and get into a more temperate and effective habit of study. . . . His forerunners at Harvard have all lived up to a good standard, and he realizes that he has a good inheritance . . . The task of making a useful and effective man out of a musical genius may not be hopeless if he is handled right![61]

Ruth mentioned a recent visit by both parents in which they "persuaded him to drop his Greek course, and hoped he would also drop the Shakespeare [English]." Roger dropped neither, however. Archibald wrote the Dean in another vein altogether.

> In Roger's case, after making due allowance for a father's bias in his favor, I am constrained to assume a share of responsibility for the action taken by the Administrative Board because I allowed him unwisely I think considering his age at the time, to enter college when he did. A certain degree of maturity, which he lacked, is, in my judgment, as necessary to a boy as ability to pass examinations, if he is to meet intelligently the duties and to reap all of the benefits of college life. . . . I refer to my own share of responsibility because I feel so strongly that he has missed some of the opportunities which I had as a student at Harvard, and that he has missed them, partly at least, because he was too young to take advantage of them.[62]

Hurlbert was not a dean for nothing; he knew what to write to each parent. To Archibald he wrote, "As I said to Mrs Sessions, I think you make no mistake in letting Roger come, for although he did not have the maturity of some College fellows, he was a good deal more mature than a great many boys much older, who entered with him."[63] To Ruth: "I know that his instructors think well of him. Only the other day, one of the teachers who has come into contact with him, spoke of his genius. He *is* a musical genius, and I want to see that genius developed."[64] (By now we should not be surprised to learn that Hurlbert had discovered he and Ruth Huntington were "far off cousins.") In response to her letter Roger wrote his "dearest Mother" that he had already determined to go to church regularly before she had suggested it. "The Dean seems to think I had been foolish, but not that I had done anything particularly disgraceful; he regards my probation as a severe *warning*, rather than a threat."[65]

His failing chemistry in his senior year put him one semester from graduating. He had wanted to drop chemistry and keep psychology, but the dean would not let him, telling him to drop psychology. He was held back in the summer of 1915, when he lived at 35 Concord Avenue, to take a summer-school course in botany in order to replace chemistry with a course from the same scientific group. Botany attracted only three students, however, and Roger was able to substitute a history course (on the Civil War and the War of 1812, a grade of C), taught by a genuine captain. Sessions loved military history and spoke of this course often over the remainder of his life. "I could have told you after that course every time General Grant lit his cigar during the Battle of the Wilderness. And just how they moved around the battlefield of Spottsylvania."[66] He had planned a spring 1918 visit to Civil War battlefields—Manassas, Fredericksburg, Chancellorsville, and the Wilderness—but that came to naught.

On February 18, 1916, he was recommended for the A.B. degree with the class of 1915. Finishing a degree after the month or year of graduation was fairly common at Harvard; a significant portion of every class was counted in their class year after the fact. When Sessions received an honorary degree from Harvard June 12, 1964, he sat on stage saying to himself: "I wonder if they looked at my academic record?" and laughed recalling it.[67]

If Sessions attended his graduation ceremony, without having received his degree, on June 24, 1915, he would have heard Oxford don Alfred Noyes set a somber tone by reading his poem that began, "Music is dead, while half the world is dying." President Lowell then told the graduates: "The future is dark. We know not whether we shall be entangled or escape being entangled in this war."[68] Henry Cabot Lodge was the principal speaker for the Widener Library dedication that afternoon. (Widener himself had perished on the *Titanic* three years earlier; the Library was a memorial.)

Meanwhile Roger had more immediate concerns that summer. He was in love with Angela Richmond, the sister of a classmate, William. Grace Angela Richmond was a year older than Roger; she was graduated from Smith with the class of 1916. Letters hint at the possibility she thought him too young for her. In order to become more physically attractive, Roger shaved off his old "disgusting" mustache and started another one ("I know I must wait till my mustache reaches the age of discretion"). He wrote to George Bartlett, "She has changed me and made a new person of me; so if I ever should approach my ideals and become a great composer, you had better write her a letter of congratulations. Gosh, I love her."[69] Shortly after that outburst Ruth wrote to Roger at Yale, typically splashing cold water on his enthusiasm. "But I hate to have you lavishing a great deal of perfectly good affection on A., because I don't feel somehow as if she were quite worthy of it. . . . I feel sure she has never cared anything about men or they about her."[70] Angela's birthday was the same as Bach's, March 21, in Roger's opinion one of the greatest days in music. Only playing certain of Hugo Wolf's songs affected him as much as seeing Miss Richmond.

At the end of Roger's four years at Harvard, he listed his membership in various school clubs in the 1915 class album. The Men's League for Women's Suffrage has already been mentioned. He also listed himself as a member of the executive committee of the Socialist Club, founded in 1908 by Walter Lippman. Another original member was Roy Dickinson Welch. The Club was not particularly active during Roger's years; but it revived in 1915. The few membership lists that exist do not show Roger's name. "I am getting to be sort of half a Socialist, although I am more or less opposed to many of the ideas," Roger had written Pater in the fall of 1912.[71]

He also listed the 50-year-old Episcopal student society St Paul's Club, which he joined in the first semester as a freshman and thought it "will be a great help to me." (He wrote to Pater, whom he knew would approve.[72]) Members included President Lowell and Bishop Laurence. This society had undertaken a social service mission to build a mission church in poorer East Somerville. The Club and its 250 members had purchased land for this purpose. Needless to say, Roger's grandfather, Bishop Huntington, had been elected an honorary member. It would have been considered mandatory, in his mother's view, for Roger to join the St Paul's Club. At the same time his brother John was attending a different Episcopal institution, St Paul's preparatory school in Concord, New Hampshire.

Roger did more than attend concerts, buy music, and study music at Harvard: he also performed once as a pianist in Boston. During his last semester at school and through some unknown connection (possibly Hill), he met Isabella Stewart (Mrs Jack) Gardner, the art patron who had helped found the Boston Symphony Orchestra. Guided by the expertise of Renaissance art evaluator Bernard Berenson in purchasing works of art, she built a Venetian palazzo on the Fenway in Boston and filled it with masterpieces. A large tapestry room served (and still does) as a concert hall where she could patronize young composers and performers and invite her friends to hear them play. Roger played for her "Salome Evening" May 7, 1915; his friends E. E. Cummings and Chandler R. Post also attended the event and signed the guest book.[73] Roger wrote to his mother:

> The notorious Mrs Jack! You can imagine my surprise mingled with consterna-
> tion . . . I played much better than usual and got through *Elektra* at a great rate.
> Whereupon and *worüber* [whereat] Mrs Jack began to enthuse, hinted that I was
> the best imitator of orchestral effects she had ever heard except [the Polish opera
> tenor] Jean de Rezke, and made me promise to go to her palace on Friday
> evening . . . and do the same by *Salome* . . . The first time she ever heard *Salome*,
> she told me airily, was when Strauss played it for her before it was finished. Jean
> de Reske taught her all the Wagner Operas.
>   I realize that to tell you all this will make you beside yourself with fear I will
> make an ass of yourself [*sic*]; but I am practicing *Salome* very diligently. . . . This
> is more or less the chance of my life . . . please don't be horrified! I would much
> rather not have played for her in the first place, but since I evidently made a hit,
> why then it's Mrs Gardner's bad taste rather than my good playing.

In a second letter Sessions reassured his mother about the May 7 performance:

> Well, Mother dearest, you may allay your anxiety completely about Mrs J., for
> I played *Salome* only before a small and select company that heard *Elektra* in my
> "brilliant and altogether masterly" interpretation. And, as *Salome* is ten times as
> easy as *Elektra*, it sounded extremely well on what is reputed to be the best
> Steinway in the world. I was surprised to hear *my* playing sound so well.[74]

During the summer of 1915, when the *Review* was not being published and Roger had only one remedial course to occupy him, he sought another venue for his prose. This time, however, it was to discuss theater, not music. *The Harvard Monthly* had been published since 1885. In the July issue containing two entries by E. E. Cummings, two by Robert Hillyer, two by John Dos Passos, and one by S. Foster Damon, Roger's essay "Euripides and Mr. Barker" (the director) was chosen as the lead article, its title in boldface. The five-page review discussed recent performances of *Iphigenia in Tauris* and *The Trojan Women* done in a translation by Oxford don Gilbert Murray. Murray's translations of the Greeks had helped generate a new interest for Greek drama on the London stage. Roger appeared as erudite on the subject of Euripides as he was on classical music.

> He is the fountain head of all important drama since his time. . . . It has remained for Euripides, a thundering voice out of the remote past, to do for us what newspaper reports, poems, statues, and other dramas have utterly failed in doing; to make real to us the horror of war and the glory of true heroism and noble suffering—not only in the war which humanity is waging now, but in that of all times and nations. . . . Among other things, several lessons were learned. The *deus ex machina* was seen to be a device of beauty, which, like the chorus, raises the plane of the drama from the real to the ideal . . . The [performances] should mark only the beginning of the death blow of classical pedantry and the restoration of Greek tragedy to its real place in our life.[75]

In 1915 Roger appears to have undergone his first spiritual crisis. To his mother he wrote: "I am now having a terrible conflict about my attitude toward life and towards the whole world in which I live. Please pray for me, because I need help, and this is so vital and personal I think that no one but God can help me, and I know I shall be led right if only I depend on Him to the utmost of my power." The next letter read in part: "I think we are all pragmatists at heart; but I should never dream of trying to justify religion in the pragmatic manner. To me, if it is necessary at all to justify religion, a very vital and lively form of the 'ontological argument' is sufficient evidence of the existence of an omniscient, omnipotent, and good Being, Whom I can only approach through Christ."[76]

This crisis may have been connected to Sessions's behavior and his self-evaluation of having been an "ass" that summer. During the crisis he ultimately turned to Father Sill for advice.

HARVARD MUSICAL REVIEW

Among the activities Roger listed in his senior yearbook was president of the *Harvard Musical Review*. He had begun his career as a published author 15 years before any of his music was printed. In July 1913 he had joined the staff of the monthly *Harvard Musical Review*, "a completely quixotic enterprise" begun in October 1912 by members of the 1914 class.[1] The *Review*'s founding president was Gilbert Elliott, Jr. He was succeeded by S. Foster Damon, Sessions, and John Burk.[2] The *HMR* cost $0.25 a number, $2 a year to subscribe. The 1914 masthead spelled out its mission: "Its aim is threefold, to furnish a musical paper with purely artistic aims, to bring to a larger number the ideals of the Harvard Musical Department, and to preserve the best compositions in the smaller forms written by Undergraduates and recent Graduates."

Spalding wrote of its inception:

> This was a direct example of cause and effect; for so many Harvard graduates had gone into musical criticism during the last half century, that it was natural for students to found a paper of their own. In this way they acquired practical experience in musical criticism just as the *Crimson* and the *Lampoon* have furnished for New York and Boston papers so many professional journalists and men of wit.[3]

Sixteen-year-old Roger published his first article, "Wagner's opinions of other composers," for the *Review*'s Wagner centenary issue (May 1913).[4] Archibald, the editor of *Ainslee's* magazine, "helped me to put it in decent shape. He said he would do it for me if I would really study it and try to learn how to write a little from it."[5] Considering Sessions's many subsequent published essays and four books, it seems he learned a great deal from his editor father, whose prose style he may have emulated. Sessions's opinions about critics, program music, "American music," and his fundamental attitudes about music, were already formed at this young age and did not significantly alter over the next seven decades.

Despite its prospectus, the *HMR* published little actual music. The editors sometimes had difficulty getting enough articles, and some were not so good. "In fact, the whole thing had a somewhat callow tone at times, and we sometimes got in trouble with alumni, not always for the best of reasons."[6] One prominent graduate, writer Owen Wister, felt the *Review* spent too much space covering new music: he submitted an article in the December 1914 issue meant to inform them that music did not start with Debussy. That fall Wister and Arthur Foote, "a very, very nice man," had invited Sessions to lunch. The war had just started, and the two did not speak at all with Sessions, only to each other. Wister read a letter he had received from Henry James about the war. Their strategy, evidently, was for the *HMR* editor to hear their views that the younger generation in the US was in danger of going to the dogs; contemporary composers were no good; Strauss was just a money-grubber; and so on. Sessions, a little taken aback, gathered that his elders did not approve of him and his colleagues at Harvard.[7]

Nevertheless, in 1951 Sessions remembered Foote, along with Hill, Horatio Parker, Arthur Whiting, and Charles Martin Loeffler, as having been supportive and given him "generous encouragement and friendly advice."[8] In a subsequent lecture he described the musical world of 1913:

> The Fourth Symphony of Sibelius was regarded with suspicion; the *Valses Nobles et Sentimentales* of Ravel were controversial; Strauss's *Elektra* seemed a shrewdly calculated shocker which the composer himself had repudiated in a much touted and likewise suspect *volte-face* in *Der Rosenkavalier*. Stravinsky was but a name; and as for Schoenberg, his First Quartet seemed quite obscure, and the *Five Orchestral Pieces* wholly incoherent."[9]

Nevertheless, a remarkable amount of ink was spent discussing both Stravinsky and Schönberg in the *HMR*. Other major composers addressed were Wagner, Strauss, Debussy, Fauré, and Mahler.

A photograph in the class of 1915 album shows the *HMR* board with Sessions at the center. The other board members were J. D. Austin, Fritz J. DeVeau, John N. Burk, D. McC. Stewart, H. M. Levy, George H. Bartlett, and R. M. Jooling. The *HMR* was financially troubled, and the writers and editors had to contribute their own money to keep it running. In February, after Sessions's second probation, which forbade him to work for the *Review*, Burk, who would write the program notes for the Boston Symphony for many years, took over the editing and ultimately oversaw the demise of the *HMR*. Viewing the four-year history of the *Review*, Sessions commented, "I think it's quite remarkable that it should have existed [at all]."[10] Sessions never kept a full set of copies of the magazine; by the 1960s, he had only one issue.

Sessions's niece described the composer: "In 1915, Roger overflowed with audacious perception and a patronizing intellect. He was impulsive, prodigal, and beguilingly radical, witty as well as wise. He had an inexhaustible drive to know everything, to be first to express an opinion, and to tell others what he knew and thought."[11] Between May 1913 and December 1915 Sessions contributed 14 lengthy articles, several short editorials, and some unsigned articles (including one under a pseudonym) to the *HMR*. His writing is characterized by strongly held opinions (not always supported) and an ability to fix upon the core of an issue. For example, in his first article, "Wagner's opinions of other composers," Sessions revealed his wide knowledge of Wagner's writings and perspicaciously concluded that Wagner was "a man who was governed by his aversions rather than by his sympathies." Wagner wrote about Gluck, Beethoven, Weber, Schumann, Liszt, Brahms, and Mendelssohn. Roger opined on Wagner's anti-semitism: " 'Judaism in Music,' . . . was prompted more by his dislike of Jews than by any special thought upon the subject . . . [and was] attributable to racial hostility and perhaps also to jealousy of Mendelssohn's success." The importance of Wagner's opinions "lies in the extent to which they have influenced contemporary musical criticism. His favorable estimates have, strangely enough, made little impression upon the musical world; it is his hostile criticism which has counted most."[12]

In this first article, Sessions revealed his *bête noir*: music criticism. He regularly read

Ernest Newman, George Bernard Shaw, W. J. Henderson, H. T. Parker, and other not-able contemporary critics. Even in these authors, and much more so in the general run of music criticism, he perceived bickering, name-calling, and lack of open-mindedness; this struck a nerve. Long before he himself would be subjected to criticism, he fired a salvo at the entire field, which he perceived as hostile to new music. He attributed part of this to the residue of the recent Brahms–Wagner controversy (he was firmly planted on Wagner's side) and another portion to the typical unwillingness to embrace the new. The *leitmotif* of his criticism of critics, however, reveals a deeper anger toward them than at merely what they exhibited in the professional musical world. Thoughtful, logical, and erudite himself, Sessions had difficulty reconciling himself to the seemingly arbitrary power of critics who could not themselves write music. Perhaps the undignified proceedings in the newspapers offended his gentlemanly New England upbringing, but possibly he rebelled at the idea of being judged by inferiors.

As a pre-emptive gesture he wrote "The case against professional musical criticism." Here he raked over the critical establishment beginning with W. J. Henderson. His objection was the critics' perceived lack of objectivity: "there is almost invariably some prejudice which will influence the forming of any opinion." He called prejudice by what he considered its true name: gossip. Sessions condemned critics, for example Brahms's disciples, for spoiling good causes and for making personal remarks against composers. Although he mentioned Bernard Shaw, Olin Downes, and Ernest Newman in a positive light, he concluded "problems in artistic appreciation should be discussed as if they were problems in morality. But we must guard against the great danger of taking professional criticism too seriously, for as it now exists it is utterly useless—nay, harmful, except when considered purely as a means of making a living."[13] Discussing critics who cannot find form or melody in revolutionary modern music, Sessions wrote:

> Music requires, perhaps more than any other art, logical statement of ideas, but it is first of all an expression of emotion or thought, and as our emotions and thoughts are not of the type that are readily coerced and measured out according to the prescription of others; neither can their physical expression be fitted into the mould which others make for them, no matter how competent those may be.[14]

And, "Professional criticism also hinders thought in that it has established and fostered what is known as 'good taste,' which Bernard Shaw has very correctly called a form of snobbery." He did praise "purely objective biography or digest." Lawrence Gilman's guide to *Salome* comes in for commendation, as do Philip Hale's Boston Symphony program notes. Sessions wrote to his mother about this article: "Only when I see a piece of first-rate criticism, do I begin to doubt myself. But the good criticisms are so few and far between that the person who has not heard the music cannot tell the good from the bad."[15]

Anonymous editors at the daily *Harvard Crimson* took issue with his views:

> [Mr. R. H. Sessions] would be more effective were his tone less sweepingly denunciatory. . . . The music critics, like the poor, will presumably be always with us. What is needed is not a campaign for their extermination, but for their improvement. . . . The nervous, chip-on-the-shoulder, lustily contemptuous attitude will never convert the unbeliever, whose objections will not be brushed aside with a cool 'One need not reply to the above mentioned criticisms.'[16]

The last sentence was invented out of whole cloth: his article did not even imply such a statement.

Although Sessions was somewhat hotheaded in this article, nevertheless he and his friend and editor Felix Greissle maintained this negative view of music critics for their entire lives. Sessions often pointed out that music journalism is "for the day; that's what the word [*jour*] means." Prausnitz noted the contradictory position in which this view placed Sessions: "Sessions' appetite for a public [artistic] identity contended painfully with an already well established unwillingness to acknowledge the judgment of the marketplace."[17]

The next issue of the *Review*, December 1913, did not retreat an inch. An editorial described

> the case against musical criticism as it now exists; that is, the present slap-dash method by which an unskilled journalist is often enabled to vaunt before the public haphazard judgment, often seriously affecting the mode of reception of a new work. Too much stress cannot be laid on the incompetence of most critics of today; the real trouble being that since music is the most intangible of the arts, the general public is frequently unable to decide which are the competent critics and which are the charlatans.

Unsigned, this editorial stressed all of Sessions's points and was quite possibly written by him.[18] Indeed, an unsigned review on the same page—of the American premiere of *Der Rosenkavalier*—concentrated more on the poor critical notices than on the opera. "This lazy, contemptuous attitude of many critics toward men who after all is said and done are manifestly their superiors, is a thing unjustifiable from the standpoint of good taste, good manners, or good journalism." Sessions again?

In "Our attitude towards contemporary musical tendencies" in the January issue, Sessions took on several "isms": conservatism, radicalism, iconoclastism, realism, pessimism, and others. For example, he listed four types of views held by conservative critics: 1) a "bitterness against the legendary materialism of modern conditions," 2) the belief that "music has had its day," 3) the contempt held by some who have a musical education over those who do not, and 4) those who "believe that operatic music is *per se* of an inferior genre." The critics' "profession is of a destructive rather than constructive character . . . Destructive criticism is less work, as well as more fun, than constructive appreciation. The tearing down process may have a certain air of romance; but a ruin is a rather ugly object." Sessions was altogether too positive and optimistic to tolerate this. He ended, "Let us adopt a constructive attitude toward art and life in general. Not until we have done this will we begin to realize the infinite possibilities of the present and future, as well as the constantly-increasing beauties of the past."[19] He wrote to Ruth: "Most people think that you must be either radical or conservative; but I see very good reasons for being neither. The extreme radical is no more harmful than the extreme conservative; but I think he is often less sincere as there is a certain romance in iconoclasm which everybody experiences sooner or later."[20]

Responding to an article about ragtime that appeared in the same issue of the *Review*, Sessions commented:

> Ragtime is, it cannot be denied, typical of America, and a great sign, to my mind, that America is a distinctly musical nation. But this theory, if widely adopted, could not but result in the active discouragement of attempts in other

styles. . . . Not till the advent of a genius, who shall, as a genius, be unhampered by prejudice of this kind can we have a true American music; and the sooner we realize this, the better.[21]

In the same article he attacked Ernest Newman for viewing Elgar and Holbrooke as greater composers than Debussy and Strauss.

In a February book review Sessions suggested that some modern symphonies should be added to those listed in *Symphonies and Their Meaning* by Philip H. Goepp. He viewed Goepp as belonging to the group who still nourished the Brahms–Wagner controversy. Pieces Sessions wanted included were Liszt's *Orpheus, Die Ideale*, and tone poems *Also Sprach Zarathustra, Don Quixote*, and he lamented that only one (the Fifth) of Mahler's symphonies was included. He would have replaced Bruckner's Second, Fourth and Fifth symphonies with the Seventh and Eighth. American composers that Goepp had mentioned included Hadley, Strube, Chadwick, and Loeffler, but MacDowell was "scarcely mentioned."[22]

Writing of "New Boston Opera House Productions," Sessions reported that Fevrier's *Monna Vanna*, Montemezzi's *L'Amore dei Tre Re* (substituting for Zandonai's *Francesca da Rimini*), and *Die Meistersinger* received first Boston performances.[23]

In 1914 Sessions was absorbed with Wagner's last music drama: "As for the music of *Parsifal*, too much can scarcely be said in its praise." (He later wavered in his opinion of the work.) He defended it against those who denounced it on moral grounds and as anti-feminist. Noting that the *Parsifal* craze was dying down in America while a *Tristan* mania ascended, Sessions pointed out that "Wagner during his later life fluctuated between the ideals of passion, as typified by *Tristan*, and asceticism, as portrayed in *Parsifal*."[24]

Sessions was made editor of the *Review* in the fall of 1914. As he became editor, Frederik van den Arend, class of 1917, and later George Hodges Bartlett (1918), joined the board of editors. In four pages of editorials Sessions touched on topics that would concern him throughout his career. For example, "Originality is not the criterion of genius. . . . No genius can be more than, at best, four or five per cent original." He cited Goethe, Shakespeare, and Bach as examples of those who had borrowed ideas. In reply to Wister's letter to the editor, Sessions pointed out that

> the supreme authority of the older generation is just in this age beginning to be questioned. Nevertheless, Bach was of the older generation when he wrote the *Passion Music* and the *Mass in B Minor*, and most of the other great men of the world have done their finest work *between the ages of fifty and seventy*. [emphasis added] . . . It is easy enough for the younger generation to proclaim that the world is to be revolutionized, that the ideas of its fathers and grandfathers outworn—all of which is absurd; it is equally absurd for the older generation to be righteously shocked when the younger generation indulges in idealism and tries to express itself in its own glorious way.[25]

The formal published response to Wister was written under a pseudonym, "Ragnar Brovik" (the quotation marks included). Brovik noted that Wister opined "that an older man is a better judge of the *sine qua non* of art." Sessions again dealt cleverly with generational conflict: "A genius is always old and young; every personality of genius is to a certain extent a child."[26]

In "A new Wagner essay" Sessions reviewed Ernest Newman's *Wagner as Man and*

Artist.[27] Today Newman is often criticized for glossing over some of Wagner's less desirable traits, but Sessions took him to task for impugning the genius at all. Some of Wagner's characteristics that Sessions defended will be seen in his own behavior in this book. Whether Sessions was subconsciously emulating his idol, or simply shared (to a far lesser degree) some of Wagner's worst faults, is hard to determine. It is fascinating, however, to read Sessions, in his teens, defending Wagner's treatment of his first wife and his borrowing of money from numerous friends. Regarding Minna Wagner, "it is certainly more rational to pity her than to condemn Wagner, or for that matter, to lay specific blame on anyone." And "Wagner eventually paid off his debts, [!] a fact which Mr Newman fails to mention, even though he notes that Wagner was a professional borrower. Even if he had not paid off his debts, it would hardly indicate that he was a swindler; it would show that he was a very bad business man." Further, "the idea of considering others never occurred to him. He would recognize no obstacle to his wishes." And—as with Ernest Bloch—"Everyone who was not Wagner's friend, ready to take up the sword in his behalf, was to this uncompromising Siegfried a foe." Finally, "[Wagner] never considered his public for an instant, and the world is infinitely the richer."[28]

"The psychological basis of modern dissonance" investigated, somewhat technically, Helmholtz, Lipps, and Stumpf's theories on consonance and dissonance based on ratios, overtones, and perception of sound. Sessions translated and quoted at some length Schönberg's *Harmonielehre*: "It depends entirely on the growing capacity of the analyzing ear how much one can become familiar with the far lying overtones, and thereby increase one's conception of the artistic effects so far that the whole natural collection of tones can have a place in it." Sessions placed a rejoinder as a footnote: "This sounds better as a theory than it works in practice. Prospective converts should examine Schönberg's *Drei Klavierstücke*, op. 11, or his *Funf Orchester-stücke*, op. 16."[29] Sessions concluded the 16-column article with a historical view of dissonance citing specific passages by Monteverdi, Beethoven, and other composers (including Schönberg) to demonstrate that dissonance is in part a function both of context and of history.

In an editorial for the December 1914 issue Sessions inveighed against chauvinism, a result of the war. In reading a London paper Sessions found little discussion of Delius's music, but "criticism" of whether—because of Delius's German birth—to program his music at all in England. This he attributed to French and English jealousy of German music. In addition to mentioning the "colossal and all-inclusive horror [of the war] (and it is impossible to exaggerate this)," Sessions found time to take to task critics for remarks "which even if just, do violence to courtesy and good breeding."[30]

He gave his opinions of Brahms, Tchaikovsky, Mahler, humor, and program music. A fervent Wagnerian, he continued to find fault in Brahms: "In reality the sonata form is Brahms's master." He cited the first movement of the Fourth Symphony and the Violin Concerto, but rejoined: "Those who find nothing but form in Brahms are surely beyond help!"[31] Milton Babbitt claimed that Sessions used to like Brahms until he realized that his mother had met him. Later, Sessions changed his mind about Brahms. In a conversation with Luigi Dallapiccola, they did not discuss Brahms,

> because he didn't really like Brahms. Of course, I do love certain works of Brahms very much. When I was very young, you either were for Wagner or for Brahms. For instance, the idea prevalent in the teens was that Wagner was wonderful with the orchestra and that Brahms simply was not. This was nonsense. As a matter of fact, around that time I read an interview with Maurice

Ravel in which he was talking about Cesar Franck, who was supposed to be a good orchestrator. (God knows why; I think that was certainly one of his weaknesses.) But Ravel said, "Of course, Brahms was a far greater man, even by his tremendous gift as an orchestrator." Coming from Ravel, that puzzled me and I thought, "Wait a minute, yes, that's really true; it does sound wonderful on the orchestra."[32]

Sessions's close friend, van den Arend (Van), wrote "The retort courteous," his only *Review* article, also lambasting music critics. He began by citing a review that quoted Josef Stransky, conductor of the New York Philharmonic Orchestra,

who after hearing one of Schönberg's pieces in Berlin, turned to the composer and said: "I have learned a new word in America—*bluff*. You cannot bluff me!" ... When critics make such remarks (and they are very common) one wonders whether the people who condemn criticism may not be in the right after all. ... The one safe way to expose a humbug is to prove him wrong. If you merely call him names, he will beat you at your own game; but closely scrutinize a bluff and it will succumb.

Van pointed to W. J. Henderson's view that critics can play a constructive and important role, but "One still looks forward to the time when the critics will give up asking the public to be blindly intolerant, when they will indulge no longer in irrelevant squabbles, when they will cease hurling epithets at composers and, silliest waste of all, at each other."[33]

Sessions was editor from May through December 1914. That fall the new Music Building opened, which incorporated accommodations for the *HMR*. Until the building opened, Sessions had run the business of the magazine from his dorm room, 19 Matthews Hall (office hours: Tuesdays, 1:45 to 3:30).

Sessions's lack of efficiency and organization reared its head here, too. When Sessions was placed on a second academic probation in December 1914, John Burk, who also attacked music critics, became the editor during Sessions's last full semester at Harvard. We should presume that Sessions felt guilty for letting down the board of the *Review*. He had also let down his father, the editor who helped him on his literary path. Perhaps in an effort to expiate his guilt and help the *Review*, Sessions published a second set of three articles on Strauss *after* he had left Harvard and was a student at Yale. These appeared in the October, November, and December issues of the *Review* in 1915, and demonstrate a remarkable *volte-face*.

In the 1914 set his praise of Strauss was absolute: "The most striking characteristic of *Don Juan* is its absolute perfection of form." And, "It is difficult to praise *Tod und Verklärung* too highly."[34] *Feuersnot* contains "one of the greatest love scenes in music."[35] Sessions mentioned that Strauss's Symphony in F minor was performed often in this country by Theodore Thomas, one of the composer's early American champions. Possibly some of his positive view of Strauss was instilled by Archibald and Adeline who had sung under Thomas.

Tchaikovsky, according to Sessions's first Strauss article, "can never really move us; he gives us a sensation of acute physical pain rather than spiritual conflict or sorrow."[36] And,

Strauss's nearest competition in modern times is probably Mahler. Mahler's canvas was gigantic, his emotion profound; but he was incapable of the refine-ment of a Strauss; beside those of Strauss, his melodies and harmonies seem almost absurd in their obviousness. And Mahler's spirit was narrow; he was the musical metaphysician. Strauss is the more universal artist, the painter of human emotions and destinies.[37]

Sessions felt *Till Eulenspiegel* should be regarded as absolute music rather than as program music, and this led him to examine the ingredients of comedy.

Generally speaking, comedy consists of two elements—wit and humor. True humor is an attitude toward life—an emotion, as it were; a sense of humor consists in a thorough insight into, and sympathy with, the workings of human nature. . . . The truly humorous man is on intimate terms with humanity, and is able to appreciate more deeply its sorrows as well as its joys and follies.[38]

And finally: "Strict program music is just a source of amusement for people who do not understand music."[39]

William Blake appears linked with Strauss. "We have often wished that there were a second Blake to illustrate Nietzsche's *Zarathustra* in colors, just as Strauss has in tones."[40] In these initial three Strauss articles Sessions described the tone poems and their programs. Discussing *Elektra* he pointed out that "The critics found fault with the principal motive of the drama—the motive of vengeance. But, strange as it may seem, these are the same critics who would pronounce Hamlet—which has virtually the same plot, except that the protagonist is a man, and that there is much more bloodshed—the greatest drama ever written."[41]

A little more than a year later, after he had fulfilled his A.B. requirements and was a student at Yale, Sessions published a second set of three articles in the *HMR*. Sessions's opinions about Strauss had changed drastically in the interim. That summer he had read Romain Rolland's *Jean-Christophe*, in which Strauss is taken to task (see below). In this series Sessions announced that Strauss is "of the past." One "need only turn to the tone-poems and the one-act operas to realize the gulf that lies between the former and the present Strauss."[42]

Sessions was doubtless also influenced by the generally held opinion that Strauss had turned backward after *Elektra*. Indeed, Sessions felt that Strauss should have continued writing tone poems rather than operas. Sessions considered that Strauss's music tended toward what "Wagner termed *Kapellmeistermusik*—in the vernacular of our time, 'hack-work.' "[43] Strauss had lost his "self-assurance." And, "We feel that he is now no longer a conqueror, but a slave of his success."[44] Sessions put himself into something of a quandary seen from today: how could he still be pro-Wagner and at the same time pro-Stravinsky, while now expressing anti-Strauss views? These would appear to be contra-dictory positions. Sessions analyzed Strauss's technical failures, particularly those in his harmony: "He is but an amateur in post-Wagnerian harmony," and "He applies his method of harmonization to commonplace themes merely in order to make them sound unusual."[45] Later in life Sessions would never have agreed with his earlier self on this point. Some music works perfectly well without being harmonically or thematically unified: witness *Rhapsody in Blue* or any Renaissance motet.

Critics again came in for criticism, this time for "slip-shod attempts at analysis" and dwelling on "the shortcomings and mak[ing] the successes incidental." Sessions also described program music, ultra-realistic passages, and form. He quoted Horatio Parker on the subject of complexity, and asserted that Brahms's melodies are, like many of Strauss's, "long-winded and diatonic."[46]

In his second essay Sessions again traversed the tone poems one by one, starting with *Aus Italien* and continuing with *Macbeth, Tod und Verklaerung, Guntram* (an opera), *Till Eulenspiegel, Sinfonia Domestica, Also Sprach Zarathustra, Don Quixote,* and *Ein Heldenleben.* Remarking that both Beethoven and Strauss had written their heroic symphonies in the key of E flat, Sessions compares the *Eroica* and *Ein Heldenleben*:

> Both are heroic in the highest sense of the word. But, aside from any purely musical discussion, it is evident that the two characters are widely different. Beethoven's hero is a figure of the awakening of the nineteenth century—a rebel; Strauss's is a superman who fights against the pettiness of the world. Beethoven's hero is the more classical—a leader of men and a doer of great deeds; Strauss's is an individualist—like Guntram, he is "ewig einsam," [forever alone] a proud dreamer of heroic dreams that are above the common herd. This is, perhaps, the weakness of the Straussian hero, in contrast to the splendid child of Beethoven's revolutionary ardor. But Strauss's hero is none the less heroic; his heroism is of a different type, a type truly representative of the spirit of his time, and brings us a glorious, crystal clear message, albeit in some sense a ruthless and cheerless one. Beethoven's hero is the more human, and, perhaps, the better balanced of the two; but both are of the same nobility of soul.[47]

The last essay, written just prior to the first performance of the *Alpine Symphony,* concentrated on *Salome, Elektra, Rosenkavalier, Ariadne auf Naxos,* and *Das Josephslegende.* The last is "doubtless one of the worst scores ever put forth by a composer of genius," resulting in "a sickening effect of colossal artificiality."[48] As if to justify Sessions's assertion that "Strauss is no longer a creative force in music," a somewhat negative review of the European premiere—"void of soul and heart"—was reprinted without comment at the conclusion of his article. Sessions could not have known this, but the *Alpine Symphony* was to be Strauss's last tone poem.

Several events produced Sessions's harsh judgment of a major composer: first and foremost was the profound influence of Rolland; then the nearly universal agreement of critics and modernists that Strauss had turned his back on modernism; the atmosphere at Yale and the influence of Parker and of Sessions's new colleagues (now nearly his own age); his falling into the trap for which Sessions elsewhere chastises music critics, that is, their sweeping statements; and, combined with the above, a suspicion that Strauss had sold out his artistic values for financial success and popularity. Such is the snobbism of the not-yet successful toward the successful.

The *HMR* limped along for another three, short issues under John Burk. The editors struggled to keep it afloat; George and Van still worked at the *Review.* Even infusions of money did not help. It had already been under attack from the "older generation," graduates such as Francis Rogers 1891 (chorister of New York's Harvard Club) and others, such as Wister and Foote, on the Graduate Advisory Board, for discussing new music too often. Now another unsigned attack was hurled from the *Harvard Crimson.* This article responded to "men [such] as the musical critic of the *New York Tribune*" to the effect that "as an authority on art the *Music Review* has little value. The majority of articles are contributed by undergraduates, and the views supported are the product of minds inexperienced and without breadth." The *Crimson* quoted from the original stated mission of the *Review,* but avoided the more recent mission statement: to represent the undergraduates and recent graduates in the music department. It wanted the *Review* to alter what it had been for the past four years; it advocated for "articles by men of reputation, preferably alumni." The *Crimson* ended by advising the entire enterprise to change its stated course: "There is at present no standard musical paper in the country, as there was formerly no standard law periodical. The high position which the *Law Review* has attained indicates that a similar place is open to the *Musical Review* under a revised policy."[49] The *Crimson*, wittingly or not, hammered the last nail into the coffin of the *HMR*. It ceased publication that month—March 1916.

Chapter 2

YALE THROUGH THE CLEVELAND INSTITUTE

YALE

The summer of 1915 was a turning point for Sessions, as might be expected of someone finishing college. He wrote to George Bartlett, who had visited him in Northampton in late August.

> I have been going thru a revolution this summer, and have made it miserable for everyone with whom I have come in contact. You see, as soon as the revolution is over—and I think it will be soon—I will be no longer a child; and I think you will like me better than you did this summer, for, I must admit, I have been an ass. So please forget the unpleasant times, and remember the pleasant ones—the long constitutionals we took—especially the first one. I should hate to think you took seriously all I said about my family, for instance. But, the truth is, I have been going thru a violent reaction this summer, and as soon as I stopped working mentally, chaos appeared. Amen. However, I think you will find me a little less disagreeable thereafter.[1]

We are curious to know what Sessions had confided about his family. In September Nan wrote about the family situation, doubtless referring to Ruth. "I felt better after I got on the train on Sunday, and decided that I was a goose. We'll have another good talk about all that sometime, but I want you to be sure that I see more clearly than you can how entirely it and other similar things are my fault. There's a great deal that we *must* allow for, or we will regret it later on."[2] Nan was to suffer Ruth's sudden outbursts, which were sometimes violent; Ruth hit her 28-year-old daughter so hard it cut her lip.

This drastic change, or "revolution" as Sessions called it, shortly became quite visible on his person. Sessions's appearance suddenly altered from that of a youngster to a rather middle-aged man in only two years at Yale. His mother had commented on the physical change, and photographs show direct evidence. By the time Sessions was 20, he had already acquired the physical stance, posture, and body shape (slightly bulging in the front) familiar to his friends later in life. He now appeared considerably older than his classmates, and, photographed with Quincy Porter in 1917, looked as though he could easily be Porter's father.[3] Then 20, he had a full head of longish hair, but within only a few years he would be partially bald, which aged him further. Such a speeded-up aging process must have been disconcerting. Sessions never looked like a young man; he went directly from youth to middle age.

An earlier letter to George during Sessions's delinquent summer at Harvard (1915) reveals that he had completed the entire 1577-page novel *Jean-Christophe* in five days. He was probably inspired both by the awarding that year of the Nobel Prize for Literature to its author, Romain Rolland, and by Rolland's historical books about Beethoven and Handel.

> Pardon me if I say it is by all odds the greatest novel I ever read. I could not put it down for a second, hardly. I spent all Sunday reading and eating, as I had no collars to wear to church. I wept over certain parts of it, as I wept over *The Trojan Women*. As you know, it is in ten parts, each complete in itself. You will recognize the souls of all your friends that are worth writing about; for everybody that is living today is there in all essentials. There are some valuable musical ideas there, too. Above all, you will find a clear and keen analysis of the Germany and the France of today, and, if books mean anything to you, I think that you will find, as I did, that the book clarifies many of your ideas, and helps you and inspires you to live the kind of life and think the kind of ideas, and have the kind of opinions and emotions, that you want to have. *George, this is not a sermon!*[4]

Once described as the world's greatest musical novel, *Jean-Christophe* illustrates Rolland's tendency to think in high-sounding, idealistic, but vague analogies, which deliberately confuse the hero with the work—life with art. Rolland adhered to what he felt to be justice and truth, producing a novel that exerted a deep moral influence in its time. "The unifying factor is that most of the characters, at one point or another, ultimately turn against the hero," wrote Louis Auchincloss, "because there is something about genius and personal integrity on such a scale, that creates in them a passion to belittle it, or even to extinguish it. So glaring a light shows them up, warts and all."[5]

Rolland taught music history at the Sorbonne, and stressed that cultural history should investigate the moral and spiritual atmosphere of the time. He invested sensation as the source of knowledge ("I sense, therefore I am") and attributed the basic cognitive role to intuition rather than reason. Beethoven's musical greatness was therefore seen as a function of his greatness of spirit. Rolland felt the artist was the intermediary between the sensations of his own era and the timeless stream of human feelings. A hero possesses greatness of heart and of faith (not necessarily religious faith), resistance to suffering and disappointment, participation in life-force and in nature, and an unvanquished spirit even in the face of inevitable defeat. Handel, who scorned the limitations of nationalism, provided one heroic model for Jean-Christophe. Beethoven was clearly the other. The term "force" appears frequently in *Jean-Christophe*, as it does in Sessions's early letters, referring to a personal force, a physical and emotional strength, as well as the power of one's ideas.

Rolland set up conflicts between vision and virtuosity, between the internal world and worldly success. Christophe would rather see all past classics destroyed than have them be worshipped at the expense of the continual development of musical creation. The individual creator ought not to become petrified. Sessions used to say that every ten years one should take out the contents of all one's mental files, that is, intellectual categories, and spill them on the floor in order to shake up one's codified assumptions. Consolation is not to be had in stability or awards, but in the artist's certitude of the continuity of his Becoming, that is, his development in the future. The process of Becoming must continue until death. Rolland inherited this idea from the French philosopher Ernest Renan. *Deviner* (French for Becoming) does not envision final perfection, rather the movement of Becoming is the end in itself; the final victory is the sum of all of the processes. The notion of Becoming, an arrival at the status of greatness and a trust in the future, is the novel's main theme. One interpreter wrote, "As Christophe becomes more aware of the nature of Becoming, he loses the illusion of future stability, concentrating on the continuation of the life-process without reference to any goal. He gives up the thought of interrupting his development long enough to allow the public to catch up to him."[6] Another author explained that Rolland had provided Sessions with a tool for coping with the reality that his and his contemporaries' music was ignored: an explanation for the time-lag between the artist and his public.[7]

This theme of Becoming, as well as the novel's individual characters, spoke powerfully to Sessions. This novel about a musical genius provided Sessions with guideposts to follow in his own life. Similarities can be found between him and his family and that of the fictional German composer. Christophe's parents seem ill-matched; he loses his beloved grandfather while he is young; he experiences a crisis of faith; and he loves nature, particularly mountains. (Winding mountain paths are a major metaphor, along with rivers, for the path of Becoming. Rolland lived in Switzerland, and Sessions would find consolation and transcendence while hiking in the Alps, in Leichtenstein, and in the White Mountains of New Hampshire.) At the summit of a hill, Christophe has a vision: he "rises above the struggle for success and recognition in the 'feverish and sterile world' of Parisian culture, as well as the search for a national artistic identity for the country [France] of his adoption."[8] Uncle Gottfried, Christophe's mother's brother, is a mysterious poor wanderer of profound intuitions, deep religious sentiment, and unperverted simplicity. "Music," Gottfried tells Christophe, "must be modest and sincere—or else, what is it?"[9] (One can hardly not think of Father James Huntington.) "Uncle Gottfried's influence is unmistakable: a work of art must find its motivation in primary physical sensations."[10] Rolland himself was influenced by Tolstoy, particularly "What is Art?," an essay that Sessions also urged on friends. The Russian also stressed sincerity as the goal. Politically and artistically Sessions felt "more in sympathy with France and Russia than I am with the United States; and I cannot consider that an influx of Russian or French culture could do us much harm. But I consider German culture of the past."[11]

Paul Anderson has analyzed the influence of *Jean-Christophe* on Sessions.

> Five themes permeate the writings of Roger Sessions, each appearing in multiple contexts throughout his life. First, he believed that integrity is the ultimate virtue, outweighing in importance the social virtues. This premise led him to advocate the isolation of the artist from corrupting associations. Second, he held that musical experiences may be either genuine or false, and that not all people are equally equipped to make accurate aesthetic judgments. Third, he believed that genuine art is based upon physical sensation, although his early emphasis on pure impulse evolved into a more balanced view that basic sensations must be shaped and refined in order to become art. Fourth he considered the creative process to be essentially deterministic in its workings: the composer has no guarantee of success in his effort, but his success is only feasible within the relatively narrow bounds dictated by the music itself. Finally, because the outcome of the creative process is dictated by specifically musical constraints, the composer must avoid placing himself under obligation to non-musical constraints, including generalized conceptions of form.
>
> Each of these themes appears in some form in the writings of Romain Rolland. These premises further matured in Sessions' mind through his interaction with others, including Ernest Bloch and Arnold Schoenberg. Although Sessions' aesthetic thought evolved throughout his life, these five basic premises persisted in some form.[12]

As Jean-Christophe casts off successive cloaks of his creative personality, he experiences shame, scorn, or hatred for what he has been in the recent past, a pattern repeated in Sessions's early years. Rolland forgives falls from grace, however: a fall creates a reaction to carry one's moral development further than had a fall not occurred. An artist must experience the imperfect and conflicting stages that lead to Becoming.

"In his youth, Christophe is haunted by terrors associated with falling, night, obscure corners, closed rooms, and turns in the road."[13] Christophe tries to kill himself out of sheer indignation at the injustice of his schoolmaster's treatment of him. We have no evidence of suicidal thoughts by the young Roger, but his reaction to headmaster Green's treatment was severe and life-lasting. Significantly, perhaps, for Sessions, Christophe loses a sibling, a namesake who dies in infancy. Indeed, the intervention of death informs the entire novel. The deaths of Jean-Christophe's family and friends operate as Rolland's chief transitional device. Christophe carries the spirits of departed family and friends with him; they provide the impulse in his development. Sessions could not know this in 1915, but in his long life, he would see the deaths of his entire immediate family and of many close friends. These experiences, beginning with the deaths of the Bishop and Hannah Huntington, as we shall see, had profound influences on him. Rolland finds inspiration in Italian art, and Jean-Christophe achieves a kind of intuition or epiphany, a mystical experience of universal love, on the Janiculum Hill in Rome. The American Academy in Rome sits, as did Sessions's apartment there, atop the Janiculum, the highest of the hills inside the walls of Rome. Another Rollandian pattern is that of transcendence through resilience: no one would deny that Sessions was resilient.

"The structure of [Rolland's] music aesthetic rests on the premise that music exists by its own internal necessity, without essential influence to external causes or purposes," wrote one scholar. A better summation of Sessions's own aesthetic could hardly be found. And "the process of artistic creation represented for Rolland a necessity stronger and more real than the artist's commitment to the world of men."[14] Jean-Christophe's Uncle Gottfried thinks music must be an instinctive expression of man's emotions at a given time. To him any music created out of the mere desire to obtain renown is incomprehensible. Rolland combined this view with the Wagnerian idea of the composer's special moral status, and appropriated for the novel Wagner's love life, his avoidance of obligations, and unashamed sponging. The result is a portrait of what Nietzsche foresaw as the *Übermensch*. That larger-than-life subjectivity and distended ego of the musician–hero are reflected in the novel's distorted proportions and non-literary techniques and structure.

Jean-Christophe could not tolerate Brahms. Rolland also changed his opinion of Richard Strauss in his articles on Germany, music reviews, correspondence, and diary. Christophe is at once a reflection and a fictional contemporary of Strauss. Rolland lambasted Strauss's *Sinfonia Domestica* for its literal attempt to depict events and people rather than emotions, as well as its attempt to tie music too closely with a program. The timing of Sessions's own reversal about Strauss can be traced to his exposure to Rolland's views on Strauss (see section "*Harvard Musical Review*"). At mid-century Sessions was to read another novel about a composer by a Nobel-winning author—Thomas Mann's *Doctor Faustus*. This time, however, he knew the author personally.[15]

The influence of Rolland's novel on our composer was profound. At the impressionable age of 18, Sessions found comfort in becoming acquainted with another musical genius—even if fictional—and in taking Rolland's lessons and aesthetics to heart. Overwhelmed, Sessions thrust the novel on friends, explaining that they could not understand him unless they had read it. These friends included Van, George, John Burk, Elmer Newton, William Greene, Robert Hillyer, and S. Foster Damon.[16] His sister Nan and future fiancée would also read the novel. For the rest of his life Sessions would never abandon this conception of art and the artist. It provided him with the long view, the notion that a composer is always developing, and the comfort that the future would see him differently from the present.

As he had done at Harvard, Sessions spent a good deal of time reading. Here follows a partial list of books he read at Yale: *Rhoda Fleming, Lord Ormont, Evan Harrington, Beauchamp's Career, Vittoria, The Egoist, Richard Feverel*, and *Sandra Belloni*, all by George Meredith, Galsworthy's *The Freelands*, Wells's *The Research Magnificent*, and Artzibasheff's *Breaking Point* and *Sanine*. Also Dreiser's *The Genius*; *Homo Sapiens* by Przybyczewski; the periodicals *The Little Review, The New Republic*, and *The Masses*; E. B. Holt's *The Freudian Wish* (he had read most of Freud's major works); Strindberg's *Miss Julie; Spoon River Anthology*; and C. E. S. Wood's *The Poet in the Desert*; Rolland's *Vie de Tolstoi* and Tolstoy's "What is Art?" and *Anna Karenina* inspired Sessions to begin studying Russian grammar. He reread *Jean-Christophe* in French. In 1916 the list included Walter Pater's *Plato and Platonism*; he then read Plato in the original Greek and Goethe's *Wilhelm Meister* in German. Sessions also read Henry James and Santayana, who "will be appreciated much more after he has been dead a few years."[17] Ruth recommended Wells's new book, *Mr. Britling Sees it Through*.

Because a collection of letters stored in a tin box begins in the summer of 1915, it is then that we meet some of Sessions's closest friends and learn details of their relationships, their travels, the music they heard, and the books they read. While at Harvard together, there had been little need to write letters, but because Sessions missed them in the summer of 1915 and later at Yale, their correspondence is quite voluminous. His mother, too, wrote often. After Sessions left Harvard his friends George Bartlett and Frederik van den Arend roomed together. Sessions wrote to and heard from both frequently. The subjects of their letters concern topics of the day: the war in Europe, pacifism, the movie *The Birth of a Nation* (which Sessions saw four times), contraception, books, music, as well as arrangements to visit each other's families. Sessions wanted to visit George, but, as usual, had no money to do so. "You know me well enough to know," he wrote, unwittingly echoing Wagner's credo, "that I will not let a mere trifle like cash prevent me from enjoying myself if I want to. I will get it somehow."[18] Sessions offered George by way of enticement, in addition to a written invitation from his mother, the Connecticut river "nice and high, and we have two automobiles—I mean one automobile, one Ford, a tennis court, and a riding horse, besides poultry, cattle, and pigs to play with."[19]

George Hodges Bartlett, the oldest of five children, was born February 3, 1897, less than two months after Sessions, into a prominent family in Webster, Massachusetts. He was named after his mother, Georgia, rather than his father, Paulding. In 1908 he had suffered a heart infection. Before graduating from Harvard, he had traveled to England. He finished his courses in February 1917, just turned 20, having been excused from final exams because of his fine record. He was graduated in three and a half years, whereas Sessions took four years and a summer school. (George received an A in the music course in which Sessions had received a B.) George had even learned the music of the *Ring* cycle before Sessions had. Pianist and organist George was the business manager, starting in February 1915, of the *Harvard Musical Review* and a member of the Circolo Italiano. John Burk wrote of him as "shy and quiet spoken" with a "quickness and humor," "a quick and sensitive musician" to whom "piano playing [was] a delight."[20] George's letters reveal him as refined, humorous, well-read, sophisticated, and very smart. Photographs show him to be good looking. Bartlett idolized Bach and Franck, and those who knew George idolized him.

The equally handsome Frederik van den Arend, known to his friends as "Van," was born in Holland two years before Roger; he became a naturalized citizen in 1909.[21] His architect father was Dutch, his mother born in New York City, and the family lived in Colorado Springs. He had attended Kent School from 1909 to 1913; therefore he overlapped with Sessions for two years (1909–1911). He later studied architecture. Volatile in correspondence, where his spelling was atrocious, Van expressed his views forcefully. Van declared in a letter from Colorado, "I am a pacifist and Im willing to fight for it. But what the devil is there in the ideal—or the actuallity—of nationalism worth fighting for. Its just geographical snobbery so far as I can see."[22] After serving as an ambulance driver in the war with their mutual friend "Dos" (John Dos Passos), Van discovered he liked travel to exotic places and worked for a while in Madagascar. He would marry Gertrude Drain, and be divorced in May 1946 in Reno. His relations with Sessions in the late teens were testy.

An editorial in Max Eastman's *The Masses* struck Sessions. He wrote to George "on their attitude toward religion—and it has encouraged me a good deal about their attitude toward Christianity. Their revolt, they say, is not against Christianity. They believe in Christ; but they hate the false religion which has sold it to the ruling classes for money. Now, this is the way I feel—I explained it to you, you remember in Hadley."[23] Ruth fretted, "I shall thank God when you get to a steady and permanent faith, for I never know just what phase you are passing through; one letter will announce that you believe in the foundations of the Christian religion—then you come home and confide to your sister or me that you have no faith in it or perhaps in the church—another time you take quite a different point of view."[24]

Figure 16 George Hodges Bartlett.

Figure 17 Frederik van den Arend.

Later in 1916 Sessions wrote to George,

> If I believed in God I should have much to thank Him for. As it is I am sometimes almost constrained to believe in Him, though my reason says No. But I can not help having faith in *something*, and my first desire in life always has been, and will be, to create something for humanity as a whole, and to help achieve real progress in a genuinely and nobly popular art—popular in the best sense. Gosh! but that sounds priggish and egotistical. But I can't help feeling in revolt against many tendencies in modern art and wanting to be a force that shall do its modest part in helping obliterate them. Not that the great composers mean any less to me than they ever did. But hereafter they all must soon be classed as of the past, from which a new art shall arise that shall be more truly representative of the soul of humanity. Otherwise I don't correctly interpret our generation or our century.[25]

Sessions had heard Elgar's *The Dream of Gerontius* in New Haven. He disliked the poem but thought the music Elgar's greatest work. "I wouldn't mind being a Catholic so I could create a hell for Messrs Roosevelt, Root, Lloyd-George and the Kaiser. I am afraid that the Gerontius is too typical of modern Catholicism of a certain type. But I think the worst thing engendered by Christianity is its brooding on Death, and its supernaturalistic egotism."[26]

After having to forsake the plan to study with Ravel in Paris, he had considered moving to New York or remaining in Cambridge. Yale was Sessions's fourth choice. Yale's department of music was similar to a small-scale conservatory. Founded in 1890, the music school then considered itself at a post-graduate level, although it granted a Bachelor of Music degree: students often already had a B.A. and subsequently pursued a B.M. at Yale. The faculty numbered a dozen, and about 175 students attended. Arthur Hadley was president and Horatio Parker dean of the School of Music. William Haesche taught instrumentation.

Sessions had arrived at Yale with a reputation for his Harvard publications; his opinions had been discussed as far away as New York. He therefore found it socially easy to make friends. One new friend, composer Douglas Moore, was trying to get Sessions into the Elizabethan Club, an honor. Another was pianist Bruce Simonds, an exact contemporary. Simonds taught from 1921 to 1973 at Yale and, during the years 1941 to 1954, was dean of the Yale School of Music. (He named his son Roger.) Other friends included violinist/composer Quincy Porter, Mike Elliot, Richard ("Buzz") Cuyler, and Frederick ("Fritz") Anderson (class of 1915), who taught Italian, French, and Spanish. Sessions, Elliot, and Anderson labeled themselves the Trinity—Father, Son, and Holy Ghost.

Sessions was later to compare Harvard with Princeton: "Harvard is liberal, but Princeton is free." For Sessions Yale of 1915 was neither as free nor as liberal as Harvard, but the musical life was better. As a bastion of liberalism Yale had, in Sessions's view, a long way to go to match Harvard: "Yale undergraduates, however, are lords of creation. Woman's place is in the home; Socialism is rot."[27] After some effort a Socialism Club was founded at Yale and Sessions became a member.

Sessions, who lived during the first year at 1214 Taylor Hall and the second at 124 Wall Street, undertook the B.M. degree at Yale, where he studied exclusively, although not privately, with Horatio Parker; with him he took classes in music history, both strict and free composition, advanced orchestration and conducting. According to the 1917–1918 catalog, five (of the eight offered) music courses were meant for third- or fourth-year students: no. 4, History of Music, whose text was Waldo S. Pratt's *The History of Music*, was taught two hours a week by Parker. No. 5, Strict Composition, involved harmony in five or more parts, three- and four-voice counterpoint, three- and four-part fugues, canons, and free treatment of different kinds of thematic material (a prerequisite for no. 6). Parker taught this course two hours weekly. No strict composition (or any other) by Sessions appears in Yale's files of pieces written for these courses. No. 6, Instrumentation, was taught by Haesche and dealt with the nature, compass, and tone color of all orchestral instruments. It is likely that Sessions did not take this course, since he had had two years of orchestration/instrumentation at Harvard.

The two exclusively fourth-year courses included no. 7, Free Composition, in which smaller forms of free instrumental and vocal music were composed and studies made for larger compositions (if their material merited). An extended work, probably in sonata form, was required at the end of the year. This course was also taught by Parker. Nos 5 and 6 were prerequisites for no. 8, Advanced Orchestration and Conducting. Students studied Classical and modern scores and orchestrated original or other compositions. How to select and perform orchestra repertoire and choral works was taught, an opportunity to conduct was provided, scores were necessary, and the class met one hour a week with Parker. Because Parker conducted the New Haven Symphony, he could offer the conducting opportunity to students. He encouraged composers to conduct their own works, and he himself had a solid technique. We do not have Sessions's grades for any of these courses.

Organist Horatio Parker had studied with George Whitefield Chadwick. Parker had been chair of the department of music at Yale since 1894, partly as a result of the success of his 1893 oratorio *Hora Novissima*. He founded and conducted the New Haven Symphony Orchestra and had been Charles Ives's teacher, from 1894 to 1898. Sessions had not heard of Ives at this time, but was doubtless attracted to Parker because of his success in opera: his *Mona* won a Metropolitan Opera prize and was given four performances there in 1912, and *Fairyland* won a similar prize and was produced in 1915 in Los Angeles. Like Ives, however, Sessions rarely credited the Yale dean as his teacher.

In 1951 Sessions described Parker as "next to MacDowell the most significant figure in the American music of that time," who, "especially in certain religious works, displayed not only a mature technique, but also a musical nature and profile which were well defined, even though they were not wholly original."[28] According to musicologist Gilbert Chase, Parker "personified the Anglo-American work ethic, which resulted in his demise at the age of fifty-six."[29]

During his first semester at Yale, Sessions wrote:

> I like Parker immensely. He scares most people; but I have decided not to be scared by him. I was terribly so at first; but now that I know more of him, I like him better. He certainly is magnetic, and I expect to be worshipping him later—as a teacher. He certainly is a wonderful teacher, and one who both inspires and stimulates. I have *determined* to win consistent praise from him the rest of the year. He hates to praise people, and has an awfully strong will; but I am going to be the stronger hereafter. It is wonderful, though, to be under such a man. . . . I can't help comparing Parker with Spalding. The standards are so much higher here that one would not imagine the two to be both college music departments.[30]

Later Sessions commented on Parker:

> He was a very sad man, really; this is the way I always think of him, as a very sad man, a very good musician, but very lonely. The day before Commencement, when I got my Bachelor of Music degree, I went to spend the evening with him. He was extremely nice and he said, "Well, don't ever spend more than four years in the same place. I'd have done much better if I hadn't spent so many years at Yale." Mrs Parker said, "Oh, I don't think you would have composed any more." He said, "I didn't say I would have composed more, I said it would have been better."
>
> I think he was discouraged and disillusioned; he had never been able to give the students what he wanted to give, and he'd sort of given up trying. He taught in an extremely traditional, conventional way, which wasn't always accepted very wholeheartedly by his students.[31]

Sessions also characterized Parker as "a very shy man. I was really very fond of him, but I never felt that I knew him."[32] Whether by design or—more likely—by accident, Sessions took Parker's advice and did not stay at any school or in any one place more than four years for the next 20 years of his life. "I think he was not a stuffy man at all. . . . But some of his students disliked him very much, because he had a very brusque manner at times. . . . At that time, an American composer was a much lonelier person than he is today [1962]."[33]

Archibald continued to support Sessions's artistic aspirations. As an editor and would-be author himself, he understood his son's goals better than most parents of aspiring composers. Sessions's letters persuaded Archibald that Yale was the right school. He empathized with Sessions.

> There isn't any wonder that you find that creative work comes hard. But I'll tell you—I hope for your encouragement—that it wouldn't be creative work unless it did. It's the hardest thing there is and nobody knows anything about it till he

has tried it. And when one has found that out and thoroughly convinced himself that there aren't any short cuts to results in creative work he's won about three quarters of his battle, for he's established himself so that discouragement and disappointment don't weigh with him nearly so much.[34]

Sessions studied piano during his first year only. This was partly because of financial considerations and the advice of his father, who was paying for his education. Archibald wrote in October,

> If I understood your letter this morning correctly, you are taking lessons on the piano and on the viola both . . . I disapprove of it most emphatically. In another way it is a repetition of the mistake I think you made last year in undertaking too much. . . . I cannot give my consent to it unless it is endorsed by your instructors. . . . The financial side is to be considered also, for both of them are extras.[35]

Of course, the steadfast Archibald relented, and let Sessions study both, saying "You needn't have the slightest hesitancy with me on the subject of money matters."[36]

Despite the fact that Archibald alone paid for Yale, Ruth also admonished Sessions about money. "I am scrimping and saving just now too, very carefully, because of the $1,500 that has had to go to the farm, which is going to cripple me for a good while to come."[37] She suggested the two share a single copy of *The New Republic*, rather than both subscribe (or rather all three of them, since Nan also subscribed). Sessions had other sources of funds; he borrowed money from George and Van; he repaid some of it by sending contributions to *The Masses*. Ruth and Archibald probably did not know of these debts. His brother John, meanwhile, was becoming quite popular—he played football—at Harvard, where George and Van were still students.

Sessions's opinions continued to be expressed at length and a bit rashly, for example, concerning Brahms, about whom as a Wagnerian he seemed ambivalent: "To me he is a man of great nobility and true genius—though no greater than some other men. As for his form, that is often calculated, and he is a slave to it; it is his chief limitation."[38] Shortly afterward: "I am getting to hate Brahms with a righteous hatred . . . just as Jean-Christophe did, because he was such a petty and self-satisfied little personality himself, and because the Brahms illusion is one of the G-damnedest lies that ever was gotten off, while César Franck, an infinitely bigger man, is just beginning to be appreciated." He admitted that he worshipped Brahms fanatically at one time, but "It's not his music I dislike; I often like that very much. It is the personality revealed in his music."[39] Then over a year later, in February 1917, Sessions wrote, "I am developing a deep affection (God save the mark!) for—Brahms; especially his short piano pieces. I think my pretended dislike of him was more a matter of principle than anything else."[40] By May he had played through the Brahms horn trio, op. 40, with a cellist reading the horn part: "It is really as fine a thing as Brahms ever wrote, and would be played more often if the combination were not unusual."[41]

In October of 1915 Sessions was already planning his first symphony; it would be in E flat. He wanted to tell only George and Van about it, as a secret. Indeed, secrecy is a theme that, beginning at least with keeping his age secret at Harvard, ran for many decades in Sessions's letters to various people. Archibald understood Sessions's need for secrecy about the work: "I know how it is from my own experience, one does feel, in a way, committed when one has spoken of his idea."[42]

Parker viewed Sessions's symphony's first movement as "a creation of considerable originality and power."[43] In fact, Parker saw little of this new symphony. Sessions wrote to Ruth, "I think you will like my symphony. Of course I have not begun it yet; but the plan is growing clearer, and I expect to really make something of it. The only thing I dread is having Parker see it periodically: for that will obscure my ideas and help to botch things generally. I am going to try and fix it so that I can work things out more or less by myself, however."[44] In March 1917 he wrote to his mother about "dodg[ing] Parker." Another composition teacher—and probably Sessions himself in the future— would recognize this behavior not as trying to preserve independence, but rather as avoiding judgment. Although it is somewhat perverse to attend a music school and not show your work to your major teacher, such a thing happens when students are insecure.

By November 1915 Sessions had obtained his first teaching job, at the Kent School. He taught music and coached the musical club every two weeks for $15 plus travel fare. He sent W. H. Cummings's *The Rudiments of Music* to Father Sill as a textbook for the Kent students' Saturday one-hour class with him. He felt that learning the fundamentals of music would help the boys in their rehearsals for, among other events, a Thanksgiving concert: "Teachers of 'practical' music are always getting more and more sensible of the necessity of a certain amount of knowledge in what is clumsily called 'theoretical music.' "[45] George's younger brother, Samuel, was a student of Sessions's at Kent. Naturally Ruth was proud of this job on several levels; she thought it "manly" to be earning money, and of course she had a strong familial and religious association with Kent. Sessions taught all year and the following summer, but did not continue at Kent when back at Yale in the fall of 1916.

Sometimes Sessions's behavior toward Archibald was inexplicable. This could be chalked up to a certain amount of "flakiness" both suffered from, rather than to any rebellion on Sessions's part against his father. For example, Archibald sent a ticket next to his own seat at the Harvard–Yale game. He asked for a telegram confirming that Sessions would be there: no telegram came. Archibald attended the game—Sessions was nowhere in sight—and he was "terribly disappointed." In addition, he worried what had happened. Sessions *was* at the game, with a friend, and had not looked up his father. (He had wanted desperately to take Angela Richmond to the game, but she went with her brother.) Although Archibald wrote on December 28 about taking Sessions to *Prince Igor* and *Parsifal* during Christmas break, he forgot to mention Sessions's nineteenth birthday.

At Thanksgiving Sessions rode in a car driven by his old Kent friend "Junior" (Azel) Hatch. A Ford ran into them and knocked all three passengers out of the car over a bank and into some woods. Sessions sustained a cut under his chin, some bruises, and a torn lip. A kind lady picked them up and delivered them to Springfield. Once in Northampton, Sessions, looking the worse for wear, met for the first time his future brother-in-law, Paul Shipman Andrews, the scion of the Syracuse Andrews family Ruth had noted. Ruth, this time understandably, dramatized the car accident and thanked God that Sessions was saved. Archibald, not with the family at Thanksgiving, wrote in quite another vein. A New Yorker, he wanted Sessions to keep out of automobiles: "I think automobiles and automobiling are damnable and demoralizing things."[46] George, too, was upset to hear this news, but responded reasonably: "I was quite alarmed to hear about your automobile accident. I am sincerely thankful that it was no worse."[47] George himself had had a more serious accident a year and a half earlier: He had been hit by a trolley car and was taken unconscious to a hospital where he stayed overnight.

Possessing enough self-awareness to grasp what he was doing, Sessions realized he had "idled away those times when I should have been getting a technique, merely indulging myself instead of doing real work."[48] In addition, the notion of becoming a doctor, first arising in his sophomore year, resurfaced during the first spring semester at Yale. "I wonder if such an arrangement would not make me a better doctor as well as a better composer, than would a purely artistic or purely scientific life. The question is, would there be time for both. After all, musical creation seems to be an essential part of my life."[49]

For Christmas that year Sessions received books and scores he had requested from his father: orchestral scores of *Tannhäuser* and *Rienzi* (thus completing his Wagner set), d'Indy's *Cours de Composition* and *Life of César Franck*, Rolland's *Life of Beethoven*, Maeterlinck's *Sister Beatrice* and *Ariane et Barbe-Bleue*. Also Russell's *Why Men Fight*, Santayana's *Winds of Doctrine*, and Verhaeren's poems. For his birthday three days later he received only one present: the picture of Romain Rolland that was to hang on many future apartment walls.

Still undecided concerning *Parsifal*, he wrote,

> I am in doubt about it, I must confess. Some places seem to me to be merely theatrical stuff, though undoubtedly there is much that is sublime. Also I am not sure that he does not in some places write sex music instead of religious music. For, while I am convinced of Wagner's sincerity, I am not sure, that this music is not perverted, though I am far from sure that it is.[50]

Two weeks later, laid up most of that time with grippe, Sessions, perhaps reconsidering Amfortas, "changed my mind about *Parsifal* again, after careful and conscientious study of it. . . . I must confess to a little surprise at how I could have felt the way I evidently did."[51]

In January 1917 his mother wrote expressing her happiness that he was waiting tables at Yale, which he began on the 15th. Sessions wrote Father Sill, "My father has always treated me so wonderfully well that I recently came to the decision that it was up to me to do my part, too."[52] Ruth saw this in political terms: "It is a big and broadening thing to have joined the army of independent workers, and I can't help feeling that what you have to give to art, and to the world through art, will be doubled in value by your getting, in this way, near to the people and the people's difficulties and needs."[53] By the next month, however, Sessions had lost the job. Given his personal habits—lateness, forgetfulness, distractedness—it is not hard to see why. Ruth bemoaned this by pointing out that his father did not earn $3,000 a year, of which he gave Sessions more than a thousand a year. (Archibald was also paying for John to attend Harvard.) For a while, Sessions ushered at New Haven Symphony concerts.

Ruth's sister Arria, after almost 50 years of service to others, suffered "from a nervous breakdown and great despondency."[54] She was taken to a private sanitarium near Syracuse. The blow to her sister Molly, with whom she had lived, was severe. Molly gave up their apartment and came back to Forty Acres every summer. Arria died two years later in March 1921. The hilltop cabin the two aunts shared, where Nan had found it less of a familial strain to stay than with her mother and where we first encountered our composer on a dark and stormy night, was then nailed shut.

During Sessions's second semester at Yale, his father not only fell ill, but Ruth also worried, justifiably, about his play, *The Iron Horse*. She intuited David Belasco's "dishonesty and trickery" would cause a "fearful blow" to Archibald, whom she had begged to see a doctor.[55] Ruth also had been having physical problems that caused a "dangerous condition." Because Ruth and Archibald had children late in life, they were older than most parents of Sessions's college classmates and perhaps suffered more physical ailments than might be typical of the parents of the other students.

Ruth understood Sessions's supposed loneliness at Yale in her own terms; she likened it both to the three winters she spent in Europe and to the two years St Paul spent in the desert of Arabia. She viewed these periods as necessary tests for anyone who is trying to accomplish "big things in the world."[56] Unhappy about the state of Sessions's religious observance, she wrote, "I wish I knew what you do on Sundays, and whether Lent means any slightest thing to you. Ever your loving Mother."[57]

Sessions, whose letters frequently contain lists—of composers (Teutonic vs non-Teutonic), his favorite composers, pieces, and books—also compared his own progress with that of other composers of the past. He compiled a list of 22 composers from Palestrina to Schönberg he wished to study. "Beethoven did not begin to compose masterpieces until he was about seven years older than I . . . Wagner wrote *Die Feen* when he was four years older than I, and did not write his first decent work till five years later . . . The source of all art is faith in one's art and oneself."[58] He continued to pour out his concerns to George.

> I know I have talent, and also something to say, and I have even got conceptions which are unreasoning and quite inevitable. For instance, I have got, someday, to write a dance of gigantic proportions for the orchestra, something gargantuan and Dionysian; but my musical ideas have become so confused that I have no idea as to just how it is to be done. The music, even, is vague and very incoherent as it now runs thru my head; yet it is there, and it has got to be released. I shall never feel happy until I have created something; and for this very reason I have never been happy since I entered college. . . . I feel as if I could have made ten times as much out of my time for the last five years if I had tried. Please pardon this tiresome egoism![59]

Acting as though he were still the editor of the *Harvard Musical Review*, Sessions criticized how it was being run regarding both the content and the business side, while still contributing long articles. His friend John Burk was now the editor. Even after the magazine folded, Sessions wanted to resuscitate it from New Haven, hoping he would have enough money to offer to its cause (which he never did).

Meanwhile his mother opposed Sessions's plans to continue to teach at Kent School during the summer of 1916. To Sessions it would be time to compose. Ruth felt it would mean freedom for self-indulgence, something she criticized in others perhaps because of her own tendency to self-indulgence. Archibald needed more time to think about it, but proffered some advice: "You ought to turn your attention from habits of self-analysis and begin to *act*. . . . Stop thinking about yourself or listening to talk about yourself. It's paralyzing. Get the idea of action into your head and psychology and ethics and sociology out of it for the time being any way."[60] Unusually, Ruth lost this battle to Sessions and his father, but not without delivering a stern lecture. "I want you both to know that I deeply regret your taking the step. I think that physically, mentally, and morally, you would be bettered this summer by leading an active life, in some responsible employment."[61] Sessions worked on a violin sonata that summer, finished it in June and sent it to Parker, who praised the work; it is nevertheless not among Sessions's acknowledged works. Archibald had written to Ruth to try to persuade her of the reasonableness of Roger's plan; he was also continuing an allowance and paying for the rental of a piano at Yale, although Sessions was being paid to teach and lead musical performances at Kent. Sessions's use of money was still problematic. Frustrated, Archibald asked for a weekly accounting of how the money was being spent as well as for Sessions's bank account statement every two weeks. Sessions, who agreed, nevertheless neglected to send the accountings or the statements.

Because of a spreading polio contagion, Ruth asked Archibald not to visit Forty Acres during the summer of 1916, and both parents warned Sessions about swimming for the same reason. By the fall of 1916 Archibald had written at least five plays, including one called the *Superfluous Husband*.

During the same summer Sessions sent an outraged letter to the editor of the *Holy Cross Magazine* about an article on pacifism during the war. The anonymous article, which Sessions described as "frivolous and somewhat sacrilegious," was titled "Is the Church prepared?"

> But the writer in question offends most in his attack on the pacifists. No, the pacifists are not ready to give their lives for America unless they are sure that in so doing they will serve the world. Like Telemachus they rush between beasts of prey, guided by a Christian ideal, in the face of a hostile public opinion. To do this requires moral courage of a kind that stands on immortality. And if we do not agree with the pacifists, it ill befits us to sneer at them. Such an attitude is the more unbecoming in a magazine which is devoted to preaching with austerity the ideals of Christianity and the tenets of Christian faith. It plays into the hands of those extremists who accuse all Christians of insincerity. It makes us wish we could be pacifists of the extremest type. Faithfully yours, Roger Huntington Sessions.[62]

Despite Sessions's absent-minded treatment of some of his friends, and even his parents and Father Sill, everyone continued to value his friendship. His personal charm, his erudition, and his genuine concern for others endeared him to people. He commanded devotion, and would do so all his life. John Burk, for example, who might have had reason to be miffed about Sessions's interference with his editorship of the *Harvard Musical Review*, asked Sessions to be best man at his wedding, December 20, just before Sessions's twentieth birthday. Much was because of pure admiration. John had written, "Your habits of thought are quicker and more brilliant than mine."[63] And Van: "You are both [Sessions and George] shockingly well read and I quake before ye."[64]

After George had visited both Van in Colorado and Sessions at Hadley in August 1916, Van and George roomed together from the fall of 1916 through spring 1917 at 26 Mt Auburn St in Cambridge. Van, irritated with Sessions, still liked him. When Sessions visited Cambridge in October and December, Van made himself scarce, then wrote Sessions to praise the new violin sonata. "Kindly do not consider this Note in the least conciliatory. I would be glad if my attitude happened to please you, but feel obliged to go my own way even if I must go without your decidedly pleasant and lively company. As for your preachements [*sic*]—bosh. Affectionately—of course—Van."[65]

Sessions's views of women continually changed, depending on the company. "I fall in love with every woman I happen to be with, just at present, if they are anything like my style."[66] Another love interest was on the horizon, one Irene Drury, although by March 1917 he was already disillusioned with her. He compiled another of his lists, this one his long line of infatuations that led nowhere: Sybil (the child in Northampton), Elizabeth, Margarethe, Celeste, Rebecca, Grace, Alice, Jessie, Priscilla, Betty, Jeannette, Marion,

Angela, Peggy, and Irene, "I often think I shall never fall in love with a woman—in any real sense I mean. For they are all so unsatisfactory; and yet I have a terrible weakness in that direction."[67]

Despite this weakness, Sessions was deeply emotionally involved for a long time with George Bartlett, to whom he wrote plainly and on more than one occasion, "I do love you dearly." He had a hard time expressing himself to George, and felt

> Friendships are not intended as things to be worried over, but as quite the opposite; and your friendship means more to me than any other, by far. As to the issue which has come up between us twice, I think it is settled now; although I think we will probably not either of us want to take advantage of its manner of solution very often; though of course I don't mean that we shouldn't if we feel like it.[68]

The emotional peak of their friendship was Sessions's dedication of his Yale Symphony to George, January 31, 1917 (he had first thought of dedicating it to Rolland).

> George, I want so much to dedicate my symphony to you. Of course it is still but in the making but, in spite of what I said to you about Rolland, I feel that it is yours, and I want you to feel so, too, even if I don't embarrass you—and I fear it would—by actually writing your name on the copies. In a sense all my work—and what is best in my life, is sincerely dedicated to you; for my love for you, George, is the noblest as well as the most profound thing in my life. I know you will not misunderstand me; I say it with all reverence and sympathy for your own thoughts and feelings; and while the vulgar fashion of the day frowns on such love as mine, it is none the less real because it looks beyond the pleasures of the moment. I know, George, that you are human, and my love is rooted in disillusion; but it reaches to the ideal and its roots are only its strength and its reality. As I look back over the past two years I see what a pitiable and sorry figure I have cut in all my relations with you; and I beg you to forget the errors of a very selfish child, who even now has everything to learn from life. My feeling is too ardent and impassioned to be expressed in words, which look strange and cold as I write them, and there are awkward and heart-rending moments when I feel speechless in your presence. If these words, too, seem labored, hackneyed, and ridiculously sentimental, please remember that I am utterly carried away + can only stammer like a child. My music, too, is utterly inadequate to express the real + glorious madness which you make me feel; but some day I may compose something that comes nearer to it than anything I can do now. Please try to realize that I feel this with my whole soul + body, and that I offer you my symphony in the deepest kind of sincerity. I will try hard to make it worthy of the enthusiasm which inspires it. Will you accept it?[69]

George wrote back, but asked Sessions to burn his letter, which he did. It appears, reading between the lines of their many letters, including the ones quoted above, that they had engaged in sexual relations in Cambridge and Hadley. Although the physical relations did not recur, the emotions raised lingered for years, while both struggled to remain friends. For his part, Sessions still loved George and continued to say so. He wanted George's affection, and eventually hectored him for it; George started to pull away. A year and a half later, in July 1918, George wrote an explanation of his own position.

From you I learned far more at Harvard than from the things which got me my degree. You introduced me to the music which I was already to love but could not find for myself. You showed me Meredith, Jean-Christophe, Bertrand Russell and the dozen other men whose work has been a constant source of real pleasure and exultation. Moreover you introduced me to Cuthbert [Wright], Van, John Burk, who may have led me from you but who made Cambridge stand for a great deal more than Harvard. . . . You know the rest—I fell in love with [Van] as I do with many charming people with vigorous personalities. His presence made me feel happy and last spring when he left I felt an agony which was truly deep—and which I thought at the time would be irremediable. . . . As for our relations dating from August—or we may say February 1916—I was wrong in entering into them, because I realized partially then as I realize fully now that they were not undertaken in the proper spirit.[70]

Although it is not possible to learn Van's feelings toward George from the extant letters, Van had purposely avoided Sessions when he came to visit them in Cambridge and called Sessions's preachments "Bosh." Despite distance and awkwardness, here, too, Sessions was ultimately able to retain Van's friendship during this three-sided love affair. His tact and patience brought them all together despite the real possibility of hurt feelings. It is likely that what Sessions had once so urgently wanted to discuss with Pater (whom he doubtless knew was gay) were feelings of homosexual desire toward George. We cannot know Pater's advice, which would have been given in the context of a confessional.

Sessions decided to return to Yale in the fall, which meant writing a new symphony to be performed. "I have been planning one for years, and have never lost sight of the original plan of what I wanted to do so it ought to be good when it is finished."[71] Sessions lived at 124 Wall Street, in a room with electric light and running water, more elegant than he had been used to, especially in Hadley where Forty Acres had neither.

In Amherst Sessions became friendly with Mme Martha Bianchi, the niece of Emily Dickinson and a lover of music and Russian art. Ruth Huntington had known Austin Dickinson's son and daughter, Ned and Martha, who were her age. "We heard many stories of Aunt Emily and Aunt Lavinia [of whom they had occasional views], who were then old ladies living in the mansion next door. . . . Emily's white gowns gave her distinction as one dedicated to the spiritual and immortal, but never the air of perpetual mourning."[72] Lavinia had come to Forty Acres. Their niece Mme Bianchi had married a genuine Russian captain—a swindler it turned out—and had lived in Europe. After Lavinia Dickinson's death, Martha Dickinson Bianchi became the only remaining member of the family and inherited numerous Emily Dickinson manuscripts. She began in 1915 to try to ignite interest in Dickinson's poems. Bianchi published four books of Dickinson and translated Russian poems into English, including those by Pushkin, Lermontoff, and Tolstoy.[73]

Sessions wrote, "Mme Bianchi said I had the vulgar idea that an artist must do all sorts of vile things in order to rise above them in his art. But of course that isn't so; nobody had a right to act like a scoundrel and it will not improve his art in any way if he does; that is a peculiarly detestable form of priggishness."[74] Later, when teaching at Smith College, Sessions made occasional trips to Amherst to visit the Meiklejohns and Mme Bianchi, "nice and sincere when you get her alone; but incorrigible in company."[75]

Invited to speak at Smith in December 1916, Sessions wanted to present a program of Russian music. Ruth, however, "would decidedly suggest taking out some of the

Rimsky-Korsakoff and also some of the Stravinsky."[76] In November Sessions saw the Ballet Russe in New Haven, witnessing *Les Sylphides, Sheherazade, Afternoon of a Faun*, and *Prince Igor*. The Faun was danced by Vaslav Nijinski, "certainly a wonder," but Sessions would have preferred to see him in *Petrouchka*.[77]

Discussing Balakirev's *Thamar*, Sessions remarked concerning the Mighty Five, "As I conceive it, the members of the 'Invincible Band' died in the order of their greatness— Mussorgski in 1881; Borodin in 1887; Rimsky-Korsakov in 1908; Balakirev in 1910; and poor old Cui is still living."[78] Sessions's lecture at Smith in mid-December went well, but took two hours instead of the planned hour and a quarter. Besides Russian music, during his second year at Yale, Sessions bought and played through Ravel's *Daphnis et Chloe*, Franck's Quintet, d'Indy's *Istar* and *Souvenirs* (arranged for piano), Mussorgsky songs, and Schönberg's first quartet, as well as a four-hand arrangement of Beethoven's Ninth Symphony.

Sessions copied his violin sonata, sent it to George, and wrote about the symphony and a cello sonata he was planning. He then worked on a trio—the cello sonata reincarnated—although, " 'My hawt is not in' the trio." The trio had reminiscences of Debussy and Schönberg's D minor quartet. He started conducting lessons and once referred obliquely to his boxing.

> But as soon as I begin the symphony, I will keep you posted as to its progress. I will probably begin it about Jan. 1st and finish it along in the middle of April [1917]. Then begins the terrible job of copying score and parts for performance. But it will be much easier than writing it will be. Please don't expect too much. It will be the best I can do; for I am far more at home—strange as it may seem— in an orchestral medium than in any other.[79]

Sessions found he had to give up teaching at Kent during his second year at Yale. He wrote to Pater, "But I have to exercise a great deal of self-restraint even staying here; + going up to the school so often would simply mean another interest, of which I must fight shy if I am to concentrate properly. I do miss my contacts with the boys, though, for it was an inspiration to see the school as closely as I did, and to feel so much a part of it; it made me feel *very* humble." He continued on the subject of teaching music:

> Musical instruction is generally carried on in schools in so slipshod and unappreciative a manner that it would be a worthwhile thing if Kent could set a new mark—something which would consist chiefly in selecting an alert and genuinely progressive teacher who could really rouse enthusiasm for all that is finest in art; and indifference to all that is mediocre. That is a much better and more desirable kind of teacher, it seems to me, than the general run of music teachers—the man who will teach the boys just what a fugue or a sonata is, or how old Berlioz was on his 30th birthday, without rousing any real enthusiasm at all. That is what I should have liked to try to do myself, had I gone back this year; but I have other duties.[80]

In January 1917 Sessions "tore up my trio in disgust" and began the symphony.[81] In a familiar Rollandian pattern, Sessions cast the recent past as non-productive, but held much hope for future progress. "The year 1916 produced nothing but that dear anaemic little violin sonata. But 1917 will see better things, because I am older and more self-possessed." The harmonic and time signature plan for the symphony was outlined:

"D major–Introduction, Largo–D minor. 1st theme introduced with fugal exposition, D major, 3/4. 2nd theme, A major 4/4, etc. etc."[82] It was scored for three flutes (one interchangeable with piccolo), two oboes (one interchangeable with English horn), two clarinets, bass clarinet, two bassoons, four horns, two trumpets, three trombones and tuba, kettledrum, harp, strings, and "possibly bassdrum and cymbals." "Last night I went to Parker's to supper, and took my symphony as far as it is done. Parker didn't like it at first, but got fairly enthusiastic after looking it over carefully."[83]

In March of 1917 Sessions envisioned being in Boston the following year, plans that circumstances altered. On April 24, 1917, Sessions and George played a two-piano concert of French music in Webster, George's hometown. It consisted of the last movement of Chausson's Symphony in B flat, the first movement from d'Indy Symphony in B flat, Debussy *De l'aube à midi sur la mer*, and the slow movement from the cello sonata by Albéric Magnard (1865–1914).

In the inescapable background, running like a continuo bass line, was the war in Europe, which would have significant consequences for Sessions, his friends, and his generation.

WORLD WAR I

In January 1917 Yale students had voted 1102 to 286 in favor of compulsory military training; Sessions made a point of voting "No." He wrote his mother, "I could not help praying that we should keep out of the war and not inflict more terrible wounds upon the face of the bleeding world than has been done already."[1] Van wrote in March, "You attach much greater significance to the Russian revolution [of March 1917] than we do—and I hope you are right . . . it will be, as you say, the biggest event since ninety-three."[2] (It was the second revolution, in October 1917, that installed Marxism.)

Ever since May 7, 1915, when the British ship *Lusitania* was sunk just before Roger was supposed to graduate from Harvard, it was clear from the reaction to the deaths of the 120 Americans on board that it would be impossible to stem the tide for revenge. Anti-German propaganda saw Germany as having a hidden agenda to undermine democracy and the United States. Submarine warfare that had sunk the *Lusitania* resumed in 1917. President Woodrow Wilson spoke of a "crusade to make the world safe for democracy." The German foreign minister's message that attempted to provoke Mexico and Japan into attacking the United States, decoded by the British, swayed America into action.

Ruth was in 109 Elm on Good Friday, April 6, 1917, when Roger came in holding the newspaper and said, "in the quiet tone that always reminded me of his father, 'I hate to tell you, Mother, but *war is declared*.' And I remember saying solemnly, 'That is the end of Wilson.' "[3] Ruth was steadfastly anti-war.

The US entered the Great War in April 1917. Telegrams and letters among Roger, George, and Van flew back and forth discussing Wilson, the war, pacifism, and the inevitable conscription, which began May 18, and what they would do about it. On April 9 Roger wrote George, "I expect to be exempt, but if I can't get out of it, I shall probably seek work in the Medical Corps, and try with all my might to get it; and if I fail, I will simply have to take the consequences—prison or even death." This may sound melodramatic, but soon pacifists were rounded up and imprisoned, and in one publicized case a conscripted man was put to death. Sessions continued,

> I am prepared to do my bit for non-resistance and freedom of conscience. Certainly the latter is one of the eternal principles, if the former is not. As I said before, I admire Mr Wilson with all sincerity; and I desire with all my soul to work for the same ends as he, in their larger aspects. But I don't see how these can be fulfilled by my offering my conscience on what seems to me an altar of folly and wanton cruelty. I am willing to risk my life for any principle of ultimate good, but I am not willing to do what seems to me to be harm in so doing, or, if possible, to help take the lives of others who may be—and many of whom undoubtedly are—in my position.[4]

Sessions was graduated in May just as the first American troops were being sent to Europe.

Pacifist Ruth advised her son: "I have been rather worried lest you might have kept up pacifist talk since the declaration of war. That would be somewhat dangerous."[5] She had devised her own solution for Roger, one that fitted nicely with her innermost desires that Forty Acres and Phelps Farm continue in the family. She reasoned that there would be a need for an increased food supply, so Sessions should come in the summer to Hadley and grow vegetables and study farming, thereby supposedly contributing to the war effort. She even leaked this story, naming Sessions, to the local newspaper; he and others were to cultivate food products this summer. With spectacular circular reasoning she ended the same letter by saying how glad she was that he was undertaking the agricultural work.[6]

On April 24, 1917, Roger and George played the two-piano concert of modern French music. Roger wrote George, who wanted to go abroad with Van and work for the Red Cross, "If anything should happen to you, George, it would be the hardest blow I have ever had to bear, and one of the very hardest I ever will have to bear; and my life, as you know, hasn't been exactly a happy one. . . . I am perfectly sick with anxiety, George."[7] George had met all of the members of Sessions's family. For his part, George found his parents would not fund his working in the ambulance corps in France, and Van left on May 27 without him. (Sessions went to New York to see Van off, June 9, 1917.) Dos Passos followed shortly afterward. George, too, was sick with worry:

> Now that [Van] is gone I realize what a deep affection I really have for him—a love more intense than I have ever had for a woman. . . . I meant never to tell this to anybody, least of all to Van himself, but it is such a relief to write to someone who really understands my feelings. Of course to have told Van how I really feel

Figure 18 George Hodges Bartlett.

toward him would make him not only uncomfortable but perhaps ironical so I have to let it remain an idealistic and unconsummated love, which is perhaps best after all."[8]

It is hard to see how this letter could have comforted Roger, as it did not return his feelings. On the other hand, he may have been relieved that George and Van's relationship was unconsummated: "Your letter, which would have plunged me into utter despair [two weeks prior, when he saw George in Cambridge], has made me very happy. . . . I have realized for some time how much you care for Van; and I can see how much you are missing him. . . . For we could not possibly live if our disappointments and sorrows lasted forever."[9]

During May, the same month that conscription was enacted and the relationship with George had come to a crisis point, the Symphonic Prelude was premiered at Yale. The piece looks on the page like César Franck's organ music. He had not completed the work, so only the first movement was performed. The nervous Roger asked Parker to conduct it, "as I am afraid I would gum the show."[10] Parker felt it no reflection on Sessions, whose unexpected stage fright may have been in part the result of a fervent desire that the music not disappoint George. Nevertheless, proud Archibald had given Sessions his prized Theodore Thomas baton with which to conduct the concert. The concert was held on Thursday, May 24, in Woolsey Hall at Yale and included works by 14 composers. Six new pieces by Yale students were interspersed among works by Handel, Viotti, Chopin, Schumann, Mendelssohn, and Liszt; four of the premieres were conducted by their composers.[11] Before the intermission and the Sessions piece, an announcement was made of three prizes and scholarships, including the $100 Steinert Prize, which Sessions won. Roger's family was present, as were George and Van. Aunt Addie had come, and Archibald brought a Mr Armstrong, a friend of Loudon Charlton, the representative of pianist Harold Bauer, violinist Jacques Thibaud, and conductor Josef Stransky, and other artists.

Immediately after hearing the concert Sessions felt he needed professional advice. He wrote to the composer Philip Greeley Clapp, a Harvard alumnus who had been a teaching fellow at Harvard during Roger's first year. Clapp had conducted his First and Third Symphonies with the Boston Symphony Orchestra and in the spring of 1917 taught at Dartmouth. Sessions sent Clapp the Symphonic Prelude and asked for technical advice.

Sincere in his praise and credible in his criticisms, Clapp wrote a detailed criticism of the movement. We can glean from this letter the problems a young composer often experiences writing his first orchestral piece. Although Clapp did not use this phrase, his advice amounted to what Strauss said of Mahler's music, "It's over-instrumented." In other words, Clapp pointed to places where the instruments cover each other; he concentrated in particular on the woodwinds, bass clarinet, and English horn, who on occasion get drowned out.

Clapp easily detected the influence of other composers: d'Indy, Chausson, and Ropartz and other Franckians.[12] At one transition he could "feel the joint." Although his criticisms had almost entirely to do with orchestration and miscalculations of balance, he reminded Sessions that nobody yet has written an orchestral work—especially a first work—with perfect orchestral color; his example was Sibelius's first symphony. It was, nevertheless, the orchestration, the course Sessions took twice with Hill, that Clapp found most praiseworthy:

The scoring [on page 10] is audacious, but I should think highly effective. . . .

On page seventeen, you have some very novel scoring which should be effective under a careful and competent conductor. . . . The working up of your first theme beginning on page 30 is exceedingly effective and the return of the second is equally so.

Although Clapp felt Sessions had not broken from his French models,

the imitation is [a] very honest sort of imitation and also very intelligent. You already show an exceptional feeling for orchestral color. . . . You further show distinction of style, and, what is still better, distinction of feeling. . . . The statement that you have not yet attained a complete individuality of style must be immediately qualified with another, that you are rapidly attaining it and that the style promises power and fineness.[13]

Sessions acceded to his mother's plans (which Archibald supported) and farmed at Phelps Farm that summer. "Things are better than I dreaded they would be. I have impressed my mother with interest in the farm, hence the possibility of a visit to Webster," George's home.[14] Van wrote expressing the hope of "the clearing up of the family troubles and the descided [sic] improvement of your Mother's health."[15] "Family troubles" were alluded to in various letters to and from Sessions, but not spelt out. George and Van had evidently had an earful in person. Sessions visited George over the weekend of July 27.

Sessions was growing fond of his older cousin Barrett Huntington (his uncle George's son). He lent Barrett books on Freud, but Huntington disapproved. Sessions felt Barrett "must have forgotten his own youth," and that "Freud's most contested discoveries seem so utterly evident to me—because of my own experience—that I would stake my life on their truth."[16] George, meanwhile, was spending the summer tutoring a younger brother for his Harvard exams, playing the organ several hours a day, and reading *Sons and Lovers*. Van would leave Colorado, travel to New Haven to hear Sessions's Symphonic Prelude, and embark for Paris shortly afterward. George wanted to go as well, but could not. Van wrote Roger he "strongly resent[ed] the attitude that some have taken—as if I were dragging George to certain death."[17]

Van, John Dos Passos, and Robert Hillyer worked in the Norton-Harjes volunteer Ambulance Corps in Paris in Section Sanitaire 60. The three companions, who had walked all over Boston together in search of good restaurants,[18] did the same in Paris: They called themselves Athos, Porthos, and d'Artagnan, "The three omeletteers," or the "The grenadine guards."[19] After July, Van and Dos signed up for the newly founded American Red Cross Section I in Italy. (The two spent a great deal of time walking around Italy, too.) Such non-governmental work did not guarantee that on their return to the United States they would not be imprisoned for escaping conscription. Indeed, both Dos Passos and E. E. Cummings were imprisoned for what they had written in letters (opened and read by the censors).[20] The robust Van found "everything, except the slaughter[,] is exhilarating."[21] He wrote to Roger,

You don't answere [sic] my letter. You damnable ingrate. The only way I see, to teach you gracious behavior and rear in me solidity of character, is for you and me to stray together, earning and stealing our daily bread as suits the whim, talking old languages, knowing different people for better for worse, and generally escaping the smug, moral, stunting routine life reserved for stay-at-homes.

So pack a bag half full of your clothes and half full of [George's], and come with me the two of you. We can turn later to teaching and preaching and fathering for solace in our potbelly-age. Just now come away and take a chance. Caged birds don't sing, Roger.[22]

How much this prospect may have appealed to Sessions is difficult to determine. Part of him, surely, wanted to see Europe, escape his family, and be with his friends. Despite the example of these friends, Sessions did not, in his subsequent letters, bring up such a possibility for himself. Such a trip would have to be privately funded—as volunteer work, not part of the services—and it was possible that neither Ruth, despite her pacifist principles, nor Archibald, who believed in the war, was willing to send their son. The unanswered question is whether Sessions had asked them to.

His Yale friends Bruce Simonds and Quincy Porter gave a series of recitals that summer in various New England towns for the benefit of the Red Cross (see the opening of Chapter 1). Both Sessions and his mother became ill at the beginning of August 1917. This restricted his diet and included doses of castor oil. None of this prevented Sessions voracious reading, which this time included Artzibasheff's *Breaking Point* (a second reading), Kuprin's *The Duel*, Hardy's *Life's Little Ironies*, and Plato's *Symposium, Phaedo*, and the *Republic*.

Although Sessions's summer of 1917 was spent relatively quietly at the farm reading Diderot and Montaigne, his friends abroad were alarmed to read disquieting reports about him. Robert Hillyer had written to Van that two Yale students, one of them Roger Sessions, were arrested for distributing anti-conscription literature.[23] Dos Passos had heard this, probably from Hillyer, now a uniformed army lieutenant, and twice asked urgently in letters, "What about Roger Sessions? Did he get arrested or anything?"[24] In Paris, Van was simultaneously proud of Roger and upset over the incident. Roger wrote of this supposed arrest to George: "First time I heard of it!"[25]

In these letters Sessions waxed on about his favorite music of the moment: Hugo Wolf songs and short works by Brahms. The French influence from Harvard may have been waning in his music when he wrote, "There is in the greatest German music a depth, and inherent sense of having been lived, that I find absent in most French music." And "Brahms's music is more the music of a *people* and has more the folk-quality [than Franck]."[26] Many letters to George ended sentimentally: "By merely existing and being yourself you make it easier for me to endure the incessant stupidity of human nature—including my own. But words are empty, and someday I will tell you in music how you make me feel. Even if I dedicate my [already premiered] symphony to M. Rolland, the second movement will always be yours, and I will try hard to make it as worthy of you as possible."[27]

Within days, by September 1917 Sessions decided to dedicate the entire Symphony to George.

I hope [my previous letter] will not deter you seriously from accepting my symphony. . . . While you must not think that I am ashamed of such senti-ments, which make life worth living, their expression on paper is a little ghastly and absurd; though I really suppose that there was no other way of letting you know what I wanted you to. Nevertheless everything we do is absurd—so much so that even solemn asses like myself must see it and revel in it. Also remember that we solemn asses are sometimes so inspired by beautiful creatures like your-self that we could dance ourselves to death in our superabundant vitality.[28]

George accepted the dedication. "I am so glad that you will accept my symphony—to put it mildly, and that is an incentive to my very best work," Sessions wrote.

> You know I have an idea that when one conceives a work of art, it already exists, but the artist's task consists in finding the exact means of expression. That is a mystical way of expressing what actually does take place. Every note is—to speak figuratively—predetermined, and our only task is to find the right notes—a frightfully difficult task, which has never in history been wholly successfully carried out.[29]

In July 1917 Sessions learned that he had been hired at Smith College, and therefore would not be moving back to Boston. Because of his age (20), he was to be an assistant at $800 a year. He was in full charge of the orchestration course and half of the composition, and was asked to play the bassoon in the Smith orchestra. His mother still ran the off-campus dormitory at 109 Elm Street in Northampton, where he grew up, Sessions House. Ruth may have been instrumental in obtaining Sessions the job; Ruth was close friends with Mrs Sleeper. He was hired on the strength of having won the Steinert Prize at Yale for the first movement of his unfinished D major symphony. Henry Dike Sleeper's one condition for the Smith job was to complete the piece.

Sessions first lived at Mrs Day's house, 36 Paradise Road, and later moved to 7 College Lane. This room was the nicest Sessions had ever had to that point. He did not, as previously, post on the wall reminders of his "past sins" such as the *Harvard Musical Review*, degrees, and pictures of his two grandfathers and the class of 1915. Rather, his four framed pictures were of d'Indy, Stravinsky, the recently deceased poet Emile Verhaeren, and a Monet landscape.[30]

William Allan Neilson, recently made president of Smith, had taught at Harvard. He was "always a very good friend of mine who gave tacit support to me."[31] Friends on the faculty included Roy Dickinson Welch in the music department, who introduced him to Neilson and would later ask Sessions to join the Princeton faculty; Arthur Ware Locke of the music faculty; Rafaello Piccoli, visiting Professor of Italian literature (1919–1920), whom Sessions felt understood him better than anybody else; John Spencer Basset, who taught history and Latin; organist Wilson Moog; and Margaret Thorpe (Farrand) of the English and Journalism faculty. He also got to know Bessie and Senda Berenson, head of physical education at Smith, Bernard Berenson's sisters. They would introduce Sessions to the art critic.

The music department consisted of Welch (who taught from 1914 to 1925), Blanche Goode (from 1913 to 1922), Rebecca Wilder Holmes (1903–1936), Arthur Locke (1915–1952), and Mary Creusa Tanner, class of 1915, who was an assistant in music from 1915–1919. The head of the department was Sleeper. Sessions and his faculty friends met for drinks on Saturday nights; they discussed politics and much else. This group consisted of Everett Kimball of the history department, Sidney B. Fay and John Bassett of the Greek and Latin department, Paul Rober Lieder, Alfred V. Churchill, and Locke of the music department. The group was considerably older than Sessions, and, as Ruth learned by being interrogated after the war, they were considered radicals.

Sessions had first met Welch, 12 years older, casually at a rehearsal Welch attended with his first wife. "By the time I went up to take my job, a couple of weeks before the term [at Smith] started, his first wife died. It was really a terrible tragedy for him. I mean, he was absolutely shattered by it. . . . I guess Roy came back [from the war] the third year that I was there."[32]

Hired first as an assistant for $800 a year (not an assistant professor), Sessions became an instructor in his last year (for $1,200). The $800 was at the lowest end of the salary scale at Smith; most of the 19 music faculty earned $1,500, while Sleeper, one of two full professors, made $3,500. Some of his students were also older than he. During Sessions's first year at Smith he taught two courses in orchestration (elementary and advanced), composition, and music appreciation. Sessions referred to each of the four years as his freshman, his sophomore, junior, and senior years.

Ivan Gorohkov, the former assistant choirmaster of the Moscow Cathedral, gave a performance of the Mozart Requiem. Sessions, struck by it, wrote for the *Smith College Monthly*:

> Russian music differs from that of other nations chiefly by virtue of the fact that it is the music, not preeminently of great individuals, but of a whole people . . . The Russian ballet represents the upper class of Russia only, a class which fell with the Tsar [the previous year] . . . In the liturgical music of the Russian orthodox church is embodied an art which has no parallels in the music of other countries. . . . The Russian service is even more largely musical than the Roman; and unlike the Roman service, its music is the work, not only of tradition, but of the finest Russian composers. . . . Profoundly emotional, yet at the same time dignified and intensely religious, it has neither the somewhat inconsequential solidity of most Protestant church music, nor the complex formal beauty of the Roman contrapuntal and Gregorian music.[33]

Sessions let himself get carried away with grandiose plans involving both Gorohkov and one of the greatest masses written.

> In the spring of 1920, in honor of Beethoven's 150th anniversary we are going to give a big Beethoven festival here, the principal event of which will be a performance of the Missa Solemnis, which Gorohkov and I are going to work on together, i.e. he will train the chorus I the orchestra. Rehearsals will begin next February or March, in order that the performance may be as perfect as possible. But think of the opportunity for me, or starting my career as a conductor with the greatest of all works. I sing in the chorus under him.[34]

For whatever reason, although both Sessions and Gorohkov were still teaching at Smith in 1920, the concert never occurred. Sessions continued his habit of announcing to others concerts and pieces long before the preparation and work were finished. We therefore hear more about what he *wants* to do than what has been accomplished, a pattern that persists for another decade. For example, during the second semester, Sessions and Locke planned a Friday evening series of lecture-recitals on modern orchestral music. The two began with *Tod und Verklärung*, playing it on two pianos. They planned also to do the d'Indy and Chausson symphonies, *Heldenleben, Afternoon of a Faun*, the Brahms First, the Beethoven Ninth, Berlioz's *Romeo and Juliet*, and Bruckner's Seventh. It is difficult to learn, however, whether these subsequent lectures took place.

His views on religion were also changing. Sessions ordered ten copies of the *Masses* both to distribute and to needle his minister. "Of course I shall not go to his church," he wrote to George, "if I ever go to church, it will be the R.C.; though I expect to sleep Sunday mornings."[35] George, too, considered joining the Roman Catholic Church in Webster to rise above the fray. Cuthbert Wright had lent plainchant to George, who had accepted an offer from Father Sill to teach at Kent School. He replaced Cuthbert in English history, when Wright joined Dos, Van, and Hillyer in France.

Sessions took teaching seriously, and advised George, who had solicited advice after having been invited to teach music at another preparatory school, Loomis. In a lengthy typewritten letter Sessions outlined his views regarding teaching music.

> I don't know whether you really can take much interest in teaching or not. I do myself, as far as the teaching of individuals is concerned, where I can get some real insight into the workings of people's minds and points of view, though in interest it is confined a little strictly to those who are really interested in what I have to give them. If you do enjoy it I think its disadvantages can be minimized if not entirely overcome. They lie in the intellectual pride and intolerance and self-satisfaction which comes from having one's word accepted as gospel in a very small world, and a consequent condescension toward the really important world without. When one is flattered to that extent one naturally gets the idea that one[']s small world must be right—more so than any other world, and this is what is called provincial mindedness. . . .
>
> What is most important, though, is that you should aim high, and not be content with merely teaching, especially in a prep school. I think that you could make a very good teacher of music if you really want to; but you should first become a musician in the real sense of the word. The thing that I object to in our department here [at Smith] is that so many of the highest men in our depart-ment are not. . . . [I can see] that you are at least on the way to a thorough understanding of music from the technical side . . . We Americans are too prone to confuse technical proficiency in an art with academicism, which is certainly odious and stifling; but no one has the real right to call himself a musician who hasn't at least a critical knowledge of the various elements—some of them wholly neglected in most musical instruction—in the technique of the art. . . .
>
> You obviously mustn't try to become a teacher of anything unless you have a deep faith in what you are teaching, and without such faith it would be disas-trous for you to undertake such a thing. . . . But unless you can give yourself to your music quite unreservedly there is worse than no use in taking it up; you will end in disillusion and despair, or what is far worse, in amiable futility if you do. D'Indy's words about the necessity to the artists of the three Christian virtues (what is the technical name?) are as true as they can be. . . . And, remem-ber that where art is concerned it must be absolutely a labor of love.[36]

As had also occurred when George asked for advice in writing an *HMR* article, it appears that Sessions intimidated him by imposing his own high and unrealizable ideals as prerequisites. (George was certainly qualified to teach music at a preparatory school.) Cowed, George never published again in the *Review*, remained at Kent, and never taught music.

During his "sophomore" year at Smith, 1918–1919, Sessions first tasted the internal political problems nearly always present among members of a college faculty. During an argument about teaching methods, Sessions said heatedly, "Any musician would agree with me." Henry Dike Sleeper called him "a young upstart."[37] Sleeper also accused him of not finishing his symphony (which, of course, was true). The implication of this altercation was that Sessions had lost his job; fortunately, Neilson backed him up. Despite the fact that Sleeper was subsequently voted out of his position as Chairman by

Sessions and his friends, Sessions's problems at Smith did not end.[38] He felt misunderstood and "wasn't really among musicians at all in my sense of the word. It was not a real musical life."[39] He felt constrained academically as well: "I was supposed to ask the students to write little pieces about the snow on the campus and that sort of thing instead of teaching them harmony and counterpoint."[40] Ultimately, he was not satisfied talking about music; he wanted to make it.

Sessions's feelings about the war varied. President Burton of Smith had signed a telegram urging President Wilson not to declare war, and Burton may have said something to the effect that Sessions should be careful. Sessions said, "At first, I was very much against the war. In fact, I won't say I got into trouble, I didn't really, but . . . I was looked upon askance in certain quarters, because I signed petitions and that sort of thing."[41] Ruth remembered:

> But from that time on he was more or less under suspicion, and the accusations against me for being "pro-German," as it was put, were occasionally strengthened by attacks on my children. I learned not to be surprised when told that my son was said to be a degenerate, a drunkard, and later a draft-dodger, when he had been rejected by the draft-board because of an eyesight-deficiency for which he had worn glasses since early [sic] boyhood. Those things were simply effects of war-hysteria, and I always asked not to be told who had reported the untruths.[42]

Burton left Smith in the fall of 1917 and was replaced by William Allan Neilson, who counseled young men, including Roger, to help them maintain a balance of liberal thought even while feeling conscientious objections to military service.

During the first winter of the American participation in the war (1917–1918) a family event drove home the divisions over the subject. Nan married Paul Shipman Andrews on December 3, 1917. They had been engaged more than a year, and Paul was expecting to be sent to France. She went to Camp Devens in Ayer, Massachusetts, where Andrews was stationed. From September to December 1918 Nan was assistant to Ellen Emerson in the Red Cross. After the war, from May 1919 to September 1924 the couple lived outside of Paul's hometown, Syracuse, New York, in Onondaga. Sessions played a march on the piano at the wedding, while Ruth accompanied a violinist. The service ended dramatically: Sessions performed the *Star-Spangled Banner* on a large trumpet. Ruth recalled, "But the spectacle of the musician, his cheeks full and tense as he solemnly pumped air into the unaccustomed instrument, brought a fit of amusement which I could hardly control. This supreme sacrifice of our pacifist predilections and agonized musical sensibilities upon the altars of Hymen and Mars was too much for pent-up emotions."[43] Archibald kept a straight face, a consistent patriot, but Roger and his mother exchanged amused looks.

Sessions considered himself a pacifist and a conscientious objector. Although the Smith faculty vociferously welcomed a local boy "done good" by joining them, he found two disadvantages: "To be the son of the foremost woman citizen is to be somewhat of a public character, and my pacifist opinions may cause me a good deal of discomfort. Though the war seems remote, Northampton is almost solid behind it; in fact, I don't believe there are any out-and-outers except my mother and I in the city." He had received a note from a French professor, Mlle Louise Delpit, enclosing a *Northampton Times* editorial on the subject of misguided zealots duped by pro-German propaganda, which she asked him to read and carefully meditate on its lesson.[44]

> I had to explain [in a letter] that I was neither a propagandist, nor a pro-German; that I was not even an "American pacifist"; but that I was an internationalist, influenced almost wholly by Europeans—among whom was her own countryman Romain Rolland. . . . I am, of course, perfectly willing to have people cut me on the street or denounce me from the pulpit if they want; but it is rather disagreeable at first, as I can't tell just who is friendly and who is hostile; though I have not encountered any really hostile people yet.[45]

It is noteworthy that, given both his subsequent identification with the term and his sympathy with Europeans, Sessions in 1917 had already proclaimed himself an "internationalist."

Sessions was friendly with anti-war leaders and read their publications. In early September 1917 he dropped by the office of *The Masses* in New York where he talked with Merrill Rogers. *The Masses*, a socialist periodical that began in 1911, ceased publication with the Espionage Act of 1917, which allowed the Postal Service to refuse to mail "seditious" literature. Its editors, including Merrill Rogers, were tried twice for anti-war activities in 1918, with both trials resulting in hung juries. Seeing Rogers's trial could easily have scared Sessions, since he was intellectually allied with Rogers and a subscriber to and distributor of *The Masses*.

Sessions also read Thorstein Veblen's *Inquiry into the Nature of Peace and the Terms of Its Perpetuation* published in 1917. He wrote,

> Mere moral objection to war does not satisfy me. If the war is the lesser of two evils really, I cannot see how I am possibly justified in not supporting it, even though I do so with tremendous qualifications—in fact, I could not support it otherwise. But I haven't yet been able to see things as most other people do; and that bewilders me either because I have perhaps too often been accustomed to look to the majority for support in crises like this, or because [his two Yale friends, Mike Elliot and Fritz Anderson] with whom I think so much in common, seem to be in favor of it. When I argued in favor of war in the now remote past (February and March 1916 and before) it was because, of course, I saw war as only the sentimental idealists saw it; for I still feel that the so-called "war-like virtues" are valuable. But even if modern warfare called them forth—and it does not—it would not be worth it.[46]

Sessions wrote to George in January 1918, "Of course I am glad, especially as my oculist, who is on the exemption board, says there is no danger of my being conscripted. I must say I am glad, though it deprives me of a problem to solve. But I fancy there will be others in life."[47] Although President Wilson never used the term, "100 percent Americanism" describes his adminstration's pro-war propaganda to "make the world safe for democracy." The ultimate musical effect was to criticize German performers and repertoire. German Kultur was seen as decadent; orchestral musicians rushed to apply for US citizenship; and the Metropolitan Opera performed German operas in English for one season. Walter Damrosch and Josef Stransky began to open each New York concert with the *Star-Spangled Banner*.

Although the *Star-Spangled Banner* was not officially the national anthem until 1931, the fact that BSO conductor Karl Muck had not performed it in Rhode Island led to a ban on the Boston Symphony playing in Baltimore, where the anthem had been written. On March 26, 1918, Karl Muck was to have given a performance of the Bach *St Matthew*

Passion, which Muck regarded as the crowning performance of his career. Sessions, en route to hear the performance, learned that Muck had been arrested. (Ernst Schmidt took over the concert and the remainder of the season.) Muck had been arrested the previous day without charges; he resigned from the Boston Symphony five days later. Even Henry Higginson, the Civil War veteran and founder of the symphony, could not protect the conductor. Muck was imprisoned at Fort Oglethorpe, Georgia, as an enemy alien and, after 17 months, deported nine months after the war was over. A naturalized Swiss citizen, Muck had been principal conductor at the Royal Opera House in Berlin, where he had officially worked for the Kaiser. Twenty-nine other BSO members were also interned.[48] Also in March 1918, a US court martial sentenced a youth to death for refusing to report for military duty when drafted.

This treatment of Karl Muck must have terrified Sessions. Here was a man whose artistic abilities had formed Sessions's own view of orchestral music. To see Muck, whom he admired enormously, and 29 other members of the Boston Symphony arrested and interned must have frightened him to his core. (Sessions was later told a story about Muck's being interned in order to avoid a scandalous affair with a girl from Brookline.) But the clash of two of Sessions's most cherished ideals—music and politics—must have rattled him. If artists of this caliber could not escape war hysteria, who could? Certainly not a lowly Smith College music faculty member. By April 1918, the next month, Sessions had changed his mind entirely, later saying that "Wilson talked me around." Acting on this less-than-sincere *volte face*, he now tried to enlist and was disqualified for poor eyesight, which he had known since January would be the case. From a November letter, we learn that Sessions's change in attitude toward the war "came very suddenly one afternoon last spring; but I have felt since then as if I were gradually awakening from a long trance in which I had been led aimlessly about, devoid of will and of faith."[49]

Now Sessions resolved whatever discouragement he had at not being accepted into the service with the view that "we whose prospects of getting in are very small, have a very definite and great responsibility on our shoulders, and we can draft all our energies more and more exclusively for the disinterested service of mankind, and so I think it is now more than ever not only our privilege, but our duty in the strongest sense of the word to work and stand for the truth and the right as we are led to see it."[50]

Years later, during the beginning of the US's involvement in World War II, Sessions wrote "A letter to an imaginary colleague," the subheading for an article published as "Artists and this war."[51]

> It is also true that at the beginning of the last war I was a pacifist, and remained so until Mr. Wilson "talked me around." Let me say that I have since remained firmly convinced that Mr. Wilson was right. . . . When I made up my mind, therefore, that I must get into the fighting, if possible, I did so with the most unheroic feelings imaginable. What impelled me to do so was simply the sense that I would have been unable to live at peace with the self that had willingly allowed others to leave me behind in offering their lives in a cause in which I was vitally interested.[52]

Sessions's brother John, meanwhile, was on leave from Harvard to spend a term at the Yale Artillery School for military training. He was eager to be trained on guns. Nan, Paul, John, and Archibald considered themselves patriots for the war. Only Ruth never wavered, but of course she did not have to face the draft. Sessions later observed, "My mother was a violent pacifist, although she wanted the Allies to win—it wasn't very consistent of her. She even got furious when I decided that I *wasn't* against the war. She said I was betraying her. She had lived in Germany and was very anti-German, and of course there was a terrific spy hysteria during that time. It was a lot of nonsense."[53]

During the summer of 1918 Ruth had written Roger a scathing letter about his finances. She threatened him emotionally in a "new and unexpected way" (we do not have the letter). Roger wrote to Archibald requesting advice on how to deal with his mother. On July 14, 1918, Archibald typed a three-page reply. Decades of experience spoke in his remarks about Ruth:

> As you doubtless realize she is a woman of an uncommon amount of resource and determination and doesn't hesitate to use both . . . a strong, enterprising, dominating character. She doesn't easily give up the ascendancy over the minds and actions of others that she has been accustomed to. . . . Admitting as you do that you have deceived her . . . you may perhaps, understand how the conviction that you have . . . grown away from her helped to increase the soreness that she feels . . . [you] conceal[ed] from her complications in money matters, which she has found out . . . her first impulse is to do something to retain her influence with you and she does it by means of an appeal to your affection for her. . . . the manner in which she has made her appeal, is a mistaken one, but it is just what is to be expected from a person of the type to which she belongs. Nevertheless . . . the manner, surprising and disconcerting as it is, is not to be regarded. . . . Put yourself in her place, even to the point of assuming for the moment her life-long habit of control of the minds of other people and perhaps you can get an inkling of how she feels . . . your mother's unhappiness [occurred] because you have developed your independence of her . . . You may expect . . . to be met with something in the nature of a discouragement; you will probably be reminded again of your shortcomings . . . she is really reaching out to you for a manifest-ation of your regard for her . . . you need not hope to be entirely free for some time to come from her interest and activity in your affairs. And you have got to take account of the fact and decide between a definite break with her and a course that will mitigate the friction that is inevitable in relations with her as much as possible. . . . I wouldn't magnify the seriousness of this episode if I were you. That it is serious is true enough, but people usually make the mistake of always enhancing the importance of whatever happens to them. Always your loving dad.[54]

By August 1918 Sessions had completely converted to the war. Working at the Soldiers' Club House at Camp Devens he wrote to Father Sill:

> When I was at Kent I was in the throes of a long and rather painful process of thinking about the war and my own relation to it. When one's convictions are strong it takes a long time to change them, and if I had been drafted and physically fit just at that time I might have acted rashly and in such a way that I would have regretted it. As a matter of fact I tried to enlist in April, but was found disqualified for any form of service then also when I came up for the draft, my eyesight being only 15/200 normal. I don't consider myself any less a pacifist than I ever have been—and if I thought that any good could be done by it I could find many things in the policy of this country which seem to me to be utterly wrong and which at any other time I should use my tongue against with

the utmost vigor; but, although I still see all of these things, I think that now the war must be won as quickly as possible, and what is just as important, the foundations of a secure and permanent peace laid. And so I have been, of course anxious to help win an end to the war; and if the physical standards should ever be changed so as to include those as near-sighted as myself, I shall be among the first to enlist. . . .

That is my state of mind at present; and I am sure you will agree with it. It is very hard indeed to be out of the war itself—and that very feeling at times becomes a source of discouragement, where it ought to be a spur; for when one is perfectly able-bodied it is a torture to have to realize that one's capacity for usefulness is limited by dependence on two little round pieces of glass. But I do feel that there is a place for all of us, and so I struggle hard, and, I hope, victoriously, not to let such feelings get the better of me.[55]

Father Sill agreed with Sessions: he himself had wanted to serve. Given a chance to go to Europe, he then told himself that at no other place than Kent could he keep in touch with the 150 Kent alumni in the service. Pater wrote Sessions that Van was back in the United States and "seems to be in a very troubled state of mind."[56]

Sessions answered Pater's September letter from Smith almost immediately, and wanted to visit Sill. "But I am dead broke, and as I want to get down there ever so much, I wonder whether I could possibly ask you to lend me the money [ten dollars] until November or December. . . . But it still is hard to see one's brothers and friends going out and sacrificing themselves and yet be unable to share their sacrifices with them, in the real sense."[57] The friend he mentioned was not Van—he did not inquire about him—but Junior Hatch, who had told Sessions of his experiences abroad (and who was, perhaps not incidentally, married).

The ever-reliable Pater sent Sessions the ten dollars, and Sessions visited him at Kent twice that fall. He felt the trip necessary because

For some time I have felt the need of a good talk with you, such as I have not had since I left school, on religious matters; as you know or may have guessed, I have had a great many difficulties of that sort during the last years, and I feel that the time has come when I can and must clear them up. I have some very funda-mental things to learn, or relearn, and I need help which I feel that you could give me better than any one else.[58]

In May 1918, Sessions had arranged for a performance on which he and Locke first played his symphony—insofar as it was completed—on two pianos, then the Smith College orchestra performed the revised first movement. The concert may have been put together at the last minute; there is no program for it at Smith. Naturally the dedicatee, living in nearby Kent, was invited. In his first letter to George in four months Sessions expressed his change of view on the war. "I don't see how the world is to be fit to live in if the Germans should win. On being sure of myself on this point I tried to enlist; I was examined by the head of the local Medical Advisory board, who informed me that my eyes rendered me unfit for any form of service, even under the draft. I hope you will regard me as regenerate. I am still a conscientious objector."[59]

George knew that Sessions was already well aware before he tried to enlist that he would be turned down; a letter in January had established that fact. Perhaps George was unhappy about the perceived hypocrisy he had witnessed in his pacifist friend. He himself would register on June 5, although he felt sure of an exemption for a chronic problem. Perhaps he did not want too overtly to be accepting Roger's token of love, the symphony, since he was more emotionally involved with Van, whom he did not "suppose will ever come back again unless he has to." Perceptive and sensitive George realized that something had indeed changed in Roger. Highly uncharacteristically, George did not attend this performance of his symphony. The next month he apologized, writing stiffly, "Dear Roger—I have treated you in a thoroughly ungentlemanly manner and I am heartily ashamed of it." He gave a lame excuse for not sending a telegram explaining his non-appearance. One reasonable cause of his behavior came at the end of his letter; "I feel as if you had dropped me with a thump ever since that visit I made to Northampton in January—one of the nicest times we ever had—too."[60] Indeed, four months had gone by without a letter from Sessions until the May invitation. During those four months, while George moved to Kent and began teaching, Sessions continued to teach at Smith, changed his mind about the war, worked on the symphony, and, in March, also met a new love interest.

Sessions responded from the Harvard Club in New York, where he spent time with his father before going to work at Fort Devens for the summer. The symphony performance had gone well and Sessions was disappointed that George did not hear it. By this time Sessions had been thoroughly turned around by President Wilson's arguments:

> My heart is where it always has been on that subject; but I think that it becomes clearer every day that Germany must not win—that Prussian militarism must be crushed, if the creative forces of the world are to have free play in the future. And the only way in which that can be done is through the victory of the Allied cause—a military victory if necessary, a peace by reconciliation if it should ever be possible—I am afraid it will not. Those are Pres Wilson's views and they are mine; and I could not, holding these views, refuse to do anything which might contribute to the ends desired.[61]

As to who broke off the relationship, Sessions declared that George had done so. He felt that two springs had gone by without their understanding each other, and that had caused him "suffering." Sessions again asserted his love for George, but added bitterly "but to you I was merely a substitute for someone else." George responded that "I have always felt that you cared little about my affairs but I was glad to share yours because I felt that they were greater and more important than my own. I don't really feel that way but you must remember that you were a much older mind than I when we first met."[62] (The two were the same age chronologically.)

Camp Devens was not so arduous that Sessions did not have time to read George Brandes's book on Shakespeare and those of the Bard's plays he had not previously read. George declined another invitation to see Sessions, but almost immediately, in July 1918, wished he had not. He dropped a bombshell: "I was examined for the Draft on Friday, and put in the class of 'limited and special military service.' There was a rumour last night that I was to be sent off this week in a medical corps, but I can hardly credit it."[63] This was a blow to his mother Georgia, who felt he would never be drafted. Sessions wrote the next day: "I am not only sorry, but surprised, to hear that you have been accepted for limited service; for my eyes disqualified me from any form of service."[64] The self-absorption in the second half of that sentence is a little hard to stomach.

George drove to Hadley to see Roger at the beginning of August; John and Alberta Burk were staying with Ruth, but this time it was Sessions who did not appear. Sessions was hiding something that, if he saw George in person, he would betray. Now George regretted his absence in May. "You know I feel dreadfully about your symphony performance. It was a busy time at Kent but I could probably have gone if I hadn't felt that you didn't want me. Your letter had something in me [*sic*] that kept me from coming."[65] Sessions's response was even more conflicted than previously. Disavowing anything in his May letter that could have given George that impression, he then demanded no less than

> complete frankness and trust on your part. . . . So I look to you to play the part of a true friend and to meet me on absolutely my own terms. . . . So I implore you to realize the importance of all these considerations and to consider very carefully what must be done to save our friendship not only from danger to which it is liable in itself, but to save it from the sinister influence which it might all too easily exert upon other relations of our lives.[66]

What "sinister influence" did he mean?

In the same letter Sessions mentioned that he had visited Claremont, New Hampshire, and walked in the woods. Here Sessions was exhibiting far less than "complete frankness." Although he declared that "the whole difficulty may be that I want you too much," he also wanted a woman who lived in Claremont and neglected to disclose this. Sessions's "own terms" seemed to consist of requiring love from two people, while not confiding in either that he also loved someone else.

George's attempts to visit Hadley were foiled, and in the meantime Van returned to Boston face the draft. Sessions's new roommate at Smith was Frederick Dietz, an American whose German name would put him under suspicion. Sessions had gone to Kent for a heart-to-heart talk with Father Sill, and there had had a conversation with George, whom he wrote again in September. In that letter Sessions told George something he could not say in person: He was in love with "Miss F_____."

> Imagine the purest, humblest, and yet the strongest of spirits—strong enough to sustain and redeem a chaotic bundle of serpents like myself—which finds its expression in the most beautiful of all mediums—a wonderful speaking voice, which is commented upon by everyone and for which its possessor is famed everywhere; a spiritual beauty so overwhelming that one cannot wholly tell whether she has physical beauty of not—though to me she is most beautiful in every way. . . . I have no right to assume that she cares in the least for me—I merely have hopes."[67]

The last sentence is somewhat disingenuous, for Miss F_____ had invited Sessions to her family's home in Claremont that summer. He had known her since March—the midpoint of the otherwise mysteriously silent four-month period of non-communication with George.

A great calamity hit that fall: the famous 1918 influenza epidemic. Ruth's house at 109 Elm had 14 cases in the first ten days. Every house, on or off campus, was quarantined. Emergency infirmaries were filled, so Ruth turned one of their rooms into a ward. The epidemic lifted as quickly as it had descended; classes resumed, and many wanted to forget the illness and the death toll.

In the midst of this, Sessions ran in and out with news. One morning, November 3, 1918, factory whistles blared from Easthampton, Holyoke, and Springfield. Ruth grabbed the telephone to ask the operator what happened: "Treaty of Peace with Austria!" The telephone lines crowded while flags went up. Just then Sessions appeared and was asked to play something:

> "The Ninth Symphony, of course," he responded promptly. "There couldn't be anything better; wait and I'll run over and get it while you do the singing and praying." He did fetch it, and played it completely through, adagio and all, the girls moving about meanwhile in restless excitement. When he came to the Hymn to Joy, however, they stood about the piano and beat time with hands and feet.[68]

The staid old town of Northampton went wild. A leaderless mob marched up Elm Street, and cars tooted their horns. Although later dispatches arrived, saying that peace must still be arranged, this did not discourage people. The official announcement came seven days later.

Early on the morning of the Armistice, November 11, George wrote from the Kent School, "The bells are ringing again—I guess it is over at last. Cuthbert and the rest are saved, Van will probably not be sent to prison."[69] Sessions wrote on the 12th:

> Yesterday was a wonderful day for me. The morning Miss F_____ and I spent walking the fields of Hadley . . . the killing is all over, and that once more we can sing "Alle Menschen werden Brüder Wo dein sanfter Flügel weilt." Of course it was wonderful to be with her. On the way home we stopped in the cemetery, and I could not help wishing with all my heart that the dead could come to earth again even if for but one day. [Among those buried there were his grandfather the Bishop, his grandmother, his uncle George, and his sister Mary.] A few more such walks will be more than I can stand. As it was, the emotional tension was at some moments almost unbearable. But I never in my life had such an intense feeling of oneness in spirit with anyone. . . . Tell [Pater] that I spent a great deal of time in the Kent chapel in spirit yesterday.[70]

Hundreds of young men (F. Scott Fitzgerald—Sessions and Dos Passos's exact contemporary—was among them) were disappointed not to go to France to fight. President Wilson was the object of intense negative feelings, and a reaction set in against those suspected of anti-war activities.

In 1918 Dos finished his novel about the war, *Three Soldiers*.[71] When published in 1921, this third novel established Dos Passos as a major writer; it was one of the important American novels to come out of World War I. The parallels to the three friends—Van, Hillyer, and Dos Passos himself—have to be recognized. The character of Chrisfield seems, in this author's opinion, to be partly based on Van, while the main character, John Andrews, is clearly autobiographical with elements of Dos's Harvard friend Roger Sessions added. A biographer of Dos Passos points to Sessions as the model for the character John Andrews. In the next breath he also relates the Andrews character to *Jean-Christophe*, although after reading the Rolland novel Dos Passos turned against it.[72] Andrews is a Harvard-educated composer who, "When he had been a child . . . had lived in a dilapidated mansion that stood among old oaks and chestnuts, beside a road where buggies and oxcarts passed rarely to disturb the sandy ruts that lay in the mottled shade."[73] In addition, Andrews wants to study piano in Paris in order to support his dependent mother and aunt in the style to which they are accustomed. Later the blocked fictional composer explains,

> "But my mother taught me to play the piano when I was very small," he went on seriously. "She and I lived alone in an old house belonging to her family in Virginia [Dos Passos grew up in a mansion in Virginia] . . . Mother was very unhappy. She had led a dreadfully thwarted life . . . that unrelieved hopeless misery that only a woman can suffer. . . . She used to spend hours making beautiful copies of tunes I made up. My mother is the only person who has ever really had any importance in my life."[74]

A novelist of Dos Passos's caliber had a great deal of insight into Sessions's life.

Dos had read the manuscript to Van in Italy, and Van admired the novel because it "tweeked self-righteous America by the nose." The book was controversial when it appeared in 1921, considered to have "insulted the Army" by its raw portrayal of the American experience in the Great War. Van wrote to Dos, whom he felt had succeeded "in making America see how dreadfully she bulldozed herself with phrases, how pitifully she is ridden with the same vices for which she reviled the Germans, how brutally she squashes individuality." Van felt that the book did more to increase humaneness and decency than had the "glorious company of whiny liberals."[75] He finally understood why Dos had been "so bent upon volunteering" for the Army. Dos Passos wrote of Van in his memoirs: "Robert and I had both liked Van in college. He was one of a cozy group who lived in the same rooming house and called themselves the Family . . . Van was contrary, irascible and comical when he wanted to be as any blue-eyed Dutchman you ever saw."[76] Van and Dos Passos remained close. The only person to whom Dos wrote, in the summer of 1929, that he was to marry was Van. The unmarried Van's response, however, was flippant.

At Smith in 1918–1919 Sessions continued to work for the Red Cross. The second week Smith was put in quarantine from the influenza epidemic. All that meant to Sessions was more time to spend working on the symphony. Miss F____ went back to Claremont after a stay at Hadley where the two of them sat on the Connecticut River bank a half mile south of Forty Acres, "the most inexpressibly blissful moment of my life."[77] Needless to say, Sessions had prescribed that she read *Jean-Christophe*.

Sessions had fallen in love, again, and became engaged to marry. In that eventful March Sessions had met a student violinist, who was then a sophomore. She would later live at 26 Green Street and in the annex to Ruth Sessions's house during her senior year. The mysterious Miss F____.

BARBARA FOSTER

Of the many characters populating this book, the most mysterious and opaque is Barbara Foster. Even photographs of her are blurred and indistinct; it is hard to tell what she looked like, although she was described as beautiful.[1] The dim memories people have of her conflict; there is agreement, however, that Barbara had "a sad life." Some of what was said about her is purely hearsay from biased sources: Sessions's niece Sarah Chapin said Barbara was "crazy," "manic-depressive," and had "epilepsy." Catharine Huntington, Sessions's cousin, told Sarah that Barbara had difficulties with her mother who was "also psycho."[2] Sarah's own reaction to Barbara was that she was "beautiful and scary."[2] Barbara's sister Rosamond, however, saw her as "brilliant" but in "delicate health."[3] Both Ruth and Roger remarked that Archibald was quite fond of Barbara, while Ruth called her "brilliant and fascinating."[4] George spoke highly of her.

For 50 years most people who met and knew Sessions had virtually no contact with Barbara. In 1977 Ernest Bloch's daughter Suzanne was one of the very few who remembered her: "Barbara was a lovely young, young girl. I remember my mother used to say, 'How does an American woman look so neat? She always looks so neat.' She still does."[5] Opposites must have attracted: Barbara was "neat," Roger messy.

Sessions did not save Barbara's letters (with one significant exception), whereas she kept his numerous letters to her up until 1925. Any subsequent letters from him she might have saved were destroyed in a house fire in the 1970s. Therefore we inherit little of her prose on which to judge her personality. Ruth's autobiography is sketchy about Barbara, about whom presumably she could have said a great deal. Prausnitz concluded that Ruth did not perceive Barbara as a real competitor for Sessions's affections: she was still the center of his life. Sessions said nothing against Barbara—indeed, he felt real sympathy toward her—but told this author that she was not in good physical shape in a nursing home at the end of her life and that not much could have been gleaned from talking to her.

Here are the bare facts we know about Barbara Foster. She was born in Claremont, New Hampshire, on June 22, 1899, and died of a heart attack there July 4, 1980. Two and a half years younger than Roger, she was the second daughter of bank cashier Frank H. Foster of Keene, New Hampshire, and Inez E. Fairbanks of Brattleboro, Vermont.[6] Inez may have been brought up in a convent. Barbara's older sister was Eleanor Stewart Foster, an accomplished pianist who later married and divorced flautist and engineer Jan Merry Cohu.[7] The hearsay from Sarah Chapin is that Eleanor may have committed suicide. She spent most of her long life in Paris and died there. Rosamond Foster (later Sayre and Sheldon) was Barbara's younger sister by eight years and an aspiring pianist.[8] Before attending Smith College, Barbara had attended Stevens High School in Claremont. She studied the violin.

Figure 19 Barbara Foster.

Barbara's family was Episcopalian. Later in life she converted to Roman Catholicism: "Why stop at the vestibule when you can get to the source?"[9] Part of the cause of this conversion was her immersion in medieval art and early Christian churches; she worked with the prominent art historian Wilhelm Koehler.[10] Barbara Sessions, who sometimes wore a turban, was known in the art historical world as Koehler's assistant. That she was his lover as well is merely rumored and cannot be verified.

Roger and Barbara started seeing each other shortly after they met in March of 1918, during Roger's "freshman" year teaching at Smith College and Barbara's sophomore year as a student. Needless to say, the administration opposed romantic fraternization between faculty and students. This impediment led to difficulties for the couple, and at one point Roger had talked Barbara, an excellent student, into leaving school. The need to keep the relationship secret was crucial until they could become engaged. Roger proposed marriage on December 17, 1918, a month after the war was over.[11] The engagement ring he had bought her did not pass inspection with Ruth, however, who ridiculed it. Mortified, he got another ring. Ruth was frequently "sarcastic and condescending" to her children to maintain control over them. Although the courtship was brief—March to December 1918—the engagement lasted longer than anticipated, a year and a half, because it met with opposition from Ruth, who "hammered" Sessions with the fact that he was financially not stable enough to marry, from faculty at Smith, and from Barbara's parents, who erected several timing hurdles.

Roger wrote to Barbara's father formally requesting the hand of his daughter in marriage. Frank Foster responded not entirely enthusiastically:

I little imagined when I went to the train last evening to welcome Barbara that she was bringing home such a charge of high explosive with her luggage. The bomb however proceeded to go off shortly after her arrival. . . . You will I am sure, easily understand that it is not wholly easy to adjust oneself to a situation so little anticipated and which involves so deeply a dear child's future. . . . I am sure you will not take it amiss if I add that such acceptance must, for the present, be somewhat conditional. I feel that Barbara should finish her college course for one thing . . . And then too your own proffessional [*sic*] career must be considered and not handicapped by prematurely assuming marital responsibilities. . . . If we must give Barbara to you we shall grasp at all the available compensations and one of the chief ones, I feel, will be the privilege of knowing your mother and that soon I hope.[12]

The Bishop's daughter somehow infiltrated every possible aspect of Sessions's life. The Fosters' insistence that Barbara stay in school would mean a year-and-a-half wait until the marriage. Therefore Sessions started a campaign to undermine her parents' wishes. Even Aunt Molly was in on the plot, later offering her hilltop cabin as a place for the two to live, and then becoming guilt-ridden about hurting Inez Foster's feelings.

Despite the secrecy surrounding Sessions and Barbara's relationship, Sessions did reveal the secret engagement to at least two people close to him: George and Pater. He wrote George a week after becoming engaged and tried to finesse the fact that he himself had not been entirely forthcoming with George while having demanded "complete frankness" from him. Indeed, he tried to blame George, in part, for his not telling him the truth.

> George, can you realize what it means when I tell you that I am engaged? I told you a little of how I felt, and I told you that it was the first time I had ever really been in love; and yet you had heard me say that very thing so often before that you chuckled inside—I felt you doing it—and set me down as having made an ass of myself once more. Perhaps you still think so; the consciousness that you felt that way prevented me from talking much about it, and you cannot have seen what was in my mind all the time. At any rate, no one was ever more in love, more profoundly moved by the greatest of experiences than I am, and it is because of this that I hesitated before telling you, lest you, who stand in the peculiar relationship to me of one who knows intimately one of my former selves, yet who seems to have lost touch with me since because of that very knowledge, should not understand what has come into my life. You see, we outgrow our old selves much faster than we realize it; and while I was at Yale and even later I had not learned to catch up with myself while I was with you. And you know very well that we have lost touch with each other since then. So I am telling you this because I want you again to be my friend, or rather our friend, for I have already ceased to think of myself as one person.
>
> . . . I was wrong when I wrote you and told you that I was not willing to meet you half way. I am, and I hope you will forgive me for having said that, which may have been the whole cause of our misunderstanding. . . . I can only tell you that she is about my sister's height, with light brown hair, blue eyes, very delicate skin and the most beautiful speaking voice in the world. . . .
>
> I am sure, George, that I am glad I told you; and let us forget the past and be natural, not self-conscious, with each other.[13]

George rose to the occasion with generous friendship. "I little realized that it would come so soon but I have long hoped for such a letter as I had from you yesterday. . . . I burn with a flame far less powerful than yours but it never languishes and it has stood the test of years." George gladly acceded to Roger's request to write to Barbara, but Sessions's letter also evoked some self-examination on George's part.

> You know, it worried me for weeks to have both you and Pater say, within a few days of each other, that I was sure to be a debonnaire old bachelor—intimating (in Pater's case), saying frankly in yours that I lacked all enthusiasm including my power to love truly and wholeheartedly. The truth of the matter is that I don't know where I am. I lack oneness of purpose . . . Your path was somewhat plainer to embark upon[,] I imagine[,] however much depression it may bring on at times.[14]

Enormously relieved by George's reply, Sessions wrote on New Year's Eve 1918: "You have come back to me—or is it I who have come back to you—the real you, I mean? . . . Whenever you care to 'bother' me with your troubles you will find me a willing listener and eager to help you or be of comfort in any way that I can."[15] George did write to Barbara, stiffly he feared, but a trip to Northampton to meet her was temporarily out of the question, since the influenza quarantine was still in effect. She wrote a friendly letter wanting to meet George and see Kent, but could not travel there for the same reason. Finally the quarantine was lifted, and George came to Northampton to meet Barbara, February 2, 1919.

The previous month Barbara and Eleanor had made their first trip to New York, where they met Archibald without Roger. Archibald was duly impressed, "[Barbara] is one of those very rare persons who makes the life of every one that knows her richer + in my case she has not only done that, but she has brought to me a new reval[u]ation of you. For if such a girl could give you what she has, you must have something in you that, with all my affection for you, I had not suspected."[16]

Sessions wrote to Father Sill of his engagement, again willing away Frank Foster's objections.

> Pater, I have never in my life had cause to be so thankful for anything so much as for the fact that the years of my manhood have been clean ones. Will you pray that I may be helped to be worthy of this great happiness and that I may give her the very best that a man can give? . . . [P.S.] You can see how important it is that, since girls' colleges are in spirit *a little* like girls' boarding schools, this should be kept in the *utmost secrecy*. It would make it very hard for us if the girls should get news of it; so I will ask you to mention it to no one except with my permission. George Bartlett knows, but nobody else at [Kent], and unless there is a very good reason I don't want anyone else to know but those I have told.[17]

We may make two assumptions regarding Sessions's views of sexuality from this letter. First, he did not consider intercourse with George to count against keeping his manhood years "clean." Second, that he had not yet had sexual relations with Barbara. Despite his request for Pater's prayers, and those prayers themselves presumably offered, Sessions did not keep his vow to remain a virgin until marriage.[18]

Roger and Barbara did not return George's visit by going to Kent, where they were expected at Easter. First, Sessions had fallen down a fire-escape and scraped skin from the left side of his face, then caught a cold that turned into the flu, which hospitalized him.

Most important, however, was that "Barbara's family objected to the Kent trip on the ground of conventions." To appease them, they postponed it indefinitely. "It is revolting to have to do this, but defiance, in which we could perfectly well indulge, would mean a complete break and would involve a good deal of suffering for them . . . It is a terrifically difficult relationship, as you may guess, and all has not gone well by any means."[19] Inez Foster would not even let Roger and Barbara take a walk together in Claremont. Indeed, Barbara did not see Kent until August 1920, more than a year later—and after their marriage as propriety demanded.

In June 1919 Sessions wrote George that he had heard from John Burk, who had "seen Van and that V. and I are apparently permanently estranged."[20] Sessions thought this in part because Van did not reply to his engagement announcement; Van, however, was ironic about all marriage.

Also in June 1919, Foster wrote again:

> I am going to be perfectly frank and tell you that the proposal seemed to present not only the traditional two horns that every dilemma wears but several subsidiary ones. If I undertook to veto the plan [of marrying at Christmas time] I was confronted with the prospect of making you both certainly very unhappy, and very probably resentful and if I consented it meant a considerable wrench both to Mrs Foster and myself to have Barbara abandon her college course to which our ambitions for her were very thoroughly committed and even more difficult for us is to reconcile ourselves to her marriage so much sooner than we had thought of, with the difficulties of providing for her in this short half year, even the minimum of the things she ought to have in the way of outfit and equipment. Then too from what Barbara tells me it is going to be not at all easy for you to provide out of your salary the many necessary things that will be essential for beginning housekeeping even on the most modest possible scale.[21]

Because Barbara had at this point lost interest in college, Foster gave in on that score, but he granted permission for the following Christmas conditional on the duration of her grandfather's serious, helpless condition, a burden on Inez Foster. He would prefer Easter or the following June (1920). Again he mentioned Ruth and the "great treat" of seeing the whole family together. For her part, Ruth had made an aborted plan for Archibald to come in the summer of 1919 and travel to Claremont together to meet the Fosters. "Mother, I think, is anxious to show that we are a united family."[22] Archibald had attended Nan's wedding. Ruth, perhaps hypocritically, wanted to "*show*" a "united family," while, of course, they would not *be* a united family. The Sessions family had been severed for two decades.

Like perhaps all romantic relationships, this one was based on neurotic needs, particularly Sessions's. His "nervousness" is a subject that came up a great deal in his love letters to Barbara. He even read a book by Dr L. E. Emerson on the subject. He felt that marriage to Barbara would steady him. The nerves were a result of his relationship with Ruth; she had, by frequent and unexpected outbursts of criticism (and violence?), undermined his self-confidence. Although Ruth's moods passed quickly, they wreaked havoc: "I do everything in order to keep the peace with Mother," Sessions wrote. He found it difficult to sleep at night; old demons haunt him. He tells Barbara, as well, that he loves Nan but fears his mother.[23]

"The hardest thing in my life to conquer is the self-depreciation," he wrote, the doubt of his own strength. "And if for many years she tended to undermine my faith in the ways of which I have told you, yet I am—with your blessed blessed love, dear—regaining it a thousand-fold." And, "Like most of my talks with Mother, it [the conversation] threatened to become a *contest*—it was, in fact." He even attributed his "fear of life" to "too much maternal influence."[24] One three-page letter contained 16 emotional "Pleases," most underlined, a great deal with which to burden an undergraduate. Indeed, there are also references to having hurt Barbara and causing her suffering; she is subject to his "moods." She, too, felt insecure. He refers to his "emotional domination" of her and her "emotional subjection" to him: Sessions said he had an "impulse to dominate," which may have come from his mother. Four years after their marriage, Sessions hoped "no vestige of an inferiority complex—that most damnable, pernicious, insidious of all worms—should trouble you any more."[25] In 1922, he wrote "whenever we have seemed fundamentally to disagree, you have almost always stood on the side of real intelligence, I on the side of impulsive action."[26]

The letters are otherwise notable for their air of secrecy. In one, written on a train, Sessions twice switched to French when a passenger sat next to him, English when the person left. Second, his hyperbolic style, while understandable in the first stages of love, lasts for six years' worth of letters. His neediness for her love and assurances of his own seem forced; the more endearments and underlines he uses, the less persuasive he becomes.

Several letters to others stated that Barbara would leave college and that they would be married, first at Christmas time 1919 (George was to play the organ, while John and Alberta Burk would represent the only other non-family guests), then in March 1920. Barbara was to graduate in June of that year. Sessions strongly recommended that she abandon all her previous extra-curricular activities (working on the school periodicals, playing in orchestra) in order that she spend her free time preparing for the wedding.

In December 1918 Sessions was, as usual, hard up for money. He decided to sell some of his books and sent George and Van a list of titles and prices: they purchased the books, and John Burk lent him money. Archibald continued to pay monthly installments on Sessions's bills. And Sessions had a salary, although small, at Smith. Sessions worked on a long article on Berlioz which he wanted to submit first to *Musical Quarterly* for two reasons: for the money and because he felt Berlioz still needed championing. The March date was a particularly sore issue with Father Sill. Sessions wrote, "I am afraid the marriage will have to be in Lent, as that is when the vacation comes—I am sorry, but we do not share Fr. Huntington's feeling, + you can understand the exigencies of the college year."[27] Sill wrote back,

> I am sorry you are obliged to set the date for our wedding in March for the simple reason that I am ever so anxious to show the generation ahead of me, of men like Father Huntington, that we respect their feelings. But it has been a queer thing in your family that each generation seems to have done something, or adopted a point of view, which was hard for the generation ahead to swallow. Your grandfather was undoubtedly a source of grief to your great-grandfather Dan. Father [James] Huntington did many things which his father had to put up with, and now the fourth generation is apt to do things which Father Huntington's generation, no doubt finds hard to bear. You are a most interesting family. I only hope that if you ever send a son to me I shall be able to train him so that the thing about all else he will desire to do is to bring joy to the heart of his parents and older relatives.[28]

Father Sill had many remarkable qualities, but no one would have called him a soothsayer. Reader: tuck his last sentence away in your memory for future recall.

It is difficult to see any other reason for an early marriage—Barbara was only 19—than purely selfish motivations on Sessions's part. He already had two college degrees and seemed not to care much about them. She, however, was doing quite well as a Smith student (considerably better in terms of grades than Sessions had done), while he was working to persuade her to give up her studies, and presumably her career, in order to devote herself solely to him. In addition, he was not financially situated to marry. Most of Archibald's many weekly letters over the years had dealt with trying to get Sessions to budget his money. When approached as to whether he would subsidize their marriage, Archibald drew the line: no, he could not. He considered Sessions as having a "practical psychological problem" regarding the monthly money sent him; he begged Sessions not to borrow any money and run into debt. His request that Sessions keep him abreast of his accounts was ignored entirely. In this way Sessions was like his mother at a young age, completely oblivious to money, anticipating a marriage while unaware even of how much women's clothes and household items cost. He romanticized poverty, thinking it could be a "blessing," whereas Barbara saw debt as "something degrading."

Then there was the inevitable sexual tension between any two young people in love, which Sessions clearly felt could not be deferred for a year and a half. His behavior during their engagement was a harbinger of his future treatment of her interests and career.

Meanwhile, he was more than evasive when introducing the subject of George to Barbara: he wrote in an undated letter soon after their engagement,

> I think I told you about George—he is the only one of my good friends who is younger than I am; and he is, in a way, not a friend in the real sense, for I find it difficult to have any *exchange* with him. But he is *very* lovable; and the fault has been mine, for I was too blunt once, and muddled things by disapproving in a very evident manner in a case where I should really not have meddled, and where my meddling only aggravated matters + though I think he still has a real affection for me, as I have for him. He is not in the least a vigorous person— he has had heart trouble and his family have rather suppressed him for that reason.[29]

This is hardly an accurate version of their relationship, the "meddling" distorts Van's connection, and "vigorous" was the term George used to describe Van.

In the summer of 1919 the *dramatis personae* stood thus. Roger, reading a great deal of Freud and supposed to be working on his symphony, and Ruth were getting along better than ever and living in Hadley at Phelps Farm. Barbara was home in Claremont with her parents and sick grandfather. Archibald had resumed sending funds from New York to Roger, but did not always receive the agreed-upon acknowledgment. Van had quit teaching at Kent (in a huff) and moved to North Carolina to farm a new property his parents bought. Pater was furious with Van over a political incident at Kent, one in which, philosophically, Roger took Van's side. George was practicing the St Anne fugue for the wedding and came to visit Hadley in August. Sessions wrote him, "And while I am as fond of you as ever—it seems the height of intemperance to mention that now, but please forgive—it is not with the greedy kind of affection that wants to devour you, soul and body, that it was, for instance, summer before last."[30] In the same letter, which purported to inform George how much he had changed because of his love for and intimacy with Barbara, Sessions brought up old devils: that intimacy "has freed me so wonderfully from the ghouls that have haunted me since I went to Cloyne. Although the[y] have not all disappeared they can be quickly banished, and when we are married and living together they will be mere memories and romantic legends."[31] (In the throes of romantic love, he had not interpreted Freud accurately: marriage alone could not dispel the "ghouls.") Nevertheless George did acknowledge a change in Sessions, "I have not felt so near to you for nearly five years. Barbara must be a wonderful stabilizer—like the governor on an engine."[32] A year later he described Sessions in another mechanical metaphor: "I had a glorious week in Hadley with Roger and his wife. Roger is a wonder. I get more refreshment from him than from any other soul in the world. He is a regular charging station and I have had my batteries refilled."[33] For his part, George never referred, except we presume in the letter that was burned, to their affair. Sessions, however, continually returned to the subject, even if it was "the height of intemperance."

Barbara wrote after George left Hadley that she would indeed return to college that year. At least one reason, Sessions gleaned, was "that things were so uncomfortable at home for her that college would be by far the less of two evils."[34] Barbara began writing to Ruth and receiving extravagant thanks for the letters (and mysterious injunctions like "Better tear [my letter] up into tiny pieces"). Ruth wrote to them both, "You know I always feel more comfortable when I can introduce a little pathos into a situation!"[35] Ruth enjoyed being privy to so momentous a secret and, while disapproving, defended the couple by taking their side against the Fosters.

When their engagement was announced, in the spring of 1919, Barbara's friends at Smith, George had heard, "were quite startled . . . because they had always considered [Roger] shy and given over to music! What a world this is."[36] Foster's endorsement of this marriage was conditional on Barbara's finishing college. Inez Foster, whom Roger considered unalterably hostile to their marriage, had taken an extreme measure to split the couple: she announced that she herself was pregnant and that Barbara could not marry because she needed her to take care of the new child. (There was no new child.) The wedding was again delayed until slightly before Barbara's graduation, which she planned not to attend because it came during their honeymoon. Her teachers and parents, however, hearing of this and, unlike her, knowing that she would graduate *summa cum laude*, persuaded Roger to bring her to graduation to accept the surprise of her honors. The wedding was finally held at 11:00 a.m. on June 5, 1920—not in a church because Sessions refused—but in the Foster home on West Pleasant Street in Claremont, with only the two families present: Ruth and Archibald; Roger's siblings, John and Hannah; Barbara's parents, Frank and Inez; and her sisters, Eleanor and Rosamond. The presiding minister, who lived in Claremont, was (somehow this will not surprise us) Rev. George Huntington. Neither George Bartlett, who had frequently been asked to play the organ at the ceremony, nor John and Alberta Burk could attend. Roy and Sylvia Welch married, June 16, 1920, days after Sessions's own marriage.

George had written on May 22 that he was unable to say whether he could come, and not to count on him. "You see, I have had unaccountable heart palpitations for a week which forces me to keep pretty quiet. . . . I ought to stay here and try to recovery my equilibrium before I go abroad."[37] An amateur psychologist might read a psychosomatic meaning into his not attending the wedding. (Sessions was seriously considering teaching at Kent after his "senior" year, 1920–1921, at Smith.) The usual letters mentioning books and music now flowed between both Barbara and Roger and George. Too many books are mentioned in each letter to be recounted here; all three read the same works and sent them to each other. In August 1920 George wrote to Father Sill about Barbara, hoping the two of them would come to Kent to teach,

> She is without exception the most wonderful girl I have ever known. She will be as great an addition to the school as Roger. Among other things she is a brilliant scholar and could help teach in almost any course if needed. . . . But [Roger] has a gigantic intellect and tremendous energy which is bound to be a stimulus. As a musician there is nobody comparable to him.[38]

Rosamond Foster remembered the wedding and the white-haired Archibald, the only person besides Sessions himself with whom this author spoke who had met Archibald: she liked him a great deal. She also clearly remembered the "very domineering" Ruth, whom she would know for a quarter of a century. Her observation spoke volumes: "I wouldn't have wanted to have had her for a mother."

Barbara was indeed "brilliant;" her grades at Smith make this plain. She was elected to Phi Beta Kappa in 1919 (in her junior year), and, as mentioned, was graduated *summa cum laude* (one of three students). She majored in English and minored in history, although most of her courses were in music. In addition to courses in these three subjects, she took Latin, French, astronomy, botany, Bible, psychology, and Italian. The only course she did poorly in was first-semester, sophomore-year, required physical education (Senda Berenson's course), where she earned a C+; she converted it to an A- the following semester. Her older sister Eleanor did not attend college; she studied at music conservatories. Rosamond, who followed Barbara to Smith and also majored in English, class of 1928, earned mostly Cs, with some Ds and an occasional failing grade. Unlike Barbara, she took art in addition to music.

The Sessionses honeymoon was spent in the most romantic place (and the cheapest— money was always a consideration) he could devise: the aunts' hilltop cabin near Forty Acres. Michael Paul St Agnan Huntington, uncle George's son who had graduated from the Episcopal Theological Seminary in Cambridge, remembered Barbara in his diary in somewhat censorious terms; he evidently had not adjusted to the "new woman" of the 1920s. In August the newlyweds and their Huntington relatives went swimming in the Connecticut River, exactly one mile from the cabin. "Barbara, who's rather that kind, went in in a one-piece seductive bathing garment—hardly a suit! Openly risqué and giddy and scant material, it showed too much of her girlish form. Refreshing swim, but glad to cover her up with cloak on way up."[39] The Sessionses returned in the summer of 1921 as well. Indeed, until 1925 they frequented the old farm every summer.

Sessions continued work on the Symphonic Prelude to complete it as a symphony. He added a new dedication, "R.H.S. to B.F., December 17, 1918," thus transferring his offering to George to his new love, Barbara. Archibald Sessions, through his friend Mr Armstrong, had shown the unfinished work to Josef Stransky, Mahler's successor as conductor of the New York Philharmonic, which gave concerts in Northampton. Stransky promised Archibald to give the Sessions work a private reading in October of 1919 and to perform the completed piece with the New York Philharmonic in January 1920. "The tone that [Stransky] took in his talk with me indicated, as I interpreted it, an anxiety to do everything he could to further your plans and your interests. . . . in order to put things through with him, one has to be right on the dot."[40] Sleeper added to mounting pressure by his prodding.

Sessions now faced what was for him an extremely uncomfortable situation. While others may have seen a golden opportunity, this situation unveiled all of Sessions's

Figure 20 1921 tea party on porch at Forty Acres: Ruth Huntington, Catharine Huntington, Barbara Sessions, and Roger Sessions.

insecurities as well as revealing once again his innate inability to organize his time. Fear of success again reared its ugly head: the fact was, he was not emotionally ready for this success, success being far scarier than failure. Not for the last time would he become his own worst enemy when confronted with an important opportunity. Despite many announcements that he would finish the symphony, the piece was not yet completed more than two years after its 1917 premiere at Yale. Indeed, rather than working on the symphony, Sessions set about arranging Berlioz's *Symphonie Funebre et Triomphale* for organ, five trumpets, trombone, two pianos, and percussion: bass drum, cymbals, and the regular small military drum. As usual, he tried to arrange performances before this work was done; he hoped to give it at Smith the following year. He asked George to propose to Pater a performance in memory of the Kent men who fell in the war.

His problem revolved around his sense of his technique as a composer.

> I guess it was in my third year (my "junior" year), I decided that I couldn't finish this piece the way I wanted to. I didn't really know what I was doing, and I needed some more studying. I tried to do some work by myself for a long time, and that wasn't sufficient, so—but I had to get out of this obligation. I knew that any mature musician, who I thoroughly respected would tell me to do this, and study some more. I was really quite desperate about it.[41]

In October 1919 a performance of Sessions's symphony was announced for that Philharmonic season. Stransky evidently felt that enough time had elapsed for Sessions to have completed the work.

Sessions never would respond well to the pressure of a deadline; it only blocked him more. He became bogged down in the second movement, the movement meant especially for George. He attempted to resolve the creative crisis by studying Cherubini's *Counterpoint* and Vincent d'Indy's *Cours de Composition*. Sessions was able to identify difficulties fairly precisely: in two letters to Barbara in the summer of 1919 he explained, after a morning in which he had only written three measures, that

> Transitions are the hardest thing in music to write; for logically they ought to be in the nature of quite direct progressions; but here I have an important idea to develop as well—the theme of the first movement, its second movement form; it is going to become increasingly important as the movement progresses; and its statement must have a marked character of its own, in addition to its transitional character. Modulations, as usual bother me; and I have to use a good deal of will-power in keeping the thing in check.[42]

And, "One vow I have made—never to orchestrate again till a complete sketch is finished; for I have lost 4 orchestral pages." He literally lost music as well, finding a much-needed old sketch in the Smith Music Hall. In it he found "a motif which comes in the 2nd theme presentation which I had forgotten but tried to reconstruct; and found it different from and quite superior to my reconstruction."[43]

Rather than working on the Symphonic Prelude, Sessions spent time and effort in the campaign to remove Sleeper as chairman of the music department. His friendship with Neilson and Welch was useful in this endeavor. Roger set the stage for George in world political terms:

> Miss Holmes, Miss Goode, and myself—Gorohkov, I think, too—represent the extreme left of the department, while Sleeper and four others whom you never have heard of occupy the right. Welch and Locke are fairly near the left. . . . Sleeper is Tsar; Moog is Milyukoff, Locke is Krensky, Miss Holmes and myself are the bolsheviki. The issues are the character of the concert programs, the music in chapel, fair play for Gorohkov (that is an especially sore point with Sleeper, and is what really precipitated the revolution), and finally the present curriculum, which needs revision from top to bottom. While I can't claim credit exactly for starting the revolution, yet I think that I helped in rather large measure to precipitate it.[44]

By late January 1919, the little revolution was enacted. It turned out Moog was not Miyukoff, Sessions admitted, but a Bolshevik, and was now chairman of the department. Sessions succeeded in removing Sleeper, the man who had hired him; but he did not succeed in finishing the symphony.

He realized in November 1919, past Stransky's October reading date with the Philharmonic, that he needed to discuss his musical problems with another composer. Given his insecurities, he also desperately needed validation. He felt he could rely on the European Ernest Bloch. He also felt that Bloch's word would carry weight with Sleeper and help extricate Sessions from the obligation to Stransky.[45]

Sessions's turning to Ernest Bloch was as much running away from Stransky and the unendurable opportunity to succeed as it was a cry for professional help. He needed someone to reassure and stabilize him, and here Sessions jumped from the frying pan directly into the fire.

Sleeper managed to persuade Sessions that it was not polite to keep Stransky dangling and to write him, finally, that the work would not be completed. Sessions's letter, however, could not erase the consequences of his inability to finish this symphony. Unfinished pieces, like unfulfilled promises and unpaid debts, do not disappear into the ether. They hover, lingering, waiting for a time—of course most inconvenient to the debtor—to manifest themselves. Then they strike with devastating consequences, much worse than what could have resulted from a promise fulfilled, a debt paid, a work completed. Later, when the abandoned symphony was almost forgotten, it would take revenge on its maker; it would collect its principal, as well as accumulated interest. Sessions would be permanently scarred and forever haunted.

GEORGE BARTLETT

That fall of 1919 Sessions moved to 40 State Street, while Barbara lived in Ruth's annex. Ruth sent them to Boston to hear the Boston Symphony, including d'Indy's new symphony, on October 17, 1919. They stayed with the Burks; John Burk was now the program annotator for the Symphony and gave Roger tickets. The two might have heard Ernest Bloch's *Psalms 137* and *114*, November 14–15, 1919, conducted by Pierre Monteux, that fall.

Having tried Roger's oboe, George was now attempting to learn the violin. He thought Marjory Parsons, the only woman he mentioned in a letter, was closer to becoming his fiancée. Delighted that George was considering marriage, Roger could not resist advice. George had heard the Symphony concert in which Bloch conducted his *Three Jewish Poems*, March 23 and 24, 1917. On December 17, 1919, Sessions wrote George a lengthy letter about his interview with Ernest Bloch.

> The week that I telephoned you I had decided to go to New York to see Ernest Bloch on the subject [of the symphony] . . . The week before I went down I got some "Psalms" [22, 114, 137] of his for voice and orchestra, just published by Schirmer—also a string quartet; and was so carried away by Bloch's intellectual and emotional force that I kept the Psalms with me for two or three days, and did practically nothing but study them and play them over. They made a greater impression on me than anything else in modern music—by far. . . .
>
> If Bloch's music inspired me, Bloch himself did and does still more. . . . He suggested millions of things to me, and I have been a new man ever since. Indeed, his personality is such that one weighs his every word, to absorb it into one's mind and let it achieve a new and individual growth there. The result is that I have given up the symphony, and have gone back to the roots of composition in my work with him.[1]

When he first visited Bloch, Sessions stayed overnight with Van, who was working in an export house in New York City, where—as Sessions wrote to George—he "had one of the best visits with him that I ever had. We have both grown older—and wiser; and you are no longer a bone of contention between us, as you once were, on my side at least . . . And I have gained two very good friends again." He planned to stay with Van for a week after Christmas. Sessions's personal charm fed his ability to make and keep friends. Otherwise, it would have been difficult to foresee that both Burk and Van—not to mention George—would have returned to him better friends than ever. Concerning his approaching wedding Sessions wrote, "I must admit I'd rather have you than some members of the family."[2]

George probably did not know that Roger had rededicated the symphony to Barbara. Generously, George understood about the abandonment of his symphony in Rollandian ("Becoming") terms.

> What you say about yourself and your technique is, I suppose true, but it is hard for undiscerning people like myself to see it. Of course your technique has got to be developed, and you know its limitations better than almost anyone else. What I feared, as I saw you from time to time revising your Symphony, was that you would never be content to let it go as long as the whole thing did not represent the point you had reached in your development when it was finished. At that rate, of course, you would never finish it. For that reason I am glad that you have given it up at present, although I am really very fond of it, almost as if it were partly my own. It still represents you as you once were, like the cast off clothes of a dear friend, and it has a meaning for that reason.[3]

In the same letter George confided his feelings about Marjory Parsons:

> I was really in love with Miss Parsons and it had taken me twenty years to find it out. You see, when you grow up with a girl it is hard to define your feelings for her. . . . I felt perfectly sure of her, particularly after the Harvard–Yale Game when we had a marvelous day together. A week later she wrote to tell me of her engagement to a cousin of mine. I was never so taken aback in my life. . . . I am convinced more than ever that I loved her, now that she is lost forever. Every time I think of it I have a terrible feeling of emptiness.

Circumspection had prevented him from confiding more about his feelings for Marjory to Roger, "the one person in the world whose sympathy I really wanted."[4]

Engaged couples often indulge the urge to play matchmaker for their friends, and the Marjory story prompted Roger and Barbara to a series of plots to set George up with someone else. Roger even implied that, since Barbara knew Marjory, they were a little worried about George and her. Returning to the symphony, he wrote,

> Thank you very much for what you say about the symphony. It touches me very much to have you say about it what you do, and to care about it. I must go onward however. The first movement is the part of me which you knew the best, a poor weak, bewildered creature with high thoughts, who had not yet found himself or learned anything of the meaning or possibilities of life. But you know how the second movement troubled me; and the fact that Mr Bloch thinking that it would worry me to have him speak so frankly, told me very cautiously what I had known to be the trouble all along, is of some significance, Don't you really think so?[5]

Now it was George's turn to wait four months, from January to May 1920, to write to Sessions. He planned to sail to France and visit northern Italy after Marjory's June wedding, at which, ironically, he would serve as an usher. He saw an "element of diabolical humor" in that situation, a "reproach to my priggishness."[6] More important, however, was George's determination to form with his brother Samuel their own boarding school, based on his observations of Pater's both good and bad points as a headmaster. A few months, later he and Sam found some buildings at South Kent in the Berkshires that were being used as a school for mountain boys, but which would be abandoned the next year, 1921–1922. Samuel Bartlett, Richard Cuyler, and Father Sill founded the South Kent School in 1923. Cuyler served as director of curriculum and Bartlett as headmaster until 1954. His son George was headmaster from 1968 to 1989.

The year 1920 was an election year, one in which Archibald seemed the only family member truly interested; he was voting for Warren Harding. Sessions voted for Eugene V. Debs and would rather have seen James Cox elected than Harding. Despite his political conversion, Archibald had a highly perceptive grasp on his own and the next generation. He could almost predict the artistic flowering of the Roaring Twenties.

> Though it may seem strange, it is the thinking of the people of your generation that interests me most. I get the impression that they are the only ones who have anything really vital to look forward to. The men and women over thirty have all of them, so far as my observation goes, been swallowed up in a morass of materialism—most of them much sooner than they ought to be, and sooner than they were fifty years ago. What impresses me more than anything else about 20th century humanity is its lack of sophistication; and that the problem before your generation is, chiefly, to bring it back to us. . . . You people in your second and third decades, intellectually and spiritually, own the world and the question is—what are you going to do about it?[7]

Roger and Barbara traveled to New York to hear the first performance of Bloch's viola suite with Bodanzky and Bailly as soloist, November 5 and 7, 1920. Could George join them? He also asked George to play the *Sacre du Printemps* with him at Smith, trying to "inject a little pep into things here by having evenings of modern music." (The first concert was *Pelléas*, however, which George attended.) In this same letter of October 1920 Roger first mentioned to George the idea of his going to Cleveland with Bloch (instead of to Kent; he asked George not to mention this to Pater). "[Bloch's] plan is to take seven or eight of his most promising pupils with him—whom he thinks are all exceptionally talented and original, and build up an American 'school' with us as nucleus, just as the Russian school was built up from the Invincible Band. That seems about as inspiring to me as anything could be."[8]

Other issues arose on the Bloch front. In January 1921 Roger and Barbara visited his in-laws in Claremont.

> That visit impressed upon me the absolute provinciality of most Americans. The Fosters are anti-Semitic to quite an extent—they fear that the Jews are getting an undue influence in the country and will corrupt our institutions. It is not hysterical—simply, reasoned fear, the fruit of absolute inexperience. Barbara tells me that her father has never known a foreigner or a non-Anglo-Saxon intimately, and has not known any at all except for the Russian workers and Jewish tradesmen in Claremont. The fear is not only of Jews, but of all foreigners: Mrs Foster asked me, for instance, whether Bloch in becoming an American citizen did so as one who is contented and pleased with "our institutions and ideas" or whether he had brought a lot of revolutionary ideas from Europe! . . . Mr Foster is a man of very unusual intelligence, and would undoubtedly know better if he had ever lived outside of New Hampshire and Vermont, and the kind of town and background which makes these states so provincial; for he is an unusually fair person within his own sphere. It is not opinions that one has to fight, but prejudices

inculcated from childhood, which are bound by unenlightened training to the most generous impulses. So I think the most important thing is the development of an enlightened technique—intellectual, moral, and spiritual, and, of course, physical.[9]

Sessions's new enthusiasm was Gian Francesco Malipiero, whose *Sette Canzoni* he bought. He saw him as "an Italian Mussorgsky," and "Next to Bloch I think he is he greatest composer of the present generation—always leaving Stravinsky out of consideration, as I don't feel that I am familiar enough with the *Sacre du Printemps* to judge him."[10]

Sessions could not pay George for the Stravinsky concert they did play at Smith. Sessions was already in considerable debt—he mentioned "the large sum I owe you"—to his friend. Nevertheless, George sent Roger what we assume from his thank you letter was an extravagant Christmas/birthday present, probably books or scores. In January 1921, however, Sessions had not only not repaid the debt, now $50, but asked George for an additional $500 in two installments, $200 needed that month. "I can't tell you how much I hate to take advantage of our friendship and your generosity in this way."[11]

Although Sessions had started three and a half years earlier at Smith earning $800 a year, by this time his salary was $1,500. Therefore $500 represented one third of a year's salary. The Fosters were proved right that Sessions could not afford to set up a household and take care of a wife. In any case, Barbara, now graduated, was working for the Smith College music faculty (her name appeared on its letterhead). In addition, Archibald continued to send money to Sessions, as he did to both Nan, who was also married, and John, still a Harvard student. Promises to George that Sessions had learned his lesson about being "reckless in regard to finances" proved worthless; he would repeat these mistakes again and again. Perhaps it is useless to question where the money went, or for what it was needed. Sessions did often eat at restaurants rather than at his boarding house. Bills for books and music were run up. He was not contemplating a large purchase, such as a house, or car, or an extended trip. One question lingers: did Ruth or Archibald, much less the Fosters, know how much Sessions was in debt? George would have been absolutely dependable when it came to discretion, although he was never asked in a letter to keep the loans a secret.

George Bartlett, while from a relatively wealthy family, was not so rich that he could come up with $500 on short notice. Unlike Roger, he had attended public school and was a scholarship student at Harvard. He answered immediately that he could send Roger $22 as soon as his Kent salary was paid him, another $100 at the first of February, and another $200 in the middle of March. "Pay me when you like. I am only too glad to be of any use."[12] George felt somewhat depressed about teaching and thought himself a failure: "So much so that several boys have told me that they think I am far from well—which means, far from being the cheerful, hapless person they knew two years ago."[13] At Kent, George had a talk with Roger's "forbidding" uncle, Rev. James Huntington; they exchanged books. "I am always a little afraid of him, because I never know just how far I can go."[14] Father Huntington was in fact canonized; for his selfless generosity, perhaps George ought to have been too.

Barbara and Roger both wept when they read George's letter, "You are so unspeakably good to do it, and to put it the way you do. If you have the slightest idea of how we feel toward you, know that if there is anything in the world that we can do for you, we will feel badly if you don't ask us. You have always been the best friend that anyone could be, and you may be sure that we will never fail you in the slightest degree."[15] Nevertheless,

Roger immediately failed George in one small degree, which was to send this letter of thanks—it lay on his desk for four days while he absent-mindedly forgot to mail it.

George's birthday was February 3, and Roger wrote a longer letter the previous day. He tried to cheer George up about teaching and invited him to come to New York with them to hear the National Symphony Orchestral play Bloch's *Schelomo* conducted by Mengelberg. On the 20th, Bloch's violin sonata was played for the first time, under the auspices of the Friends of Music. Barbara would stay with one of Archibald's sisters. Here, again, Sessions failed his friend in a small way: this letter hid unmailed in Sessions's pocket, missing George's birthday by four days. George had already gone to New York to hear *Tristan* and Harold Bauer playing the Franck Prelude, Chorale and Fugue, and the Waldstein Sonata, as well as Schumann and Chopin. George wrote he hoped to spend the next year abroad studying school systems for his own school. (Of course, he enclosed a check.)

Roger's mid-February reply contained an invitation to Northampton to give George some rest. "I am very sorry to hear that your heart is cutting up again. For God's sake take care of yourself."[16] When George did not write back about coming to Northampton, the worried Sessionses telephoned Kent to learn that he had been taken home to Webster sometime after the 9th. Barbara wrote a long, newsy, and concerned letter, inviting him to stay under their care, and Sessions added a short note, assuring George "how very, very much love we send you. In haste Roger."[17]

George's illness came at a busy time for Sessions, who has been informally invited by Bloch to teach at the new Cleveland Institute of Music. He would make $2,000 there, perhaps more. In New York Bloch took Sessions to see Steiglitz's photographs, which Roger described in detail to George. In addition he wrote about the Malipiero quartet. This letter, March 19, was written in New York and sent from New Haven, therefore Sessions had not seen the March 14 letter from Georgia Bartlett to Barbara. Her news was devastating: George's heart valve, whose chronic leakiness should have kept him out of service, was now infected, but "Do not suggest [in letters] that he will not soon be himself again."[18] George was much sicker than even he himself knew: George was dying.

Barbara wrote long, entertaining letters, while Roger's first impulse was to enclose a line of music, from *Die Walküre* Act I, Siegmund's Spring Song.[19] Later he ended a letter with instrumental version of the Woodbird's Call from Act II of *Siegfried*. He had not done this for six years, since their letters of 1915 in which many handwritten music examples appeared. Long intimately attuned to nature at Hadley, Roger sent George a juniper twig, a red maple blossom, as well as a pussy-willow from Forty Acres. Sessions waxed philosophical, referring to a two-volume novel by Jacob Wassermann, *The World's Illusion*.

> Our minds are so confused, these days, by the "winds of doctrine"—little winds and big gales—which blow us hither and thither; and by attitudes which we strike, under the compulsion of one petty urge or another, that we cannot see the truth. That has been my experience, and it has set me against mankind in general and made of me a living example of what mankind suffers from. It is so wonderful to know a person like you who is so untroubled by follies of that kind and can see the truth with a clear eye, and understand human nature instead of nourishing a puny spite against it, like my own. But perhaps I, too, will be assured someday. People like you and Barbara redeem the world by your very existence.

In the midst of a fairly mundane discussion of music departments in the same letter, Roger's emotions suddenly got the better of him, and he blurted out, "Oh, wouldn't it be so much nicer if chaos would come to the world in sections, and not attack all human interests at once? We could then tackle it in regard to one thing at a time."[20] Sessions's emotions cannot but have been stirred by the fact that George sent more of the promised loan, literally from his death bed, where he had lain for six weeks. George felt, "If my fever would only leave me I would get well very soon."[21] He still looked forward to his European trip.

The chaos attacking all human interests at once at that time included, in addition to George's illness: the fight Father Sill was waging with TB; the death in March of Roger's aunt Arria; the possible move to Cleveland; the fact that Roy Welch suffered a break-down and Sessions had to take over his classes; that Ruth, after 20 years, had sold 109 Elm Street to Smith and moved to Phelps House; that his sister was to have a baby (Nigel Lyon, born May 24); that his brother was about to graduate from Harvard; and the introduction of Mina Kirstein into Sessions's circle.

Barbara wrote George about meeting more of the somewhat older Huntington cousins. "It is very interesting to me to meet 'the family,' and study their varying degrees and types of Huntington-ness. In appearance, too, they make a striking group, with such very strong resemblances. Have you ever noticed their hands? Almost without exception they follow the same broad lines, with rather blunt fingers, and a sharp angle at the base of the thumb. Roger's are by far the best."[22]

On April 29 Sessions wrote George a long letter, part of which attempted to amuse him by proposing a contrapuntal theory based on smell:

> [We had] the joyful news that you are having a taste of spring from your porch. I hope that there are apple trees near by, so that you can get a taste of the delicious odor—which alas! reaches us only in combination with the odor—somewhat ubiquitous in Hadley, I'm sorry to say—of cow and pig manure. I think there must be great artistic possibilities in odor—I have a theory even of a scale of odors, resulting from my observation of the peculiarly contrapuntal way in which these smells reach us, a much more poly-odoriferous effect than one would imagine from a knowledge of the possibilities of combined timbres. The apple blossoms are wafted deliciously (like the highest tones of the solo strings) over a deep bass accompaniment of pig-manure (weird arpeggio effects on the muted tuba) or the more spring-like and really fresh and animal cow-manure (contra-bassoon). You probably won't find my description in the least entertaining, but I assure you they describe my impression with some accuracy.

This letter continued in a musical vein: Bloch's *Israel*, Di Lasso's *Penitential Psalms*, and musical world generally.

> It is the independents, like Bloch, who must struggle for recognition today; it is they who refuse to make the sensation which would bring them recognition in the musical world today; for they must face a double enemy; those, on the one hand, who still are pious traditionalists and pedants (God knows why any of them ever compose at all, since what is good has apparently all been done generations ago, in their view); and those who make a fetish of new sensations and cultivate a manner, as is done in the little Mutual Admiration Society which is contemporary musical Europe. . . . I have made my vow—just as Bloch made his thirty years ago; only

mine is somewhat less the product of an impressionable child than was his made at the age of eleven. *My vow is not simply to devote myself to composition; but also to keep myself pure and my individuality intact.* [emphasis mine] God knows there was never a harder place to do this than contemporary America; for our nouveaux intellectuals are, in the end, as deadening as our Puritans and Philistines, and the only thing a vigorous individual can do is to keep his mind grimly aloof, and to love the truth fanatically, and without respect to personalities or to the whirlpool, in the calm center of which the truth and reality lie. . . .

Please don't try to answer our letters; there will be plenty of time for that and for much more than that later on when you are stronger. Affectionately as ever, Roger.[23]

This was the last communication Sessions had with George. Six days later, May 5, 1921, he died. The funeral was May 9. George Bartlett was 24 years old.

The worst that could happen had happened. The "beautiful creature" to whom "if anything should happen . . . it would be the hardest blow I have ever had to bear, and one of the very hardest I ever will have to bear" (as Sessions had written exactly four years earlier) had died at a tragically young age. Sessions, also 24, would never completely recover from this blow, one that left a hole in his life. How many emotions vied for dominance in his grief? Guilt, at borrowing money and having never paid it back. Longing, to retrieve his best friend for the past seven years and keep him for the rest of their lives. Regret, that he was not at all times completely honest with George, while George was never duplicitous. Feelings of mortality, to have someone his own age die. More regret, that the symphony dedicated to George had not been completed and could not stand as a memorial to him. Sorrow, that someone he had loved who had loved him in return was gone for good. Loneliness and loss, that part of his life had permanently been cut out of someone's memory. Sessions began to set Whitman's *Leaves of Grass*.

We know little directly of Sessions's response to this tragedy. Sessions may have equated George with Olivier Jeannin, Jean-Christophe's doomed best friend (whose son was named Georges). Perhaps he closed off that portion of his experience, attempting to dress the wound. His sister Nan (but not Archibald or Ruth) wrote Sessions a condolence letter: "George was such a sweet person—of course, that is a banal thing to say—I have always felt that your friendship was different from most those between men, + it was lovely that Barbara could share it too."[24] Sessions spent part of the summer of 1921 in the hilltop cabin typing all of George's letters to him, as well as George's letters to Father Sill. That summer Sessions, Barbara, and their Smith colleague Mina Kirstein commiserated on long walks. Of what we inherit from Sessions, the many letters, lectures, books, interviews, only a couple of direct mentions of George occur after his death. One, a year later, was when he wrote to Barbara from Hadley that hearing the train whistle made him sad, because it was the train on which George used to arrive. Another, also to Barbara, will be quoted here (see p. 180). The last one will appear eight years later in a letter to another close friend, also homosexual, Aaron Copland. In all his written prose and extensive interviews, with Columbia in 1962, Edward T. Cone in 1965, this author from 1974–1980, Frederik Prausnitz in the mid-1980s, and occasional others, Sessions never brought up George's name. He never mentioned George to his children. This author originally came across George only as the dedicatee of the Symphony. Prausnitz's book on Sessions does not mention him at all.

For all Sessions's considerable ability to make and keep friends, he found he could no longer bear to correspond with Van, and Van never wrote to Sessions again. Indeed, Van had abruptly disappeared; Sessions had already received a postcard from Africa. We can only guess what Van's reactions to losing his college roommate must have been. Whereas Sessions tended to internalize his pain, Van acted: he moved to Madagascar and spent the rest of his life in Leipzig, Indonesia, and Brazil.

In my 1992 *Correspondence* this author first posited "an association between [Sessions's] symphonies and the death of loved ones may have begun here."[25] I shall continue this theme when we encounter the first four numbered symphonies. Although Roger had told George he felt most comfortable writing for orchestra, it would in the future be both difficult and take considerable time—in one case two decades—to overcome emotional hurdles. For Sessions, writing any symphony could not escape association with his first symphonic effort and its fatal consequences. Sessions not only had the demons of Cloyne to deal with and his mother's unreasonable demands and sudden criticisms, but he now also had the memory of George to haunt him.

It was not only the money Roger owed George, although that should have caused guilt enough, but the money was also a metaphor for the emotional arrears Sessions had permanently incurred. George, like Sessions's sister Mary, would remain as an idealized figure frozen in death. Sessions had placed himself in an impossible situation regarding George: quite simply, now he could never repay him, by any means. Decades later, he would try.

Memorials other than the Sessions Symphony were offered for George. The $2,000 Harry Hall organ that he had picked out for the chapel at Kent was dedicated to his memory; it lasted until the 1950s. Father Sill had instituted a fundraising effort to pay for the organ: George had been the first to contribute. A plaque in the (new) chapel commemorates George: "The organ in this chapel is in loving memory of George Hodges Bartlett Born February 3, 1897 Died May 5, 1921 Master of English, German and History 1919–1921. He was the first to use the organ and in the work of praise and worship gave generously of his time and talents. Requiescat in pace." The Kent School published an editorial about George in its *Kent Quarterly*, and the yearbook for 1921 devoted a page with a photograph, his dates, and the caption, "In Loving Memory the Class of 1921 wishes to express its gratitude and affection for his devoted and untiring services to Kent School." Part of the editorial read: "That his rendering of the [Beethoven] Second Symphony and the unusual thoughtfulness that he introduced into the *Liebestod* could open a sudden vista of things that were worth while, even to those who could not understand music, is significant. Significant not of musical greatness so much as a rare penetration of sympathy and tremendous understanding that cannot be forgotten."[26]

Father Sill (the "Old Man", George called him to Roger) wrote at length about the teacher who had arrived when only twenty. He is partly quoted here.

> His heart had burned for social justice. It was the great desire of his life to see a more perfect equalization of opportunity in the different classes of American society. . . . He had a remarkably brilliant intellect. Yet with all his brilliancy he was never other than humble. He had positive and radical ideas but when he differed from others it was always in such a happy, sweet way that there was no sting about it. [He never "crabbed" at faculty meetings.] . . . I remember standing with him on the field, watching the maneuvers of our military companies and seeing tears in his eyes as he spoke of the German and French and English boys, as young or even younger than some of ours, who were being sacrificed daily in the terrible carnage of the war. . . .

He generally had a word to say about the sermon as he came down from the [organ] gallery and it was always said with the sweet smile which was so characteristic of "G" that it seemed to remain on that beautiful countenance even in death.

"G" loved music. The organ meant a great deal to him. He could not get on without his piano. He knew what music can do for the soul and did all in his power to encourage it in the School.[27]

In a small memorial booklet, an anonymous author wrote, "To know him slightly was a pleasure. To know him at all intimately was an experience that meant a fundamental awakening, and left one never quite free from the memory and influence of his valourous spirit. He lived intensively, in understanding with fine things: he tasted life and love and the glory of them, and then he died—in May. J.G.C."[28]

Another legacy of George's, in addition to the South Kent School, could be considered the letters he wrote to and received from Roger Sessions, parts of which are reproduced here. The alert reader may have questioned the presence of letters *by* Sessions in the Tin Box Collection; it would seem logical that letters he received would be stored there, not those he wrote. Georgia Bartlett, after the funeral, returned to Sessions all of his letters George kept for six years. Those letters were saved, along with the many that Sessions received from Van, John Burk, his parents, Sill, and others, in the Tin Box. The Tin Box was then left at Phelps House in the attic after 1925 when the Sessionses went to Europe. Perhaps Sessions felt he could also box up his emotions and leave them behind. Depending on the Ruth's discretion regarding reading others' mail, to store intimate letters in such a place might have been a slightly dangerous act (except that a letter was "a sacred thing"); they remained in Ruth's house for more than half a century. Sessions and Barbara appear never to have gone back to retrieve those letters, or reread them. Only in the late 1980s did his brother John's daughter, Sarah Chapin, after the departure of her mother, go through the attic and discover the Tin Box containing these hundreds of letters vividly outlining the life and concerns of Roger Sessions from 1915 to 1925. As a service to scholarship, she typed up almost all the letters and published them. From those letters, we learn an invaluable amount about Sessions during a formative period in his life. Without those letters, we would never have met the handsome, brilliant, musical, and generous George Bartlett.

ERNEST BLOCH

The opportunity to have his symphony played at Smith by the New York Philharmonic in the fall of 1919 paralyzed Sessions. "I wanted to consult somebody whose musicianship was so uncontestable that I could absolutely trust him that he wouldn't give me any nonsense. The only person I could think of in this country at that time was Ernest Bloch."[1] Sessions desperately needed validation. Dvořák and Mahler had returned to Europe some years earlier; it would be a long time before Stravinsky and Schönberg came to live in the US. The only major European composer in New York besides Edgard Varèse was Bloch.

The second violinist of the Flonzaley Quartet, Alfred Pochon, had encouraged Bloch to emigrate, which he did in 1916. The Quartet played his String Quartet No. 1 in the United States on December 31, 1916. This successful premiere led to performances with orchestras. Bloch conducted the Boston Symphony March 23 and 24, 1917, performing the Boston premiere of his *Three Jewish Poems*. The Symphony did not travel to New Haven with this program, therefore Sessions must have gone to Boston from Yale, if this was indeed the first Bloch piece he heard, as Prausnitz claims.[2] The Symphony also played *Two Psalms for Soprano and Orchestra* (Psalms 137, "By the Rivers of Babylon," and 114, "When Israel went out of Egypt," with soprano Povla Frijsh) in Boston on November 14 and 15, in 1919, with Pierre Monteux conducting. Within a week of *that* performance Sessions had written to the Swiss composer. In March 1921 Sessions wrote Bloch, "I can never tell you what an overwhelming effect your music had on me. . . . I am one of the millions who will always be grateful without measure for your wonderful music."[3]

Entirely the opposite from the genteel Parker, Bloch was an expert at self-promotion. In this he was helped considerably by writer Paul Rosenfeld, who promoted him unceasingly in his *Musical Chronicle*. Sessions wrote of the critic: "It is impossible to overestimate Rosenfeld's contributions as a writer [for *The Dial*, 1920–1927] and as an enthusiastic propagandist for [Bloch and] the contemporary music of his period, and for the development of music in this country."[4] Bloch's "Hiver–Printemps" (Winter–Spring), Two Poems for Orchestra, was premiered in Boston April 29 and 30, 1921, with Monteux conducting.[5]

Bloch taught from 1917 to 1920 in New York at the Mannes College, which had just opened its doors. The New York Society of Friends of Music sponsored a full program of his works, May 3, 1917. Both Bloch and Arthur Bodanzky conducted the concert: *Schelomo; Psalms No. 22, 137*, and *114*; the "Israel" Symphony; and the *Three Jewish Poems*. The Philadelphia Orchestra performed a similar concert in 1918. "Israel", a symphony with two sopranos, two contraltos, and bass, was first performed May 3, 1917, in New York with Bloch conducting. Bloch's Symphony in C# minor was performed by the New York Philharmonic, May 8, 1918, again with Bloch conducting. In addition, his

Viola Suite won a $1,000 prize for chamber music offered by Elizabeth Sprague Coolidge in 1919. Bloch's success and music were hard to miss; he was already famous in the United States after having been in the country only three years.

Bloch had arrived in 1916 with a reputation; he brought a letter from Romain Rolland that praised his music highly. Bloch had made friends, given a big concert, and gotten a lot of attention. The Rolland connection—the author of *Jean-Christophe*—could only have cemented Sessions's admiration for the man. "I associated him with everything I'd read about Europe, of course. And I just wanted the 'cold dope.' I just had to have it."[6]

The October 1919 deadline with Josef Stransky for the reading of the symphony had passed, and the strain of not fulfilling expectations must have burdened Sessions. The symphony was in trouble; now it would certainly not be done by the New York Philharmonic. This deadline and lost opportunity stirred something—finally—in Sessions, to seek a teacher's help. He had deliberately kept the work from Parker, and he had received valuable criticism from Clapp. Now he needed the judgment of someone he trusted, and he was willing to expose himself and his music to scrutiny. He had little idea how difficult this scrutiny would be.

In preparation for the meeting in November 1919, Sessions bought some of Bloch's music, published by Schirmer: the *Psalms* for soprano and orchestra, *Psalm 22* for alto or baritone and orchestra (1914, dedicated to Romain Rolland), and the First Quartet. Excited about meeting the European composer, he also experienced those complicated emotions all music students share who "switch teachers." Sessions felt he was betraying Horatio Parker, even though he had not formally studied with him for two years. His sense of guilt must have been amplified by unlucky timing. Only weeks after Sessions let everyone know he had started with Bloch, Parker died suddenly on December 18, 1919. Sessions would continue to harbor some guilt over leaving Parker for Bloch.

Bloch made the first appointment with Sessions at his Lexington Avenue apartment. (This apartment, at 955, where Bloch lived between 1918 and 1921, was between

Figure 21 Ernest Bloch in 1925.

69th and 70th Streets on Lexington Avenue, near the Mannes College.) Sessions stayed overnight with Van at 358 West 23rd Street. Bloch answered the door and sat Sessions down; Sessions had brought the Symphonic Prelude with him. Bloch said, "Well, now, of course, you're very young, and I suppose you know everything." Sessions, getting into the swing of things, responded, "Yes, of course." Bloch asked him to sit at the piano.

> He treated me very roughly. I wasn't prepared for this, but I did want someone on whom I could rely to give the whole business right from the shoulder. Afterwards he told me that he did that just to see whether I could take it or not. He had had other young people who came to study with him who could not. But that was what I wanted, and I told him so. I was in the clouds when I came out of that meeting. I wrote it all down in a diary [the minute he left Bloch's apartment], which I destroyed years ago. I wrote it all down word for word, and one day when Bloch was in my study, years later, I said, "Sit down. I want to read you something." And I read him the whole thing. His jaw dropped, and he said, "You make it sound as if I didn't like your music." I said, "You gave me no reason to think that you did."[7]

> Well it seemed to me that he shouted at the top of his lungs the name of every composer of whom he found traces in my music [d'Indy, Franck, Debussy, Wagner, and Strauss]. And after a while—I mean, I wasn't fazed by it because I knew this was true, you see, and because I was after the real thing. Afterwards he said, "Well now, look. It doesn't disturb me at all that there are other composers in your work. Of course, every young man has that. The important thing is that you yourself should be there." [Then Bloch said,] "Now, I think you've got to make a big resolution and give this [symphony] up for the present. . . . You must study for two years, and in two years, I think I can tell you, you can be able to do everything you want."[8]

The two sat down and began working right away: they analyzed the first eight measures of Beethoven's Op. 2, No. 1. Bloch emphasized the role of the ear as opposed to that of a system. This lesson took hold; Sessions frequently spoke of the role of the ear for the composer and prescribed Roberto Gerhard's term a "willing ear" for the listener. "I think I learned more in the ten minutes that remained of that hour than I have learned at any time since, because he made certain connections between what I had learned already and the music that I wanted to write, that I didn't know existed."[9] Bloch explained how the harmonies built to an important rhythmic point, how the bass line ascended, and how the motifs shortened as the climax approached. This opened Sessions's eyes; he thought to himself, "All that harmony that I studied does make sense after all."[10] Later, in Cleveland, Bloch told Sessions the symphony was one of the most gifted things by a young composer he had seen. But he would never treat an American student like that again, he said, because Sessions was literally the only one who knew how to take it. As a teacher himself, Sessions never treated a student roughly.

Sessions returned to Northampton thrilled, but his mother was not happy; she "made a very long face about this." Barbara had maintained the view that the two should get away from Northampton into a better musical atmosphere. Sessions had always countered with three reasons for staying: Roy Welch, his job, and his mother. Roy Welch understood Sessions's excitement about Bloch and tried to cheer Ruth up. Neither was Smith College's Sleeper pleased about the abandonment of the symphony. Nevertheless

Sessions, while still teaching at Smith, studied for almost two years in New York with Bloch. (Thus the symphony was abandoned a year and a half before George died.)

Sessions wrote to his fiancée about his second lesson, in December 1919. "Finally he said 'now, we have just begun; I prophecy that in two years you will be able to do anything you want to do—that is, to write in the most effective way—for orchestra, or anything else. Whether you can say anything original or not is another matter—that depends upon other things—upon your life; but you will be able to write what you want in the most effective way.' . . . I then told him I was going to be married—he was very enthusiastic at first; then he spoke of the responsibilities + cares that marriage brought with it. But, he said, it is life."[11]

Sessions went once a month or every six weeks to New York to take a lesson from Bloch whenever he could scrape together the money to pay for one. As usual, he borrowed money from friends. The two did not work on analysis of contemporary music: they spoke about Wagner. Bloch's analysis concerned classical form. He later discussed counterpoint by using examples by Orlando di Lasso and other late Renaissance composers. At the first interview Bloch had asked Sessions whether he ever looked at music—what he called studying the anatomy of music—from the point of view of a conductor or a composer. The exercises that Sessions wrote for Bloch from 1919–1920 covered three technical aspects of music: fugue, counterpoint, and musical form. Evidently Sessions's harmony was good enough, because of his summer-school course with George Vieh, that he did not need to study it again.

Bloch had studied in Frankfurt with Iwan Knorr, a German composer who had studied in Russia. He is often ranked with Reger as one of the greatest masters of counterpoint and fugue of his time. Knorr published four books, two on fugal writing.[12]

Bloch's teacher in Munich, Ludwig Thuille had, with Rudolf Louis, written a *Harmonielehre* in 1907. As a teacher himself, Bloch completely eschewed textbooks in favor of drawing deductions from actual music. This was the technique that Thuille and Louis had promulgated in their text. Later Sessions would challenge this inherited view of how to teach counterpoint; he would not feel that the right approach was to start with composers' music, then deducing rules from what they had done.

Fugal writing was the largest portion and the most revealing of the three subjects found in Sessions's 150-page folio devoted to his study with Bloch.[13] This study culminated in five complete fugues by Sessions. Bloch and Sessions and were clearly using Bach's 48 fugues from the *Well-Tempered Clavier* as a point of departure. Sessions wrote over 40 original fugal subjects as exercises. The problem was then to compose countersubjects and to master invertible counterpoint. Bloch dictated that one of the subjects, in E minor, be turned into a three-voice fugue. It is perhaps revealing that, of the 40 subjects, the one in E minor was most suited to this treatment. Its model appears to be the E minor fugue from Book I of the *Well-Tempered Clavier*, the only one of the WTC 48 in two voices. Sessions was later drawn to the key of E minor in his tonal music: both his First Symphony and his First String Quartet are in E minor. Sessions systematically explored the possible uses of the subject, countersubject, and counterpoint for this fugue with Bloch. The final ink version of the fugue did not contain a true countersubject, but included a presentation of the subject in the key of the dominant—not previously attempted in the sketches.

Sessions was glad for a chance to escape from Smith to what he considered a more professional atmosphere at Kent. Smith was too rarefied; he wanted to work in the dirt, as it were. He wrote to Father Sill, "I should be glad at any time to explain to you the many ways in which I have found a college teaching position incompatible with real artistic achievement; they are all conditions which, I think are inherent in the college faculty system, since they are almost universal, and which do not exist at Kent."[14] The teaching offer from Kent included two courses in Latin or Greek in addition to music, for a salary of $1,500. In addition, Sessions volunteered to take "any other two courses which you may suggest" and noted he had kept up with his Greek more than the Latin.

After four years of Smith, Sessions was to have left to teach at Kent in the fall of 1921. He wrote to Sill in April 1921 for the last time. (George's death may have been why Sessions permanently severed his correspondence with the long-lived Pater.[15]) Sessions was moving. He had another offer.

> I have accepted a position with the Cleveland Institute of Music next year, as I told you I might last fall. I hope you understand that it is the chance of a lifetime, since it means intimate association with a man whom I consider, and who is becoming more and more generally to be considered the greatest composer living today, and perhaps indeed the greatest that has lived for a good many years. The Cleveland Institute under Bloch's leadership is I believe destined to do a work the importance of which it would be difficult to exaggerate. So, while I shall miss being at Kent, I am afraid that my destiny calls me elsewhere. It is going to be very thrilling and stimulating work, and I think that I would rather be there than anywhere else in the world.[16]

Before moving to Cleveland, however, came the spring and summer of 1921, the two seasons that provide the only extant letters from Sessions to Bloch. In one he asked Bloch to take as a student his Yale friend Quincy Porter. In the same letter Sessions informed Bloch that he had persuaded the Letz Quartet to read Bloch's Quartet. "I can never tell you what an overwhelming effect your music had on me . . . nor what joy it gave me to see that the others understood + loved it too."[17]

Bloch gave Sessions something of an assignment: make a four-hand arrangement of "Israel." He worked on it with the intention of trying it out with Miss Goode of the Smith faculty. Returning to his aunts' hilltop cabin near Forty Acres, Sessions and Barbara evicted two families of squirrels, one family of field mice, and four large and aggressive families of wasps from their winter homes. The Sessionses moved into what had been their honeymoon home. Arria had died that spring and Molly moved out. He wrote to Bloch in late June of what he hoped to accomplish that summer.[18] Nowhere in his letters to Bloch does he mention the death of his best friend in May or the fact that he was mourning him. It is entirely possible that Bloch knew nothing of George, whose symphony he had advised Sessions to discard. Sessions tried to slam shut that chapter in his life, and to move to another state would help achieve that. By July, however, the work on "Israel," as well as on his own music, was going quite slowly: "I am trying hard to give the two players as much liberty as possible without injuring the sonority and balance; also to keep the phrasing and the part-writing clear. It is really quite a problem!" As always, he was optimistic: "I am beginning to *see things clearly*, and I have great hopes."[19]

By late August, however, he told Bloch, he had "done very little work." He castigated himself before Bloch might have a chance to.

> During the last few weeks I have come to a realization of my own incompetence, and have been seeking a way out. The truth is that I am utterly without self-discipline, in my whole life; and this has thwarted me and frustrated me at every turn. To give one instance: the work that I have done for you has been *false*,

simply because I have put so little energy into it—through sheer lack of force of will. When I started out with you I wanted with the utmost sincerity to do my work justice; but my forces scattered themselves, and the work which I have always done for you is more than unworthy of what I could and should have done. This is humiliating and discouraging to me because of my failure to make the most of my association with you and the teaching you have given me—without which I would have become almost desperate in Northampton. But this is only one way in which I have failed; the disease affects everything I do.[20]

A year and a half of studying with Bloch was completed, and Sessions still felt "a failure of technique. . . . Fortunately I never have lost beyond recovery my faith in myself; and I think I am speaking soberly in saying that I know that I shall cure myself." Indeed, in spite of frequent failures to live up to his own, and others', expectations, Sessions was consistently and remarkably optimistic: next year will always be different; things will work out then (shades of *Jean-Christophe*). If Ruth was Scarlett O'Hara regarding Forty Acres, Sessions shared the character's motto, "Tomorrow is another day." Considering his limited success as a composer—he had yet to complete a catalogued work—he had remarkable faith in himself and in his ability eventually to overcome those factors that inhibited him. Ultimately, he would succeed in conquering his own worst enemy: himself.

CLEVELAND INSTITUTE OF MUSIC

In April 1920 a small group of patrons each contributed $1,000 to establish a music school in Cleveland; studios at the Hotel Statler sufficed until a facility could be found. The Cleveland Institute of Music opened December 8, 1920, at 3146 Euclid Avenue, a three-storey house known as Nellis House. Among the first faculty were pianist Nathan Fryer, a pupil of Leschetizky; Louis Edlin, concertmaster of the Cleveland Orchestra; and Victor de Gomez, its principal cellist. By 1921 Beryl Rubinstein and Ruth Edwards had joined the 22-member faculty, which included violinist André de Ribaupierre, organist Edwin Arthur Kraft, and, in March, Jean Binet teaching Dalcroze Eurhythmics, an important study at the Institute. Sessions was joined in Cleveland by his Smith colleague, violinist Ruth H. Willian. Sessions was hired in the summer of 1921 to teach theory, music history, and music appreciation at a salary of $2,250, which, during his first and second year there, meant he taught about 20 hours a week at $5 an hour. Sessions began performing on faculty concerts with Ruth Edwards, accompanying soprano Edna Williard and flutist Weyert Moor on December 17, 1921. The young and enthusiastic faculty had the notion they were building an institution from scratch, which, of course, they were.

Bloch found what he called the Middle West extremely crude, a kind of wilderness. To travel to New York took 14 hours by train, and he commuted regularly. At the time Sessions had never been farther west than Syracuse. He had the idea there were no hills between the Allegenhies and the Rockies—he thought one could see straight across!

In a letter to his colleague Jean Binet, Sessions listed his address as "Cleveland, *Filth City*."[1] Euclid Avenue

> was the big old street which was a very famous thoroughfare in the nineties, and I guess in the early years of this century. By the time I got there, it was somewhat run down, and in fact the conservatory, the institute where I worked, was down on Euclid Avenue, near old 34th Street, I think. . . . If I walked across to school from Euclid Avenue itself, I got my trousers covered with burrs. That's what I mean by being run down. There were all sorts of these big old houses which—oh, looked like nothing I'd seen anywhere.[2]

The Sessionses first lived in an apartment house on Euclid Avenue. The original idea had been for the two couples—the Blochs and the Sessionses—to live either together or quite near each other. The next year, 1922–1923, the Sessionses lived on 87th Street, where *The Black Maskers* was composed. Streets were numbered outward both east and west from the center of town. Except for six weeks, the two lived on the west side, on a bluff on Lake Erie. The Institute also moved in November 1922 to 2827 Euclid Avenue, the Chisholm Residence.[3]

In the fall of 1921 both of Sessions's parents wrote: Ruth was snobbish about the sorts of people one might meet in Cleveland. "Of course the ordinariness of the mass of Cleveland people is inevitable."[4] She also wrote a severe letter to Barbara about the debts the Sessionses had left behind in Northampton.[5] Archibald got the impression from letters that they "were in a thoroughly congenial atmosphere—even though it is Hebrew." He was being bogged down with work, which literally doubled when *Ainslee's Magazine* shifted from a monthly to a bi-weekly.[6] He had taken no summer vacation, reserving his vacation days for the expected rehearsals by Belasco of one of his plays.

Now that Roger and Barbara were too far away to visit or help her, Ruth discussed her health for the first time in letters, attempting to put a classic guilt trip on the two. One December letter details

> one of the horrid nervous spasms . . . tingling of every nerve . . . could not shake off the terror and misery all day . . . The worst of it was that I felt convinced we could not have you come for Christmas—that Aunt M[olly] could never cook for so many of us, and that even if you were here I should not be able to stand the excitement and might not be allowed to see you . . . terribly nervous nights, they are not epileptic seizures, by the way, and no brain-symptoms whatever, only the horrible sort of all-over-nerve-pressure that is so hard to stand. . . . I can't yet use my arms at all.[7]

Whatever was medically the matter with her should not really have prevented Roger and Barbara from visiting at Christmas, yet Ruth raised this straw man.

Sessions's salary was a considerable increase over his salary at Smith. Bloch received $20,000, a salary comparable with other conservatory directors. He tried to get Sessions

Figure 22 The Cleveland Institute of Music, the Chisholm Residence.

as many teaching assignments as possible, but Sessions's own insecurities interfered. As he had avoided teaching woodwinds at Smith, he also backed away from teaching oboe and conducting in Cleveland. Theoretically, he should have been able to teach both; he had studied oboe in Cambridge and conducting with Horatio Parker, but he had never conducted—neither his own piece at Yale nor any Beethoven at Smith.

The manager of the Institute, Mrs Franklyn B. Sanders, had already been asked to find the Sessionses a place to live. Martha Sanders was a force to be contended with. Her financial backing was crucial to the Institute, but more important was both her willing-ness and her ability to do the work necessary to start a conservatory. (She would eventu-ally run it.) Sessions had trouble with controlling women. The very few times Sessions had something unpleasant to say about a person in decades of letter writing, that person was always a powerful or wealthy female, a reflection of Ruth Sessions. The prohibition on criticizing his mother was too strong; he could, however, strike out at substitutes. Mrs Sanders, "slightly annoyed," had reason—from Bloch himself—to expect Sessions to teach conducting. Sessions wrote to Bloch: "I shall answer her in my most oily manner! I really find these little feminine endearments rather amusing—except for the waste of time they involve."[8] Sessions's condescending attitude (evidently shared by Bloch) about "women control" was ironic, since his own deficiencies, not hers, were at issue.

Sessions left for Cleveland around September 15, and Barbara began a job teaching on the 21st. Once in Cleveland, Barbara became annoyed with the social life where after a dinner people played "silly games." "They can not make me try to make a social *monkey* of my husband—*I will not!*—I will try to do my best to help him with what he feels necessary for the Institute—but *nothing more!*"[9] An aspiring art historian, Barbara had little use for Cleveland's art museum, seeing nothing there that would make her want to return. She took classes with Bloch and played the violin. Both of the Sessionses missed the countryside.

Occasionally, they met someone important in the musical world. Bloch and Sessions had lunch with Siegfried and Winifred Wagner. To hear Siegfried speak of "my father" must have sent shivers up Sessions's back. He also saw Nadia Boulanger on her first visit to the US; she introduced Sessions to Stravinsky (see section "Stravinsky").

Sessions was impressed by the Cleveland Symphony Orchestra, but less so with its conductor. The Russian-born Nikolai Sokoloff had settled in the United States in 1914, studied violin with Loeffler in Boston, and played in the Boston Symphony Orchestra. He had been music director of the San Francisco Philharmonic from 1914 to 1918. The Cleveland board tried to promote him as the next Stokowski. The Orchestra performed in the Masonic Auditorium, built in 1920 with a seating capacity of 2,190. (In 1931 it moved to its current home, the famous Severance Hall.) According to Suzanne Bloch, "the problem was that the two society women who ran the two big music organizations, the Institute and the Orchestra, were rivals. [Adella Prentiss Hughes], who ran the Orchestra, just boosted Sokoloff very much and Mrs Sanders, of course, boosted my father as much as she could."[10] Cleveland in the 1920s was nevertheless not a musical city. Suzanne continued: "They would go to concerts together. . . . when something really was bad with the orchestra, Roger and my father began to comment on it not very tactfully or send each other messages."[11]

During their first summer, in 1922, Sessions was Bloch's assistant in summer school: he earned $500 teaching summer school in 1923 and 1925. He taught five hours on Monday and Thursday, seven on Tuesday and Friday, three and a half on Wednesday, and one on Saturday, which left him little time for piano practice. (He spent more time writing letters to his wife, away trying to earn money, than at the piano.)

In some ways Sessions's teaching was more elementary than what he had been doing at Smith, "but much more solid, at least."[12] The enrollment varied: the school began in 1920 with seven students, which increased to 69 by the end of the year. These increases were repeated in each of the four years Sessions taught: 1921–1922 enrollment increased from 118 to 254; 1922–1923 from 156 to 325; 1923–1924-from 216 to 390; and in Sessions's last year, 1924–1925, from 289 to 483. That year the theory classes alone had 184 students. In November 1925 the Institute had 456 pupils.

The student newspaper, *The Outpost*, published Sessions's occasional short essays. In his 1922 "A teacher views a problem," Sessions wrote,

> Every teacher is tempted, from impatience or vanity or some other cause, to pose as an omniscient and infallible prophet of the one true faith; while on the other hand a natural intellectual laziness too often gets the better of the pupil and causes him to accept and even demand ready-made conclusions, definitions, rules, etc. But the pupil ought to be using his brains in a search or demand for the explanation of fundamental causes. Thus teaching may cease to be the exciting intellectual stimulus which it should be, and become the dullest kind of routine; the teacher sinks further and further into the rut of barren self-satisfaction, and the pupil ends in disillusion or mediocrity.[13]

Sessions liked his colleagues, many of them students of Bloch, as well as those who were professional performers. Bloch's students, colleagues at the Cleveland Institute, included Bernard Rogers, Herbert Elwell, Quincy Porter, Theodore Chanler, Hubbard Hutchinson, Isabel Swift, Jean Binet, and Anita Frank. (Binet left in 1923, but a life-long friendship with Sessions had already been cemented.) Quincy Porter replaced Hubbard Hutchinson at mid-year, 1922–1923, as a theory teacher; he remained until 1928, having been made head of the theory department in May 1925. The Williams College-educated Hutchinson, always torn between music and writing literature, had just published a novel, *Chanting Wheels*, and would publish *From Rome to Florence*.[14] Sessions's opinions were confided to Binet: "Hubbard [Hutchinson] and I have become quite intimate . . . I don't find it at all hard to appreciate his very fine *qualities*; at times he seems like the one human being here among a bunch of tiresome + self-centered egoists."[15] He and Sessions shared the same birthday, December 28, 1896. Hutchinson, however, suffered from leukemia and, after three years (1931–1934) of writing music criticism for *The New York Times*, he died at 37.

Sessions did not continue working privately in composition with Bloch longer than a year; he attended Bloch's classes, however. Bloch's daughter Suzanne also studied at the Institute, taking composition and counterpoint with Sessions. Suzanne considered him "really a relative." She noted that the small classes were mostly girls and a few boys; a photo of Sessions teaching at the Cleveland Institute shows five girls and one boy.[16] She remembered the early days in Cleveland:

> Now Roger and my father had very much in common, and they also had the most wonderful Rabelasian minds. And what went on in my father's office was something incredible. The stories that they told and the jokes they had! And the classes were absolutely wonderful, because Roger, though not devastatingly exciting, you know, he has a great sense of humor and knows music. Anything he can play. He doesn't have to give much explanation. He goes to the music and plays it for you and, with his sort of grunting way, brings out all the essence of it.

Figure 23 Bloch and his pupils at the Cleveland Institute of Music, 1922. From left to right: Jean Binet, Hubbard Hutchinson, Ruth Willian, Quincy Porter, Roger Sessions, Barbara Sessions, Aaron Bodenhorn, Isabel Swift, and Anita Frank.

[Hutchinson] and Roger were the two people teaching theory and ear training and so on. And Hubbard was very handsome, you know, with red hair and dressed fit to kill. Here comes Roger, you know, with soft collars, kind of a little bit lumpy. And Mrs Sanders said to my father, "I have to talk to you. There are complaints by parents saying Mr Sessions goes and teaches with soft collars. He doesn't dress formally." And Father said, "Is that so?" Father next day only came wearing soft collars![17]

Whatever self-doubt Sessions harbored about his ability to complete his music was somewhat allayed by his teacher. By the spring of 1922 the list of incomplete pieces included another symphony, a smaller orchestral work, a piano sonata, and three smaller movements that might find their way into the longer ones. Sessions wrote to Ruth:

[Bloch] has often had the same lack of confidence and the other difficulties which I have in my composing, and told me very freely about things that had helped him, and expressed his entire confidence that I would be able to do something really fine. It was so encouraging to have such a talk with him, and will really help me a great deal. Lack of self-confidence such as I have is an American disease; Bloch assured me that there was no reason for it in my case, & it did me no end of good to talk with him about it; for it is the worst disease that an artist can have, especially at the outset of his career, for there are millions of things to discourage him after the career is under way.[18]

None of the six pieces he worked on in 1922 survive in the composer's catalog.[19] Indeed, we have yet to encounter any piece he considered worthy of his catalog. Nevertheless, in 1923 his works were performed on faculty recitals. On March 13, 1923, the faculty string quartet (de Ribaupierre and Willian, violins, Porter, viola, and Aaron Bodenhorn, cello) performed a Bagatelle by Sessions and a Prelude by Binet, as well as folk-song arrangements by Porter and Rogers. (The Bagatelle was repeated December 7, 1923, paired with a Nocturne by Chanler.) On April 25, 1924, three excerpts from *The Black Maskers* were performed piano four-hand by Ruth Edwards and Beryl Rubinstein: "Wedding Music," Song, and Fire Music (Closing Scene). In addition, on March 28, 1924, his *Lento moderato* was performed by Sessions's sister-in-law and new faculty member, pianist Eleanor Foster, with Porter on the viola. The two also performed Bloch's viola suite on this concert.

Eleanor had not gone to Smith as had her two younger sisters, but had been a piano pupil of Heinrich Gebhardt and Adelaide Proctor and studied Dalcroze and solfège at the Longy School in Cambridge. Her faculty biography stated that she had made public appearances in Boston and other eastern cities. At Cleveland she taught not only piano but also theory and ensembles. She left Cleveland after two years (1923–1925), in the year Sessions, Barbara, and Bloch left. Eleanor, too, went to Europe.

The 30-member Institute String Orchestra also performed, as did the all-girl quartet. Barbara Sessions played violin in both. One String Orchestra concert drew an audience of 600. Her quartet played the Menuet from Schubert's A minor Quartet, op. 29, on January 30, 1925, in the ballroom of the Hotel Statler, where most of the major concerts were held.

The 1923–1924 year was difficult, in part because Bloch's indiscreet remarks about Sokoloff resulted in the conductor's decision not to play Bloch's music that season. Unlike Sessions, who virtually never lost his temper, Bloch was unable to control his. Sessions thought Bloch's new secretary, Lillian Rogers (the first wife of Bernard Rogers), would help calm him. It had been an ill-considered political move on Bloch's part, however, to replace Mrs Sanders—thereby demoting her—with Mrs Rogers. Sanders was a board member and helped build the Institute. Bloch would need friends and he was losing them. Bloch traveled frequently to give master classes during the summer of 1924 in San Francisco and at the Eastman School in January and February of 1925. Mrs Sanders wrote to him asking, in effect, why the Eastman School's advertising materials about their guest did not include mention of the Cleveland Institute. Bloch, along with André de Ribaupierre and Sessions, went to New York on November 8, 1923, to hear the premiere of Bloch's Quintet, given by Harold Bauer and the Lenox Quartet.

Sessions was quoted in an article in *Topics*, an Institute magazine:

> For our musical salvation in this country we need more background. A discriminating taste does not necessarily follow from the recognition of a few chords of Bach and a much played composition of Beethoven. Good music should be part of our living. On the continent people sing Schubert in their homes. There are numberless friendly groups performing chamber music in pleasant informal way. There, beautiful music is taken for granted.
>
> It takes background of this order for a basis from which to enjoy modern music. You can't very well be thrilled by a departure from orthodoxy if you aren't aware that there has been departure.
>
> Another point, modern music is today in an experimental state. It's fair to call it musician's music[,] for composers are often simply trying out material to achieve effects. When they use their results to express the basic emotions of their people then we shall have great things from them.[20]

Financial problems continued to rear their heads. After Sessions left Hadley in the summer of 1922 to return to Cleveland, he had a "frightful *crise de nerfs* [fit of hysteria] over a mistake in my bank accounts which had resulted in a bad check, and a threatening letter from the Ohio Bell Telephone Co., which I received three weeks after it was sent."[21] At a board meeting in March 1924 Bloch read a letter from Sessions asking for more money. Sessions had evidently discovered that he was being paid substantially less than other faculty. The board voted to give him a bonus of $500, to be paid immediately, and to offer him a salary for the following year (1924–1925) of $4,000.

Sessions's successful public lectures on the *Ring* cycle (Bloch had asked him to lecture) led to his giving a talk with musical illustrations at the piano the week before each of the 12 Cleveland Symphony Orchestra concerts. The series cost $10, and the price of an individual talk was $1.25. After the Wagnerian Opera Company presented in Masonic Hall during the week of November 20, 1924, the *Ring* cycle, *Tristan*, and *Tannhäuser*, on which Sessions had lectured, he wrote a review for the school paper *The Outpost*. Sessions had known Wagner's music well for more than a decade, since his paper at the Kent School, his essays on Wagner for the *Harvard Musical Review*, and his lectures in Cleveland. While bemoaning wrong entrances, certain cuts in the operas, the lack of Wagner tubas, and some poor conducting (*Tristan* by Stransky), Sessions praised Moerike, the conductor of *Walküre*, and Ernest Knoch's conducting of *Siegfried*. He wrote, "The joyous ecstasy of the music, this drama, became for us the most powerful of realities; the faith which inspired such a magnificent performance became reflected in our renewed faith in the power of art which remains great even in the midst of a sick civilization." *Tannhäuser*, Sessions felt, "scarcely held its own beside the greater works of Wagner," but in *Die Götterdämmerung*, "Not a measure, not a chord, is lost in bringing home to us this crushing sense of universal destruction." Sessions ended, however, by asserting that "His art already belongs to the past, and our effort must be to keep it vividly in mind as one of the great worlds which human imagination has created."[22]

Sessions's Wagner lectures were publicized in the local newspapers. Suzanne Bloch continued,

> I remember for the first time after the First World War the Wagner Company from Germany came. . . . they gave the whole Ring. The whole Institute stopped to prepare for that. That was the beauty about this Institute. . . . And the excitement, you know. It was so wonderful, because in th[ese] so-called small towns where there was never music, never like in New York, a thing like this is an event. Here now we have how many concerts? You get blasé. But in Cleveland when something like the Wagnerian company came for a week. And I always remember Roger said he would give lectures on the Ring. And that was something. He gave lectures and he played, of course. You know how he plays, he can really dig. He played all the themes and he told us about these wonderful keys that made things extraordinary. . . . I remember we were so stunned—it's the way he did it. Now you know Roger, when you talk to him he doesn't exactly seem to project great excitement, and yet he does something . . . Oh. We were all so thrilled. And then to hear the stuff, it was just too, too much! He really did, he was really extraordinary in that way.[23]

Although at the time Bloch was undergoing a "terrible crisis," according to his daughter, which affected the entire Institute's atmosphere, many wonderful events made Sessions's experience memorable. "Roger looks back, as he has told me one day, he said, 'You know we thought it was pretty bad. When I think now how wonderful it was.' It was a human school compared to some of the schools that are big, well-organized . . . factories. This was a human thing with human beings with the good and the bad, but it was all the time alive."

Ultimately, and inevitably, Sessions's relationship with Bloch in Cleveland became

> more and more complicated. . . . I was extremely fond of him always, but I began, in the absolutely ruthless way that a young man does—because it was so bound up with my own problems, I suppose—well, scrutinizing my whole feeling about Bloch as a human being, as a composer—well, very carefully, and I began to be very critical of some things about him. As I say, this is all part of the process of getting free of this personality, you see. And I did—Bloch obviously didn't like my being interested in any other composer, and I was. . . . Bloch, as I say, was an extremely vivid personality. He was a man of tremendous curiosity. Well, perhaps I wouldn't quite put it that way. He was a man of tremendous gifts, no question about it, much greater gifts than I think ever came really to fruition. One reason for that was a very, very complex personality. He grew up in Geneva, and when he was—well, he grew up in a bourgeois Jewish family in Geneva. He was a very, very gifted young man, and a very gifted personality, tremendously ambitious. He wrote an opera, *Macbeth*, which was produced in Paris [at the Opéra-Comique November 30,] 1910, with great success. I met later the man who wrote the text of *Macbeth*. (I'm not referring to William Shakespeare.) . . . I met [Edmond Fleg] in 1924, I went to spend the summer in Europe and met him in Paris, and by that time I was on the road to, I won't say, disenchantment, because this was not what it was at all. It was simply a very, very strong dependence, and I'd become, as I say, very critical, in a certain sense. . . . This man told me that after the success of *Macbeth*, which was really rather spectacular, Bloch did everything that he could to destroy his own success, you see. In other words, Bloch was a very, very complex personality who was very much at war with himself.[24]
>
> Then he found that there was a lot of friction. I mean, there were reactions against the success. Well, every musician has gone through this and knows about it, but Bloch's reaction was sort of to withdraw from a great deal that he considered contemporary music. He was very fond of Debussy, who was very nice to him, but he was suspicious of Ravel, very suspicious of Stravinsky. Stravinsky was an emerging young personality in Paris at that time, and I think Bloch assumed a hostility on the part of these people, and adopted a kind of an attitude of aloofness, if not hostility. In fact, the hostility became much stronger later on. . . . I mean that Bloch was a highly gifted man. . . . He had at the same time a background of French culture which gave him an ironic streak, a very sardonic streak in his nature. These things would fight with each other. I mean, I've known several people in my life who were their own worst enemies, and Bloch was one of them. . . . Well, Bloch didn't almost kill himself physically, except once—a very, very extraordinary incident in Cleveland, in which he almost did kill himself. In fact, I never was sure whether he really intended to kill himself or just scare the hell out of everybody around him.[25]

Openly unfaithful to his wife Marguerite Schneider, Bloch kept falling back in love with her. From 1923–1925 he had an affair with his student, then made a teacher, Anita Frank. When his wife learned of this from others, she became angry. Anita lived in the apartment next door to the Sessionses on Euclid Avenue, where Bloch would visit her. Marguerite Bloch wrote for advice to Lillian Rogers, who had left Cleveland for New York. Rogers wrote to the girl, who was depressed by the letter; when Bloch asked her about it, he heard that his former secretary had written that he had a mind like a sewer. This struck Bloch deeply. Bloch then told Sessions privately that he had resigned from the Institute; he felt that bottom had fallen out of his world. Suzanne quoted her mother, who "used to say, 'If only there were more people like Sessions around my father instead of all these kind of adoring females and people who had no minds of their own.' This was a man who was on equal terms with my father."[26]

Shortly afterward, Sessions, Barbara, Bloch, and Anita Frank attended a performance of *Salome*, and Bloch's depression came to a head. He saw the world in Manichean terms: people were either on his side or great betrayers. Now he felt betrayed. He then took a huge dose of the barbiturate veronal, and fell into a coma, hovering between life and death for a couple of days. Sessions recalled,

> Then he gradually came out of the coma. He was quite incoherent for a while, and then became coherent again. He was in a very exalted frame of mind, which impressed everybody, moved everybody to tears. He made a speech. Absolutely extraordinary occasion in Cleveland—I mean, an occasion of a performance of his [Violin Sonata]. He'd told me that he wasn't going, asked me to make the speech about the piece that he was to have made himself. I dropped in on him on the way to the place, and he suddenly decided to go, and he said, "I'll speak for just a minute, because I'm really not strong enough. And you get up and analyze the sonata." Bloch stood and spoke for half an hour and unburdened his soul, and made a public confession of all his sins. Then you can imagine how I felt getting up to analyze the sonata, after this, oh, absolutely religious revival occasion. Then the piece was played. Bloch was quite a showman, too, you see. There was this side of him. Then afterward everybody came up and congratulated him. . . .
>
> Bloch had worked up this tremendous emotional situation, and then he simply couldn't sustain it afterwards, you see, because he had sort of keyed himself up to the highest pitch of moral tension. I mean, he had a number of people ready to go with him to the ends of the earth, if you like. And then his ironical side came out. It was very educational, you see. I mean, he obviously couldn't sustain it. At first, he was going to—he told the Board of Directors, got them all worked up, too; he told them that he was being paid too much. He was going to work for much less money. Then when they tried to follow that up later, he said with disgust that they were trying to profit by that veronal affair.
>
> When he was under the influence of the veronal, he told me that he had dreams, and one dream was—and this has been distorted, and I'll tell you the accurate version as I heard it from him, and I wasn't the only one who heard it, but it's a tale that has grown, you see—one dream was that he went to Heaven, and he met, was ushered into the presence of his illustrious colleagues of the past, and they all greeted him as one of them, Mozart—yes, Mozart was there, and Beethoven was there, I think Wagner wasn't. There was one very great composer who was absent. I never could quite understand why, but maybe he was actually reporting an absolutely bona fide dream that he had. Anyway, he asked Mozart why he wrote his superficial last movements to his work (which, if I may say so, is nonsense); Mozart said he did it to make people happy. So this

led to a great examination of conscience on Bloch's part. He realized he'd been a great egoist all his life and so forth.

Another thing was that he'd met God, and God sent a personal message to me, and the personal message from God to me was that Stravinsky was a nice man and a gifted composer, but he was on the wrong track. This sounds absolutely ridiculous when I tell it, and does no justice to this man who was really quite a person—I mean, I knew, quite an extraordinary person. But, on the other hand, it was rather a shock.[27]

This episode took place during the 1923–1924 school year. Bloch, however, did not discontinue the adulterous affair, which the next year got him fired from the Institute.

THE BLACK MASKERS

In February 1923 Samuel Eliot, Jr, Sessions's Harvard friend at Smith College, renewed his request to Sessions, now living in Cleveland, to write the incidental music for the three-evening senior dramatics. Eliot, the grandson of a former Harvard president, had been a member of the Washington Square Players from 1914 to 1916, where he presented Leonid Andreyeff's *Love of One's Neighbors*. He had translated Franz Wedekind's *Tragedies of Sex: Erdgeist (Earth Spirit)* and *Pandora's Box* (the sources of Berg's *Lulu*).[1] The previous Smith productions Eliot directed were *The Yellow Jacket* (1919), a take-off of Chinese drama for which Sessions had supervised the writing of the music, and *The Merchant of Venice* (1920; Sessions had also supervised the composition of its music), done instead of Eliot's own choice, Percy MacKaye's *Sappho and Phaon*.[2] In 1921 he had chosen *False Gods* by Eugene Brieux, which was produced, and in 1922 *A Winter's Tale* was done—rather than Eliot's choice, Edward Sheldon's *Garden of Paradise*; for a second time he was overruled by the senior class.

Sessions, who had already read Andreyeff, was probably not fully aware that the choice of Andreyeff, too, was controversial at Smith. The senior class had voted overwhelmingly in December to premiere the 1915 translation of the expressionist and fatalistic *The Black Maskers*. A "hot campaign against it," however, resulted in a reconsideration meeting in February, where the vote was 130 in favor to 100 opposed. Claiming that he had "had very little influence over the choices in the past five years," Eliot recalled that he "merely stated that I would not care to produce any other play . . . for the class."[3] After the production the Chairman for the Class of 1923 wrote: "It was, obviously, a new tradition in art, a play which derived its dramatic intensity from the presentation of internal rather than external action. . . . The story itself, with its infinite gradations from the objective to the subjective could not but fascinate eager imaginations. . . . We would give a play which would contribute to the dramatic achievements of the United States."[4] One letter from a Czechoslovakian exchange student was positive, but three alumnae jointly complained they were not sufficiently "entertained;" after all, they had paid for their tickets in order to be entertained.[5] In the November issue of the *Smith Alumnae Quarterly* two more letters appeared, which defended the play and criticized the idea that the dramatics should be "amusing."[6]

Eliot wrote,

> I don't recall when I first read Andreiev's *Life of Man* and *Black Maskers*, but already I regarded him as the world's top dramatist after Strindberg died in 1912, and enough leaders of the Class of '23 agreed with me, so the first American production of *Black Maskers* began in the fall of '22. I designed the sets: on stage right, great steps rising to a balcony where pretend-musicians

played (the real ones were beneath it) and to a doorway into a great tower, symbolizing Lorenzo, up which the final fire roared and great blocks fell in; up left-center tall windows at which black maskers scratched and whined, and down left the big door thru which everyone entered—one girl I remember wore a mask of round-eyed astonishment which as she entered made spectators titter, only to gasp with horror when she turned to look at them. Off-stage, left, was a semi-circular platform, set with a half-dome and two recesses so that one got the idea 'twas the inside of Lorenzo's skull, which was wheeled to stage-center for Scene 2; but Scene 4 was (I think) done with draperies, the living Lorenzo standing, back to audience, beside the dead one.[7]

The 30-year-old Eliot directed and designed the masks, the scenery, many of the costumes, as well as devising the elaborate lighting with torches flaring and falling, and spots shining from one side only.

A literary critic described Andreyeff's work: "Few writers of any age have surpassed Andreyeff at depicting a mental state that recurs repeatedly in his stories: that transitional movement when a desperately sick mind, on the verge of snapping, expresses an intolerable apperception of horror in a maniacal laugh. Frenzied cachinnation turns up so regularly in his pages as to constitute something like Andreyeff's signature."[8] Remembering the death of Andreyeff's wife, Alexandra Mikhailovna, just prior to the writing of *The Black Maskers*, may help us to understand Lorenzo's frequent ravings, "I have lost my wife," despite the fact that she is present in the play. Even the villa in which Andreyeff lived sounded from Maksim Gorki's description to be similar to the set of *The Black Maskers*.[9]

The play was expressionistic and "ultra-modern at the time."[10] Sessions described the story: "It's a play about an Italian Renaissance [actually twelfth-century] nobleman, the son of a Crusader, supposedly. And he comes upon a document [in scene 2] which convinces him that he is really the offspring of an affair that his mother had with a groom, probably. And that unhinges him, you see, as far as his sense of identity."[11] Smith students feared for the sanity of the audience and some had "visions of a line of ambulances conveying audiences and players to Hospital Hill." The *Smith College Weekly* published an outline of the play and two pages of explanation of its "inner meaning."[12] Eliot wrote, "I knew nothing, then, about psychiatry, but when I did learn about Manic-Depressive Psychosis it was obvious that the play came out of that, as Andreiev experienced it—and how wonderfully he did dramatize it."[13] The play dealt with insanity, split personality, identity crisis, symbology, a fire as redemption, and, of course, scary black maskers, reminiscent of those Thanksgiving costumes that so frightened Sessions at 417 Washington Avenue. Sessions outlined the play and described it in detail in *Conversations*.[14]

The Black Maskers bears a strong resemblance to Poe's *The Masque of the Red Death* and *William Wilson. The Masque* and the Andreyeff play share common features of a masked ball in a castle, an orchestra, and the presence of a terrifying guest whose mask cannot be removed. When William Wilson's *Doppelgänger* appears the candles instantly become extinguished; similarly the Black Maskers cause the lights to go out. At a Roman masquerade ball, where both William Wilsons wear a black silk mask, the evil character murders the good one, who tells him that in so doing, "thou has murdered thyself." Failing to understand the black maskers, representations of his own soul, Andreyeff's Lorenzo splits into two, the one self slaying the other. This duality leads to his tragedy: insanity. At the same time, by killing the double and thereby renouncing the evil in his soul, Lorenzo has attained the knowledge of God and perishes in the same moment.

Elliott Carter cites Mittner's definition of Expressionism, which constitutes a prim-ordial utterance (*Urschrei*) and the imposition of geometric structure on reality.[15] Andreyeff's play fits both these definitions. In scene 3 Lorenzo "utters a wild cry and falls:" at that moment the black maskers break into the castle (his soul) and usher in chaos.[16]

An abstract structure is also present because the varied recurrence of the same events makes it impossible to determine which scenes are "real" and which exist only in Lorenzo's crazed imagination. The play is in two acts and five scenes (three in Act 1 and two in Act 2). Arguments could be forwarded for least three different chronological orderings of these five scenes: 1) that the action proceeds from scenes 1 through 5 in order (this seems fairly doubtful, and much is done to dissuade the audience from this conclusion), 2) that the second scene, in the tower, actually occurs first (Sessions appar-ently believes this to be the case, given his own description of the action), or 3) that the ball in the last scene represents the *only* reality in the play and, in fact, happens first. Scenes 1, 3, and 5 take place at the ball where their similar action is varied. Scenes 2 and 4, away from the ball, are the only ones in which both Lorenzos appear simultaneously. Scene 3, where Lorenzo utters his primal cry, acts as the fulcrum of this geometric, palindromic structure.

Sessions's music for *The Black Maskers* exists in two forms: the 13 numbers of the incidental music itself, and a five-movement suite drawn from the incidental music. One must consult eight sets of sketches and manuscript scores in four different locations, plus the two published versions of the suite, in order to piece together the order of Sessions's composition of both works.[17]

The incidental music became the suite thus: the Dance (no. 1 in the incidental music) became the first movement of the suite; the wedding music (2) does not appear in the suite (it sounded too much like Stravinsky's Dance of the Adolescents); (3) stayed as Romualdo's Song; the next three scenes and interlude (nos 4–7) were eliminated. Music for Scene 3 (8) lost its initial 12 measures and is combined with Lorenzo's Song (9), the new bars between rehearsal numbers 60 and 68, and the close of scene 3 (10) to form the second movement of the suite. The Prelude to Scene 4 (11) became the Dirge, the suite's third movement, while Lorenzo's last-act song (12) was eliminated. The Closing Scene (13) of the incidental music became the fourth movement of the suite, Finale.

One of the major differences between the incidental music and the suite involves the ending of the play. About this matter Eliot and Sessions disagreed. Eliot wanted a loud grandiose ending, while Sessions defended a pianissimo close. For the production Sessions wrote in a loud chord dying out, but in the suite he reverted to his original idea.[18]

Four times Andreyeff in his play specifies instruments; these Sessions dutifully incorporates (all numbers from the suite): 1) castanets for the Old Woman, no. 6ff (Sessions wrote crotales, high-pitched metal disks, meaning castanets, and Monteux later corrected him); 2) an organ for the funeral in scene 4, no. 79ff; 3) trumpets in scene 3, two bars after no. 68, echoed in the Dirge at nos 75 and 79; and 4) the trumpets announcing the death of Lorenzo at no. 81. Bloch raved about the orchestration, sure he had heard two contrabassoons.

Sessions was not as literal when it came to the words of Romualdo's Song; he changed a few to make them more singable. His most inspired change was the omission—three times prior to the last section of the song—of Andreyeff's word *black*, thus saving it for "black depths of my heart" and "black depths of my thought" and rendering that last passage far more dramatic.

Sessions worked on the music from February 11, 1923, through the day of the dress rehearsal, June 9, 1923. He began at the beginning of the play, the first ball scene. Although the entire work took four months to write, Romualdo's Song was written in one night at Forty Acres, and the Dirge in a day. (Because the song was not altered for the suite, it is the earliest catalogued work by Sessions.) The opening piece, the Dance, however, took a long time to write; he showed it to Bloch before the performance. As already mentioned, this music may have been the fulfillment of the dream he had confided to George about writing an enormous dance movement. From the beginning Sessions thought of much of the work in terms of a full orchestra. Smith had to import instrumentalists from Boston and New Haven.

In order to get from Cleveland to Northampton for the performance, Sessions and Carl Buchman rode Quincy Porter's motorcycle; his own motorcycle, Kundry, had been left in Cleveland "on the urgent advice of friends."[19] (He had already been in an accident on it.) "We must have cut quite a figure on the roads; and we certainly attracted attention," he wrote to Barbara.[20] The trip appears to have taken four days. The two stayed at Forty Acres and Phelps House, both of which could house quite a few guests. Sessions wrote three numbers at Forty Acres and Buchman copied out the orchestral parts. Sessions wrote to Barbara, "Oh—will you call up Aaron [Copland] on Tuesday or Wednesday + ask him whether he has heard from Miss Kidder and wire me if he has? Bixler can't come—+ so that leaves us very short on cellos. He promised to write to Miss Kidder yesterday."[21] Next to arrive was Barbara, who quickly summed up the situation—they would not finish in time for the performance—and sent out "an S.O.S. call to New Haven for Quincy." Porter joined Sessions the day before the final rehearsal; he brought Hope LeRoy Baumgartner, a Yale instructor. The four worked on the parts, which were finished "in the nick of time."

The production took place June 14–16, 1923, at the downtown Academy of Music, "so named because in 1892–93, when it was built, many descendants of Jonathan Edwards' parishioners were still leery of the word Theater."[22] (The college had no place to stage dramatics.) The kettledrum player, Katharine Abbot Wilder, recalled the chemical smoke from the burning castle coming backstage during rehearsals. During the performance the orchestra sat under the stage right set. (The smoke was just as bad there.) She was nervous about keeping the drums in tune amid such modern sounds, but the composer/conductor told her it would not be too bad if the drums were a bit off. The thrill of hearing the conductor say "Well done" was remembered 50 years later. Whenever a major orchestra played *The Black Maskers*, Wilder took pride that she had played in the premiere. She also attributed to that performance her lifelong improvement in counting and coming in on time when playing the piano.[23] One cellist, Caroline (Bedell) Thomas, remembered playing and at first hating the wild modern music for *The Black Maskers*. She would rush to Music Hall to play Bach to "wash her mouth out." As rehearsals progressed, however, she liked it more and more.[24] The production involved 115 students, all seniors, plus an orchestra of 40 players.

Faculty member Leland Hall trained the student performers and Crucita Moore prepared the rehearsals; some of the orchestra consisted of faculty members; violinist Quincy Porter was a ringer. An overture written by Miriam Stevenson (1923) was performed for the production. "The expense was so great (each torch had to have its own dimmer, operated by someone who could watch when a B[lack] M[asker] put it out and a servant relighted it) that the class of '23 was in debt for quite a while."[25]

On Wednesday Jean and Denise Binet had their first glimpse of the New England countryside in America: they were shown all the details and told all the stories about

Figure 24 The original program for *The Black Maskers*, Smith College, 1923 (drawing by Adeline Boyden).

Forty Acres and Phelps Farm. On Thursday, the day of the first performance, "the Misses White of Heath, not to mention 'Uncle Archie'," came to Phelps Farm.

Sessions tried to synchronize the music with the play. "You've got to time it in your imagination."[26] "The [first] performance was by all odds the least [good] of the three, and quite unsatisfactory in many ways. The music was so placed as not to be well heard, the orchestra players missed various cues, and the play ended before the conflagration music was half finished," Sessions wrote in the Forty Acres diary. More guests arrived the next day, including Bloch. The group went to visit the hilltop cabin and signed the aunts' old guestbook: Bloch under the column for residence put "Somewhere on the Planet Earth," Binet copied Bloch and under "remarks" wrote "(married too)." Porter remembered his "Noah's Ark" comment and this time wrote "Better weather this time."[27] Porter and Sessions had spent that morning arguing over where to place the orchestra to be better heard; and more rehearsals were held, but at that night's perform- ance "the fire music was still too slow; my inexperience as a conductor was responsible for that."

The Foster family also came, Eleanor having arrived via motorcycle, and stayed in the hilltop cabin. So did Bloch's friend from Cleveland, Isabel Swift.

The Saturday performance was by far the best of the three. The orchestra missed fewer cues; Sam Eliot arranged matters so that the prelude to Scene IV, in some ways my favorite number of the nine, was better heard; and the conflagration music came out at such a tempo that for the first time it was heard in its entirety. Barbara and I stayed for the banquet afterwards, and were driven home by two of the Black Maskers.

Later, another party was held for all the guests in the north parlor of Phelps House. The motorcycle and its sidecar managed to support the Binets' large suitcases, Porter's two instruments, and people. "I do not remember how much there was, but do remember the impression that Denise was buried under a mountain of luggage." Supper was a picnic near Phelps Farm and the evening entertainment was held in the Long Room at Forty Acres with Bloch giving "a graphic account of the various intrigues attending the performances of *Macbeth* in Paris." After Marion Code, Mrs Jones, Bloch and Isabel Swift, who left together, had gone, the remaining party "vegetated, slept, talked of Harvard (a great descent from earlier conversations!), and felt a pleasant sense of relaxation." Sessions left for the Cleveland Institute's summer school (his summer school classes that year had a large enrollment, earning him an extra $329), cousin Catharine left for Provincetown, and Barbara went to Claremont for a week and then to Martha's Vineyard for July, where she was to be a paid companion. Sessions concluded his diary entry: "This is not the place, exactly, to speak of the decisive experience which this has been for myself. But no setting could have been more perfect for a decisive experience of any kind."

The score was dedicated to Bloch, who told Sessions, "I could not sleep all night after your *Black Maskers*."[28] Nevertheless, within days of the performances and after playing the piece at the piano for the first time since the production, Sessions wrote to Barbara, "It is the mood, the play, which I have gotten away from; the music still seems to me beautiful and moving—as much so as it did before!"[29] Despite its success, and its position as the only acknowledged large work of the Bloch period, Sessions felt "it lacked inner coherence. I realized that I had written something real; but I still needed to learn to write without a program."[30] Given that Sessions allowed that he never understood this expressionistic drama, coherence may not have been entirely feasible.

The *Boston Evening Transcript* stated that it was "without question the most important dramatic production ever given at the college," and described the music as "in extremely picturesque, modern style."[31] Part of the success of *The Black Maskers* arose from the critical attention it received in the press. As often is the case, some critics were more influential than others, and Paul Rosenfeld was one. He collected his essays in book form: *Musical Portraits* (on 20 composers, 1920); *Musical Chronicle* (covering New York seasons 1917–1923); *An Hour with American Music* (1929); and *Port of New York* (1924). Rosenfeld's *Port of New York* article about *The Black Maskers* originally appeared in the October 1923 issue of the *Dial*.[32] Despite the "I-was-there" quality of the prose, Rosenfeld did not attend a production; at Bloch's prompting, Sessions played the work for him at the piano in Westport, on the weekend of August 11. Rosenfeld began his *Black Maskers* review with praise for Eliot, one of "the race of American college professors who have not yet permitted the environing elements to annihilate intellectual curiosity and courage." By securing "a certain unknown young composer," Eliot "made himself the immediate producing cause of one of the most important events in the life of music in America." Rosenfeld continued:

The nine numbers supplied by the composer brought perfectly to Andreyev's drama the extension through music required by him. They are a re-creation, in a sister medium, of the play itself; flowing from a vision of it so profound and exact that it seems the composer must have stood while composing close to the point at which the dramatist stood when he made the dialogue. . . . They have indeed the wild sinister pulse of Andreyev's dolorous phantasy, the sardonic and anguished cries, the flow of inky depressive current. Their tones utter, too, the chaos, the sorrow, the baffled frenzy of the mind which can no longer harmonize its visions, its many cruel, irreconcilable truths, and lies disrupted in doubt. . . .

The [composer] is an artist. His workmanship declares him marvelously in control of his resources, capable of producing hard form which reveals itself the larger the more it is heard. Broken as it sounds, elusive and mysterious as it is in outline, full of abrupt brutal resolutions and strange new sounds and sudden suspensions and blinding blurs, his work has a fine clarity and solidity of form. There is not a consonance in the work; the ideas are subtle and delicate; nevertheless, we do not go lost in the free, ultramodern style.

. . . There is great strength in the movements; powerfully pulsing rhythms; long melodic lines that flow and continue and extend in beauty; no padding, no waste. The orchestral dress, too, is masterly.

But the Andreyeff music constitutes an Opus 1 . . . we had been wondering whether the arrival of a musician with enough of chaos in him to make a world were truly possible in America. . . . And yet, that golden gift is among us to-day . . . the music of Roger Sessions is suffused with the state of those for whom the world to-day is dangerously near a vast bare barrack, and on whose lips the savor of life is brackish. It speaks their hundred ironic, conflicting, pensive, crisscross moods. And we feel strangely at home with it, strangely rich and released. . . . The composer may find himself more richly in the absoluter forms. . . . He himself is good luck.[33]

Sessions reacted to reviews a little shamefacedly, annoyed with himself for the curiosity he felt in regard to publicity. "In any case I am sure you," he wrote Barbara "have faith enough to know that this sort of thing has no effect on my real mood or on my attitude towards myself or towards life. I have resolved very firmly to be prepared for the 'crucifixion' which Bloch says will come and which I have long had the sense to foresee."[34] Sessions mentioned Rosenfeld in a 1951 lecture:

True, Rosenfeld had little understanding for the real and characteristic tendencies of the period between the two wars, and his ideas remained *au fond* those of postromanticism, with a strong admixture of American nationalism. There is no doubt, however, that he played a significant role in the formation of the musical generation of the twenties. The present author belongs to that generation; Rosenfeld was not in complete sympathy with him, but Rosenfeld's interest and his willingness to discuss issues were of the greatest possible value to all who came in contact with him. One found in him, as in few others of that time, a genuine awareness of the issues, and a desire to understand the motivating forces behind them.

The foregoing notwithstanding, Rosenfeld was in no sense of the word a music critic. It may seem paradoxical to say that he possessed neither authentic musical knowledge nor, very probably, strong musical instinct.[35]

Within a week after the production, Roy Dickinson Welch commented on *The Black Maskers*.

[Sessions] has thought himself into Andreyeff's bitter tragedy and he has brought the resources of an individualized and thoroughly mastered musical idiom to bear with telling effect upon the drama. It is in the most "advanced" style, this music. Like the drama, of which it means to be a part, it probes and lacerates the senses. But, if one may venture a judgment upon one hearing . . . it may be said Mr Sessions has produced a work of high importance, and one that will be recognized as a significant contribution to modern music. This music must be heard for its own sake and it is to be hoped that Mr Sessions will arrange it in concert form and make it available for orchestral repertoire.[36]

This may have been the first suggestion that Sessions turn the work into an orchestral suite; if it was, Welch had pushed Sessions in a direction that would bring him more attention as a composer. The orchestral suite to *The Black Maskers* (1928) continues to be the most performed of Sessions's works.

However much critical success *The Black Maskers* garnered for its composer, its director Eliot had the opposite experience. Most of the Smith community who saw the production hated it, including the older alumni and the trustees, who had just given him a second three-year appointment. President Neilson advised him to do no more senior dramatics until he was sure of obtaining tenure. Eliot staged no plays in 1924, 1925, and 1926.

In a letter to Romain Rolland, Bloch wrote of his pupil:

For me, he is the *first American* who truly has a *creative gift* in music. The music he wrote last year for the *Black Maskers* of Andreyeff, that I heard in Northampton, is a *masterpiece*. He must play it for you (he plays atrociously, but it doesn't make any difference!). There is in this music a talent of fantastic imagination, a life, an irony, a suffering I have been seeking in vain among the acrobats of our time. Ultra-modern! My music seems pale beside it! But classical, logical, well-structured, strong. *Nothing arbitrary*, nothing forced; no preoccupation with astounding the experts, or inventing something "new." You will find influences, as is normal in a young man (but of great maturity, nonetheless)—a little of Stravinsky, of Wagner, and not a little Bloch!—But there is *great hope*, and personally I would give all I know of Schoenberg and Stravinsky for some pages of his work. I think Sessions is an authentic genius. I know him, I have looked out for him, I have fought for him, here, for he does "not belong," and gives not a f . . . for success, or money, or notoriety, and he is not "good-looking!"[37]

The Fosters, Quincy Porter, Jean and Denise Binet, and numerous family members such as Ruth and Archibald were able to witness his success. Bloch sent a telegram to the Institute, which Mrs Sanders posted: "Sessions music the most prodigious thing I have heard here. He is a great genius and America should be proud of him."[38]

After several opportunities to conduct had passed Sessions by, he finally made his conducting debut with *The Black Maskers*. He had even whittled his own baton. The audience could not see him, since he was underneath some of the sets, which may have allayed his nervousness, though, as we have heard from him, his inexperience showed. Suzanne Bloch recalled,

Now in 1923 when he conducted *The Black Maskers*, my father went to Smith College to hear it. And his descriptions of Roger Sessions when he came back—I can see that—he said, "Do you know, at the rehearsals there was Roger Sessions with his beautiful work conducting with a lollipop in his mouth?" He was moved to the thing. He met the family, wonderful mother, aunts, the whole family, he just fell for this New England family and loved it.[39]

In May 1924 Bloch continued in his letter to Rolland.

> But he is a human being of the first order. He is the only one here who under-stands me. Upon hearing his *Black Maskers*, played by a miserable orchestra of thirty-five amateur musicians, which he conducted (he is as bad a conductor as he is a pianist!), I was *overwhelmed*. I could not sleep the following night! I cried in my bed. I felt that this man is the only one who can say all that I have not been able to say myself. A spiritual son, closer to me than my own son. If I have been able *to help* a single person to develop himself and give to this country the immense music that will symbolize its problems and destiny, well, my struggles will not have been in vain.[40]

Suzanne Bloch remembered her father was upset that *The Black Maskers* was not swept into the repertoire. He had wanted the initial success to lead to further success, so he showed Schirmer the score, trying (unsuccessfully) to get the work published. He also went with Sessions to Mrs Harriet Lameer, a great lady in the musical world, who had founded the Friends of Music, whose orchestral and chamber music concerts had pre-sented the concert that had helped to establish Bloch. The fact was, however, that Sessions had not written enough music for a concert, unless it was a production of *The Black Maskers*. As we have seen, Bloch had also brought Paul Rosenfeld's attention to the work.

A year after the production, in June 1924, Sessions played *The Black Maskers* for Nadia Boulanger.

> Nadia was tremendously impressed with the B.M., which I played her through no. 5a, and which I am to finish tomorrow night. She was more enthusiastic about it than any one except Ernie, and saw what I consider its strong points immediately. That was a great encouragement to me, as you can imagine; for it gave me confidence in myself in relation to Europe such as I had not felt certain of before . . . She said she considered it not only a very fine work, but a very important work![41]

After the next night, when he played the Dirge and the "fire music" (the finale), Sessions wrote,

> She said it was the most significant score she had heard for a long time. We went over it together after that, and she looked at some details. She evidently is a quite superb score reader and has a splendid eye for details, as she appreciated my intentions in a minute. I told her about Stokowski and she advised me to make an appointment if possible to play it for him next fall. She pointed out the fact that she had no idea what the play was about, but that the music seemed not only impressive, but absolutely clear, to her, logical not only in the separate parts but in the succession of the parts.[42]

By September 1924 Sessions had

thought a good deal about the *Black Maskers*, and in fact started out in what seemed to be the most logical way, by trying to estimate its ultimate worth, its weaknesses, its limitations, its shortcomings, as they appear to me. I realized that in spite of its beauties it represents in many ways a point beyond which I don't want to go any further, in the same direction. But I wanted to formulate absolutely clearly to myself the direction in which I do want to go.

In the first place, it is *psychological* music. That is certainly not in itself a weakness, and I believe, too, that in the *Black Maskers* it most of the time avoids becoming one. . . .

What I feel is, to be brief, that the B.M. expresses a phase of my life which was entirely or almost entirely intellectual, which nourished itself on thoughts and images of a *purely* imaginative character, and that it gets its power from this source which is as far as possible removed from the sources of being. This makes it perhaps less universal, less truly vital, even though it certainly does not condemn it. The music that I dream of, and must create now, is music which is fundamentally of the *body*; that is based first of all on a direct appeal to the senses, the nerves, the muscles. *The Black Maskers* has of course this element, but I believe infinitely less than my music must have. I want to base my musical language on this absolutely elemental appeal.[43]

Lacking confidence, Sessions withdrew the incidental music to *The Black Maskers*, but wrote incidental music for Cleveland performances of Carlo Gozzi's *Turandot*, May 8–19, 1925. (He revised it that summer.) And Eliot had suggested an opera on Poe's *The Fall of the House of Usher*. Sessions began this project and sketched quite a bit of the story before discovering he was not really interested in doing it: it was left incomplete. Combined with the aborted 1922 Nocturne for Orchestra, the performed Bagatelle for quartet, and an *Adagio* for organ completed in Europe, these works represent the sum of the Cleveland and Bloch period. The only subsequent performance of the incidental music was on March 15, 1931, at the Broadhurst Theater in New York, Hugh Ross conducting, during the 1930–31 Copland–Sessions season. Copland's *Music for the Theater* was given on the same concert; Sessions was not present.

The first performance of the newly completed Suite was to take place in Cincinnati, April 13 and 14, 1928. It was rescheduled for November 23 and 24 of the same year. That, too, was postponed, although Sessions, in Rome, did not learn of this for several months. The Cincinnati Symphony performance with Fritz Reiner was finally held December 5, 1930. Sessions wrote to Aaron Copland, "The male critic was excellent; but the two ladies found it gruesome + repulsive. Apparently it sounded well on the orchestra, in any case; + that is all that matters to me, as far as that piece goes."[44] For this performance Sessions rewrote the Finale, since the original rearrangement was somehow lost between New York and Cincinnati. "So I made another rearrangement—a still better one. There are theoretically three versions of the last movement."[45] The Reiner performance with Cincinnati represents the premiere of the Orchestral Suite.

The publication of the Suite by the Viennese house of Waldheim-Eberle was announced in 1931–1932. Cos Cob in the United States, however, published the Suite in 1932 because of Copland's efforts. Leopold Stokowski gave it with the Philadelphia Orchestra on November 4, 1933. At this early date the press had already begun reacting to Sessions's music in the manner all-too-typical of later journalistic criticism. "In influence, The Black Maskers seems Stravinskian, and in essential identification cerebral rather than emotional, as is the play," *Musical America* reported.[46] Even so, the piece may not have been finished by then. As late as May 11, 1946, when Leon Barzin conducted the NBC Symphony, *The Black Maskers* was referred to as "technically finished, with authoritative instrumentation."[47] Only three movements, however, Dance, Dirge, and Scene, were played. The first recording, issued by subscription by the American Recording Society, was only in 1952.

Important later performances of *The Black Maskers* follow. Otto Klemperer conducted *The Black Maskers* with the Los Angeles Philharmonic Orchestra, March 8 and 9, 1934. Fabien Sevitzky performed the work with the People's Orchestra of Boston, in February 1935. It was this performance, in part, that got Sessions in hot water with Serge Koussevitzky (see Chapter 3). Sevitzky, later the conductor of the Indianapolis Symphony, played *The Black Maskers* in the 1948–1949 season. When Sessions was composer-in-residence at Tanglewood Music Festival, in July 1955, the Boston Symphony performed the work there under Pierre Monteux. *The New York Times* reported,

> It has power, atmosphere and more than a touch of profundity. It is not so difficult to absorb as some of Mr Sessions' more recent works, and it ought to be on American symphonic programs more often. The only drawback is that it requires enormous virtuosity from the instrumentalists and the kind of reliable musicianship from the conductor that Mr Monteux could bring to it. The Boston Symphony rose to the occasion, playing with tremendous drive and with relish for the interesting colors and sonorities the composer imagined. The composer and the performers were recalled repeatedly.[48]

In the fall of 1958 Sessions, along with Peter Mennin, Ulysses Kay, and Roy Harris, were sent by the state department on a cold-war cultural exchange to Russia (see section "Symphonies Nos 3 and 4"). On October 15, 1958, the Suite, minus its first movement, was played in Moscow, something of a homecoming for the Russian-inspired work. Northwestern University held a Sessions festival organized by Paul Fromm, from January 26 to 29, 1961, and presented eight of Sessions's works, including *The Black Maskers* Suite. On December 1, 1984, at the Foro Italico with the RAI Orchestra of Rome, Massimo Pradella conducted it on an all-American program, probably the last time *The Black Maskers* was performed in Sessions's lifetime.

FRIENDS

Both Jean Binet and Bloch had been pupils of Jaques Dalcroze. Binet had moved from Switzerland to the US in 1919, studied with Bloch in New York, and founded its Dalcroze Rhythmic School. Hired in March 1921 at the Cleveland Institute to teach the Dalcroze method, Binet resigned in June 1923. Sessions described this method: "Jaques Dalcroze was a Swiss musician who evolved a system of teaching rhythm which became almost a cult, an educational cult, let's say. It was very, very good. He taught rhythm by means of physical movement, you see, which has led many people to think it's a kind of dancing. And it isn't primarily dancing at all; it's just simply expressing rhythm in terms of bodily movement."[1] After leaving Cleveland, Binet taught Dalcroze Eurythmics in Brussels for six years and spent the remainder of his life in Switzerland promoting Swiss composers. Sessions would visit the Binets and meet Jaques Dalcroze in Switzerland in 1924. He later described and credited Binet: "I owe to Jean more than perhaps to any other person—certainly more intimately than to any other—whatever knowledge I have of Europe itself . . . No human being ever existed who was less capable of malice, and it was difficult if not impossible to sustain malice towards anyone whatever in Jean's presence."[2]

Two very different, but both rich, people entered Sessions's life in the early 1920s before he went to Cleveland; he remained friends with them for many years. Mina Kirstein Curtiss (1896 to 1985, Sessions's exact contemporary) was the sister of the ballet patron Lincoln Kirstein and daughter of a partner in Filene's department store in Boston. Her other brother George published the *Liberal Weekly*. Born in Boston, Mina earned a B.A. from Smith in 1918, attended Radcliffe, and received an M.A. from Columbia University. From 1920 to 1934 and again from 1940 to 1943 Curtiss was associate professor of English at Smith, where Sessions met her in 1920. She wrote radio scripts in 1942–1943 for the Office of War Information, and, from 1935 to 1939, for the Mercury Theatre of the Air with Orson Welles and John Houseman.

As Ruth had done by leaving Archibald in New York and going to Hadley, Sessions also left Barbara behind during CIM breaks to visit his mother there. In terms of his marriage, this behavior was almost as devastating as Ruth's had been. During the first of these lengthy separations, and following in the dubious and indiscreet footsteps of his teacher, Sessions began an affair with Mina in Northampton. (She was in London in August 1922 and the summer of 1923, so it is likely that their affair began sometime in the spring of 1922.) Sessions gave her one of the several holograph scores of *The Black Maskers*, inscribed "For Mina with my love—Roger."[3] She later became connected to the Bloomsbury group in London through meeting David "Bunny" Garnett, with whom she had an affair.

Kirstein's letters to Sessions are not dated; their order is therefore conjectural. A free spirit, she revealed far more than Sessions did in letters. In one letter Mina referred to "our episode of some weeks ago today. To me it had a very rare quality of impersonality and generosity about it. By generosity I mean that it had none of that rather agonizing sex-conflict, desire-for-power-over-another-person element. I don't really feel that I know you any better because you have made love to me nor do I feel that you necessarily know me any better."[4] Sessions and Barbara had been married only two years and he was already unfaithful. Later Mina wrote that when she first met Garnett in 1923–1924, she professed surprise at his sexual interest because, according to her memoir (in which Sessions is not mentioned) of her "deeply ingrained belief in the sanctity of marriage. In my innocence I assumed that no married man could express the feelings he did."[5]

Although we do not have many of Barbara's letters to Sessions, from his responses we can assemble some of her thoughts. In a letter of July 1922, after telling the insecure Barbara about picnicking with Mina, Sessions wrote, "The fear that you speak of—that I may leave you behind—is quite groundless, of course. . . . For however much I might be in love with [Mina], there is a final intimacy which I never could desire with her, and which I do desire and very profoundly, with you . . . We both agreed that you were a very marvelous person, not half-appreciated; and also that you have very great talent."[6] Mina and Barbara spoke in the summer of 1922, and Mina breezily sailed to Europe on the *Homeric* on August 19. Sessions's counsel to Mina of discretion and tact, especially around Barbara, appears not to have been heeded. Indeed, she forgot the advice altogether: "The only thing you may have advised me that I can remember was to cease being a virgin and that advice I followed."[7] Nevertheless, she asked Sessions not to tell anybody, because her parents did not know.

In London Mina heard the Bloch suite, read *Babbitt* and *The Wings of the Dove*, and attempted to smuggle a copy of *Ulysses* to Sessions. Mina, too, felt somewhat useless in comparison with Sessions's determination to compose.

> What [should I] do next year and the year after and the year after that. With you it is different. You have talent and a genius you must obey. But I, I have nothing but a mind and body that know how to amuse themselves. . . . I don't understand Mr Bloch's allusions to my masochistic influence but I am afraid he's right. . . . My feeling about you, Roger, dear, is odd. I admire you so much more than most of the men I know. But that very admiration keeps me aloof in a way. I couldn't bear to risk having some triviality come between it and our friendship. . . . Oh, well it's lucky for the calm and peace of Smith College faculty circles that we're not here together. The very best part of me is yours, Mina.[8]

In 1926 Mina married Henry Tomlinson Curtiss, who died tragically the next year. Ultimately, Curtiss need not have worried about her contributions. She edited an anthology, *Olive, Cypress and Palm* (1930), and a collection of enlisted mens' *Letters Home* (1944). She translated and edited the letters of Marcel Proust (1949). From the Proust work she became interested in Georges Bizet, tracked down and purchased the Bizet archive of letters and other documents, and wrote a major study of the composer, *Bizet and His World.*[9] Through her interest in Bizet, in 1953 she published an article on opera composer Fromental Halévy.[10] She referred to herself as a "literary detective or an eclectic adventurer in the kingdoms of the mind" on the dust jacket of *Other People's Letters: A Memoir*. For her translations, editing, and writing she was awarded the French Legion of Honor. She also became friendly with Virgil Thomson, who "drew" her musical portrait, called "With Fife and Drums: A Portrait of Mina Curtiss," for piano on June 15, 1941, in Ashfield, Massachusetts.[11]

Financial problems continued to plague the Sessionses. After *The Black Maskers* performance two of his checks had bounced. Sessions tried to get a handle on their monetary affairs: he saw this as a warning

> direct from God himself (figuratively speaking) that there are certain things which have *got* to be reformed in our life, beginning now. By that I mean that I realize at last in this matter, as in others, that we have an appalling lack of self-discipline, and that we must both, in sack-cloth and ashes, decide once for all to put our first efforts towards getting out of debt, keeping out of debt and *saving*. One of my first tasks this summer will be to make out a list of debts and actually figure out our total deficit.

He proposed that he and Barbara each keep an accounting of money spent and live by a budget. Only then "we will be in a position to go abroad, have children, and do a hundred other things that we haven't the slightest prospect of doing now. . . . I am terribly afraid this letter so far sounds like a sermon preached by the prince of hypocrites."[12]

Barbara was clearly upset by this lecture on budgeting and money. In his next letter Sessions wrote,

> I do feel, however, that you have underestimated the seriousness of the situation when you begin by feeling hurt at something I have said. If you want me to admit full responsibility for the past I will; I reproach you for nothing, and consider the question of guilt or innocence as of no importance whatever. . . . When I say that we must *never again*, whatever the cost, give a bad check, I am not accusing you of irresponsibility . . . This doesn't lessen my love for you in the least. . . . I want this to be as *impersonal* a matter as possible; and you can help me tremendously by not feeling that you *have* to justify yourself.[13]

Barbara was working as a paid companion in Martha's Vineyard while Sessions taught summer school in Cleveland. Barbara's July 30 financial news was not good. "It isn't a terribly great comfort to know that you can't provide the $50 probably," Sessions wrote, "and I thought I made it quite clear in a letter written three weeks ago that it was this summer that I would want it. I do wish you had let me know. . . . Don't pay *any* bills, darling, or spend a cent more than is necessary until I see you, then we can make some kind of plan." Sessions even considered selling Kundry, his motorcycle, but decided it "would be a bad investment in the end. . . . We will be very poor this winter, but we will have each other, and that is everything; so long as we have that, we can sell all our possessions and got to live in a garret if necessary. Meanwhile we will have to borrow . . . $250.00."[14]

Reading *The Brothers Karamazov* for the second time did not provide enough physical sustenance for the composer, teaching summer school in Cleveland in 1923. To save money he avoided solid food, went on a "milk diet," and postponed doing the laundry. The departure of Jean and Denise Binet for Europe that June weighed on Sessions and appeared at the time to close a chapter in his life. The lack of food brought on a depression that took the familiar form of phantoms, this time of a financial nature. The depression lead to a self-examination:

In so many ways my precocity has made me feel that I have missed many things from youth which the normal person needs, for instance; and these things—the religious problem, and the moral problem with all their issues, complex and manifold, have to be thrashed out by the individual who on his side has no basis, no discipline, to keep him together in the process. Well, these are going to be adventurous, and in a sense, thrilling weeks. I am re-learning many sides of myself which I had forgotten or ignored, and which are the signs of an inner chaos—a chaos not as much of the mind as of the spirit and emotions; the result doubtless of years of inhibitions combined with a temperament that is not too tranquil.[15]

The "inner chaos" came directly from his experience with *The Black Maskers*. One antidote helped his upset state—playing through *Die Walküre* on the piano. After summer school he drove Kundry from Cleveland to meet Barbara in Hadley, but had an accident that left a permanent scar on his head.

Theodore Chanler had studied at the Institute of Musical Art in New York City from 1914 to 1920, without receiving a diploma. There he studied composition and counterpoint with Percy Goetschius and piano with Ethel Leginska and Richard Buhlig. Ruth knew about Chanler. "The mother is the R[oman] C[atholic], the father an Episcopal churchman, so that in their marriage arrangement it was decreed that the girls should be brought up in her church, the boys in his; and I don't know how Theodore happened to get into the other fold!"[16] The mother, Margaret (Daisy) Chanler, was reputed to be brilliant and musical; the house in Geneseo, New York, wonderful and big. The Chanlers also had an apartment on Fifth Avenue and one in Paris. Chanler had gone to the Cleveland Institute to study with Bloch; he did not receive a degree there either. He was given a similar assignment to the one Bloch had given Sessions: to make a piano arrangement of Bloch's music, this time the *Three Jewish Poems*. Later Chanler moved to Paris, studied with Nadia Boulanger for three years, traveled extensively, and attended Oxford University. He is known exclusively for songs.

Chanler wrote Sessions from New York City where he was having a fine time sleeping late, dancing all night, cultivating critic Paul Rosenfeld, attending parties with his friend F. Scott Fitzgerald and many others. Letters rarely include the year with the date, so some of the timing here, too, is conjectural: the time frame, however, is from 1921 to 1923.

In a letter to Sessions, dated January 15 (possibly 1923), Chanler reported on a party at Rosenfeld's where the guests included Carl Sandburg, Dos Passos, Edmund Wilson, Sherwood Anderson, Ethel Leginska, Leo Ornstein, and Darius Milhaud. Milhaud, clamoring to hear some blues, got into a tiff with Ornstein, who had never heard any blues and did not know what the term meant. Ornstein had told Chanler that he ranked Bloch even higher than Ravel. Somewhat to Chanler's surprise, all Dos Passos wanted to talk about was Roger Sessions and hear news of him. Chanler had gotten to know Milhaud long before Sessions became Milhaud's friend. Chanler sent Sessions Milhaud's *Le Boeuf sur le Toit* to play through with Binet. He also met Vladimir Dukelsky, an exact contemporary whom he considered had the "great advantage of being a completely equipped musician."[17]

By January 1924 Chanler, in Oxford, missed Sessions. He had been studying with Boulanger and gave Sessions a description of her approach:

I studied with Nadia Boulanger who has just renewed an old friendship with Ernie—he may have told you about her. She's an excellent teacher and started me on a new kind of exercise which worked wonders. You were probably cured of your hesitation and overscupulousness by the *Black Maskers* but the work I tried to do on the *Pantomime* last summer only made mine worse. So she told me I must begin to keep a musical diary, writing some kind of a piece every day and not caring in the least if it's bad—so long as it's finished. . . . Nadia Boulanger teaches very much as Ernie [Bloch] does only she's not so brilliant nor so fastidious nor so full of herself. . . . She thinks Fauré the greatest living composer, but she says no one appreciates him before he's thirty.[18]

Chanler would go to France during the summer to study with her. Meanwhile he wanted Mina Kirstein's London address from Sessions to look her up.

In one letter Chanler referred to both a symphony and the Nocturne on which Sessions was working.[19] His parents did not want him to return to Cleveland. Other problems concerning Chanler's parents affected Sessions directly.

Then besides (this will seem tactless but I may as well admit it) your financial difficulties did become rather a strain on me. It wasn't really your fault at all, because of course I gave you the impression that I was in full control of my father's fortune and that a word to my mother or even to Mr MacVeigh would bring back any required sum by the next mail. I knew it the back of my head (and not really very far back at that!) that it wouldn't work as smoothly as I made you think. I must get over my unfortunate habit of deceiving myself. It seems to make trouble all round, besides getting me into profoundly unhealthy states of mind.[20]

On another occasion Chanler asked for the return of $25 he spent on Bach cantatas for Sessions. Once again Sessions found himself in a position asking a friend to lend him money. Chanler had spoken at great length about Sessions to his mother, a cultivated lady who played the piano weekly with Poulenc when she was in Paris; she was eager to meet Sessions. For his part, Sessions was purported to be scared to death of her.

As might have been anticipated, the meeting between Margaret Chanler and Bloch, in Cleveland, did not go especially well. Bloch spoke continually about himself rather than of Chanler, and Mrs Chanler did not understand a note of Bloch's music. She was more impressed with Sessions and Barbara: she liked *The Black Maskers* and arranged for the composer to play it for the conductor Eugene Goossens. (It was hoped Goossens would play the work in Prague, but he did not.)

One Chanler letter written from Geneseo mentioned Aaron Copland twice in passing and "I've been reading *Sons and Lovers*. It's a very beautiful book. Miriam seemed slightly overdone, though perhaps I only thought that because of the resemblance she bears to Aaron—and I don't think Aaron's quite so bad."[21]

Chanler would turn against Sessions in the mid-1930s, the nadir of his career, reporting to the powerful newspaper critic Virgil Thomson that it was Sessions's negative opinion, rather than his own, Chanler had expressed in a review of *Four Saints in Three Acts*. This caused the glass-jawed Thomson to drop his hostility to Chanler and instead hold a grudge against Sessions—about which our composer never knew. Sessions, innocent of Chanler's two faces, always considered Chanler "a dear friend" despite Chanler's snubs.

By January 1924 Archibald was still giving Sessions money and still hoping that Belasco would produce his play. He was also concerned for Barbara's health: "I'm greatly relieved to hear that Barbara is on the mend. I was really worried about her. I want you to promise me that if she should have any recurrence of the trouble, or any other trouble, to see that she gets the best care to be had—and that goes for you, too—and not think about expense, for that will be taken care of."[22] We do not know from what Barbara suffered at this time, however Archibald's concern would prove prescient.

SUMMER OF 1924

"My style and my attitude toward music changed that summer. Or, let's say, I began to write somewhat differently than before."[1] Finally, at the age of 27, Sessions went to Europe and encountered first hand the culture that had already influenced him so profoundly. That summer truly marked a change in Sessions, one of which he wrote often to Barbara. This change delineates the end of his first period of creativity. Sessions was not alone among the Cleveland Institute faculty in traveling to Europe that summer. A June 1924 picture shows seven faculty members linked arm-in-arm: Carton Cooley, Beryl Rubinstein, Sessions, Victor de Gomez, Ruth Edwards, André de Ribaupierre, and Dorothy Price. Most of these people would see each other again in Europe.[2]

Most likely because of lack of money, and possibly also because of Barbara's ill health (she had some kind of operation in April), Barbara was not able to accompany Sessions on his first trip to Europe. Her fear that he might leave her behind was being literally realized. In May Sessions wrote to Mrs Sanders requesting an advance of $900 on his next year's salary "in order that he may go to Europe this summer and be here for the summer school next year [1925]."[3] The sum of $900 would seem enough to support two people for three months abroad, compared with the price for the two living in Europe the next year, $3,000. There may, however, have been debts to pay first. We can only speculate about their discussions as to whether to wait until the two could travel together. Possibly Barbara was too upset with him or too ill to go, but we could equally well assume that she was self-sacrificing and Sessions was too eager to wait. That Sessions would leave Barbara behind tells us his priorities. He already had reason to feel guilt around his wife: embarking on this trip may have exacerbated it.

Barbara spent the summer of 1924 as a paid companion on Martha's Vineyard to Mrs Malcolm MacBride, as well as in Claremont, Hadley, Webster, and Boston. On June 14 she saw Sessions off on the White Star Line's *S.S. Olympic*. She greeted his return in mid-September, at the same Brooklyn port, while staying there with his Aunt Adeline. (Sessions returned on the same ship as Mina.) Sessions had had some difficulty obtaining a passport: the change of name at his birth was an obstacle. When Archibald sent Sessions's birth certificate, with "Pitkin" listed as his middle name, the passport office would not accept it—doubtless because Sessions asserted his middle name was Huntington (he did not know about the birth certificate). Archibald then got the baptismal certificate from St Mary's Church in Brooklyn with its "Huntington," which satisfied the customs office, although the baptismal certificate presented other problems since the year of birth was incorrect (1897).

Barbara kept all of Sessions's letters from that summer, but none of Barbara's daily letters survive. While normally it is possible to reconstruct some of the other side of a correspondence by reading only one side, here it is difficult because Sessions's letters,

Figure 25 Roger Sessions portrait, signed June 1925 to Quincy Porter (Standiford Studio, Cleveland).

although laced with hyperbolic expressions of love, are incurious about Barbara's life. Since each letter would take ten days to reach its addressee, three weeks would elapse before one correspondent could receive a response to any remark from the other. There appears to have been a mutual agreement that he deliberately try to limit his letters to impressions of Europe, to confiding his own thoughts (evoking shades of writing "a good letter" to Ruth), and not burdening her with his emotional problems. In addition, Sessions had to make up for the fact that he was going and not she, as well as to try to dispel her unhappiness about his extramarital affair with Mina Kirstein. (It could not have helped that he would see Mina in London. Sessions swore, however, that he had been faithful to her that summer.) These letters reek of guilt, as well as self-castigation for past behavior and an effort to earn back her trust. His incessant referring to her as "darling," "infinitely precious one," and "beloved one" begin to seem a little forced. In repeatedly reassuring her of his love, he only points to the fact that she had reason to doubt it. His hyperbole may have been wounding, such as numerous iterations of "you have no idea"—how foreign the French countryside looks, for one example—and about many other things.

Sessions traveled second class for the week-long voyage, which meant that he could not go to the front of the boat. A steward gave him a tour, however, and first class impressed him as "more magnificent than any hotel I ever saw! turkish baths, a swimming pool, squash courts—all in the height of luxury. . . . I am determined to make Mina invite me to at least one meal in the *à la carte* café in the *Majestic*, when I come back."[4] He discovered his college friend Richard Cuyler's mother and sister in the same class and found Dostoyevsky's *The Possessed* in the British ship's library; he read the entire novel during the crossing. He wrote of Dostoyevsky, "It is so hard to believe that he died in 1881. Of course, the marvelous thing about him and about the book is the uncanny psychological insight with which he builds his characters. Well, this is a platitude—you know, on reading over my letters, I sometimes recognize my grandfather [Huntington], the old man of the tribe, to an alarming extent."[5] This impression grew: "Do my letters even seem to you to read like—well, let's say, like sermons by the Rt. Rev. Frederic Dan Huntington, late bishop of Central New York? . . . Perhaps I have that in my blood, too."[6]

It was difficult for Sessions to strike up conversations, "I have no art whatever in the way of meeting and getting to know strangers—it is my damned shyness."[7] His shyness in meeting even other composers he knew prevented him from approaching George Gershwin, who was on the same ship but in first class. "I have a perhaps foolish scruple against approaching a first class passenger, especially one whom I know so little."[8] On board, Prohibition did not apply: he could drink with impunity. An example of the kinds of statements typical of future letters: "A trip to Europe is so infinitely casual so informal, one gets an entirely new conception of the world; mankind seems smaller and less important than ever, and Matter, Energy, Force—the mechanical driving power of the world and the universe infinitely greater."[9]

Being aboard a ship brought memories of the not-so-distant past: "So, as we drove through a heavy fog last night, I had a hard time putting down the thought which came into my head—the *Titanic* disaster, which made such an overwhelming impression on me at the time [1912]—I was in New York when the *Carpathia* which came to the *Titanic*'s rescue, came [in] and it worked rather vividly on my imagination at the time."[10]

His first step onto European soil, June 21, 1924, was at the port of Cherbourg, "a delightful and quaint old place, but infinitely more foreign than I had any idea France would be."[11] At this late moment Sessions became a little anxious about not having written "Aaron," who was supposed to arrange for his stay in Paris. On his first night he attended *The Magic Flute*.

When he reached Paris, he took a taxi to 269 Rue St Jacques, in the fifth *arrondisement* on the left bank, which turned out to be the Scola Cantorum, while the hotel was next door. Aaron was Copland, who was already friendly with both Theodore Chanler and Herbert Elwell. Copland had been living in Paris with Harold Clurman since June 1921. The two received $20 to $25 dollars a week from their parents, a considerable amount that kept them well provided for. Clurman observed first hand that Copland knew how to save money.[12] In this, as in so many other ways, the two composers differed. Sessions had met Copland in New York music circles in the late teens before Copland's departure to Europe in 1921.[13] Copland arrived and spent the rest of the long day showing Sessions around Paris—the Quartier Latin, the Jardins du Luxembourg, and Notre Dame. They took the *métro* to go to eat, were accosted by a "painted lady," and strolled back across the Place de la Concorde to Sessions's hotel. Copland, who had sent off for Bloch's Viola Suite and songs, was soon to leave Paris for the US. The next day Sessions found Beryl Rubinstein, from the Cleveland Institute, staying around the corner. That night Sessions and Copland went to the Paris Opéra to hear . . . *The Magic Flute*. Although the performance was "ghastly," the music was so divine that Sessions wept about "twenty times" during the performance.

The following afternoon, while Sessions was at Copland's rooms at 66 Boulevard Pasteur, in the fifteenth *arrondisement* (also on the left bank), Theodore Chanler showed up and stayed for dinner. Chanler proposed they go immediately to Nadia Boulanger's apartment. Mlle Boulanger was not at home, but her "sprightly" mother, who lived there with her, spoke with them. In 1962 Sessions credited Chanler, "also a very close friend, who died last year," as taking him to meet Boulanger.[14] She lived at 36 rue Ballu in the ninth *arrondisement* on the right bank near Montmartre. It was arranged that Sessions and Chanler see Nadia herself at 2:00 p.m. that day. It was a short meeting, at which one later that week was arranged for Sessions to play his *Black Maskers*. Boulanger's fourth-floor apartment, reachable by a rickety elevator, was notable for the presence of two grand pianos as well as an organ (Mlle's instrument) in the living room.

That night Sessions attended the Russian ballet, where Chanler pointed out Auric, Poulenc, Milhaud, and Stravinsky in the lobby. Sessions, too shy to speak to any of the composers, was happy to talk instead to his old friend Dos Passos. In his first week he would hear the Mozart Requiem, *Les Noces* three times, *Pulcinella* twice, the *Sacre, Petrouchka*, Satie's *Parade*, Auric's *Les Fâcheux*, Milhaud's *Le Train Bleu*, and Poulenc's *Les Biches*. Sessions "really felt very much impressed by [*Les Noces*]; it seems to me as great as the *Sacre* and really a very beautiful and moving work."[15] Sessions was one of the four pianists in the recording of *Les Noces*, so it is fascinating to note how highly he regarded it upon first hearing. After having seen a rather bad ballet performance of the *Sacre*, he observed, "I feel that Stravinsky has done things of which it is quite possible that we cannot yet estimate the significance; yet I have the feeling that he has a terribly destructive influence on everything around him, as perhaps all great personalities are bound to have."[16] (He might also have been thinking of Bloch.)

A day later Sessions had lunch with "Teddy" Chanler and met another American, although a native Russian: Vladimir Dukelsky. Gershwin later advised Dukelsky to change his name to Vernon Duke, under which name he became known for composing popular songs including "April in Paris." Dukelsky, only 20 and "rather attractive," was ambitious. He suggested that Sessions play his *Black Maskers* for Henry Prunières, the founder/editor of *La Revue Musicale*, along with Gershwin and himself, "to persuade Prunières that there is something decent and vital in America."[17] This did not happen.

Sessions viewed Dukelsky as a disappointment personally. He felt Vladimir spouted Stravinsky's ideas as if they were his own and projected an attitude "of somewhat callow superiority." Sessions reflected, "He himself doesn't matter in the least; he is obviously out to 'make a success,' and thus our aims are different. I thought many times of what Bloch told my mother after the performances of the B.M.; I realized how completely alone one must be if one has individuality of any sort."[18] Sessions was strengthened in his view, "clearer to me than ever—the importance of going absolutely straight ahead, perfectly ruthlessly, on my own path."[19]

A few days later Chanler confessed to Sessions a "fatal passion" for Dukelsky, who was bi-sexual ("trente-et-une" or "ambidextrous" in the jargon of the time). "I tried to give Teddy sage advice; I really think Dukelsky would be utterly bad for him and would lead Teddy a hell of a life, as I have gathered, both from my own impressions and from Beryl, that he is a thoroughly vain person."[20] The "experience was depressing to me, not from a musical so much as from a personal point of view. A person with a great deal of assurance, even when he is Dukelsky's age is always difficult for me to deal with, and always upsets me at the time more than he or she ought to."[21]

Other friends in addition to Copland and Chanler took care to see that Sessions had a good time. On several occasions Mark Brunswick and his family took Sessions to dinner. Brunswick, who studied with Bloch starting in 1923 and with Boulanger until 1929, would remain one of Sessions's closest friends. Despite the amount of time he spent with American friends, Sessions, once in Florence, had time to reflect on the French themselves: "I don't like the mixture . . . of the desires for unbounded admiration and homage on the one hand, and pity on the other. But fundamentally they are a marvelous people."[22] A performance of Cocteau's version of *Romeo and Juliet* left Sessions with the view of the "whole thing [as] terrifically conventionalized and 'arty'—awfully poor." He compared it with Maxfield Parrish or Mary Raymond Shipman Andrews, a dig at his sister's mother-in-law. "The fact that the [French] can appreciate the real thing—Stravinsky and Picasso—is what saves them."[23]

Sessions sent Barbara a copy of *Ulysses* for 60 francs (about $3); Chanler smuggled it into the US. In addition to eating and drinking in the open-air cafés of Paris with Dos Passos, Sessions also saw Herbert Elwell, another friend of Copland's and a student of Bloch's (1919–1921) and of Boulanger's (1921–1924). Meeting Brunswick and Elwell for tea somewhat depressed Sessions, who was sensitive to Elwell's situation: "The spectacle of this boy, who has apparently had to go on with his music in spite of the opposition of his family, who has very little money indeed, who apparently is not strong physically, and who besides seems lonely and sad perhaps in the extreme, was a terribly touching one to me. His face shows suffering of the most intense kind." In addition, Sessions considered Elwell's project of trying to apply Hambridge's theory of Dynamic Symmetry to music a "pathetically wasted effort." He liked Elwell's music, however. His quintet "has much more individuality than Quincy's [Porter's] quartet, without quite Quincy's mastery. I asked him to let me take the score and parts back to Cleveland with me, so that we might have it performed."[24] Elwell won the Rome Prize in 1923 and went to Rome in the fall of 1924 for three years. He would have a long career in Cleveland as a music critic.

Many letters fervently attempt to bolster Barbara's self-esteem.

> If you could have any idea of the joy and confidence and absolute admiration with which I think of you, you would have no more doubts about yourself, my dearest, darling person. . . . Of course, I realize what you have to contend with; it is chiefly something which I have done to you. . . . This summer, [may free] both of us from a past which still has, or did have, too great an emotional significance for us . . . when you say that your only worry about me is for fear that I will be prevented by nervousness or excitement from getting the full benefit of every experience, I want you with my whole soul to realize that that is no cause for you to worry; that these things are a part of my experience, and that they are something for me to control, and for me to strengthen myself in controlling.[25]

His disavowals to the contrary, his wife knew him extremely well; she had seen how nervousness had obstructed the path of his compositional career. She had witnessed the creative blocks that prevented works from being completed or performed.

Sessions also saw Jean and Denise Binet in Paris, if only for three hours spent at the customs house. Sessions would see them in Geneva a week later. Taken to another expensive restaurant by the Brunswicks, Sessions saw the Cleveland Orchestra conductor, Nikolai Sokoloff to whom he expressed his high opinion of *Les Noces* as approaching the *Sacre*; the conductor could not agree. The promised meetings with Mlle Boulanger came to pass; Sessions's immediate memories of her reactions to *The Black Maskers* are recorded in that section of this book. He was, of course, delighted that Mlle thought the work "not only a very fine work, but a very important work."[26]

After he played for her the remainder of *The Black Maskers*, the Dirge and "fire music," at his last interview with Boulanger, the two had a long talk. She had advised him to make an appointment to play the work for Stokowski.

She had expected to be interested, from Bloch's letter, but that "of course one person's reaction is not the same as another's" and that she had been quite prepared for possible disappointment. Then we talked for about an hour, about Bloch, about Elwell, about the six, and their ideas. . . . She said that the present fashion of gaiety is undoubtedly a reaction from the horrible experience of Paris in war time and gave a very vivid description of the black nights, and the dread that hung over everything, in spite of the fact that life went on as usual. I could understand her very well, of course, I told her every thing about Bloch, while making it clear, of course, that I was his friend. She was extremely sympathetic and just as nice as she could be. She is coming to Cleveland when she travels in America next winter.[27]

In London Sessions saw Mina Kirstein, who lived in Trevor Square. She had written to him in Paris in great distress over both how she found things in London and how much her psychoanalysis with Ernest Jones was taking out of her. Sessions wrote to Barbara, "Well, I had already made up my mind that I didn't want her at all, that I had come to realize what my love for you really was, and that I was yours, darling and yours only . . . There was some restraint, of course, between us, a little embarrassment which would naturally be the case."[28] At lunch at Mina's her brothers Lincoln and George Kirstein were present.[29] Mina, George, Lincoln, and Sessions all went to the opera together—*The Magic Flute* (for his third time in Europe!) with Goossens conducting. (Despite Margaret Chanler's urging, Sessions did not show Goossens *The Black Maskers*.) He also attended Shaw's *Saint Joan*, about which he was so "thrilled" he wanted to send Barbara a copy. Sessions was a little disappointed, "a slightly raw deal," not to have had, through Mina, a glimpse of novelist David Garnett, art critic Clive Bell, or any others of the Bloomsbury group. Bell had published *Since Cezanne* (1922) and Garnett had just published the fantasy novel *The Man in the Zoo* (1924) that Barbara read and that was dedicated to Mina. *The Man in the Zoo* concerns a man, who, in a fit of spurned love, arranges to be what his lover declares he should be—an exhibit in the zoo.

Huntingtons appeared in London as well. Sessions saw Constant (uncle George's second son); his wife Gladys he met for the first time. Gladys asked Sessions directly whether he had any children, and he reported that he blushed vividly. (Nevertheless, in letters to Barbara he referred to contraband birth control devices that could be smuggled back.) All the Huntingtons, including the one whose middle name was Huntington, went sightseeing.

Sessions was considerably more excited about Geneva than about London. He spoke English with Jean Binet, but French with Denise, her sister, brother, father, and brother-in-law. Sessions's French was improved by constant use: Denise observed that his "tempo ha[d] increased, from *Largo* to *Andantino*; and I really can always succeed in making myself understood."[30] (The fact was that all his life his speech was slow, no matter which language he spoke.) His friends tried to connect him with people who would play *The Black Maskers* in Europe. Fernande Peyrot wanted to have it played, but Ernest Ansermet was not in Switzerland at the time to approach. Sessions disposed of his second letter of introduction (one was to Boulanger) in going to see M. Alfred Boissier, an Egyptologist. In Geneva he also called on Jaques Dalcroze and on George Templeton Strong, an American (and friend of Edward MacDowell's). Sessions had almost nothing to say of the two. It was exciting, however, to drive through Lausanne and Morges, both on Lake Geneva, where Stravinsky's *Renard* and *L'Histoire du Soldat* were composed.

Sessions's love of nature was fulfilled by numerous mountain climbing excursions, and he relayed lengthy, detailed descriptions of sunrises, flowers, birds, and all things natural.

> The sunrise this morning, for instance, I haven't half described. I imagine the most stupendous crescendo, slow and inevitable, with new colors and new instruments always, going from the darkest, most sombre, most mysterious colors to the lights and most intense brilliance—sunlight on snow and ice. I thought of a huge musical form, a symphony or a fugue of the most abstract but the most intense kind—the musical equivalent of this scene.[31]

This love of nature began at Forty Acres, and in this he closely resembled his mother and his grandfather. In addition, in *Jean-Christophe* much credit is given to the Swiss countryside as restorative to the "force" of the title character. Binet and his family had a house facing southeast to Mount Blanc. Sessions was completely enamored with the Swiss countryside and mountains, which helped explain his adamant letter to Copland a few years later that he *must* get out of Paris and come to Switzerland. An accommodating Copland did so, but it was not clear that Copland—like Archibald fundamentally a creature of the city—valued the countryside as much as Sessions.

His friendship with the Binets would last a lifetime, although they never returned to the US. Sessions literally adored Jean: "Jean is his always incomparable self. If I were in the least homosexually inclined I would be violently in love with him. But the fact that I haven't a trace of such feeling for him convinced me that such things are impossible for me."[32] Since Barbara was aware that Sessions had had much more than a "trace of such feeling" for George, and since she needed bolstering in any case, in the next sentence Sessions assured her that she was the only one he loved. Surrounded by the companionable Binet family reminded Sessions of happy and congenial American families—not his own, of course; he cited the Bartletts as an example. Indeed, the Bartlett family had gone to Martha's Vineyard and seen Barbara there.

The day after this letter a catastrophe struck the Binet family. One of the nephews, aged three, fell down two flights and was killed. The boy's mother was expecting another baby, and a distraught Jean left to be with his own mother during the crisis. Such a terrible event for the Binet family left Sessions feeling altogether unable to be of help. Although he had been trying to spare Barbara his own emotions, this event made him break his resolution.

> You have no idea what a struggle it has been, sometimes. If I have not written you of my terrible fits of homesickness, of self-distrust, of apprehension, it is because you know only too well that side of me, and because it is absolutely necessary for me to conquer myself in all these ways, and to cease dissipating my energies on what are in actual fact merely symptoms; it is also because, if I let my emotions tyrannize over me, they tyrannize over you also, especially if I write them to you, or tell you about them. And I am sure that one of our greatest difficulties has always been just that.
>   . . . Your problem is, of course, absolutely different; I think that it would be a very great mistake for you not to tell me *all* of your doubts and your emotions, for I can help you very much, and want desperately to be more of a help than I have been in the past. Furthermore, all of your problems are my creation, my *ruinous* influence which I only can counteract effectively if you are *really* to be happy with me and love me . . . while you understand me marvelously well, I

haven't understood you—dear, dear, dear darling—nearly so well . . . I have been too selfish, too blind, too clumsy.[33]

He found a seven-leaf clover, which Binet said must certainly mean he would have good luck, but (typically) forgot to enclose it in his letter to Barbara. While writing these long letters, Sessions was simultaneously keeping a diary—unfortunately destroyed some years later. Some of the content of those diary entries doubtless made its way into these letters. Evidence of Sessions's guilt for his treatment of Barbara is apparent:

Of course darling, I think you have overrated your "timidity and servility." I have been responsible for this so much, in taking an attitude of hostility so often towards impulses which were neither timid nor servile on your part . . . when you speak of your real nature as being "essentially free and self-sufficient," you are only saying what I have always known to be true, really. But I have been your worst enemy in this respect as in so many others.[34]

Sessions hoped that Barbara's impulse to write would return.

And, dearest darling, if I have ever done anything to discourage you or to hinder the free development of your sensibility, I am ready to go down on my knees and beg forgiveness for what has been my egoism and my weakness, which I am determined to overcome and which I think I have gone a good way towards overcoming. And yet, how can I really say it? What I have done is so bad that *anything* that I can say must seem an impertinence.[35]

Could he mean more than his infidelity here? We do not know.

André de Ribaupierre had a home in Clarens, Switzerland, visited by the faculty from Cleveland who arrived that August. The guests, whose photograph appeared in the *Musical Courier*, included Beryl Rubinstein, Ruth Edwards, Binet, Mrs de Ribaupierre and their daughter Annette, Sessions, and Mrs Charles G. Hickox, a founder of the Cleveland Institute.[36]

Rubinstein and Edwards were also in Paris. CIM faculty Dorothy Price and Hubert Linscott also visited Clarens. Beryl would marry, in 1925, Else Landesman, a Cleveland native. Rubinstein had written to Sessions that he had spoken with Sokoloff about *The Black Maskers* in Paris. Nevertheless, Rubinstein was hurt by something (not identified) in Sessions's attitude toward him, and Sessions determined to repair the friendship.

Ribaupierre transmitted the news that Bloch, contrary to expectations, was not going to send his wife and daughters back to Switzerland for the following year. Sessions wrote,

I must confess to a selfish joy that we will still have Lucienne [Bloch] and to an equally selfish chagrin that we will still have Suzanne. . . . I can't believe that Ernie's reasons are genuine but fear he has simply weakened at the idea of being lonely. I am sorry for Lucienne—after all, she is the one person in the family who *really* matters; but then she will always be Lucienne.

Other emotions concerning the Bloch family occupied Sessions:

I don't intend to have another winter ruined by other people's heroics and emotionalism, as the last one was. The whole thing makes me blush for Ernie and seems the final death blow to the "veranol affair." I'm afraid [Bloch's son] Ivan isn't very happy about it, and wish there was something I could do to help him with his very real problem. . . . If it weren't for Ernie and Lucienne and my very real attachment to both of them, I would feel *quite* cynical about it all. . . . I simply don't intend to go through another farce like that of last year.[37]

Barbara was "apparently inclined to be more charitable to Ernie, than I . . . But I feel more than ever that we must not for a moment let ourselves become involved with the emotions of the Bloch family. It is a contagious disease, and once one has been afflicted with it, the only wise thing is to avoid it."[38]

Although Sessions and Binet took a car to Villeneuve, at the opposite end of Lake Geneva, where Romain Rolland lived in the Villa Olga, "we did not have time too see R. R., though; and really didn't feel too much inclined to; he receives very few visitors, if any, and I, curiously enough, have no inclination to see him except to discharge an obligation to Bloch."[39] This may be disingenuous. Here was an opportunity to meet his literary hero, the author of *Jean-Christophe* and numerous other works Sessions had read. Bloch had already written Rolland about Sessions: "For me, he is the first American who truly has a creative gift in music. The music he wrote last year for the *Black Maskers* of Andreyeff is a masterpiece."[40] Sessions's shyness, activated at learning that Rolland received few visitors, may have dampened his desire to see the author. Once again, personal demons and Puritan New England manners interfered with his innermost desires. This avoidance was exactly what Barbara had feared—that Sessions's "nervousness and excitement" might prevent him from receiving the full benefit of his European experience. Bloch, as well, who had gone to the trouble of writing a letter of introduction, may have been disappointed.

Finally, Sessions traveled to Italy, his ultimate destination. His first reactions to Florence were ecstatic: he wrote to Jean Binet early August, "It is almost too beautiful, because it doesn't seem at first sight entirely real. On a stroll I saw the splendid Cathedral, statues of Michelangelo and others; the house where Dante was born; I walked on embankments that cannot be described, they were so full of varied colors."[41] Two days later he gushed to Binet, "So far I have done practically nothing, from the sheer intoxication of this place—its color and its atmosphere—just wandered around the streets, where there is so much to see, even on the outside! Also I have been reading a little of the history of Florence, which I found quite indispensable."[42]

In Florence, dripping with August perspiration, Sessions wrote to Barbara again of how he envisioned their future relationship. He admitted to having lost sight of the person she really was since the beginning of their engagement in 1918. "I feel . . . sometimes that you are still a little afraid of me—that you are not quite able yet to speak to me with absolute boldness."[43] Evidently, Barbara had felt that Sessions was "unconscious" of her in company. This sounds completely plausible; he once left his ten-year-old niece running after him in a train station because he had completely forgotten that he was responsible for her during the trip.

Europe came to represent the past, America the future, and Sessions's sense of being an American was naturally heightened. He wrote about the US: "I have far more than ever a feeling of responsibility toward the *whole* country and not toward any particular group."[44]

High-altitude thoughts such as these were sometimes brought down to earth by a letter from Barbara. This was especially true of one concerning her visit to the family at Phelps House. "I am very sorry indeed [Sessions wrote] that you found the situation so distressing. The combination of my mother and sister is one of the worst I know, my sister brings out all that is worst in my mother, and I guess my mother doesn't bring out the best in my sister, either. Even at that however you can't imagine what it used to be like in the past."[45] And "I feel badly that the Hadley situation has irked you so much . . . of course a good deal of your difficulty comes from my relationship with it all, and the feeling that that gives you."[46] It is difficult for us to diagnose Ruth's and Nan's relationship to each other, since Ruth's own behavior is so hard to deduce from the careful descriptions of others. In letters to her brother, Nan tried to excuse her mother's verbal and physical violence by saying Ruth was not really responsible for her behavior. Ruth seemed not to know—after her outbursts of mean-spiritedness and even striking Nan— what she had just said or done. Nevertheless, it was Ruth who accused Nan of being mentally unstable, abnormal, and slightly unhinged. (There is no evidence of this.) Nan, like Archibald, disassociated herself from Ruth, thinking of her impersonally as she had done her Red Cross patients.[47]

Family tensions were never far from the surface of Sessions's thoughts, as much as he would try to suppress them. In some deep psychological sense these tensions still interfered with Sessions's creativity. "Did I tell you"—of course, he had not—"that I wrote some time ago to Mrs [Claire] Reis telling her that I had decided to give up the idea of writing the piece I had planned [and announced] for the L[eague of] C[omposers]? I know you will be disappointed."[48] Mrs Reis had written May 9 asking "for a piece to be done at the Library of Congress for vocal quartet or double quartet with accompaniment of a small ensemble consisting of a string quartet with four woodwinds and battery, or if preferred string quartet alone."[49] His name had already appeared in the publicity. Sessions was still struggling with "so many things which precocity and other influences of my early life obscured." He contemplated larger issues and reverted to his list making:

> What is the present? I tried to think of many things which characterized it: I even made a list, one night at St. Cerque, of the various present day movements, personalities, events, psychological reactions, etc. which characterized it—The war, the various things arising from the war and then manifestations— Psychoanalysis—the Einstein Theory—Picasso, Stravinsky, Proust, Joyce, etc.— Machinery—American business—Revolution—Reaction—the Orient, etc. etc. etc. These too one must understand, and I felt that I understood it very little, much less than I really wanted to. But as I thought it seemed not by any means the essential thing; nor the place that I wanted to live in principally. It seems to me that this world of the present day is simply the stage, so to speak. One must know it and live in it; most of one's activities will take place with it as a background. But it is not the play itself.[50]
>
> What I crave *above all else* is a greater experience of the most elementary sensations; a closer touch with nature, with all the fundamental facts and conditions of our existence—the elementary sensations of the organism and the most intense and vivid experience of them. . . .
>
> Well—here is the central thing, after all, I have a gigantic task to fulfill in my life; I need all the resources possible to perform this task. The task is simply to be true to the promise which I feel so strongly in myself, and not to disappoint those many others who have felt it, too—in other words to *write great music.* But music, like everything which lives, is based on the most profound facts of the universe; as some one has said—the *movements* of the soul—it must be made first of all of those most elementary sensations of which I have spoken. Our

knowledge of the past, our experience of the present, are the things which help us to give form and design to these elementary sensations; they are necessary parts of the whole. But they are not the *material* out of which life is made. And as for me personally I need all three of these things and want them all to a far greater degree than I have ever had them before; the *permanent* things. This summer I have gone a very long way toward getting them; although in a very fundamental way. I cannot get the third and most important really completely until I am with you; though I have had some wonderful and absolutely unforgettable experiences of that kind such as the ones I have told you about.[51]

Among Sessions's favorite locales during his nearly four weeks in Florence was the Sagrestia Nuova in the right of the transept of the Cathedral Santa Maria del Fiore, which he visited three times and found hard to pull himself away from. The church of San Lorenzo with Michelangelo's allegorical statues for Giuliano de' Medici ("Dawn") and Lorenzo de Medici ("Night") reclining on their sarcophagi, the twelfth-century church (a rare example of Florentine-Romanesque architecture) of San Miniato al Monte, the town of Fiesole, and the Pitti and the Uffizi galleries were also draws. (The bad lighting in the museums was hard on Sessions's eyes, a frequent subject of mild complaint. He thought the overuse of his eyes brought on nightmares.) Because he knew no one in Florence, no time was spent socializing, and all speaking had to be in Italian, his first attempts to make himself understood in this third language. At first he could only understand the language with difficulty and could not read the newspapers. (Sessions also spoke German, but did not travel to Germany or Austria on this trip.)

Despite the numerous resolutions to be disciplined about finances, Sessions had such a good time in Florence that he ran out of money and had to abandon his planned trip to Rome. Sessions followed his original plan to return via the Simplon tunnel to Geneva to see the Binets. From there he traveled back to Paris. He had skipped both Rome and London on the way back; he stayed in Florence until August 30, took the train back to Geneva, where he saw the Binets again and met Jaques Dalcroze for a half an hour, and traveled to Paris arriving September 4. He and Boulanger took a long walk together in the countryside. He left Paris on the 11th and sailed from Cherbourg on the *Majestic* on September 17.

Barbara had written about the possibility of having a baby, which she did not then feel in a position to have. Sessions urged her to go ahead; they would come to Europe in two years (1926) and plan to have the baby in the spring of 1927. He also said it was her decision.

Further attempts to persuade Barbara he had changed (indeed, he lost 15 pounds on the trip) in personal ways that could allow her to start fresh with him, pepper every letter.

> You are the only person who ever *really* has been able, even partially, to understand me. Even George—and you know how much I loved him, I think—never *understood* me; I craved understanding so much at the time, and my love for him was so great, that I sometimes let myself believe that he did. And Jean believes in me and appreciates certain sides of me; but neither of them *really* went further than that. . . . I am fully conscious of your sufferings, and your revulsions, darling . . . and in spite of your marvelous unselfishness and devotion your impulses have cried out more than once under the neglect with which I treated them—and sometimes I just add with great regret and humiliation, the scorn also.[52]

To assure her that life from now on would be different and better for her was a tall order. This same lengthy letter attempted to outline fundamental changes and philosophical attitudes Sessions now intended to adopt. Although lengthy, the quotations below represent only a fraction of the girth of this final letter from Europe. They attempt to lay out his attitude toward the future, and if the self-evaluations seem audacious, we must remember they were expressed for his wife's eyes alone.

I suppose my renewed self-confidence is simply the most obvious spiritual result of this new energy which I feel within me. But I want you to understand exactly what it means. For it means infinitely more than that I know that I can become a great musician, or that I have confidence in my own strength of will. It means that I have come to realize not only the greatness of my gifts, but the extent of them; to realize that while music is without doubt—at least, so it seems to me now—the most important of my gifts, it is by no means the only one. And that, to fully realize myself, which means to be really satisfied or to approach satisfaction with my life I will eventually have to become much more than a musician. . . .

In other words, darling one—and I say it to *you* without the least concealment of hesitation—I have come to realize that I am a *supremely* gifted person; that I have within me possibilities which cannot be overestimated, but which have been largely unrealized for a variety of reasons, some of which have been due to causes outside myself, others *undeniably*—and these the most important—to causes in my character or the state of my development. One of the causes has of course been the very variety and richness of my impulses, which have tended to nullify each other, as any single day out of my life would have been able to testify. . . .

And, in spite of the absolutely purist aesthetic attitude which I had adopted, I could not in the name of music renounce all the claims of general development and for want of a better term, though I use it with all the intensity and profundity of its original sense—*culture*. I mean, to be specific, I cannot ultimately deny myself the development of my body save insofar as I preserved my good health, or the activity of my mind except in musical problems. I crave, as I wrote you, the intimacy with nature, which I regard as the absolutely fundamental thing in life, which comes from intense and primitive physical sensations of all kinds; I must have a body in the first place whose vigor will enable it to react strongly and intensely to those sensations—a *first-rate* machine, in other words. Do you understand me, my dearest one? Secondly, I crave a general understanding of life in its varied aspects, including everything except mere theory; I can never again conceive of shirking an interest in contemporary affairs, for instance, as I rather prided myself on doing before, or of going through life *merely* as a musician. I feel the need of a mastery of a hundred things, of a general understanding—and above all of a whole new personality, which will express what I really am—what I really have it in me to realize . . . the one thing that I needed more desperately than *anything* in the world, and that before I could even go on thinking I must have this—order, iron discipline and efficiency in my thought and in my work . . . to plan my life according to the strictest logic and discipline. . . .

These thoughts [of writing for posterity] came back to me with great force while I was in Florence; it is *eternity* that matters, in art as in every thing else, and only that. . . .

The music that I dream of, and must create now, is music which is fundamentally of the *body*; that is based first of all on a direct appeal to the senses, the nerves, the muscles. *The Black Maskers* has of course this element, but I believe infinitely less than my music must have. I want to base my musical language on this absolutely elemental appeal. . . . Even if my work should prove to be small in quantity, it must be *first rate*, in the absolutely strict sense of the word— *perfectly* realized, ultimately. That my personality and genius are sufficiently great so that I can aim with complete confidence at perfection, always. Perfection, that is, in the sense of *absolute* realization, as far as such a thing is humanly possible. . . .

The kind of music I want to write is above all the expression of the kind of person I want to be. . . . I ask of you only one thing: your confidence. I don't ask it on the basis of the past; I could not respect myself for a moment if I even suggested that. . . . I must follow that path unquestioningly and uncompromisingly myself; I ask you to regard my decisions as to every detail of that path as considered and final, *as not involving you in any way* but to be unquestioned by you as far as *I* am concerned. I ask you also to feel yourself free, of any responsibility whatever for me, whether that of trying to modify impulses or emotions in me which you fear may be dangerous, or of shielding me from any influence whatever. . . .

First of all my teaching. . . . I have, however, the intention of aiming always at being absolutely concrete—of proceeding from facts and not from generalities— but of deducing the generalities from the facts; of making my pupils depend— teaching them how to depend—on their own senses, and cultivate them. . . .

Finally, as to *personal* relationships. First I have spoken of my desire for *solitude*. This is only partly a matter of *physical* solitude; I must have *spiritual* solitude as well. . . . I don't intend to get involved *in any degree whatsoever* in the spiritual crises or the personal situations of other people! In the first place this is a matter of self-preservation; but in the second place I believe that composure, self-command is the only attitude that can be of use in any situation whatever. . . . Other relationships [besides those with equals: Barbara, Bloch, and Lucienne]—with the unintelligent, the simply more or less egotistical, or the not wholly sympathetic, require too much energy for their maintenance, and I shall not go any further than ordinary courtesy demands. . . .

Your *madly, passionately, gloriously* devoted Roger[53]

Almost as an afterthought Sessions mentioned an "extraordinarily increased interest in painting." He did not relate this to her work or interests, but vowed to go as often as possible to museums.

Suddenly, Sessions began composing: alone in a country whose language he did not yet speak fluently, he turned simultaneously to religion and to Bach in the form of a piece for an unexpected instrument, the organ, based on the harmonic scheme of Bach's "Jesu, meine freude" (Jesus, my Joy). The work, significantly in E minor, was finished in Florence on August 19, revised in Cleveland April 10–14, 1925, and dedicated to Douglas and Emily Moore. Douglas Moore was an organist, as were Boulanger and George. Sessions had written for the organ in the Dirge of *The Black Maskers*, and would complete two other pieces for this set, as well as write a Chorale for Organ in 1938, and an organ version of *Psalm 140* in 1963. Nevertheless, by 1975, Sessions thought the organ was "not my instrument."[54]

At the time he judged *The Black Maskers* "very harshly;" only much later thought it a good piece. This new work, to be published with two later works for organ, represented the "only abrupt and conscious change I have ever adopted." He startled himself by choosing to write a severely linear, sober piece for organ—almost a "physical refreshment" to turn from *The Black Maskers* to the "basic joys of line and movement." During the period from 1924 to 1928 he embraced Neo-Classicism with intensity and fervor. He wanted to shed superficialities, to concentrate on the large line rather than have the details buried in a "general free-for-all"—the reverse of so-called Expressionism. When detail is related to the line as a whole, it takes care of itself.[55]

Largo, the second of what were to become three organ pieces, was finished in Paris, May 27, 1926, and dedicated to Theodore Chanler. The third, Ben Ritmato, dedicated to Bloch's friend Dore Landau, was also completed in Paris that May. These latter two preludes are, however, considered part of his next period.

Upon his return from such an exotic foreign trip he encountered that which greets many who have been away from "reality" for long: problems. In this case, the realization by Archibald that David Belasco was in fact not going to do his play, but rather had sold it as his own creation to a movie studio as the script to *Building the Union*. Archibald hired a lawyer, but the situation was never corrected, and the betrayal had to have left him—and Sessions, too—highly disillusioned.

The summer of 1924 in Europe had cemented Sessions's sense of himself and his sense of belonging to a larger world than New England and Cleveland. Jean and Denise Binet would live in Europe for the rest of their lives and with them remained part of Sessions's emotional life. If he wanted to reconnect to this life and to the art he so admired, he would have to find a way to return to Europe. In the fall of 1924 that seemed only a remote dream.

STRAVINSKY

During the summer of 1922 Sessions obtained the orchestral scores of Stravinsky's *Petrouchka* and *Le sacre du printemps* (published in 1921). He had known their four-hand arrangements since 1914, when he played *Le sacre* through with Edward B. Hill and later performed it with George Bartlett. The orchestral publication of *Le sacre* transported Sessions for four days—he thought of nothing else during that time in Hadley, even reading the score at the blacksmiths when the horse was being shod—and it confirmed what Sessions thought the music meant. He became enormously influenced by these two pieces, which did not please Bloch: "I could never sell Stravinsky to Bloch at that time. It came by itself many years later."[1] Suzanne Bloch remembered her father adored the early music of Stravinsky, but not the later music, "and he felt that really Roger kind of turned his back on him, which is a very human thing, egocentric thing."[2]

Sessions had spoken about Stravinsky quite a bit during his Cleveland years, 1921–1925, even lecturing on his music at one of the Cleveland Orchestra lectures. Stravinsky's music was still problematical for the public. Sessions saw him as a "somewhat legendary figure," much to Bloch's annoyance.[3] Stravinsky had already conducted the Philadelphia Orchestra, January 30 and 31, 1925, in a concert devoted entirely to his music. He came to Cleveland to conduct its orchestra in three of his own pieces, February 12 and 14: *Fireworks, Le Chant du Rossignol* (The Song of the Nightingale), and *Firebird* (Sokoloff, conducting Tchaikovsky's Sixth Symphony, filled out the concert).

In 1924 and 1925 both Bloch and Sessions gave well-advertised, free, public lectures at the Institute. Bloch chose topics such as "Oriental Music," while on Wednesdays at 2:00 p.m. Sessions dwelt on the programs the Cleveland Orchestra did the following day: he gave 17 lectures relating to the concerts during the 1924–1925 season. The day before Stravinsky was to conduct, Sessions gave his regular Wednesday lecture on the program, as well as an additional talk that night, a special lecture on "Stravinsky, the Man and his Works." Sessions spoke about the *Rite of Spring* and played excerpts at the piano, explaining the music as he went along. He told the audience that the fact that each new work of Stravinsky seemed completely different from the previous one was what made it hard for them to understand him. They had just absorbed one style when a completely different one appeared next. Stravinsky ought to be commended, Sessions asserted, for his independence of style and for the gamut of his musical expression. Because of his public lectures on Stravinsky, Sessions thought he was seen as "slightly crazy in the eyes of Clevelanders."[4] When Stravinsky came to conduct, all his friends were invited to meet him, but not Sessions.

Nadia Boulanger came to Cleveland to give both an organ recital at the Museum of Art and a lecture, February 13, 1925, at the CIM on "Modern Music and its Evolution." She illustrated her talk at the piano by playing orchestral works and piano pieces by

Fauré, Florent Schmitt, Ravel, Roussel, and Bela Bartók. Boulanger had dinner with the Sessionses, and they went to the concert together. (Sessions did not know that Mrs Sanders had that month recommended Mlle Boulanger to the board as a possible successor to Sessions.) Boulanger said, "This is absolutely absurd, you must meet Stravinsky. In fact, you're the one man in Cleveland who really must meet him."[5]

> So after the concert, she took me out to see Stravinsky. Stravinsky was very nice, but said that he had so many social obligations that he just had not time for what he called "les gens interessante." [All of Sessions and Stravinsky's conversations were in French.] "But," he said, "I'm going to Philadelphia to play my concerto." I told him that I was very glad to hear Le Chant du Rossignol and Feux d'artifice [Fireworks] and Oiseau de Feu [Firebird] but what I really wanted to hear was some of his later music, specifically his Piano Concerto. He said, "Well, this is all right for you, Monsieur, but not for the general public. I'm going to play it in Philadelphia on Sunday, and I'm going to take such and such a train, why don't you take that train and come to Philadelphia, and come to a rehearsal and the concert?"[6] So I did. I had a very nice time on the train with Stravinsky. He had a bad sinus, and he wanted to go to bed early, but I of course thought he was bored and I was scared to death anyway. But he said, "I'm going to the Hotel Sylvania in Philadelphia. Why don't you go over there and take a room, then stay there, and we can see each other?" So I did. I went and took a room at the Hotel Sylvania and went up to my room. I thought, "Of course I can't bother Stravinsky; if he wants me he'll call me," so I spent the morning by myself. Then I went down and had lunch. Having nothing else to do, I had lunch quite early, and when I was coming out of the dining room I met Stravinsky, and Stravinsky said, "Have you had lunch?" and I said, "Yes." He looked at me from head to foot as much as to say, "What a strange young man, here he has a chance to have lunch with Stravinsky and he goes and has lunch all by himself." Well, I still was scared to death. I was petrified, of course. I had no idea what to do.[7]

Sessions had falsely assumed anybody in Stravinsky's position would be what he called "a stuffed shirt." Upon becoming a formidable figure himself, Sessions "got used to the fact that older men, no matter how famous they are, like to have younger men around them, and are very cordial and friendly, instead of just feeling the younger men are a nuisance."[8] Having been brought up a gentleman, naturally Sessions wrote Stravinsky a thank-you letter (in French).[9]

And yet Sessions was ambivalent about Stravinsky. Although he had other opportunities to see more of him, "at that time I didn't want to, you see. I didn't want to get too close."[10] In addition, he later told Milton Babbitt that, although he liked certain pieces of Stravinsky's, he "basically didn't like [the Piano Concerto] very much."[11] Sessions would see Stravinsky in New York occasionally, and in 1947, when he gave a pre-concert talk on Stravinsky's music, they had a lovely time after the concert. Sessions asked whether Stravinsky remembered the Philadelphia incident—which he did.

From 1947 to 1959, however, Sessions had no contact with Stravinsky. In New York in 1959 Stravinsky sent a message "that he'd like to see me, and I went to see him and had a wonderful time."[12] In 1959 Stravinsky gave a concert in the Town Hall on December 20, 1959, in which he conducted Les Noces (The Wedding) and asked four composers to play the piano parts. Lukas Foss played the first piano, Sessions the second, and Aaron Copland and Samuel Barber played the other two parts. The work was recorded for

Figure 26 Samuel Barber, Igor Stravinsky, Lukas Foss, Aaron Copland, Roger Sessions during a rehearsal for *Les Noces*, recorded December 21, 1959 (photograph by Don Hunstein).

Columbia (MS 6372) with Mildred Allen, soprano, Regina Sarafaty, mezzo, Loren Driscoll, tenor, and Robert Oliver, bass, with the American Concert Choir, Margaret Hillis, director, and the Columbia Percussion Ensemble.

Sessions twice wrote about Stravinsky's *Œdipus Rex* in 1928.[13] He had heard Koussevitzky conduct it with the Boston Symphony Orchestra and the Harvard Glee Club February 24, and 25, 1928. (It had been premiered, unstaged, in Paris, May 30, 1927.) "Those who heard the inadequate performance in Paris last spring will agree that Mr Koussevitzky gave *Œdipus* virtually its world premiere."[14] He referred in *Modern Music* to "*Œdipus* [a]s the direct result of a certain aesthetic faith, a faith which regards works of art as objects existing in and for themselves apart from the limitations of purely personal emotions."[15] Although Sessions never mentioned the term *Neo-Classicism*, a term that came into common use later on, he described it well. Sessions had heard yet another Paris performance, in late May 1928, conducted by the composer. He wrote to pianist and composer John Duke later that week:

> *Œdipus*, however was the really great experience of that evening. I was surer than ever of the greatness of this music, hearing it done by Str. himself. The contrast with Koussevitzky was extraordinary, + really illuminating. I was quite aware that K—is careless with his tempi; but at the same time I realized he was trying tremendously hard to do it as he thought Str. would like it. The extraordinary thing was that under Str. it was far warmer + richer than under K—obviously the man felt this music in every fiber of his being—felt it *as music* in all of its significance, without losing any of its impressiveness it became lighter, more

tense, and far more dramatic. . . . However—I have had again, an enormous impression from Stravinsky—both his playing + his conducting have improved enormously since I heard it last. In his playing of the concerto one felt, above all, a simplicity + dignity so extreme that, while one felt that, all the time, he was merely *presenting* the music without interpreting or underlining a single note, the impression was enormously forceful—its extreme impersonality + objectivity were in themselves *forces*—they seemed the nth of musical feeling, controlled and disciplined through its very strength. I assure you it was a surprise, for I have never considered Stravinsky a good performer; and it was, probably by reason of this surprise, a very significant experience for me.[16]

He wrote to Nicolas Slonimsky, "I meant to write you, too, about Stravinsky's *Œdipus Rex*, which I heard in Paris in June [May]. Of course you have seen the score; it seems to me a most remarkable work—one of the very finest that S—has written."[17]

Copland wrote to Sessions about Sessions's *Hound & Horn* article on *Œdipus Rex*: "Am I right or isn't it better even than the *M{odern} M{usic}* one?"[18] Copland was correct according to his own lights about the difference between the two articles. The *Hound & Horn* was shorter, more vivid, and more to the point than the one written for *Modern Music*.

The 1928 *Hound & Horn* article stressed the connection between Stravinsky and Handel's oratorios: "monumental in conception, dignified and stately in mood . . . polyphony is always a result of harmonic necessity . . . [the] harmonic scheme is, as with the Handel, of the utmost simplicity." And "In *Œdipus*, the harmonic structure, simple as it is, is more elastic than the earlier Stravinsky; the experience of the *Octour* and the piano *Concerto* shows its print in the extraordinary continuity, the ease of transition, which characterize *Œdipus* to a far greater extent than is the case with either the *Sacre du Printemps* or *Les Noces*." Sessions went on: "The interruption of the music by the spoken word adds, too, an almost liturgical suggestion—a more profound expressive element than may at first appear."

Sessions's ultimate compliment had to do with closeness to nature, another kind of Adoration of the Earth: "The tremendous power of his musical personality, its vigor and 'closeness to the earth,' are all the more intense for being harnessed and directed into impersonal channels. . . . Let us content ourselves with our homage," Sessions ended the essay, "to the power and self-criticism of an artistic nature which, having discovered certain tempting and beautiful novelties of expression, has been able without sacrifice to renounce them in the interest of a more impersonal, more universal ideal."

In *Modern Music* Sessions wrote that the music of *Œdipus* was built on a strictly harmonic basis; in this respect it stood in striking contrast to the other recent works of Stravinsky, which were primarily contrapuntal. He pointed out that in the work, "the harmonic axis is nearly always a tonic triad," that is, a "persistently reiterated D minor harmony." Rhythm, Sessions felt, "is superficially at least, far less striking in *Œdipus* than in either *Le Sacre du printemps* or *Les Noces*." A great compliment, coming from a New Englander, was "The emphasis was entirely on the work, not on the composer."

Years later Sessions was to share billing with the Stravinsky when, in January 1976, Georg Solti conducted his cantata *When Lilacs Last in the Dooryard Bloom'd* on the same concert with *Œdipus Rex*.[19]

Chapter 3

THE EUROPEAN PERIOD
1925–1933

FATHER FIGURES

Back from Europe, Sessions lived during the 1924–1925 school year at 1464 Lee Road. During this year Bloch and the Cleveland Institute would sever their connection. The CIM had begun a string orchestra conducted by Bloch. Barbara Sessions played violin in this orchestra of about 40 students and faculty. Violinist Albert Spalding, visiting a rehearsal in November, complimented them: "Never have I seen such beautiful bowing by so large a body of strings."[1] A second visitor later that month would also prove important in Sessions's future: Cesar Saerchinger, a friend of Bloch's, was a guest lecturer.

André de Ribaupierre's policy was to place one "girl" as second violin in each year's student quartet. The students, and most likely Barbara Sessions, took umbrage at this policy and, in the fall of 1924, in a move "which may signify a feminist movement in music circles" formed an all-girl quartet, the only such entity in Cleveland. The members of the "Girls' String Quartet of the Cleveland Institute of Music," pictured in both *Musical America* and the *Musical Courier*, were Lois Brown and Barbara Sessions, violins; Ione Saastemoinin, cello; and Marie Martin, viola.[2] They must have played well: The following year Brown and Martin joined the string faculty as assistants.

Sessions could not long refrain from prose writing. He had been publishing for almost a decade and continued to write more prose than he did music. For *Musical America* he contributed "Will tomorrow bring retracing of steps in musical creation?"

> Yet with the emphasis placed upon experiment and discovery, little room has thus far been left for the mastery of material which creative genius needs for its fulfillment. The true master does not need to experiment, and too great pre-occupation with material novelty hampers the development of his thought. . . . It is evident, however, that "ultra-modernism" has fulfilled its purpose and that the problem is now one of order, organization, form. Dissonance and rhythmic freedom are now no longer live issues, and the excitement as well as the useful-ness of unorganized novelty has passed. . . . Already there are signs of a partial retracing of steps, with a greatly enriched vocabulary, toward the principle of tonality. The polyphonic and melodic principle is reaffirming itself by reaction against the harmonic and coloristic tendencies of yesterday.[3]

In the spring of 1925 the Cleveland Playhouse gave a production of the play *Turandot*, for which Sessions was asked to write incidental music. Sessions attempted a Chinese flavor in this piece, scored for two pianos and eight percussion instruments. The per-formances took place May 8–10; the score was dedicated to Mrs Joseph Russell. Sessions appeared onstage as an actor in another of the Playhouse's productions, F. J. Turner's *The*

Man who Ate the Popermack. Sessions explained, "a popermack was an oriental fruit, which was absolutely delicious, but if you ate it, you smelled so badly that no one wanted to come near you. I portrayed a Chinese philosopher. They chose me because of my voice, mainly, and I had very provocative and shocking words to say that scandalized the Cleveland public. But very wise."[4]

As was mentioned previously, Bloch was fired at the end of the 1924–1925 school year. Sessions said, "He was caught *in flagrante*. His girl friend was . . . very indiscreet, very exuberant. Probably meant nothing to him, but he was fired. Furious!"[5] It became a great embarrassment to the Institute's trustees. Bloch had been quite publicly re-engaged around Christmas time in 1924, but fired in May 1925. The school had difficulty raising money in part because of this open scandal. Already unhappy because Bloch insisted on the French fixed *do* system (where *do* is always C) rather than the moveable *do* system (where *do* is the tonic pitch) taught in the Cleveland public schools, the board also felt he was not an effective fund raiser. Bloch's own overwrought diary entries about his dismissal neglect to mention his affair or to take any personal responsibility for what happened.[6] Some of the faculty resigned in protest. Sessions would have done so were it not for the inconvenient fact that he was obliged to teach summer school because of the agreement made when the Institute gave him the $900 advance on that year's salary. In any case, he needed the money. His protest was therefore somewhat muffled. Mrs Sanders became the director for the next seven years and was succeeded by Beryl Rubinstein. After Bloch's resignation, Quincy Porter was appointed the head of the theory department and taught until 1928, resuming for the 1931–1932 year. Porter became the star composer at the Institute.

Bloch made a scene over which faculty stayed and which left; betrayers were again invoked. Sessions's departure was, however, not entirely because of loyalty. "I can't pretend that my motives were completely unmixed. I was already glad to get away from Cleveland, where I never felt at home."[7] Leaving Cleveland, Sessions "wanted to get to a larger place, where I could measure myself against the musical world, I suppose, more than I could in Cleveland, which was, at that time a desert. I wanted to go to some center."[8] Bloch's firing had come at the end of the school year, in May, rather late for Sessions to find another position. Sessions felt that most schools would tolerate a considerable amount of scandal within their walls, but as soon as there was publicity outside a school that threatened the reputation of the institution, then they could act quite brutally. In addition to Bloch, he knew personally of three other people caught in these types of situations, which had to do with philandering "of a fairly normal kind, quite normal, I would say."[9] He used to say that the minute Bloch left, he would, too: it was bad enough in Cleveland with Bloch, without him it would be impossible. Later he thought this view rather unjustified.

Sessions spent the evening of June 26, 1925, with the Blochs. "I was surprised at the absence of any bitter raving or saying what a great man he was . . . He really was his very best self last night—the person that I haven't seen really since the New York days."[10] Bloch gave him a death mask of Nietzsche. Watching the preparations that summer for a new administration, Sessions became philosophical over the Institute and Bloch:

> It may be that in some inexplicable way we all of us failed, through weakness,
> perhaps rather through inexperience. Ernie of course failed and it is more than
> possible that he was in a certain sense the cause of the failure—his inadequacies
> and lack of appreciation of what an inestimably valuable thing he had. After all
> he was frankly our leader, and I feel that he dodged a great many of the responsi-
> bilities of leadership. But in looking at the thing frankly, I can see that some,

perhaps all, of *us*, too failed to realize what we had, and that a really big opportunity escaped us.[11]

Sessions had dinner on the Fourth of July at the Bloch home, from which they watched fireworks. "There was no pettishness, no vainglory, no pronunciamentos."[12]

Some of Sessions's summer was spent reading Walter Pach's *Masters of Modern Art*, Havelock Ellis's *Analysis of the Sexual Impulse* and *Love and Pain*, Schweitzer's *Bach*, and Boccaccio as a possible source of "opera, ballet, 'melodrama,' pantomime?," on which he wanted to collaborate with Barbara.[13] Another source was Poe's *The Fall of the House of Usher*. Regarding the Ellis, Sessions tried to be honest with himself:

> I must confess I find it in some respects difficult to read much of the time. I suppose it stirs too many complexes, and that that fact makes me a little restless when I read it; and yet for that very reason it is perhaps rather fascinating, and makes me wonder if I have lost temporarily the faculty of being honest with myself in regard to these [sexual] things—the faculty that Mike Elliot always admires so much in me. But I trust not—after all it is easily recovered if one has once had it.[14]

Five days later, working on his music, Sessions tried to analyze himself:

> My problem seems to me to be above all one of coordination and regulation, and above all perhaps one of controlling the tempo of my nervous rhythm. . . . Perhaps I can explain matters better by saying that I find myself rather in the position of a pianist or a violinist who has made the mistake of practicing too fast, and who has thus wasted a great deal of energy and formed awkward habits; he then must practice again slowly in order to gain real mastery. Or perhaps I am more exactly like a man who has, as an infant prodigy, been forced ahead of his normal age, and who must eventually stop and grow mature before he can really amount to anything. Thus my nervous reactions are too quick and I am faced with the problem of reeducating them to act with precision.[15]

One nervous reaction doubtless arose upon the receipt of a letter in July asking for the complete parts so that the Philadelphia Orchestra could privately read *The Black Maskers*. Sessions had taken Boulanger's advice and sent or given his score to its conductor, Stokowski. The work would take Sessions several more years to complete. Parts are normally extracted from the score for each of the orchestral performers after a performance is secured. Stokowski and the orchestra eventually played the Orchestral Suite on November 4, 1933, eight years after the receipt of this letter. (The Suite's premiere had been given by the Cincinnati Symphony in 1930. See section "*The Black Maskers*.")

Sessions's sojourn in Europe in 1924 had given him a greater appreciation of art, and reading *Masters of Modern Art* helped crystalize certain connections.

> It is extraordinary how certain parallels with music can be drawn. Stravinsky, perhaps, could be likened to Cézanne in certain respects, and Scriabine to Redon. Bloch of course to Gauguin. Stravinsky resembles Seurat, too, in certain respects. But—perhaps because I know it so much better than painting—it seems to me that music—even the most daring—has deviated far less than painting from tradition—simply because so many of these aesthetic problems do not exist for

it. The problems of music are practical ones in the main. The boldest innovator in music can not, if he would, deviate very far from tradition since music is in its whole essence so abstract and so flexible.[16]

Finally, after spending too much time on his incidental music for *Turandot* and having already received assurances of the necessary money for the European sojourn that fall, Sessions spent his last evening, July 23, 1925, with "Ernie." Bloch had greeted Sessions and, after a few minutes' conversation, then somewhat rudely gone back to making photographic enlargements, which kept him busy until 11:30 at night. Sessions spent the time waiting by talking with Suzanne. Finally Bloch stopped his own work and the two "had a *most touching* farewell. You see it was a somewhat ironical occasion in some ways, even to the end. Not that I mind in the least; it was the final thing in my relationship with him, and in every way a typical one."[17]

Sessions and Barbara left for Europe in the fall of 1925, and Bloch moved to San Francisco. Archibald was left behind in New York. Thus both father figures, real and surrogate, under different circumstances departed Sessions's life at this time. (A few years earlier Sessions had stopped writing to Father Sill, another father figure, at Kent.) Part of the problem Sessions had with Bloch, aside from the natural weaning of himself from a strong father–teacher figure as any son or student has to do, was that "Bloch and I belonged to different generations, and there'd been quite a change in the whole musical point of view between these generations. I mean Bloch belonged definitely to the prewar generation. I belonged definitely to the postwar generation. . . . World War I was a tremendous cleavage."[18]

Suzanne Bloch remembered, "There's no question it was a personal thing. [Bloch] felt like Roger was his child, and his musical creative child had gone away to the Schoenberg thing, which he didn't approve of. No, he felt there were great things [written in the Schoenberg method] and I think he was right."[19] Sessions found it very hard to speak about Bloch because "if you like I'm ambivalent about him. I not only had to become independent, I reacted very much against him, in a certain sense. . . . I found myself being rather ruthlessly critical at times. . . . There were certain things in his point of view about music which I just couldn't accept, and which I felt—well, accounted for things which I felt as weaknesses in the music itself."[20] He continued, "Bloch really in a sense belonged to a sort of Wagnerian tradition. In other words, he thought of himself as more than a musician, you see, as a kind of prophet, which is a very hard thing to describe without making it sound very unsympathetic."[21] And "Bloch thought of himself as . . . a person with a kind of a philosophical or moral or religious message, through his music. And I felt, and I came to feel very much, not without reason, that he gradually grew more interested in the message than in the music."[22] In 1927 Sessions wrote of Bloch, "It is as though in becoming more conscious of his personality, his 'message,' he had almost deliberately thrown aside the serenity—one is even tempted to say the universality—of his native musical impulse . . . His role is prophet or orator, rather than lyric poet; least of all is it creator of objective aesthetic worlds."[23]

In the same article Sessions surveyed all of Bloch's music to date. He assumed Bloch to be an American composer, since he had become a citizen in 1924. Sessions discussed *Macbeth* and the Jewish Cycle (*Trois Poèmes Juifs*, the *Psalms* for soprano and orchestra, *Schelomo*, the *Psalm 22* for baritone, and the symphony "Israel"). He defined the "Jewish" character of the music as

above all sumptuous and grandiose; rich and exuberant in color, luxuriant and full-blown in form. Its austerity, if such it can be called, is a pagan austerity of mood; intensity and concentration rather than essential restraint, a quality of his soul rather than of his art . . . attributable before all else to this extraordinary directness and intensity of feeling . . . What he has done is to allow his imagination to play on the embodiment of a truly Jewish spirit in music.[24]

Then Sessions approached the works that followed the Jewish Cycle: the Quartet, the Suite for Viola and Piano, the Sonata for Violin and Piano, and the Quintet.

In these later works his dominant moods are those of pessimism, irony, and nostalgia . . . Bloch no longer writes as a Jew, but rather as a solitary individual . . . The violence of his later music is ruthless and mechanical . . . Irony . . . becomes one of his characteristic moods, manifesting itself above all in a fondness for the grotesque, for caricature; the *allegro ironico* of the Suite, like its Lisztian prototype, is the embodiment of the "Spirit that denies." . . . The nostalgia . . . grows out of this disillusion. . . . [There are] rare moments in the Jewish works when the European and the oriental elements in the music seem to clash with one another.[25]

Lastly, Sessions dealt with what Bloch had written at the Cleveland Institute:

most illuminating; from a distance it assumes the form of a sort of panorama of American provincial life in its most characteristic phases, thrown into clear if lurid relief by the apparition of a personality such as Bloch's . . . Cleveland's rejection of Bloch was a rejection precisely of the best that he had to give—that, as all who were with him can testify, he wanted so passionately to give. His very geniality, his force of conviction, his ironic laughter—his richness of temperament and culture, in other words—stood in his way.[26]

Sessions felt that, because of the defeat in Cleveland, in Bloch's Quintet he could detect that the composer was somewhat more on his guard, and "little [wa]s intrinsically new."[27] Much later Sessions told his student Milton Babbitt that Bloch was "a compositional genius who never composed a composition of genius."[28]

Sessions quoted Bloch regarding a passage in *De Profundis* of Orlando di Lasso, " 'I can conceive of a day when Beethoven will seem old-fashioned; even Bach may one day seem old-fashioned, while Wagner has begun to seem so already. But this can never grow old.' "[29] Sessions concluded, "And if the effort of a different conception to assert itself has temporarily seemed to isolate [Bloch], to deprive him of adequate recognition, there can be no doubt that the adjustments of history will restore to him his true place among the artists who have spoken most commandingly the language of conscious emotion."[30] Always a faith in Rollandian posterity. Sessions wrote an appreciation for a Bloch Festival held at the Juilliard School of Music, November 14–15, 1947. He called the three all-Bloch concerts "a symbolic vindication of the career of one who has had the courage to remain always a completely individual and even a solitary figure."[31]

Sessions remembered having seen Bloch for the last time around 1949 or 1950. Bloch said, "You've got a wonderful wife, wonderful family—and a wonderful mother-in-law!"[32] Sessions saw him in Paris once, but never in Switzerland or Italy. They saw each other occasionally in San Francisco. "We were never on close and intimate terms again."[33] Sessions did keep up with Bloch's two daughters, Suzanne who taught Renaissance music at Juilliard, and Lucienne, a well-known artist.[34] Ivan was the third child. Suzanne Bloch remembered that her father went to a 1958 concert in Berkeley, "and he said [in his diary], 'I heard a [String] Quintet of Sessions; horrible, horrible.' And the next week, he said, 'I went back to it the second time the Quintet. I was wrong. There's something in it.' "[35]

Near the end of Bloch's life, in 1959, Suzanne pleaded with Sessions to visit him, but Sessions never did.

> And he didn't get in touch with [my father] at all. And when he was at Agate Beach [Oregon] he never visited. And as I said, near the end, when father was dying, I met him when he was at Juilliard. I said, "You know, Roger, father is dying. He has cancer. I don't know how long he'll last. I wish you'd write to him." He didn't. And I felt very sad. I wish he'd written, because *really* it would have meant so much to my father.[36]

Nevertheless about a month after he died, Sessions was in Oregon and wanted to see Mrs Bloch. He called her, but got the feeling she did not want to see anybody from the past just then. (Sessions, always too late, may have misinterpreted Mrs Bloch's reaction.) Suzanne and Lucienne had both their parents cremated. The two sisters waded into the Pacific Ocean and tossed the remains in the air and into the sea, declaring, "Now you two can fight it out for eternity!" In 1976 the sisters put up a memorial tablet on Agate Beach (moved in 2005 to the Newport Performing Arts Center), which had a profile bas-relief of Bloch by Lucienne and read, "Ernest Bloch, Composer, Philosopher, Humanist, lived nearby with his wife Marguerite (1939–1964) 'Give me solitude, Give me Nature' Walt Whitman." Reflecting on Sessions's not visiting Bloch, Suzanne said, "It all comes back to you, the good and the bad."

After the farewell between Sessions and Bloch in the summer of 1925, Sessions turned to Archibald, the hero of that year. Archibald's Harvard Class report for 1933 stated,

> For Street & Smith he started a new magazine known at first as *People's*, then *People's Favorites*, and finally as *Complete Story*. In 1916 he was editor of *All Round* and lived at 15 West 29th Street in Manhattan. Still later, in addition to the editorship of this magazine, he developed two more, *Sports Stories* and *Sea Stories*. During these years he wrote many book reviews. The magazines were successful largely owing to his ability to pick out articles with wide appeal. Naturally he came into contact with many well-know writers, some of whom he was the first to recognize. This was true of O. Henry, with whom he formed a personal friendship and for whose Biographical Edition he wrote the preface.[37]

Archibald's success in his literary career is hard to assess; perhaps the lack of evidence is silent testimony. Although he published no works of fiction, he worked steadily as an editor of fiction at *Ainslee's* and elsewhere. In the first decade of the century, he and O. Henry visited bowling alleys and shooting galleries on Sixth Avenue together. In a note preceding O. Henry's *The Voice of the City: Further Stories of the Four Million*, Archibald writes of him: "I have always thought that the dominant trait in O. Henry was his sensitiveness. By that I mean his extraordinary perception of delicate and subtle shadings of character in other people and the instantaneous reaction they produced in his own mind."[38] Here Archibald listed three "rebuffs" that O. Henry met with trying to get his stories published, although he noted "it is perfectly true that he escaped most of the discouragements experienced by the average run of young authors."[39]

This comment touched upon the catastrophic experience in 1924 in Archibald's own literary life. Ruth claimed to have indulged in wishful thinking about living with her husband once his literary success was achieved and after such a long separation. She never lived with her husband again, but that was not because of the success or failure of his creative work. Ruth wrote

> Another interest had come into my husband's life. He had begun to do some writing of plays, for which he had only evening-time, but which promised real success. He was working with David Belasco over one of the plays, which they were planning to produce together. The two were excellent friends; Belasco very enthusiastic over its possibilities, and over the subject-matter, a bit of American history not yet appropriated for drama or fiction . . . The enterprise filled him with hope, the hope he had cherished for twenty years of being able to provide, after a little longer waiting, not only for the needs, but for extra indulgences which we had not been able to achieve thus far. With our children all self-supporting [!] and no longer in need of financial help, we could make a home together again in some quiet spot, and live simply; the success of the play would put us on a footing of ease, if not actual luxury.
>
> . . . A friend once said to me; "Have you no villain in your book? No story is complete without a villain." I laughed and said that villains were boring to write about. But there was one, of whom I could not write; the false friend who stole, and sold, my husband's play and broke his heart; the heart that had withstood the ravages of the great blizzard thirty years before, but was not proof against mortal treachery. We try to forget the crime and remember only the happy visions that were never realized.[40]

Archibald wrote to Roger in Cleveland in the fall of 1924:

> I have been rather surprised, from what the various members of the family have said about the play fiasco, at the sensations I have experienced myself, for it almost seems as though I have been rather callous about it. If it were not for the fact that I have really felt very badly about it on Belasco's account—as I explained to Barbara—I should suspect that I had grown so old that I had lost my capacity for feeling of any sort. But being as sorry for him as I have been it seems to me that my emotions haven't been so dulled as all that.[41]

The "false friend" was John Russell, who in 1924, along with David Belasco had sold to Fox studios, where he worked, the claim that he himself had written *The Iron Horse* (the title comes from an Emily Dickinson poem about the locomotive), which was made into the movie *Building the Union*. Archibald had worked on the play with a collaborator, Mrs Wilson Woodrow, not with Russell. In the spring of 1925 Russell had invited Archibald to spend a couple of months this summer with him on his houseboat on the St Lawrence, "But I fancy that his plans for that are likely to be changed when he discovers that he has been made a defendant in a case in which I am plaintiff, particularly when he find that he is charged with 'falsity' claiming that he is one of the authors of *The Iron Horse*."[42] In 1925 Archibald wrote to his son that he and his lawyer were sanguine about winning their copyright suit against Bill Fox. The case, however, was to drag on past Archibald's death. At one point the Fox Film Corporation had offered a settlement of $2,500 to be divided between Archibald and his co-author. That was not accepted, and in the end the two got nothing. In 1934 Paul Shipman Andrews wrote to Mrs Woodrow that he had contacted Mr Russell, then living on the West Coast, but with no success. In June of 1925 Sessions wrote to Barbara regarding his father, "The whole trouble is that I know him so little or rather that I see him so little that we have so often misunderstood each other, and that so many times, alas! Mother misquoted him that I have impressions which are certainly false, sometimes."[43]

At this time Sessions, on the advice of Copland, was applying for a grant from the Guggenheim Foundation, which had just stated operation. Sessions's materials were sent on June 25, 1925. Evidently he was nervous about obtaining the grant and with reason: 15 winners drawn from 74 applicants were announced the previous month, on May 28. Sessions was again too late. Copland had been asked to apply and was the only composer to win one of the grants of $2,500.[44]

Bloch's enthusiasm for *The Black Maskers* might have helped Sessions.[45] The irony, which Sessions may not have known, was that Bloch himself, now out of the Institute job and with three adolescent children to support, had applied for the same Guggenheim while writing Sessions a letter of recommendation. Bloch was turned down due to his age. He did not tell Sessions this, but did reveal that he had written for Sessions instead of other students—"G. Antheil, B[ernard] Rogers, and de Leone"—who had asked him. In the same letter, written in French to Sessions in Italy, Bloch expressed his joy and even envy that Sessions is now his "own master." Bloch continued,

> It is normal, natural and necessary that at a certain moment the seed has to detach itself from the plant and live its life. Do you remember a morning, in Cleveland, in the "Old Building," when you asked me what you should do with your students, and I sent you, "packing!" I already felt then, that it was necessary for you to bring out your own personality . . . I knew that it was there, latent in you, but a constraint, an "inhibition," as they say here [in San Francisco], interposed itself between you and others . . . It is always a joy for me to see beings emancipate themselves, musically—for sentimentally, I would never permit myself to judge . . . To each his experience! For they also are necessary. It is almost indispensable in life to take sometime the "wrong way" in order to appreciate the right, later.[46]

Days after the Guggenheim application was sent, in July 1925, Sessions wrote his father a long 12-page letter asking for $1,800 for himself or $2,500 for both him and Barbara to go to Europe. He applied psychological pressure on him by accusing Archibald of having no confidence in him. Archibald defended himself in a letter of July 17, 1925, and on July 22 wrote the anxious Sessions, who had evidently not told Archibald the Guggenheim "scholarship" was out of the question.

> To the first part of your letter all it seems necessary for one to say is that I guess we understand each other, and always will . . . Supposing you and Barbara go ahead and make your plans as though the two scholarships had already been awarded to you. I understand from you and from her that you are certain of $500 from Mrs MacBride. I am quite sure that I know where I can get $2,500 for you, which will make up $3,000. I gather from what you say in your letter that this amount will take you both to Florence and keep you for a year. If I am right

about that I don't see why you shouldn't plan for it. I told Barbara something of the sort when I saw her in Hadley. I understood from her that the work she would have with the Smith College people in Paris they would be only too glad to have her do whether they could raise the money to pay her or not. So it resolves itself into this, that if you and she can swing the proposition on $3,000 for the year, you can go ahead. Of course, if the scholarships come across you will not need these advances from Mrs MacBride and through me. Let me know how this strikes you.

I wonder if you could tell me when Stokowski will have his rehearsal of the *Black Maskers* and whether he would let me hear it.

Always your loving dad.[47]

The funds were not in any sense an "advance;" this was a gift from Archibald to the couple. Sessions and Barbara sailed on September 2, 1925, on the *Mauretainia* at reduced rates, but with "truly splendid accommodations."[48] The pressing question, however, is, where did Archibald find the huge sum of $2,500? Perhaps he relied on his own family for financial support, possibly Edwin Hooper or Adeline Sessions.

Sessions's enthusiasm for Europe was tempered by a realization that he could not truly be an expatriate. He wrote at the time:

I shall spend the next year and also in all probability the following three or four in Europe, devoting myself mainly to composition. I do not believe, however, in the necessity, or, for myself, the possibility, for American artists to live permanently in Europe. While the shortcomings of America from this point of view are evident to anyone who regards the matter intelligently, I believe that it is on our own soil that the only genuine possibilities for the future of American art ultimately lie.[49]

Without Archibald's requested financial support Sessions would never have experienced one of the pivotal periods of his life, the European years and the subject of this chapter.

FLORENCE

Jean Binet was ecstatic that the Sessionses were coming to Europe in 1925. He had already dedicated, in December 1924, a work to Barbara and Roger Sessions: "Inconstant Lovers, Words by William Shakespeare, Music by Jean Binet, for Voice and String Quartett."[1] The title alone suggests very strongly that he knew of Sessions's infidelities.

The first year in Florence the Sessionses lived on 25 Via dei Bardi, at the edge of the Ponte Vecchio, subsequently destroyed during the Second World War. The Germans had destroyed all the bridges across the Arno except the Ponte Vecchio. Sessions remembered the Italian attitude was "Those pigs! They think the Ponte Vecchio was really the most beautiful bridge. Of course, we Florentines all know that Ponte Santa Trinità was much more beautiful, but it didn't have all these little shops on it."[2] Instead of destroying the Ponte Vecchio, the Germans bombed the streets just at its entrance, the Via dei Bardi and the Borgo San Jacopo, to make it difficult to cross. Both streets were rebuilt. Eventually, the Germans blew up the Ponte Santa Trinità, which was rebuilt using the original stones. Sessions felt that the square at the Palazzo Vecchio, where a replica of Michelangelo's David stands, is—he repeated this—"The most wonderful place in the world."[3] He drank many a vermouth looking up at the Palazzo Vecchio.

Sessions knew two of Berenson's sisters, Senda and Bessie, from childhood and from Smith College. Senda had married Herbert Abbott, whose prominent Connecticut family knew the Huntingtons of Forty Acres. Mary Berenson's sister, Alys, had married Bertrand Russell. Both sisters had already introduced Sessions to Berenson.[4] Sessions may have known of Berenson through other sources as well. Berenson had been editor of *The Harvard Monthly* before Sessions came to Harvard (and published in the *Monthly*). Isabella Stewart Gardner, for whom Sessions had played, was a beneficiary of Berenson's authentication of Renaissance art works, as were Charles L. Freer in Chicago, Henry Frick in New York, Henry Walters in Baltimore, and Baron Edmond de Rothschild of Paris.

Berenson had lived in the Villa I Tatti since 1900, when his sister Senda found and leased it. A rural villa that dated from the sixteenth century, I Tatti was in the valley of the Mensola riverlet southeast of San Domenico below the village of Settignano, in whose postal boundary it fell. A previous owner had dammed up the Mensola and created a tiny lake, known as the Laghetto, in a grotto. About five hundred feet above I Tatti on the crest of a hill arose the enormous Castle of Vincigliata. Within the villa's entrance gate stood a stone chapel used by earlier inhabitants. There were also solid stone outbuildings, a stable, and plastered houses for the farm workers. Eventually the estate included 70 acres. Berenson brought a player piano with a supply of piano rolls of Bach's music. Of the many paintings that decorated I Tatti bought by Bernard and Mary

Berenson was an altarpiece for the Church of San Francesco at Borgo San Sepolcro painted by the Sienese master Sassetta. I Tatti became a repository for both art and art lovers.

Guests could stay at his estate's villinos as long as they did not disturb Berenson's work. Sessions had loved Florence so much that his ideal future, expressed to his father, was to return there. Since Berenson's death, Harvard University has owned the property, known as the Harvard University Center for Italian Renaissance Studies.

When Barbara arrived in Florence, Mary Berenson let the couple live in the Villino Corbignano, recently vacated by Kenneth Clark. The Sessionses lived there on and off for two years, that is from 1926 until the end of 1927. (Sessions came back to the United States, leaving on December 27, 1927, for six months in the first half of 1928.) Berenson had numerous guests, and art students such as Barbara were given the complete freedom of his library. In 1926 Senda and her husband Herbert were guests in the villino. During that winter other guests whom Sessions met included Walter Lippmann, Ruth Draper, Kenneth Clark, Hutchins Hapgood, Umberto Morra, Robert Trevelyan, Carlo Placci, Alberto Moravia, and Cyril Connolly. One of the people who visited and lived with them for a month or more was Lucienne Bloch. Needless to say Lucienne had a wonderful time.[5] Mary Berenson was having the nearby clock tower rebuilt during their first-year stay.

When Sessions stayed with the Berensons, "People asked, why? Berenson told them 'because I like talking to him.' "[6] According to Berenson's biographer, life for the art critic was

most intensely lived in talk, in the friendly duello of words across the tablecloth

Figure 27 Villino Corbignano in Settignano where Sessions and his wife lived in the mid-1920s on Bernard Berenson's estate I Tatti (courtesy of Martin Brody).

or in the circle about the fireplace, in the art of conversation, of which Berenson was a master. . . . They shared allusions as if they were all partners in an intellectual joint-stock company. If they were writers like Berenson, it was thus they tested their insights on a jury of their peers. Such talk became an established ritual at I Tatti, and Berenson would preside like a latter-day Dr Johnson.[7]

Berenson's answer regarding Sessions makes perfect sense to those many who have conversed with the composer. *Simpatico* (as the Italians say), fluent in languages, erudite, witty, never showing annoyance or anger, warm, lovable (in Ruth's words), wise, and friendly, Sessions struck almost everyone he met as someone worth speaking with. His lifelong ability to make and keep friends has already been remarked on. Bernard Berenson's generosity to Sessions is a further example.

While Sessions was living in Settignano, Luigi Dallapiccola was pursuing his education at the conservatory in Florence. In the same region at the same time, they did not meet, an age difference and their social circles keeping them apart.

In 1926 Sessions applied again for a Guggenheim. His references were Ernest Bloch, Nadia Boulanger, Paul Rosenfeld, Douglas Moore, Roy Welch, and Carl Engel. Sessions received the first of his two successive Guggenheims in 1926; Copland's $2,500 fellowship was renewed that year, and Leopold Damrosch Mannes also won a fellowship in the same competition. (Mannes and Moore had been awarded Pulitzer scholarships for composition of $1,500 in 1925.) When Sessions applied for a renewal for the following year, 1927, he did not name Serge Koussevitzky as a recommender; however, Henry Allen Moe, the chief executive of the Foundation, wrote to Koussevitzky for an opinion. Bloch responded generously to the news of Sessions's Guggenheim. He reflected, however, "I am a romantic fossil lost amidst this epoch that I do not understand, that I do not like, and . . . do not envy."[8]

At Harvard, in 1913 or 1914, Sessions had heard Charles Martin Loeffler's *A Pagan Poem*, based on a poem by Virgil. A review stated that the poem was not as good as a similar poem by Theocritus. Sessions, intrigued with the idea of the original story, bought a copy in Greek, but his Greek was not good enough to translate it at the time (he later read it in Greek). When he found an English translation, written in the 1870s, he was disappointed by the tameness of the love scenes. While waiting for a plane to take him from New York to California in 1952, he found a collection of Greek poetry at a bookstand. The translator was his old friend from the days at I Tatti, Robert Trevelyan. Sessions was "bowled over by it," and thought he had to set the entire poem to music. The result was the *Idyll of Theocritus*, almost 50 minutes long, composed in 1954.

Sessions wrote to Copland in 1932 on the subject of critics:

> I have always noticed, with Berenson, for instance, his tireless seeking to find some new light on the real nature of the painter's, or the musician's real activity, + have discussed the thing with him a hundred times, his attitude always being "You have nothing to learn from me, but I can learn always from you"—that, I mean, with every "creative" artist with whom I have ever seen him.[9]

Two factors interfered with Sessions's desire to remain in Florence in 1925. First, Barbara had received the $500 from Mrs MacBride to do work in art history in Paris. That arrangement was part of the financial backing the two needed to live abroad. Barbara left Florence after a month to go to Paris to study at the Sorbonne; she concentrated on the artist Paolo Uccello. Barbara, as any art historian would do, fell in love with Paris and did not want to leave. It was, after all, Paris in the 1920s: exciting, new, filled with artistic celebrities in all fields—Picasso, Matisse, Diaghilev's Ballets Russes, Cocteau, Gertrude Stein, Nadia Boulanger, and many more. There were no other composers at I Tatti and no concert life as there was in Paris. The leading composers in Paris were Ravel and Roussel, as well as Les Six: Georges Auric, Louis Durey, Arthur Honegger, Darius Milhaud, Francis Poulenc, and Germaine Tailleferre. It is more than understandable that Barbara, having spent four years in Cleveland, would want, on her first trip to Europe, to stay in Paris, not only for the city's own sake, but out of the duty to her fellowship. The next year her sister Eleanor married a French flutist, Jan Merry: she would remain in Paris most of her life.

Referring to Barbara, Sessions once told this author, "Paris in the 1920s was a heady place for a young woman." Her recalcitrant husband insisted on moving to Italy, away from the art and music capital of the world. His decision to leave her in Paris would have serious repercussions. Barbara, whose husband had been unfaithful to her, was romantically involved with another art historian and became pregnant. Sessions urged her by letter to have the baby, which was, he thought, very probably not his. By the time he reached Paris, however, she had had an abortion in late May 1926. The operation had not gone well; she became infected, required hospitalization, and would never be able to have children. In this author's opinion, Nadia Boulanger and Copland, as well as the Binets, knew of this situation while it was happening. Boulanger became quite attached to Barbara. Barbara wrote to her: "Your kind messages of sympathy + encouragement have meant so much to me that I can't leave Paris without thanking you for them—and also for other things of which it is more difficult to speak."[10] Telling Copland, "there aren't too many people with whom [I] can talk," Sessions, discussing Barbara's health, wrote "The summer has been pretty well upset, + I have a been a good deal under a strain since the end of May with all this on my mind."[11]

After Sessions's first year on the Guggenheim Fellowship, 1926–1927, the Foundation Report wrote up his activities (which it did not for the renewal, 1927–1928). He had submitted the "plans for a work including an opera, *The Fall of the House of Usher*, and a symphony—both in process of composition." The tenure was twelve months starting from September 1, 1926. The list of compositions he reported to the Guggenheim was: "Music for Andreyeff's drama, *The Black Maskers*, 1923, performed at Smith College; incidental music for Vollmüller's *Turandot*; three Choral Preludes, for organ; several small works for piano, and a string quartet."[12] Only two of the Choral Preludes and the First Symphony were written during the year's fellowship. *Turandot*, as well as the withdrawn string quartet, had already been performed in Cleveland. The "several small works for piano" seem to have disappeared.

Sessions returned to the United States for the premiere by the Boston Symphony of his First Symphony in April 1927 (see section "Symphony No. 1"). After that, he stayed in the country for several months. Ruth returned to Europe with Sessions; Barbara was ill in a hospital in Switzerland. Ruth and Sessions first went to Paris, then to visit Barbara in Switzerland, and subsequently to Vienna and Venice. In June Sessions left Ruth in Venice after one day and returned to Florence to see his wife. The couple spent most of the next summer of 1928 in Juziers, outside Paris, as well as ten days in the Swiss Alps.

The musical politics of Paris and the Boulangerie were as nothing compared with the genuine political situation of the day. Germany was living under the short-lived and vastly creative Weimar Republic. In 1922 the Fascists had gotten control of the government of Rome. Berenson, both a Jew and a foreigner, had doubts about Mussolini's claims. He did not keep a low profile: his friend Gaetano Salvemini, an historian and anti-Fascist, "was arrested in Rome and incarcerated in the Florence prison. Two thousand Italian scholars and writers published a protest in Turin and letters of protest poured in from abroad."[13] After a scheme to lend Berenson's passport to Salvemini came to naught (the two looked superficially alike), Berenson's position was more difficult. Salvemini was released (and ended up teaching at Harvard), nevertheless Berenson asked the American vice consul, Henry Coster, to stay at I Tatti and protect the estate while he went to Sicily in 1927. That year, too, talks were begun with Harvard to give the estate to the University on Berenson's death. Berenson was almost alone among his circle in holding these negative views of the Fascists: his neighbor Edith Wharton reported that her Paris friends were all Fascists, like those of similar income in the United States. Il Duce, evidently, appealed to the wealthy.

Berenson made his anti-government views known at dinners. Sessions knew that mail could be opened and read, and therefore waited until he could mail Ruth a long letter from Belgium. He gave her one view of the leader.

> I said I would write something about Italian politics, and this is difficult because my own feelings are so complex and so really conflicting that I find it hard to unravel them. It is in no sense an easy situation to judge, especially as it depends as much on the character of one man who is all the time being subjected to tests and temptations of the most difficult kind; and of course the future only can tell how he will ultimately meet them. . . .
>
> They apparently expect other nations to give their colonies for an outlet of their surplus population; and at the same time have passed laws taxing bachelors very heavily, and abolishing the spread of birth control information—in other words, forcing as great an increase of population as possible. Finally—and this goes most against the grain for me—they are trying more and more to control education and thought, in a way that has actually alienated the most intelligent spirits—at least the ones I know—and that will in the end, if it goes much further, make of the Italians a race of parrots.
>
> That of course is one side. The other is Mussolini's personal influence in not only introducing *discipline* but in being a really intelligent factor. The latter he certainly is; and one appreciates the value of these things which are far more important in a *poor* country like Italy than in a rich one like England or Germany or above all the United States. The last thing I balk at, I doubt if it is possible to build a new order without using what was best in the old; and the fact that so many of the highest types of Italian—[the philosopher] Benedetto Croce for example—are all but persecuted by the Fascists, makes me pause very long before regarding the good they have done as completely compensatory. . . .
>
> Don't in any case answer the part about Italian politics. I don't mean that it would be really dangerous; but it is much wiser for foreigners living in Italy to keep mouths tight shut.[14]

While in Rome Sessions had an opportunity to hear the dictator speak. In a letter whose date is difficult to determine (it is a fragment), he wrote to his mother:

> I must tell you about Mussolini. It was an extraordinary experience; I was so intent while he was there in the hall that I didn't realize till after he had left the hall, what a really strong and deep impression he had made on me. I felt, first of

all, enormous power, extraordinarily perfectly directed, and used at each movement with the utmost economy . . . His whole being is of the utmost simplicity; of the fierce expression of certain photographs there isn't a trace, as everyone agrees who has even seen or talked with him. Several times, over his face came the most [illegible] and winning smile that I have ever seen. Not a trace of vanity in his bearing or his face, and at the same time enormous pride and consciousness of power. An impression of inner solitude, of absolute self-reliance—the man who accepts all responsibilities and assumes even great ones—I cannot tell you how enormous was my impression.[15]

"Simplicity" was one of the highest compliments a New Englander such as Sessions could pay. From a performance perspective, he could appreciate great oratory. On the other hand, one political development should have disturbed him. The Lateran Treaty between the Vatican's Pope Pius XI and Mussolini's Fascist government was negotiated in 1929. Both Pope Pius, the successor to Benedict XV, and Mussolini had come to power in Rome in 1922. Benedict's support for the Christian Workers Party was withdrawn; its leaders exiled or jailed. The Christian Democrats, another political party, also fared badly, as did the Christian Socialists, considered no different from Marxists. Under the Treaty the Pope gave his blessing to Mussolini as ruler of an officially acknowledged Catholic Italy, and, he said, "gave Italy back to God," while Mussolini gave the Pope sovereignty of the Vatican's 44 hectares and declared the Pope "a good Italian." Sessions did not write about this conflation of religion and politics, but considering his oft-stated religious position as "crypto-Catholic," here he could easily have found discomfort in both his religious and his political views.

Back in the United States, Herbert Hoover had been elected in 1928 and became president in March 1929. About this event Sessions wrote to his mother, "Public affairs seem to be in a thriving state, just now—I suppose [brother-in-law] Paul is very happy that Hoover is at last really president; and I can't be seriously depressed, in spite of Berenson's rather apt remark that Hoover's election was essentially 'the victory of the "stick-in-the-muds" '!"[16]

Once in safer Switzerland, staying at Chalet Favre-Pernet in Vaud, in July, August, and September of 1929, after living at the American Academy in Rome for almost a year, Sessions wrote to his mother at length about his political views.

Rome, has quite thoroughly changed my impressions of Fascism. The atmosphere there is much *tenser* than in Florence. . . . Rome, however is quite different + I have to confess that I found that my impressions of the whole thing had been mistaken in certain important respects. It is not that the *theory* on which Fascism is based disturbs me any more than it ever did; I mean that I can accept dictatorship + even admit that it is necessary under certain circumstances. It is rather what Fascism is in the Italian spirit that I find intolerable. Rome, intellectually, I find stuffy, narrow, + provincial to the last degree. . . . And the musical world of Rome is full of men who are using the regime to further their own interests . . . that artistic values are wholly destroyed in a mass of nationalistic propaganda, undiscriminating praise for everything Italian. . . . You see I can admit even nationalism when it means a legitimate pride in the nation's achievements; but when it consists in an extravagant claim for *everything* produced by one's own people, a rather childish vanity about the most everyday things, and in frowning on all criticism, no matter how sincere + well-intentioned, even from one's own fellow countrymen, I find it intolerable + actually destructive of all that makes for real + solid development.

At all events, after a year in Rome, I am convinced that it is not idealism of any kind that is at its root, and that its benefits to the Italian people are largely material ones. About Mussolini too I have changed. Undoubtedly he is an interesting person + a powerful one; but "greatness" is a *big* word, and especially after the Concordat with the Vatican I have felt less + less inclined to use it on him. . . . Not only did Mussolini make two vulgar, clumsy + irreverent speeches on the occasion of the ratification of the treaties, but he suffered a real diplomatic defeat in so doing. The Holy See, I am afraid, is not so easily outwitted, and one has to be pretty clever in order to escape defeat at its hand, once he begins to raise issues and [secretary of state Cardinal Pietro] Gasparri knew how to make the most of Benito's blunders. . . .

P.S. Naturally it would not do if it were too generally known that any American felt this way—also I still have as little sympathy as ever for the *Lateran!* + still believe the more violent enemies of Fascism are a pretty bad lot.[17]

From a musical point of view, Mussolini had a great influence. Il Duce claimed a godlike omniscience in music. Rome's main opera house, Teatro Costanzi, was nationalized, while the venerable Augusteo, a concert hall built atop the tomb of Augustus, was torn down and not replaced. Bernadino Molinari conducted the Rome orchestra from 1912 to 1943. Influential Italian composers during this period were called *la generazione dell'ottanta*, the generation of the eighties. They comprised conservative composers born between 1875 and 1885: Casella, Malipiero, Pizzetti, Respighi, Franco Alfaro, and Riccardo Zandonai. In early September 1930 the first Venice Festival was held in combination with the Biennale. Casella was the vice-president and Labroca and Malipiero were on the executive committee. The Schoenbergians were excluded.

SYMPHONY NO. 1

Sessions had tried three times to write a First Symphony: the Yale Symphonic Prelude was not completed, then withdrawn; another symphony begun in the early 1920s in Cleveland was also withdrawn. Originally a piano quintet, the third and newest effort had morphed into a symphony in Florence. The first movement of the Symphony in E Minor, Sessions's first catalogued symphony, was completed December 5, 1926; the second, January 3, 1927; the third was "the first big movement I had in which ideas came to me in Italy itself," was finished on January 31, 1927.[1] He burned the sketches.

Sesssions played the work in Paris for Boulanger, who thought the recapitulation in the first movement too long. After the work was performed, Sessions agreed and made cuts as well as other changes that Koussevitzky suggested. Sessions's later antipathy to Boulanger caused him to repress the memory of having given her the autograph score.[2]

The second movement was written rapidly. Sessions had received a telegram stating that his father was seriously ill. He wrote quickly through a night, obsessed by the irrational thought that when he finished the movement, he would receive another telegram saying that his father was better. The next telegram, however, contained the news the Archibald Sessions had died, January 5, 1927, a week shy of his sixty-seventh birthday. Sessions then dedicated the symphony "to my father." For the second time a symphonic work of his was indelibly associated with the death of a loved one.

The composer, who had days earlier turned 30, had no one in Florence with whom to share his grief; Barbara was in Paris. The only surviving letter in which Sessions mentions his father's death to someone outside his family was to Copland. On February 25 he confided,

> The one really dark moment of the winter came with the death of my father early in January, he was the member of my family whom I cared the most for, + with whom I had the most in common; and the loss is a very great one indeed—and for Barbara too, since she adored my father and he her. I am comforted in some measure by really wonderful memories, and the consciousness of his influence, which was of a kind that will be with me as long as I live.[3]

These memories could have been a comfort only "in some measure," since, because of Ruth's leaving Archibald, Sessions had not spent the normal amount of time with his father that a child and young man ordinarily would. Copland responded to the remainder of this letter neither expressing condolences nor mentioning Sessions's loss.[4] To someone whose first preserved letter outside his family, written at 13, was one of condolence—to Father Sill upon losing his father—Sessions had to be somewhat taken aback by Copland's seeming lack of both sympathy and social etiquette.[5] He never mentioned his father again, however, and continued to confide in Copland.

Copland had recommended that Koussevitzky perform Sessions's symphony. As was typical of Sessions, he was late getting the score and parts to the Boston Symphony. (At one point he used Barbara's illness as an excuse.) Although the Symphony was promised to Koussevitzky for the first week in January, he did not complete the last two movements until that month.

Sessions left Florence for Paris to see Barbara and doubtless to commiserate over Archibald's death. The same spring of 1927 Sessions's sister-in-law was married in Paris. Eleanor Foster married flutist Jan Merry (Cohu), and Sessions gave the bride away. He also gave Merry a solo flute piece, Pastorale, perhaps a wedding present; the piece is now lost. On February 10 he sent his mother a letter to Boston that dealt with Italian politics, Berenson, Boulanger, and the symphony.

> While I was in Paris I played the Symphony to Nadia Boulanger, who was tremendously enthusiastic. She said it was not only a very beautiful but a very important work—the first work showing the Stravinsky influence which is at the same time absolutely personal and individual—and later she told her mother and some guests who were there that it was *"une oeuvre tout à fait remarquable"* . . . I can assure you that it is an infinitely finer, more beautiful and more human work than *Black Maskers* . . . Bloch will like it less well; it is less picturesque and less superficially striking; but it is *solid* both in its structure and in the fresh and perfectly authentic impulses which lie beneath the surface; and while, as I grow older, I shall doubtless write more perfect works—more easy and finished, I shall never write one that is more genuine or more truly spontaneous, in every movement.[6]

Sessions did not relay Boulanger's reservations. In any case, Ruth would hear the symphony for herself. She, Rosamond Foster, and other family members attended the April 22 premiere in Boston. Barbara had stayed in Europe for two reasons: she was still ill, and the Sessionses could not have afforded her boat fare. Sessions was in the US from March 15 through April 30. Copland traveled with him by boat back to Europe. It was Copland who secured the publication of the work, by Cos Cob press in 1929. The excitement of Sessions's debut at his beloved Boston Symphony was dampened by the fact that he saw his family for the first time after Archibald's death and visited his father's grave. The one person who had made the symphony possible, Archibald, never heard any of his son's work performed by a major orchestra.

Another audience member, Elliott Carter, a teenager who would not meet Sessions until 1964, was "immensely struck. . . . I followed his work from then on, going to concerts where his music was performed, collecting scores and reading articles with consuming interest."[7] Carter was "always deeply impressed by his integrity as a man and musician." He wrote, "Slowly over the years he has developed his own style. His development has been by conquest and mastery of the whole art rather than by the cultivation of personal mannerism." Carter continued, "Indeed Roger can perhaps be considered one of the very last composers to have formed his outlook in the pre-first-world-war time and to have held to the standards of that period—as did Stravinsky, Bartók, and Schoenberg."[8] Carter was influenced by this Sessions work in writing his own First Symphony in 1942.

After the symphony was performed, Sessions made the changes Boulanger and

Figure 28 Igor Stravinsky and Roger Sessions.

Koussevitzky had recommended, mostly in the first movement.[9] The only two versions of the symphony that exist in Sessions's hand are the first two movements in piano score in ink and an orchestral score of the entire symphony in pencil. (The manuscripts come to us from Boulanger; Boulanger's gift to Harvard will be discussed in the section "Boulanger and Copland.") The penciled orchestration is marked in red and blue. Those marks represent Sessions's drafts toward a re-barring of spots which he, or Boulanger, or Koussevitzky (who was notoriously challenged by works with constantly changing beat-patterns) considered needlessly complex. Just before rehearsal number 77 in the last movement, for example, the pencil orchestration has three measures—5/8, 2/4, and 5/8. In the published version these are rebarred as two measures of 7/8, easier for conductor and players. At rehearsal 80 two bars of 3/8 become one bar of 6/8. In addition 5/8 and 2/8 are frequently combined to make 7/8. These shorter groupings are found in the *Sacre* and *L'Histoire du Soldat*—where they were also a bad idea. Doubtless Sessions was influenced by Stravinsky, nevertheless all the red penciled corrections appear in the score published by Cos Cob.

The orchestral score expands the music of the piano score in the first movement; however, some of that new music was later cut (writing this work taught Sessions to trust his first instincts). A total of 23 bars was removed.[10] Some music was written later and added on the advice of Boulanger and Koussevitzky.[11] Twenty-four bars are crossed out in the orchestral manuscript and 15 new bars were composed on Koussevitzky's advice.[12]

A transposition up occurs four bars after no. 21 until one bar after 22 in the published score; the original piano version had those eight bars down a perfect fourth. In the recapitulation it is transposed back down. Some of the movement markings and metronome markings were altered between the orchestral manuscript and the published version. The first movement in the manuscript reads quarter note equals 116 to 120 (rather than the 116 in the published version). At no. 28, we find *Doppio movimento, un poco più tranquillo*, but both the early piano and the orchestral versions read *Con espressivo non esagerata, e senza rilasciare affatto il tempo giusto* ("with not exaggerated expression, and without quite releasing the strict tempo"). The *senza rallentando* the measure before no. 38 was added later. The second movement, "Largo," was originally marked eighth note equals 40 to 44, but for the published version he changed it to eighth equals 52. The third movement was also sped up between the manuscripts and the published version: a quarter note equaled 126 in the manuscripts, but appears as 138 in the Cos Cob edition.

Not only was Stravinsky's Neo-Classicism prevalent in the 1920s, but American jazz also permeated the musical air. Asked whether he thought of jazz in composing the Symphony in E Minor, Sessions responded,

> I never thought consciously in terms of jazz. Naturally I heard a lot of it, and I feel that both in this [first] movement and the last movement, there is a certain trace of jazz. And curiously enough, when people hear this work nowadays, it's that that strikes them more than any relation to Stravinsky. Ragtime became jazz just about the same time as I was writing the symphony. Jazz was something very, very new. It was a new word. I think that they just suddenly began calling it jazz, that's all. I think (this isn't anything beyond a guess) that when people began to be a little self-conscious about syncopation and that sort of thing, that they began calling it something special. Jazz, actually. For instance there was a piece, a popular piece, it was just a c-major scale, but played . . . they called it "Ragging the Scale."[13] That was a late precursor, or early example of jazz. That was in the twenties sometime. . . . When I came back from Europe in 1933, I felt that the popular music that I was hearing all sounded like Ravel. Of course jazz and ragtime have influenced European composers. Milhaud [wrote] *La Création du Monde*. It was ragtime rather than jazz. And Stravinsky wrote Piano Rag Music and Ragtime [both 1919] in the 'teens.[14]

The Boston Symphony Orchestra, having just completed a three-concert series in March devoted to the centenary of Beethoven's death, premiered the Symphony in E Minor April 22, 23, and 26, 1927, under Koussevitzky. To add to the composer's nervousness, it was announced in New York papers that WJZ, WBZ, WBZA, and KDKA radio stations would broadcast the performance live. Four Boston papers reviewed the work. *The Boston Evening Transcript*'s H. T. Parker came to the performance twice and wrote two reviews, the second more positive than the first. The audience also received the second performance better than the first. Parker began, "In Roger Sessions Mr Koussevitzky has discovered a notable composer." He reviewed the composer's program notes as well as the piece: "For, by rare exception in his calling, he has the gift of words as well as tones." Later he wrote that the symphony "teemed with rhythmic life, because it was in incessant, vibrant, irresistible motion; because it stripped music to the quick as a logical pattern of sound in movement; because it was directed by mental power and technical resources into concentrated mental impressions. . . . He writes a music from the mind to the mind by rhythms propelled."

In the second review Parker noted that Sessions "had overcome the nervous embarrassment of Friday." Little had he known that on Friday, Sessions, nervousness overwhelming him, had thrown up backstage before being led on to take his bows. In addition, Saturday's performance produced neither the previous night's hisses from the audience nor a prodding for applause. Parker felt "the sonata form had received a new lease on life, born of an American spirit. The first movement bears not a mark of nationality." And "The Finale, in particular, gained in gusto of gayety. The vigorous rhythms, the forthright instrumental phrases, the exuberance and the exhilaration of the musical progress carried all before them. . . . The Finale, however, teems with the robustious, rolicking, devil-may-care gayety [attributable] to the American temperament, masculine and on a spree." In the same breath, he mentioned Copland, whose Piano Concerto had recently caused an uproar in Boston, reporting that intermission gossip had them born on the opposite ends of the same Brooklyn street. In Parker's opinion, the First Symphony was "a work of close mental concentration, no small inventive power and keen command of orchestral technique."[15]

Paul Rosenfeld, who had already championed *The Black Maskers*, was almost as enthusiastic about the E minor Symphony. Writing in the *Boston Globe* an article whose sub-headline read "Roger Huntington Sessions notable composer," Rosenfeld described the work as "showing notable talent and not a little promise." He continued,

> Rhythmic polyphony, reinforced by polytonal or atonal harmonic effects, with a continual flow of interweaving strands of melody devoid of points of repose except at the end of movements, characterize Mr Sessions' style. The slow movement, much of which has remarkable beauty and nobility, proves Mr Sessions' native feeling for harmony to be at least as strong as his rhythmic impulses. Ideas and expression are here felicitously blended. The first and last movements are based on salient and individual ideas. The working out is skillful, yet not devoid of spontaneity of effect.

He noted the orchestration: "Mr Sessions seemingly is convinced that there are too many strings in the usual orchestra, and that composers habitually give them too much to do." He pointed to the use of the piano in the percussion section and stated, "The wood winds are his mainstay."[16] Rosenfeld called for a repetition of the symphony on future concerts; however, as was the case with the Third Symphony commissioned much later by the Boston Symphony, the Orchestra never played either work again.

"There are in this symphony jazzy sounds as well as jazzy rhythms," *The Christian Science Monitor* wrote, "but one does not feel, as one did, for example, with Mr Copland's Concerto, that they are inserted to satisfy a demand for jazz in the concert hall. Rather, they seem to be incidents of an elaborate, contrapuntally rhythmic musical scheme, which is perhaps a natural product of an anti-romantic period." Noting that "Mr Sessions, though of excellent stock, may well be a dangerous fellow," because Chadwick's Ballade "Tam O'Shanter" was "affectionately greeted" (Chadwick was present) while Sessions's music hissed. The author reminded the reader that Strauss had been hissed in Boston the previous generation.[17]

One periodical interviewed the composer. Here Sessions contradicted his own program notes and felt the Bloch's influence was almost wholly lacking. "Sufficient it is that he uses syncopations in a manner in which no one before Gershwin, Berlin and Copland . . . could have done."[18]

Philip Hale in *The Boston Herald* had reservations about the first movement only, which he felt had "no regard for the orthodox sonata form. . . . It is in this movement, which we wish Mr Sessions would rewrite, that we find the influence of Stravinsky in his more mechanical movements." The two subsequent movements were, however, "where uncommon musical ideas are expressed in an uncommon manner; there is an ingenuity in the instrumentation [in the second movement] not so observable in the other movements. The frenzy of the finale is not distasteful: on the contrary here Mr Sessions writes with gusto; also in demoniacal vein."[19]

Six reviews were published in Boston. All but one praised the work; Hale's negative remarks were confined to the first movement. Nevertheless only the negative comments from the Hale review were picked up and repeated at length in *The New York Times* May 1 report, which identified the composer as "Robert Sessions." "Mr Hale found the first movement of questionable value;" the anonymous reporter summarized, then quoted longer passages. Only in the last paragraph did he admit that "The press as a whole was favorable and encouraging to the composer." Calling H. T. Parker "the doughty reviewer of the Transcript," the article closed by misquoting him.[20]

For the first time, but not the last by far, the *Times* seems to have set its mind against Sessions. Not only did it report only the negative portions of one Boston review, but it would also do so again with the bad European reviews of the same symphony performed in Geneva, conducted by Ernest Ansermet in 1929. In an effort at damage control with his mother, Sessions wrote to her about the *Times*'s translation of those French reviews: "The translator changed it in just such a way as to turn it from a really rather good thing, to which I in no way could take exception, into a slightly condescending—and I must add, at the same time rather stupid one."[21] When the Philadelphia Orchestra under Alexander Smallens gave the symphony in December 1935, the *Times*'s coverage consisted of two paragraphs describing only the boos and the fact that audience members walked out.[22] The *Times* had not sent its own reviewer and misquoted or mistranslated only the negative remarks of other reviewers—all this for three separate performances of the same piece. (If Sessions were prone to the composer's occupational hazard—that is, feelings of persecution—he might in this case have had cause.)

The April 6, 1929, Geneva performance at the International Society for Contemporary Music in Victoria Hall was conducted, as mentioned above, by Ansermet. Sessions traveled to Geneva for the performance at the seventh meeting of the ISCM, arriving April 5, only one day before the concert and in not enough time to hear rehearsals. The performance also suffered from being moved to first on the festival, by a not-so-good orchestra, and from three parochial Geneva critics who lambasted the new music. The *Journal de Genève* wrote, "The Symphony No. 1 by Mr Roger Sessions is of such musical poverty that no one could have failed to notice . . . The work is completely lacking in unity, and each of the three movements has its own style, if I may dare to call it that."[23] The *Courier de Genève* read "The Largo was the best part, truly grand as it expressed, tastefully and calmly, much sadness and suffering. . . . The first movement is monotonous in spite of some outbursts in the winds. . . . The last movement opens with a lively and gay theme in the flute. The whole lacks cohesion, and one could wish that its vivacity would stretch from beginning to end without the padding."[24] The *Tribune de Genève* outdid the other two. Naming all of the individuals on the ISCM jury, it asked, "For what reasons did the jury accept this work which does not allow the slightest glimpse of an interesting personality."[25] Sessions wrote his mother that three of the orchestra members took pains to apologize for their city.[26]

Otto Klemperer had told Sessions "he wouldn't dare conduct it." Sessions felt the performance in Geneva was excellent, but Ansermet was having a hard time, because "at that time it was a very difficult work. A very difficult work. I asked Ansermet if there was anything I could do to make it easier and he said, 'No, no. You can't simplify the truth.'"[27] One notable critic from outside Geneva, H. H. Stuckenschmidt, said of the symphony "Roger Sessions is perhaps the most talented, yet the most crepuscular of [the composers represented.] His symphony . . . surprises one at times by its strokes of genius."[28]

Later that month Sessions wrote to Copland,

Ansermet played it splendidly, as I say. I was delighted with the way the first movement, above all, went; delighted because for the first time I felt thoroughly happy about it, and convinced that it *could* sound as I wanted it to and even better! The rhythms were alive and always *pushing ahead*; and at the same time Ansermet kept the men splendidly in hand, so that not for a moment did they hurry or drag, as they always tend to do in that movement. The other movements suffered a little because the Orchestre Romande of Geneva is not the Boston Symphony; especially one notices this in the tone quality. On the other hand Ansermet understood these, too, marvelously; and I also found him during the rehearsal much more responsive to my suggestions than S. K. had been.

. . . The symphony made a very satisfactory impression on *musicians*; all of those for whose enthusiasm I cared were *really* enthusiastic, and I made many new friends.[29]

In November 1944, on the first public concert by the Radio-diffusion Nationale in Paris after the expulsion of the Germany army, the work played was the American Roger Sessions's Symphony No. 1.

More than 20 years elapsed before the symphony received a New York performance. On November 4, 1949, the newly appointed conductor at the Juilliard School of Music, Jean Morel, gave the work with the school orchestra. *The New York Times* then reported,

Mr Sessions's composition is full of the excitement and tenderness of youth, expressed in the staggering variety of rhythms and tonal colors for which its period—and its composer—is noted. The brash patterns of the first movement, the suave, sustained brass sonorities in the second and the pagan humor of the third were once cause for wonder and resentment. Today these things are no longer shocking, but the music retains its vitality, and each movement is integrated in a flow of counterpoint that remains satisfying. The relation between movements, however, may be less convincing.[30]

The work has fared better in subsequent performances. Almost exactly 70 years after Sessions finished his First Symphony the New York Philharmonic programmed it for the first time as part of their new American Classics series. Neeme Järvi conducted the symphony in concerts on February 20, 21, 22, and 25, in 1997. The loyal Sessions symphony fan, Dennis Russell Davies, programmed the First with the American Composers Orchestra for January 11, 1998, in Carnegie Hall. The *New York Post* wrote, "The First Symphony is a happily bright piece of Americana, breezy, open, full of catchy, syncopated rhythms. Blindfolded, you would guess Copland."[31] *The New York Times* simply called it "brash, uncharacteristic and now more than 70 years old."[32] In September 2005 Leon Botstein conducted the American Symphony Orchestra in New York in a performance. The *Times* now saw the second movement as "anticipat[ing] Barber as well [as Copland]: the sumptuous string writing in the Largo edges toward the Barber Adagio, composed in 1936."[33]

The recording of the symphony took a long time, in this case over 30 years, to appear. Sessions's former student Eric Salzman wrote "Never too late" in 1960 announcing that fact.[34] Released later on CD, it remains the only recording of the highly accessible work. Unfortunately, it is not a good representation of the piece. Sessions said of it, "The recording of [the first movement] is much too fast, much too fast. It should be played not staccato, but tenuto by the brass. I was worried about that recording but it was made in Japan, and there was nothing I could do about it."[35] The metronome marking for the first movement is 116 to the quarter; the recording takes it at about quarter = 154.

The New Yorker's usually excellent Alex Ross gave a cursory preliminary examination of the Philharmonic's American symphony project.[36] While dealing with Copland, Harris, and Cowell, he neglected even to mention Sessions as a possible candidate for the Great American Symphonist. A *New York Times* Sunday article dealt with all nine composers played by the Philharmonic: Copland, Harris, Hanson, Randall Thompson, Piston, Barber, Ives, Schuman, and Sessions. The author described "Sessions's First is a Stravinskian romp with an American accent: Petrouchka at the hoe-down."[37] This quip upset the composer's daughter: this author was even more bothered by the omissions. All eight other composers were represented by photos (Ives the previous week), but there was none of Sessions. Much worse was the omission, in a sidebar called "On CD, Americans on Parade," of the massive performance and recording project of Sessions's symphonies undertaken by Dennis Russell Davies. At a minimum, mention should have been made of the previous year's release of Symphonies Nos. 6, 7, and 9 by the American Composers Orchestra on Decca. The author omitted Sessions—while acknowledging Hanson, Thompson, and Barber—as Fellows at the American Academy in Rome. While Sessions himself viewed *The New York Times* with irony and equanimity, his friends and relatives were not so generous. It seemed not to matter in which decade, or by which author, Sessions's music was treated; according to the newspaper of record his music was almost always seen as "knotty," "cerebral," or "academic." That tradition started in the 1920s with this review of the First Symphony. His consistently bad treatment by the *Times* became a standing joke in his circle. The composer used to kid that if he ever got a good review from the *Times*, he would start to worry about his music.

In Sessions's First Symphony the second movement has a long cantilena much like that of a Bach aria. (His Piano Sonata No. 1 opens with a similar gesture.) This interest in melody and the line of the whole work (*le grande ligne*) is a signature feature of Sessions's music from the beginning and is related to Wagner's "endless melody." Even though his First Symphony owes something to Stravinsky's *Petrouchka*, the piece cannot be dismissed as simply derivative. The uniqueness of Sessions's sense of line remains in the memory and separates him from the Russian master. (One Russian element, however, is the use of the piano in the orchestra.)

It is worthwhile to speculate about this influence of this work on other pieces in addition to the Carter work. For example, in the first movement the syncopated thirds in trombones accompanied by a raucous timpani are similar to patterns one hears later in Copland's *El Salon Mexico*. Given this symphony's memorable melodies and rhythmic energy, the fact that it is not played more often remains incomprehensible.

BOULANGER AND COPLAND

If it is written in places that I studied with Nadia Boulanger, it's not true.
I knew and saw her often; furthermore, when I first met her I thought I would
like to study with her, but I was very young and inexperienced and did not know
the rest of Europe then. I came to disapprove of Nadia. She was really a busi-
nesswoman, not a disinterested musician at all. Nadia was overworking for her
students. People don't realize it, but there were musicians who had nothing
to do with Nadia Boulanger. And she had some strange ideas about the U.S.
She thought it was a young, inexperienced country that did not know its way
around and should have a guardian, and that France should be its guide. I soon
discovered there were other countries in the world.[1]

Sessions's relationship with Nadia Boulanger, one of the most powerful women in music
in the twentieth century, began amicably, but was fraught with differences in view-
points. Like the CIM's Martha Sanders, Boulanger became a substitute for Ruth Sessions,
someone it was permissible for Sessions to dislike openly. Her promotion of her students' music flew in the face of his Rollandian belief that art must survive in the world
on its own. Suzanne Bloch, who studied with Nadia Boulanger at the time, felt that
Boulanger and Sessions "got along . . . Roger is very good at meeting people, [and an]
exchange of great minds."[2] When Suzanne married in Paris, Sessions and Boulanger
were the two witnesses. While philosophical and behavioral differences never affected
his friendship with Aaron Copland, Sessions found Mlle Boulanger less tolerant of such
differences.

Boulanger lived with her mother, Princess Raissa Mychetsky. Sessions's 15 and
Barbara's nine letters frequently asked after the health of Mme Boulanger. By the summer of 1926 Sessions had placed himself in a position with Boulanger familiar to his
friends: she had lent him 1,200 francs.

Along with Serge Koussevitzky, Boulanger had written, February 15, 1928, on behalf
of Sessions to the American Academy in Rome. Barbara wrote out and kept a copy of the
letter. Boulanger expressed an admiration for Sessions's music and character, and that his
admission to the American Academy in Rome would be a "great thing" both for him
and for the Academy. She cited the First Symphony as the cause for her view of Sessions.

Sessions kept the other of two letters from Boulanger in a file marked "Curiosities." It
can be dated to the period of the ISCM competition jury for the June 1933 Amsterdam
Festival at which Sessions was a judge. Much later Sessions mentioned this letter often,
flabbergasted that she had dictated to him whom to vote for in the competition. They
were mainly her students: Copland's Variations; the Neugeboren Trio; Marcelle de
Manziarly's Concerto; a quartet by the Swiss composer Schulé; the Dutch composer

Beers's Sonata; Lennox Berkeley's Sonata or songs; and anything by Jean Françaix. She also mentioned Igor Markevitch and Jean Cartan and underlined the word *worthy* three times, as well as one underline for "I count on you."[3]

The fact is that Sessions did study with Boulanger, seeking her advice and approval. He did not pay for lessons, however. Boulanger once generalized about her students in the third person, "There were three kinds of music students, the kind who had money and no talent, and those she took; the kind who had talent and no money, and those she took; and the kind who had money and talent and those she never got."[4] Sessions wrote Copland he was to study piano with Boulanger the summer of 1928.[5] Despite Sessions's later avowals that he did not study with Boulanger, the question can only be semantic. Perhaps he did not pay her for lessons because she knew he could not afford it (since she lent him money). Aside from an exchange of money, however, of what do composition lessons consist? Repeatedly showing the teacher one's music. Getting advice and taking that advice. Returning to the teacher with every major work: *Black Maskers*, Symphony in E Minor, three chorale preludes (for organ, her instrument), the Piano Sonata, and the Violin Concerto. Not only do we have letters—some already presented here—attesting to the fact that Sessions showed her his work, but he also gave her the manuscript of the First Symphony and inscribed to her copies of all of the pieces he wrote during the European period. Boulanger's collection came to Harvard University after her death. Many are signed: manuscripts of Chorale Preludes No. 2 and No. 3 and a photocopy of the first Chorale Prelude; the Cos Cob large edition of the Symphony in E Minor (inscribed "*À Mademoiselle Nadia Boulanger avec mes sentiments d'admiration et de profonde affection. Roger 21 Septembre 1929*"), plus the holograph manuscript; the Schott edition of the Piano Sonata ("To my dear friend Mlle Nadia Boulanger with deep affection Roger H. S.—Juziers, July 19, 1931"); the large score published by Cos Cob of the Orchestral Suite to *The Black Maskers* ("To Nadia Boulanger most affectionately Roger, Paris, September 24, 1932"); and the miniature score of the Violin Concerto published in Sessions's hand by The Edgar Stillman-Kelley Society ("To Nadia Boulanger, with all affection, Roger, January 1937").[6] Sessions was indeed a Boulanger pupil.

In old age neither Sessions nor Aaron Copland remembered when they were first introduced. The two had very likely met in the late teens: John Burk's letter mentioning getting "Copeland" a ticket to a BSO concert Sessions was also invited to seems to clinch it.[7] As we have already seen, by June 1923 Copland was being called upon to supply a cellist for the premiere of *The Black Maskers*. Copland had shown Sessions around Paris (see section "Summer of 1924"). He had already read Rosenfeld's *Dial* article on *The Black Maskers*.

On the surface Sessions and Copland would not seem personally suited to be close friends. Their many differences might seem to outweigh any similarities. While Sessions was born into one of the oldest American families and considered himself a "closet Catholic," Copland was the son of Jewish immigrants. Coincidentally, both were born on Washington Avenue in Brooklyn. Each had been born to parents late in life and relatively late in birth order (Sessions third of four and Copland fifth of five), each had a strong and adored older sister, and each first learned the piano from his mother. Two of Copland's siblings were musical, while John Sessions briefly considered a career as a singer. Their four-year age difference was to appear wider partly because of Sessions's educational head start. Copland did not attend college upon graduation from high school, but studied privately with Rubin Goldmark starting in 1917, whereas Sessions had obtained two degrees in music, from Harvard and Yale, by 1917. That fact, plus Sessions's premature physical aging and baldness, the baldness already apparent in 1920, could only have made him seem much older to Copland. Each was short and had large ears, and if one were forced to choose, one would judge that Sessions was slightly better looking—not much of a compliment since Copland was famously homely. Significantly for Sessions, Copland had read *Jean-Christophe*.

Whereas Copland was gregarious, open, and made friends easily, the essentially shy and reserved Sessions nevertheless shared his ability to make and keep friends. By all accounts Sessions was a complicated personality, while Copland's great gift was to be simple, so to speak. These personal characteristics would manifest themselves in their music.

Copland, completely un-neurotic, was goal-oriented, efficient, purposeful, and ambitious. Whatever faint ambition the highly nervous Sessions possessed had been undermined by his habit of dithering and a lifelong inability to meet deadlines. Sessions settled into teaching for decades, a career he took seriously, whereas the peripatetic Copland never obtained a permanent position and taught only in the summers at Tanglewood. Sessions became well known as a teacher, Copland as a conductor and for many other musical activities.

Both composers made very little money during the first several decades of their adulthood. Possibly Copland's parents, who ran a department store in Brooklyn, earned more than Archibald, who had tried to succeed as a fiction writer and playwright. Sessions earned very little and mishandled the money he did have, which forced him to borrow frequently. He never owned his own home, having always rented or lived in university housing. On the other hand, Copland was frugal. Only in his forties did Copland begin to make real money: his final house is now a retreat for composers. Copland's mother and father would die within the two years before Ruth's death.

At a deep level of identity, however, was their difference in sexuality, Copland being a confirmed homosexual while Sessions was—mostly—heterosexual. That meant that Copland remained single while Sessions married and had two children. Their sexuality, which might have distanced the two to some degree, was, surprisingly, one of their most personal points of connection. In a letter we do not inherit, Sessions apparently wrote something "glib" about homosexuality; Copland had recently come out to him. In an equally irretrievable letter Copland mildly chastised Sessions for his perceived lack of sympathy. The incident was a misunderstanding, and to clear it up Sessions confided in a November 29, 1929, letter to Copland information that he had not told anyone save Barbara and probably Father Sill.

> Thank you also for your particularly nice letter, + for answering mine so fully. How curious the whole incident was!—and how obvious its whole explanation! Of course, the truth of the matter is that I have always taken "sexual" problems in the *general* sense very lightly, though I have never taken my own experiences—however happy + free they have been—lightly at all. I have often shocked even people who consider themselves liberal through this fact. It may be for this reason that you found me flippant or as you say glib. What I mean to say that if I had found myself in your position—or indeed, at the time when I did find myself partly though of course not wholly in your position, it never was to me any more than a practical problem; and that it was for me simply something that I developed out of—something that, from causes which are as much a mystery to me as they could be to anyone, passed definitely out of my life with the death of a certain person nearly ten years ago, + which have never shown the least sign of coming into it again—for this reason especially I am glad that it is

no longer, as you say, a "problem" to you; for though it never would occur to me, from my own experience, that one must struggle to accept oneself in that way I believe I can imagine—both from your experiences + from that of some other friends, that it must be or have been a pretty difficult experience + I have indeed had enough difficulties in accepting myself in other ways to know what it can be. I don't remember citing experiences of my own, of that kind, to you in our conversations together (the "scandal" I referred to was of course, of another kind—when I spoke of it I still thought you were talking literally of your relations with women) but whether I did or not I might easily have done so. As for the postcard I imagine it was simply that I was hoping for a letter![8]

This reference to the unnamed George Bartlett, who had died eight and a half years earlier, would be Sessions's last recorded mention of him. (It is a remote possibility, but not outside the realm of the plausible, that Copland had met George in Boston.) Note, however, that Sessions expanded the time frame backward to a decade, placing George's death before his marriage. It should be taken as a sign of their extremely close friendship that Copland and Sessions could write and speak so freely of their personal sexual experiences and even "scandals." The letter also tells us that Sessions had developed out of that stage in his life. What remained of it, however, was a true sympathy for and understanding of his many gay students, who felt they could safely confide in him and not meet with judgmental scorn. As a favor to Copland, in 1934 Sessions gave Copland's lover, Victor Kraft, composition lessons for free.

The courses of Copland and Sessions's compositional development illuminate another contrast. Copland had developed what might be described as regularly, in that he began studying composition seriously at college age; developed rapidly in his twenties and thirties; produced masterpieces in the forties, fifties, and sixties; and retired from composing in his seventies, and died at 90. Sessions followed an irregular path of development. He started composing seriously at age twelve, produced almost no music in his teens and very little music in his twenties, thirties, and forties; and became most prolific during his fifties, sixties, seventies, and eighties. Sessions was writing music until his death at 88.

The crucial area in which they differed was in their music. Sessions's music was frequently described as "cerebral," or "academic," while many of Copland's pieces were considered "accessible" Americana. Both composers had begun, however, by being influenced by Expressionism: Sessions with *The Black Maskers* (1923) and Copland's *Grogh* (1922–1925). Each adapted the twelve-tone system, and Sessions became known as a prominent American representative of the Viennese system, a mistaken view. Copland incorporated jazz, which never appealed to Sessions for use in his music (in part because he had had too much respect for "folk song" as an indigenous art form to appropriate it).[9] Copland frequently wrote for the dance and for several movies, which Sessions never did. He preferred the European models of symphonies, concertos, and sonatas. Copland represented the apex of Nadia Boulanger's French approach, whereas Sessions was the foremost American representative of German formalism between the wars (despite his own view of himself expressed below).

A correspondence between them began in 1926 that lasted until the 1970s, but was concentrated in the decade 1926–1936: of the 107 extant letters between them fully 90 fall into this decade. We inherit only 17 letters by Copland, although there had been many more. A lopsidedness is also found in the content and style of the letters. Copland tried to get something accomplished or acquire information with each letter. Once he signed himself aptly, "Yours efficiently, Aaron." Sessions, on the other hand, took the writing of a letter as an occasion to philosophize in ways similar to his essays published in *Modern Music* at the time. His considerably longer letters are more literary than Copland's, but not much is accomplished in them.

These letters detail not only the inner workings of their important concert series, the Copland–Sessions Concerts, but also their opposed views on the notion of an American music. Sessions wrote in his first preserved letter to Copland (August 24, 1926) that "I can't pretend that I think I have risked your friendship in speaking so frankly," but

> you deserve hell, and worse, [for] your assumption of the title and, let us say, the obligations of a "New York composer," or even a "young American composer." You are quite aware, I know, that I feel a certain irony in regard to schools and groups, and, in music at least, a respect for individuals who stand by themselves in the most profound sense. And if I found your [Organ] symphony not only far bigger and more impressive, but in the real sense more *original* and more perfect than the Theatre-music, the nocturne, + the serenade, I feel that it is because the others are the result, or perhaps the expression of a *parti pris*, a deliberate attempt to mold your thought along lines which are not only *not* your own, but something far less than what you have in yourself. I mean that I find the music of Aaron Copland speaking for himself, incomparably finer that of Aaron Copland the New York Composer, quite aside from the pleasure and amusement that the latter gives me.[10]

Copland's admiration for Sessions's music was couched somewhat less polemically. Referring to Sessions's First Symphony, Copland wrote May 26, 1927: "But I must say that only since that week on the boat do I really seem to know you. And the reflection of the real you I find completely expressed in the second movement (one part of 'you' anyhow). I've played it over and over again and it seems to me more lovely and more profound each time."[11] (Sessions had also used the phrase "the real you.")

The genuine affection between the two is easily seen in these letters. Their many differences in personalities and careers also become readily apparent. It was Copland, with his ambition and savvy, who helped Sessions's career more than any other single person was to do, whereas Sessions could not aid Copland's career in any way. Copland, the first person to hold the Guggenheim Fellowship in music, had suggested in 1924 that Sessions apply for a Fellowship and live in Europe as he was then doing. Copland recommended Sessions to the head of the Guggenheim Foundation.

Copland also recommended Sessions as a writer for Minna Lederman's *Modern Music*. Sessions would write a series of articles for her periodical. Copland was even able to coax Mary Churchill and Lederman into giving Sessions money. He persuaded Serge Koussevitzky to commission and perform Sessions's First Symphony. Played by the Boston Symphony Orchestra in April 1927, it was Sessions's first important performance, and "launched me in the world" (see section "Symphony No. 1"). Barbara acknowledged Copland's importance to Sessions: "What would we do, Aaron, without your worldly wisdom—to say nothing of all the reasons we shall have for missing you far too much, that alone makes me tremble to think of putting an ocean between us."[12]

The most ambitious of Copland's schemes was his 1927 idea to form a society to play younger composers' music in New York. He enlisted Sessions to lend his name and support to the Copland–Sessions Concerts, which lasted from 1928 to 1931. Composers whose pieces were performed on the series included Delaney, Porter, Crawford, Weiss,

Rudhyar, Lopatnikoff, Cowell, Wagenaar, Blitzstein, Antheil, Lipsky, Dukelsky, Harris, McPhee, Milhaud, and Thomson.

The three-year Copland–Sessions Concerts connected these two composers in the public's mind. Yet each approached the concert series in his own distinct manner. In New York, Copland was eminently practical: he secured financial support, contracted for the halls, arranged the publicity, obtained the parts, recruited performers, and acted as host at the reception. Sessions and Barbara were living in Northampton and then in Rome at the American Academy during these years. He helped choose the pieces, but could not complete his own Piano Sonata in time for the first—or the second—concert. He vetoed suggested titles for the series, equivocated about certain choices of pieces, and did not appear at the concerts. The co-sponsors' friendship survived the many travails of long-distance concert presentation.

Sessions rejected the suggested title "Laboratory Concerts," but did not offer an alternative, as asked. Barbara wrote a draft of a prospectus for the series. After much correspondence the society was named the "Copland–Sessions Concerts"—in part because, as Copland wrote in 1928, "I don't feel able to swing such a thing all by myself, without at least your moral support in America. I think it would look presumptuous on my part to want to run a society entirely alone—and it would look thus in the eyes of the public."[13] After the initial concert was planned for the spring of 1928 Sessions learned that he had won the Rome Prize and would be living in Rome. This left the burden of organizing the concerts entirely on Copland's shoulders. The burden would have fallen on Copland in any case, since during the spring of 1928, when Sessions was in the United States teaching at Smith College, he did little to help, and some things to hinder, the project. The almost daily exchange of letters between Copland in New York and Sessions and Barbara in Northampton reveals the brinksmanship Sessions engaged in while attempting to write his Piano Sonata in time for the first Copland–Sessions Concert, April 22, 1928.

Typically, Sessions had his eyes on the big picture, rather than working on immediate goals. "Furthermore, my head is full of certain projects which I want later on to discuss with you; projects which can + must wait until our concerts are pretty well established, + also until we are ready to start on them, which may mean several years hence; but things which will certainly, if they are at all possible, mean incalculable things for music + for America."[14] The practical Copland wrote a week later:

> The latest excitement is that I am engaged to play my [Piano] Concerto at the Hollywood Bowl on July 19th. Charming, *pas?* They wanted Gershwin, but had to take me instead. This means I see New Mexico and America! Now will you be good. I'll probably return a rampant [America] affirmer. My plans are to leave on May 15 for Santa Fe and remain there for two months, then to California and back to the MacDowell Colony for August and September. This all seems very far from you, worse luck.[15]

Sessions answered: "Please don't worry about my not seeing the music. I trust your judgment entirely." He even asked Copland for advice as to how the Sonata ought to be announced on the program (simply Sonata or with the movements): "The truth is that I need a NURSE!"[16] (This was an unconscious echo of his mother's distress after childbirth; she was indeed provided with a nurse.) Only ten days before the concert, Sessions assured Copland: "*Don't worry about the sonata.* It isn't finished, but I *swear* to you it will be ready in time—you can count on it absolutely. Also, I like it—it is much better than the symphony."[17] Barbara included a message on the same letter. But the next day, she secretly mailed another letter to Copland and asked him not to tell Roger. She was

> a little worried about the sonata. . . . As a mater of fact, I think he is himself secretly in a state of panic which he can't admit to you because he has some kind of feeling that the more declarations he makes the more his will-power will be spurred by the feeling that he *has* to get it done at the risk of utter disaster . . . if you can possibly find it in you to be that generous and forgiving—write him as encouragingly as you can and don't hint at any alarm. Aaron, you have no idea what *hell* he goes through.[18]

Copland was able to rise to this difficult task. He wrote on April 15:

> Last week, when no letter came saying the " 'Sonata' was finished" I naturally began to suspect trouble. Your letter therefore was reassuring. Don't worry twice underlined, should satisfy anyone. However, you most certainly have my sympathy. I think writing a work to order for a set date excellent—when one has finished it. But of course, the situation you are now in is horrible and my feelings as a fellow-composer and as a concert-manager are at war with one another. As the former, I should like to say, don't *you* worry; after all it's the Sonata which is important and not its being ready by a set date. But, as co-director of the C-S—Concerts I should like to see the public get what it is promised. (As the other co-director, I know you feel the same.) O Hell—I hope I don't sound as if I *were* worried. I refuse to be like the famous cook who blew out his brains because the fish didn't arrive in time for the king's dinner.
> All things considered, it would seem highly desirable that the Sonata be finished, however. You have until five minutes before the concert—24 hour a day.[19]

Not only did Sessions not finish the Sonata (it was replaced by the Chávez Sonata), but he did not appear at the concert. Copland wrote to him the next day, April 23, and Barbara answered. Copland:

> I'm really sorry you weren't with us—I should have liked you to have been there so that we could have discussed the music (particularly Chávez), so that you could have passed on the spirit of the concert which I didn't think quite satisfactory, so that you could have helped out at the party, which was a dismal affair, etc. etc. People asked for you both and the moral responsibility of the occasion was rather heavy on my slim shoulders. But I'm a man to accept the inevitable— and everything that happens in connection with the two of you I always place in that category![20]

Two movements of the still incomplete Sessions Sonata were performed on the May 6 concert by John Duke, the teacher of its dedicatee, Rosamond Foster. It took Sessions two more years to finish the work by writing the third movement. Claire Reis, the Executive Director of the League of Composers, was still trying, by October 23, 1928, to persuade Sessions to send even the incomplete work to Walter Gieseking. She had already asked Copland to send a similar letter to Sessions and counted greatly upon having Gieseking play it on the League's program in February. (Needless to say, this did not occur.) During that time Sessions showed the Sonata to Boulanger. Any frustration Copland might have felt over this episode was entirely absent from his enthusiastic *Modern Music* review of the work in 1931: "To know the work well is to have the firm conviction that Sessions has presented us with a cornerstone upon which to base an American music."[21]

Their close friendship was to continue along these lines for eight more years after this concert. The two saw each other quite often in various European countries, took vacations together (Copland went to Switzerland to visit Sessions in August 1929, for example), and Copland continued to arrange concerts with Sessions's music on them. When Sessions moved back to the United States in 1933 and taught in New York, he again depended on Copland, now his *de facto* publisher, for everything from sending out parts to finding a place to live. Many more letters in the 1930s amplify this scenario.

So what happened in 1936 to bring to an end this friendly and helpful exchange? Because each had long before accepted the other's foibles, it seems unlikely that, much belatedly, Copland would become irritated at what Sessions referred to in a 1973 letter as his "antics." And there is no evidence that Sessions ever changed his opinion of Copland as a composer or as a friend.

Copland quoted in *The New Music* a manifesto Sessions wrote in 1927:

> Younger men are dreaming of an entirely different kind of music—a music which derives its power from forms beautiful and significant by virtue of inherent musical weight rather than intensity of utterance; a music whose impersonality and self-sufficiency preclude the exotic; which takes its impulse from the realities of a passionate logic; which, in that authentic freshness of its moods, is the reverse of ironic and, in its very aloofness from the concrete preoccupations of life, strives rather to contribute form, design, a vision of order and harmony.[22]

As fresh, young, and perhaps indisputable as this sounds, it begins a philosophical difference between the two composers. Sessions said,

> Also I felt at that time that one very strong drive behind the movement was that some of my colleagues wanted Europeans to recognize them as "Americans." Europeans haven't the slightest idea, for the most part, what *is* "American" unless they have been here a lot. . . . With Americans it was also the question of identity. I never felt that my identity was bound up in showing people that I was "American," according to some preconceived idea. The main thing is to be completely oneself—the "national" character is a by-product.[23]

Sessions also recognized nationalism as the root of political problems in Italy and Germany.

Copland's biographer, Howard Pollack, and Paul Anderson think philosophical disagreement was the reason this close friendship dissolved. Discussing "The aesthetic thought of Aaron Copland," Anderson traces six basic premises in Copland's writings to four ideologies: French Symbolism, the writings of André Gide, American Progressivism, and Pragmatism. Anderson's close reading of both composers' prose leads him to conclude "in contrast with Sessions, Copland focused primarily on the form of a piece as opposed to its content."[24] And "Together with breadth of emotion, and in contrast with Sessions, Copland prescribes originality and the avoidance of 'influences.' "[25] Copland's "pluralism, of course, contrast markedly with Sessions' universalism. Whereas Sessions' convictions presupposed the existence of a single unifying truth undergirding all things, Copland's imply the reverse: a basically chaotic existence in which systems of order govern within specific but limited contexts."[26]

Copland's biographer sees "the decline of [this] relationship [as] long beset by deep artistic and temperamental differences. Among other things, Copland had begun to find Sessions's music 'almost too difficult,' while Sessions seems to have felt just the opposite about Copland's. Other factors no doubt played a part as well, including Sessions's possible resentment over Copland's growing success."[27] Sessions addressed this question in 1983: "I don't understand how anyone can say there was jealousy between Aaron and myself. How can you be jealous if someone is doing something different from you? If Aaron and I had a dispute, I don't recall it now, so it could not have been very import-ant. I have always liked Aaron very much even though we haven't seen each other often in recent years."[28]

Pollack provides one possible explanation for the dissolution of this friendship that describes Copland's relationships with both friends and lovers. These followed "a recur-rent pattern of a year or two of intense intimacy, a year or so of drifting apart, and the settling of the friendship onto a stable but cooler footing."[29] The friendship with Sessions, however, sustained throughout almost two decades and a problematic concert series. Copland had viewed everything to do with Sessions and Barbara as in the category of the inevitable. This author does not think that the philosophical differences between Sessions's internationalism and Copland's Americana separated them, and I shall posit an alternate, highly human, therefore more likely, explanation.

The answer lies in circumstances involving two of the other *dramatis personae* men-tioned in this section. The central event in Sessions's life in 1936 was his divorce from Barbara, his wife of 16 years, in order to marry Sarah Elizabeth Franck (see section "Marriage and the Violin Concerto"). When Sessions lived in Italy, both abortion and divorce were outlawed. (Divorce was finally legalized there in 1970.) During the sum-mer of 1936 Sessions wrote from Reno, Nevada, to his student David Diamond in Fontainebleau *not* to tell Nadia Boulanger that he was to remarry. Diamond, however, had already told her. The Roman Catholic Boulanger wrote to Sessions imploring him not to divorce. (We do not have this letter, which Sessions sent to Barbara to deal with.) For his part, Sessions considered this none of Boulanger's business, and his frequent and affectionate letters to her abruptly ceased.

> The breach came at the time of my divorce [in 1936]. She didn't want me to be divorced. She didn't know anything about the circumstances at all. . . . She made many things her business that were not her business, and furthermore, there was more to it than that. . . . I think the root of the whole business is that she never forgave me for going to live in Berlin instead of coming to live in Paris. I think it's as simple as that. I think she regarded my generation of American composers as her domain, and as a matter of fact, a lot of things that happened to me—a lot of unpleasant things, let's say, or unpleasant situations, not personally unpleasant but musically unpleasant—stemmed perhaps not from her directly, but from her entourage, you see. For years, I was classified as a "Central European," belonging to the Central European tendency. Well, this is of course absolutely absurd, from the point of view of an American musician— completely absurd. But still I was tarred with that brush, if you like, and I don't blame her personally for it, but you know disciples are always the worst people. They make all the trouble.

Actually, I think, that was the essence of the thing. The thing that caused the final break was the way she treated my wife, my second wife, when she met her first in Washington [in April 1937], which was unpardonable—especially since my second wife had nothing to do with my divorce at all.[30]

It is easy to believe that Boulanger let her dismay be known to others. She had been on extremely friendly personal terms with Barbara (she probably knew about Barbara's operation and she continued to correspond with her). Possibly Boulanger had even recommended the doctor whom Barbara saw, and may have felt responsible for the catastrophic result. In any case, as Ravel had learned from experience, it did not take much to be stricken from her orbit. Sessions and Boulanger became permanently estranged over the divorce. It is considered likely by those who knew her that Boulanger dictated that others follow her course of excommunication. This left Copland with the uncomfortable task of choosing between his friend and his former teacher. Thus two casualties of his divorce were Sessions's loss of his close friendship with both Boulanger and Copland. This meant a severe blow to his career both because of the loss of Copland's private support and because of Boulanger's public disapproval. Only after 1936 did Sessions speak negatively about Boulanger.

Sessions burned several bridges behind him, but he was willing to sacrifice a great deal—as he must have guessed that he would have had to—in order to remarry and have children. Never again were Copland and Sessions on the intimate terms of the 1926–1936 years. Later letters are widely spaced over time, deal with business issues, and sometimes contain genuine but distant affection. Their friendship survived this crisis and moved to a different level of mutual respect, while each composer avoided depending on the other.[31]

Friendships do not founder on differences in philosophy or compositional styles. Sessions and Copland had made their positions clear about American music from the beginning, while each admired the other's music. Friendships always dissolve for *personal* reasons. Friends of divorced couples frequently find themselves aligned with one or the other of the couple (and not necessarily the one through whom they met the spouse). So, for example, both Nadia Boulanger and Theodore Chanler cut Sessions and his new wife in public. It is likely that Copland, like Boulanger, possessing the secret knowledge of Barbara's operation, subsequent illness, and resulting inability to conceive a child, felt sympathetic toward her. It is also plausible that he liked her a great deal—many others did. On these intimate and personal shoals Sessions and Copland's friendship foundered. Each was in his mid-to-late thirties when this occurred, and each acted like a mature adult by maintaining a professional and distant front and never denigrating the other composer. Others were left to imagine and promulgate some notion of animosity between them.

On at least two occasions were the Copland–Sessions Concerts remembered. Thirty years later Charles Schwartz organized a Composers Showcase concert on May 11, 1958, dedicated to both men with whom he had studied. The audience crammed into a small art gallery on 6th Street included Carlos Chávez, Elliott Carter, Alan Hovhaness, Stefan Wolpe, John Cage, Ralph Shapey, and Milton Babbitt. William Masselos played Copland's Piano Fantasy and Max Pollikoff the Sessions solo Violin Sonata. A reporter noted that "neither composer could remember exactly the site of the concerts of their series" and that Sessions had only attended one of the concerts.[32] At Tanglewood in 1980 a similar concert commemorated the series. Here the Copland Piano Variations and his 1950 Quartet were heard, while Joseph Silverstein played the Sessions solo Violin Sonata and Yehudi Wyner the *Pages from a Diary* piano pieces.

In *Our New Music* Copland wrote of Sessions as the consummate, painstaking craftsman of "tactile sensibility," limited melodic inventiveness, and textural complexity, creating, at his best, "music of ineffable pessimism—resigned, unprotesting, inexpressibly sad, and of a deeply human and nonromantic quality."[33] In 1980 Copland remarked that Sessions's importance lay in "his seriousness, solid culture and broad musical background and knowledge," as well as his influence on a sophisticated elite, but his music did not present "an especially striking stylistic profile" and he had made "comparatively little dent."[34]

In his Italian lectures, published in 1956, Sessions granted that Copland defied pigeonholing, rather he summarized prominent trends in American music while remaining "a strong and well-defined personality, easily recognizable in the different profiles his music has assumed."[35] Ultimately, Sessions felt, as Milton Babbitt quoted him as saying, that "Copland was more talented than he realized."[36]

Sessions wrote to Copland congratulating him on his seventieth birthday in 1970, and Copland attended an all-Sessions concert in 1973. Copland thanked Sessions in 1974 for an inscribed score of *When Lilacs Last in the Dooryard Bloom'd* Sessions had sent him: "Dear Roger: I was pleased and touched at receiving the inscribed copy of your Whitman Cantata. It's obviously a major accomplishment, and I look forward to getting to know it petit à petit, and to learning it in the Spring of '75. Many thanks for sending it. All best to Lisl and yourself. As ever Aaron."[37]

Copland and Sessions saw each other for the last time at a performance of Stravinsky's *L'Histoire du Soldat* in September 1981 in which, with apt casting, Sessions read the Narrator, Copland the Soldier, and Virgil Thomson the Devil.

THE AMERICAN ACADEMY
IN ROME

Sessions and Barbara had spent their second $2,500 yearly Guggenheim stipend eight months before completing the second year's Fellowship. They left Europe on December 27, 1927, and he taught at Smith to earn the needed money. They lived at 15 Adare Place in Northampton and saw Ruth frequently. The Copland–Sessions concert series began that spring. After the debacle with Piano Sonata on the first and second of the Copland–Sessions concerts, the couple left the US in May 1928 for Paris, lived at 20 Rue de Berne, and spent the summer of 1928 in Juziers, 15 miles outside the capital. On June 26 Sessions heard Stravinsky conduct Œdipus Rex (see section "Stravinsky"). Between September 10 and 15, the two attended the ISCM festival in Siena where Bloch's quintet was performed. Possibly, they then went to Florence.

Having spent two and a half years in Florence, Sessions wanted to remain in Europe. Felix Lamond, founder of the music program at the American Academy in Rome, suggested that he apply for the Academy Fellowship known as the Rome Prize. Sessions's three recommenders were Serge Koussevitzky, Nadia Boulanger, and Roy Dickinson Welch.[1] The application for the Rome Prize stated: "NB VISITING STUDENTS WILL BE EXPECTED TO REMAIN UNDER THE DIRECTION OF THE ACADEMY FOR AT LEAST EIGHT MONTHS OF THE YEAR." All applicants had to sign and agree to this stipulation. The prize would amount to $1,500 a year for three years and a traveling allowance of $500 per year. Housing, meals, and a studio were provided in the palatial McKim building on top of the highest of the hills inside the Roman walls.

Charles Follen McKim had founded the American Academy in Rome in 1894 for architects. The Rome Prize in music was first awarded in 1921.[2] Composer Edward MacDowell, an incorporating trustee of the American Academy in Rome in 1905, had urged the establishment of a music program but died a few years later. The British Felix Lamond lectured at Columbia, where he might have met MacDowell, and was a music critic for the New York Herald from 1909 to 1915. Lamond had suggested to trustee Daniel Chester French in 1913 that a music fellowship be established, but not until after the Great War was money available for such a project (some of it furnished through the efforts of Lamond's daughter). Harry Harkness Flagler offered $25,000 toward a fellowship in the name of Walter Damrosch, providing the Academy would match the amount. Frederick Juilliard contributed money in his own name (money that he had inherited from an Academy patron, his uncle Augustus).[3] A third, smaller fellowship amount was raised in honor of Sessions's teacher Horatio Parker. Three "unmarried" American men would occupy the fellowships in overlapping three-year periods. Fellows would be required to use their travel allowance to visit other places in Europe.

The first three fellows were Leo Sowerby (1921), Howard Hanson (1921), and Randall Thompson (1922); Quincy Porter had won Honorable Mention. Between those three and Sessions's first year at the Academy (1928) Wintter Watts, Herbert Elwell, Walter Helfer, Robert Sanders, and Alexander Steinert had won the Rome Prize. Sessions, the Damrosch Fellow, was the ninth fellow: he overlapped first with Sanders (Parker Fellow, 1926–1929) and Steinert (Juilliard Fellow, 1927–1930), and later with Normand Lockwood (Parker Fellow, 1929–1932) and Werner Janssen (Juilliard Fellow, 1930–1933), plus Herbert Inch (a traveling fellow, 1928–1929, who later won the Prize). Sessions had applied on February 29 and learned on May 8, 1928, that he had won. Ten contestants, including Bloch's student Robert Delaney, had applied, an increase over six the previous year. The jury that picked Sessions was chaired by his Harvard teacher Edward B. Hill, along with John Alden Carpenter and Leo Sowerby. (This appears to be the only occasion long-time trustee Walter Damrosch was not on the committee.) Sessions's Fellowship started in October 1928 and would be renewed through the summer of 1931.

Sessions was an unusual choice for at least two reasons. First, he was two years older than the stated age limit of 30. Second, in contradiction to the terms of the Fellowship and the Academy, he was not "unmarried." The French Academy in Rome had in 1927 eliminated the celibacy stipulation and even had women fellows. Alexander Steinert and his wife Sylvia had broken that barrier in music at the American Academy. Sessions and Steinert could not live at the Academy's McKim-designed building, however, because of their status. Sesssions and Barbara lived nearby at the Villa Sforza, Via Garibaldi 31—in an out building no longer standing that had a fabulous view of Rome. Barbara worked in the Academy library.

Alexander Steinert, who overlapped two years with Sessions, was extremely wealthy: his grandfather had founded the New Haven Symphony and M. Steinert & Sons, a piano manufacturing company in Boston. Sessions had been aware of him since his years at Harvard, when Steinert's family guaranteed $18,000 for a stadium production of *Siegfried*, and Sessions had won the Steinert Prize at Yale. He had already met Steinert in Paris, where the composer had lived lavishly, studying music at the Conservatoire and entertaining Toscanini, Paderewski, Piatagorsky, Koussevitzky, and his teacher Ravel. Steinert worked with Gershwin and Cole Porter, later conducting Gershwin's music including the first revival of *Porgy and Bess*. There is, however, almost no mention of Steinert in Sessions's correspondence. In addition, Werner Janssen became the "star" of the Academy and an important conductor while in Rome and later in the US (his performance of Barber's music helped Barber win the Rome Prize). Sessions failed to capitalize on either of these two potentially valuable professional associations.

Rather than write music, Sessions took the opportunity to learn Russian, since the two ladies who ran the Villa Sforza building were white Russians. He bought a first edition of *War and Peace*, read it in the original Russian, and wrote to Koussevitzky and Nicolas Slonimsky in their native language. Sessions gave a talk, March 27, 1929, about "Some aspects of contemporary music" before fellows from other academies in Rome.

Initially, Sessions liked Rome enormously; he wrote to Copland how superior it was to France, which he thought "fundamentally alien to him."[4] "The shades of Hanson and Sowerby still hang over the [Academy] to a certain extent; but this has not seemed to affect either my status or my peace of mind!" He also thought Lamond "more than kind" and "a man of the world, which means a great deal."[5] Even before Sessions and Barbara reached Rome in October 1928, he had begun a campaign to persuade Copland to apply for the Rome Prize, in order that Copland be in Rome during part of their stay. Copland, however, wanted to stay in New York.

The Sessionses arrived at the Academy October 5, 1928, and stayed until December 15.

From December 15 to February 1, 1929, they spent in Florence and came back to Rome February 1 staying through June 30. Director Gorham Stevens noted in his diary on June 12 an "unusual amount" of typhoid in Rome. From April 5 to 10, 1929, the dates of the seventh ISCM Festival, Sessions and Lamond traveled to Geneva for the perform-ance of the First Symphony in Victoria Hall (see section "Symphony No. 1"). Sessions spent a total of nine months of his first year of the Rome Prize at the Academy.

Trouble was brewing in 1929 at Forty Acres and Phelps House. Back in the 1890s the Bishop had bought Phelps House from his relatives for Ruth as a summer home. In the twenties many changes took place at Forty Acres, seen from the short distance of Phelps House, where Ruth had spent her summers since her retirement from Sessions House at Smith in 1920. Forty Acres had passed to George Huntington's children in 1910. Barrett first took it, but gave it up in 1918. It stood deserted, the rooms filled with colonial antiques and silver, but considered haunted. This situation must have been unbearable to Ruth. Electricity and indoor bathrooms were finally installed in 1921. The other Huntington brothers were helping to make it habitable, particularly Dr James Lincoln Huntington, who wrote a book about the house.[6] His mother, George's widow, Lilly St Agnan Barrett Huntington, lived there for four years, dying in January 1926.

Then several calamities occurred, which to some degree forced previously unaddressed family questions about the fate of Forty Acres. No sooner had John Sessions gotten married in July 1927 than that winter (1927–1928) a flood caused by heavy snow crept into its basement, and the entire back "stoop," the spacious verandah, had to be rebuilt. Ruth pressured John to leave his job and move to Forty Acres and Phelps House in 1929. In January 1929, within weeks of John's arrival on the property at Phelps House, the caretaker's cottage burned to the ground and had to be rebuilt. After this disaster James Huntington's brothers and Catharine gave or sold their shares to James.

James Huntington's first action must have dismayed Ruth enormously: he decided not to continue farming on the land. That meant dealing with the fire hazard of the 1783 barn, in "shocking condition." A local man, Clifton Johnson, was interested in copying the barn to build a farm museum. James gave him the barn in 1929, if he could move it off the property to his location two miles away. The Hadley Farm Museum on Route 9 opened May 27, 1931. The spot where the barn had been was replaced with a sunken garden, a lily pond literally in the place of the manure pit. Ruth was determined that the ancestral land remain farmed, and persuaded her Harvard graduate son—Roger was useless, living in Rome—to move there from New York state and take up dairy farming. John tried manfully for more than a decade to please his mother, running a milk route—his mother sometimes at his side. In 1939 he went back to Harvard to earn an MBA—and returned to Phelps House.

During the summer of 1929, at a time when its future was in doubt, Sessions was feeling possessive about his family home. Meanwhile, Dohenny (Dawn) Sessions could see the situation clearly. Ruth had relayed to Sessions Dawn's no-doubt accurate remark that Ruth treated John as a "hired man."[7] Ungraciously, Sessions was outraged and took entirely his mother's point of view: then pregnant and living on the property, Dawn should have no say-so in the family into which she had married, he declared. Sessions supported Ruth, who lived during the winter at 121 Sedgwick Street, in Syracuse: he felt it was "quite intolerable that Dawn should consider herself entitled to be a party to any conversation you may have with John, in regard to either the farm, or anything else that concerns the property—or in fact anything you wish to discuss with him!"[8] If this was truly Sessions's attitude about spouses, as opposed to possibly posturing to try to please his mother, such a view also left Barbara without influence.

In the same letter Sessions regretted he had "never been able, in the last years, to quite reach [John], much as I have longed to do so." He always proclaimed his devotion to his brother, but Sessions had been living in Italy for four years; how could he "reach" John in those circumstances? The disposition of the property at Forty Acres had touched a raw nerve. He was living abroad, unable to influence events, and felt keenly the possible loss of the family homestead. Having been made by Ruth over the years to see Phelps House as his real home, now he could not bear to see it run by his sister-in-law. Possibly he thought he would inherit it himself: he reminded his mother, "I never forget that I am your oldest son, or cease to want to be to you all that that should mean." If this was a fantasy of inheriting the property, it was a complete self-delusion; Sessions could never successfully have taken care of either Forty Acres or Phelps House. His uncle George's capable sons had tried during the 1920s to save Forty Acres. Only when James Huntington gave up his medical practice in Boston and moved there in 1943 was there any hope of keeping that house. Sessions could invoke primogeniture, but he was not in any sense able (or willing, if he were honest with himself) to take over the farm and house at Phelps House. Somehow, Dawn, the person living and working there, possibly unwillingly, was cast as the villain. It is perhaps therefore ironic that Dawn Sessions should be—almost 60 years later—the sole family member remaining at Forty Acres and Phelps House after more than 200 years.

Two major floods, in 1936 and 1938, caused severe damage, the first invading the house at Forty Acres by several inches. Before anyone else could reach the house at Forty Acres during the March 1936 flood, John and Dawn Sessions had "labored for hours to protect what they could from the rising flood," they carried furniture and other belongings upstairs.[9] Personally and professionally 1936 was already Sessions's worst year (see section "Marriage and Violin Concerto"); it was as though his problems were being externalized by the calamities at Forty Acres. Both ancestral home and composer were injured and aching for a solution in 1936. Ruth had the manuscript to *Sixty-Odd: A Personal History*, finished in 1920, lying around and might have felt that, with the damage at Forty Acres, the old days were completely over—she may as well publish a post mortem on those decades.

During the 1938 hurricane, in addition to the second flood, numerous old trees were felled or limbs torn off by the strong winds. One tree fell onto the east porch, destroying it, the same porch on which photographs of the clan had been taken for forty years (see Figures 12 and 20 [pages 38 and 125]). It was rebuilt.

In 1942 John sold the milk route and took a job at Mount Holyoke (while still living at Phelps Farm) where he was the assistant treasurer and assistant comptroller at Mount Holyoke College. He was beginning to free himself of Ruth's overbearing influence.

James Huntington was responsible for the preservation of the Porter-Phelps-Huntington house and other buildings. Various members of the family wrote to Dr Huntington for medical advice, including Barbara Sessions. Across the road was Ruth Sessions, still living at Phelps House, with John and Dawn and their two daughters.

In 1955 Forty Acres, the family's home for six generations, was donated, with its entire contents, to the Porter-Phelps-Huntington Foundation, Inc. It is now a museum run by the private foundation. Its many letters, diaries, and papers were placed on loan to the Amherst Archives. Dawn Sessions would continue to live there until 1988. (Elizabeth Wheeler, Edwin Wheeler and Clara Sessions's daughter, had been associated with the Porter-Phelps-Huntington Foundation since 1978, and lived for a while in Phelps House after Dawn moved out.) When Dawn moved to a nursing home in 1988, her daughter Sarah went through the Phelps House attic. There she found a tin box filled with hundreds of letters by Roger to his wife and George Bartlett, including numerous letters to Roger, many of which have been quoted in this book.

Forty Acres is still a museum and Phelps House has stood uninhabited since 1988. Ruth's determination that both remain in the family and occupied by family members came to naught. She sacrificed her son John on this chimera. John was to die just three years after Ruth, at the age of 49. Largely because of Ruth's demands on his brother to care for Phelps Farm, Sessions always accused his mother of "ruining" John's life.

From July 1 to October 1, 1929, the Sessionses stayed at Les Diablerets, Switzerland, saw the Binets, and traveled to Paris before returning to Rome. He worked on a new symphony, not catalogued, and went mountain climbing. The Fosters came *en masse* to visit them in Switzerland, and he persuaded Copland to visit as well.

In Rome Sessions eventually redeemed himself concerning the Piano Sonata. Frank Mannheimer,[10] who had played the two movements in Florence in 1929, gave a semi-private performance of the completed two movements of the Sonata on March 3, 1930, at the Academy's Villa Chiaraviglio. He played the Sonata again in 1931 on the radio in London, February 24; in Rome, March 12; in Bad Homburg, July 7 (Sessions did not attend this performance); and in Oxford on July 23, for the ISCM Festival. It was there that Copland first heard the finished version. The Sonata was published by the German firm of Schotts Söhne, a publication deal arranged, no doubt with Klemperer's recommendation, during Sessions's six-week stay in Berlin in the spring of 1931, an unusual sign of acceptance of an American in Europe.

In late April of 1930 Barbara was hospitalized in Rome for 10 to 14 days for complications related to her operation four years previously. She was prescribed a course of mineral baths, which she took in June in Tuscany; it prevented her return to the US.

Frank P. Fairbanks, a Fellow from 1912, painted Sessions's portrait, along with 34 other arts (as opposed to classics) Fellows. These originally hung in the billiard room of the McKim building, and for decades have been hanging behind the Academy bar, where they can still be seen. Fairbanks also painted a large mural for the map room, recently removed, that displayed Sessions's name prominently.

During the second year of Sessions's fellowship he stayed at the Academy from October 1 to December 14, 1929, and then traveled to Florence, December 14 to February 19, 1930, and returned to the Academy February 19 to stay until July 16, 1930. He lived for seven and a half months at the AAR and sailed to the US on July 18, 1930. The remainder of the summer (starting August 1, 1930) he spent the time in Hadley, not Europe. Perhaps he had again run through his *stipendio*. He saw a great deal of Copland during this hiatus and remained in Hadley well past the AAR October 1 deadline to return for his third Fellowship year. Possibly Ruth pressured him to stay with his brother at Phelps House.

Academy Fellows were referred to as "students" on forms, and, although that is no longer true, outsiders sometimes still think Fellows are studying a discipline rather than working creatively in their field. Sessions wrote to his mother,

> It has not been wholly pleasant for instance to be called always, in Roman society, a "student" at the Academy, and to be asked if I have a good teacher, etc.—since the general public cannot be expected to know that one can easily be technically a "student" there without being in any sense a pupil; and I don't by any means always have the opportunity to explain that I finished my so-called "studies" eight years ago. One has to achieve some things . . . without allowing

Figure 29 Roger Sessions portrait at the American Academy in Rome, painted by Frank
P. Fairbanks, FAAR '12.

oneself to be affected one way or the other by one's fancied "position" or by the
props which might come from outside oneself.[11]

British organist Felix Lamond (1863–1940) lectured at Columbia and was a music
critic for the *New York Herald*. The creation and administration of the music program at
the Academy was largely due to his efforts. Lamond submitted annual reports for
the two decades he ran the Music Department (1920–1940). Requirements included
completed pieces, works played on annual Academy concerts, and general evidence of
availing oneself of the advantages of the prize including abiding by its residency and
travel requirements. The degree FAAR (Fellow of the American Academy in Rome) was
awarded upon completion of the Fellowship. Lamond reported on numerous performances, publications, reviews, and other activities by the three current music Fellows, but
in these annual reports Sessions stood out as having not accomplished anywhere near
that of his contemporaries. He had never availed himself of the professional quartet, in
residence weekly in order for Fellows to write for and hear performed their (and others')
works. On none of the *three* annual concerts—the most important musical event at the
Academy—did Sessions's music appear.

By far the most significant musical opportunity for Fellows was the possibility of
being performed by the Augusteo Orchestra. Both Hanson and Janssen had conducted
it. Steinert composed for his graduation from the Academy a "Leggenda" for full orchestra, not only played at the Augusteo but also by the Boston Symphony. Lockwood
composed a Sonatina for piano and a three-movement symphony played at the annual
concert. In addition he wrote a Choral Symphony, "Drum-Taps in four movements on
Whitman." All that Lamond could report of Sessions during that year (1928–1929) was
that his "work comprised a revision of his piano sonata and a Ballata, Illustrative of

scenes in Boccaccio's 'Decameron.' He also prepared sketches [begun in 1927] for a Violin Concerto."[12] The Ballata was never completed and was withdrawn; the Violin Concerto remained unfinished for eight years, which left the Piano Sonata, still not quite completed after its partial premiere two years earlier.

As mentioned, at the end of the second year Sessions continued to stay in Hadley from August 1 to the middle of November 1930, rather than return to Rome by October 1. He wrote to Copland: "I have been inwardly cursing + almost weeping at the utter irrationality of my leaving the U.S. at this time. [. . .] I don't intend by any means to waste this next year; but neither can I see any reason for spending it in Europe, when I would rather be at home, especially as I have decided to pass the rest of my life in America."[13] The pressure of the Copland–Sessions Concerts may have been weighing on him.[14] Ironically, this third year in Rome—at four months his shortest yet (despite his signed pledge to spend eight months)—would alter his life and career; it changed his mind about returning to the US.

He finally returned to Rome on December 14, 1930, and stayed until March 17, 1931. During Sessions's last, abbreviated year, he was reported to have continued work on the concerto. Lamond, falling into the familiar trap of believing Sessions when he said he would finish a work soon, announced, "This work, on completion of the orchestration will be performed in Berlin during the coming season by Max Strub under the conductorship of Otto Klemperer. It will also be played in Rome." Neither of these concerts came to fruition. Lamond wrote, "He had made considerable progress on an orchestral work, entitled 'Strophe.' Sessions has contributed a song, entitled 'On the Beach at Fontana,' for a volume 'The Joyce Book,' which is to be published by Oxford University Press as a mark of homage to the Irish poet, James Joyce."[15] "Strophe" was never completed, and the Violin Concerto would take much longer. The tally of music begun and completed at the Academy in three years of funded compositional activity: one song, "On the Beach at Fontana." Ironically, Sessions misinterpreted the poem, thinking it about a homosexual relationship, when in fact it concerned a father–son relationship.[16] The only Sessions piece performed at the Academy was the Piano Sonata, played twice, March 30, 1930, and March 12, 1931, neither publicly nor on an annual concert.

A graduation piece was still required. By November 1931, after Sessions's Fellowship had technically ended the previous August, Lamond had still not received the orchestrated Violin Concerto and therefore did not consider Sessions's prescribed work as finished. Irritated, he wrote in 1938 that Sessions "was in Rome for three years, principally owing to my efforts, and in spite of many 'urgings' did very little work."[17] Despite promises from Sessions to send him the orchestration (and the fact the work was published in 1935, which Lamond may not have known), by 1938 Lamond had still not received the score to the Violin Concerto that, if submitted previously, would have allowed Sessions to receive his diploma. (The score is now in the Academy library.) The fact is that Sessions, along with Wintter Watts (who earlier had not been asked back after two years because he wrote so little), did not meet the Academy's expectations and did not formally obtain the recognition of the Rome Prize, the degree FAAR. Like his mother, who never completed her three years of certificate work at the Leipzig Conservatory, he did not complete his three years at the Academy and had a good time in Europe instead. Also like his mother he found it more fun to learn another language than to work on music. He assumed he had been belatedly awarded the Prize when he sent the Academy the score of the Violin Concerto in 1938: on a later résumé, Sessions listed his Rome Prize degree as 1938.

Sessions had not learned the hard lessons of Harvard, the Symphonic Prelude, the first Copland–Sessions Concert, and numerous other times when he let others down because he could not finish his music by allowing other intellectual distractions to redirect his energies—a fatal combination of enormous insecurity and a sense of entitlement. Lamond would have agreed with what Rosamond Foster told this author was Sessions's dominant characteristic: "frustrating."

Sessions never attended Milan's La Scala, although he frequented the Rome Opera and operas in Florence. He did hear Richard Strauss conduct his "Alpine" Symphony and *Don Juan* at the Augusteo, and sat behind him during *Ein Heldenleben*. Needless to say, Sessions never introduced himself to Strauss. In Rome Sessions saw composer Alfredo Casella, whom Sessions had first met at Bloch's house in Cleveland. Sessions spent considerable time with Casella and with Mario Labroca. Labroca then wrote a highly flattering account of Sessions for the *Christian Science Monitor*, which so closely represented Sessions's views that he might have dictated it.[18]

During Sessions's last months in Rome, December 1930 through March 1931, Cesar Saerchinger also came back into his life. Saerchinger was a European representative of CBS living in London. His mission to Rome was almost outlandish in its audacity: he was to persuade the Pope that, since he promised to broadcast over NBC, he ought to broadcast over CBS as well. A tough proposition; Saerchinger never got to see the Pope, but made important-sounding phone calls to New York every day. *Al improviso*, all of a sudden, as the Italians say, the CBS deal with the Vatican came through.

Saerchinger had lived in Berlin after the Great War and was active in musical circles there. He introduced Sessions to several musicians, including Pierre Monteux and Otto Klemperer while they were conducting in Rome. Klemperer had heard only Sessions's Piano Sonata on March 12, 1931. Events moved rapidly thereafter. Three days later, March 15, the Sessionses had a musicale at their Villa Sforza apartment, perhaps to celebrate the day *The Black Maskers* was being played on a Copland–Sessions Concert in New York. Klemperer was so taken with Sessions (and Barbara) and so persuasive that, *al improviso*, two days later, on March 17–19 (the travel took two days) the Sessionses left Rome for six weeks in Berlin (through May 1). Influenced by the magnetic Klemperer, Sessions liked Berlin so much he decided he wanted to live there. He moved to Berlin in the fall, after staying in Rome only one more month (May 8–June 13) and Florence for a month (June 13–July 12) at Berenson's guest house.

He traveled to England where his First Piano Sonata was heard July 23 at the ISCM in Oxford. (They could not afford for Barbara to go. Indeed, Sessions then owed Copland 200 marks.) He left England August 1 and spent the summer on the Baltic Sea halfway between Kiel and Lubeck, then went to Hamburg for three weeks, then Berlin, where the couple would live for two years. For the first year Sessions lived on a Carnegie grant, "and I guess that there was some money left over from that, because we lived there for two years. I don't remember where all the money came from, but I only had one year of the Carnegie grant. At that time, I was having too good a time. On the other hand I felt, during that year, that I'd been in Europe long enough, and I was very anxious to come back to the United States."[19] Barbara earned money as a translator.

To leave the Academy in 1931, after his final year, was propitious from a financial point of view. Because of the Depression, the Academy had to cut fellowships to $1,200 and travel stipends to $300. Its summer school was also canceled. By June 1933, when Sessions eventually returned to the US, he was considered a European by Americans.

BERLIN

In the summer of 1931 the Sessionses settled in Berlin, which, before the advent of the Nazis, was considered a place of extraordinary politeness in all social and business transactions. This aspect must have appealed to the well-mannered New Englander. The one-year Carnegie grant paid their expenses.

During the last years of the Weimar Republic, culture was valued; people cared passionately (either positively or negatively) about new works. The 50-year-old Berlin Philharmonic Orchestra, conducted by Wilhelm Furtwängler, produced no operas, but championed works by the Second Viennese School. Erich Kleiber conducted the Staatsoper, where he produced *Wozzeck*. The Civic Opera (Städtisch Oper), conducted by Bruno Walter along with associate conductors Fritz Stiedry, Paul Dessau, and Fritz Busch, did contemporary opera, including operas by Bartók and Janáček. The short-lived Kroll Oper (1927–1931) was underwritten by the state: Otto Klemperer conducted it along with associate conductor Alexander von Zemlinsky. At the time Sessions was in Berlin, Furtwängler, Klemperer, and Walter were considered the three leading conductors. Klemperer and Furtwängler were opposite poles—a little like the situation with Schoenberg and Stravinsky—although Klemperer introduced Sessions to Furtwängler. Sessions did not view Erich Kleiber as equal to those three.

Klemperer had made his Berlin debut with an all-Schoenberg program, and the composer himself taught at the Prussian Arts Academy from 1926 through 1933. Meanwhile, Hindemith, who came to Berlin in 1927, taught composition at the Hochschule für Musik. Sessions probably heard the premiere of Otto Klemperer's opera *Das Ziel* ("The Goal"), given in concert version April 19, 1931. Sessions said, "Klemperer did a very, very great deal for me there. He introduced me to people, and also, I never paid for a ticket to the opera, for instance."[1] He felt that Klemperer was a greater conductor than Toscanini, whose renditions of Beethoven Sessions did not care for (although he did admire his conducting of Italian opera). "What is tremendous about Klemperer is not so much what he does with the orchestra, but what he does with the music. Tremendous vitality, tremendous mastery of the music. I've heard very very few performances of Beethoven symphonies that can compare with Klemperer's performances of the Fifth and Seventh and the Eroica and the Ninth, and his performances of Mozart—fantastic!"[2]

The couple lived in the apartment, at Lützowufer 10, of Max Strub, Klemperer's Kroll concertmaster, where Copland also stayed in the fall of 1931. Klemperer himself lived two doors away. Strub was separated from his wife at the time and spoke no English; the Sessionses spoke German. Strub also gave them concert tickets. The second year the Sessionses lived at Kurfürstenstrasse, 126, possibly the studio owned by a Jewish family whom Sessions never saw again after January 1933. Barbara was earning money by translating from French to English Princess Marie Bonaparte's work on psychoanalysis. According to Prausnitz, Barbara may have had an affair with Klemperer, and Sessions became involved with another woman.[3] In the spring of 1932 Strub had a breakdown, the reason Sessions gave Boulanger and Copland for his not playing the Violin Concerto (which, in addition, was not finished). Always the optimist, Sessions felt the Concerto would be done the following season.

Because of Copland's organizational skills, Sessions's First Symphony was performed in Berlin by the Berlin Symphony Orchestra, Ansermet conducting, on December 9, 1931. (Copland's First Symphony was played as well.) It was sponsored by the International Society for Contemporary Music.

"It was a fantastic time in many ways. In the first place, there was a kind of cultural activity that I haven't seen the like of anywhere else, at any other time."[4] He attended Wagner operas he had not heard before; *Rienzi*, for example. "I always describe it as the most unrewarding evening I ever spent. It's not quite so bad as that."[5] He also heard *Das Liebesverbot* and *Der fliegende Holländer*, which completed the catalogue of Wagner's operas: Sessions not only owned all the scores, but he had now also seen productions of them all. It was during his time in Germany that Sessions, because of the political use the Nazis made of Wagner, turned against the composer (see below).

On October 22 Stravinsky conducted the premiere of his Violin Concerto, with violinist Samuel Dushkin, in Berlin. Sessions saw Stravinsky again through their mutual friend Dushkin. More world premieres followed: Hans Pfitzner's opera *Das Herz* had simultaneous premieres in Berlin and Munich, November 12, 1931; Hindemith's oratorio *Das Unaufhörliche* was given November 21. Sessions heard Edward Steuermann and Rudolf Kolisch play the Berg Double Concerto.

Sessions saw *Wozzeck* in Vienna, not in Germany, where Hindemith and Kurt Weill were the reigning composers. Naturally, Sessions heard quite a lot of their music, including *Mahagonny*. Another Kurt Weill opera, *Die Bürgschaft* ("The Pledge"), was given March 10, 1932. Stravinsky playing the piano and Dushkin the violin gave the first performance of his *Duo Concertant* on the Berlin radio October 28, 1932. The next day Franz Schreker's opera *Der Schmied von Gent* was premiered. Two days later Prokofiev, as piano soloist, gave the world premiere of his Fifth Piano Concerto with the Berlin Philharmonic under Furtwängler. (Sessions met the Russian composer.)

Cesar Saerchinger was a friend of Artur Schnabel, about whom he would write a book, and he introduced Sessions to the pianist: "I was scared to death of him at the time. He seemed to me to be a formidable person. I met him, he was extremely nice to me, but I didn't feel really close to him until years later, when he was in this country [the US]. I was very close indeed to him for several years."[6] And "In a sense I knew him as well as I knew Klemperer; but I got to know him so much better later on. I mean, he really was my best friend, you know, as far as musicians are concerned."[7]

Later, in the States, when Sessions went weekly to New York to teach, he always had lunch with Schnabel. He also visited him in New Mexico in the summer of 1941. Schnabel came to California and the two spent time together there. In 1947 the pianist had a heart attack and was never quite the same after that; he did not play as often, and Sessions continued to see him.

> He was a very, very great pianist, in the first place. He was perhaps above all a very, very great musical mind. He was of course also a composer. I have to be a little reserved about that, because although he was—you see, when his biography was written by this friend of mine Saerchinger, who also founded the Schnabel Society, of which I was president for a couple of years. Saerchinger

asked Ernst Krenek (who's a friend of mine; a contemporary of mine very close to Schnabel also) and me to make studies of Schnabel's music. I had the orchestra music, Krenek had the chamber music. This music is full of strokes of genius, that's all, but it's still very problematical, in the sense that it's the work of a man for whom composing was never the main thing. It may have been what he loved the most—I'm not sure—but it was not what he dedicated himself to. I think he dedicated himself to playing especially Beethoven, and Mozart and Schubert.[8]

Saerchinger also introduced Sessions to Hindemith. Sessions heard Hindemith only in concerts, never at the opera. Hindemith's *Philharmonisches Konzert (Variationen für Orchester)* was conducted by Furtwängler at the Philharmonic for the orchestra's fiftieth birthday. Sessions wrote to Copland that Hindemith, only a year older than Sessions, reminded him "so strongly of my brother, that I had the feeling I know him very well."[9] Sessions was not especially drawn to Hindemith's music, although he admired it. A young American man studying with Hindemith asked to study with Sessions. Evidently, Hindemith had blown up at him during a lesson, and he was shattered by it. Sessions would take him for the summer on two conditions: one, that he go back to Hindemith in the fall, and that in the meantime, if Hindemith agreed, then Sessions would talk to him about the student. After Sessions's "very nice talk" with Hindemith, the young man studied with him for the summer. (Sessions, being tactful, declined to identify the student.)

In the fall Sessions explained to Hindemith some of the facts of American musical life:

> I said to Hindemith, "You see, the difference is that whereas in Germany you have conservatories which are comparable to our law schools and our medical schools"—in other words, the standards may not be as high as you would like or as I would like for that matter, but if a person has a degree you can count on the fact that he's accomplished a certain amount. You know that you can rely on a certain amount of achievement and background and competence. "But in the United States, you can't. In some places you can, in other places you can't. You've got to judge this boy a little by that standard."[10]

(The student had a master's degree—Sessions would not say from where—and he had success in a small town.) Hindemith had probably told him that he had no talent, and he had never heard that before. Sessions did not think a teacher should say that to anyone. The boy did not know harmony and had to study it. He returned to Hindemith and his lessons proceeded well after that, and Sessions saw him in the US once in a while. By 1962, however, Sessions considered Hindemith an unsympathetic person.

Later Sessions also saw Hindemith in the US, where sometimes in the company of Sessions's German friends Hindemith appeared evasive and embarrassed. His fellow Germans judged Hindemith harshly (and so did Sessions). Hindemith *did*, after all, return to Germany and Switzerland. Later Sessions evaluated himself rather harshly for having judged Hindemith, whose situation he could not fully step into. "I've come to a conclusion, especially since the war, that I'm not going to judge individuals until I have been in that situation myself."[11] Sessions also observed the German political scene.

> I had one very good friend who was a British journalist [for the *London Morning Post*], who, either just before or just after Hitler came to power, took me down one night to the Taverne, the cafe table where the foreign journalists all got

together in the evening, and from that time on I was the most faithful attendant at that table. I heard a great deal about it, heard a great deal of discussion. Sometimes Germans came to the table. There were even spies who came to the table, and I talked with them. When I say spies, I shouldn't say—they weren't secret at all, everybody knew who they were. For instance, a man who came several times was named ["Putzi"] Hanfstängl, whom I had met at Harvard years and years and years before. He was a graduate student, and he was the man who used to play Wagner for Hitler [Hanfstängl ranked high in the regime]. They came and were genial and so forth, but I think they knew where everybody stood.

I remember one night I got into a long argument with a German who wasn't a Nazi but who was trying to justify the whole thing, and the argument lasted till after the cafe officially closed. It had begun filling up with Nazis. They got fairly restive when they heard heated conversation going on, with the names of Einstein and Thomas Mann and other people being mentioned by me. But they couldn't do anything about it, because the press—they were treating the press well, they were trying to—well, get the United States and England on their side, and certainly not succeeding with that crowd at all.[12]

That journalistic "crowd" had its own vision of what would happen. They all felt the French, the Poles, or (perhaps) the British would intervene long before anyone else did. They felt that at any moment the French and the Poles would bomb Berlin. For Sessions's part, he was indiscreet in his pronouncements at the journalists' regular table (*Stammtisch*) at the Taverne on the Nettleborkstrasse in Charlottenburg section of Berlin: "Ich bin Kulturbolschewist!," the term the right wing used for so-called *entartung* (degenerate) art. Overhearing this, one German journalist asked Barbara, "Ihr Mann ist Jude, nicht wahr?" (Your husband is a Jew, isn't he?).[13]

Sessions visited Paris for two weeks at the end of September in 1932. He saw Boulanger there, who was upset that Sessions and not she had been picked for the ISCM jury to meet in Amsterdam in December. (It was for this competition that she wrote Sessions the list of whom to vote for.) Soon afterward Sessions wrote in French to Jean Binet.

So—should I confess that Germany deceived me? I don't have the *feeling* of having been deceived, but when I think of my state of mind the last time I was with you, I do have to admit it. Sometimes I think the only way, at least for me (perhaps it's the normal way) to understand things is to fall in love with them; and so last year I fell in love with Germany, and was doomed to disappointment.

. . . I've seen very strange things; for example, in September I spent two weeks in Paris, and when I returned I had to acknowledge some rather extraordinary about-faces on the part of some friends of mine—they were communists on September 15, Nazis on October 1st! But it was above all striking because I'd been away. Here, even a little more than elsewhere, one sees the growing triumph of the stupidest, most cowardly elements, and in general of the blindest prejudices and the most petty resentments; and the increasing disruption of the strongest and best friendships.

. . . This seems to me to be a neurotic folk—without any internal strength because of a lack of moral education, without confidence in themselves—with all the characteristics that go along with that; a distrustful bunch, uncertain, sometimes submissive and sometimes brutal, and above all putting their trust in dreams, in theories, in books rather than in realities and in experience. Now that they are missing *men* and real traditions of authority and discipline one has the impression of an *extremely* weak populace, and in spite of everything they say, it seems to me almost unbelievable that in case of a grave international crisis they would be able to stay afloat. The radical movements have no *positive* strength of conviction, instead they are outbursts of resentment, lacking inner discipline and missing any individuals of real ability.

. . . There is an *astounding* lack of taste, sometimes; sometimes one has the impression that no one can tell the difference between one kind of music and another, provided it falls into the framework of German convention.[14]

While in Berlin Sessions met Arnold Schoenberg at the home of Hans Stuckenschmidt. They both later taught at the Malkin Conservatory in Boston; but because they taught on separate days and Sessions commuted from Hadley, they did not see each other at the short-lived school. Schoenberg was to have conducted a program of his work at the Boston Symphony, and Sessions was to speak to Schoenberg at the intermission, but Schoenberg was indisposed, and Richard Burgin conducted the Bach-Schoenberg Preludes and *Verklärte Nacht*, January 12–13, 1934.

After the letter to Binet in the fall of 1932 Sessions re-evaluated his desire to live in Germany. "Even before Hitler I had decided that that would be my last year, although when I first went there I wanted to settle there. Those were strange years. Berlin was a very exciting place all during the Twenties, and these years were the tail end of all that . . . Exciting musically, and exciting intellectually, and exciting every other way."[15] During the months after Hitler became Chancellor in January 1933, much changed as drastically on the musical front as on others. On March 11 the director of the Berlin Civic Opera Carl Ebert and Fritz Stiedry, its conductor, were summarily removed from their positions as "non-Aryans." Four days later Berlin radio announced an absolute ban on "Negro Jazz." In April, as a response to prominent American musicians protesting the exclusions of Jews, the radio announced that none of the American composers' pieces or the musicians' recordings would be played, including those by Walter Damrosch. Furtwängler wrote a famous letter, April 6, to Dr Goebbels, the Nazi Minister of Propaganda, asking that Max Reinhardt, Otto Klemperer, and Bruno Walter not be excluded from German cultural life. Goebbels rejected the letter.[16]

Sessions responded in *Modern Music* in the fall of 1933,

In practice, Germany has been deprived of such personalities as Walter, Klemperer, Schnabel, Busch, Schoenberg and dozens of others, whose offenses range from *Kulturbolschevismus* and "non-Aryan" descent to unorthodox opinions in regard to Wagner or Beethoven or merely to personal affiliations of an unorthodox nature. . . . Other musicians, who had taken little or no interest in politics, found themselves in a position of the utmost and most painful moral uncertainly through being forced to come to terms with a set of conditions and standards entirely extraneous to those which had previously concerned them, as performers, composers, teachers, or critics, in the practice of their art. Musical education has been weakened, and the situation of the musicians affected made incomparably more difficult, by the denial to Jewish musicians even of licenses to engage in private teaching in their own homes; while discrimination on racial or political grounds in the matter of the payment of royalties and the fulfillment of contracts of all kinds has become increasingly general with the virtual cessation of legal protection for persons belonging to the affected classes.

After quoting Goebbels's letter to Furtwängler in order refute it, Sessions stated,

> The conception of art as propaganda appeals either to the type of artist who is so childlike as to be incapable of self-analysis, or to minds so academic, sterile, and tortuous as to be incapable of any but purely interested reactions. . . . An artificial shutting off of "foreign contacts" will not therefore necessarily deepen the indigenous ones, nor will it give roots to those who have not got them. If a healthy art cannot absorb "foreign elements" it will throw them off spontaneously, and without external and self-conscious pressure. . . . It is Wagner, not Bach or Mozart, who is the spiritual father of the National Socialist musical ideal; only one of several Wagners, moreover, and that the most purely subjective, visionary, and barbaric one. Beethoven is conceived according to the Wagnerian tradition as the foreshadower of Wagner rather than as the heir of Mozart and Haydn. The Nazi movement, then, is, from a musical standpoint, the victory of a distorted Wagnerism; its spiritual "enemies" includes whatever fresh impulses have been alive in the world since Wagner's time.[17]

When Sessions left Germany in the spring of 1933 he traveled through Florence. The "First International Music Convention" met there in May and included a congress of musicians and music historians who were to discuss opera. Sessions was asked to speak about American opera, which he did in Italian. There Sessions met the French composer Darius Milhaud, who would become a lifelong friend. He also saw many of his Berlin friends in Florence who had already left Germany and were not going back. One was Klemperer: he had thought himself too important to be vulnerable, but suddenly reversed his position and left immediately. He appeared at I Tatti with a letter of introduction from Sessions to Berenson. The whole musical world seemed to be in Florence in May 1933: composers Arnold Schoenberg, Alban Berg, Richard Strauss, Ernst Krenek, Bela Bartók, Zoltan Kodály, and Egon Wellesz; Italian composers Francesco Malipiero, Pizzetti, Respighi, Casella, and Labroca; and writers Edward Dent, Henry Prunières, Alfred Einstein, as well as many others.[18] Sessions was invited to lunch with Malipiero, Berg, and Wellesz, and two Italian composers. He remembered,

> My only other contact with Alban Berg really, was one morning, a beautiful May morning, I wrote a letter to my wife [in Berlin] and went to the post office to mail it and there was Alban Berg, who was a very tall man, striding along. He looked very happy, and we greeted each other. He said, "Let's have a cup of coffee together." [The conversation was in German.] And we went out in the square, sat outdoors, and drank coffee. He asked me what Germany was like, because I had just come from there. And I sang him the Nazi song—not the words. But it was not a very consequential contact—it was a very pleasant one. Schoenberg was the one that I really knew of these [Viennese school] people.[19]

Sessions had met Webern earlier, but was so shy he only shook hands with him.

By 1962 Sessions kept few photographs of his friends posted on bookshelves, but among them were photographs of Schnabel, Bloch, and one of him with Berg and Malipiero at a party in 1933 in Florence. The only other one was a drawing of Schubert.

Figure 30 Sessions, Gian Francesco Malipiero, Alban Berg, Egon Wellesz in Florence, 1933.

Years later Sessions recalled, "When I came back to this country for years, until we entered the war, I was very, very much concerned with this [German] situation, because it seemed to me that nobody in the United States would face up to what was really going on. I won't say nobody, but most people."[20] In 1941 Sessions defended European émigrés in a debate in *The New York Times*.[21]

Sessions went from Florence to Naples then to the US in June 1933 without Barbara. He and Leopold Godowsky sailed on the Italian *Vulcania*, arriving in New York on June 11. No sooner were they on American soil than they spoke out. "Mr Sessions said there was not an opera house in Germany that had not been adversely affected by the ousting of Jewish conductors and musicians," the newspapers reported the next day.

> He said that after the burning of the Reichstag on February 28 he had witnessed beatings of Jews in the streets by brownshirted mobs. "The open violence lasted about five days," Mr Sessions said, "but it did not stop after that. The outrages were conducted behind doors or in the secrecy of the night. I have heard people compare the Nazis to the Fascisti, but there is no comparison. I lived in Italy for six years and in Germany for the last two years. It is not the single atrocity that matters, but the crude and intolerant spirit of Germany, which is incredible to an American."[22]

On June 27 Lincoln Kirstein had lunch with Barbara, still in Berlin. Barbara simply ignored the fact that her husband had had an affair with Kirstein's sister a decade earlier. Kirstein noted in his diary that Barbara warned him: "Every Jew should leave as soon as he can."[23] Sessions did not return to Germany for almost 30 years.

Chapter 4

THE DECADE 1936–1946

MARRIAGE AND THE
VIOLIN CONCERTO

Sessions's personal and professional life got worse before it got better. The nadir and turning point of his career both occurred in late 1936. In 1933, after 13 years of marriage, Sessions and Barbara, who had returned from Europe separately, lived together in Northampton. Then Sessions moved to New York while Barbara stayed in Northampton, separating just as his own parents had done a third of a century earlier, also at the 13-year point in their marriage. The pattern of his parents' marriage was repeating itself. After 1934 Barbara lived in Washington, DC, and in Maine. Sessions's later explanation was that Barbara was enamored of the glamour of Europe and had difficulty readjusting herself to the austerity of Depression-ridden America. Another major problem, however, had reared its head: Sessions decided he wanted to have children and Barbara could not provide them. Ultimately, the decision to divorce was mutual, and he never spoke of her with bitterness.

Sessions then became involved with a student from Smith College, 17 years younger than he. Barbara remarked with irony, "So you're in love again?"[1] This unidentified girl was not stable and caused her friends and Sessions a great deal of worry. She was placed in a mental institution and fell in love with another patient, which let Sessions off the hook. While discussing this relationship Sessions evaluated himself bluntly: "I've been a sinner and I've been a fool,"[2] a comment repeated on other occasions.

Bloch or Albert Elkus may have arranged that Sessions teach summer school at the University of California at Berkeley in the summer of 1935. There Sessions met Sarah Elizabeth Franck (November 15, 1906–July 9, 1982), a student in his Music Literature class who eventually became a private pupil. Lisl, as she was known, hailed from Spokane, Washington. Ten years younger than Sessions (28), she herself was the daughter of a second marriage. Her parents were Hermann Franck, a successful banker who had emigrated from Holland to this country in 1895, and his second wife, Ruby Marble Franck.[3] Ruby was born in Nebraska, while her father came from Maine and her mother from Arkansas. Hermann and Ruby had two children: a son, Robert E. Franck (born ca. 1903), a manager of a contractor's firm who married a native of Iowa, Rhoda. Lisl was Robert's younger sister. She and Robert had a half-brother from Hermann's first marriage, Tom Franck, whom she almost never saw. Lisl told Sessions she planned to work at the New York Public Library in the fall of 1935. She came east, but found the library job too strenuous. When Sessions returned to Berkeley for summer school in 1936, she drove across the country with him to visit Robert in San Francisco. Evidently, Lisl had planned her travel around Sessions's movements. Nothing resembled a whirlwind romance, but Sessions and Lisl decided to get married.

Extremely well read, Lisl eventually worked as a librarian at a boys' school in Princeton. She devoted the next nearly half century entirely to her husband's needs and career.

Sessions needed a wife desperately (he once had told Copland he needed a "NURSE"), and Lisl was willing to fulfill this role without outside pursuits to interfere with her single-minded concentration on him. She remained entirely supportive of and loyal to her husband. Their son recalled, "Her ironclad precept—that with regard to my father's psychological well-being anything that wasn't part of the solution was part of the problem (a precept that if I may say so went so far as to include both her children) took over her life completely."[4]

Divorce is never easy: one is divorcing one's entire life, Sessions once pointed out. In 1936 and subsequent decades, divorce was relatively rare and bore more of a social stigma than it does today. None of Sessions's ancestors for hundreds of years nor his immediate family and his descendents ever divorced, only Sessions.[5] He spent August and September of 1936 at a ranch outside Reno, Nevada, where one could obtain a divorce after six weeks' residency. In August he sold Josephine, the car he used to drive to Nevada, in order to pay for the divorce, but that left him with neither the means nor the money to get back east. Despite his physical distance from the family and the musical world, Sessions would during these six weeks face all of the powerful women in his life: Nadia Boulanger, Elizabeth Sprague Coolidge, Barbara, aunt Adeline, his sister Nan, cousin Catharine, and most of all, Ruth. Perhaps he considered Boulanger and Coolidge as stand-ins for Ruth, and he managed to enrage all three.[6] Nevertheless, this was an entirely epistolary drama.

The state of Nevada would grant a divorce only on the grounds of adultery; Barbara agreed she would be the "guilty party," although he was already ensconced with Lisl. Barbara meanwhile was looking forward to a position in her field in Washington, DC, at Dumbarton Oaks. Hannah felt that the divorce was "absolutely [Barbara's] choice."[7] Hannah's husband, lawyer Paul Andrews, gave Roger legal advice.

The marital separation had caused Ruth to feel that Roger had returned to her; she would again take up her role in guiding him. He had other plans, however. He intended to keep his relationship with Lisl completely secret, so that Ruth would not learn of her until the divorce was final and the marriage almost accomplished. Lisl had met Hannah

Figure 31 Lisl Sessions (courtesy of Elizabeth Pease).

by letter and Catharine in person, but she was studiously kept away from Ruth. Sessions enlisted both Hannah and Catharine as allies. Ruth would have no say about these two decisions, and she would not be allowed a chance to "pass" on Lisl. He had brought Lisl to Hadley without Ruth's being there, secretly introducing her to both his brother John and sister-in-law Dawn. Even Barbara had helped prepare the way by telling Ruth, "I hope and expect Roger to marry again."[8] The family's solicitude was entirely on Ruth's account; none was offered to Barbara.

Sessions stayed at the TH Ranch at Pyramid Lake in Sutcliffe. Nadia Boulanger, having been told by David Diamond that Sessions was divorcing, wrote to Sessions from Paris, urging him to reconsider. Sessions thought this none of her business and forwarded the letter to Barbara to deal with.[9]

Family troubles were not far from the surface. First, Nan had still been attempting to reconcile with her difficult mother, who visited her in Syracuse in April 1935. She wrote her brother, "I felt such a complete lack of contact with her that her departure left me with no emotion except for a general sense of relief from an exacting & physically exhausting round of regrets."[10] Two months later, their uncle Rev. James Huntington died, June 29, 1935; he was buried at the Holy Cross West Park, New York, rather than in Hadley with the rest of the Huntingtons. Soon after his uncle's death, two of Sessions's beloved aunts died in 1936: Molly Huntington and Adeline Sessions. Aunt Adeline, after having sent Sessions $100, then died suddenly on September 10, 1936, in New Canaan, Connecticut. All of the Sessions family, including Barbara but except Sessions, who was awaiting his divorce trial and could not leave Nevada, attended Adeline's funeral. Ruth may then have begun to suspect they knew something she did not. She was having a difficult time, not so much over losing her sister-in-law as with the editors of her autobiography who wanted to cut portions she wanted to keep. The day after the trial, September 22, Sessions wrote Ruth a long, contradictory, even illogical letter from Salt Lake City, dropping the bombshell that he intended to marry soon—someone she had never met.

Prausnitz described much of the fateful letter as seeming "patently untrue."[11] Sessions put an entirely upbeat face on the failure to complete his quartet, the commission from Mrs Coolidge, and his consequently not receiving the $500; he did not mention borrowing from Adeline (he even stated all his debts were taken care of). Gradually he let slip that everyone else in the family knew about Lisl and that he was about to remarry. Reading between the lines, one gleans that Lisl had pursued Sessions, who had kept knowledge of her existence from Ruth for well over a year.

His description of meetings with Barbara the previous winter ring true: "the times we saw each other were infrequent and unsatisfactory + often very painful; we didn't seem to know how to act towards each other, + she was obviously not wanting to come too close to me or to encourage me in any way." And, "You will be tempted to think, I know, that I fell in love with Lisl 'on the rebound.' " Nevertheless he claimed, not entirely convincingly given the rest of the letter, that Barbara "needed only to give me a sign in order to bring us back together." Finally, "what [Barbara] + I had together, to recognize that in many ways my life with her was not *right*. If it had been, perhaps we would not be divorced—when I say not right I mean, of course, not always built on the solidest of bases. What I truly want, now, is to build my future life absolutely solidly; + it is the fact that Lisl can + will help me to do this that has, perhaps almost more than anything else, influenced my decision to marry her." He closed, "I know I have your love, + I pray also that I may have your understanding in this—I know I will have it eventually."[12]

Sessions then avoided Ruth altogether; he returned directly to Princeton for fall classes and left Catharine to deal with the fallout from this letter: she wrote to say that the news was not easy for Ruth to take. (Catharine had lent Sessions $30, to be paid back in $10 increments; sometimes reminder notes were necessary.) Ruth's first documented reaction was to question the need for a separate sitting room for Lisl in Roger and Lisl's anticipated new Pennington rented house (as opposed to an apartment), since Sessions would need a study. Ruth forgot entirely how demanding she had been of Archibald when she insisted on the "necessary" expense of live-in nurses.

Sessions and Lisl married at Phelps House in Hadley on Thanksgiving day, November 26, 1936. It was a small wedding, and in addition to the double celebration, Ruth upstaged events somewhat by presenting copies of her newly published autobiography, *Sixty-Odd: A Personal History*, to the assembled guests. David Diamond received a signed copy (see section "David Diamond").

Sessions's son John recalled the bond between Lisl and Lisl's mother, Ruby Marble.

> I feel very strongly that anyone who didn't know . . . [my mother] before the death of *her* mother in late summer of 1962 really had very little sense of what she was like. The two were extraordinarily close (my mother was even born on my grandmother's birthday [November 15, 1879]), really in many ways like sisters. Certainly I feel I was "brought up," essentially, by the two of them. When my grandmother died, a crucial part of my mother's identity and, rather soon, her vitality and ability to cope with a good many things, went with her.[13]

Ruby Franck was by then Hermann's widow, and she lived in Palo Alto, California. Sessions, too, had enjoyed seeing his mother-in-law when they lived in Berkeley.

Despite the important attempt to break Ruth's dominance over his life, Sessions was still emotionally invested in his mother, still tried to keep the peace between them. He wrote to Ruth in the fall of 1936, "And you see too, there is no reason at all why you and I shouldn't, really, understand each other better than we have ever done, + I for my part am determined that we shall, + will do everything that I possibly can do in that direction."[14] Ruth's control over was Sessions was still in effect; it would be for fully 50 years.

Serge Koussevitzky had suggested to Sessions, after the 1927 premiere of the First Symphony, that he write a violin concerto, another golden opportunity.[15] Copland wrote to Barbara and Sessions that summer hoping Sessions had almost finished his Violin Concerto. Another early mention of the piece was in a letter from Sessions to Slonimsky stating that he had gotten started on a number of pieces including a Violin Concerto.[16] Although years later Sessions would postdate the beginning of work on this piece to his years at the American Academy, it had been begun in the summer of 1927.

By June 1928, just after the Piano Sonata's partial premiere, Sessions confidently told Copland that he would "finish the sonata + work principally on the Vl. Concerto + and other large symphonic work I have in mind. Also the Nightingale + Usher!"[17] Two months later he wrote to Copland, "I am now working on the violin concerto in an effort to get some of it ready to show S.K. next month."[18] These two letters from came Paris and Juziers; similar reassuring sentiments about the completion of the concerto were sent from Rome during his three years there. Nevertheless, he postponed the concerto to work on a new symphony for the deadline of the RCA Victor prize, May 27, 1929.[19] Not only was that symphony not completed by the deadline, which Sessions should have known could not be accomplished, but he also abandoned work on it altogether.[20]

Meanwhile, Koussevitzky, whose ability to program works with relatively short notice within one season was unlike the situation with major orchestras today, was still waiting to see both the symphony and the concerto.

By the spring of 1931, when Sessions met Klemperer, he excitedly wrote to Jean Binet that Klemperer would conduct the Violin Concerto—when it was finished—and that his concertmaster Max Strub wanted to play it with other orchestras as well.[21] Sessions mentioned a deadline of March 1, 1932, for the completion of the concerto in order that Strub play it. By May, however, Strub had had a "breakdown" and could not play it that spring. Strub's situation furnished Sessions an excuse to tell others why the work was postponed; of course, it was still not completed.

In September 1932 Sessions met with Koussevitzky in Paris to show him the first two of the three movements of the concerto. Koussevitzky could not say much since the work was not finished. He did want, however, his concertmaster and assistant conductor of the BSO, Richard Burgin, to be the soloist. And Koussevitzky took Sessions at his word that the piece was nearly complete: he announced to the newspapers that he would perform "one untitled work" by Sessions with the Boston Symphony.[22] On October 15 Sessions had sent the violin part and the piano arrangement of the first and second movements, promising, "It is almost finished now." He wrote, too, "I am very glad Burgin will play the concerto for not only do I know he is a wonderful musician but I also have the impression that he's got a style which my music needs—a strong tone, a deep 'breathing,' *piena voce* [full-voiced] expression."[23] Note that at this late date in the composition Sessions was planning only three movements. The concerto now has four movements, so the idea of adding another movement must have come after the fall of 1932.

The reader will not be surprised to learn, as Copland must not have been, that by Sessions's return to the US in the summer of 1933, he had still not completed the work; he had missed the entire Boston Symphony season. As we have seen, his failure to turn in a completed score of this concerto to the American Academy in 1931 meant he did not formally receive the Rome Prize.

In the winter of 1934 Sessions wrote to Klemperer, now conductor of the Los Angeles Philharmonic, "I am nearly through with the concerto and have been looking on [*sic*] other things as well."[24] Klemperer had performed the Suite from *The Black Maskers* in March and wrote to Sessions about the response.[25] Uncharacteristically, Sessions had written an article for the Sunday *New York Times*; several months later he would publish a letter praising Klemperer's performances of Beethoven's Fifth Symphony on New York Philharmonic concerts, October 11–14.[26]

Meanwhile, the League of Composers embarked on a huge project: they commissioned eight composers for eight performing organizations to present their work during the 1934–1935 season.[27] Four were commissioned for orchestral works: Sessions, Louis Gruenberg, Roy Harris, and Walter Piston, and Sessions was paired with the Philadelphia Orchestra under Stokowski, perhaps because he had just played *The Black Maskers* in November 1933. The Sessions, Randall Thompson (originally commissioned for a choral work), and Piston symphonic projects were held over to the 1935–1936 season.[28] By the following season, the League ceased pursuing Sessions to complete his commission. Sessions never completed a work for Stokowski. Another opportunity with a major orchestra was wasted because of his chronic psychological inability to live up to his commitments.

Copland could only have shaken his head at the news in a spring 1934 letter that "the Concerto will be mostly ready."[29] In the fall of 1934 Sessions gave Burgin the violin part of the concerto, while Sessions was orchestrating the last movement, which he thought would be ready shortly. A November exchange of letters between Sessions and Koussevitzky settled some matters. Sessions wrote that

> I hope you will understand my attitude, when I tell you frankly, that a perform-
> ance in Boston, and especially in New York, would be of great importance to me
> at this time, since I have recently returned to this country and begun my work
> here. It is a curious fact that while my music has been played widely in America
> and Europe, I have not yet had a major performance in New York, and I believe
> that there is a real desire here to know my music better. So, I should naturally be
> not only pleased but very grateful if you could find it possible to put it on your
> program this season.[30]

Koussevitzky could not change the season's schedule at that point, but wrote that he would definitely do the work in both New York and Boston during the first half of the 1935–1936 season. On receiving this letter, however, Sessions made a blunder based on both his lack of trust in Koussevitzky and his ambition to have a better-known violinist play the solo. Glad to wait until next season, but not happy with the bird in his hand, he immediately suggested

> that it might be better for the work if this were entrusted to a violinist who
> could play it later with other organizations. With this in mind, I wonder if you'd
> object to my taking up the matter with Mr [Joseph] Szigeti and Mr [Albert]
> Spalding, both of whom have expressed their interest in the work and desire to
> see it. Mr [Efrem] Zimbalist and Mr [Bronislaw] Huberman have also shown
> considerable interest in it, but I believe there is little or no chance of their
> actually wanting to play it.[31]

Koussevitzky replied that he had shown Sessions's letter to Burgin who had no objec-
tion to Sessions's showing the concerto to other violinists. (Indeed, in September 1935 he announced in the newspapers a violin concerto by Sessions "with Joseph Szigeti the probable soloist."[32]) That Burgin was gallant enough to relinquish a premiere for which he had already been practicing the part may have influenced Koussevitzky's contradict-
ory postscript: "Incidentally, I just learn [*sic*] that the 'People's Symphony' are playing a work of yours at one of their concerts in Boston, and must tell you that I avoid giving works of composers whose names have appeared on their programmes."[33] The People's Symphony Orchestra was conducted by Koussevitzky's nephew, Fabien Sevitzky, who was planning to do the Sessions First Symphony. Sevitzky was a thorn in Koussevitzky's side; Koussevitzky considered his nephew was cashing in on his fame and forced him to change his surname. The People's Symphony, however, did not present serious competition to the BSO. Koussevitzky may have been more annoyed than he let on that Sessions rejected his choice of soloist and used the ill-feeling toward his nephew to escape the performance altogether.

Alarmed by the postscript, Sessions wrote back. He tried to distance himself from the People's Symphony, saying his symphony was published and out of his hands; he would never bring a work in manuscript for them to premiere. He even doubted their ability to play the First Symphony (and indeed they substituted *The Black Maskers* Suite). Nevertheless, it was in part his own fault for still not having completed the concerto and for attempting to secure a better-known soloist. Sessions's actions would lead to a professional catastrophe.

The two major areas of his life, personal and professional, collided in the same month, November 1936—the month before his fortieth birthday. He married Lisl on Thanksgiving, which ended a difficult personal chapter happily. The marriage had also meant, however, the considerable cooling of his relationships with Boulanger and Copland and a subsequent mar on his career. The fate of his largest work to date, much discussed but not yet heard, was now in the hands of one of the violinists Sessions had picked, one who had agreed to do it. This was a huge mistake.

The Violin Concerto was finally completed in August 1935, just before Sessions left Berkeley for the East and four months before the completion of the Berg Concerto. Despite the fact that he had met Lisl that summer, Sessions dedicated the work to Barbara. In October Sessions sent the piano score for the first two movements to Albert Spalding and suggested that "we should not feel committed to Koussevitzky if there is an acceptable chance for performance elsewhere." Sessions's reason was that Koussevitzky "has on several occasions previously, made me unsolicited promises which he then failed to keep and I have no reason to think that he may not do so again." Sessions also confided that Klemperer has given "more than a nibble," and Sessions "would love to have [him] give the first performance." In addition he thought Eugene Ormandy might be interested.[34]

The Boston Symphony had scheduled the work for November 1936, and the concerto was announced in the papers as late as October 11.[35] One interested audience member, violinist Louis Krasner, appeared at Symphony Hall only to read the word *Canceled* over the Sessions concerto on the poster. Spalding had asked Koussevitzky to postpone the performance—in effect canceling it—because he and Sessions could not come to an agreement about the fourth movement, which Spalding wanted changed. Sessions found he could not alter the last movement, a tarantella played punishingly fast throughout. Although Spalding could not point to anything unviolinistic, he clearly did not have the technique to bring it off. Strub had gone over the first three movements with Sessions, who took his advice seriously. (Spalding, the heir to the sporting goods manufacturer, tried to make amends to Sessions by offering to pay for expenses incurred: there were none, however.) In addition, Serge Kotlarsky had played the violin part, with Sessions at the piano, in a private performance, November 22, 1935, that Diamond and Gideon attended, and at the Murray Theater in Princeton, January 26, 1943. The solo was difficult but playable—as any violinist nowadays could testify by looking at the part. The soloist does not have to compete with other violins; there are no first or second violins scored in the concerto.

A year later, after no public performance, a chastened Sessions wrote to Koussevitzky attempting to revive interest the concerto by the BSO. He mentioned that both Jacques Gordon and Nicolai Berezowsky would be happy to play the work. He even said he would be satisfied with Burgin. Koussevitzky, however, had two American concertos planned for the 1937–1938 season (by Edward Burlingame Hill and John Alden Carpenter) and, in an unwelcome gesture, released Sessions so that other orchestras could play the work.

Koussevitzky may well have been furious after almost ten years of waiting for a composer who continually dithered. We know for a fact that he never scheduled any work by Sessions again for the nearly two more decades he conducted the BSO. This in itself was a huge blow to Sessions, who had always written orchestral music with the BSO sound in his ear. Worse, however, was the rumor that the work was unplayable, even unfinished, although it is easy to understand how the second part of such a rumor could have spread. Once taken hold, gossip like that is almost impossible to conquer. For example, an anonymous *Time* magazine author, reviewing the Second Symphony in 1947, wrote inaccurately, "He is probably the most difficult of U.S. composers. His twelve-year-old violin concerto bogged down all but one of the many violinists who tackled it."[36]

In a manner he neither could have predicted nor desired, Sessions had a certain third-party revenge on Spalding. This came obliquely in 1937 via composer William Schuman, whose Second Symphony won the Aid to Spain competition. Sessions was the only judge to have voted against the piece. Schuman visited the older man in Princeton, where the two hit it off personally. Sessions changed his mind about the symphony, and encouraged Schuman to continue work on it, but Schuman discarded the piece. So soon after the cancelation Schuman must have heard an earful about Spalding. Sessions did not know he was confiding in the future (1945) President of the Juilliard School of Music, or that Schuman would, in the first semester there, summarily dismiss Albert Spalding from his 12-year position on the violin faculty. Schuman also fired Sessions's good friend Frederick Jacobi. As director of G. Schirmer, he saw to it that Schirmer published Sessions's Second Symphony. This was the only work Schirmer published; Sessions's works were mainly published by Edward B. Marks and (later) Theodore Presser.

Louis Krasner finally met with Sessions and received a long explanation of the Spalding episode from Sessions's point of view.[37] Sessions played the work in the summer of 1939 with violinist Robert Gross, at Colorado Springs. He wrote to Miriam Gideon, "We played really quite well—*far* better, beyond all comparison, than the New York performance which you heard. It was very satisfying to find this work, which has in a sense been so unlucky, still better than I had realized + to again be excited + moved by it. I believe it is the best, or at least the most complete + and characteristic work I have written—the test, that is, from the Sessions point of view!"[38] He expressed similar sentiments to Krenek. Gross played the work with the WPA Illinois Symphony in the Blackstone Theater, in Chicago, Izler Solomon conducting, January 8, 1940. This constituted the true premiere, since it was played with orchestra. Benjamin Britten attended this concert (and did not like the piece).[39] In 1941 the National Youth Orchestra, under Leopold Stokowski, with Gross as its concertmaster, played the first two movements of the work.

Sessions had played the work in a piano arrangement at the University of Oregon in the spring of 1947, and violinist Patricia Travers performed the piece in Germany. Krasner, who had premiered both the Berg and the Schoenberg concertos and had played each with the Minneapolis Symphony, wanted to interest its conductor, Dimitri Mitropoulos, in the Sessions concerto. Once Sessions had Krasner's concert date for Minneapolis, November 14, 1947, he wrote immediately to Koussevitzky to disabuse him of his reported impression the work was still not complete.

Tossy Spivakovsky wrote to Sessions in 1949 of his admiration and love for his concerto. He had evidently persuaded Mitropoulos to conduct the concerto with himself playing "next season" at the New York Philharmonic. The violinist expressed his praise to Sessions: "The originality, nobility and loftiness of thought in your work fascinated me at once, and I am convinced that it will not take long to be recognized as one of the few great violin concertos."[40] Spivakovsky gave the New York premiere of the Bartók Violin Concerto, the only time the composer heard the work. This projected performance, however, did not come to pass.

Finally, on February 15, 1959, 24 years after its completion, Spivakovsky premiered the Violin Concerto in New York with Leonard Bernstein conducting the New York Philharmonic.[41] The concerto was also republished, this time by Edward B. Marks.

Gunther Schuller conducted in a 1968 recording (CRI 220) with Paul Zukofsky, still the only recording of the work. As a gesture of homage, David Diamond hid quotations from both Sessions's Piano Concerto and the Violin Concerto in his own Ninth String Quartet (1966–1968).

Elliott Carter, a long-time admirer of Sessions, reviewed the New York performance:

> There are obviously many degrees of similarity possible between phrases controlled by the same directional motif, and when directionality is used with other kinds of remote relationships such as imitation of outline, ornamentation, and simplification, directional inversions, etc. The play of these could be likened to the use of metaphor and simile that results in the fascinating effects described in Empson's *Seven Types of Ambiguity*.
>
> More and more the notion of extended, continuously flowing sections during which ideas come to the surface, gain clarity and definition, and then sink back into the general flow has characterized Sessions's unique style, and he seems to have striven for this first here. When Sessions wrote this work, the twentieth-century concerto had reached a rather fixed stage of development through the combined efforts of Stravinsky, Prokofiev, and Hindemith. Shunning the Classical opposition of solo and orchestra, it had turned, of course, to the Baroque form for assistance in finding a way to organize concertos in which the solo was the prime mover and in which the orchestra is used mainly to intensify and amplify the solo part. Sessions carries this method further than any of his predecessors. The violin dominates the orchestra in every sense, playing almost continuously a part of prime thematic or figurational importance; it is never dwarfed or overwhelmed in volume of sound, intensity of expression, or brilliance by the orchestra. Yet the orchestra has a typical life of its own. This remarkable feat not merely reveals high skill but must be the result of careful choosing of characters, themes, and all other devices with the final end in mind.[42]

Sessions thought Carter's remarks were remarkably insightful, "almost uncanny," and "brilliantly discerning."[43]

This entire experience reconfirmed one important lesson in Sessions's mind. Already highly hesitant to promote his own music because of his personal insecurities and his New England background, Sessions now had evidence that supposedly confirmed the futility of doing so. The Koussevitzky episode was the last time Sessions would ever try to influence a conductor or a performer to play his music.

In 1937 Hannah Andrews tried to convene a family council about supporting Ruth. Nan and her husband planned to supply her with a yearly income, and they thought that, despite moments of forgetfulness, Ruth should live alone, as she wanted, without an attendant. Nan wrote to Lisl, intuiting that she was the person to talk to about money and family property rather than Roger. Nan wanted to discuss a plan to try "to retain all the land permanently."[44] Indeed, Lisl took firm control of all the Sessions family finances—a wise move. Their daughter Elizabeth has said concerning his use of money, "If it weren't for my mother, Dad would have been in the slammer!"

Sessions had written to his first wife in 1937, on his first wedding anniversary, that Lisl was pregnant. Barbara's reply was the only letter of hers he kept, perhaps to assuage any guilt. Barbara had written,

Your letter at Thanksgiving time took of course, a little while to be assimilated, and I could not write at once. I know you understood much of how it could not but make me feel. But in the most healing and happy way there has finally come for me a sense of deep satisfaction that for you this fulfillment is ahead. It is difficult for me to explain why this should be; it's an impersonal thing, in a way, outside ourselves. Yet I can think with real joy now of there being a child of yours, and I am profoundly happy that it is to happen. Please know this, my dear, and that I mean it with all my heart. I write stiffly because that is the only way these words will come. But I know you will forgive that and understand.

Perhaps to remind Sessions—and herself—of her own attractiveness, the remainder of the letter was devoted to an Italian friend of Berenson's who had given her "a whirlwind campaign of gallantry in the most stereotyped Italian manner."[45]

Barbara lead a useful life as an art historian, never remarried, and continued to suffer from ill health. In 1934 Barbara had lived at 2021 Q Street NW DC. She wrote on June 20, 1936, to Dr James Lincoln Huntington, Sessions's cousin, about her medication, a continued use of Luminal, a "marked sedative and depressant," that was prescribed the previous fall by a Dr Reynolds. In addition Barbara was concerned that her sister Eleanor needed a "heart man," to keep her blood pressure down. In this letter, she confided that she had accepted a position (rather than take one with "the Boston Museum") with the private collection of Mr and Mrs Robert Woods Bliss in Washington DC, where she would be doing "primarily research."[46] In June 1936, she was at the Walker Art building at Bowdoin College in Maine.

In August 1941 Barbara wrote to James Huntington of her "own difficulties [that] do not seem to have cleared up entirely," and she mentioned that she had "had no more of the attacks (evidently slight convulsions) . . . [since] four of [which] occurred between October of last year and early June of this."[47] Barbara also thanked James for having treated Eleanor, who was well enough to return to France to work for the Friends Relief Committee. Barbara herself now wanted to consult Huntington again professionally. She had been working with art historian Wilhelm Koehler at Harvard, which as an institution had been good to her concerning her health problems.

In the early 1950s she told Huntington of her "terrific struggle against my illness has had to be waged on a rather a new plane—with increasing success, I am thankful to report. In fact, there is no doubt that I am really better now than I have been at all since my breakdown in Providence."[48] She wanted to shed "the whole psychoanalytic attitude, as well as the anti-convulsant medications I have been using for so long."[49] She concluded her problem was a simple one of basic morale. That did not prevent her doctors from prescribing phenobarbital and anti-convulsants. Clearly, she suffered from protracted bouts of ill health involving some sort of seizures.

All three Foster sisters found themselves unmarried and living in or visiting New England. In "Return of the Natives," an article in the Claremont *Eagle-Times* in 1975, Barbara, at age 76, was described as "delicate and gentle in a rose-plaid suit," her sister Eleanor as "vibrant in green jersey and colorful scarf." Eleanor had been divorced from engineer and part-time flutist Jan Merry in France, where she was required to return to her maiden name. She returned to Paris shortly after the interview. For 18 years she was the musical organizer and scriptwriter for a Masterworks of French Music radio program, heard on 300 American radio stations. She had stayed in Paris during the German occupation, working with the American Friends' Service Committee. A love of dancing and an investigation into a method of improving "centered coordination" led to a series of exercises she evolved that strengthened a belt of muscles in the solar plexus region. She wrote a book in French on the subject, *The Solar Center of the Body: Source of Energy and Equilibrium.* The interviewer noted that Eleanor was her own best advertisement: "At 78 she moves like 40; her enthusiasm glows like 20."[50]

Barbara was described in the same article as having made Bernard Berenson's acquaintance and having done a considerable amount of research for him. Her life was spent mostly in libraries and museums. She had studied art in Paris, Florence, and Rome living with Sessions. In Washington, DC she helped prepare the Dumbarton Oaks collection for transfer to Harvard University. Working with Koehler, she researched the history of medieval manuscript illuminations. For eight years in the late 1960s and early 1970s she was curator for the Andover, Massachusetts, Historical Society. In June 1975 she returned to Claremont, and, because of poor health, lived in the Tolles Home on Sullivan Street.

Sessions saw her again at least once. He and his family moved to Cambridge in the fall of 1968 to take up the prestigious year-long position of Norton Professor of Poetics at Harvard University. These lectures were published as *Questions About Music.* For whatever reason, Sessions felt it incumbent upon him and his wife and two children to travel to Claremont, New Hampshire, to visit Barbara in the Tolles Home. Elizabeth Sessions remembered the excursion vividly, thinking that the whole experience and conversation was "very civilized." One must wonder, however, what prompted Sessions to visit his former wife. He had been, since 1936, and would continue, paying alimony at the rate of $500 a year (which Lisl resented, but Sessions did not). Did he want to introduce her to his two children, ages 20 and 22? It was doubtless meant in kindness and friendship. Sessions remained on good terms with almost everyone in his life. We do not know whether Barbara ever heard the concerto dedicated to her.

Many aspects of Sessions's life had been difficult, and the birth of his first child was to be another. John Porter Sessions was born eleven weeks prematurely on March 5, 1938. The medical emergency was traumatic for both parents; indeed, the baby was not expected to live, since at that time extremely premature babies did not often survive. The baby was kept in the hospital for an extended period and needed special formula when he came home. The dog Popo kept John company when he finally left the hospital. Sessions, a first-time father at age 41, wrote a piano work, *Little Piece (for John, Age 1, 1939).*[51]

> We had to watch him very carefully. We couldn't let him cry at night, because he had a slight hernia, which was dangerous. So I would get up and walk the baby on my shoulders every night. And then finally after a year and a half, we were told we should let him cry now. The first time he cried for a good hour, then he suddenly stopped. After a little while my wife said to me. "Do you suppose he's still alive?" And I said, "Well, I think he is." I didn't get much work done between '36 and '41, I guess.[52]

Fortunately, John lived and grew to be taller than his father. During 1938 Sessions found the time to write a Chorale for Organ, in his own way turning to religion during this crisis: he dedicated it to his wife Lisl.

Suzanne Bloch remembered seeing Sessions in Princeton later; she had a son, Matthew, and Sessions was with John. "And he was so impressed. He would say, 'You know, listen. He can go [sings] 'Jack and Jill went up the hill.' There was Roger Sessions teaching his little boy to do Jack and Jill! Ah, it was so lovely, you know."[53]

So upsetting was this near loss for Roger and Lisl that their next child, Elizabeth Phelps Sessions, born September 5, 1940, eventually felt that all the parental attention had been directed to her older brother, and that she was not as cared for (by her mother; her father always stood by her) as the delicate baby had been. Elizabeth was born when Sessions was 42, a little older than the age of his own parents when his brother John was born.[54]

Both children had Huntington family middle names, Porter and Phelps, and their first names also came from the family heritage. John was Sessions's fraternal grandfather's name as well as that of his brother. The name Elizabeth went back at least seven generations and was also her mother's name.

John attended the Episcopal Kent School (where he was confirmed). Father Sill had long before noted that each generation of the Huntington family became problematic for their parents and expressed hopes that Sessions's son, once sent to Kent and under his influence, would reverse that legacy. Pater's hopes were in vain. John later attended Princeton University (class of 1959), and studied cello in New York at the Manhattan School and in Cologne. A call from Sylvia Welch ensured him a job at Smith College, where he taught music for many years and received tenure. John married an Italian Catholic, violinist Giovina d'Aprile, another Manhattan student. Elizabeth, who was not confirmed and did not attend a religious school, received a B.A. from Barnard and earned a Ph.D. in Slavic languages from Princeton (class of 1968). She taught Russian at Brandeis for a few years. Elizabeth married widower Robert Louis Pease at her parents' Princeton home, 63 Stanworth Lane, in May of 1970. Pease, a theoretical physicist who taught physics at the State University of New York at New Paltz, died in 1994.

The symmetry Sessions's sister and brother had already provided—Nan had two boys, John two girls—was continued by Sessions, who had a boy and a girl. That symmetry

Figure 32 Elizabeth and John Sessions at the Matterhorn (courtesy of Elizabeth Pease).

Figure 33 Roger and Lisl Sessions (courtesy of Elizabeth Pease).

was extended again when John Sessions had a daughter, Teresa Alba, born June 24, 1966, and Elizabeth Pease had a son, Roger Daniel (named after his mother's father and his father's father), born May 5, 1974. (Sessions's grandson's birthday was on the fifty-third anniversary of George Bartlett's death; perhaps Sessions did not remember his former friend by this time. In any case, he never mentioned George to Elizabeth.) Teresa Sessions enrolled in Georgetown and returned to study at Smith, then married Robert Peacock in 1992. Roger Pease attended Georgia Tech and followed in the footsteps of his father, becoming a computer chip designer. Sessions would have become the great-grandparent of three children by Teresa. His last name, however, was destined to die out in his grandchildren's generation. Neither Roger Pease nor Teresa Peacock would carry on the Sessions name.

DAVID DIAMOND

David Diamond may first have heard Sessions's name at the age of 12, in 1927.[1] His family had moved to Cleveland, where he began two years' study at the Cleveland Institute of Music, which Sessions and Ernest Bloch had left in 1925. By November 1934 Diamond was enough aware of Sessions to want to study with him and with Paul Boepple in New York.

Diamond vividly remembered first meeting Sessions at the New Music School and Dalcroze Institute at 9 East 59th Street in the winter of 1934. Sessions's voice was "unforgettably deep and resonant of unmistakable culture. He was robust then; imposing; not so much tall as stocky and sturdy, like some great oak tree. He was only thirty-eight years old but seemed older because of his large head with its impressive calvity. With swarthy skin, full sensuous lips, he seemed to me like some fabulous oriental potentate."[2] Suzanne Bloch remembered, "David Diamond in those days cleaned the floors. Every morning when I arrived [at the New Music School] to give my lessons, he was there sweeping the floors in the school to pay for his lessons with Roger. He was also a bartender, I think."[3]

After Diamond's first year of study a correspondence began when Sessions congratulated him on winning the Elfrida Whiteman Scholarship that allowed him to continue his studies at the New Music School. Following a second year of study with Sessions, Diamond traveled to Paris in the summer of 1936 to work on the ballet *Tom* with Léonide Massine. Sessions prepared the way by writing to Nadia Boulanger: "I am sending this by my friend + pupil Mr David Diamond; I know that when you meet him you will understand why I think so very much of him, + feel that he is one of the truly few. [. . .] But it is, truly, a real joy to me to send you this friend, than whom I cannot imagine a more truly satisfying representation of myself."[4]

During the summer of 1936 Sessions wrote to Diamond from Nevada:

> But I have thought of you so much, + hope that the summer has been a good one. I had a letter the other day from Nadia B. + she spoke so very nicely about you—only said you had not shown her your music—+ she was disappointed. How come? [. . .] Lisl + I will be married in the fall, but neither of us yet knows just when. I have had a rather severe blow, financially, [the failure to complete the Coolidge commission] about which I won't go into details just now; but this *may* force us to postpone our marriage till the Christmas vacation. In any case, we want you to be at the wedding—as one of the witnesses if my brother should *not* be there, since of course I suppose he will have to act as witness if he is. But the two people we really want with us that day are you and my cousin Catharine Huntington. Also—I wish you wouldn't say anything much about the fact that I

am to be married, just yet in any case; I shall tell very few people, in any case, probably, as we want it quiet.[5]

Since Sessions could not leave Nevada until after the divorce trial two days later, he made the burdensome request that Diamond hire movers and move all his belongings out of his New York apartment to Princeton by the end of the month. Dutifully, Diamond performed this "great favor," obeying Sessions's desire that it be done "as cheaply as possible."

Although his student was almost 20 years his junior, Sessions and Lisl accepted Diamond's friendship, which was particularly valuable to Sessions at a time when many others were deserting him because of his divorce. When Sessions married Lisl, in November of 1936, Diamond was one of the few invited to Hadley for the ceremony. Ruth greeted Diamond dramatically as "friend, musician, idealist."[6] Diamond would witness and sign the marriage certificate.

Diamond freely acknowledged that their 50-year relationship was stormy at times, which is confirmed in letters. Diamond did not follow Sessions to Princeton, as both had hoped, but rather went to Paris to study with Boulanger, which was difficult for Sessions to accept. When Diamond returned to France in the summer of 1937, he was in the tricky position of continuing to study with Boulanger, the woman whom Sessions never forgave for her interference in his divorce and the renowned teacher whose pull on the gifted student was undeniable. The tension between the two older figures forced Diamond to try to please both of them, an almost impossible task. This summer produced seven of his eight preserved letters to Sessions.

Sessions wrote to Diamond at Fontainebleau:

> And don't *you* let *me* down! By which I don't mean, certainly any course of action which anyone—including myself—can [illegible[7]] even in [illegible] most insidious guise of "opportunity" dull your sense of what you *have* to be + do. I dare say this seems like nonsense to you but you will understand some day. However it is one of those things which it does absolutely no good to say, since, if you really have in you what I have always believed, you need no advice—+ if you shouldn't have the strength nobody's advice could save you.[8]

Diamond wrote to Sessions a month later, first raving about his lessons with Boulanger, then asking, "Do you feel, that if for some reason, Nadia can find a way to have me stay in Paris until she returns to America because I am so unsettled about a way to live in New York this winter. Shall I stay on? I want *really* to come back in October, but what will I live on, where will I live, and how will I work?"[9] Sessions responded at great length to Diamond's letter, dispensing advice but worrying that "When I [compared myself] to N[adia] + A[aron] I felt that nothing I [could] say at this time would carry any real [weight] with you + felt too that you had [made] up your mind." He continued,

> However, I must tell you [one] thing very definitely; it isn't [easy to] tell you, but for your sake [as well] as my own it has to be [acknowledged] that [what] you have said about com[ing back] to me—both before you left [N.Y.] + since you have been in Paris [—you] have spoken as if your coming [de]pended on Nadia's decision + no[t on] yours—[and] on her intentions regarding [you, not] on yours regarding her. If I had chosen, I might have [drawn] very obvious conclusions from this—[and] the result would certainly not have [been]

a favorable one as far as the [abi]lity of your continuing [to study] with me is concerned. And I hope this [is] plain; if you come back to work [with] me it must be because I am your [first] not your second or third choice; + [while] I shall not ask [you] to proclaim this [from] the housetops I shall expect it to [be per]fectly clear + unequivocal between you [and] me and anyone else whom it may [concern].[10]

Diamond wrote back:

Firstly Roger you must never feel I am or ever did consider returning to you as a second choice after Nadia, for going on with Nadia is entirely out of the question and has always been so. [. . .] The real solution was for me to return to America and seek a cheap place somewhere along 3rd Ave. between 59 + 72 Streets. If this does not work out to return to Rochester until I can raise enough money through loans to keep me in New York through next spring. I understand so well the importance of my return to New York, but I don't ever want to go through the horrible conditions I faced in 1934 or last winter's jerking sodas from 9–3 for $12 a week on top of a stomach disorder. It was no joy, that I'm sure you know. And I certainly don't feel myself to be an opportunist! If I come back it's because I know definitely I must continue the good promises I've accomplished, and the loyal friends I have in New York are worth more to me than any kind of arrangement that could be made here by Nadia. [. . .] [Be]sure always dear Roger, though I'm not very good at handing bouquets, that being with you (aside from lessons) is one of the greatest joys I've felt. Often I think of the nights we've had boiled eggs + toast together + I'd give up a great deal to do it *this evening*.[11]

Sessions responded:

Of course all this, I realize depends on the sources of income which you have. If you *have* a source of income, well + good; otherwise the only thing for you to do is to find a job which will assure you a living—+ give you as much free time as possible for your work + study. Please don't think I consider this an ideal solution; but it is life, + what hundreds of others—including the very greatest—have accepted as a matter of course. And all really first-class men (and a lot who are not first class) have managed to survive it + do their work just the same. Above all, it is life + reality—the only healthy basis for any life or career. [. . .] But you see what I *don't* like is your writing me that your decisions depend on my, or anyone else's, answers to your questions. I am not—as I told you in the spring—the least interested in bidding for you against N. B. or otherwise offering you inducements to come back to study with me. I told you months ago—before any of this arose—that I would teach you without charge if you wanted to go on. [. . .] So, mon cher, in the kindest + friendliest possible spirit—please try to grow up! It seems incredible to me that you should not have seen in advance that the money for your return was far from guaranteed—it all came from the fact that you were anxious to go to France + very anxious, too, not to antagonize N. B.[12]

Although Sessions's advice was down-to-earth and realistic, Diamond might have thought that it did not quite resemble Sessions's own career. Sessions had received two

Guggenheims, the Rome Prize, and a Carnegie grant that kept him and his wife afloat in Europe for seven years. He had never worked at a menial job, as had Diamond. Diamond, always impecunious, had not set aside money for his return. Although Sessions had done exactly the same thing in Nevada the previous summer, he nevertheless scolded Diamond for lack of foresight regarding money, a case of the pot calling the kettle black.

Quick to defend himself, Diamond wrote Sessions:

> Your second letter came this morning and truly after the perfect suggestions of the first one, I was a little aghast at what you bring up in this one. Honestly Roger have I been so much a deceiver that you cannot clearly see how deadening the whole business is? [. . .] Now to come back to New York to face the possibility of finding another horrible job like soda jerk is beyond my remotest wish. You speak about my growing up and facing reality. Very well Roger I'll face it clearly with your most honest answer. Can you say I have not had my share of reality (at its rawest state) from all I've had to do the last 3 years from the Dalcroze School to last winter's work? [. . .] I've had my fill of your *reality* and my life's been in my hands all my life long, but it's up to my neck. The fake + pretense which exists in America stifles me. [. . .] I've music to write + progress to make + I'll be damned if I'll be stopped by bad finances. I shall come to New York and barnstorm until I can raise some money for myself. Then we'll resume our work. How long it will take I don't know, but always keep faith in me.[13]

Sessions wrote in some exasperation, "I will only say now that you misunderstand me utterly in thinking that it is a question of whether N.B. has taken or could 'take my place' or that that could ever have other than a sentimental importance to either of us."[14] Within two months of Diamond's return to the US, however, he asked Sessions for a letter of recommendation for a Guggenheim fellowship to study with Boulanger. Sessions dispatched the letter and then wrote to Diamond: "I feel, on the basis of your attitude since last summer and before, that we no longer agree on fundamentals sufficiently to make it fruitful for either of us to try to go on together. You remember, I wrote you in August the conditions under which I felt that we could go on. I said that if you came back I expected it to be a real choice, made with *real conviction.*"[15]

Despite what might not have been an entirely enthusiastic recommendation by Sessions to the Guggenheim Foundation, Diamond did receive a Guggenheim fellowship in 1938. The epistolary relationship continued, but their letters became much shorter and more businesslike. Diamond briefly described his problems with Sessions in a letter to a fellow Sessions student and Rome Prize winner, Charles Naginski: "How I wish R. would not feel bitterly towards me. One day, perhaps, he'll see my decision to study with B[oulanger] was for the best."[16]

In March of 1939 some of the misunderstandings were cleared up, however, Sessions expressed one specific regret about his behavior. Whether this regret was justified is hard to know. We have no evidence that Diamond ever took offense. It may be an example of overly scrupulous self-criticism such as Sessions applied to his music:

> I can remember attitudes—quite unconscious + irresponsibly exaggerated—on my part which may have made it extremely difficult for you to be frank with me. I mean, not only that I spoke more freely + less seriously that I should have done, in regard to certain people; but I spoke about homosexuality, for instance in a

way that must have seemed to you quite obtuse + insensitive; in a way that, certainly, misrepresents my real attitude *entirely*. It is just, you know, my habit of letting off steam + though you could not have been aware of that at the time, meant precisely nothing.[17]

Diamond was openly homosexual. Sessions also wrote: "I'm sorry I seemed 'cold.' I certainly did not, + have not, meant to be harsh with you, + do not mean to be now. You ask me 'surely our friendship is not through.'—The truth of the matter is that it has seemed to me that, on your side, it has been through for some time."[18]

Diamond moved quickly to repair the situation: he met with Sessions in early April 1939 in New York. Sessions was again seduced by Diamond's charm and wrote "what a good time I had with you yesterday morning."[19] All was temporarily forgotten while Sessions's evaluation of Diamond's music rose in tandem with his personal estimation.

A year later, in the spring of 1940, however, grievances appeared again. Belatedly, Diamond asked for the return of the violin he had left in Sessions's care in 1937. Had he been more aware of Sessions's foibles, he would not have been so foolhardy. Sessions moved out of his apartment and absentmindedly left the violin there. The incident of Diamond's missing violin produced enough blame to go around, and the instrument was never found.

More misunderstanding arose the next year when Diamond asked for Sessions's reaction to an outline for a set of lectures Diamond proposed to give at Smith College. Sessions's response upset Diamond and Sessions wrote again to try to explain himself.

> You are facing very much what I had to face twenty-three years ago [in 1918], with certain differences, some of them favorable to one, some to the other of us; I know fully well both how hard that is, and am fully acquainted with the various forms of torture that one goes through. But you really ought to know, and I am sure you really do know, that *security* nowadays simply does not exist— it is nowhere to be found, in my life any more than in yours. The best we can hope for is that by a gigantic and multiple effort we can somehow help to restore it to the world. Of course I am very, very sorry that as a "hero" I have "never quite measured up," as you say. But does it seem entirely sophistical when I ask you whether any one ever can, conceivably, measure up to some one else's demands? One is obliged first of all to measure up as far as possible to one's own, and I doubt if any one ever succeeds at that, even.[20]

This breach was similarly repaired. Sessions wrote to Diamond asking him to come to Princeton to talk, which Diamond did in early April. Sessions wrote again, "It was *very* good, I thought, Sunday, + I hope you feel reassured about everything. Believe me, you have every reason to do so."[21]

The next month, however, produced another contretemps. As president of the American section of the ISCM, Sessions had secured a performance of Diamond's *Music for Double String Orchestra, Brass and Timpani* at the Festival in New York May 7–27, 1941. Sessions wired Diamond to not ask for money, since the performers were not being paid; Sessions begged him to cooperate.[22] Nevertheless, Diamond withdrew the work from performance because, as he remembered in 1988, he "was not allowed to attend a rehearsal."

The 1940s were a decade of both productivity and recognition for Diamond, which helped relieve his daily struggle for money. He was awarded a second Guggenheim

Fellowship and a $1,000 Rome Prize in 1941. (He could not go to Rome because of the war; the next year the Fellowships were suspended.) He also received a commission from Dimitri Mitropoulos to write *Rounds* for string orchestra. The Koussevitzky Foundation commissioned Symphony No. 4, and he was awarded a National Academy of Arts and Letters Grant. His String Quartet No. 3 (1946) won the New York Music Critics Circle Award. Recognition and success came to the composer while in his late twenties and early thirties.

From his new position on top of the world in 1950, Diamond turned on his former teacher by severely criticizing Sessions's Symphony No. 2 in print. The work had garnered some bad reviews (see section "Symphony No. 2"), and Diamond jumped on the bandwagon:

> The first movement is far too long—far, *far* too long—and too busy for its materials. The recapitulations seem to be the result of calculation rather than inevitability for fulfillment of the structure. The second movement is entirely too short, and of a charm bordering on the banal, a quality heretofore not recognizable in Sessions' music. The third movement is the best, most convincing, but again, too long. And the last movement fails mainly for its inferior material . . . [and] incessant din. The last measures fail to bring the work to a conclusive termination . . . The orchestration of the entire work lacks variety, especially in textures and sonorities.[23]

In 1951 both Diamond and Sessions had Fulbright fellowships to Europe and both landed in Florence, where the two saw each other fairly often. Evidently Sessions forgave and forgot the review. One of Sessions's friends, Mario Labroca, seemed politically too far to the right to suit Diamond. When Sessions explained that Labroca had his good points, Diamond responded, "I suppose you can find *some* good in *anybody*." Sessions returned in 1952 to his "lame duck" year at the University of California at Berkeley, while Diamond remained in Italy for the next 15 years. When he returned at the age of 50, he taught at the Manhattan School of Music (1965–1967). Resuming a long-moribund correspondence, Diamond wrote to Roger and Lisl Sessions, November 26, 1966, congratulating them on their thirtieth wedding anniversary. The two were "surprised and touched" that he should have remembered the event.

Two years later Diamond again tried to resurrect the relationship, this time with an even grander gesture. His Ninth String Quartet was not only dedicated to Sessions but also contained hidden quotations from Sessions's own Piano Concerto and Violin Concerto. In August 1968 Diamond sent the Quartet to Sessions along with a hint of the quotations. Sessions wrote back,

> That [the quotation] escaped me until I really read the work through for the third time is a tribute to the fact that the piece is *really* yours, and that the fragment in question is thoroughly integrated into the whole—as one would, after all, expect. But I am very much touched, nevertheless, by the quotation, and delighted and honored by the piece itself. It is beautifully written for quartet—very transparent in texture, and, it seems to me, very clear in the general design. Excuse me—I hope this sounds as it is intended to sound, and I assure it is not meant as an ex-teacher putting an ex-pupil on the block! As you know very well, the qualities I have spoken of are neither very common, or are they at all easy to achieve![24]

He ended the letter with the hope that the two would see each other again sometime that winter.

The last preserved letter from Sessions to Diamond is dated December 9, 1972. Afterward, letters would not be necessary: Diamond joined the Juilliard composition faculty in 1973, where Sessions had taught since 1966, and they saw each other weekly until 1983. Diamond spoke eloquently at a memorial concert for Sessions in 1985 and later published "Roger Sessions remembered." Here he looked back on the 50-year troubled relationship: "When, a half century later, we would find ourselves together at Juilliard, the far past came into its proper perspective, and we were finally the colleagues we were meant to be, free of rancor and anxiety, and yes, he would even own up that, as I had been hotheaded and impulsive in my youth, so had he been egotistical and shortsighted."[25]

The publication of their letters in *The Correspondence of Roger Sessions* gave rise to further evaluations of this relationship by book reviewers who rarely failed to notice the uniquely intense quality of the Sessions–Diamond correspondence. The anonymous *Publishers Weekly* reviewer interpreted the problems as based on Sessions's "ill-concealed jealousy" of his younger student. Such an interpretation had not occurred to Diamond or myself, but seemed at least plausible to us. On the other hand, George Tsontakis, who knew both composers well, wrote in *The Musical Quarterly*,

> Diamond's letters reveal the shortcomings of youth; they display a seemingly insatiable need for attention aimed at Sessions, who appears to grow increasingly weary with each missive. [. . .] Even so, the relationship, if sometimes thorny, provided a certain support for Sessions. [. . .] Throughout, Sessions remains genuinely concerned for the younger composer's welfare, even when admonishing Diamond to stand on his own two feet.

Tsontakis described the letters of the 1950s as written "to and from the now more mature, gracious, and reasonable Diamond."[26]

The magnetism of Diamond's personality, his knowledge of personal events in Sessions's life, and the investment of time and energy the older composer gave him all pulled Sessions irresistibly toward his talented student. Diamond described Sessions's "music, for all its problems, [a]s the work of a relentlessly obsessive mind chained to the demands of an equally relentless intellect. He composed not out of ambition, but because he could do nothing else."[27] No matter how problematic the relationship became, Diamond was always able to salvage and preserve this valuable friendship, while Sessions repeatedly forgave him. And it was Diamond's encouragement and help that prompted me to write both *The Correspondence of Roger Sessions* and this biography.

PRINCETON

"If somebody had told me, just before I landed in New York," Sessions mused 42 years later, "that when I came back from eight years of living in Europe I would be teaching at a university within three years, I would have tossed him overboard or jumped overboard myself, because it was the last thing in the world that I wanted to do."[1] Sessions said,

> I had a job in Boston with [the Malkin] conservatory which had just been founded. It started out with a great flourish. Unfortunately, shortly after I'd been engaged to teach composition there [on Thursdays and Fridays], I found that they'd engaged Schoenberg, also. This excited me but also dismayed me a little because I didn't see how I was going to make much money if Schoenberg was teaching there, too. As a matter of fact, neither of us had any pupils to speak of and the conservatory didn't last very long.[2]

Nicolas Slonimsky, whom Sessions had seen daily in Berlin, endorsed the idea of Sessions moving to Boston. Sessions, however, rented a house in Northampton, where he lived with Barbara during the 1933–1934 school year and from which he commuted to both New York and Boston every week. The couple separated in the fall of 1934, and he moved to New York, living at 149 East 61st Street off of Lexington Avenue for $45 a month. The means of the commute was a car named Annabelle, whose successor was the Plymouth, Josephine. Europe now seemed remote: "I felt when I came back from Europe: 'Well, Europe is out of my life completely.' Because I could see nothing but destruction coming near."[3]

At the same time Sessions was engaged to teach at The Boston Conservatory of Music, located directly across from the Boston Symphony, at 256 Huntington Avenue. The Malkin Conservatory was on Beacon Street. Circulars with Sessions's photograph were sent out. The text read: "The Boston Conservatory of Music announces the engagement of Roger Sessions, Distinguished American Composer. Mr Sessions will conduct courses in Theory of Composition (Harmony, Counterpoint, Instrumentation, Composition) Classes now forming."[4] Despite the advertising, by October 2 Sessions had no pupils. One person contacted the school about meeting with Sessions, but he was not a student. Alan Chamajians, recently renamed Alan Scott Hovhaness, wanted to show Sessions his music. The president, Albert Alphin, did not know whether to charge, since Hovhaness said he was a friend of Sessions. Sessions never had any classes or students there. By August 1934 Sessions had accepted a position at yet a third Boston school. "I had a job also at Boston University. I gave a couple of courses there for several years, I forget how many."[5]

He taught as a lecturer at the New School for Social Research in New York City; as a lecturer at Boston University College of Music; as a teacher at the Malkin Conservatory in Boston; and in New York at the Dalcroze School of Music, all four—in two different cities—from 1933–1934. He later estimated his total income from these four jobs as $2,000.[6] At the New School he taught Beethoven: the Sonatas opus numbers 101 and 109, and the Op. 59, no. 1, and Op. 131 quartets, for which he gave Schenkerian reductions.

Copland arranged a Yaddo Conference during the fall of 1933 in which Sessions participated. Clarifying his position on music schools, Sessions gave the *Herald Tribune* his views about the efficacy of composers griping. "There is, so far as I know, no cause to 'complain' of the attitude of the established music schools toward the American composer, nor did I voice such a complaint either on my own behalf or in behalf of others."[7] And "It seems to me that a complaining attitude on the part of the composer, aside from its general inappropriateness, does his cause the worst service possible."[8] The New England gentleman had spoken.

In the second semester—winter 1934—Jean Binet, who had previously taught at the Dalcroze School in New York, recommended Sessions to Paul Boepple. Boepple asked Sessions to join him in a partnership. He suggested forming a new institution to be called the New Music School at the Dalcroze Institute that used the Institute's building at 9 East 59th Street.[9] Sessions began the proceedings in late January with a lecture "The composer and musical education."[10] Pianist Lydia Hoffmann gave the New York premiere of the completed Piano Sonata at the New Music School, October 24, 1934. Among the faculty were Suzanne Bloch, Ada MacLeish, Harvey Pollin, and Israel Citkowitz. Problems began almost immediately, however, because Sessions was not completely committed to the Dalcroze method. Boepple hired another teacher whom he later married, and she and Suzanne Bloch, who taught there on Sessions's recommendation, did not get along.

According to Suzanne,

> Mr Boepple was trying to have us teach in the style of the Dalcroze method that he had taken. And he had invited people like Roger and me and Ada MacLeish [who had sung at the Paris Opéra], wife of Archibald MacLeish, to tell us how to teach *do, re, mi.* And I remember Roger kept passing me little notes about how awful it was. We didn't last very long, because he wasn't paying us either.[11]

They gave up the New Music School in the middle of its third semester, spring 1935. By March Sessions had decided to quit—which can hardly be viewed as anything but a failure on his part—and went back to private teaching, for which he tried in vain to get a Carnegie grant to support himself. The next year Boepple succeeded Margarthe Dessoff and conducted the Dessoff Choirs for the next 32 years. Sessions also published his ideas in two articles about opera and music criticism, the latter bore the subtitle "Composer's concern with journalistic criticism a sign of his immaturity."[12]

Milton Babbitt first met Sessions in the late summer of 1935 by climbing the several flights up to his "dark attic room" in the Granberry Piano School building apartment (Sessions had no affiliation with that school). Sessions had so little room in the studio that he had to sit on the edge of the bed to examine Babbitt's compositions. Babbitt perceived Sessions's "removal and isolation [as] a pervasive one." He and his colleagues described Sessions as "the lone Roger."[13] Arthur Berger also observed Sessions "stood alone . . . he was not a joiner."[14] Sessions said, "This was the worst period of my life. I felt totally alone, because I was entirely opposite the current that was going around here. . . . I mean those were awful years really. I had no friends really among American musicians at all."[15] His friends were Krenek, Karol Rathaus, Schnabel, Klemperer, Kolisch, Steuermann, Hans Weisse, and Stiedry. Miriam Gideon, who had debated between studying with Schoenberg or Sessions and chosen Sessions because he was likely to stay on the East Coast, remembered him as having "been in Europe for so many years that he was practically an expatriate."[16]

Babbitt had few publications of Sessions's works to consult: the Piano Sonata was published by Schott (according to Babbitt, against the wishes of many in the publisher's hierarchy). The Symphony and *The Black Maskers* Suite were both published, via Copland through the largesse of Alma Wertheim, by the Cos Cob Press. The Edgar Stillman-Kelley Society published the 1935 Violin Concerto. Sessions did not have a real American publisher. The situation with recordings was worse: the first, and for a while only, recording of Sessions was of the 1936 String Quartet by the Galimir Quartet.[17]

Author Paul Bowles studied in a harmony class of Sessions's beginning in February 1935. A Young Composers Group met for a while in Bowles's apartment.[18] In 1935 Sessions was evidently working on a viola sonata (no longer extant) for Marcel Dick, later a violist in the Cleveland Orchestra.[19] Other students and composers sought out Sessions. Ross Lee Finney was teaching at Smith College in the mid-1930s, and drove to Phelps House to show Sessions his music. Vivian Fine worked with him at the Dalcroze School, along with Miriam Gideon, David Diamond, Hugo Weisgall, Irwin Heilner, and Lehman Engel. This group, as well as Babbitt and Princeton students, would represent the first generation of Sessions's students in this country.

Miriam Gideon arrived one day for her lesson at the Village apartment to find a note on the piano: "From this time on, I want all my students to call me 'Roger.' "[20] Gideon also offered Sessions her 410 Central Park West apartment (17F) for him to teach. Sessions had changed studios several times: first the East 61st Street studio, later Gideon's apartment, and then a tiny studio in Greenwich Village. He also taught lessons at Alma Wertheim's apartment, and in the early 1940s Mark Schubart's mother provided an apartment at 38 Grove Street for Sessions to teach.

In the summer of 1935 Sessions was asked to teach summer school at the University of California at Berkeley. Both that summer and the next he lived at 2600 Ridge Road in Berkeley. "I'd never been south of Washington or west of Cleveland before, and I got in my car one morning and drove down to Macon, Georgia and then turned to the right and went to Jackson, Mississippi, where I visited a pupil of mine [Babbitt], then drove down to New Orleans and from New Orleans out to Los Angeles, and from Los Angeles up to San Francisco and Berkeley, spent the summer there and then drove back."[21] He finished his Violin Concerto in San Francisco in August 1935, the night before he started driving east.

> During that summer [of 1935] I was offered a job teaching two courses in the New Jersey College for Women, what is now known as Douglass College, and I went and taught there. I at least had an assurance of some money, because that whole spring before then I don't think I had any money at all. I don't know exactly how I managed. Maybe I ran up some bills. I'm sure I did.[22]

His parents had also done so living in New York in the 1890s. Sessions was hired by Dean Margaret T. Cowin to teach at the New Brunswick college.[23]

The music departments at Harvard, Yale, and Columbia had been founded in the nineteenth century by John Knowles Paine, Horatio Parker, and Edward MacDowell, respectively. Princeton, however, did not have the advantage of a strong composer committed to incorporating music into higher education until the mid-1930s with the advent of Roy Dickinson Welch, frequently referred to as the "Father of Music at Princeton."[24]

Welch, who we have met at Smith College where he was chair of the department of music from 1924 to 1934, had received two Guggenheims (1930 and 1931) to Austria and Germany. In the 1934–1935 year he had been invited by Princeton President Harold Willis Dodds to report on the wisdom of establishing a music department. What little there was of a music department was then under the Creative Arts Program; later it became subsumed under the Department of Art and Archaeology.

Welch had less in terms of money, faculty, and facilities than did Martha Sanders when she helped found the Cleveland Institute of Music. The CIM was in far better shape as a musical institution when Sessions arrived there in its second year than was Princeton in 1935, the second year of Welch's efforts and the year Sessions was hired. Despite its Ivy League status, Princeton did not have much to offer music students or faculty in the middle of the Depression. Indeed, 20 years earlier Smith's music department had been much more substantial than Princeton's was now. Sessions was again on the ground floor of an enterprise, like the Cleveland Institute and the New Music School, which could fail. Almost 40, he was starting over once again, teaching elementary harmony to freshmen.

"In the Fall of 1935 I had a telephone call one day from Roy Welch, who said that a man named Ralph Downes, who taught [at Princeton], had been offered a big job in England [as organist of the Church of the Oratory in London] and was going away. Would I come and finish up the term with his courses?" The British Downes was the first organist and choirmaster for the Princeton chapel, dedicated in 1928, and taught the freshman course in harmony. Downes resigned, November 19, 1935, during Welch's first full year. Welch remembered his young colleague from Smith of almost 15 years earlier, Roger Sessions. Downes had received $5,000 a year, but Sessions earned $1,200, since he replaced Downes only as lecturer. An organist and choirmaster was needed to fulfill Downes's other duties; J. Earl Newton of the New Jersey College for Women held the organ position temporarily, while Sessions took over Downes's teaching of harmony. "For the first term I was paid by Ralph Downes, officially, not by Princeton University."[25]

Welch was allowed to select two faculty members for the Music Section: he chose Sessions and musicologist Oliver Strunk, who had been chief of the Library of Congress Music Division. The Music Section's facilities consisted of a tiny office for the chairman and a still smaller office for the secretary. The students met in the basement of Alexander Hall, the Peking Room of Murray-Dodge (shared with Theatre Intime), and the crypt of the Chapel. The library was stored in McCormick Hall, and there were no practice facilities. Babbitt recalled, "No member of the teaching staff had an office, or even a desk, and students were met on stairways, chapel crypts and street corners. During World War II there was no functioning Music Section. Roger taught an occasional [American] history (not music history) course in service programs, and served as an auxiliary policeman; Oliver Strunk taught German."[26] Sessions also taught History 109, Modern European History.

In 1935 the "Section in Music" had 35 students; by 1941 it had 380. The entire three-member faculty taught the two courses: 1) Polyphonic period, Strunk; and 2) the Romantic and Modern Periods, Welch and Sessions. In this Sessions had to compete with Welch, who was frequently honored by students as one of Princeton's "most inspiring lecturers."[27] Recognition as a teacher counted more heavily in the music department than did achievement as a creative artist.

Sessions still needed to scramble to teach elsewhere to supplement his income. In the fall of 1936 he joined the new Cecelia Music School of the Madonna House Settlement in New York City, run by Heidi Katz. The faculty included Edgard Varèse, and Sessions was to teach advanced composition and counterpoint. This school may have fizzled out, along with Sessions's job, when in the fall of 1937 another school for students of limited means was founded by Heidi Katz and Samuel Chotzinoff. This was the Chatham Square Music School at 211 Clinton Street, and its faculty included Sessions, Miriam Gideon, and Samuel Barlow.

Sessions's position at Princeton from 1935–1936 was visiting instructor. The next year he became half-time instructor in music. From 1937–1940 he was assistant professor of music (his official title in 1937 was assistant professor of harmony and counterpoint), and from 1940 to 1942 lecturer in music. In 1942 he was promoted to associate professor of music, a position he kept until he left for Berkeley (which offered him full professor) in 1945. Ironically, that year Welch finally established a Department of Music at Princeton. When Sessions returned—he referred to this Princeton-Berkeley-Princeton period as his life's ABA form—in 1953, he was made, along with Arthur Mendel, professor of music. From 1953 to 1965 he was the first William Shubael Conant professor, and from 1965 until his death he was William Shubael Conant professor emertius. Welch wrote of Sessions that he was fine as a teacher of graduate students and upperclassmen, but, "in the pre-war years, he had outlined the work to be covered and left the teaching to his assistants. . . . As a classroom instructor on the whole, informal, but systematic and provactive."[28]

In the late 1930s Sessions was busy with his new position, wife, and two children. Nevertheless some of his music was being performed. He was supposed to have had a one-man concert at the New School for Social Research during the 1935–1936 season, but this did not come to pass. In 1938 he worked on a Symphony on A minor, never finished. In November 1939 the WPA Composers Forum-Laboratory at the Lenox Art Gallery of the New York Public Library presented a program devoted to "the provocative music of Roger Sessions, a composer whose awareness of his times and boldness of expression have greatly influenced modern writing."[29] The works played were the Piano Sonata (John Kirkpatrick), "On the Beach at Fontana" and "Romualdo's Song" from *The Black Maskers* (soprano Lodema Legg; probably Sessions as accompanist), a collection of short piano pieces (probably those for children and the Pages From a Diary) played by Sessions, and the E minor String Quartet performed by the Galimir Quartet.[30] At the conclusion a public question-and-answer period with the composer was held.

John Duke continued to perform the Piano Sonata, once in November 1936 in Princeton; Paul Stassevich conducted *The Black Maskers* Suite for the League of Composers at Town Hall, with Harriet Eels as soloist (she sang "Romualdo's Song" on her vocal recital April 20, 1936; it was also done in May 1936 by the Brooklyn Symphony conducted by Chalmers Clifton); and the Chorale for Organ was played on Lazar Saminsky's Three Choir Festival at Temple Emanu-El in late March 1939. Sessions's largest work during the late 1930s was his first String Quartet, premiered in March 1937 in Washington and New York by the Coolidge String Quartet. On the same concert was the winning work by Jerzy Fitelberg, for whom Sessions had voted as a member of the jury for the Coolidge Prize. (The other adjudicators were conductor Eugene Ormandy, Oliver Strunk, German critic Paul Bekker, and violinist Jacques Gordon; 263 composers entered.) Sessions also served on the Rome Prize jury for two years, 1938, the year his student Charles Naginski won, and 1939, when it was awarded to William Denny from Berkeley. Sessions also performed himself; with cellist George Barati he gave a concert of cello music by Beethoven, the two sonatas, op. 102, and Bagatelles, op. 126.

Politically, Sessions was active in two ways. He joined the Musicians' Committee to Aid Spanish Democracy by judging a competition that would award a commission for a new orchestral work. The other members of the jury were composers Copland, Harris, and Bernard Wagenaar and conductor Alfred Wallenstein. The committee "raised funds for the purchase of an ambulance, which will be used by the American medical units on the Madrid and Aragon fronts in Spain."[31] He was one of 160 musicians in 1939 to sign a petition to President Roosevelt to denounce the embargo against Republican Spain as serving "only to aid the forces of aggression and international lawlessness which are already threatening our sister republics of South America."[32]

In 1941 a new presence was added to Princeton's Music Department: Rosamond Foster Sayre, Sessions's former sister-in-law and the dedicatee of the Piano Sonata. She became the music librarian, department secretary, and general factotum. She typed Sessions's business letters and kept carbons, initialed "RS: rfs." Her husband, Daniel Clemens Sayre, had been hired that year to plan and head the new department of Aeronautical Engineering.[33]

During late 1941 poet Wallace Stevens read his poetry at Princeton. Afterwards, Henry Church and his wife held a dinner party in his honor. Stevens was afraid he had insulted everybody and would never be asked back. (This unjustified self-blame was common in him.) He wrote to Church several months after the event, convinced he had lost the Churches as friends. "Then too, Roger Sessions worried me to death. I thought that possibly my bearing toward him had not been what it should."[34] Church reassured Stevens on all points, including Sessions: "I'm sure of Sessions you made a real friend for you made him sit down at the piano and play again his own composition—That rarely happens to him—That was just before the evening broke up—I dont [sic] know what else you could have done to him—I am deeply grieved that you have had so much *mental torture*."[35] It is likely that Sessions played some or all of the *Diary* pieces. At least he met Stevens; his friend Vincent Persichetti set Stevens's *Harmonium*, but Stevens had not attended two performances in New York. Persichetti never met the poet of one of his best works.

Edward T. Cone joined Sessions's composition class in 1936, and received a B.A. in 1940 and M.F.A. in 1942. Cone remembered the pieces he studied in Sessions's classes: Bach's *Well-Tempered Clavier*, Beethoven's op. 59, no. 1, *Nuages* and *Fêtes* by Debussy, Mahler's Sixth and Eighth Symphonies, and Schoenberg's opp. 11 and 23. One entire semester was spent on the *Tristan* prelude, which Sessions played at the piano from memory. Cone and Babbitt were to remain in Princeton for the rest of their careers.

Andrew Imbrie recalled his first meeting with Sessions; Imbrie was 16 and just back from studying with Boulanger at Fountainebleau. He entered Princeton in 1938 and was graduated in 1942. He studied in a group of 10 to 12 students, clustered around a piano. Such public exposure of a teacher's remarks about a student's work could easily result in hurt feelings, but Sessions was always so tactful in his corrections that students' egos went undented. "The disarming informality of his teaching never interfered with our sense of the keenness of his perception of musical discourse. His ability to pinpoint the hesitancies and obscurities in our music seems to us nothing short of uncanny."[36]

During Imbrie's senior year at Princeton, the class spent an entire year on Beethoven's quartet, op. 132—without getting to the last movement.

Roger's teaching was maddeningly discursive: one thing would remind him of another, this would trigger an anecdote, and so on for perhaps ten minutes. Then he would pause, place the palm of his right hand behind his left ear, and say, "BUT . . ." and would return to his original topic. The curious thing was that this topic now had acquired a new depth of focus brought about the apparent digression.[37]

Sessions was still speaking out politically. For *The Princeton Herald* in 1944 he wrote a front-page article entitled "Why I oppose a change in administration." "I shall work for Roosevelt . . . because between the two I prefer Mr Roosevelt on every issue that seems to me to be really important." Sessions wanted to discuss the "vast and complicated problems of war and peace." He mentioned the implications of the atomic bomb and

the real issue, which is not the abstract willingness to join a world organization [the UN] which might or might not be effective. The issues involved are: first, recognition of the question in its real and urgent necessity; secondly, the willingness to face candidly and to attack patiently and with understanding the enormous difficulties involved—moral, economic, political and finally, willingness to accept the sacrifices necessary if such a world organization or any program whatever is to succeed.[38]

Sessions was to teach summer school elsewhere besides Berkeley. Black Mountain College, a highly experimental, "progressive" college, had begun in September 1933 under John Andrew Rice.[39] Located 15 miles from Asheville, North Carolina, the school occupied vacant YMCA summer camp property, and in 1941 moved to nearby Lake Eden. There were no credits, no grades, and the college never had more than 50 students at one time. The faculty was usually paid only room and board: they served out of personal desire. Nevertheless, because the creativity of the artists who came as both teachers and students, Black Mountain achieved a position in the world of the arts out of proportion to its actual size. Its influence in art, dance, music, and poetry was considerable and lasting.

The first major figure in the school was the painter Josef Alpers, who had arrived from Europe when his institution, the Bauhaus, was closed. Later, important European and American artists taught or studied there, including Robert Motherwell, Ben Shahn, Helen Frankenthaler, Cy Twombly, Willem and Elaine de Kooning, Franz Kline, and Robert Rauschenberg. Merce Cunningham represented the world of dance; his company was founded there in 1953. Music in the school's later period was heavily influenced by the presence of John Cage and David Tudor. In 1946 at Black Mountain musicologist Edward Lowinsky completed his controversial study of *musica ficta* (chromaticism) in the Renaissance. Lou Harrison taught for two years and was replaced, in 1953, when Stefan Wolpe joined the faculty and remained until the school closed in 1956.

The period immediately preceding the 1944 Black Mountain Summer Institute had been uneven, to say the least, with regard to music faculty. The first semester, in 1933, a young composer/violinist named John Evarts applied to teach there: he confessed to not knowing the bass clef. Evarts was a protégé of Thomas Whitney Surette, director of the Concord Summer Music Institute, whose credo might be summarized as "Learn as much as possible through doing: through singing and through playing an instrument . . . Music is not only important as a field of study, it should become a part of daily life."[40] This almost communal approach to music fitted snugly into the collaborative artists' colony atmosphere fostered at Black Mountain. Nine music majors, however, could hardly be called an orchestra; twice as many students enrolled in folk dancing.

In 1935 Henry Allen Moe, secretary to the Guggenheim Foundation and advisor to Black Mountain, consulted with Surette to find a composer-in-residence. Their usual discernment abandoned them when they chose Dante Fiorillo. Prolific, Fiorillo produced pieces with Black Mountain and the names of its founders in their titles. One author gave a dramatic explanation for Fiorillo's abrupt departure. He had solicited many pieces from European colleagues telling them he would play their works in the United States. At one concert composer Alan Sly detected a strong similarity between a work by Fiorillo and one of those European scores. He reported the plagiarism to Moe and Surette, and Fiorillo was let go.[41]

European painters or architects had long been a major factor at Black Mountain. The musicians, the British Sly and the Italian Fiorillo, had not lasted. Black Mountain's doors opened to European emigrants who could not otherwise find teaching positions in American universities. Jewish émigré musicians associated with the Second Viennese School came: violinist Rudolph Kolisch, pianist Edward Steuermann, composer Ernst Krenek, and conductor Heinrich Jalowetz. The esteemed Schoenberg pupil (1904 to 1908) Jalowetz had also studied with musicologist Guido Adler, knew Mahler, and conducted the Cologne Opera, leading works by Schoenberg, Berg, Webern, and Krenek. He went straight to Black Mountain in 1939 and stayed at the college until his death in 1946. "Just as significantly for the fate of Black Mountain, he seems to have had the character of a saint."[42] He and his wife Johanna embraced the communal life of the college. Duberman stated categorically, "Jalowetz . . . was probably the single most beloved figure in Black Mountain's history."[43]

Sessions, who already knew many of these musicians, did not take Surette's ideas too seriously; however, he responded to an invitation, probably from Jalowetz, to the first Black Mountain Summer Institute, held in celebration of Schoenberg's seventieth birthday in 1944. The war in Europe and Japan was still raging. Jalowetz thought the time had come to "reconstruct our shaken world." The stage was set for an unprecedented meeting of "virtually all of the prominent" European Viennese school in the United States and the major American modernists to talk, perform, and bond personally in the great out of doors that is the North Carolina Appalachian mountains.[44] Schoenberg, although not physically present, was spiritually omnipresent that summer at Black Mountain.

Jalowetz and Frederic Cohen had organized the Summer Institute. Performers included pianist Steuermann and his students, singer Lotte Leonard, and a quartet assembled by Kolisch. Composer Mark Brunswick was invited; he had lived in Europe from 1925 to 1938 where he was associated with Webern. In the United States he was chairman of the National Committee for Refugee Musicians (1938–1943), through which he was responsible for saving and transporting to the US a large part of Austro-German musical culture. He taught at City College of New York for 21 years. Roger Sessions was the other American composer invited. Like Brunswick, he spoke German fluently.

Sessions so enjoyed himself that summer that in September he wrote to *The New York Times* enthusiastically:

> The college, which is situated in the Blue Ridge Mountains, was founded in the early Thirties by a group of idealists who believed that education is a kind of collaboration between individuals differing in experience and knowledge but between whom barriers arising from positions of authority are minimized to the

Figure 34 Black Mountain 1944 Summer Music Institute faculty. Seated on grass from left to right: Frederic Cohen, Elsa Kahl, Marcel Dick. Seated: Johanna Graudan, Heinrich Jalowetz, Lotte Leonard. Standing: Nikolai Graudan, Rudolf Kolisch, Lorna Freedman Kolisch, Edward Lowinsky, Mark Brunswick, Edward Steuermann, Ernst Krenek, Trudi Straus, Roger Sessions (photograph by Barbara Morgan, Barbara Morgan Archive).

utmost extent. In practice this results, as I was able abundantly to observe, in an amazing freedom of discussion which to one coming quite unprepared from the outside world, is extremely impressive in its testimony to the maturity and seriousness of which young Americans [students] are capable.

. . . Those who participated in music at Black Mountain this summer will never forget the experience and will certainly do all in their power to keep it alive both there and elsewhere.[45]

Sessions sent birthday greetings, along with a copy of his summer lecture, "Schoenberg in the United States," to Schoenberg.[46] Schoenberg responded with a *cadeau* of the first page of the manuscript of *Die Jakobsleiter*.[47] This was the beginning of their friendship as well as the beginning of the thaw in Sessions's opinion of the master and of twelve-tone music. Black Mountain exposed him to talented European musicians who were entirely devoted to Schoenberg. Already identified with Europeans, Sessions at Black Mountain became even further embedded with them in the public's mind.

Sessions's enthusiasm for Schoenberg and the friendships with Europeans he made and renewed at Black Mountain never wavered. But his excitement about Black Mountain itself was transferred to a spin-off of the avant-garde school. At the end of 1944 Frederic

Cohen resigned and asked Sessions and Brunswick to join him at a rival summer institute in 1945 at Kenyon College, in Gambier, Ohio, where they spent that summer. Black Mountain embraced John Cage in the summer of 1948, and some American modernists had already decamped. With a new leader, Black Mountain emphasized poetry and continued its experimental tradition—turning from a school into more of an artists' colony—before its demise in 1956.

Back at Princeton the next year, Sessions encountered "office politics." Babbitt recalled,

> One early morning in wartime 1945, I had just finished teaching a calculus course, and was walking across the campus toward breakfast, when Roger came dashing dangerously, breathlessly, and angrily out of the Art (music) building, shouting, "They gave Oliver Strunk an office, but not me! I am going to Berkeley." He insisted I accompany him to the Western Union office, before breakfast, to wire acceptance of the offer from Berkeley which he had before not weighed very heavily. Five minutes after firing off the telegram, Roger, over coffee, already was having misgivings, but there could be no turning back to no office.[48]

SYMPHONY NO. 2

President Franklin D. Roosevelt died April 12, 1945, while Sessions was in the midst of writing the slow movement of his four-movement Second Symphony. The first and last movements were only partly finished at the time; indeed, the two middle movements were completed before those two. "The slow movement's very dark, and I felt very much in the mood to dedicate it to Roosevelt, simply because his death was very tragic, a terrible loss to the world, of course," Sessions recalled. "In a very real sense I think a great many people, including myself, felt it as a kind of personal loss as well. Then the symphony of course was written in wartime, mostly. For me, I would not like to say it reflects the war—it didn't consciously—but I feel it's associated in my mind with it. It was."[1] The climatic passage in the last movement Sessions called "the atomic bomb," associated in his mind with the bombing of Japan in 1945.

The First Lady, Eleanor Roosevelt, had written in a 1962 etiquette book that when one addresses a professor one should say "Professor Sessions." "I was a little bit surprised, because I don't know Mrs Roosevelt. There must be another [Professor Sessions] some-where."[2] Mrs Roosevelt may have been well aware that Sessions's Second Symphony was dedicated to her husband's memory. Sessions marked the score "Princeton-Gambier-Berkeley, 1944–46." During the summer of 1945 he had taught in Kenyon College in Gambier, Ohio. Almost two decades had passed since the First Symphony.

Sessions continued, "It's sort of the culminating point of a life that begins with my First Quartet, perhaps. That's the way I looked at it at the time, although I'm not sure . . . but I feel that my Second Sonata, much more than the symphony looks ahead to the works that came later on."[3] Both the Second Symphony and the Second Sonata were finished near the end of 1946, the turning point in Sessions's life and music.

The Second Sonata, completed December 1, 1946, was premiered in Berkeley by Bernhard Abramowitsch, then played on May 16, 1947, by Andor Foldes at the Museum of Modern Art, its first New York performance. Edward T. Cone and others who attended Foldes's performance felt that the Sonata broke a new path for the composer. Sessions said in response, "Well, that's very interesting, because I wasn't so aware at the time. I wrote the Sonata very, very fast, comparatively speaking. I really wrote it in about six weeks. And I wrote it too fast to notice this."[4] Sessions felt that Cone played it better than Foldes, who later admitted to Sessions that the piece was incomprehensible to him.

"Milton Babbitt pointed out once, he said to me, 'Do you realize you're on the fringe of the twelve-tone system?' I said, 'Well, no, I didn't think of it. Not consciously.' He said, 'Look, there's lots of things. For instance, you realize the bass, at the beginning of the slow movement, is a retrograde version of the melody in the right hand.' "[5] Because many of the motifs appear both melodically and harmonically, Cone felt a deep unity between melody and harmony. He pointed to the way the first theme of the second movement grew out of the tremolo at the end of the first: from the cluster of two notes a melody emerged.

Ruth Sessions, 87, died on December 2, 1946, the day after the Sonata was finished, several days after the completion of the Symphony. For almost half a century—Sessions would turn 50 four weeks later—Ruth had dominated his life. Now she was gone; Sessions was finally free of trying to please her. He did not dedicate the Sonata to her. (It was first dedicated to Foldes and the dedication accidentally removed on publication; Sessions did not reinstate it.) He had considered dedicating the Second Symphony to Ruth, but when Roosevelt died months before she did, changed his mind. He never dedicated any of his works to Ruth.

Sessions's chronic lateness also affected the premiere of his Second Symphony. The Alice M. Ditson Fund of Columbia University, controlled by Sessions's Yale friend Douglas Moore, commissioned the symphony. The Ditson Committee had difficulty getting the work performed, because Sessions was late in getting the score to the committee's chosen conductor, Leon Barzin. Barzin felt he did not have time to prepare the NBC Symphony Orchestra for a May 1946 performance. Moore transferred the rights to the premiere to Monteux for a New York premiere, which did not come to pass. The next idea was that Alfred Wallenstein conduct it in New York with the Los Angeles Philharmonic (February 7, 1947); but Wallenstein felt three rehearsals were insufficient. The Ditson fund finally released itself from the premiere rights and asked Sessions to accept any invitation he might receive; indeed, Monteux had done the work in San Francisco a month before this formal notice. Despite all this, the work won the Music Critics Circle of New York award as the outstanding new orchestral composition by an American citizen played during the 1949–1950 season. On May 17, 1949, it won a Naumburg Musical Foundation award (Welch was on the committee), which meant it would be recorded.[6]

Andrew Imbrie remembered preparing the parts for the Symphony before the San Francisco premiere, January 9–11, 1947.[7]

> Along with my colleagues [I] was willingly conscripted for the correction of the instrumental parts before the rehearsals began. . . . We stayed up late at Roger's house the night before the first rehearsal, Roger himself doing the string parts. At about four in the morning he discovered an omission of perhaps ten measures of music for the first violins, which of course had to be corrected in each individual part. There ensued a string of Anglo-Saxon monosyllables, punctuated by "Excuse me, gentlemen." . . . As the rehearsals progressed, the sense of the music miraculously began to take shape, like an unfinished Michelangelo. The sculptural simile is intentional: I do not recall ever hearing music that had such a tactile quality: the ideas and their transformations unfolded for me with a breathtaking palpability; yet of course they were constantly in motion. They rocketed around me, echoing through the vacant auditorium of the San Francisco Opera House like guided missiles. The eloquence, the excitement, and the luminous triumph at the end left me in a daze. I haven't recovered.[8]

Sessions's program notes for the premiere dwelt on the importance of the key of D minor (the key of the first movement) and described the other movements as in F minor, B flat minor, and D major. By this time, however, tonality was no longer completely functional in his music.

The premiere performances of this symphony were not well received by the press. *Musical America* reported that the audience was "offended" and "verbally vindictive." To the reviewer, "It seemed to express the epitome of all that is worst in the life and thinking of today."[9] Yet one of the performers, violinist Michael Mann, son of the novelist Thomas Mann, wrote to Sessions an admiring letter.[10] Sessions's notes state his position: "It must be remembered that for a composer musical ideas have infinitely more substance, more reality, more specific meaning, and a more vital connection with experience than any words that could be found to describe them."[11]

Just before the New York premiere, perhaps thinking of the bad reviews four years earlier, Sessions inoculated himself somewhat by publishing in *The New York Times* "How a 'difficult' composer gets that way."[12] Using the Berg Violin Concerto as an example, he demonstrated that the public does catch up to the work once its idiom becomes familiar.

The New York premiere, with the New York Philharmonic on a concert broadcast from Carnegie Hall on January 12, 1950, also received bad notices. It drew fire from *Time*: "A few in the placid audience just couldn't take it. As Dimitri Mitropoulos flailed the orchestra through the first movement, sharp, hard and dissonant, they got up and walked out. The survivors were rewarded. The slow movement was just as uncompromising, but more elegiac, occasionally reminding them of melody. The final movement, like the first, was a rouser."[13] Diamond's negative reaction has already been cited. Perhaps he had read *The New York Times* review, which hedged its bets: "For us it is a painfully studied and artificial piece of writing . . . this may be a mistaken estimate of the work."[14] An enthusiastic minority in the audience called him back repeatedly. When the piece won the Naumburg recording award, another critic from the *Times* liked it better.

Mitropoulos's interest in the work had developed in a purely Sessionsesque manner: "In a visit to Mr Sessions' home in California last summer [1949], the conductor asked about the composer's piano sonata. The latter went hunting for it in the basement. When he returned, Mr Mitropoulos, who had casually picked up the score of the symphony and had read through a good deal of it, began to ask questions about the way to handle the slow movement."[15] Sessions felt that Mitropoulos played the second movement more deliberately than he wanted it.[16] Nevertheless he cited Mitropoulos with Jean Martinon as two of his most loyal conductors. On June 9, 1948, at the ISCM Festival in Amsterdam the Symphony was given its European premiere by the Concertgebouw Orchestra.

Sessions ultimately thought he should have called the second movement an intermezzo. Program annotator Michael Steinberg felt the second movement

> gives us the shortest and lightest movement he ever put into a major work. One of the things "lightest" means is that, so unlike Sessions's usual way, the first tune is unvaried upon its returns, though the continuations are full of delectable surprise. It is an ambling, wryly good-humored scherzo, whose slightly off-center chords remind me a bit of the delightfully tilted harmonies in Nielsen and Prokofiev. It takes less than two minutes and disappears in a puff of air.[17]

In recent years the Second Symphony has been played with some regularity. André Previn led the Pittsburgh Symphony December 10, 1982. San Francisco played the work again February 7–19, 1990, and August 12, 1990, in Davies Symphony Hall; and on tour to Regensburg (August 20), Besança, August 31, and East Berlin, September 8, 1990, all under the direction of Herbert Blomstedt. The Minnnesota Symphony Orchestra gave two performances of the Second Symphony, March 17 and 19, 1993. The Boston

Symphony Orchestra presented it November 23, 25, and 26, 1994, under Seiji Ozawa, as part of the BSO's musical survey commemorating the fiftieth anniversary of the end of World War II. The American Composers Orchestra performed the Symphony on January 12, 1997, in Carnegie Hall. One reviewer felt the music "really gripped me . . . solid, conventional stuff." The *Wall Street Journal* critic continued,

> Sessions often is described as "rugged," maybe because his music bristles with atonal complications, but that's not what I hear in it. First, I hear transparency. Here's a man who knows how to write for orchestra. There's a lot going on, but everything has light and air around it. Next I hear melodies that are rapt, motionless and utterly ravishing. Mr [Dennis Russell] Davies, a Sessions special- ist, phrased them with detailed care, and the orchestra responded like the superb thoroughbred it mostly is . . . There's something odd about this music, though. Like any good classical symphonist, Sessions starts and ends his work with fast movements, saving the slow parts for the deep interior. But these quicker movements don't really move. The rhythms sound as if they ought to be pro- pulsive, but somehow aren't maybe because they sound a little forced. . . . Had Sessions found the right bottle for his wine? I didn't think so; his symphony form was *too* conventional. That made me feel as if I'd floated into limbo.[18]

The New York Times felt, "This is tough music: earnest, energetic, colorful. And it was played in that manner. The marching finale suggested a missing link between the Berg of 'Lulu' and Shostakovich. This was music embattled, tumbling over with things to say."[19]

Bard College's summer Copland Festival included Leon Botstein's performance of Symphony No. 2 with the American Symphony Orchestra on August 21, 2005. Again the *Times* weighed in: "The [Copland] Third Symphony was placed in a fascinating context next to Roger Sessions's Symphony No. 2, a dense and challenging work that engrosses with its Schoenbergian complexity but fails to tug on the primal emotions in the way that Copland's symphony so effectively does."[20]

The end of the year 1946 was pivotal in Sessions's life. Both this symphony and the Second Sonata represent a significant turning point in Sessions's career: After Ruth's death he was able to write music much faster and with more fluency. A weight was lifted: he no longer lived under her judgmental pressure. Perhaps this is the moment to try to explain Sessions's personality in terms of psychological motivations. The follow- ing analysis, necessarily speculative, draws upon vocabulary found in Karen Horney's *Neurosis and Human Growth*.[21]

Sessions's parents were opposites: his mother was domineering and self-indulgent, his father passive, slightly absent-minded, and indulgent toward his children. Sessions, at age three, could not help but have felt abandoned by his mother's removing the family from New York, leaving Archibald behind. His entire life he was at pains to explain his parents' relationship, especially because they did not divorce. Sessions was almost entirely under the control of a highly neurotic and unpredictable woman. He needed to tread on eggshells.

Being sent to an English-style boarding school may have made him feel further unwanted by the remaining parent, unloved and not worthy of either parent's attention. Whatever "neurotic claims" he possessed began in Northampton. The violence of emo- tion that resurged whenever he discussed his bad experiences at Cloyne—being publicly humiliated and teased—indicated that remembering this period of his life still opened wounds. His success in persuading his parents to send him to another school cemented Horney's "neurotic claim" of feeling special, as though he "should" be treated differently from other students. Certainly, he was told from a young age how bright he was.

Roger's connection to his mother was the cornerstone of his emotional life. Controlling if and when the children would see their father, she became all-powerful. Ruth's neurotic claims for attention—usually asserted by her own sudden physical distress or by attacking others—kept everyone constantly attentive to her needs. Sessions felt it essential to keep the peace with his mother. Considering her leaving Archibald, her frequent fights with Nan, and the fact that Sessions considered Ruth to have "ruined" John's life, it was more than likely that she punished Sessions emotionally, too. A remarkable, but emotionally expensive, achievement was Sessions's ability to remain in her good graces. When she lashed out at him, perhaps physically, he remained still and said nothing, bringing on her display of remorse. Maintaining the relationship and her necessary emotional support took a huge toll: only her death 50 years later lifted her hold on Roger. The hostility he suppressed toward Ruth had been displaced onto other powerful women: Martha Sanders and Nadia Boulanger, for example.

Reared in a religious New England family, Roger found any desire to demonstrate what he knew or could do fundamentally unacceptable: one simply did not brag, and personal ambition was seen as a failing. The Huntingtons demonstrably helped others, not themselves. Perhaps the definition of genius is someone who knows something or can do something for which neither his background nor education has entirely prepared him. These moments of discovery are wondrous and revelatory, and in the case of Sessions such moments had started at a young age. This author once prodded him at length as to when he realized he was so different musically from everyone else. After much evasion, finally he answered, "Well, in the first place one can tell that by just looking around and seeing what goes on in the musical world."[22] Here was a conflict: he *knew* he was different, but could not acknowledge it socially or publicly. For the same reason this meant, on the other hand, he could not pursue his family's self-sacrificing, religious path.

In order to assert himself at the age of 12, he informed his parents he was to become a composer. (He always knew he would be a composer; it was not a decision per se.[23]) Here at least two factors were at work. First, composition gave him a means to escape feelings of worthlessness; he could summon his intellect and musicality to the rescue of his fragile ego. It was an abrupt declaration, striking in its firmness: he never swayed from what amounted to a distress signal sent to his parents. The second factor may have been a striving for "vindictive triumph" over Ruth and Archibald (and Adeline and Grace, for that matter). He would outdo them, become a better musician than they ever could have been. Not only would he become a musician, but he would *control* music as a composer.

While all Sessions's emotional claims were activated in the first decade of his life, his college experience could only have reinforced them. Pushed into Harvard at so young an age, he could not have escaped the notion that he was different, in effect special or entitled. Here he began the second part of his "neurotic solution:" he became detached, absorbed in his work and intellectual pursuits, and resigned to not expecting much from people. Possibly Parker subconsciously reinforced this. *Jean-Christophe* paralleled some of his experiences and provided a template on which to pattern his beliefs.

By the time he was teaching at Smith College he had achieved most of his solution. The parts were in place: he had succeeded at Harvard and Yale in music, he had married a student, and he had a job teaching music. Nevertheless he still needed to replace his absent father. He chose a substitute whose own need for attention exceeded Sessions's. It is difficult to avoid the conclusion that neurotic needs determined much of Bloch's and Sessions's student–teacher relationship. Bloch needed loyal followers (indeed, his world divided cleanly into "enemies" and "friends") and Sessions needed a strong father figure to admire. Now Sessions's leaving Smith College takes on a new perspective. To follow Bloch to Cleveland Sessions had to cut himself off from his mother in both actuality and symbolically. His second act of self-assertion was to sever himself from the Harvard–Yale–Kent–Smith axis with its suffocating past. Part of that past were painful memories associated with George Bartlett.

In a sense he jumped from the frying pan into the fire. Sessions was now subject to the vagaries of Bloch's personality. When Bloch got himself fired from the Cleveland Institute of Music, Sessions's dependency on him dictated no other choice but that he should also leave. In doing this, however, Sessions realized that he must break with Bloch. Significantly, he turned to his father for the means of escape and self-actualization. Archibald gave his son enough money to live in Europe for at least a year. But in 1927, during Sessions's sojourn, his father died without their ever becoming fully reconciled or Archibald witnessing any of Sessions's success as a symphonist.

Resentment toward his mother—which could never and would never be openly acknowledged—still fumed, and Barbara suffered on this account. He had affairs with other women, and because Barbara could not have children, he eventually divorced her. When Sessions remarried in 1936 and in a conscious attempt to free himself from Ruth, he went behind his mother's back to keep his bride-to-be a secret. His mother had published an autobiography, which, strikingly, omitted any mention of her son's accomplishments.

By now, however, Sessions, perhaps tired of the turmoil of his life and still staggering under the weight of his neurotic claims, resigned himself to a fairly cynical attitude. He continued his strategic position of amused detachment from everyday issues, with the notable exception of politics. (A sample of this detachment from, for example, popular music, occurred at the death of John Lennon in 1980. Sessions's Juilliard students, who always took him to a birthday dinner in December, expressed considerable dismay over the recent loss, and Sessions tried hard to be sympathetic. He had not, however, ever heard of the former Beatle.)

Sessions's experiences in the practical world of trying to get music performed, especially his experience with the Violin Concerto, made him retreat to his Rollandian, long-held attitude of aloofness. Because any rejection touched on his fundamental feelings of rejection by his parents, he needed to construct a position denying that a rejection had taken place. While he maintained a private artistic conviction of the worth of his music, it coexisted with a neurotic desire to escape current public judgment. His "shoulds" were: to be above the estimation of his contemporaries (only something as remote as "history" could be allowed to judge him); loudly to denounce music criticism as an opinion that should not matter; not to have to participate in the political work of getting pieces performed, published, or recorded; and not to have to obey deadlines. He was able to postpone gratification for decades—even past his death—in order to maintain these "shoulds": it should not matter what others said about his music as long as he himself considered it genuine and sincere. Needless to say, this particular neurotic solution greatly appeals to serious artists in the US today, and indeed the American view of the arts might have helped foster Sessions's self-protective attitude.

Let us examine the effect of this solution on his children and students. John had not escaped the pattern of his father's life. He became a musician and taught at—of all places—Smith College. Friction between John and his father had been longstanding, and at one point the two of them visited a counselor. Sessions's parental guilt was assuaged when the psychologist told him, "Parents don't make mistakes. They try as hard as they can." Paradoxically, John both sought his father's help in his career and distained having his reputation as a cellist determined by his father's fame. Receiving help with his career was fruitless—and John resented that—because Sessions's own neurotic solution forbade careerism. This split only worsened at the end of Sessions's life.

Elizabeth avoided direct competition with her father when she gave up piano studies partly because of her father correcting notes when she practiced. Despite considerable ability in languages, mathematics, and business, hers is Horney's "self-effacing" solution. She was intimidated by her overpowering mother and scared of her grandmother Ruth. Highly attached to her adoring father, she named her only child Roger.

To a lesser extent Sessions's students have felt a similar effect to that of his children. In the realm of purely musical matters they learned a great deal from him; but in the practical day-to-day aspect of establishing a career in music, Sessions was of no help whatsoever. None of the students queried about studying with Sessions responded that he had helped their careers in any direct way. He would never campaign on behalf of a student (for example, at Juilliard he did not attend scholarship decision meetings), a performer, or for himself. He rejected symbols of accomplishment or status, which made him unable to derive pleasure from his 1982 Pulitzer Prize. The high ideals he espoused were in fact unattainable, which students rarely realized.[24] To obey the dictates of Sessions's neurotic commands they had to eschew ambition and success entirely, which they were unable or unwilling to do.

On the other hand, the decades of difficult psychological work it took Sessions to achieve his sense of self paid off for his students. He was often able to instill in them the self-confidence that he himself had once lacked. Earl Kim put it simply, "He made me feel important."[25] Many others assert that he gave them confidence in their own instincts. He made them believe in themselves, and they loved him for it.

What is remarkable about Sessions's career is not that his music is not as well known as it ought to be, but rather that—considering his obedience to a stringent idealized self-image, a psychological block toward careerism, as well as a genuine lack of business ability—it is known at all.

Chapter 5

THE TRIAL OF LUCULLUS THROUGH *MONTEZUMA*

BERKELEY

At the end of World War II enrollment in higher education increased significantly: the University of California doubled to more than 25,000. In 1945 the United Nations was born in San Francisco. Antonio Borgese wrote a suggested world constitution. During the 1940s and 1950s several prominent composers taught or lived in California: Schoenberg taught at USC and UCLA, Milhaud at Mills College, Bloch lived in Oregon and taught summer school at Berkeley, Stravinsky lived in Los Angeles, and Krenek moved there in 1947. Sessions, who had taught at the summer school at Berkeley in the summers of 1935, 1936, and 1941, was to join them on the West Coast. When Sessions arrived in Berkeley in 1945, Milhaud lived only ten miles away, and the two saw each other frequently. Sessions described the move:

> I was [in Princeton] virtually through the war—the German war ended before I left. In the fall of 1945 I was offered a job in Berkeley. I had spent three other summers in Berkeley in the meantime and I wanted very much to go to the west. I didn't like the Princeton climate too much and my wife hated it. But mainly I had a feeling of adventure. I wanted to move to another part of the country. There were other elements in it, too. One was that it was made very clear—and I'm not blaming anyone for this at all, it just was the [Princeton] university policy—that the composer *did* interest them in California. That was probably the decisive thing. It wasn't that I had suffered any particular hardship at Princeton—but—there were no concessions made. I couldn't ask for anything on the ground that I needed time for my own work. One consequence was that my own work didn't flourish at all. I wrote one big work more or less by the skin of my teeth all the time that I was in Princeton [the First Quartet, 1936]. I wrote little pieces, and I wrote my Duo for Violin and Piano in 1942. I got started on a big symphony [No. 2]. But the minute I got to Berkeley, I began producing. I finished the symphony, which was very much of a turning point in my career. I wrote a piano sonata [No. 2] immediately. I wrote an opera immediately, which was produced there. Actually, there were three years when I didn't produce again. I wrote a book instead, which I regret although the book is quite successful.[1] It wasn't only for this reason that I did it. It was also a period when I needed to take stock.[2]

Sessions did, however, write 20 articles during his decade in Princeton. Evidently, he needed the money and also had something to say, especially about the published writings of theorists Schenker, Hindemith, and Krenek.[3]

Sessions's salary increased considerably when he moved to Berkeley. At the end of his

Princeton decade he was earning $4,500 (some extra work brought in more). That year he began at California with a full professorship and a $6,000 salary plus $500 to aid in moving. That salary steadily increased ($7,800 in 1948–1949, for example, $8,820 in January 1951). By the time he left in 1953, he was earning $9,924. The amount was frequently adjusted upward in the middle of the year.

The Sessions family lived from 1945 to the beginning of 1947 at 2137 Rose Street in Berkeley. Then they rented a house at 107 Tamalpais Road, on a hillside. Sessions and Lisl played four-hand arrangements of symphonies and tried to give their two children happy childhoods. At least John was happy; Elizabeth, five when her parents moved to California, was teased by her classmates. Her mother replied to her complaint that her classmates did not like her with "What is there to like?" Elizabeth's father, still vividly remembering the teasing and traumas he had suffered at Cloyne, was a constant source of support during her girlhood.

As often was the case, the cause of Sessions moving to a new job involved a specific individual. In this case that person was Albert Israel Elkus. Elkus's mother was a distinguished pianist and patroness of music, and his father a businessman and mayor of Sacramento. Elkus studied piano first with his mother, then with Harold Bauer in Paris and Joseph Lhevinne in Berlin, among other teachers. From 1916 to 1928 Elkus conducted choral societies in Sacramento and San Francisco. Beginning in 1923 he began a series of academic appointments including at the University of California in 1931. He conducted the University's symphony orchestra starting in 1934. In 1937 he was appointed chairman of the department, a post he continued until 1951. After becoming chair his compositional life ceased. The attitude about the creative side of music at Berkeley differed from Princeton's because Elkus viewed composition as compatible with teaching. He appointed a remarkable faculty: Randall Thompson, Arthur Bliss, Manfred Bukofzer, Ernest Bloch, and Roger Sessions. An historian might be asked to teach music theory and a composer a music history course.

All this had been made possible by the support of Monroe Deutsch, a Classics professor at Berkeley who became Provost. Deutsch had given Elkus a free hand to bring the level of the music department up to that of Classics and other departments. When Deutsch retired in August of 1947, Sessions and other composers contributed to a memorial album of music. While others submitted previously published music or works written for other occasions, Sessions wrote a short untitled piano piece "For Dr Monroe Deutsch with admiration and sincere affection (and apologies that it is a somewhat gloomy piece!), Roger Sessions, Berkeley, August 1947."[4]

From 1933 on Elkus was a member of the Board of Governors of the San Francisco Symphony Orchestra and probably was a force behind the premiere of Sessions's Symphony No. 2. Sessions had known Elkus since the summer of 1935. Having met his second wife, Lisl, at the University was also a powerful draw, as was her close attachment to her mother Ruby, still living in Paolo Alto. Elkus's personal charisma, in combination with a "final straw" moment at Princeton concerning the lack of an office, drew Sessions to California. Sessions dedicated his String Quintet (with second viola) to Elkus, a piece requested for the dedication of Berkeley's new Hertz concert hall, in 1958.

Elkus gave up the conductorship of the University Symphony Orchestra in 1946, the year before it performed *The Trial of Lucullus* under Sessions. Although he was truly loved by both students and faculty, Elkus retired at the age of 67 in 1951 during the Loyalty Oath controversy (see below). He became Emeritus and immediately assumed the directorship of the San Francisco Conservatory of Music, a position Bloch had held almost three decades earlier and one in which Elkus served until 1957. Unlike universities or colleges with pension plans then dictating age limits, conservatories had no mandatory retirement age. Elkus continued both to teach piano at the Conservatory and to lecture in the University Extension division until his death in 1962.

Immediately after his mother's death, Sessions wrote *The Trial of Lucullus*, during the winter and spring of 1947, in what was noticeably record time. After *Lucullus*, between 1947 and 1951, Sessions made sketches for two big works, one of which was later completed and the other not. "It harked back to the 1930s, the work I'd had in mind at that time in the middle thirties, and I just felt it was too late to write that piece."[5] He made numerous sketches at the time. One became his Fourth Symphony.

For a while, Sessions was a member of the American Musicological Society and listed it on his résumé. Under the general chairmanship of Gustav Reese, a joint meeting with the Society for Music in Liberal Arts Colleges was held on December 29, 1949, at the New York Public Library. Roy Welch chaired a session with Raymond Kendall, Paul Henry Lang, and Sessions speaking. At the same meeting were old friends Nicolas Slonimsky, Oliver Strunk, and Edward Lowinsky. Nevertheless, perhaps because of his personal difficulties with Manfred Bukofzer, with whom he shared a large office at Berkeley, Sessions soon gave up membership in the organization. Bukofzer was unpleasant to Sessions's students (because of Bukofzer's jealousy of his students' success, Sessions thought), and he once insulted Lisl, who "got very angry at him, because she's an inflammable lady."[6]

Sessions taught at Berkeley from 1945 to 1953. His schedule generally meant teaching three, three-unit courses: Introduction to Harmony, Musical Analysis, and Composition. One then-freshman at Berkeley, Gordon C. Cyr, remembered the excitement on campus over his arrival.[7] Sessions had brought with him some of his graduate students, Andrew Imbrie, Leon Kirchner, and Earl Kim. Leonard Rosenman and David del Tredici studied with Sessions then, too. The students organized a Composers Forum to promote their music, an activity that included Composers Forum Workshops, public readings of student compositions with questions from the audience. Ultimately these expanded into a season of three or four concerts, about which there was considerable enthusiasm. Darius Milhaud's Mills College graduate students, such as Leland Smith and William O. Smith, were also involved, but when both Milhaud and Sessions attended, students were "considerably inhibited."[8] In addition to presenting new works by student composers and area musicians, the Forum performed music by Stravinsky, Schoenberg, and Copland. It outlasted Sessions's stay at Berkeley, well into the 1950s.

Sessions's music was performed on its concerts: Bernhard Abramowitsch performed the Second Piano Sonata, February 10, 1948; on March 20, 1950, violinist Nathan Rubin and Abramowitsch played the Duo; and in June 1951 the West Coast premiere of the Second Quartet was given by the California Quartet (whose Khuner was a former member of the Kolisch Quartet). The Solo Violin Sonata was done at the San Francisco Art Museum on June 8, 1953, and the First Symphony's first performance in San Francisco was September 18, 1955, by the California Symphony, Murray Graitzer, conducting. Joseph Kerman conducted Sessions's Kent Mass with organ, March 26, 1957. Students threw themselves into performances of Sessions's music. The University Chorus sang his *Turn, O Libertad*. Berkeley violinist Barbara Rahm, with Sessions at the piano, performed his Duo. Much more of his music was performed at Berkeley in Sessions's first two years there than had been done in the previous decade at Princeton.

At Berkeley Sessions's analysis classes often amounted to a detailed study of Stravinsky's Symphony in Three Movements, Bartók's Concerto No. 2 for Violin and Orchestra, and Schoenberg's Fourth Quartet. (Sessions had met Bartók when he gave a piano concert at Princeton, February 7, 1941.) Cyr observed of Sessions's teaching style,

Whether in informal conversation or in the classroom, Roger Sessions' speaking style was deliberate, tending toward the ponderous. He always chose his words with care, ever in pursuit of *le mot juste*. In appearance and bearing, he seemed the prototypal New Englander . . . and aristocratic in the best sense. . . . But Roger was certainly not without his strong antipathies. He was intolerant, for example, of the so-called "American nationalism" then in vogue, which he felt to be artificial, self-conscious, and—worst of all—pandering to an illegitimate taste.[9]

Between the opera (1947) and the Second Quartet (1951) came that "God-damned book," *Harmonic Practice*. Suggested by a Princeton student of his, Christopher C. Reid (class of 1947), the son of the Harcourt Brace textbook editor, James Reid, the book took Sessions at least two years to write. He composed hundreds of musical examples, as well as the text. He thought he could write it quickly, but

> I could write a harmony book very quickly, but I couldn't write a harmony book by Roger Sessions quickly, that's all. . . . Furthermore, I wrote, I think, around 800 exercises for the book. That took a certain amount of time, you know, because you have to sort of do every exercise as you work it out. Otherwise you'll find that you're demanding in Chapter 2 something that doesn't come until Chapter 14, something like that.[10]

Somewhat to his surprise the book paid him royalties—about $1,000 a year—for many years.

Elkus's son related an oft-repeated story about an end-of-the-year Romantic era class.

> The scene, that lower-floor classroom of the old [music] building, with its own outside entrance. Time, 11:59 a.m. of a blue-skied, late spring, last day of classes. Doors and windows are wide open. Students begin to cap fountain pens and close notebooks. Sessions says that he'd like to take his final minute to speak about the three great post-Romanticists, Debussy, Strauss, and Mahler. Pens are uncapped and notebooks re-opened. "Debussy said, 'The world is vile, mankind wicked. There is no hope. But at least on a nice afternoon we can lie on the grass with a flaxen-haired girl and watch the clouds.' Strauss said, 'The world is vile, mankind wicked. There is no hope. But at least we can all make a little money.' Mahler said, 'Goodbye.' " Whereupon the Campanile's hour bell chimed twelve.[11]

Sessions's interest in liberal politics never abated. His name appeared on an open letter to the National Institute of Arts and Letters on the House Committee on Un-American Activities.[12] He also lent his name and his effort to sponsor a concert of Hanns Eisler's music at Town Hall the night before Eisler was deported from the US.[13]

Although Sessions was progressive in his politics, he was also practical. In January 1948 he severed his connection with the Progressive Citizens of America because, "The third party movement which the P.C.A. has chosen to support, seems to me not only inept but irresponsible, and Mr Wallace's position untenable from the standpoint of the progressive cause. . . . I shall continue to work, according to my best lights, for the cause of international understanding and peace abroad, and civil liberties and the economic well-being of all the people at home."[14] On the same day during the 1948 presidential campaign, he wrote directly to the third-party candidate, Henry A. Wallace.

I am writing you as one who lived under fascism in Italy for six years, who witnessed the rise of Hitler in Berlin in 1931 to 1933, who voted for Roosevelt as often as his voting status permitted and took an active part in the campaigns of 1940 and 1944 . . . I cannot refrain from expressing my deep consternation at your latest move in heading a third presidential ticket. I have weighed carefully all the pros and cons of the situation and cannot help coming to the conclusion that you have dealt the cause of both peace and what I believe you as well as I consider democracy a serious blow, of which the consequences are at best incalculable, but at worst may well prove to be catastrophic.

Sessions went on to disagree with Wallace that the Marshall Plan had divided the world into two camps. Neither could he agree that President Truman and the Democratic Party had become "completely reactionary." Sessions argued that the Republican Old Guard was being given aid and encouragement by the third-party movement. Finally, he related the third-party movement to what he had seen in Germany, "a policy of catastrophe as led the Communist Party of Germany in 1933 to allow Hitler to come to power rather than to combine in a united opposition to him." And

while it is always argued in favor of such a policy, that a reaction against the abuses of a conservative regime will inevitably redound to the advantage of democracy, such a calculation seems to me to be a deliberate toying with the forces of history, which have a way of their own and do not follow the laws of the billiard table. . . . In the atomic age we simply cannot afford to take such chances. I am therefore, with deep regret, obliged to bend my small efforts to opposition with the movement of which you have assumed the leadership, and to hope very earnestly that you will eventually be persuaded to withdraw from what seems to me a disastrous adventure, before the harm done is irreparable,
  Very sincerely yours.[15]

Wallace responded from the offices of the *New Republic* in New York with a two-page typed letter. He could not accept Sessions's position that the third party guaranteed the election of the Old Guard Republicans. He was counting on a large turnout to elect progressives to Congress; in this he agreed with Senator McGrath, chairman of the Democratic Party. He felt confident that during the election season Sessions would find that his analysis had excluded several historical factors and was premised on essentially speculative theses.[16] Truman, not Wallace, won the election of 1948.

Sessions, along with his colleague Joaquín Nin-Culmell and many others, became involved in the 1952 Presidential election by writing to colleagues an "Appeal to members of the academic profession to support Adlai Stevenson for president." The printed letter, with scores of names printed in the margin and dated October 1, 1952, stated, among other things, that Stevenson "has refused to debase the discussion of complex problems into slogans, catchwords and epithets. . . . Perhaps you have read his courageous message to the Illinois legislature in defense of academic freedom and personal liberties."[17] The letter appealed for funds to buy radio and television time in California. Sessions was one of the ten signers.

During the early years (1949–1950) of the McCarthy period, University president Robert Gordon Sproul proposed, and the Regents of the University of California approved, on March 25, 1949, that employees be required to swear an oath stating that they are not members of the Communist party. Earl Warren, governor of California, supported it. In addition to the usual affirmation to support the Constitution of the United States and that of the State of California, the "Loyalty Oath" read:

> Having taken the constitutional oath of the office required by the State of California, I hereby formally acknowledge my acceptance of the position and salary named, and also state that I am not a member of the Communist Party or any other organization which advocates the overthrow of the Government by force or violence, and that I have no commitments in conflict with my responsibilities with respect to impartial scholarship and free pursuit of truth. I understand that the foregoing statement is a condition of my employment and a consideration of payment of my salary.[18]

This requirement of the faculties and staff of the University of California system caused considerable outrage. Meetings and discussions were held, choices deliberated. Should the faculty as a body decline to sign? Living in Princeton and lecturing at Juilliard that summer, Sessions signed the oath, one of about half the faculty who had signed by August. California was to be hit especially hard in this era of blacklists; many careers in the film industry were ruined. Sessions, asked if he believed in "private enterprise," replied that "Of course—composing is the most private enterprise there is."[19] But the matter could not be laughed off.

The next summer, 1950, was even more problematic from the point of view of the California faculty. Sproul had broken with the Regents and sided with the faculty, but some Regents—Neylan and his supporters—were virulent against the faculty. When, on June 25, 1950, North Korea invaded South Korea and war began, the issue became more volatile. Doubtless with a sense of self-preservation Sessions signed his yearly contract (that contained the oath). Sessions felt some guilt over signing it, since that summer 31 "non-signer" professors and 157 University of California employees had been dismissed for not signing. (One of the "non-signers," David Saxon from UCLA, became president of the University a generation later.) After a lawsuit and the addition of new members to the Regents (which lost the suit against them), by October 1951 the Regents voted to rescind the Oath requirement. In the meantime, 55 courses were not being taught since their faculty were fired, and 47 people offered faculty positions at California declined in part because of the Oath. The University had suffered a blow, and Albert Elkus decided to retire in 1951.[20]

Sessions's old friend Aaron Copland was having his own political difficulties, which he addressed in a letter in February 1953 to the Board (of which Sessions was a member) of the League of Composers. The League had publicly protested the cancelation of the performance of Copland's *Lincoln Portrait* at the inauguration concert for Dwight Eisenhower. Copland's letter was read to the board: he denied that he had ever been a member of any political party, Republican, Democratic, or Communist; and stated that the only organizations he joined were those whose primary purposes were the musical and cultural interests of America. "I don't think I need to comment on the implications of this little episode, for its sinister overtones must be clear to everyone. We, the intellectuals, are becoming the targets of a powerful pressure movement led by small minds. It is surely a sign of the times that a musical organization like our own should have become involved in an affair such as this."[21]

Copland (and later David Diamond) was called before Joseph McCarthy's Senate Permanent Subcommittee on Investigation on May 26, 1953, and would somehow rate an FBI file that lasted from 1950 to 1975. This meant Copland was constrained in getting passports. Both the cost of legal representation and the emotional strain of feeling pursued were considerable. Later, several performances and awards for Copland were canceled. Although music critics for the *Washington Post* and *The New York Times* came to his defense, the *Herald Tribune* critic, Virgil Thomson, remained silent, declining to defend either Copland or Roy Harris. Copland's own reaction was stated unusually strongly for the even-tempered composer: "My 'politics'—tainted or untainted—are certain to die with me, but my music, I am foolish enough to imagine, might just possibly outlive the Republican Party."[22]

Soon after, composers would encounter other elements of McCarthyism. In April 1953 Senator McCarthy prodded the State Department to enact security hurdles for sending music and recordings to libraries abroad; "any 'derogatory' allegation made against a composer—whether substantiated or not—meant an immediate barring of the composer's work from any of the 196 official American libraries around the world. Such allegations could include a signature in defense of Republican Spain . . . they blacklisted not only Copland but Gershwin, Sessions, Thompson, Harris, Thomson, and Bernstein."[23]

In the same period twelve-tone music gained something of a reputation among the right wing as being un-American, having been imported by European refugees. Sessions was seen as on the wrong side of this divide as well.

Sessions described the music department as having "exploded" after Elkus's departure in 1951. Although Sessions was in Italy during the 1951–1952 year, he heard stories about Nin-Culmell, the brother of Anaïs Nin, who became the next, and highly unpopular chair. During his "lame duck" year of 1952–1953 Sessions was able to observe Nin-Culmell first hand. Sessions said of the situation:

> It was a very nice place to teach because everybody liked each other. [Nin-Culmell] really wrecked the department the minute he became chairman. As a visiting professor he seemed very nice and able to get along with everybody, but then the minute he became chairman, he took over. He was a rather weak man, and he leaned on people and then would throw them over rapidly. It became impossible. The department was in a way disintegrating. The department had always been very harmonious until Albert Elkus retired in 1950 [*sic*], but then it exploded.[24]

Sessions had been awarded a Fulbright scholarship (established only four years earlier and derided by Senator McCarthy as the "half-bright program") for the academic year 1951–1952. In addition to completing the 1951 spring semester, he was getting *Harmonic Practice* ready for Harcourt Brace. After the semester he had gone to Princeton on his way to Florence—with the teenaged John Harbison in tow.

Sessions had been sounded out by Whitney J. ("Mike") Oates, chair of the Princeton Classics department, in May of 1951. Sessions was staying with the Kolisches in Madison, Wisconsin, where his Second Quartet was premiered, on the 28th. After the war, Oates (another Classicist, like Monroe Deutsch) had conceived, found the money for, and initiated a cross-continent recruitment of high-caliber faculty for Princeton. This project grew into the National Woodrow Wilson Fellowship Program. In 1953 Oates was also responsible for the establishment of Princeton's Council of the Humanities. Sessions was going to be in Europe that summer, and would see him in the east to explain his terms regarding salary. The fact that Elkus had left as Berkeley chairman must also have been a factor. (He did not tell Oates that he wanted to come back; Sessions had learned some negotiating skills by this time.)

I really wanted to get back east, because this is where I belong. It's near New York. See, I went out there partly because I felt that other parts of the country were *too* dependent on New York. I had had the feeling that something indigenous was getting started out there. That was a disappointment when I found how essentially provincial it was. And yet the university is a *very* impressive place; the whole university is very impressive. I would say that California and Harvard were the two really great universities in this country—but totally different.[25]

Sessions had seen Roy Welch in the summer of 1949, which he had spent in Princeton and lectured at Juilliard. (The lectures were a result of his former student Mark Schubart being made dean.) When his Second Symphony was performed in New York in January 1950, he was in the east and saw Welch for the last time; he died a year later. Welch had mentioned the possibility of Sessions returning to Princeton, and so had Edward T. Cone. Sessions saw Mike Oates again in July of 1951. In order to obtain the sabbatical (with two-thirds pay) to take his Fulbright, however, Sessions had had to promise Berkeley to return and teach one more year after the grant, that is 1952–1953. Telegrams from Princeton and Berkeley flew back and forth. While in Florence he received a telegram from President Harold Dodds asking him to return to Princeton. Sessions hoped that Berkeley would not make him an offer that would make it impossible to leave. The dean at Berkeley, meanwhile, implored the administration to meet Princeton's offer of $11,000. Berkeley allowed Sessions to leave after another year; they were given little choice. "And I became even more productive after I got back to Princeton."[26]

In the fall of 1953 the Sessionses returned to Princeton, where he was now given a full professorship. There is evidence that the University of California tried to exceed Princeton's offer to Sessions, once they discovered it was valid, but they did not write to Sessions soon enough; he had submitted his resignation more than a year in advance. He had written to President Sproul on April 19, 1952, from Florence saying he had accepted Princeton's offer; he received $11,500 from Princeton.[27]

For one and a half years, starting in the summer of 1953 the Sessionses lived at 57 College Road West. From 1955 for ten or eleven years, they lived at 70 Alexander Street. After Sessions was retired, he and Lisl moved into graduate student housing at 63 Stanworth Lane. Sessions never bought a house. Lisl, who had graduated with a Bachelor of Library Science from the University of Washington, had held her first official librarian position in the main library of Portland, Oregon, then at a large public school in Spokane, Washington. She retired from librarian work while her children were being reared and returned once they were in elementary school. In 1953 she joined the staff as assistant librarian at the Princeton Public Library before working at the private Hun School library beginning in 1960.

Milton Babbitt, who had stayed at Princeton during Sessions's years at Berkeley, noticed a difference in Sessions's teaching upon his return. "The Roger who returned to Princeton almost a decade later taught differently and even thought differently. Now he wished to be influenced by only his own thought, and that as it manifested itself compositionally, so his private teaching seems to have consisted almost exclusively of considerations of the students' compositions."[28]

Changes had occurred at Princeton during Sessions's sojourn in the West. In 1945 the music section attained departmental status and was given Clio Hall for a home; music was finally under one roof. The first Ph.D. in music was conferred in 1950. Another change was the building of Woolworth Center in 1962 devoted to music. Both the popular Record Lending Library and concert activities increased in number. The death of

Roy Welch on January 8, 1951, had been much felt. The Bach scholar Arthur Mendel came to Princeton in 1952 and served as chairman for the next 15 years. Others joined the faculty and contributed to the musical life: Walter Nollner directed the Glee Club from 1958 to 1973, when he became choirmaster as well. During the 1960s and 1970s, when Kenneth Levy, Lewis Lockwood, and Peter Westergaard were chairmen, the Princeton music department expanded, especially with the addition of women to the all-male college.

After his return to Princeton, Sessions began writing in his new scalar-constructed dissonant style. The first piece done this way was the Solo Violin Sonata (1953). The twelve-tone method is used consistently only in its first movement. The Scherzo does not incorporate it, while the Trio obeys it very strictly. "That was the first work in which I used the row in a thoroughgoing way. The next work in which I used it at all in this way was my Third Symphony. . . . In *Theocritus* there is a row, but the serial technique is used very episodically, maybe less so than I think at this point, because I don't give a hoot for that particular kind of analysis."[29] When asked by Cone in 1962 what led him to experiment with the row at all, Sessions replied,

Remember the remark about Mount Everest that Kennedy quoted in one of his speeches lately? [Because it's there.] The row was there. And I think the row yields resources, in a certain sense—yields, I won't say another dimension, but it

Figure 35 70 Alexander Street, where Sessions lived when he taught at Princeton.

yields resources . . . It would be very hard to say exactly what those resources are, but I mean, I used the row a great deal vertically, harmonically. I feel in this respect very much, the row has a lot to yield. . . . But you don't always have to give a complete statement of the row, nor do you have to give it necessarily at the beginning of the piece.

I often tell my students that grown up men don't obey rules. They've learned the rules long before that, and the rules have been a great help to them, but nothing one does as a mature man is done because there's a rule that says it should be done, in any field whatever. It may be that the rules are replaced by wise and shrewd ethical conduct, so to speak, and I would say the same is true of music.[30] . . .

It's just exactly like a man who says he wanted to write books like *Finnegans Wake*, so it's not necessary to learn English grammar. I think the parallel is extremely, very close there.[31]

In 1955, when Sessions was invited by Copland to join Boris Blacher to replace Copland for a summer at Tanglewood, he met the Argentine composer Alberto Ginastera. Ginastera invited Sessions to his own country in 1965. Sessions taught young composers in Buenos Aires. Sessions also visited Santiago, Chile, and Lima, Peru, after two days

Figure 36 Composers (seated left to right) Douglas Moore and Roger Sessions (standing left to right) Aaron Copland, Elliott Carter, Wallingford Riegger, William Schuman, and Walter Piston, ca. 1958.

in Rio di Janeiro. He spent time in Mexico City, the setting for *Montezuma*. He received an invitation to Japan, which he declined since they were doing none of his music. Other travels took him to Scandinavia, Liechtenstein, and Franconia in New Hampshire.

So busy was Sessions that he described his life in May of 1958 as "a kind of stretto in a quintuple or sextuple fugue."[32] In 1958 he traveled to the USSR. He, Roy Harris, Ulysses Kay, and Peter Mennin went to Moscow, Leningrad, Tiflis, and Kiev—Sessions's Russian came in handy. *The Black Maskers* Suite was performed in the homeland of its author, Andreyeff (see section "Symphonies Nos 3 and 4").

Sessions would later ask Mennin for a job at Juilliard, according to Prausnitz. In March 1965 Mennin announced Sessions's hiring on the faculty to replace Vittorio Giannini, who left to head the new North Carolina School of the Arts. The other two appointments were pianist Rudolf Firkusny and composer Luciano Berio. After his mandatory retirement from Princeton at age 68, reached on December 28, 1964, he retired on June 30, 1965. After a year of teaching at Juilliard, Sessions received both the Bloch lectureship at the University of California and the Norton lectureship at Harvard.

Despite four years at Smith College, 23 years at Princeton, and the seven at the University of California at Berkeley, Sessions never felt truly comfortable in an academic setting. About teaching he remarked, "Whatever success I have as a teacher has been due to the fact that very gifted people have been around me always. I suppose I can take some credit for the fact that they're willing to stay around."[33] Four years at the Cleveland Institute of Music and 16 years at The Juilliard School were far more congenial to him. Academe, he declared, was filled with "vipers and slugs."

THE TRIAL OF LUCULLUS

The most ambitious project Berkeley undertook was Sessions's first opera. Because of a difficulty in reaching agreement with the Bertolt Brecht estate, one of Sessions's greatest works is neither published nor performed nowadays.

Between 1937 and 1945 Bertolt Brecht wrote many of his most important plays. He was in exile from Germany, having left the country in February 1933 immediately after the Reichstag fire. According to the editors of the older Brecht edition, "*Lucullus* was commissioned by the Stockholm radio in 1939 and completed in a fortnight; Hilding Rosenberg was due to write the music but it never got done and the broadcast did not take place."[1] The second complete Brecht edition specifies that *Lucullus* was written in Scandinavia in six days in November 1939.[2] Two years previous to *Lucullus*, Brecht had written a pro-Soviet *Lenin Cantata* (1937) with former Schoenberg student Hanns Eisler. Brecht wrote both the first version of *The Life of Galileo* (November 1938) and *Mother Courage* (1936–1939) just prior to *Lucullus*. Margarete Steffin was his collaborator for all three. Possibly Brecht intended Lucullus to resemble Adolf Hitler. "The play itself can be seen as a by-product of his [unfinished] Caesar novel [*Caesar*], or at least Brecht's reading for it, which had included Plutarch, Dio Cassius, Suetonius, and Sallust, now reviewed in the light of the Nazi invasion of Poland and the Anglo-French mobilization."[3] In January or February 1939 Brecht wrote the prose "Lucullus's Trophies."[4] The play *Lucullus in Court* (*Lukullus vor Gericht*) was first broadcast by Studio Bern of the Swiss–German radio Beromünster May 12, 1940, while Belgium and The Netherlands were falling to Hitler. This earliest version is referred to here as the 1940 version. There was no music for this performance.

In 1945 Brecht's anti-Nazi drama *The Private Life of the Master Race* was given its world premiere at Berkeley's Wheeler Auditorium.[5] The Drama Department's Henry Schnitzler, the son of Arthur Schnitzler, was responsible for the production. For his spring 1947 show, he wanted a Sessions work to fill a double bill with Stravinsky's *L'Histoire du Soldat*. The music and drama departments at Berkeley in 1947 occupied the same small clapboard building. Bukofzer and Sessions shared a spacious corner office next door to Elkus's office, and Henry Schnitzler was nearby in the quaint building (see Figure 37). Sessions wrote first to Brecht. Schnitzler, who directed, then wrote to Brecht, who had arrived in California in July 1941 and was living in Santa Monica, that he would like "eine kurze Schuloper" (a short school opera), a play like the children's work *He Says Yes*.[6] Brecht's wife sent the radio play *Das Verhör des Lukullus* (*The Trial of Lucullus*) and its English translation by Hofmann Reynolds Hays. Hays (1904–1980) was Brecht's friend and first wholly American translator (including the poetry). He had probably acted on Hanns Eisler's suggestion to translate *Lucullus*. Hays taught playwriting and had been head of the drama department at

Figure 37 The music and drama building at Berkeley.

Fairleigh-Dickinson University, as well as writing plays, poetry, novels, and literary criticism.

Brecht seemed to have had in mind a musical setting from the beginning, because in the first radio script a page appears that outlines one to five songs for each of his fourteen scenes; some are called "songs," others "quartet," "trio," "recitative," "duet," and "chorus."[7] Sessions agreed: "But both the German and English version were offered to me . . . and on a number of grounds I could not imagine its performance as a spoken drama on the stage."[8] Sessions subtitled his work "Opera in one act, for radio or stage performance." His was the first opera based on the new medium of a radio play, as well as the first English-language setting of the play. Brecht took no interest in Schnitzler and Sessions's opera, whose performance occurred in the same year he was planning Charles Laughton's *Galileo* and his family's return to Europe, to Zurich, that fall (1947). That move was prompted in September and October 1947, when Brecht and Eisler and several Hollywood writers were called before the Committee on Un-American Activities; Brecht was blacklisted. Their collaboration on *Galileo Galilei* was premiered in Los Angeles in 1947.

Lucullus, written extremely quickly for a student production, was Sessions's first dramatic work since *The Black Maskers*, almost a quarter of a century earlier. Despite being one of his finest and most immediate works, two major hurdles stand in the way of publication and recording. First, Sessions assumed that he had the rights to set it. Both he and Schnitzler failed to get permission in writing from Brecht. (Evidently Brecht forgot—or wished to forget—that Sessions had composed an opera, because he announced in the program notes to the 1949 version by Paul Dessau that this was the first opera made on his text.) Second, Sessions had not secured the rights to the Hays translation. Two English translations of the play exist, as do several versions of the German text. The earliest translation is Hays's, but in the first complete Brecht edition Frank Jones is the translator. The firm that originally published the Hays translation has been long defunct, which also complicates the copyright problem of the text.[9] (The 1940 version was originally published in German in the USSR by the Comintern's magazine *Internationale Literatur*.) The failure to secure these two sets of rights had long-term, disastrous consequences for the opera. There appears also to have been a concerted effort on Brecht's and Paul Dessau's part to promulgate their 1951 version of the play (see below) and suppress the 1940 version.

The score is easily the messiest Sessions ever produced, because of the haste of its composition. This complicated matters for his publisher, Edward B. Marks, whose 1950 piano–vocal score is littered with mistakes. After three subsequent productions were mounted between 1955 and 1966,[10] the music publisher's lawyers discovered that the lack of permission was an insurmountable obstacle to publication and performance. Brecht died in 1956. No financial accommodation could be reached with Brecht's son, Stefan, still living, and the publisher and composer were forced to withdraw this opera from his catalog. *Lucullus* has not been performed in over 40 years.

Sessions remarked, "I myself feel that, in many respects and from many directions, we are developing new conceptions and new criteria—dramatic, musical and theatrical—of opera in this century. I regard *Lucullus* as part of my own—and also, I believe, Brecht's—contribution to this development."[11] Questioned about these "new conceptions" of opera, Sessions responded: "The subject matter and the whole tone—interpreting political events on a broader scale" characterized twentieth-century opera in Sessions's eyes. On that subject he thought immediately of *Moses und Aron, Wozzeck*, and Dallapiccola's three operas, *Il Prigioniero* (*The Prisoner*, 1944–1948), *Volo di notte* (*Night Flight*, 1937–1939), and *Ulisse* (*Ulysses*, 1960–1968). Going out on a fairly secure limb, Sessions named *Così fan Tutte, Don Giovanni, Le Nozze di Figaro, Die Zauberflöte*, and *Falstaff* as the "five perfect operas." Close in the running in his opinion were *Otello* and *Pelléas et Mélisande*.

"Fundamentally *The Trial of Lucullus* and *Montezuma* are about the same thing: the futility of conquest."[12] In addition to the similar political tone, a technical feature is shared by both operas: a narrator provides commentary. The roles of the Herald and Court Crier are Brecht's devices to visualize the action to the intended radio audience. (In productions the Herald of the first six scenes became the Court Crier for the remainder of the opera.) *Montezuma* takes place as a series of flashbacks visualized by the onstage Bernal Dìaz, an historical figure who participated in the conquest of Mexico.

Since *The Trial of Lucullus* and the 1940 version of the play are not easily available, a synopsis will be provided here. Sessions followed the Hays translation religiously. Very little is cut and only a few words changed. Sessions could have changed them, or subsequent directors may have been responsible for the substitutions. The play consists of 14 short scenes, each telegraphing quite different emotions in spare and direct language. Both the full manuscript and the published score join scenes 13 and 14, hence the opera's scenes total 13 without omitting any scene.[13] The great Roman general Lucullus (ca. 117 BCE–56 BCE) has died before the opera begins. His trial in Limbo shall determine whether he will be allowed to proceed to the Elysian Fields. Scene 1, in F minor, The Funeral Procession, involves a great number of people: the soldiers carrying the cataflaque, a chorus of Romans, slaves hauling a frieze, and individuals with opposing views of Lucullus's achievements. Scene 2 consists solely of the Herald's description of the return to normal daily life after the procession has passed through.

In scene 3 a children's chorus recites, in B minor, what they learn in school about famous generals. They strive "to write our names one day on the tablets of immortality." Lucullus's burial is allegorically portrayed in scene 4. When the procession arrives at the wall, a Hollow Voice instructs the soldiers to "set it down" for "no one is carried. Behind this wall a man goes alone."[14] Lucullus's lawyer's attempts to intervene are quickly overruled by the Voice, who instructs the general to take off his helmet in order to crouch through the low gate. The chorus of soldiers (scene 5) sings both individually and together an unmournful goodbye to their general; they are more interested in going drinking and to the races.

Scene 6 contrasts sharply in mood with the previous scene. The Hollow Voice orates on the subject of waiting and observes that the newcomer "seems not to have learned to wait." Lucullus, angry that he was not met, paces and demands to be escorted away. Silence answers his protestations. An old woman kindly tells him what she knows of the proceedings: "A person's usefulness counts the most" and the jurors are "little people who fully understand how hard life is for us in times of war." A Threefold Voice calls for the old woman, whose trial takes only a moment. The Threefold Voice calls "Lakalles!," a name that irritates Lucullus for "only in the slums . . . in the unwashed / Jaws of the vulgar, of the scum / Is my name Lakalles."

Scene 7, Choice of Sponsor, begins with the Court Crier assuming the Herald's task of narration. He identifies the five jurors as formerly a Farmer, Teacher, Fishwife, Baker, and Courtesan. The Judge of the Dead asks Lucullus to call a spokesman from the Elysian Fields, but to Lucullus's astonishment, his choice, Alexander of Macedon, "is unknown here." He proposes that the frieze of his gravestone be called; the slaves turn to shadows and drag the frieze through the wall. In scene 8, Bringing the Frieze, the Crier describes the figures: a captured king, a strange-eyed queen, a man with a cherry tree, a golden god, a girl with a tablet that names 53 cities, a dying legionary, and a cook.

The Hearing, scene 9, begins. Lucullus tells of his swift battle with the King, who questioned by the Teacher, corroborates Lucullus's story of lightning and devastating attack. The Courtesan asks the Queen how she got there. The Queen was vanquished by 50 men while she bathed in the River Vienne, Lucullus's triumph being that the King could not "protect his property From prodigious Rome." The Girl with the Tablet testifies, "One day at noon an uproar broke loose / Into the street swept a flood / Whose waves were men . . . In the evening / Only foul smoke marked the spot that once was a city." The slaves who hauled the golden god tremble and cry answering the question "What was carried off?": "Us. Once happy, now cheaper than oxen / To haul away booty, ourselves booty." Lucullus claims he had their god carried away "So that the whole earth might see our gods / Were greater than all other gods." The slaves quickly point out that the god weighed 200 weight in gold. The Baker records only "brought gold to Rome."

Scene 10 is a recess in the trial. Lucullus rests and hears the talk of new shadows, slaves, behind the door. Missing the real world, Lucullus asks whether there's wind above. The answer: "There may be in the gardens. In the suffocating alleys / You don't notice."

The emotional peak of the opera and play occurs in scene 11 in the confrontation between the general and a juror, the Fishwife, who interviews the Legionary. Lucullus protests that war cannot be judged "By those who do not understand it." In a long soliloquy, which Sessions thought could be set in nothing but A minor and whose music has been transposed and sung separately, the Fishwife describes waiting at the dock for her son to return from the war. She caught a fever, died, came to the Realm of the Shadows still seeking her son, Faber. The gatekeeper had told her that the many Fabers there had all "forgotten their names / Which only served to line them up in the Army . . . And their mothers / They do not wish to meet again / Because they let them go to the bloody war." The Judge announces, "The Court recognizes that the mother / Understands war."

In Scene 12 Lucullus again overhears shadows talking through the wall, now about the recruitment of soldiers to fight in Gaul, a country they never heard of.[15] At the beginning of scene 13 the Judge warns the accused not to anger them any longer with his triumphs, but to recollect his weaknesses, which may serve him better. From this point the testimony becomes more favorable, the atmosphere and music lighter. The Baker asks the Cook how he came to be in the procession. The Cook thanks Lucullus, who let him cook to his heart's desire. The Baker understands the Cook's happiness because Lucullus had let him be an artist. The Cook also testifies that in Greece, full of art treasures and books, Lucullus, with tears in his eyes, charged his soldiers not to set fires. After the customary silence while the jurors consider the testimony, the Farmer discovers that Lucullus's Treebearer brought the cherry tree to the slopes of the Apennines. The Farmer's tribute to "The finest of all your trophies" is set descriptively by Sessions in B flat major. The Fishwife's song and the Farmer's scene were Sessions's two favorites in the opera. As with much opera, the contrast of keys helps create dramatic contrast between scenes and characters.

The Verdict in scene 13 (it appears as scene 14 in the original numbering) is left for the audience to determine. The Judge summarizes Lucullus's case pointing out that his most splendid witnesses were not the most favorable to him, while the small ones prove his hands not entirely empty. David Drew called this last scene "an apotheosis without theism."[16] The tribunal, the chorus, sings of "the ancestors of the joyous world to be" and withdraws. Both Sessions's opera and Brecht's original play end there.

Berkeley staged *The Trial of Lucullus*, in which 144 students participated, with only one professional involved, baritone Edgar Jones, who sang the role of the Judge. (Two other musicians petitioned the union to be able to play for free.) Imbrie, Kirchner, and Kim divided up the coaching tasks for both singers and instrumentalists. At the premiere April 18–26 (six performances), 1947, Denny Trevor sang the role of Lucullus, and soprano Martha Long sang the Girl with the Tablet.[17] The opera is perfectly suited for student performances: because of its numerous roles, nearly everyone gets a chance to sing a solo—thus giving many students a chance to perform. And almost everyone remains on stage for most of the opera. Twenty-eight named roles appear in addition to seven soldiers, a chorus of slaves (baritones, basses), a chorus of school children (soprani), and the Three-fold Voice (chorus, behind the scenes of soprani, mezzo-soprani, and contralti).

His student Cyr remembers, "The epic quality of Sessions' score took hold from the beginning and was maintained with a near inexorability throughout. *Lucullus* is plainly of the same stuff we find later in the winding funeral train music of Sessions' cantata, *When Lilacs Last in the Dooryard Bloom'd*."[18] The French horn player, S. Earl Saxton, who drew the scene as a cartoon and later became first horn in the Pittsburgh Symphony, remembered Sessions as "such a genuinely great and wonderful person. Unbelievably plain and humble, unpretentious, soft-spoken and kind, and all of us would readily have given anything for this opportunity to work with him. There were so many moments of fun, even hilarity, sprinkled throughout the rehearsals."[19]

The instrumentation for Sessions's opera reflects what was available on campus. Apparently Berkeley had few violins, since there is no second violin section; however, Sessions's 1935 Violin Concerto had no violins at all. Nevertheless, numerous students were involved in the production as singers or players. The minimum possible number of orchestral players was 30, the maximum 46. The concert hall had no orchestra pit, and a single framework set was used. In the summer of 1947 Sessions copied over the score in Crescent Lake, Washington, adding more percussion. That spring's performance in Berkeley used only a *tambour provençal* (military drum), which Sessions had used in practically every score. In the revised score two players are required to play the additional tambourine, tam-tam, bass drum, and cymbals. Ultimately, Sessions thought "*Lucullus* has much more relevance to my later music than *Rienzi* had to Wagner's later music."[20] The opera was an immediate hit.

Alfred Frankenstein, who also reviewed *L'Histoire du Soldat* on the same bill, wrote for the *San Francisco Chronicle*,

> ["The Soldier's Story" is] at the furthest imaginable pole from the grand style, the big, complex, somber resonances, the humanity and dignity and clangorous drama of "The Trial of Lucullus." Perhaps its most remarkable feature, from a purely esthetic point of view, is the unparalleled suppleness of its vocal declamation. There is little or no lyric melody in the vocal parts, but, through an exquisitely perfect adjustment of tone and word, Sessions achieves an incredibly sharp musical characterization of individuals, so that the music of each role projects its personality with the utmost clarity and point. . . . It is a drama in music as well as a drama with music. It moves with a vast, tidal urgency, both in the whole and in the contrasts of crest and trough on its surface. It is one of the things one would like to have remembered from the era after World War II.[21]

In Oakland a reviewer wrote: "This modern work on a classical subject marches with the majestic pace of classical drama, the impressiveness of a historical pageant, and carries about as much dramatic punch as the recent Passion Play. The orchestra score is interesting in texture, and easier to 'take' than the composer's recent Second Symphony."[22] Rumors reached *The New York Times* of a Tanglewood production that summer, which did not come to pass.[23]

One composition student at Stanford, Richard Maxfield, upon hearing *Lucullus*, was so impressed he transferred to Berkeley to study with Sessions. Later he studied with Krenek in Los Angeles, went to Princeton (1954–1955) to study again with Sessions, and got a Fulbright to study in Florence with Luigi Dallapiccola. He later became involved with the Cage contingent.[24]

Schnitzler, like Samuel Eliot before him, had subsequent problems with the administration, in his case the head of his department. He lost his job at Berkeley and moved to Los Angeles, because, according to Sessions, he was too much of a professional and his colleagues were jealous of him.

The current text of *Lucullus* differs from that which Sessions set. Brecht had given the play to another composer. At the ISCM in New York in May 1941 Paul Dessau belabored Sessions with questions about whether Dessau ought to be composing modern music "at a time like this."[25] Dessau met Brecht in New York in the spring of 1943: he had written the music for the 1938 Paris production of 99% and for the 1954 *Caucasian Chalk Circle*. Brecht invited Dessau to Hollywood to supplement his collaborations with the ever-busier Kurt Weill and Eisler. Dessau wrote the music for *Mother Courage* songs, and Brecht gave him *Lucullus*, leading Dessau to conclude "he wanted *Lucullus* turned into an opera."[26] Brecht, however, had Stravinsky in mind as a possible composer, for he asked Dessau if he could interest the Russian, also living in Los Angeles, in the work. Stravinsky was too busy. In 1944 Brecht had felt Dessau's music "useless" for his epic theater.[27]

Brecht and Dessau returned to East Germany before Christmas 1948. Brecht then hoped Gottfried von Einem would compose a *Lucullus* opera.[28] In 1949, two years after the Sessions version had been produced, Dessau, in the hope of a large advance, began work on his own opera and persuaded Brecht to make textual changes. Dessau thought that the events of the ten years since the 1940 version—the impact of Nazi war crimes, the revival of Socialist Realism, pressures of the Cold War—invalidated the original ending; its pacifism would be contrary to the new East German Democratic Republic's policy. "And in making an opera for a very different Germany after the war it would suffer a sea-change more notorious than any other transformation of [Brecht's] often variable works."[29] The alterations became news.

Thorsten Preuss numbers the first Dessau version as the radio opera of 1949; the second the opera of 1950; and the third as January 1951 (none of these three was ever played). The controversial March 1951 premiere he counts as the fourth version, and the October 1951 performance the fifth. The authorities in East Berlin had allowed a closed performance of the Brecht–Dessau *Lucullus* for Party members and Free German Youth on March 17, 1951, the same day that the central committee passed a resolution "Against Formalism in Art and Literature." Brecht and Dessau met with members of the government who seem to have required Brecht and Dessau to add passages exempting defensive wars from the general condemnation. Subsequent performances of the 1949 version were canceled. The new version was first performed on October 12, 1951. (One scholar argues that no changes were made.[30]) The theater critic Eric Bentley gave his opinion of the results: "Dessau's two Brecht operas . . . are indeed *called* operas. But the more effective of them, *The Trial of Lukullus*, the one on which BB collaborated, the music is pretty much reduced to percussive accompaniment of the text. Sublime sound effects!"[31]

Dessau wanted *Lucullus* described as an opera, whereas Hermann Scherchen, its conductor, envisioned rather a "musical play."[32] In Dessau's opera, *The Condemnation of Lucullus (Die Verurteilung des Lukullus)*, a title that leaves little to the imagination as to the verdict, one of the major differences from the text Sessions set lies in the last scene, The Verdict. Here each of the jurors and the judge himself jump up to shout, "Send him to nothingness!"; even the warriors from the frieze and the slaves who hauled it cry "To nothingness!" The warriors lament, "If only we / Had deserted the aggressor! / If only we / Had joined the defenders!" Dessau inserted three new arias ("Summons to Defense," "Who is Rome?," and "Song of the Fallen Legionaries") to accommodate these new passages and to redistribute the weight of the musical expression in favor of the court and against the defendant.

In the 1949 Dessau version, the roles are given to specific voices: Lucullus, buffo tenor; the Queen, coloratura soprano; the Courtesan, mezzo-soprano; and Two Virgins, mezzo-sopranos. Sessions's ranges are: Lucullus, high baritone (almost a tenor); Queen, soprano; Courtesan, soprano; The Girl with the Tablet (instead of Two Virgins), soprano. Sessions's opera is through-composed; Dessau's is fundamentally a *Singspiel* with several characters, including The Announcer, speaking rather than singing. Sessions, in whose opera this important role is designated as "The Herald," assigned it to a baritone. Dessau's version designates the role The Toneless Voice as "a musically and vocally endowed actor," whereas in the Sessions score The Hollow Voice is a bass. The published Dessau opera libretto text (1951, see below) also contains speaking parts for the "Speaker of the Court of the Dead" (the Court Crier) and the crowds of slaves, soldiers, shades, and children. Dessau's opera does not include the testimony of the stone figures from the frieze; rather the shadows represented there are summoned to give evidence. Dessau eventually sent Sessions a copy of his *Lucullus*.

In 1957 still further changes were made to Dessau's opera, and *The Condemnation of Lucullus* was performed in this version at its second public East German production, in

Leipzig, in 1957. In 1960 Dessau cut Lucullus's tribute by his cook from scene 6 and he composed a new chorus for the legionaries at the end. The changes made to the 1940 version in the 1951 *Lucullus* may have been deliberately camouflaged. The publishing house of Suhrkamp Verlag in West Berlin began a *Versuch* series of Brecht's recent works. Elisabeth Hauptmann, formerly Brecht's chief collaboratrix and also for a time Dessau's wife, was its editor. She issued the 1951 version, generally assumed to be the 1940 text; theaters were not allowed to use the previous ending.

In 2003 the second Complete Edition of Brecht's works published *Lucullus*. Its editors asked, "How could the very existence of the first and best version of Brecht's play have been hidden from our view for so many years?" They have published for the first time the 1940 version (they received the Sessions–Hays libretto from the present author) in the new complete works. Their objective "must be to bring the first of these three versions out of the cupboard and get it played as it deserves."[33]

Therefore several versions of the German play and Dessau's libretto exist: the radio play of 1940—the version Sessions set in English; the text of 1949–1950 that, revised, became the opera libretto in 1951;[34] the opera libretto of 1957; and Dessau's changes in 1960. As mentioned above, the German text of the radio play was published in 1940 in the monthly *Internationale Literatur*, the German exile magazine in Moscow. The editors of the older *Collected Plays* feel this is "the most effective" of the versions because it is shorter and leaves more to the audience's imagination.

One of the most important musical events for Sessions, once back at Princeton, was the April 29, 1955, production of *The Trial of Lucullus* (along with Monteverdi's *Combattimento di Tancredi e Clorinda*).[35] The guiding spirit behind that production was Sylvia (Mrs Roy) Welch, who had seen *The Black Maskers* done by students at Smith. Curt and Grace Graff staged the opera. Nicholas Harsanyi conducted a cast of 63 in the McCarter Theater. (Sessions could not have been closer to the McCarter at that time; 70 Alexander Street is next to the theater.) The Princeton production used dances in some of the interludes. Soprano Janice Harsanyi, the conductor's wife, became an important proponent of Sessions's music, singing the *Idyll of Theocritus* and the *Psalm 140*, dedicated to her and which she premiered in 1963.

At the time of the 1955 performance Sessions had said of the work,

> The text of "The Trial of Lucullus" offers the most fundamental requirements of living drama. The characters, from Lucullus himself down to the characters who speak only a few lines, are human beings, not puppets or symbols. This is what I have tried to embody in my music—to make each character speak with his or her own native accents, vocally first of all, and secondarily in the orchestral accompaniment underlying the declamation. There are no "leit-motifs," although a few associative musical ideas will be readily recognized.[36]

At Northwestern University, on January 27, 1961, Thor Johnson conducted *Lucullus* (and the Mass). The director of the school's Opera Workshop, Robert Gay, staged *Lucullus* on a dark set layered on several levels.

The Juilliard production in New York in 1966 gained the work the most attention. Directed by Ian Strasfogel, it had sets and projections by Ming Cho Lee. According to the printed program, Sessions was supposed to conduct the opening night (May 19), but Jorge Mester conducted that performance and the second night (May 21). The reviews were glowing.[37] Unfortunately, that was the last production staged of a major work by Sessions on a text by a major playwright.

SCHOENBERG AND
DALLAPICCOLA

In the 1920s and 1930s Sessions had appeared to be, if anything, a member of the Stravinsky camp. His teacher Bloch disapproved of the Stravinskian direction Sessions's music was taking. Meeting Stravinsky, hearing *Les Noces* and *Œdipus Rex*, and Boulanger's teaching also influenced him. Nevertheless, after hearing a piano performance in 1927 of movements, including the minuet, from Schoenberg's Suite for Piano, op. 25, and the Stravinsky Sonata of 1924, Sessions felt that in both composers' "pieces it seemed that every note was exactly where it belonged, and the impression they made was unequivocal, unqualified, and completely focused. In other words, they were masterworks in the full sense of the term."[1] Sessions thought to himself, " 'You're a young composer still, and there's a whole part of the musical world that you don't know really much about.' So I got all Schoenberg's piano pieces, and learned a great many of them by heart [opp. 23, 25, 19, and 11]. I learned these [op. 23] by heart."[2] He found he knew the works better than many he met in Berlin who raved about Schoenberg's music.

Nevertheless, when he lived in Europe, Sessions disapproved of what he saw of the "Schoenberg School." His views can be seen in his review of Krenek's book *Über neue Musik* in 1938:

> This writer's [Sessions's] antipathy for the twelve-tone system is expressed precisely in these terms, provided that by "nature" is understood not physics but the response of the human ear and spirit to the simplest acoustic facts. He is profoundly out of sympathy, therefore with the conception which Krenek boldly avows, of music as an abstract system like geometry. . . . [there is a] measurably qualitative distinction between consonance and dissonance, are psychological as well as physical facts. . . . What one hears in twelve-tone music is often plainly at variance with the conceptions that go into its construction.[3]

As often happened with Sessions, however, meeting the human being could soften his views toward his music or theory. Sessions met Schoenberg in Berlin, saw him in Boston, and renewed the acquaintance in the late summer of 1941 at the Hollywood home of Dr Caroline Fisher, a professor of philosophy at UCLA. After Sessions left Berkeley for the east, he stopped in Los Angeles to visit a friend, pianist Richard Buhlig. The two were invited to dinner at Fisher's house in Hollywood with Schoenberg as the third guest.

> I spent really the evening talking to Schoenberg. We talked about Beethoven quartets, most of the time. Of course he could talk about Beethoven quartets like no one else. Then after dinner, there was a general conversation. This was in the

summer of 1941; we weren't in the war yet. My friend Buhlig was attacking the British, and Schoenberg and I were staunchly allied defending the British and attacking the Germans, of course. Buhlig was not pro-German at all, but he was inclined to think we shouldn't do anything about Hitler, I think, a little. I was very much inclined to think we should do something about Hitler . . . it used to be said of me in New York that "some of his best friends are Gentiles!"[4]

Spending the summer of 1944 at Black Mountain surrounded by many of Schoenberg's friends must have been highly influential. Clearly, Schoenberg embodied Rolland's aesthetic criteria as expressed in *Jean-Christophe*. Sessions initially stated his admiration for him in print and letters rather than in person. In 1944 he wrote "Schoenberg in the United States" as a seventieth birthday present.

No younger composer writes quite the same music as he would have written had Schoenberg's music not existed. . . . For genuinely new ideas determine the battlegrounds on which their opponents are forced to attack. . . . Regarding [the twelve-tone] technique itself much misleading nonsense has been written. I am in no sense a spokesman for it; I have never been attracted to it as a principle of composition. But one must distinguish carefully between technical principles in the abstract, and the works in which they become embodied; even a great work does not validate a dubious principle, nor does a valid principle produce in itself good or even technically convincing work.

And "The listener must listen to Schoenberg's music in exactly the same spirit as he listens to any music whatever, and bring to it the same kind of response. . . . The [works] pose new problems for the performers—but they have this in common with much of the best music of every generation."[5]

Sessions later said, "Schoenberg is one of the very great composers, because he's a composer who always gives you something new when you go back to it. I can't feel that way about Stravinsky at all. I mean I can go back with pleasure to Stravinsky, but I don't ever find there are new discoveries in it, you know. He was a great composer, too, undoubtedly, but . . ."[6]

Sessions sent the article "Schoenberg in the United States" to Schoenberg on October 30, 1944, with the first of ten letters, this one wishing him a happy seventieth birthday.[7] Sessions was, characteristically, as late with birthday wishes as with commissioned music: Schoenberg's birthday was in September. Schoenberg himself took a month to respond, but did so unexpectedly. He not only wrote to thank Sessions, but also sent two presents: the first page of the score to *Die Jakobsleiter* and two birthday canons for Carl Engel, both puzzle canons in three voices with text.[8] (Engel had died the previous May.) Sessions appears to have been overwhelmed by the generosity of these gifts, because, although he framed the *Jakobsleiter* for his study wall and admired it every day, he did not write Schoenberg a thank-you letter for *three years*.

In the fall of 1945, when Sessions moved to the University of California at Berkeley, it was easier to visit the older composer in Los Angeles. Sessions also began teaching Schoenberg's music in his Berkeley classes, including the recently completed Piano Concerto and the Fourth Quartet. Later he got to know the Violin Concerto, the Second Chamber Symphony, and the String Trio.

When he spoke with Schoenberg about his Fourth Quartet, Sessions "told him I felt [a] very strong relationship to the key of D minor. He said, 'Yes,'—and quite rightly—'Yes, but what you must realize is that the key of D minor is not really defined, and that what you feel is simply the relationship between the notes.' This is true. It's rather hard to get across, but it's true. This conversation was about 1949 or so."[9] (The last time Sessions saw Schoenberg was in the spring of 1949.) "It seems to me that the essential fact of tonality is not the establishment of the key, but the possibility of changing the key, you see," Sessions said in 1962. "In other words, I think that the essence of tonality is the possibility of modulating. In contemporary music, since we don't have a cadence, we can't really modulate. We can get sharp contrasts, but we can't sustain that contrast."[10]

Proximity also allowed Sessions's Berkeley students to visit the older composer. His students Leon Kirchner, Dika Newlin, Roger Nixon, Jeanne Shapiro (Bamberger), and Walter Nollner all saw Schoenberg; Kirchner, Newlin, and Nixon studied with him as well. The students relayed to Sessions Schoenberg's

> tireless energy in asking of them—above all the gifted ones—that they bring into their work the last degree of resourcefulness of which they are capable. It is not surprising that under such instruction they learn to make the greatest demands on themselves, or that their love of music and sense of music is developed both in depth and intensity as a result. It is this which distinguished Schoenberg's pupils above all—their training is not merely in "craftsmanship" but an integral training of their *musicality*, of ear and of response.[11]

A second compliment to Sessions from Schoenberg was to come via Kirchner. Kirchner had played for Schoenberg an acetate recording of Bernhard Abramowitsch playing Sessions's Second Sonata and reported to Sessions the master's reaction: "Now I know how Schumann must have felt when he first heard the music of Brahms."[12] Sessions wrote to him in the summer of 1948: "I need not tell you that there is no one living whose approval means so much to me as does yours."[13] In a letter Schoenberg confirmed what he had told Kirchner: "This is a language. I mean, it conveys a message and in this respect it seems to me one of the greatest achievement a composer could arrive at."[14]

Sessions responded: "It is truly wonderful to have a word from you regarding my music and you need not doubt that I treasure it. And part of my joy comes precisely from the fact that you speak in terms of the *music* and 'language' in the sense that you—and I, too, mean—and not of harmony and counterpoint, etc. which, after all, we respect only the more for recognizing—as too many people seem not to do—that they are the *means* and not the end."[15] At the familial level, Schoenberg's ten-year-old son Ronald and Sessions's ten-year-old John played both tennis and cello together. "Both our sons were cellists and both were championship tennis players."[16] Ronald Schoenberg had been a ranking amateur in Europe and John Sessions became the under-15-years-old champion of California. The similarities between the two boys were so striking that John came to his father one day and said, "Dad, Ronnie Schoenberg and I are the same person," while Schoenberg said, "Your son is a better cellist, but mine is a better tennis player."[17] (John Sessions was to premiere the Six Pieces for Violoncello and the Double Concerto for violin and cello by his father.[18])

Another connection between Schoenberg and Sessions concerned the author Thomas Mann. Mann's son Michael, a violinist in the San Francisco Symphony, had performed in the 1947 premiere of Sessions's Second Symphony and written to Sessions an admiring letter. Sessions wrote a letter to Thomas Mann, about the novel *Doctor Faustus*, to which Mann responded appreciatively on December 31, 1948.[19] Mann wrote in German, "if an artist and someone who has so much understanding of the times as you [the great composer] do recognized the situation that I tried to present in it from his own experience, his own struggle and suffering as true and correct, then this has to be of the highest importance to me." Mann's daughter Elizabeth had wed Antonio Borgese, the librettist for *Montezuma*, in Sessions's Princeton home November 23, 1939.[20]

As is well known, Schoenberg was upset by Mann's novel; he feared readers would find Leverkühn as a fictionalized version of himself, and he disliked the implication that genius is a product of degeneration. His pressure resulted in an Author's Note appended to future published editions of the novel stating that "The twelve-tone, or row system, is in truth the intellectual property of a contemporary composer and theoretician, Arnold Schönberg. I have transferred this technique in a certain ideational context to the fictitious figure of a musician, the tragic hero of my novel. In fact, the passages of this book that deal with musical theory are indebted in numerous details to Schoenberg's *Harmonielehre*."

Sessions was caught in the middle of this debate.

> I was friends with both Thomas Mann and with Schoenberg. . . . One Thanksgiving dinner with Schoenberg the topic of Thomas Mann came up. Schoenberg remarked that he was afraid that history would credit the invention of the twelve-tone method to a little-known German composer named Adrian Leverkühn. I tried to reassure him tactfully; however, what was really going on in my mind was, "What do you care? You will be remembered for your music, not for inventing the twelve-tone system."[21]

In February 1949 Schoenberg traveled north to speak at the all-female Dominican College of San Rafael. Since Sessions had previously spoken there, he sought Sessions's advice about the level of the audience.

A day before Schoenberg's seventy-fifth birthday, Sessions sent a birthday letter with student Jeanne Shapiro. In November 1949 Schoenberg wrote to ask Sessions to help his old friend, pianist and theorist Moritz Violin, a friend and pupil of Schenker, achieve a teaching position.[22] Sessions now confronted not only his views toward Schoenberg's theories, but also toward Heinrich Schenker, about whom he had published three articles shortly after his death in 1935.[23] Schoenberg wrote regarding Schenker,

> Frankly, I was opposed against most of his conclusions, but on the other hand I have to admit that he has also made some very valuable analyses (of the Beethoven Ninth for example) and had some new ideas in respect to understand the thoughts of composers. . . . But, if you see the effect which it makes when [Violin] has explained what he does, first playing how it is usually performed and how it can be played according to his theories, then you will perhaps admit, as I have had to admit, that this is very impressive. Mr Violin is, of course, an excellent piano player. I must say, the difference is striking.[24]

Despite his essentially negative view of Schenker's theories, Milton Babbitt credits Sessions with having introduced Schenker's term "tonicization" into English use, as opposed to the more literal translation "tonicalization." By the time Sessions published his own theory book, *Harmonic Practice*, in 1951, his views on Schenker had softened somewhat, perhaps partly as a result of his contact with Schoenberg and with Schoenberg's friend of 50 years, Moritz Violin.[25]

He did meet with the pianist named Violin and wrote to Schoenberg "Incidentally he spoke very wonderfully about you and I was very happy indeed to hear such sentiments especially from a disciple of Schenker. My wife suggested too that we ask him to have Christmas dinner [1949] with us, and we will be so happy to have him here, together with a couple of my pupils."[26] Sessions was unable to secure Violin a teaching position, partly because of his age (65) and partly because his English was not good.

After the Violin episode a year and a half elapsed before renewal of the correspondence. Sessions responded from Wisconsin, to a now missing May 1951 letter, mentioning that in July 1951 the Sessions family would move to Italy for a year. He also sent greetings from Rudi and Lorna Kolisch to their old friend.

Schoenberg had sent Sessions the first edition of *Style and Idea*, which Sessions received in June.[27] He sent a thank you letter and wrote, "I have been distressed to hear that you are not feeling well this summer, and sorry to have not been able to see you, on that account."[28] Indeed, the two never saw each other again. Schoenberg died—as he feared he would—on Friday the thirteenth, July 1951.

Less than a year later Sessions published "Some notes on Schoenberg and the 'method of composing with twelve tones'." At the head of the article he quoted from one of Schoenberg's letters to him: "A Chinese philosopher speaks, of course, Chinese; the question is, what does he say?"[29] Sessions doubtless remembered performing the role of a Chinese philosopher in Cleveland. Here Sessions argued that the notoriety surrounding the twelve-tone method presented a barrier to the music itself. He argued for historical evolution of the method: "Dodecaphony—here used to mean simply the independence of the twelve notes of the chromatic scale—is the result of an impulse which has been inherent in Western music at least from the moment that musicians began to combine voices simultaneously." And "What Schoenberg achieved, then, with the formulation of the twelve-tone method, was to show his followers a way toward the practical organization of materials . . . Its significance is the greater precisely for the fact of being something far more unpretentious, but at the same time far more vital, than a new harmonic theory or a new aesthetic principle could possibly be."[30]

Parts of Sessions's Sonata for Violin, finished in the following year, 1953, use twelve-tone techniques. The influence of both Schoenberg's music and his friendship had permanently changed Sessions. Sessions adapted the twelve-tone method loosely and in his own way, for the rest of his life—40 more years. His use of hexachords as scales with added tones, however, differs in essentials from Schonberg's twelve-tone method. Analysts trying to decode Sessions's music always run up against this fundamental fact: Sessions works are *not* twelve-tone. His notes are drawn from six-tone scale patterns, such as Berg's procedure in *Wozzeck*. He explained,

> I always have made very great use of what they call the symmetrical [combinatorial] row, you see, in which the two halves of the row can be transformed in such a way that they have a certain relationship to each other. I mean, you could rearrange the notes in the second half, or the second hexachord, since there are twelve tones—six and six, you see. It's even apt, in my music—it does in the Quintet, it does in *Montezuma*—it becomes three and three and three and three, you see. Well, this is just a way of making possible the fullest possible exploitation of the material.[31]

"Of course, there was one other thing that prevented me from seeing more of [Stravinsky] in California. It's a somewhat ridiculous situation. During those years, I was seeing a lot of Schoenberg, and Schoenberg and Stravinsky represented two opposite poles. They had not been on close terms, or even any terms at all, for many years."[32] Sessions's close friend Darius Milhaud used to laugh and say that if you went to Los Angeles and saw one of them, you would have to be careful about seeing the other. Sessions learned, however, that "actually towards the end of Schoenberg's life, Stravinsky wanted very much to come into relations with Schoenberg, and Schoenberg wanted to come back into relations with Stravinsky. I've heard the story from people who were very close to Schoenberg, especially, a very good friend of mine who was very close to Schoenberg. It was an accident that they never actually did meet again."[33]

> The only thing is that Schoenberg was very isolated in Vienna. He really suffered a great deal for his musical convictions and ideas, and when Stravinsky, in the early twenties, seemed to follow what to him seemed like a very reactionary path musically, he felt abandoned, and he attacked Stravinsky . . . He wrote some little choral pieces which he called satires, and the text of the pieces was a not-too-veiled attack, not so much on Stravinsky himself but on everything that Stravinsky represented, Neo-Classicism. . . . Now, this is a complicated thing. I'm not going to try to interpret either one of them. I won't take any position at all.[34]

Almost immediately—and coincidentally—after Arnold Schoenberg's death, Sessions met another major composer who became a close friend, one who used Schoenberg's twelve-tone method in an unconventional manner, as did Sessions. Alfredo Casella had mentioned Luigi Dallapiccola (1904–1975) to Sessions before he left Rome for Berlin in 1931. Indeed, Casella was to become something of a promoter of Dallapiccola, as well as other younger Italian composers: Dallapiccola always felt grateful for Casella's help. Another member of the *generazione dell'ottanta*, Gian Francesco Malipiero, also influenced Dallapiccola.

The ISCM jury in Amsterdam, on which Sessions sat in December of 1932, had seen Dallapiccola's Partita for Orchestra. Sessions voted for it, but it was not played at the 1933 Amsterdam Festival.

Dallapiccola and his wife, Laura Coen Luzzatto, who was Jewish, were Florentines. Dallapiccola had moved there in 1922. To protect her when Nazi troops occupied Florence beginning on September 11, 1943, the two hid in Borgunto, north of Fiesole, and elsewhere with friends. After 1945 Dallapiccola had an additional career as a writer for *Il mondo europeo*.

When Sessions returned to Florence in 1951, two decades after having lived there, he saw old friends: David Diamond, Antonio Borgese, Dimitri Mitropoulos, and Mario Labroca. By this time, Dallapiccola and Goffredo Petrassi had become the most prominent post-war Italian composers. Dallapiccola had been in Tanglewood the summer of 1951, just before he met Sessions, and he visited the US for long stretches thereafter, including teaching at Queens College (1956 and 1959), at the University of California at Berkeley (1962), Dartmouth and Aspen (summer of 1969). Dallapiccola's best-known students were perhaps Luciano Berio and Bernard Rands.

During the 1951–1952 Fulbright year Sessions gave 11 lectures. In Florence from November 1951 through February 1952, he gave eight at the Accademia Nazionale Luigi Cherubini, in a series entitled "Lo stato attuale della musica nell'America del Nord." These were translated and published as *Reflections on the Music Life in the United States*.[35] The remaining lectures, "La musica contemporaneo negli Stati Uniti," were given in the spring of 1952 at La Spezia, Genoa, Savona, Turin, Alessandria, Milan, Rome, Naples, Pisa, and Venice. An additional lecture, "I giovani compositori in America," was delivered in April 1952 in Florence.

During his 1951–1952 Fulbright year in Florence, Sessions met Dallapiccola, eight years younger than he, and later reminisced:

> I spent the winter in Florence, the city that I most love, and which I had, before and during the war, despaired of ever seeing again. The evening of our arrival my wife and I met our friend Leonardo Olschki, who knew I hoped to meet Dallapiccola; he immediately proposed to call him by telephone, in order to arrange a meeting between us. The result was an invitation to spend an evening which I shall always remember, and the beginning of a friendship that has meant at least as much to me as any other, in a life that has been rich in precious relationships. I felt an instant and lively sympathy which, as the autumn, winter, and spring passed, developed into a deep affection, and an ever-growing admiration for a personality that was vivid, profoundly cultivated, and gifted, all in the highest degree.[36]

Shortly after meeting the Italian, Sessions wrote to his student Harold Schiffman: "There are some very congenial people here—among them Luigi Dallapiccola whom I see very often. He lives very near us, + I have found him most congenial—many of our trains of thought, + even our relations with certain individuals, have been uncannily parallel. He is the only musician whom I have found with whom I feel I have very much in common."[37]

This parallelism can be seen in several facets of their lives. Like Sessions, Dallapiccola had initially been influenced by Richard Wagner: after a 1917 performance of *Der fliegende Holländer* Dallapiccola became aware of his vocation as a composer. Not until 1934 did Dallapiccola gain an official teaching post (teaching secondary piano) at the Florence Conservatory, where he remained until retirement in 1967. These dates almost precisely parallel Sessions's tenure at Princeton. Dallapiccola's command of languages almost equaled that of Sessions: he spoke French, German, and eventually English. Their conversation and correspondence was entirely in Italian. His father had been a professor of Greek and Latin. Dallapiccola was also an author of numerous articles about music.[38] Like Sessions he was highly cultivated and well-read man; he, too, enjoyed Classical Greek literature and set Greek poems to music. And, like Sessions, he was, as the Italians put it, *simpatico*; that is to say he possessed a warm heart and a deep understanding of people. Dallapiccola had, again as had Sessions, repudiated most of his early work from the 1920s. His later work, particularly *Volo di notte* (*Night Flight*, 1937–1939), took the literal view of "rising above the storm." This detachment—only one part of Dallapiccola's musical personality—matched Sessions's Rollandian views beautifully. And Dallapiccola was acquainted with the Second Viennese School; he had known Berg and met Webern. He was the first Italian composer to adopt the twelve-tone method.

Dallapiccola was one of the few of Sessions's friends shorter than he. He made up for his lack of height by an erect carriage (Sessions, too, had excellent posture), a sense of authority, a warm smile, and a soft-spoken intensity of speech. Laura Dallapiccola would have liked to find a subject on which the two composers disagreed: there seemed to be none.

While Sessions was in Florence, Dallapiccola had just completed a one-act "Sacred Representation," *Job*, which had been premiered on October 30, 1950, in Rome. A

Figure 38 Luigi Dallapiccola.

broadcast of his opera *Il Prigioniero* (*The Prisoner*) took place in 1949. The Juilliard School of Music's opera department had given the American premiere, March 15–19, 1951.[39]

Feelings of friendship were mutual on Dallapiccola's part. He wrote in 1964 for the BMI Sessions promotional booklet:

> Roger knows how much I love his Fourth Symphony and how ever since its first reading I was struck by its so very singular "divergent" process: as the emotion increases, the sonorous means which are used become less. He knows that I consider his Violin Concerto a unique piece and that there are very, very few other works which I should so much like at least to be able to hear, in an adequate performance. It will tell him nothing new when I write of how much I was moved on receiving the very poetic and so inspired *Idyll of Theocritus*, by the dedication of which he chose to do me honor. . . . Roger should know that in the dedication [of the *Cinque Canti* to him], besides admiration for the inspired artist and the conscientious craftsman, is embodied admiration for his character and personality as a human being.

In 1952, doubtless at Sessions's behest, Berkeley arranged a concert of Dallapiccola's works, with Sessions translating the guest composer's French into English for the California audience. Sessions wrote to Dallapiccola about his visit to the Berkeley music department, "But it seems to me entirely possible that with regard to the type of music and musical tendencies that both of us represent—and I'm not referring to dodecaphony—the prevailing mood is decidedly 'vorrei e non vorrei' [I want it and I don't want it], without the youthful vivacity of Zerlina! We shall see."[40] In addition, Dallapiccola had been to Mexico, and Sessions was excited to hear about the trip. During

Dallapiccola's trip to San Francisco the two saw their mutual friend Darius Milhaud. Another mutual friend was Pietro Scarpini, the leading Italian pianist after the war. Scarpini disdained recording, but played Dallapiccola's music, including the *Sonatina canonica* (1943, dedicated to the pianist).[41]

Dallapiccola kept Sessions abreast of the interpersonal problems among ISCM board members in Europe.[42] Sessions, as president of the American section of the ISCM, was to explain these to Copland, the vice-president. Always tactful about interpersonal relationships, Sessions had met Dallapiccola's great rival, Goffredo Petrassi, an ISCM member about whom he wrote with restraint: "Meanwhile I met Petrassi and I conversed almost officially with him for an hour and a half. He was very friendly and it always pleases me to speak Italian even when much isn't being said. . . . With certain types of people I can converse in a civilized fashion even though there is little I want to say or hear."[43]

Many of their students traveled either to Florence or to the east coast to study with the other composer. These include Salvatore Martirano, who Dallapiccola taught from 1953–1954 and sent to Sessions; Martirano then won the Rome Prize in 1959. Sessions's student George Strum studied with Dallapiccola from 1955–1957 on a Fulbright. Donald Martino studied with Sessions and Babbitt until 1954 and went to Florence on a Fulbright to study with Dallapiccola from 1954–1956. Frederic Rzewski studied with Sessions at Princeton and won a Fulbright to Rome, 1960–1962; he met Dallapiccola through Sessions. In 1965 Sessions wrote introducing John Harbison to Dallapiccola. Henry Weinberg had studied with Babbitt and Sessions at Princeton and with Dallapiccola in Florence. Craig Shuler studied at Juilliard and won a Fulbright to study with Dallapiccola. Tod Machover studied both with Sessions and Dallapiccola. Daniel Brewbaker, a Sessions Juilliard student, moved to Italy in the 1980s and met Laura Dallapiccola.[44]

Each composer sent works to, or heard works by, the other. Letters mention Dallapiccola's liking Sessions's Second String Quartet. Sessions sent Dallapiccola the Violin Sonata (1953), while Dallapiccola sent Sessions the *Canti di Liberazione* (1951–1955). Dallacipccola dedicated his 1956 Webernesque *Cinque canti* for baritone and eight instruments to Sessions. The work has a "symmetrical row" whose second half is the retrograde inversion of the first half. Sessions dedicated his *Idyll of Theocritus* to the Italian, and sent it to Dallapiccola describing the premiere and subsequent performances.[45] Sessions could not, at the last minute, hear Dallapiccola's cantata *An Mathilde* (1955) for female voice and orchestra performed in New York, May 7, 1956, but Dallapiccola sent him the score.

Theocritus was performed in Stockholm June 5, 1956, at the ISCM with Martha Long singing and Sixten Ehrling conducting.[46] At the end of the month Sessions visited Dallapiccola in Florence. Sessions saw *Il Prigioniero*, for which he had the score, October 5, 1960, at City Center. He offered to go over the English translation with Dallapiccola, thinking he could improve it. He wrote about the work: "It is the first time I heard it at the theater and I was more captivated than ever; I still—today I read the score twice—I can't forget it. There is no doubt that it is one of the principal works of our time, and we were profoundly moved by it. I must add that the audience seemed greatly impressed; every indication points to a great success."[47]

Dallapiccola had written to Sessions in 1960 describing the Fourth Symphony as "an emotional crescendo obtained with the minimal amount of sounds."[48] Part of the time Sessions was working on *Montezuma* Dallapiccola worked on his opera *Ulisse* (*Ulysses*, 1959–1968).

The subject of the row, and the common misunderstandings surrounding it, came up often in their conversation. Sessions liked to relate one story:

> Dallapiccola told me once of a student of his at Queens College. (Every now and then we would meet in New York for a drink.) One day he told me he had met one of his students that morning, and the student told him, "Oh, Maestro, I've started using the row." And Dallapiccola said, "Oh, that's very interesting. What's the row?" This boy fumbled in all his pockets here and there, and finally he said to Dallapiccola, "Well, I haven't got it with me now." And Dallapiccola thought that was awfully funny. And it is, although that's the way some people interpret the row.[49]

In the summer of 1960, after Princeton's successful summer seminar on music the previous year, Sessions wrote to Dallapiccola to invite him to participate in that summer's festival for three weeks in August. The participants at the 1959 seminar had included Copland, Krenek, Ginastera, Varèse, Greissle, and Steuermann. Others attending the seminar were Robert Craft, John Tukey, and Stravinsky, and the Lenox Quartet was in residence. Sessions solicited their papers to be published in *The Musical Quarterly*.[50] The contributors were the editor, Paul Henry Lang, Paul Fromm, who paid for it, Sessions, Edward T. Cone, Elliott Carter, Vladimir Ussachevsky, Krenek, and Babbitt.

Sessions wrote to Dallapiccola after the November 1960 Presidential elections,

> You of course must have followed the news of the elections here—the result was extremely satisfying for us and we ardently hope that Kennedy will not betray the trust that his most ardent supporters have placed in him. Personally I would have preferred [Adlai] Stevenson, but K. is young and undoubtedly very intelligent, and it seems to me that things have already taken a turn for the better in the country. His political opponents do everything possible to make trouble—few of my compatriots are aware of what a dangerous game this is to play; but until now he gives an impression of strength and authentic courage, and I think we can allow ourselves a little hope.[51]

In January 1961 Sessions was one of 155 leading figures in the arts and sciences to be invited to John F. Kennedy's inauguration; he had to leave the Fromm Festival in his honor in Evanston, Illinois. He had conducted his Third Symphony in Oberlin and *The Black Maskers* in Evanston.

There are similarities between Sessions's *Montezuma* and Dallapiccola's *Il Prigioniero*. Both are set in the occupied lands of Philip II of Spain, Mexico and the Netherlands respectively. Both have distinct political overtones and in both the protagonists are doomed. In November 1960 plans had been laid to produce *Montezuma* in Florence: they were then postponed to the spring of 1962, which Sessions told Lisl would probably "add ten years to my life!" The production was abandoned, however, because Sessions had still not finished the score. In Europe from February through August 1961 for the planned, but aborted, performance of *Montezuma* Sessions traveled in Germany, England, Scotland, France, Italy, Greece, and Switzerland. Sessions and Lisl visited Boris Blacher in Berlin and traveled to Athens and the Greek island of Cos, the scene of *Idyll of Thecritus*. He returned through Switzerland and saw Dallapiccola in Florence around February 20; he remained there for two months at the Pensione Quisisana e Ponte Vecchio, 4 Lungarno, Archibusieri.

During a sixty-fifth birthday tribute to Sessions, in 1961, several composers wrote and spoke about Sessions. Darius Milhaud said, "I do not want to omit amongst his human qualities the faithfulness of his friendship towards other musicians, and I am happy to be one of them." Dallapiccola waxed: "Beautiful, admirable and impressive is the presence of creative artists . . . but how consoling it becomes when to these [qualities] we add the presence of artists who are also human; who know, in other words, love and understand their fellow human beings." Edward Cone repeated Dallapiccola's remarks at the close of a seventy-fifth birthday tribute.[52]

Dallapiccola wrote to Sessions in September 1963, six months after having received a letter from Sessions. He and Laura had spent 12 days in the summer traveling to Greece, on their way to Israel. His impression of Stravinsky's *The Flood* at La Scala was "something 'impossible.' "[53]

The Sessionses then returned to Berlin for the spring and summer of 1964 on a Ford Foundation grant to prepare for the premiere of *Montezuma*, April 19. Sessions wrote to Dallapiccola between performances, quite candidly, because he knew that the same company was scheduled to premiere *Ulisse*. Dallapiccola had telegrammed Sessions "Hals und Beinbruch" ("Break a leg!"), and Sessions replied, "Both the letter and the telegram gave me a clear sense of your friendship, which is one of the most precious things in my life and which, of course, I will never forget." In a letter appended to this one, Sessions brought up the linguistic issue of familiar address:

> I'd like to say one more thing that has been on my mind for some time now. Since I am not Italian, I don't exactly know the proper use of "tu." I would be very happy if we could use it but I fully understand that this is not only a national custom but also a personal one, and I have realized that being the older of the two, it is up to me to suggest it first. So, if you in your response should like to call me "tu" I would be very happy, but if you should prefer "Lei" as always, please do so without embarrassment. I have lived too long and understand too well to be in any way vulnerable in this sort of thing![54]

In this same letter Sessions cited Dallapiccola's quotation of Valéry, "A work of art is never finished, only abandoned."

In September 1964 Sessions expressed his appreciation for what Dallapiccola had written for his BMI brochure (quoted earlier):

> It would be impossible for me to express, my dear friend, how deeply your words moved me, both those in the letter and those in the booklet. I am even more moved at the thought that these words spring from a deep and faithful friendship, which is even more precious than your words of praise, given that they not only provide moral support and recognition, but also a sharp sense of one's own insufficiencies. Thank you, my dearest friend, from the bottom of my heart; your generosity and affection are more dear and precious to me than words could ever express.

Sessions had the score of *Montezuma* sent to the Italian composer. His mind, however, was preoccupied with the national politics of 1964:

> Unfortunately the current political situation here is both critical and dangerous. There is no doubt that Goldwater represents a very ugly part, unfortunately not

altogether new, of our country. One mustn't speak of Fascism or even of war but rather of politics that are not geared toward very probable or immediate *consequences*, and of a blind and idiotic simplicity. I don't think he will win, but he has fanatical and dedicated supporters, so there is always a possibility, and his defeat, in order to be completely satisfying, should be strong and crushing. The next eight or nine weeks will be awful and worrisome. Fortunately Johnson and Humphrey seem to be very capable men and there's no denying that their supporters include some of the best elements in the country with the exception of some politicians—like [Nelson] Rockefeller—who are trapped by their party's abnormal situation, but whose best interests and political future depend on a decided defeat of the candidate they supposedly support. A strange, abnormal and very preoccupying situation—but let's hope.[55]

Dallapiccola was to be in the US in the fall of 1964. His arrival would coincide with the presidential election between Goldwater and Johnson, which inspired Sessions to write, "I'll see you in New York the evening of November 4 (let's hope that in the same day we will all find out that Johnson was definitely elected, and that we will be freed from any worry as far as that is concerned!), and I am delighted."[56]

In 1966 the Arno River flooded and destroyed many priceless artifacts in Florence. Sessions wrote to Dallapiccola in 1967 of "the terrible disaster [that] struck our beloved Florence," a few days before the two would see each other in Ann Arbor, Michigan. Out of embarrassment Sessions wrote: "I can only say that my silence dates back to the beginning of the bombings in Vietnam, and to my shame, my profound embarrassment, and to the struggle against the desperation that assails me over what happened and what continues to happen there."[57] Sessions's Symphony No. 7 received its premiere on October 1, 1967, with Jean Martinon, the dedicatee, conducting the Chicago Symphony Orchestra in Ann Arbor. Sessions and Dallapiccola were guests of the department of music of the University of Michigan, commissioners of the Symphony. Sessions's former student Ross Lee Finney remembered, "The talk was about opera, or I should say, about Luigi's *Ulysses* and Roger's *Montezuma*. I have never seen two composers talk with more gusto and pleasure."[58] Sessions had heard a rehearsal of Dallapiccola's *Variations*. The Ann Arbor visit would be the last time the two composers saw each other, although Dallapiccola taught in 1969 in Dartmouth and at the Aspen Music Festival that year.

Dallapiccola would enlist Sessions in political causes involving musicians. He appealed to Sessions to persuade the reluctant American Academy of Arts and Letters (of whom Sessions was a member) publicly to ask President Johnson to intervene on behalf of Korean intellectuals kidnapped in Europe, imprisoned, and condemned; Dallapiccola referred specifically to composer Isang Yun (1917–1995). *Die Zeit* in Hamburg had published a petition that garnered 161 signatures. Sessions contacted George Kennan, the President of the Academy, whom Sessions also knew from the Institute for Advanced Study at Princeton. A political consensus at the Academy was lacking, so no letter was sent. Sessions spoke with Elliott Carter, who, along with others, was trying to appeal directly to the South Korean president Park Chung Hee. After two years' detention Yun and his wife were released, both because 23 prominent musicians wrote a letter of protest (Dallapiccola was on the list) and because of pressure exerted by West Germany, to which the Yuns returned.

Meanwhile, the US was undergoing an upheaval in early 1968. Sessions wrote, as always, in Italian.

We were shocked at yesterday's announcement that Johnson will not be a candidate for the Presidency but feel somewhat encouraged by [Eugene] McCarthy's and [Robert] Kennedy's candidacies. All these events seem to have changed the perspective—we still don't know in what way, but instead of torpor and almost desperation there are evident signs of vitality, energy, and purpose. However, it seems to me that the situation will remain uncertain for some time, and although undoubtedly a *crescendo* has begun, some surprises await us before the trombones come in. Johnson's retirement appears genuine; the efforts at negotiation [in Vietnam] seem insufficient, and we are so accustomed to disappointments and to being cheated that we are always watchful and suspicious. In all of this, the young people are truly extraordinary—they have found a reason for living, they work, they travel and [illegible]: and they have really produced some unexpected results—so, who knows?[59]

"Some surprises" did not wait long: only three days after this letter the Rev. Martin Luther King, Jr was assassinated, and in June Robert Kennedy met the same fate. The country was turning inside out. Sessions dedicated his *When Lilacs Last in the Dooryard Bloom'd*, on which he was then working, to the slain leaders.

Dallapiccola's *Ulisse* was performed in German, September 29, 1968, by the Deutsche Opera in Berlin conducted by Lorin Maazel. Seven days earlier Sessions had written encouraging well wishes. Dallapiccola had conveyed Sessions's greetings to their mutual friends at the Deutsche Oper for Sessions. These friends included singers who had created roles in *Montezuma*: Annabelle Bernard (who had sung Malinche), Herbert Melcher (Montezuma), Ernst Krukowski (Bernal Diaz the Old), Karl Ernst Mercker (Bernal Diaz the Young), and Loren Driscoll (Alvarado). The fact that both Sessions's and Dallapiccola's largest operas were premiered by the same company and sung by the same singers only cemented their indestructible friendship. Pleased with the production, Dallapiccola realized that it would take time and patience for his opera to become a little less difficult to perform. He used a phrase that Sessions frequently quoted, "Si sa che la nostra professione è la scuola della pazienza" (One knows that our profession is the school of patience).[60] He sent Sessions the *Ulisse* score, with which Sessions spent hours. Sessions immediately sent Dallapiccola his Fourth Symphony and the (then) five pieces for cello. On the subject of politics Sessions quoted Churchill, "God protects the stupid, and the United States of America."[61] Sessions, by now living in Cambridge as Norton Professor at Harvard, "fervently" hoped that the aphorism would continue to hold.

Dallapiccola and his wife, closely following the US elections in November of 1968, knew "the results have been disappointing for you." Richard Nixon had won—barely—over Humphrey. The Americans under 21 Sessions had such faith in were not yet allowed to vote. Dallapiccola felt the American situation in Vietnam and elsewhere was a problem "extremely serious and urgent: I am convinced that without such a problem the brutal and unjustified Russian oppression in Czechoslovakia would not have happened. We admire the great heroic effort of the Czech people and we anxiously wonder how long it will last."[62] The "Prague spring" was suppressed.

For the next six years—1968–1974—the two composers neither saw one another nor wrote letters, save one by Dallapiccola announcing his daughter's marriage. That letter went unanswered. Sessions finally resumed their correspondence in December 1974: he sent a letter through another former student, Henry Weinberg, since the Italian postal system was notoriously unreliable. He apologized for not having communicated on the occasions of Annalibera's wedding, Dallapiccola's own illness, and his seventieth birthday.

Sessions sent his *Lilacs* cantata, his Eighth Symphony, and the Concertino for Chamber Orchestra. Lisl, he told Dallapiccola, had fractured a pelvic bone and had a heart condition. A few months after Nixon resigned because of Watergate, Sessions wrote, "Naturally you know about what went on in our country. We replaced an inconsistent, very dangerous, lying, and irresponsible president with one who according to provincial criteria is certainly honest but, alas, is stupid [Ford]."[63]

Dallapiccola read and listened to the Eighth Symphony. He congratulated Elizabeth on becoming a mother, and the Sessionses for becoming grandparents, earlier that year. It was a feeling he could not imagine and would never experience. The letter, dated January 5, 1975, was preoccupied with the death of Carlo Levi, the founder of an antifascist movement in 1930, who wrote *Cristo s'è fermato a Eboli* (*Christ Stopped at Eboli: The Story of A Year*). This letter arrived only a month before Dallapiccola's own death at 71 on February 19.

Lisl, who wrote to Laura first, declared that the devastated Sessions now said, "I no longer have anyone to talk to."[64] Their mutual friend Darius Milhaud had died several months earlier, June 22, 1974. For the first time Sessions wrote in English—a condolence letter to Laura Dallpiccola.[65] He felt he could express himself more confidently in his native language.

Asked if there were similarities between Dallapiccola's and Sessions's own piano music, the composer responded,

> It would be very hard to say exactly what the difference or even the similarity is. Although I found him certainly as congenial a composer as I have ever met, I felt more and more that we were really not that much alike. The idea of dedicating the Five Pieces [for piano] to him came at the very last moment, before they were published. I didn't even think of no. 4 in that connection before he died. No, that's not true. The connection with Dallapiccola is purely coincidental. I never think of him as a composer for the piano especially. . . . The reference to him at the beginning of the fourth piece I put down because I was thinking of him part of the time when I was writing it. I wrote down measures 13–15 and then later thought, "Why don't I dedicate the whole thing to him, to his memory?"[66]

Dallapiccola was primarily a vocal composer and, in fact, Session was also a composer who wrote often for the voice. Sessions observed, "My meeting and friendship with Dallapiccola gave me a very great impulse to go in much more for vocal music. Naturally, in my own way and in my own language."[67] If one were to take into account all the choral and vocal works Sessions set, it could be seen that he wrote more music for vocal than for instrumental pieces. Because neither opera is recorded, and because of the lack of availability of recordings of *Psalm 140, Turn, O Libertad*, the Mass, *Idyll of Theocritus*, and the *Three Choruses on Biblical Texts*, Sessions's vocal music is less well known than the symphonies and other instrumental works. Sessions and Dallapiccola are more often praised than performed, because of both the expense of mounting their operas and the difficulty of the music. Posterity has united the two modernist composers: in death they still had something in common.

SYMPHONIES NOS 3 AND 4

Liberated by the death of his mother in 1946, Sessions started to write more prolific-ally—even working on two symphonies at once. Now fully mature as a composer and his own person, Sessions could at last come to terms in his music with the deaths of three men: two of whom had been dear to him and a third with whom he had difficult relations.

In 1957 he reflected:

> For four very important years—1911 to 1915—I heard the [Boston Symphony] orchestra at least once a week . . . and in the following years I traveled frequently to Boston to hear programs of special interest to me. These were impressionable years . . . which left me memories which are still vivid and concrete—[of] both of the classics and of the contemporary music of that time. I realized long ago that my whole conception of the orchestral sound and all that goes with it were formed by these experiences; and have often said that all of my orchestral music has been written essentially for the Boston Symphony as I heard it then.[1]

Commissioned by the Boston Symphony, the Third Symphony was completed in Princeton on September 25, 1957. The premiere, conducted by Charles Munch, was given on December 6, 7, and 10 in Boston and on December 11 at Carnegie Hall. The program annotator for the Boston Symphony remained Sessions's old Harvard friend, John Burk, for whose wedding Sessions had served as best man. Sessions still had many memories of attending the Symphony with George, Van, and Burk.

Sessions had had, however, a difficult relationship with the Boston Symphony. Because of Koussevitzky's and the composer's falling out over his Violin Concerto in 1936, the BSO had not played any of Sessions's music from 1927 until after Koussevitzky's death in June 1951. Edward T. Cone stated that up until his death, Koussevitzky was con-vinced Sessions had never finished the concerto. Sessions thought he had persuaded him otherwise by sending a score and receiving an acknowledgment. In Sessions's opinion, Koussevitzky was covering up somewhat for not having played it, by claiming it was not completed. In addition, he stated "[I] never have felt that any conductor of the Boston Symphony since Muck could touch Muck, and I don't think that Koussevitzky was as great a conductor as Pierre Monteux, by any means."[2]

A long overdue thaw between the orchestra and the composer finally began in 1955. Under Pierre Monteux the Symphony had programmed the Orchestral Suite from *The Black Maskers* in Boston, January 28, 29, and 30; in Philadelphia February 8; in Brooklyn February 11; in New York February 12; and finally at Tanglewood July 23. At Copland's suggestion, Sessions had replaced him for the summer of 1955 at Tanglewood.

Sessions wrote to Copland at the end of that summer: "It was above all gratifying to me to come once more in touch with Koussevitzky, even though it had to be post-humously. But I appreciated more than ever what he was and what he intended to do, and I found the experience an extremely moving one."[3] Sessions's stay at Tanglewood doubtless led both the Boston Symphony and the Koussevitzky Foundation to commission Sessions for a work to celebrate the seventy-fifth anniversary of the Boston Symphony, yet another example of Copland's positive influence on Sessions's career. Both Copland's own Third Symphony and Roy Harris's Third Symphony had been written for and dedicated to Koussevitzky. Sessions was commissioned to write what would be his Third Symphony in memory of Koussevitzky and his wife Natalie. Natalie had died in 1942, and Koussevitzky married her niece Olga, who outlived him for decades and with whom Sessions was friendly. This was his only dedication thus far required as part of a commission.

At the time Sessions said of the work: "It is larger in conception and scale than the [First], and does not contain the sharp and even violent contrasts of the [Second] . . . I regard this symphony as belonging very definitely among a series of works which began with my Second String Quartet (1951)."[4] He had "a lot of human associations, some of which I wouldn't dream of telling anybody about. . . . There were a lot of other things [besides the Koussevitzky connection] going on in my life at the same time and as I was writing this, they all, a lot of them come in as associations."[5] In an interview with *The New York Times* before the New York premiere, Sessions was paraphrased: "The symphony's second, lyric theme sprang from a phrase he had had in mind for forty years. During the early, baffling and often dissatisfying days of work on the symphony, the theme grew and expanded. Then one day he realized that his expanding theme had embraced all twelve chromatic notes of the scale and had become a potential tone-row."[6] This lone mention of a phrase retained in Sessions's memory for 40 years dates it to the years 1915–1917. The Third Symphony's slow movement begins with whole tones (that permeate the work) in the clarinet that bear more than a family resemblance to the English horn's opening passage in the 1917 Symphonic Prelude's second movement, the movement Sessions strongly identified with George Bartlett. In addition, Sessions would have known the English horn solo that opens the third act of *Tristan* and signifies death. This may have been one of the personal associations that Sessions "wouldn't dream of telling anybody about." He did not need to, however; the music itself reveals that while he never spoke of George, he continued to think about him. Meanwhile a commission from the BSO promoted memories of Harvard, his friends, and the Symphonic Prelude. More important was a commission in 1955 from the Kent School for a Mass to be sung with the organ George had chosen. The long-standing emotional debt to and memorial for George needed repayment—but without anyone knowing about it (until now).

As was usual for the composer, he missed the deadline, this time by two years: it premiered in the BSO's seventy-seventh, not seventy-fifth, season. The Third Symphony took a long time to incubate; nevertheless the initial ideas for each of its four movements were all sketched—uncharacteristically—at one sitting in 1950. Not until the fall of 1956, however, did he begin serious work on it. The third movement was to be called Elegy. He conceived of some of it in 1955 in Tanglewood while visiting Koussevitzky's grave in Lenox. For Sessions this symphony also recalled memories of the Lenox landscape, contained quasi-funereal passages, and reflected human existence. It was not, however, an elegy for Koussevitzky. If Sessions had meant it as an elegy for a specific person, that person would have been George. Five years later he admitted to portraying a

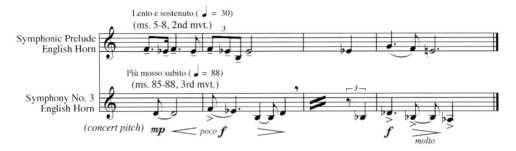

Figure 39 Symphonic Prelude compared with Symphony No. 3, English horn parts.

storm in the middle section of the first movement and the "rustlings and chirpings of whip-poor-wills" at the end of the movement.[7]

The Third turned out to be the largest and longest of his nine symphonies. Only it and the Second Symphony have four movements. In 1975 Sessions said of it, "It's a very personal work, and at the same time it's the nearest thing to an orthodox symphony that any of my symphonies are, except perhaps No. 1."[8] Before the December 1957 premiere Sessions discussed the work at lunch in New York with his old friend Aaron Copland. Koussevitzky's name doubtless came up during the conversation.

Notwithstanding all the above observations, Sessions tried to distance the emotional content from its reception,

> I do not, to begin with, consider it of any value to try to describe what is some-times called the "emotional content" of a musical work. Of course, very many feelings, impressions and experiences lie behind a composer's musical vision, but the work itself—any work—achieves by its very nature an autonomous exist-ence; it becomes something quite independent of those specific feelings and arouses in the listener feelings which are molded by the latter's own experience. What the composer actually conveys in the music cannot be elucidated; this can be really appreciated only through listening to it.[9]

John Harbison wrote that this symphony

> is very amply proportioned. It contains a song-like first movement in sonata form followed by two especially propulsive fast movements (with touches of rough-edged humor), and one of Sessions's most profound slow movements. In this work Sessions fully refined his use of the orchestra, preferring to explore myriad textures from all the different families, with the percussion as an equal partner, rather than employ the brass, wind, and string choirs antiphonally, in the manner of the "American School." Tuttis are notable for their wide registers and clarity of individual elements, and solos are set in accompaniments of great variety and subtlety. Instruments tend to play in their best registers and are seldom driven to impersonation or caricature; first violins often soar startlingly high, and unusual solo instruments such as the xylophone or contrabassoon are apt to appear.[10]

The design for the first movement is a sonata form, and the second is also in three sections, similar to a scherzo and trio. The third movement is based on a theme and two variations. The fourth has five sections, the third and fourth paralleling the first and second, while the fifth section is a coda.

The first and third movements conclude with what this author has called his "Sessions ending," in which the instruments drop out in descending or undulating note patterns, leaving a single low pitch remaining, which dies out softly. Could this be Sessions's metaphor for death? Tse-Ying Koh describes this trademark: "On reaching the climax, a tumbling motion follows, accompanied by a thinning of the texture and a diminuendo, allowing for the tension to dissipate. This downward gesture serves a cadential purpose, taking the music to a sense of repose in preparation for the entrance of contrasting material."[11] The second movement also ends softly with high flute twitters. Sessions said,

> The [twelve-tone] row is the basis of one of the ideas in the last movement. Cross my heart and hope to die, not until the very end did I realize that it ends in a sort of tonic and dominant, dominant and tonic. And I had a lot of fun writing those last measures, because at the very end that comes out. Not that the tonic has been prepared tonally at all, but that's the way the symphony ends. You have A flat and D flat in the timpani and trombones, and so you have a descending fifth at the end. That was not a joke exactly, but it was fun.[12]

The Third Symphony was the first of Sessions's symphonies to employ some twelve-tone procedures, although the reviews did not dwell on this, and because Sessions is not truly a twelve-tone composer, it is impossible to find thorough-going permutations of the row. The work still employs classical forms and devices.

The first movement is in a sonata form called *Allegro grazioso e con fuoco*. It consists of three large sections: the first section (Exposition), theme one (mm. 1–19), transition (mm. 19–27), theme two (mm. 28–52), and closing (mm. 53–56); the second section (Development) from m. 57 to m. 86—the closing (mm. 86–100) leads to the retransition (mm. 101–05); section three (Recapitulation) begins with the first theme (mm. 106–121), a transition (mm. 116–127), the second theme (mm. 127–38), and Coda (mm. 139–-52).

The second movement is marked *Allegro, un poco ruvido*, which means "somewhat rough" or "sardonic" scherzo. In 1980 Sessions pointed out that it contains a parody on "Yankee Doodle," introduced as the principal theme and first heard in the oboe and English horn in mm. 1–4, then by the oboe and trumpets in mm. 20–23. This theme recurs, thus bringing this movement close to being a musical joke (one most reviewers certainly did not get). A *tambour provençal*, or military drum, helped to create the military atmosphere, perhaps reminiscent of World War I of 40 years earlier; Koh hears "toy soldiers."[13] The movement divides into A (mm. 1–75), B (mm. 76–20), and A (mm. 121–83); each structural division is marked by a tempo change.

The third movement contains quasi-funereal passages. Marked *andante sostenuto e con affetto*, it possesses both an elegiac quality and a profound sense of yearning. Koussevitzky's gravesite brought back memories of other deaths, specifically George Bartlett's, to Sessions. The movement is a theme and two variations. The principal theme starts mm. 1–15 and concludes in m. 43, being demarked by a transition (mm. 16–20), the secondary theme (mm. 21–25), and a closing section (mm. 35–43). The first variation begins at measure 44 and lasts until measure 83. The principal theme is found at mm. 44–54, the transition at 55–62, and the secondary theme at mm. 63–67. The development, mm. 68–83, ends in its last three bars (mm. 80–83) with a coda. The second variation lasts from mm. 84–112. The principal theme appears again at mm. 84–96, and the closing section is from mm. 97–112. In the closing section the secondary theme appears at mm. 107–112 with a coda at mm. 113–120.

Sessions's program notes describe the last movement:

> The final movement is built of five sections, separated clearly by quiet and relatively static passages, in which various orchestral colors are played off against each other, and the persistent recurrence of short motifs, of sometimes purely rhythmic character, maintains the pulsation. Once again variation is the guiding principle; the third and fourth sections are extended variations of the first and second respectively. Each of the two main sections contains a number of elements proper to itself. The final section is a kind of "coda" which brings back in summary form the various elements of the opening section.[14]

Here is a formal analysis. Section I: measures 1–54, trombone sevenths, wind trills (first static passage, mm. 42–54). Section II: mm. 55–113, violins in sevenths, then woodwinds, to flute at m. 58, syncopations, then dotted rhythms with triplets in accompanying figures, and ascending lines in quarter notes (second static passage, mm. 107–13). Section III: mm. 114–219, trombone sevenths, woodwind trills, and a variation of I (third static passage, mm. 196–214; a transitional slow return to new tempo, mm. 214–19). Section IV: mm. 220–95, variation of II (the violin melody at m. 220 resembles the flute at m. 58), syncopations as before, ascending lines in quarter notes, dotted rhythms and dotted triplet rhythms at climax as before (fourth static passage, mm. 277–95). Section V: Coda, mm. 296 to end. The recapitulation of the opening is a variation mostly on I, but contains some elements of II. Quarter-note lines descend at the end (almost a V–I in D flat).[15]

Both the audience—the composer barely got two bows—and critical reaction was mostly negative. The *Christian Science Monitor*, pointing out the coolness of the applause, felt that interest was lost about half way through the symphony. "It is an extraordinary piece of writing, obviously turned out with great care, and at first it struck my ears with a kind of exotic fascination. He has composed it in something of a lyrical expressionism, as if Berg and Bartók were his artistic grandfathers, yet it is not an imitable work."[16] *The Boston Globe* was downright hostile:

> I do not believe it is music, or if it is, here is music of a curiously masochistic and perverse variety. In it is nothing of recognizable beauty, nothing of health, strength or joy. Its virtues, whatever they may be, must all be interior, concealed by a mass of unpleasant sound which in its individual parts writhes like the serpent of Medusa's hair . . . not one movement has individuality or moves in unbroken line to conclusion.[17]

Reviews in New York, one by a prominent musicologist, were on the whole better. *The New York Post* observed: "Sessions, a musician of the highest integrity together with an abundance of self-discipline and introspection, writes painstakingly because he is so critical." The reviewer was positive about the piece, but noted an audible hiss during the applause, and she polled audience members to discover they were "disgruntled."[18] Paul Henry Lang, on the other hand, wrote,

> The first impression this music creates in the listener is that of a profound conviction of the composer's high office. There lives in Mr Sessions the ancient

pride of the old craftsmen of music who believed that a score must be fitted, joined and polished until it acquires the proportions and finish of a beautiful piece of cabinet work. . . . What the new symphony proved is that he is deeply and persistently aware of life in its sensuous aspects. The work is distinguished by a light texture—at times almost chamber music like. The orchestra, though large, and not averse to climaxes, is handled with remarkable transparency, and with a very personal color scheme that was most rewarding.

The first movement, in which the outlines of a sonata structure are noticeable, impressed with its fine motivic work. All the inner voices took part in this lively exchange with alacrity. The second movement, a scherzo, is a jaunty piece with a good deal of tongue-in-cheek humor, and again displaying delicate colors, while the Andante, an eclogue, is pensive and rhapsodic.[19]

Like other reviewers, Lang had some difficulty with the last movement. Louis Biancolli, writing in the *New York World Telegram and Sun* also wrote positively, finding "Mr Sessions' symphony both daring and important. I think the mild-mannered little professor has opened a new path in American music."[20]

The New York Times stuck to its party line: "The composer has a reputation for being grim and unyielding in his music. . . . The total impression is of *knottiness*. The symphony is not quite so *gnarled* as some of Mr Sessions' other works. . . . Indeed, there is a kind of shy, hesitant lyricism in places of the first two movements, and the third is almost openly expressive." [emphasis mine].[21]

The Musical Courier managed to grasp the piece fully:

But the wonder of wonders was the electric vitality, the sheer enthusiasm they were able to instill into a composition so complex. . . . Sessions not only has something to say, but what is rarer still, that something has such magnitude and urgency that it justifies, or rather necessitates the complexity of method, which he employs. The complexity does not make the music forbidding. On the contrary, it seems to draw one into the vortex of its percolating intensity. Perhaps all of this is true because Mr Sessions' music is contemporary not only in its techniques, but also in the way its raw gnashings and wry lamentings seem to reflect the tensions of a life lived in these times so very much more incisively than most music one hears nowadays.[22]

Irving Kolodin disliked the work: "Thirty seconds of the Sessions, speaking the oboe-muted-trumpet-high-strings vocabulary, gave me the involuntary reaction: 'I don't care how well this is done, it's not for me.' . . . I would describe it as bare bones and no flesh, musically speaking."[23] Joseph Kerman wrote for the *San Francisco Chronicle,*

A new work by Roger Sessions is always especially interesting—and always a surprise, always a problem. The Third Symphony, a free 12-tone work, gives first of all an impression of abundance: excess energy, a brilliant orchestral palette, extreme contrasts, intensity and complexity to burn . . . the symphony sounds both lively and profound, both exciting and inclusive. . . . Nothing sings, though. Would it hurt? Would the tough, live organism collapse?[24]

Rather to the composer's surprise, Pierre Boulez and the New York Philharmonic performed the work at Juilliard, where Sessions was then teaching, March 5, 1976, on a concert sponsored by the Fromm Foundation. Boulez also performed the work, along with Brahms and Debussy, on a regular Philharmonic concert. By 1976, almost 20 years after the premiere, audience reaction and critical response had warmed to the Third Symphony, at least in New York. Andrew Porter, *The New Yorker* critic, had become a convert.[25] *The New York Post* wrote, "In the early movements the pungent, long-lined thematic material is especially striking. The symphony also has variety, motor energy and displays Sessions as a resourceful experienced orchestrator. The final movement—an *Allegro con fuoco*—has some sharply contrasting rhythmic motifs and at a number of points a Charleston-like dance figure is clearly discernible."[26] Harold Schonberg, retaining *The New York Times*'s approach to Sessions, wrote of it as a "superficially an impressive work. . . . It is a busy score, generous in its orchestration and rich in its sonorities. In its way it is a handsome work. What it does not have is the impress of a very individual mind. This is academic music—as academic in its way as a 19th-century score by Paine or Parker. It rides the shoulders of the big men."[27]

Dennis Russell Davies gave the work with the American Composers Orchestra more than two decades later, on April 2, 2000, in Carnegie Hall. The *Times* wrote of that performance, "The Sessions is a rigorous work, full of rhythmic drive and a compelling angular beauty, as well as a subtle sense of humor that comes through in the finale."[28] Unfortunately, Davies could not obtain funding to finish his complete Sessions symphonies recording project. He had recorded Symphonies Nos 6, 7 and 9, and, in a gesture unparalleled by any other orchestra, performed all nine of the Sessions symphonies.

Sessions's Fourth Symphony was commissioned by the Minnesota Statehood Centennial's Committee on the Arts in 1958 (according to the program for the first performance) for the state's centennial, and was premiered January 2, 1960, the year of the centennial, with Antal Dorati conducting the Minneapolis Symphony. The symphony is dedicated to the composer's wife, Lisl. The first page of the 1963 Marks score reads, slightly differently, "Commissioned by the Minneapolis Symphony Orchestra in celebration of the 100th anniversary of the State of Minnesota." On February 14 the Minneapolis Symphony played the work in Carnegie Hall.[29] After having played the Second Symphony in New York, Dimitri Mitropoulos had helped commission this work; he died in November 1960 and never performed the Fourth. Shorter than Sessions's previous symphonies, the Fourth lasts about 23 minutes. The Fifth Symphony would be shorter still.

The first sketches reach back to the fall of 1950, the time of the sketches for the Third Symphony and Sessions's work on the Second String Quartet. Most of the music for the Fourth was written in 1958, although Sessions's month-long trip to the USSR interfered (see below). The last movement, Pastorale, was composed quickly: he was told that the commission would not be paid unless he completed the work by the end of the year. The score is marked "Princeton 31 December 1958."

The Fourth Symphony's three movements reflect the three modes of Greek drama: comedy, tragedy, and pastoral. Sessions already had had the idea before the commission. He thought first of three separate pieces, then decided they could belong together. "The burlesque [the first movement, a sonata form] is a real burlesque. I mean, I felt as if I were laughing at a lot of things, including myself, not only myself but myself among other things."[30] Just before the end of the movement there is a violin solo, meant as a parody of his own Symphony No. 2.

> I thought of it as a pastoral symphony. . . . There's certainly a storm in the middle of the first movement. There are episodes in the last movement especially where there are sort of rustlings and chirpings, and Eddie [Cone] identified the

whip-poor-will. . . . There's an oven bird [he imitated the bird call] . . . In the exposition, it's the oven bird. It's high noon, and toward the end of the movement, it's the whip-poor-will.

The hermit thrush is distantly evoked three times in the woodwinds, in the flute and the piccolo's little cadenza. "There's even a bullfrog. There are insects, too. I love those things very much. There is sort of a general rustling."[31] The Fourth Symphony's second movement, Elegy, also contains suggestions of birdcalls from eastern Massachusetts. "It's an elegy, but it's more than an elegy. It's a sort of a biography, in a sense, you see—not really. I mean, not with specific references, but it's not simply a dirge, that's all. It's much more. Well, this is ridiculous, again, it's much more a kind of funeral oration than a dirge."[32] The Elegy represents "an idealized, or conventionalized, musical biography of a tragic life." The biographical subject of the tragic life is Sessions's brother John, who had spent the remainder of his life trying to fulfill Ruth's ambition to keep Phelps Farm as a farm.

John, who doubtless had as many talents and abilities as his sister and brother, sacrificed his own dreams and future out of duty to the all-demanding Ruth. John died September 19, 1948, at the age of 49 just three years after Ruth.

> My brother had just died a terrible death, a lingering death of tubercular meningitis. I've never been affected so much by somebody's death before. I was devoted to him. But we were very different. And we followed separate paths, and he was my mother's favorite son, which wrecked his life. And then I was older, and as a child I always protected him from the brutalities of the other children, and so forth. He had a very successful life in college. He was manager of the Harvard football team, but then in the business world for various reasons, things didn't seem to go well, partly because [of] things he didn't like. But finally he got a good job in New York. But then he left the good job [because of Ruth's pressure] to go up and save our property up in Massachusetts. But I was very upset by [his death], so I thought of a work, which would be an elegy for him.[33]

Lisl said that for three months after John's death, Sessions did not even smile. In his grief, he surely found it difficult not to dwell on his mother's influence on John's life, even to blame her. Sessions believed that the fact that John had whopping cough, when only one year old, had led doctors to think this might have left traces that developed into tubercular meningitis.

The Funebre section of the second movement (measures 178ff), was the first section composed. The form of the movement is: A, B (m. 56), A (m. 89), another idea at m. 111, B (m. 132), A (m. 152) Closing section: episode 1 (m. 175); episode 2 (Funebre, m. 177); coda (m. 184), which brings back the opening. The last chord is *ppp* marked *morendo* (dying out), the "Sessions ending." The final movement, Pastorale, is written in a conventional 6/8 meter, and also suggests both avian and human creatures.

In a thesis on the Pastorale, Howard Stern wrote:

> Sessions' themes, or "sections," as he thinks of them, are continuous in quality, and subject to immediate developmental expansion. Themes dramatically change character or make a departure even as they unfold for the first time. Most significantly, we shall see how successive remembrances of a theme in the midst

of a changing context succeed in suggesting an *idée fixe* which is continuously altered, as if the work were about the changing nature of memory.

For Stern "the formal technique engenders the impression of a ruminative composer on a meditative journey through nature—a kind of traversal that propels him to new material and development, even as he remains in the grip of a compelling memory."[34]

The Fourth Symphony was performed often in the 1960s, more frequently than the Third. One reason for its more frequent programming was its length: "new" music lasting less than a half-hour is much easier to program than works lasting a half hour or more. Lukas Foss, for example, had wanted to conduct the Third, but the Hamburg radio thought it too long; it wanted a work under a half hour. The Fourth Symphony was performed in Evanston, Illinois, during the Sessions festival there in 1961. Between January 26 and 29, Northwestern University School of Music and the Fromm Music Foundation presented eight of Sessions's works: Symphony No. 4, the Piano Concerto (Gui Mombaerts, pianist), *The Black Maskers* Suite, *The Trial of Lucullus*, String Quartet No. 2, the String Quintet, Four Chorale Preludes for Organ, and the Mass.[35]

Shortly afterward, his sister Nan died on March 17, 1961.[36] Paul Andrews remarried. Now there was no one left of Sessions's immediate family. Sessions outlived the last member by nearly a quarter of a century.

Sessions himself conducted the Fourth at the New England Conservatory of Music on February 23, 1962. Their usual conductor, Prausnitz, had to calm the orchestra, who felt they could not watch him. He coached the composer on conducting his own changing meters, and the orchestra rose to the occasion. Sessions was also ill-prepared in the sartorial department: he did not own a dress suit. Sent to a tuxedo rental store in Boston, Sessions returned having bought—for $18—a suit whose coattails nearly reached his ankles. Not near enough, however, to cover his brown shoes! Prausnitz described Sessions's charisma as "a curious mixture of the humble, the magisterial, the irrepressibly elated, and the unconsciously superior."[37]

The American Composers Orchestra, conducted by Dennis Russell Davies, performed the Fourth Symphony on October 20, 1985, in Carnegie Hall. *The New York Times* wrote of the performance: "Sessions' orchestra rarely glows but rather radiates with a kind of industrial gleam—bright, often abrasive sounds, but always so deftly contrapuntal and so confidently ordered and purposeful. The music's energy seemed to relax and ease through its three movements, offering a tender, simple ending in which the symphony's busy beginnings trail modestly away into silence."[38]

The (renamed) Minnesota Symphony Orchestra gave four concerts of the Fourth Symphony January 17–20, 1990, with Edo de Waart conducting. Michael Steinberg wrote of Sessions's music in general:

> From *The Black Maskers* of 1923 to the Concerto for Orchestra he completed for the Boston Symphony in 1981, whatever Sessions composed is possessed of electrifying energy, both physical and intellectual. This energy produces a densely active music in which hardly anything is neutral, in which even accompaniments become so specific as to take on an assertive life of their own. The music throws events at you at a tremendous rate, and to quote [John] Harbison once more, it is all "abundance and sublime willfulness." It is also profoundly traditional in the tensions and releases of its arching melodies, in its commitment to "the long line," in its expansive and ethical intents, its address to what Sessions called the "energies which animate our psychic life."[39]

The completion of the Fourth Symphony was delayed by an important trip. By June 1958 the Cold War had warmed to the point of foreseeing an exchange of composers between the US and the USSR. Plans had been in the air since early 1956, when Yuri Gouk, cultural attaché to the Soviet Embassy in Washington, approached the American Society of Composers, Authors and Publishers (ASCAP) about picking representative US composers; ASCAP was reportedly cool to the prospect. They then approached its younger rival, BMI, whose president was Carl Haverlin. The trip was to be jointly sponsored by the Department of State and BMI, and Haverlin recommended Sessions to participate, in part because of his linguistic ability in Russian.[40] (This was one of the arguments used on Princeton to let Sessions go for a month.) Originally, Sessions, Norman Dello Joio, Howard Hanson, Ulysses Kay, and Peter Mennin were scheduled to go to Russia, while Dimitri Shostakovich, Aram Khatchaturian, and Dimitri Kabalevsky would return the visit. The US wanted Khatchaturian, but the Russians let him leave only as part of a group. The International Educational Exchange Service of the State Department made arrangements for the five Americans, and a sixth composer, Walter Piston, was invited but could not accept; a replacement for him was being sought. The only known factor was that the Americans would leave around September 15. Twelve American educators were to accompany them.[41]

The group now numbering four—Roy Harris, Sessions, Kay, and Mennin (then in Rome)—left New York on September 17 for their 30-day trip to the Soviet Union. They had gone to Copenhagen to meet Mennin, but no visas to the Soviet Union had been issued as of the previous day. During an interview at the United Nations Sessions said, "I'm going to play it by ear, I'm damned curious about the place. Cities, the people, how things work." The three were briefed by various officials and told, in essence, to be themselves. *The Times* noted that Sessions's musical philosophy was different from the theories current in the Soviet Union. He said, "I can't imagine ever agreeing with them, but I think I have enough imagination to see there's a certain consistent picture. After all, I'm a guest. I'm going in the sheerest innocence, I assure you."[42] The trip would take them to Moscow, Leningrad, Tbilisi, and Kiev.

According to a *Pravda* report by composer Yuri Shaporin and its interpretation here, the concert of American music on October 15 was a success: Harris's Fifth Symphony, Mennin's Sixth Symphony, excerpts from *The Black Maskers*, and Kay's "New Horizons" Overture were played by the All Soviet Radio Orchestra in Moscow. On another official level, Tikhon N. Krennikov, the Union of Soviet Composers' general secretary, sent a cable to Herman D. Kenin, president of the American Federation of Musicians, expressing pleasure at the concert. The cable was also signed by Shostakovich, Khatchaturian, Kabalevsky, Shaporin, and two others. "When we were over there in Moscow, we were not allowed to see [Shostokovich], so to speak, until the very last day and when there was a lunch. I sat next to him, and he seemed to me the most nervous human being I've ever seen. He went through absolute hell under Stalin. . . . What this man was subjected to just because he was a composer!"[43]

In October 1958, the composers assembled at Juilliard (where Peter Mennin was not yet president) to describe their experience. All four agreed that composers were widely respected in the USSR, and illustrated by giving typical examples of high salaries. Numerous commissions were available, but originality and experimentation was frowned upon; modern Western music was looked down on as not conforming to "socialist realism." All works were passed on by various composers unions before they could be performed or published. Sessions noted that these unions were not actually controlled by the government; they were more like "juries of peers." The composers attended "the most moving performance I've ever seen of 'King Lear,' " translated by Boris Pasternak. Sessions spoke with Pasternak after the performance.

> As in the recent case of the author, Boris Pasternak, [Sessions] felt that the worst pressure to conform comes from the artist's colleagues and was therefore all the more insidious. It is a striking fact, however, he added, that there is a rising interest in some of the forbidden techniques among the younger composers. While some of this music is restricted to a private circulation, other pieces showing the influence of Bartók and Hindemith have been heard, and the picture may be changing.[44]

Sessions was a little less diplomatic and more straightforward with his colleagues at Princeton than he had been in New York. In two articles, one entitled "Sessions warns 'get serious' or fall behind Soviet culture," Sessions stressed that the US had better "get serious" or "wake up and find itself a second-rate nation."[45] This view was based on his impressions that the "general technical level [in music] is extremely high;" the work of younger composers is "interesting;" audiences for music, theater, and ballet were invariably "spontaneous, lively and intelligent at a high level;" Russia is a nation of "outstanding achievement, increasing every day;" and the musical educational system is "widely diffused throughout the Soviet Union on a very high level indeed." He pointed out that the US has four or five top flight conservatories of music, whereas Russia has 22, as well as a great many more musical preparatory schools. He also noted that there is "far more" contemporary work on Russian radio than on American, and that their performers get more attention. To "hold our own in the cultural world of the future," Sessions felt these things would require a great deal of "soul searching."

He concluded,

> Ultimately, though, it is not a question of "more and better" or anything of that kind. It is a question of using all the creative energy society has to offer. And in the long run that is nothing more than we should be doing anyway. Liberty is a great advantage, and we'll lose it unless we make it produce. We have to get serious now, but when we've had to in the past, we've always been able to. It's by achievement that any system prevails or goes under. We must prove ours by what we create and by the faith and energy we put behind it.[46]

When the anticipated three Russian composers arrived the following year, Khachaturian was not among them. The US welcomed instead critic Boris Yarustovsky and composers Kabalevsky, Konstatin Dankevich, Fikret Amirov, and Tikhon Khrennikov, as well as Dimitri Shostakovich. The six visited New York, Washington, San Francisco, Los Angeles, Louisville, Philadelphia, and Boston. The Philadelphia Orchestra gave the US premiere of Shostakovich's recent Cello Concerto on November 6 and 7, with Mstislav Rostropovich and Eugene Ormandy. Ormandy scheduled on the same concerts Kabalevsky's "Colas Breugono," Krennikov's Symphony No. 1, Henry Cowell's Hymn and Fuguing Tune No. 3, and Sessions's *The Black Maskers*. (The *Times*'s critic found the Sessions "the most original music of the afternoon."[47])

Cowell and Sessions were present, as were Van Cliburn, Samuel Barber, Menotti, Vincent Persichetti, and others. Sessions remembered speaking with Shostakovich in Russian.

I sometimes spoke to him at the Philadelphia Academy of Music where there are sort of recesses where the walls are thick and the windows are little. We would be there talking, and then he'd be very warm and friendly, and suddenly the head of what they call the Composers' Union would appear in the background and immediately he'd freeze up like that. I felt very badly and awfully touched, because I liked him.[48]

Later Sarah Caldwell told Sessions that she had been taken to Shostakovich's house in the USSR and saw that he had kept a photograph of Sessions on his desk.

Another article tried to describe the reality of the four Americans' visit to the USSR. "There was difficulty in obtain entrée into Soviet homes, even of friendly fellow artists."[49] Norman Dello Joio invited the six Soviet composers—to ask one was to ask all six—to his home. Copland, Schuman, Barber, Mennin, and Kay were present with Nicolas Slonimsky, who acted as interpreter. Shostakovich pointed out how few opera houses America had in comparison with the USSR; on the other hand, the US had far more symphony orchestras.

When the Russians returned home, their newspaper declared that they had "praised some American music and musicians but attacked the practice and teaching of twelve-tone music in this country." *Pravda* reported at length on their trip and doled out praise for Copland, Piston, Barber, Harris and Elie Siegmeister. Sessions's works were said to display "great originality," and Menotti was also singled out (for being evidently influenced by Mussorgsky). They did not like, according to the *Times*, "the widespread use of the twelve-tone 'system' among younger composers whose work they described as 'largely scholastic and without artistic merit.' . . . Twelve-tone music is not played in the Soviet Union because 'it is liked neither by Soviet audiences nor by musicians,' and they described it as 'spiritless' and 'mathematically developed.' "[50] Universities were censured for their teaching of young composers. It is difficult to see how they could have approved of Sessions, who not only wrote what was perceived as 12-tone music, but taught in a university.

MONTEZUMA

Charles Rosen wrote that Haydn's music is too dramatic for the stage. This might be said as well of Beethoven and Schoenberg, and it could also apply to Sessions. Sessions once remarked of the violent drama in *Montezuma* that "There aren't quite so many varieties of killing in the final version as there were in the original text, but the human sacrifice, the burning at the stake, the stabbing and the stoning to death—after all, what more can you ask?"[1]

Bernal Diaz completed his eyewitness history of Hernàn Cortez's conquest of Mexico in 1568. It was published in 1632, after his death. The subject of Montezuma had attracted eighteenth-century composers such as Vivaldi, Sacchini, Zingarelli, Graun, and Spontini (*Fernand Cortez*, 1809). Sessions's friend Darius Milhaud wrote *Christoph Colomb* (Claudel) in 1928 on a similar subject. Scored for 45 soloists, offstage orchestra, huge chorus and film inserts, Milhaud's opera was premiered on May 5, 1930. The opera was successful, but not done again for 30 years. In 1943 Milhaud wrote the three-act *Bolivar* (M. Milhaud) for the Paris Opéra (1950). Ernst Krenek's *Karl V* (1930–1933), like *Christoph Colomb*, split the stage for flashbacks, as does *Montezuma*. Staged in Prague in 1938, *Karl V* had been influenced by the Milhaud opera. Both the Milhaud and Krenek operas must have influenced Sessions.

Montezuma was written for about 110 orchestral players, as opposed to the 30 to 46 players for *Lucullus*, therefore more instrumental combinations are possible. "But the voice is always paramount, and to tell the truth, the vocal line was what I was most concerned with in writing the work."[2] There is no recitative in *Montezuma*, except a few places where Bernal speaks asides, such as "Oh, what a difficult thing it is to discover new lands!," which are set in Sessions's version of *Sprechstimme*.[3]

During Sessions's Fulbright year in Italy, he got in touch with his librettist, Antonio Borgese, then living in Milan and wondering what had become of the opera libretto Borgese had worked on for Sessions so long ago. Borgese died that year, in 1952, long before its completion. His wife, Thomas Mann's daughter Elizabeth, who translated Heinrich Schenker's *Harmonie*, helped Sessions cut the libretto.[4]

Between *Lucullus* and *Montezuma* came Sessions's *Idyll of Theocritus* for voice and orchestra (1954). The *Idyll* has a recurring vocal motive that happened to contain all 12 tones, but Sessions did not consider it a 12-tone piece. (The BBC performed *Theocritus* for Sessions sixtieth birthday.) "The vocal line in *Montezuma* is, I'd say, always very sharply chiseled, as it is in *Theocritus*. It has the same kind of—again adapted to quite different characters and characteristics—the same kind of rhythmic conception at the bottom of it. . . . From a certain point of view, *Montezuma* seems to me a vastly more complex and expanded *Theocritus*."[5]

Sessions and Lisl moved to West Berlin on a Ford Foundation grant in February, the month before *Montezuma*'s premiere, April 19, 1964.[6] For Lisl, this was to be the crowning glory of her husband's career. He had worked on the opera since before their marriage.[7] The opera has had three productions: Berlin in 1964, conducted by Heinrich Hollreiser, Bernal sung by Ernst Krukowski, Cortez by William Dooley, Alvarado by Loren Driscoll, Montezuma by Helmut Melchert, and Malinche by Annabelle Bernard; Boston in 1976, conducted by Sarah Caldwell, Bernal sung by Donald Gramm, Cortez by Brent Ellis, Alvarado by Joey Evans, Montezuma by both Richard Lewis and John Moulson, and Malinche by both Phyllis Bryn-Julson and Pamela Kucenic; and New York in 1982, conducted by Frederik Prausnitz, Bernal sung by Robert Keefe, Cortez by James Dietsch, Alvarado by Cornelius Sullivan, Montezuma by Robert Grayson, and Malinche by Hei-Kyung Hong.

In the Library of Congress Sessions collection are numerous files on *Montezuma*: the libretto and its many revisions and cuts, musical sketches, and the particell, a short score. Sarah Caldwell's Opera Company of Boston was to have ended its 1968–1969 season with *Montezuma*'s American premiere on May 18, 1969, conducted by Gunther Schuller in the Shubert Theater. Lack of funds forced the cancelation. Sessions wrote a speech on the opera, given to replace the scheduled Opera Company of Boston premiere (tickets had already been sold). Sessions told the audience about the opera.

"Let me begin with a few 'vital statistics.' The opera *Montezuma* is the result of a collaboration between my best friend, Giuseppe Antonio Borgese [1882–1952], and myself. I first met Borgese in 1933, shortly after my return from Europe, where I had resided for eight years. Six of these years had been spent in Italy, and I was already

Figure 40 US premiere in 1976 of *Montezuma*, Act I, The Opera Company of Boston. From left: Alan Crofoat, Clyde Battles, Phyllis Bryn-Julson, Brent Ellis, and Alexander Stevenson.

acquainted with the name of Borgese, through his contributions to the *Corriere Della Sera*, and his reputation as a distinguished Italian author, of Sicilian origin.[8]

"I had begun also making musical sketches. In the summer of 1937 I had in my turn occasion to visit Mexico and my fascination and involvement gained further nourishment. Meanwhile Borgese several times visited us in Princeton. He met his future wife during one of these visits at our house, and in 1939 married her there, in Princeton on Thanksgiving Day, which was also my wife's and my [third] wedding anniversary. These visits were the occasion, naturally, for further discussion of Montezuma—of characterization, of the exigencies of operatic form and treatment, and of the *dimensions* of the work. When the completed text finally arrived during the winter of 1941–42, I set to work, and in fact made during the months which followed, a very rough sketch comprising over half of the first act, a very rough sketch indeed, and to a large extent a tentative one.

"I soon found myself faced, however by two problems, which made it clear to me that this was not a work which I could finish easily or quickly. First of all, I had tried to give Borgese some idea of the appropriate length of a full-scale operatic work. When his completed text proved to be between two and three times as long, I found myself in what seemed an almost desperate dilemma. I found the text extremely exciting, and postponed for as long as possible the task of cutting it down. I even started out with the idea of setting the whole text, hoping that the problem of the ultimate length of the whole would become clearer as the musical setting took shape. Eventually, of course, I had to realize that this would not do at all; and in fact it was only after I had, on two occasions, read the entire text aloud to groups of students and friends, and become vividly aware of its enormous dimension[,] that I set myself the task of systematically cutting it down—a process that occupied in fact many years, and lasted till well after Borgese's death in 1952. The original text included four acts, which I had to decide was, already, one too many; it also contained, for instance, long speeches, much too long for plausible or even endurable operatic treatment, and scenes of astounding importance. There were sometimes also problems of the language itself—that of an enormously gifted Sicilian writer—a distinguished author of novels and plays, as well as historical and cultural commentaries—who had mastered the English language and devoured English literature, and fallen passionately in love with both—but in the very intensity of his passion sometimes strained the language to its outermost limits, making simplification imperative.

"My first efforts in cutting, therefore, consisted in slowly eliminating lines and even words which I felt could be dispensed with, and when I last saw Borgese—in Milan, in 1952, [after his retirement] he gave his enthusiastic approval to what I had done. However, the moment soon arrived when I found myself obliged to eliminate whole scenes—scenes which I had by that time sketched musically in some detail. The final stage involved a much more drastic reduction of the text. I had some help from Mrs Borgese, and also sought, and received, some very valuable advice from other friends who were versed in dramatic and theatrical matters [such as Francis Fergusson]. Each excision was made with reluctance, as it involved not only omitting some smaller scenes of great beauty, which added life and depth to the characterization, but even whole episodes which not only were a part of the main story but seemed important links in the chain of events. It was necessary to find more concentrated equivalents for some portions which were omitted. The final consideration was always that of setting the essential elements of the drama into the sharpest possible relief. When the definitive text was finished, however, I felt unexpectedly happy with the result. Not only did I feel that my cuts reduced the work to manageable proportion—(each of the three acts lasts approximately 45 min.), but I felt that, considering the work from the theatrical point of view, I had achieved, better than I had hoped, my aim of retaining, and high-lighting, all that was essential in the drama that I myself, and I believe also Borgese, wished to convey.

"I set to work on the score in the fall of 1959, just ten years ago—and with the help of very many sketches I had made, over a period of eighteen years, and finished in two and a half years the complete particell—the condensed score—of the work—the final page of which bears the date July 1, 1962. The orchestral score was completed in October of the following year after fifteen months of intense labor. In the following April [1964] the first performance took place in Berlin.

"I spoke earlier of *two* problems which I had to face before composing the work; and that of cutting down the text was only the first. Secondly—and equally important— I had felt that I needed more experience in two general directions before finally putting the work together. It is true that both my earliest efforts in composition—dating from the summer of 1909 [*Lancelot and Elaine*]—and what I consider my oldest surviving one—*The Black Maskers* [1923]—were written with the theater, and dramatic action, in view; the latter work was designed for, and performed with, a specific production in which I myself conducted the orchestra. I had also had close friends in the theatrical profession, had attended not only many rehearsals as well, in the spoken as well as the operatic theater, both in the United States and in Europe. I had even during the mid-twenties, planned and worked on an operatic project of my own [*The Fall of the House of Usher*]; after making many sketches I had abandoned it, chiefly for the reason that I found the subject one in which I could not feel the kind of involvement which I needed in order to complete it successfully, by my own standards.

"Furthermore—though I was excited by Borgese's text and found that it took musical shape in my mind very easily, I wanted to test my power more fully than I had yet done, as far as concerned both writing for voices and setting the English language to music. Thus my opera *The Trial of Lucullus*, which I composed, rehearsed, and conducted, in a space of three months in 1947, and my large work *Idyll of Theocritus*, for soprano and orchestra, completed in 1954, and first performed in 1956, were very important experiences in preparing me for the task of finally bringing *Montezuma* to completion.

"I need hardly say that during all of the years of which I have been speaking—from 1942 to 1959—I had been working also on the music of *Montezuma*. This work had involved, probably more than anything else, studying the drama and the characters and the words which Borgese had assigned to them. I read the text over and over; each time that I read it, portions of the text—speeches and episodes—would take definite melodic shape—always in the context of the character and the situation in question, and I would note those down, frequently in the margin of the copy of the text that I was using. I did not try to force this process in any way—I wanted the work to grow by itself as naturally as possible, and, at that stage of the whole process the piece did evolve in precisely this manner. I found that certain passages, and even certain whole scenes, crystallized for me in a very definitive manner, quite early in the process, and eventually found their way, with very slight change, into the final shape of the work. Others underwent considerable transformation on successive readings, as the outlines, both dramatic and musical, of the whole became more and more sharply defined in my awareness, and moved more steadily from the partially abstract to the concrete. The various characters became more and more, as it were, multi-dimensional, more and more completely alive for me, and spoke and acted their individual parts more and more as actual human beings, and less and less as mere symbolical ingredients in a dramatic design.

"Perhaps I can make my point a little clearer if I digress for a while and tell you some of my thoughts and conclusions about opera in general. I find that opera, in its history of nearly four hundred years, has assumed so many different forms and shapes (and success-ful ones)—as it still is doing, that if one is to talk seriously about it one must start with certain basic assumptions. I will give you my own.

"First of all, opera is drama; it is also music. It is not *drama with music*, but drama *in* music. Neither drama or music is merely an excuse for the other, but both are organic ingredients of a whole, and both play their complete and appropriate role in the total scheme of things. . . . Both must be completely and unequivocally present using their full resources. That seems obvious enough in the abstract, but in practice the matter is not quite so simple. Each element—music and drama—conditions the form and character of the other—and this implies problems of a kind which different times and different composers have solved in many different ways. But there could be no greater error than to think of opera as equivalent to drama designed to be spoken on the stage, simply set to music; and it would be easy to point to virtually any opera what-ever, of which the text to some extent has been taken from an already existent spoken drama, to demonstrate this fact. The criteria which are valid in the one case apply only partially in the other. Works which may seem exceptions to this rule are only partially so. . . .

"Another point I would make is that, for me, in opera, the primary focus of musical expression is always the voice. It is in other words, primarily the music that they sing, not in that played by the orchestra, that the characters reveal themselves. I have thus endeavored in *Montezuma* as elsewhere to give to each character the music which fits most clearly what he is saying, in terms of both his character and the dramatic situation at the moment. In this respect I am a disciple of Mozart and Verdi rather than of Wagner, though I do not suppose that my hearers will find the actual music like any of the three I have mentioned. My orchestra is a large one, to be sure, and plays a variety of roles. In certain cases it underlines and maintains, as it were, the general *tone* of an episode or even a whole scene—the second scene of Act I, for example, and the first scene of Act III. In other cases—most conspicuously the second scene of the third act, it creates a kind of scenic background against which the main action and dialogue takes place. Perhaps most generally, it underlines the sense of the text. There are also two very short but very important tableaux near the opening of the second act, in which there is no singing at all, and the orchestra plays alone, accompanying and underlining the pantomime which takes place on the stage. The first of these tableaus, which was Borgese's original idea, portrays the first meeting of Cortez with the Aztec Emperor, Montezuma, on the causeway at the entrance of the Aztec capital; the second, which was my own idea, a popular Aztec religious gathering in the great square of the capital, culminating in the sacrifice of human victims. This is the only part of the work in which the orchestra 'takes over'; otherwise, throughout the work, the vocal line is supreme, whether it is carried by individual singers, or by the chorus, which plays a very episodic but nevertheless important role in the whole design.

"Of all the commentaries which I read regarding the Berlin performance, the one which pleased me perhaps the most was one which laid stress on the essentially *lyrical* character of the music, and the overriding importance of the vocal line. It pleased me the more because I had felt that in the performance itself, certainly in part because the work was sung in a language other than the original English, this very important aspect of the music was not always brought out as clearly as I would have wished. The author of the review had obviously understood my intention in spite of this fact.

"Opera, once more, is a form of drama, and I have stressed my conviction that it is drama not with, but *in* music. The drama, its subject, its text, and its underlying motives, in *Montezuma*, or indeed in every text which I have ever treated musically, has been one in which I have felt myself personally and hence musically involved, since music is the world in which I most completely function. I spoke earlier of an operatic project on which I worked for a time in the mid-twenties, but which I abandoned because I could not feel this kind of involvement in it. I could state the matter in other terms by saying that in that particular case the drama never became fully drama for me.

"It is precisely because *Montezuma* had become in this sense so real for both Borgese and myself that we found ourselves so gripped by it. I do not remember even speaking with him directly in these terms, but they were implicit in everything we said to each other about it, and became more and more so as time went on, and the essential nature of our thoughts about it became more and more explicit and concrete. We spoke more and more, that is, about the characters and their motivations, in terms not only of history as such, but in terms of human beings and the forces—historical and political and religious—which moved them. Both of us—Borgese as a refugee from Fascism, and I, as one who had lived under one Fascist regime in Italy, and who had witnessed the rise and the coming to power of another, in Berlin—we both were vividly aware of, and involved in respect to, the world situation as it was developing, both before and during the Second World War; and we were aware too, of the similarities between the forces which moved the protagonists in the drama of the Spanish conquest of Mexico, and those with which we were familiar (in terms of things we had both seen and heard) in our own time.

"To be sure, *Montezuma* was for us in *no* sense an allegory, nor am I implying any idea of parallels, historical or otherwise, unless it be in terms of human nature and motivation and the tragedies that so often result from it. But the observation has been made to me repeatedly—after the fact—that *Montezuma* touches upon a surprising number of the subjects and problems which most deeply concern us today—war and conquest; tyranny and freedom; violence and revolt and assassination; confrontations of race, religion, and ideology, and, behind them all, of continents and cultures, and the destruction of one culture by another. The different forms which love of one's country, one's gods, and one's people may take. Even in a very obvious sense, psychological and technological warfare. Ultimately and perhaps above all the conflict between political sagacity on the one hand, and belligerent adventurism and greed, and finally the defeat of the former by the forces of violence unleashed and set in motion by the latter.

"Instead of giving you scene by scene description of the drama, I am going to give you a brief indication of its contents, laying my main emphasis on the principal characters. In the first place, the old warrior, Bernal Diaz del Castillo, who wrote, as an old man, the first accounts of the adventure in which he took [part] as a youth, served throughout the work—until just before the final episode of the last act, as narrator and occasional commentator. His role is that of an unseen spectator of events in which he has taken part many years before, and which he can contemplate without illusions and even with humor at times. He also sees himself—as we also do—as one of the actors on the main stage, playing a visible though secondary role as one of the youngest of the warriors.

"Each act begins with an introduction in which he sets the background of what is to follow—as he does also at brief interludes between certain scenes, in the first and third acts. He tells, at the appropriate moments, the various stages of the Spanish march from the coast of Mexico till their arrival at the gates of Tenochtitlán—the capital city. Today Mexico City occupies the same site, but at that time it was a city of fabulous beauty, as

Bernal himself asserts in a very moving passage in his chronicle, built on artificial islands in the middle of a huge lake, which was later drained by the Spaniards and of which only a small portion remains, at a distance of some miles from the city. In the third act Bernal plays a somewhat more sustained role, commenting on the various phases of the action until, overcome by emotion at the events as they approach the final climax, he fades out of the picture.

The first act is devoted mainly to the Spaniards: the landing of the Spanish force of 600 soldiers, led by Hernàn Cortez, with their horses and their cannon, both of which prove to be formidable weapons quite unknown to the Aztecs and regarded by them with superstitious awe. They raise the Christian cross and establish the standard of the Emperor Charles the Fifth. Their first encounter [is] with the native Indians—on the outskirts of a vast but loosely organized empire—[who] bring them tribute in the form of gifts and women. Ambassadors from Montezuma, the emperor whose capital is two hundred miles away on the mile-high plateau, bring them more gifts, as a token, as they put it, of "welcome and farewell." When Cortez, ignoring their message, expresses his intention of marching up the forbidding mountain-side to the "forbidden, hallowed, awful" presence of the Emperor Montezuma, and to greet him in person, they are horror-stricken: at this point a new and very important character breaks into the foreground. This is the young girl Malinche, an Indian princess who, having been sold into slavery by her mother, on the occasion of the latter's second marriage, has been given along with other women, in tribute, to the conquering Spaniards. Malinche sees in Cortez the incarnation of the legendary god Quetzalcoatl—the white god of peace and civilization who, as the legend went, had sailed away, driven by his enemies, to the eastward, but had promised to return to Mexico at an hour of need. This legend, and its hold on the minds of the Aztecs, proved to be a very important factor in the early successes of the Spaniards, and in fact the arrival of the Spaniards coincided in time not only with a period of turmoil in the Aztec empire, but with one of the dates in the Aztec calendar at which the return of the White God might be expected to take place.

"Malinche also sees in Cortez—Quetzalcoatl—a means through which she will eventually reach the palace of the Emperor, and thus, in accordance with authentic Aztec law, be released from her bondage as a slave. Montezuma's ambassadors, hearing the sacred name of Quetzalcoatl coming from the lips of a slave, are scandalized; but a Spanish show of forces terrorizes them, and they retreat in dismay.

"Before the Spaniards set forth on this march over the mountains, the Spanish priest carries out the mass baptism of the Indians. Malinche, the favorite of Cortez, is given the name of Doña Marina. She has been instructed in Catholic lore; and, after one of Cortez's important victories, she questions him regarding parallels which she finds between Aztec and Christian theology and asks him point-black whether he is indeed Quetzalcoatl, the White god of the Aztecs. He skillfully evades a direct answer, but she persists in her identification and anticipates the crucial next step in her mission—that of leading him, as the White God in person, to the city of Cholula and the great shrine of Quetzalcoatl which is situated there. . . .

"The second act takes us to the Aztec capital, Tenochtitlán, on the high Mexican plateau. The old Bernal Diaz sings of the blood, [and the] shambles which resulted when Cortez, at the holy city of Cholula, discovered an ambush the Cholulans had prepared, and turned the tables on them; and then the march past the two volcanoes which, as it were, guard the entrance to the central valley and the lake, over which great causeways lead to the city itself. On the stage we possibly see the end of one of these causeways. The Spaniards appear at the gates; and Montezuma, with his retinue, emerges from the

Figure 41 Quetzalcoatl, the feathered serpent, Aztec, ca. 1500. Stone 50 × 45 × 52 cm (drawing by Maddy Rosenberg).

city to greet them with royal cordiality. At his sign they follow him into the city. A moment after they have disappeared, the sound of deep drum begins to be heard; it is the sacrificial drum announcing the ceremony of human sacrifice; and presently we find ourselves watching the gathering of the Aztecs—with some Spaniards on the edge of the crowd. Presently a small procession of chosen victims, accompanied by the Aztec priests, crosses the stage and beings the ascent of the great pyramid, at the top of which, at the shrine of the god, the bloody sacrifice takes place. These are the two very short tableaux of which I have already spoken, and they form as it were, the setting of what follows.

"Malinche, who has conceived a child by Cortez, makes her way through the famed gardens of Montezuma's palace, to his presence. He greets her kindly, and she acknowledges him as her ruler. To his questions about Cortez she replies 'God is in him' and begs Montezuma to listen to the Christian message of peace and good-will. Cortez and his followers presently enter, bearing veiled portraits of Charles the Fifth and the Virgin Mary, on which he expatiates, trying to maintain an atmosphere of civility while at the same time keeping a wary eye open for possible dangers. To the exposition, by Cortez and the Spanish priest, [of] some aspects of Christian theology, Montezuma replies courteously in terms of Aztec belief, seeking parallels and explaining beliefs. The young Spanish lieutenant Pedro Alvarado, however, assumes from the start the aggressive and arrogant stance which has been evident in his character since the opening scene of Act I; and as this essential confrontation continues to develop, his role become an increasingly fateful one. Very quickly the leader of the younger Aztecs, Cuauhtemoc, begins to respond to his provocations, and despite the efforts of both Montezuma and Cortez to keep the situation under control, it deteriorates steadily. It is apparent that while Cortez, and his adviser, the Spanish priest Father Olmedo, aim primarily to win or cajole or eventually coerce the Aztecs to Christianity and to allegiance to Charles the Fifth, Alvarado's motivation is that of pure lust for plunder, joy in violence, and the ruthless assertion of power. At each stage in the dialogue his aggressiveness becomes more violent. Montezuma, in order to lighten the oppressive atmosphere, call[s] for dancers and for refreshment; but Alvarado, disrupting the dance, becomes more insistent in his attacks, and Cuauhtemoc on his part begins to turn even against Montezuma, who is trying to keep the situation within bounds. Eventually Cuauhtemoc draws his sword in a lunge towards Malinche, and in the ensuing scuffle an Aztec noble is killed. Recognizing that his moment has not come, Cuauhtemoc makes his escape; Cortez seizes the opportunity of taking Montezuma prisoner, ordering him put in chains but enjoining his soldiers to treat him still with the reverence due a king.

"In the third and final Act, Montezuma is still the captive of the Spaniards, though he has won their affection. His chains have been removed, under the watchful eyes of the Spaniards, he still fulfills his kingly functions; but he is forced to sign the death warrant of an Aztec noble who has been captured in an earlier ambush against the Spaniards, and to witness this noble's execution by fire. Cortez is presently summoned to the Spanish coast, to fight off a rival Spanish expedition which aims to supplant him and assume the leadership in Mexico. He leaves Alvarado in charge at Tenochtitlán. The Aztecs have been given permission to hold a religious celebration in the great square, on condition that they remain unarmed. Cuauhtemoc hopes to use this opportunity to rouse his assembled fellow countrymen to resistance against the Spaniards. Alvarado, however, regards the occasion as his great opportunity to assert his power and to mold the situation in terms of his own inclinations. He orders his henchmen to strike a stunning blow at the Aztecs while they are assembled and unarmed.

"Cortez, having defeated his enemies, returns to Mexico and, finding the Indians in a state of rebellion, and the viable situation which he, with the captive Montezuma, had striven to build up, shattered by one disastrous blow. The Spaniards, vastly outnumbered even with the fresh forces he has gained from his victories on the coast, are in a nearly hopeless position, under constant attack from all sides. Cortez upbraids Alvarado bitterly, but is obliged to leave him unpunished because he needs every available man if the Spaniards are to have any hope of extricating themselves. The soldiers, feeling themselves doomed, can only take refuge in bitter hopelessness and in nostalgic dreams of their homeland. Their only apparent hope is that rain may come, affording them a shelter under cover of which they may escape; and for this they pray fervently, with offerings to the Virgin. Cortez, in desperation, asks Montezuma to address his people, and to assure them that the Spaniards will build new ships, sail away from Mexico, and even return the loot they have acquired, if only they are granted a truce which will allow them to emerge from the palace in which they are besieged. Montezuma, skeptical, but in a hopeless position, agrees to attempt to rally his people.

"Accompanied by Malinche, who has remained at his side ever since he was first taken captive, he mounts to the roof-top. He expresses his loyalty to the Aztec gods, speaks of the dire prophecies of the wizards and prophets of his childhood, and his belief in Quetzalcoatl, the redeeming White God of civilization and peace. Under renewed pressure from Cortez he repeats the promises Cortez has made; but not believing these promises and understanding the position very well, he proposes to his countrymen a policy of reconciliation and religious tolerance in which the Aztecs shall share with the Spaniards the bounty of their soil in return for the technical knowledge of wheeled vehicles and domesticated animals, for instance—which are unknown to them; eventually to grant the Spaniards land yet uninhabited in which to live near them in peace. The Indians, respectful at first, are roused by their more violent elements to derision and hostility, and finally, as Cuauhtemoc shouts 'He is a Christian; kill him,' they stone [Montezuma] to death. While in the distance the Indians acclaim Cuauhtemoc as their king, and call for new assaults on the fortress, the Spaniards prepare to bury Montezuma. Cortez mounts to the roof, and tries to address the Aztecs; but the latter have vanished and the morning mist has enveloped everything. Only Malinche remains, surrounded by the clouds, which become articulate in a final invisible Chorus. They are not ready to give the rain that the Spaniards wish, but they foresee that the Aztecs are doomed, in spite of everything, and meanwhile go their own sportive way. Malinche, in despair, contemplates the impending ruin of her people.

"That is the story of the opera. As I have said, it follows very closely the chronicle of the old Bernal Diaz. The interpretation of the characters, especially the Aztecs, of course, is Borgese's and my own. We obviously do not and cannot know, how Montezuma and Malinche actually felt—we can know only their actions; and Borgese strove to find plausible and consistent motives for these, in terms understandable to us today. The popular image of Montezuma has often been that of simply a weakling; but Borgese and I both have felt that this image was palpably over-simplified—as indeed have many others. I do not of course wish to labor this point, and am not equipped to do so. In a similar manner Malinche is often branded as simply a betrayer of her country and her people. I know that Borgese pondered for months and perhaps for years over her character. She was in any case obviously a very young woman of quite exceptional abilities; and all of the historical elements which, in the opera, contribute to the formation of her character and actions—the power of the legend of the White God, for instance, and the Aztec law which granted freedom to the slave who should cross the Emperor's threshold, are amply documented in the various relevant commentaries.

"In any case, it was—I hope clearly—not the aim of Borgese or of myself simply to reconstruct history. If this were the case, the drama itself would not have had the meaning for us which it came to have. I have already stated that *Montezuma* is not, by intention, an allegory. But it is perhaps still more essential to emphasize also that it is not an attempt to portray or comment on life in the Renaissance. Nor is it in any sense, as it were, a *travel* document. Since it is about ancient Mexico, the exotic element is obviously there. But it is the scene and background of the drama, not to any degree its essential point. In the 'Notes on performance' which I wrote as an introduction to the printed score, my two opening sentences read as follows: 'This work was conceived by both its author and its composer as a story of human beings *as such*, rather than in their specific qualities as Aztecs and Spaniards. While characterization on the latter levels is obviously of importance, it should not be stressed in the performance, beyond the point of clear identification.'

"Regarding the music, I would say that the hardest thing that a composer can undertake to do—I believe in fact it is impossible to do in any way that is enlightening or really relevant—is to describe his own music. Composers are most likely to fall back on the actual music itself . . . I will simply answer one question, which I have been asked very frequently—'Did I make use of Aztec or Mexican themes?' The answer is, No, I did not. First of all, there is no Aztec music in existence. Some Mexican composers have made interesting attempts to reconstruct it, in imagination. I have not attempted to do this, and have not considered it my business, as a non-Mexican. I *have* attempted to give the Aztecs the musical characterization which my imagination dictated, and in doing so I have made some use of forms suggested to me by what I have read and seen. But once more let me reiterate—it is human beings and human situations that are significant in *Montezuma*; the picturesque elements are merely a by-product of that over-riding idea."[9]

The long-awaited premiere production in Berlin was disappointing on several levels. Son John maintained that his mother never recovered from the public rejection.[10] She had met Sessions the year he began work on the opera; it had hovered in the background of their marriage for almost three decades. In addition, her depression was amplified by the death of her mother, Ruby, to whom she had been like a sister. Each of the three productions (1964 in Berlin, 1976 in Boston, and 1982 in New York) garnered more dismal reviews than the previous one.[11] Sessions himself took the negative reactions to his opera with the equanimity born of decades of hard-earned self-confidence, or, in another interpretation, he brought to it a solid defense mechanism built on Rolland's "great man" principles. No one in his family of four could weather emotional hardship better than the composer himself. Only he had suffered the trials by fire of creative work, which Archibald had written was "the hardest work there is."

Although Sessions stressed that Montezuma "was for us in *no* sense an allegory" of political events, we need not feel so obliged to the composer's own views as not to read Cold War analogies into the opera. Sessions's own political awareness, not to mention Borgese's, is apparent at every turn in the opera. *Montezuma* and *The Trial of Lucullus* allowed Sessions to marry his musical ability with his deeply felt political convictions.

American performances of *Montezuma* were delayed. Sarah Caldwell's Opera Company of Boston had already sold tickets when lack of finances canceled the production in 1969. The Juilliard performance of *Montezuma*, which was to be the New York premiere and projected for 1976, did not occur—it was the most expensive production to date for the American Opera Center—until 1982. (Many of Borgese's words and phrases were simplified.) Indeed, it was the prospect of Juilliard presenting the American premiere that inspired Caldwell to raise the money to produce the work in 1976.[12]

After the performances of *Montezuma*, February 19, 20, 23, 1982, Sessions wrote to the president of Juilliard, Peter Mennin, "How can I ever express my gratitude, to you above all, but to everyone who helped to bring about such a gorgeous, beautiful, and moving production of *Montezuma*? I have been touched more deeply than I can express, by the immense—and profoundly successful—efforts that everyone concerned gave to the production; and of course this includes all of the players and singers. Thank you, from the bottom of my heart.

"With all due respect for Sarah Caldwell who did a fine job with the means at her disposal, I feel now that at last *Montezuma* has had a truly adequate performance—and this says much more than it might seem."[13]

Chapter 6

THE LAST TWO DECADES

CALIFORNIA AND JUILLIARD

After having taught only the year 1965–1966 and having seen *Lucullus* performed there, Sessions left Juilliard, then still at the 122nd Street and Claremont Avenue building, for the 1966–1967 year. He had been invited to give the prestigious Ernest Bloch Lectures at Berkeley. (Bloch had died in 1959.) The 1964 lecturer had been Ralph Kirkpatrick; the previous lecturer was Winton Dean. Joseph Kerman, along with others, had written an enthusiastic recommendation letter for Sessions to become the third lecturer in this newly created position. The University paid Sessions considerably more than he received at Juilliard for a year's teaching: $20,000.

Berkeley ran on a quarter system of ten weeks each. In the fall of 1966 Sessions gave an undergraduate course that analyzed his String Quartet No. 2. In January he taught a seminar on *Moses und Aron*. (In his enthusiasm he forgot the limitation of ten weeks. This course was also to have included *Wozzeck* and Dallapiccola's *Ulisse*.) Nine students were given one scene each from *Moses und Aron* for classroom discussion and a paper. In the spring quarter, Sessions gave his long-awaited composition seminar, in which about eight were enrolled. This seminar met once a week for three hours, allowing about 20 minutes' attention to each composer. Sessions gave tips for "composer's block." He had earned hard-won knowledge in this area, and now was able to share that knowledge with students.

At the end of the spring quarter Sessions was awarded an honorary Doctor of Laws degree; the diploma bore the signature of Ronald Reagan, the governor of California, who was involved in the loyalty oath controversy. Sessions would live to see this nemesis become president twice. Sessions's last trip to Berkeley was to hear the premiere of *When Lilacs Last in the Dooryard Bloom'd* in 1971.

A Berkeley history major, Christopher Wagstaff, and an English major, Stephen Gottschalk, came to all of Sessions's lectures on his own music, two one-hour meetings per week from October through December 1966 when the Second String Quartet was discussed. The excerpts following are taken from Wagstaff's notes, later typed as concise points. In the lectures these sentiments would have been considerably elaborated by the instructor.

> I have never composed from a theory. It's as I hear it. When composers use techniques, they don't derive sounds from their techniques, but from their imagination.
>
> The composer's job is to like the music that he likes—or the music that he loves, though that is considered a dirty word nowadays.
>
> That is his style, you see. If he has strong musical feeling, he will achieve consistency that way.
>
> You've got to be either yourself or nobody. A composer has to follow his own

musical bent—or instinct—instinct is also called a dirty word nowadays. [It] takes patience, courage, and conviction. And [it] takes a certain sense of identity which the composer has to acquire.

The composer works until he gets what he wants. This is the only principle I can give you. They get a masterpiece complex. They feel that they have to produce what will set the world on fire at all cost. He should be writing music— music he likes. I hate to use the word *expresses* something, but expresses something that he feels.

The question is, What does it do? One should ask, what is the effect and not what is the intention. One must assume that the effect is the same as the intention.

As always, the discussion turned toward terminology, and Sessions's views may not have been what students expected.

Whatever becomes the basis of association in a piece is essentially the theme. I shy away from the word *theme*.

I wish there were another word for musical form. I don't like the world *form*; it always suggests something static to me. Musical form has to do with time and movement. Even more than sound, it seems to me, music is bound up with the sense of duration. Sound is inseparably bound up with duration. Absolutely bound up with our sense of time.

Since the word *form* is associated with visual things (and musical form is really something different), the word *form* should be abolished.

Musical form—being something in the temporal dimension—is based on accumulation, so to speak. Like everything else—as in a conversation. What is said later in the conversation is affected by what one says in the beginning of the conversation. Musical form is the management of this fact.

If structure isn't expressive, what's the use of having it? I would say, real structure is always expressive. I don't even like the word *structure*. For a number of reasons. Everything is structure.

Absolute consistency leads to no result whatsoever.

I have often defined a phrase: that section that the ideal singer would try to sing in one breath. It's not a matter of breathing, so much as sustaining the tension. The point at which you can't let go. This conception was suggested to me by an edition of the *Well-Tempered Clavier*, by [Donald Francis] Tovey. There's a long line in a wonderful prelude in the second book. [Sessions played the phrase on the piano.] Tovey has this note on it. He said that the key to performance of this prelude is the ability to play up to a [certain] measure in one breath, as it were. This is about as good a definition of a phrase as I could find.

In the music generally called atonal, it isn't that there isn't any tonality. It's that there is too much tonality. Notes can point in many directions by themselves. The point is really, that in this music you do have a relationship between tones, surely. In all music. Even if the composer isn't aware of it, you are aware of it in listening to it. If you weren't aware of the relationships there would be nothing to listen to.

Sessions spoke about notation: musical notation is "an extraordinary cultural achievement. One can indicate so much that is purely relative there. It is an immense problem today. Our notation was invented in the early Middle Ages. Today, it has gotten top-heavy.

But very often, I would be very apt to notate the score [to make it] more easy for the reader of the score and make it more difficult for the players." The discussion ultimately led to musical analysis.

> Musical analysis is a very delicate matter. I feel even more shy about it when I'm dealing with my own work. One can find anything anywhere if one wants to.
>
> Analysis can go [only] so far. This is not what music is all about. I'm sorry, but it just isn't. Any more than you can judge a quality of wine by taking it to a chemical analyst. If you were a good cook and you wanted to tell how the meal came out, would you read the recipe or taste the food? Music belongs in that category of things.
>
> It belongs in the category of human experiences that are satisfying or dissatisfying, frustrating or thrilling. You can't manufacture that.
>
> The reason for the passion for analysis is that people are so unsure of themselves.

This led to an analysis, as it were, of recapitulation and variation.

> In my music—later—what may be called the recapitulation is always a variant of the first section. There are only two places in the last twenty years where I've had any literal restatement—in the third movement of [String Quartet No. 2], and the second movement of the solo Violin Sonata. In all the rest of my later music, the recapitulation is always a variant. There's something in contemporary musical vocabulary that makes literal repetition problematical.
>
> Music doesn't belong in the category of things where you can prove quality. Even in practical things, you can't prove this either. Quality belongs in human experience and that's that.
>
> This is why composers don't take critics too seriously.

The question of audience arose.

> I've been asked, who[m] do you write for? Well, this has nothing to do with the question at all. For other composers—the last people I write for. One writes because there's music to be written. One writes for oneself in the sense that one is much more strict with himself than anyone else. If I don't like it, I don't sleep; until it comes out where I do like it.
>
> Slogans get further and further away from facts. Facts are perfectly neutral.
>
> In the 1920s there were more people interested in contemporary music than in contemporary painting. The funny thing about music is—[and it's] not true of literature or painting—is that you have people complaining quite often when such and such a piece of contemporary music is played that it isn't Mozart. A great many people go and read the latest novel. They don't get out Dickens from the library shelf.
>
> There are probably 5,000 young composers today. I made a list of the composers of my generation last summer in a talk on American music in Buenos Aires. I think there were fourteen names.
>
> What do you do if you like poetry? Do you pay $8 and to go a hall and hear someone read it? You sit down and read it yourself. You don't have to read it out loud to know if it rhymes correctly. When I say that composers don't write music to be listened to but to have it performed. When you read a poem, you perform it.

You make a piece of music; it always has roots in one's own emotional life. I think what music comes from in us—very deep impulses that we have. More this than emotion. The term emotion is well-defined in terms of actual experience. Music expresses the dynamics behind this.

[When writing *Idyll of Theocritus*, I] suppose[d] for a moment I was the girl. I suppose I was in love with that girl for nine months. I told this to the singer in the Louisville performance.

Mozart's G minor symphony [is] one of the most tragic pieces ever written.[1]

Sessions returned to Juilliard for 1967–1968, but was called away again during the 1968–1969 year to give the Norton lectures at Harvard. He remained at Juilliard (relocated at Lincoln Center in 1969) from 1969 through 1983.

The University of California commissioned Sessions to write a major work for its centenary in 1964. *When Lilacs Last in the Dooryard Bloom'd* was not completed until December 1970, and it was premiered May 23 and 24, 1971. Helene Joseph sang the soprano soloist, Stephanie Friedman the contralto, and Allen Shearer, baritone, while Michael Senturia conducted. Sessions referred to *Lilacs* as his cantata: others feel it is the greatest of all of his works. Sessions quoted his friend Darius Milhaud saying about his music, "I *almost* made it. But after *Lilacs* he said I made it."[2] It was performed by the Boston Symphony Orchestra, April 12, 22, 23, and 26, 1977, and at Tanglewood August 13, 1977. The East Coast premiere was given twice in one evening at Harvard, March 24, 1975, with Diana Hogland, soprano, D'Anna Fortunato, mezzo-soprano, Alan Baker, baritone, conducted by Michael Senturia. (Leon Kirchner was to have conducted but bowed out.) It was later performed by the Chicago Symphony (January 29–30, 1976), the San Francisco Symphony, the Cleveland Orchestra, and the BBC.

While Sessions was working on *Lilacs* he and Lisl took his sketches to Ross Lee Finney's apartment in Greenwich Village. Finney recalled, "He was exuberant about his bird sounds and about how important they were for the piece. Roger was never pedantic. His roots may have been in [eighteenth-century revivalist] Jonathan Edwards, but they were profoundly American. His music often seems severe on first hearing, but in time it develops from a kind of earthy surface that gives meaning to the inner complexity."[3] The contralto soloist interprets the message of the bird in the woods and reflects on death itself, according to Sessions's program notes.

The poem for the cantata is Walt Whitman's reaction to the death (April 14, 1865) of President Abraham Lincoln. Whitman wrote of the progress of Lincoln's funeral train from Washington to Springfield, Illinois. Ruth Huntington had remembered being solemnly told, at age six, by her parents of the death of the president. Michael Steinberg considers the issues of setting Whitman.

The sometimes-inflated rhetoric can be a trap, and his recklessly large-breathed rhythms (no poet ever had more capacious lungs), based on the diction of the King James Bible, can present grave difficulties. It is just with those grand rhythms that Sessions is especially successful . . . projecting the poetry, now in simple chordal declamation, now in those long, high-arched lines of which he was the master, he conveys wonderfully the feel, the pace, and the variety of Whitman's lines.[4]

Sessions dedicated *Lilacs* to the memory of the Rev. Martin Luther King, Jr and to Robert Fitzgerald Kennedy, both of whom were assassinated during the composition of

Figure 42 Roger Sessions and Ellen Taaffe Zwilich at Juilliard, early 1970s (personal collection of Ellen Taaffe Zwilich).

Figure 43 Andrea Olmstead and Roger Sessions at Juilliard, 1976 (Stan Fellerman Photography).

his work. Within weeks of Dr King's death, the Compassionate Arts of the Fellowship of Reconciliation presented a concert at Carnegie Hall on May 24, 1968. The concert was entitled "Composers and Musicians for Peace" and included 12 American works. Soprano Adele Addison sang the Fishwife's song from *The Trial of Lucullus*.

Sessions had bought *Leaves of Grass* in 1921 and even begun some work on setting the text. Those sketches, which represented Sessions's first grappling with death, do not survive. This may well have been a reaction to George Bartlett's death in May 1921. Visiting Binet in Switzerland, in 1924, he reread Whitman. Later, while at the American Academy in Rome, he knew his fellow Rome Prize winner Normand Lockwood was writing an hour-long work for soloists, chorus, and orchestra entitled *Requiem*, "Memories of President Lincoln," on Whitman's poem.

In writing the contralto solo parts, Sessions doubtless had in mind the singer Ernestine Schumann-Heink (1861–1936), whom he had heard sing in her career, between 1903 and 1932, at the Metropolitan Opera. The Austrian-born contralto had regularly sung Wagnerian roles Erda, Fricka, and Brangäne at Bayreuth and created the role of Klytemnestra in *Elektra* in Dresden in 1909.

The nearest analog to the Sessions cantata is Paul Hindemith's setting of the same text composed in 1946 with President Roosevelt's death in mind. Hindemith sets music for two soloists, as opposed to Sessions's three, yet both composers distribute the lines between soloists and chorus identically, except that Sessions assigns "Come, lovely and

Figure 44 63 Stanworth Lane, Princeton.

soothing Death" to the contralto soloist, while Hindemith gives it to the chorus. Sessions did not know the Hindemith.

Steinberg wrote, "Sessions responds wonderfully both to the Biblical majesty and the musical fluidity of Whitman's poetry, and here, too, in the evocation of the gray-brown bird singing from the swamp and of the 'o'ver-mastering' scent of the lilacs, he gives us one of the century's great love letters to Nature."[5]

After the cantata *When Lilacs Last in the Dooryard Bloom'd* Sessions completed a Rhapsody for Orchestra (1970) and the Double Concerto for Violin, Cello and Orchestra (1971).[6] The Double Concerto, commissioned by Juilliard for its sixty-fifth anniversary (in 1970), was premiered on November 5, 1971. Its two soloists were violinist Paul Zukofsky and cellist John Sessions; the two also played the work at Northwestern University and at the Aspen Music Festival. Sessions had spent time as a composer in Aspen during the summers of 1958, 1963, and 1971. (The Piano Concerto had also been commissioned by Juilliard, for its fiftieth anniversary in 1955.)

During the summer of 1971 Sessions and Lisl took a trip to Norway, from Oslo to Hammerfest, returning through London. But Lisl's health began to give way, causing almost daily crises: she had heart fibrillations. Their summers were henceforth confined either to Liechtenstein or Franconia (NH), while she recovered from a broken pelvis.

On May 8, 1977, Roger and Lisl gave a party at 63 Stanworth Lane for his Juilliard students and me after two eightieth birthday concerts we organized at the School that spring. On one the Juilliard Orchestra gave the New York premiere of the Sixth Symphony, while a March 22 concert consisted of chamber and vocal music (Second Quartet, Canons, Pages from a Diary, Second Sonata, the Fishwife's Song, Romualdo's Song, and a scene from *Montezuma*.) These, it turned out, were the only two New York City events celebrating Sessions's birthday. More amazingly, although recorded by the BSO under Seiji Ozawa, *When Lilacs Last in the Dooryard Bloom'd* has never been performed in New York.

RELIGIOUS MUSIC

The Trial of Lucullus, Montezuma, and their predecessor *Turn, O Libertad* (1944), a choral work on Walt Whitman commissioned by the Temple Emanu-El in New York, provided Sessions with musical outlets to express his political views. His nine symphonies attest to his Rollandian "great man syndrome." Similarly, a body of works dwells directly on the "religion problem." Unlike many of his direct contemporaries—Carter, Copland, and others—Sessions wrote music based on religious forms, such as the organ prelude, or with Biblical texts, such as the Book of Psalms. Over a 50-year period Sessions turned to religion, services, chorales, or Biblical texts seven times for musical inspiration. Each time the work grew longer or used more forces. These seven works are, however, neither well-known nor recorded. This confrontation began with the 1924 organ prelude set to "Jesu, meine Freude," based on the chorale.[1] The prelude represented a shift in emphasis and a stylistic turn in Sessions's music.

Organist Victoria Sirota wrote that because of Sessions's family's religious background, "The organ, therefore, must have held extra-musical associations for Sessions, which are difficult to assess. The organ is not an easy instrument for which to write successfully, and yet all [five] of Sessions's organ pieces have a clear profile and betray a comfortable familiarity with the instrument."[2] She opines that the three organ preludes may have been influenced by Boulanger's Catholic personality and by her organ playing, and points out that the prelude's binary form was typical of the Parisian Neo-Classic of the mid-1920s.

In the writing of both the first and the second organ preludes Sessions had sought consolation when feeling alone and depressed. The first one, based on a chorale Bach had set and pivotal in his development, was written in the summer of 1924 while alone in Florence (see section "Summer of 1924"). The second was completed on May 27, 1926, in Paris. Barbara had had an abortion, an infection, and an operation. Sessions traveled from Florence to Paris to be with her; he looked gloomily upon a future with no children and perhaps guiltily on his role in her infidelity. Once again he turned to religion in the form of a chorale prelude for organ. "I was in Paris that summer. I was really quite unhappy, upset there for various reasons. I lived in a place on the Boulevard Montparnasse where my window overlooked the gardens of a convent. And there was a bell that tolled every quarter of an hour. And when I wrote this I realized this A# was that bell." (Later Sessions thought he detected a prominent A# in his Piano Sonata: he thought, "A# means something very poignant to me." The next morning he looked at it, and the A# was "all gone;" there, of course, but not with the significance of "running in my ear like a kind of knell. I suppose momentarily I was taken back to this very dark mood."[3]) He described the prelude as "a very somber one—the second one, very somber, dark. At least that's the way I thought of it."[4]

Sirota noticed that the third of the three organ preludes, also Paris, May 1926, "with its figural accompaniment based on a falling seventh motive which accents the offbeat in the pedal, is similar to the type of chorale prelude Bach includes in his *Orgelbüchlein* (see especially the pedal parts to 'Ach wie flüchtig' and 'Durch Adams Fall')."[5] "Ach wie flüchtig, Ach wie nichtig!" is the title of Bach's chorale, BWV 26; it means "Oh, how fleeting, oh, how insignificant." (After Sessions had been in Berkeley for a year, Bloch asked him how he liked it. "I think it's wonderful. I've never been in such a wonderful place," Sessions replied. "And he said, 'Yes, it is wonderful, of course. Of course, after a while you'll get to realize it's all a little *Ach wie flüchtig, Ach wie nichtig!*' "[6]) Sessions thought extremely highly of the Bach preludes, "I think that the Bach chorale preludes are like the Beethoven quartets."[7] Lynnwood Farnam performed the organ preludes.

A commission for 1955 brought back religious issues. The Mass

> was for the 50th anniversary of Kent School. I was asked to write one, you see, that the student body could sing. I was very, very skeptical about it, and warned them that they were not likely to be able to sing my music. So they decided to have the Glee Club sing it. Then the leader of the Glee Club didn't think that they could do that either, but since Kent School was, I suppose I should say, a High Episcopal rather than an Anglican school, they celebrated the 50th anniversary with a big mass at St John the Divine [in April 1956], in New York, and my mass was performed at it.

"But it had to be for unison choir and organ." This commission and its requirement to use the Kent organ could not have helped but remind Sessions of George Bartlett, who had taught at Kent and chosen that very organ. The organ, a Harry Hall of Connecticut, was in use from 1919 through 1956, the year after Sessions's Mass, when it was removed and reconditioned and a new console added, a Holtcamp. (The chapel itself had moved.) Sessions's Mass has been done by Princeton High School May 3, 1956; as the other half of Northwestern's production of *The Trial of Lucullus*; and by Charles Schwartz's Composer's Showcase in New York, but never at Kent.[8]

The question of language for the Anglican Mass was never at issue. The Anglican Mass is in English with the Kyrie in the original Greek. Kent's headmaster, Rev. John Oliver Patterson, felt that the Kyrie did "not really mean 'Oh, God have mercy upon us miserable sinners'—that comes in the Agnus Dei. But he said this is sort of 'Hail to the chief,' more like that." Sessions "kept that in mind when I wrote it. Otherwise it's a setting of the liturgy, what I really consider one of the most marvelous texts in the world, whatever your theological relationship to it is. My theological relationship to it is distinctly unorthodox, but I find it marvelous text just the same. . . . I'm not at all a good Anglican nowadays [1962]. I had too much of it as a child. Maybe it's Oedipus coming in. Oedipus and Jupiter, I mean. Saturn was certainly involved." "[Patterson] had his ideas about Episcopal ritual. I tried to follow the text. And I think it's a wonderful text of course. And then he wanted this stuff [the Appendix: Sursum Corda], which isn't in the regular text, so I put something together for that." Nevertheless, Sessions

> tried to forget the Latin. Of course I know the Latin text very, very well, too. I know Beethoven's *Missa Solemnis* by heart, Bach's B minor mass not quite by heart, but very well. . . . Of course having been brought up as the grandson of a bishop in a very Episcopalian family, I know this text rather well too. In fact, I

knew it before I knew the Latin. Of course, the Latin text of the Mass—God help anybody who tried to translate it into any other language and use the same music for it. Sanctus, all right. It's got two syllables with an accent on the first syllable. But [not] the Agnus Dei and the Credo.[9]

Asked if his unison mass were influenced by Catholic plainchant, Sessions responded, "Well, no, not really. I like plainchant. And I know just a tiny bit something about it, probably not much nowadays, as of the 1930s I did know something about it." Sessions was exposed to an alternative view from the one accepted by the post-Cecilian movement, pre-Vatican II Catholic church, which posited, based on research by the Solesmes monks, that all the notes of Gregorian chant were equal in duration. "I had an Italian friend who was a very good vocal teacher. He insisted . . . that the notes weren't all equal in length. It followed the Latin prosody, there's always a difference in length between the long and the short vowels, which makes sense. . . . But I don't blame plainchant for anything that I wrote."[10]

The Chorale [Prelude] for Organ, written in 1938 and then titled in G Minor, was a reaction to the difficult birth of his son (see section "Marriage and Violin Concerto"). It was premiered in April 1938 in Princeton by Robert Hufstader. In addition to that piece and the Mass, Sessions wrote a *Psalm 140* for voice and orchestra in 1963 and *Three Choruses on Biblical Texts*, scored for chorus and orchestra, in 1972.

Psalm 140 was commissioned from the nearby Princeton Theological Seminary. It was premiered in 1963 at the Seminary by soprano Janice Harsanyi with organ accompaniment. Harsanyi, who had sung *Theocritus* under Sessions and the Fishwife in *Lucullus* at Princeton, was a lecturer in church music at the Seminary. *Psalm 140* is dedicated to her. The work was written at the beginning of the Vatican II council, about which Sessions was optimistic. The BSO, with soprano Anne Elgar and Erich Leinsdorf conducting, performed the orchestrated version, requested by Leinsdorf, on February 11, 1966. By this time Sessions felt distanced from the organ, which he did not think could provide him with enough accent. He said about the original version of the work:

They wanted a religious text. And this is a Presbyterian institution. I'm *not* a Presbyterian at all, of any kind. I'm a Catholic fellow-traveler in a way. And I was very upset by what was going on in the world. I wanted to find something that would say something that meant something to me. The first part of the Psalm is about Senator Goldwater and people who wanted to go right to town with the bomb. The last part of the Psalm is about Pope John [XXIII]. Well, Pope John died the day I finished it and I thought of him.[11]

Sessions even thought of dedicating the work to Pope John, but reconsidered given those who had commissioned the work. Later the head of the Seminary told Sessions that that would have been all right; they considered Martin Luther King, Jr, and Pope John the two greatest men living.

Sessions frequently referred to himself as a "closet Catholic" or a "Catholic fellow-traveler." Like his many forefathers, Sessions more or less rejected the faith of his upbringing and turned to another denomination, this time Catholicism. Perhaps the fact that Barbara had converted to Catholicism partly influenced him.

For the Boston Symphony program notes for *Psalm 140* he wrote,

Also I had in mind from the beginning a certain kind of biblical text, which, as conceived musically by me, would require the full resources of a dramatic solo voice. I chose the text of this Psalm after much searching in the Bible for exactly what I wanted. The text is that of the King James version. The last pages were composed on June 3, 1963, the day of the death of Pope John XXIII, and the work will always be associated in my mind with that event, so sad and so moving for the whole Western world.[12]

To many of the symphonies and the cantata *Lilacs* can be added *Psalm 140* as a work that in Sessions's mind was connected with the death of someone important to him.

Sessions employs textual repetition not found in the Bible and repeats its musical shape five times during the Psalm: "Deliver me, O Lord, from the evil man" appears four additional times at the beginnings of the other verses. The identifiable gesture begins at the top of the staff and reaches down to below the staff on "from the," and then jumps above the staff on "evil" man.

Sessions's attitude about "what was going on in the world" came through in the music, according to the *Christian Science Monitor*:

> But Mr Sessions piece also went contrary to the mood of the psalm itself. "Deliver me, O Lord, from the evil man," sang David: "preserve me from the violent man; which imagine mischiefs in their heart; continually are they gathered together for war." Whereupon the composer unleashes his atonal energies in stabs of violence, in stirring of mischief, in explosions of war. Mr Sessions has set a prayer to music as if it were an angry prayer. But the petitioner is not angry. He is asking to be saved from the effects of anger.[13]

Amherst College commissioned Sessions in November 1968. Sessions, then giving the Norton lectures at Harvard, responded to Amherst's letter within a week and asked whether a Biblical text would be possible. Setting texts from the Bible was his idea, not Amherst's. Sessions traveled to Amherst—only a few miles from Forty Acres and Phelps House and the scene of his "dark and stormy night" escapade more than 50 years earlier —for its Commencement in 1969. He received an honorary degree and returned in the spring of 1970 to attend a Beethoven celebration and meet with the music faculty. The agreed deadline for *Three Choruses on Biblical Texts* was to be the summer of 1971, but the full score arrived over a year later, in August 1972. Numerous problems in reducing the chamber orchestra to a piano-vocal score and producing the parts meant two more years' delay. Between writing the second and third Biblical chorus, Sessions composed his Concertino for Chamber Orchestra (1972). He was also working on his Double Concerto for Juilliard (1971) and his *Lilacs* for the University of California (1970).

Lewis Spratlan conducted the premiere of the *Three Choruses* on February 8, 1975. In an Amherst publication chronicling the commission and its delays, Sessions was asked why he chose a Biblical text. He mentioned his *Psalm 140* and continued, "I wanted something both, in terms of my own feelings, relevant to the human condition and essentially non-sectarian in its implications, also not ultimately pessimistic—which I am neither intellectually nor temperamentally capable of being, and which also would be entirely inappropriate for a festive occasion!" (It was written for the Sesquicentennial Anniversary of the founding of Amherst College.) "Though Amherst is not a primarily religious school, I also do not myself think of this text as 'religious' in a particularistic sense at all—but as an expression of human experience and human feeling—of which the Bible is, after all, one of the supreme documents."[14]

Like *Psalm 140, Three Choruses on Biblical Texts* is orchestrated, and here Sessions omitted the second violin section as he had done in *Lucullus*. Again he used the King James version, "a wonderful work of literature." The piano appears only in the third of the choruses. The first and shortest piece is based on Psalm 130, "De Profundis," "Out of the depths have I cried unto Thee, O Lord. . . . If Thou, Lord, shouldest mark iniquities, who shall stand? But there is forgiveness in Thee. . . . My soul waiteth for the Lord more than those that wait for the morning." In this first Psalm "nothing is omitted except the last two verses, which are very specific religious references."[15] Those verses, seven and eight, read in the Revised Standard version, "O Israel, hope in the Lord! For with the Lord there is steadfast love, and with him is plenteous redemption. And he will redeem Israel from all his iniquities."

In constructing the text for the second piece Sessions also excised references to Israel from the first two chapters of Isaiah; he "eliminated everything that referred to Israel, not for political reasons, at all, obviously, but these are general sentiments, they're not applied to any one locality."[16] Indeed, Sessions eliminated all of Chapter 2 except verse 4, which appears at the end of the chorus. "Jerusalem," "Zion," and "Jacob" are found right before and immediately after verse 4. In Chapter 1 he set verses 4 ("Ah, sinful nation") through 7 ("Zion" is mentioned in 8), 9–10, part of 13, 14–17, 21–26 (four lines mentioning "Israel" are cut from verse 24, and verse 27 begins with "Zion"). "That's the Watergate one. Not only Watergate, but Vietnam, etc."[17] It begins, "Ah, sinful nation, a people laden with iniquity, a seed of evil doers . . . the whole head is sick, and the whole heart faint. . . . Except the Lord of hosts had left unto us a very small fragment we should become as Sodom we should have been like unto Gomorrah. . . . Cease to do evil! Seek judgment; relieve the oppressed; judge the fatherless; plead for the widow." The climax appears on the word "murderers!" It concludes: "And I shall judge among the nations, and shall rebuke many people: And they shall beat their swords into plowshares, and their spears pruning hooks; Nations shall not lift up sword neither shall they learn war any more."

In contrast to the second piece, which deals with the subject of corruption, the third is an optimistic revelation, purifying that which preceded it. "Sort of a general amnesty. I always call that my ecological Psalm. It's the whole of nature, so to speak. Including human nature."[18] It is drawn from Psalms 147, 148, and 150. Sessions wrote, " 'Praise ye the Lord' is for me essentially an expression of joy in life; and the Isaiah text hardly needs much explanation, especially in view of the times through which we have lived for most of this century."[19] The texts begin with Psalm 148:1, and then sets five verses of 147 (3, 6, 7, 8, and 9). Sessions then returns to 148, to set 3, 4, and 7 through 13. Skipping the first two verses of Psalm 150, Sessions ends with the remaining verses, 3 through 6.

"Praise ye the Lord from the heavens. . . . He healeth the broken in heart, bindeth up their wounds. The Lord lifteth up the meek; He casteth the wicked down to the ground." "Praise Him sun and moon, praise Him ye stars and light: Praise Him, ye heav'ns of heavens, and the waters. . . . Let ev'ry one that hath breath praise the Lord, Praise the Lord praise the Lord [*fff*] praise ye the Lord." The Amherst faculty, represented in print by Henry G. Mishkin, learned that "On one hand [Sessions] was always gentle, wise, compassionate . . . but at the same time his music carried a kick like a mule."[20]

A review recalls the reaction that *Psalm 140* had elicited from the *Christian Science Monitor*:

The pyrotechnic rendition of Isaiah's anger at the sins of Israel is punctuated by scolding, stabbing attacks on the vibraphone. The tenors and sopranos burst into a horrified shout on the names of "Sodom" and "Gommorrah," that is chillingly effective. It seems unfortunate that the anger continues unabated to the end of the [second] movement: it loses some of its force, like too many exclamation points on a page: one stops being moved by them after a while.[21]

Clearly, in these psalms Sessions gave utterance to his anger at the state of the world. After a performance by the John Oliver Chorale in 1989, a reviewer noted,

It is music of extraordinary darkness and density, composed in response to Vietnam and Watergate much as the Second Piano Sonata was composed in response to World War II. What is unforgettable about the Choruses is how they move from this turbulence toward an equally extraordinary absolution in the psalms of praise at the end. This music, like the "Missa Solemnis," is exceptionally difficult to perform and to hear. But it also offers rich rewards to the dedicated performer and to the sympathetic and energetic listener.[22]

Religion had played a large role in his family's life; it was only natural that it should occupy Sessions musically, as well. He had refused to marry in an Episcopal church. He had defied his mother about attending services. Sessions came to terms with religion more completely in his music—settings for organ and for voice with orchestra—than he had in his daily life.

THE SYMPHONIES

Elliott Carter wrote of Sessions's symphonies, "They represent a large, opulent world of varied expression, highly imaginative and moving." And he criticized conductors:

> When Roger was a young man, the musical world was much more on the lookout for the remarkable qualities his works show and these would have attracted serious musicians to devote whatever effort was necessary to bring them before the public in a convincing way. . . . While no other American has written such a large body of excellent music, yet Roger did not receive a Pulitzer prize until he was 85 with his Concerto for Orchestra, to the great embarrassment of many of us who won ours before he did.[1]

In 1995 Michael Steinberg, author of *The Symphony: The Listener's Guide*, wrote, "Sessions is a figure of gigantic stature on the landscape of American music." The catalog of his works, "while not extremely large, is one of remarkable weight and value." Calling the music "maximalist to the max," Steinberg described it as "a highly inflected musical language characterized by long melodic lines of great tensile strength and by a luxuriant polyphonic texture. . . . His work stands firmly in the mainstream. As Arthur Mendel once wrote about Bach, nothing is new except the notes."[2] Describing Sessions as conveying, even in his handwritten signature, an "astonishing sense of personal force," Steinberg saw him as

> a formidable intellect . . . an impassioned and demanding teacher, on occasion a more than slightly absent-minded professor, a political idealist who was profoundly depressed by evil and by the sheer folly of the world, a man who loved music and words with heart and mind and who was grandly opinionated about both. He had a rich sense of humor and, for all his settled awareness of his own worth, he was altogether down to earth.

Nevertheless, "He has always seemed to me to come the nearest of any musician in our time to being the heir of Beethoven."[3]

About the music Steinberg wrote:

> Dense, full of event, free of redundancy or routine filler, it allows no time to coast. . . . Sessions music is also unforgiving. Difficult music by some composers sounds more or less OK in an approximation (as distinct from a real performance); his sounds like hell unless everything—spiritual, technical, and acoustic—is in place. He heard many awful misrepresentations of his music and was aware that

people blamed the horrible sounds they heard on him, not on the performers. . . .
He himself remained imperturbably confident and patient. It was part of his
toughness that he never felt sorry for himself.[4]

"Whatever he composed is possessed of electrifying energy, physical and intellectual,"
Steinberg declared.[5] Sessions wrote, "Music is design and controlled movement and
time—movement in action, in imagination, in the vital processes of the human organism, body and mind. . . . What music conveys to us—and let it be emphasized, this is the
nature of the medium itself, not the consciously formulated purpose of the composer—is
the nature of our existence, as embodied in the movement that constitutes our innermost
life."[6]

The esteemed critic Andrew Porter stated unequivocally, "Roger Sessions is America's
greatest symphonist."[7] As a symphonist Sessions had few peers in the US. One of the two
great figures of the early twentieth century, Arnold Schoenberg, wrote no real symphonies. Igor Stravinsky's output in this genre, such as the Symphony in C, is remarkably
indebted to eighteenth-century models and represents more of a commentary about
other music than a work in its own right. Sessions never treated the music of the past
ironically, neither during the Neo-Classical period exemplified by Stravinsky, nor with
the post-modern tongue-in-cheek stance. He always took music seriously—too seriously
to indulge in irony: he was also fundamentally too optimistic a person. Some important
composers of the past century wrote no symphonies. Several composers besides Sessions
reached the iconic number of nine symphonies; these included Mennin, Persichetti, and
Wellesz. Sessions's ties to Beethoven and Mahler go beyond merely the number nine.
In a profound musical sense, all these symphonies form links in the Western chain of
orchestral tradition.

The *Oxford English Dictionary* defines the symphony as "a sonata for orchestra." Since
sonata form is virtually synonymous with tonality, most of the composers who abandoned
tonality abandoned its forms (and their titles). We see in Sessions a new kind of continuity
and articulation of classical forms. His motivic development owes much to Beethoven,
although Sessions's harmony is never unequivocally tonal. This explains why his harmony
sounds very much the same both before and after his supposed adoption of the 12-note
technique. His phrases constantly overlap and flow in a dream-like, psychological manner, somewhat like Wagner. Sections of his work are frequently contrasted rhythmically
with strongly accented masculine gestures balanced by lace-like, feminine lines. All
of his work is informed by both extraordinary discipline and stylistic integrity that
demonstrate his notion that the symphony was a place to say something important.

Sessions lived through the period between the wars, when critics both questioned
whether any American had produced an important symphony and simultaneously hoped
a great American symphony comparable to the masterpieces of American literature
would appear. By the 1960s a consensus emerged that Americans had indeed created the
great American symphony: the Third symphonies of Roy Harris, William Schuman, and
Aaron Copland. These three examples also exemplify American nationalism, and as such
(with the exception of the Copland) their composers' fortunes have fallen with changes
in the times. Copland lives on because we have found another use for his "Fanfare for the
Common Man" that opens the last movement of his Third. (It has also been given new
life as a signature piece of the Democratic Party.) Copland's music became American and
therefore lived on after its newness expired.

The closest parallel to Sessions as a symphonist was perhaps Dimitri Shostakovich,
who Sessions knew, and who wrote 15 symphonies. Like Sessions, Shostakovich inherited

the tradition of the symphony from Austro-German models and extended this tradition in his own unique manner. The symphonic works of Shostakovich that have most suffered have been those identified with a particular time or event in history, such as the Seventh Symphony ("Leningrad"). (Leningrad is now, once more, St Petersburg.) Like Copland, Shostakovich has found a new political audience. Many young people in the US hear Shostakovich's music—particularly the Fifth Symphony—as the statement of a quiet dissident. Whether he was pro- or anti-Soviet is still debated. Meanwhile, his symphonies have become repertoire pieces performed in all parts of the world.

By comparison, Sessions's nine symphonies are played far less often. Here, too, we have a large body of work, available to us mostly through recordings. As Stravinsky once pointed out, if Sessions were a German composer his work would be widely played and published by the most prestigious houses. But, alas, he was an American. This would indeed be a scandal if it were not so usually the case for American composers. Sessions, for his part, did not embrace nationalism openly, as did Copland, or implicitly, as Shostakovich. To understand the importance of Sessions's symphonic works, we must look outside the politics of his or our time. We must examine what Sessions himself insisted on calling "musical criteria": melody, rhythm, harmony, form, and counterpoint.

All of Sessions's lines sound as though they were—or could be—sung. This is, of course, the reason we think of Tchaikovsky or Brahms as great composers. We instantly recognize the melodic gift as being conspicuously musical. Sessions's melodies are frequently long and, at first hearing, difficult to follow. A sense of undulating, additive rhythm always supports the melody's natural flow. Exact repetition occurs infrequently. Sequences are not typical, yet Sessions's music develops a single idea. To hear how this organic development unfolds in each symphony is itself pleasurable.

The Second Symphony, for example, has a memorable melody in the short second movement. (Stravinsky used to whistle this melody.) Written 20 years after the First, this piece shows Sessions as completely his own man. We have speculated why this is so biographically. The characteristics of his mature style can be traced beginning with this piece, although listeners familiar with his work can already hear everything mentioned below in *The Black Maskers*. In the Second Symphony the long cantilena is more chromatic and the texture more of a mosaic than the First. Despite Sessions's long career as an academic and the fact that all of his music is thoroughly contrapuntal, neither canons nor fugues and very few examples of imitation are found in his symphonies.[8] In the Second Symphony an advanced contrapuntal technique serves a freely unfolding line in all parts. A boisterous use of polychords (a subtle sign of the times) appears in the last movement, which closes with a series of overlapping, descending fourths that became a cliché in later symphonies by Schuman, Persichetti, and Mennin.

The upbeat scherzo of the Third Symphony's principal motive sounds a little like a fragment from "Yankee Doodle." In the last movement an unmistakable Charleston rhythm appears. This must have been conscious. In all of Sessions's music, however, these are the only cases of possible references to folk or popular tunes or dance rhythms. The only remotely folk-like or popular element in all of Sessions's music is the sound of specific birds, important in the Pastorale of the Fourth Symphony and in *Lilacs*.

All of Sessions's symphonies are serious in tone and funereal in character. Many are memorials for deceased family or world leaders. The Second Symphony was dedicated to the memory of Franklin Roosevelt, and some of his works, especially the first four symphonies, were inspired or motivated by the death of an important figure in his life. Many of his symphonies are eulogistic and some (the Third, Fifth, Seventh, and Eighth) have quiet, reflective endings.

What this author has anointed a "Sessions ending" occurs first in two movements of the Third Symphony, and in *Montezuma*, finished a year before the Fifth Symphony. The orchestration of that symphony owes a great deal to the exotic orchestration of the Mexican opera. In works that end quietly, he has usually prepared the conclusion by sustaining one low pitch while the melodic material gradually disintegrates above it. Such is the case with the Fifth and Eighth Symphonies, *Lilacs*, and the Concerto for Orchestra. One critic wrote of the Fifth Symphony: "Sessions' Symphony No. 5, from 1964, is a radically dense structure befitting the geometric analogies Mr Botstein [conducting the American Symphony Orchestra] proposed [between 'The Abstract and Geometric Tradition in Music and Painting, 1930–1975'], but the moment-to-moment development is graceful and sneakily expressive."[9]

Sessions said that his Sixth (1966), Seventh (1967), and Eighth (1968) Symphonies were reflections on the Vietnam War. They "form in my mind a kind of series connected with events of that time. The Sixth Symphony becomes grim at the end, and the Seventh is grim all the way through."[10] The character of these pieces fluctuates between percussive violence and resigned lyricism. He uses a wide range of percussion instruments in these works, but those instruments always clarify rhythmic figures and articulate the phrase; they are never ostentatious displays of color for their own sake. The music is expressively powerful, as in the opening of the Eighth Symphony, where the maracas accompany the long line in the strings like "a snake in the grass." The listener is never reminded that maracas are a Latin American instrument or associated with Cuban dance music. The rhythmic aspect does not have an American accent and has no relation to jazz. Through the Second Symphony his music had had a more typical American rapid underlying pulse, but he moved away from that as well.

Almost never in Sessions music is there a vertical sonority—a chord—there for its own sake. All chords in Sessions are arrived at by the movement of the individual lines. This is in marked contrast to much Western music. (Think, for example, of the chords at the ends of Beethoven's symphonies.) There is almost no statement; the music is practically entirely development, that is, continuing development in a Schoenbergian sense. Statement means unequivocal clarity of utterance. (Take Copland's "Fanfare for the Common Man" as an example. Sessions came nowhere near that kind of direct declarative appeal.)

Sessions's resistance to the self-consciousness of Americana means a complete absence of populism; he did not seem to have known popular music (such as the Beatles). Sessions, like Carter, had seen or interpreted nationalism as the greatest single problem of the twentieth century. They rejected music that catered to nationalist sentiment, because they viewed it as at the root of what was wrong with Germany. Carter wanted to eliminate all nationalistic traits in his music. Supporting nationalism in their minds would be supporting evil. The idea was to create an "ideal inner world."

We have to assume that, since he does not refer to it in his music, Sessions did not think popular culture was of use to him. The idea of what you reject or throw away, artist Robert Rauschenberg declared, tells us a great deal about what you value. (Rauschenberg put value on "found art" that others threw away.) Sessions's rejection of folk/pop music has political ramifications.

Sessions's music can be seen as a critique of the politics and society of his day. The need for the artist, as in *Jean-Christophe*, to be set apart from the rest of the world made it easier for Sessions to reject so much. It also explained his difficulty in getting started. Writer's block and slowness of composition are usually based on acute self-criticism. Sessions was too intelligent for his own good, too critical of his own work; in the early decades the disparity between what was in his mind and what he had produced too great. He needed to bridge that gap—one he was later so useful in helping students to do—in order to be himself in his music. He was not only writing for himself, but also for an idealized future audience, again based on the Beethoven model. Those who called him "Olympian" may not have been so far off the mark.

In his orchestral music Sessions developed a unique and recognizable orchestral profile: a strident sonority of violins in their highest register refusing octave doubling; the blurred warmth of the brass interweaving in a dense counterpoint that cannot be untangled; black laughter in the woodwinds, which breaks off into florid *bel canto*-like solos of intense expression played by piccolo, alto flute, bass clarinet, even contrabassoon; a brittle foreground of xylophone and marimba; and ominous drums and percussion. Sessions described the orchestra as "his instrument."

Sessions's views on the Vietnam War were not confined to writing Symphonies nos 6, 7, and 8. He also wrote to Harrison A. Williams, Jr, the chairman of the US Senate Committee on Labor and Public Welfare. Williams answered in March 1971 restating his opposition to the military involvement in Southeast Asia.[11]

The commissions that were the immediate occasion for these symphonies reflect less international events. The Sixth Symphony was commissioned, however, for the celebratory occasion of the State of New Jersey's three hundredth anniversary. New Jersey budgeted $5,000 for works by two state composers, the second being Ulysses Kay (his *Inscriptions* on Walt Whitman). Sessions began writing it in the summer of 1965 while in South America—Buenos Aires, Chile, Peru and Mexico—and completed it at Tanglewood.

Figure 45 Elizabeth Sessions Pease, Roger Pease, and Suzie, ca. 1981 (courtesy of Elizabeth Pease).

Figure 46 Roger Sessions in 1982 (courtesy of Broadcast Music Inc.).

The Sixth's first movement's initial idea, a repeated major ninth, unifies the work as a memorable shape. The opening idea of the Adagio, a high violin melody with winds, recurs twice; the notes, however, vary. The similarity of its rhythm, register, and contour reveal Sessions's characteristic formal trait: continuous variation, that is, reminiscences without verbatim repeats. "In this style recapitulation in the old sense of the word would not work at all." The third movement's material is treated so freely it "almost has no theme at all, except the trumpet call at the beginning, which comes back."[12] The New Jersey orchestra, not as professional as it is today, massacred the work; Sessions recognized only one line as his music. The audience and critics "frankly disliked it and a few thought it was terrible."[13]

The New York premiere was given by the Juilliard Orchestra, Jose Serebrier conducting, March 4, 1977, a performance engineered by his Juilliard students and Peter Mennin to celebrate Sessions's eightieth birthday. The American Composers Orchestra performed the Sixth on June 16, 1993, in Carnegie Hall. *The New York Observer* noted, "God knows, the massive knottiness of this work remains awesome, but long gone are the days when I—and most other listeners, I suspect—can be cowed into submission by the sheer difficulty of a work of art."[14] *The New York Times* remarked, "The Sessions . . . was all hard-nosed energy and surefooted purpose, a piece that does not seduce but instead demands respect on its own harsh terms."[15]

Leighton Kerner wrote that the Seventh Symphony reconfirmed Sessions as "the greatest symphonist since Mahler." Kerner continued, "Music meets its audience more than halfway when it's this directly powerful, as in the symphony's outer movements, this dazzlingly orchestrated throughout, and this diaphanous and lyrical, albeit atonally so, in its middle movement and in the ghostly chiaroscuro of the finale's epilogue."[16] Commissioned in celebration of the sesquicentennial anniversary of the University of

Michigan, the Seventh Symphony was premiered on October 1, 1967, in Ann Arbor, with the Chicago Symphony Orchestra, Jean Martinon, the dedicatee, conducting.[17] The Seventh Symphony was Sessions's favorite. The usually modest composer said of it,

> The last movement is rather grim, well it's a complicated movement. It has a kind of scherzo with dark rumblings underneath and then the main part comes back. It's the most brutal [movement] except for the very end. The main part of the third movement ends in a sort of impasse with an ostinato on the horns, which gets slower and slower. And then the Epilogue was very slow. And if I may say so, that's about the best ending I ever wrote. Or one of them. It's quite unusual.[18]

The first movement divides approximately into an ABA form. The two initial ideas of the slow movement return in reverse order. The "Sessions ending" appears in the Epilogue he liked so much—several instruments drop out and never return: contrabassoon, trumpets, trombones, tuba, percussion, xylophone/marimba, and vibraphone/glockenspiel. For the last two measures only the alto flute, two horns, timpani, and double basses are playing, *ppp* and *morendo*. The last phrase (like the ending of *Lilacs*), rather than ceasing, recedes out of earshot.

Somewhat mysterious is the composer's assertion that the semi-pornographic horror novel *The Story of O* influenced the Seventh. Here Sessions's political beliefs, literary interests, and sexual side were engaged. He elaborated:

> *The Story of O* is a sort of strange mixture of cruelty and suffering, that's somewhere in there [the symphony], I know. Then there was a beautiful passage that I read one day, just a scene that I read in another book [a story by D. H. Lawrence], people sitting out in the garden in the evening, and that comes in here. I'd read from [*The Story of O*] in a bookstore because I'd heard about it and was curious. [It's] absolutely awful. This woman's very much in love with this man and then he lures her into a situation in this pornographic club where there are no holds barred. The women had to go around naked and any man can come up to them and do whatever he pleases. Then she gets involved homosexually. She's just subservient always, you see. Finally she asks permission—this man turns her over to a friend of his, I mean totally involved—and she finally asks this friend if he'll allow her to kill herself. He will and she does.

None of the references are specific in the Seventh Symphony. "There's nothing you could say refers to that and that's why I generally don't talk about these things."[19]

Publication of Sessions's post-1965 music went slowly. The Seventh Symphony (written in 1967) was published, by Edward B. Marks in 1977, after the Sixth Symphony (written in 1966 and published by Theodore Presser in 1975), *Three Choruses on Biblical Texts* (written 1972, published by Presser, 1976) and the Five Pieces for Piano (1975, also published in 1976), and before the Double Concerto (1971, published 1979), the Rhapsody (1970, published 1981), the Divertimento (1960, published 1982), and Symphony No. 9 (1978, published 1984). Such are the lengths of time composers typically endure before their music is published. Sessions's friend and Juilliard colleague Vincent Persichetti had persuaded the composer to switch from Marks to Presser, where Persichetti himself was an editor. Recordings took even longer. The Seventh Symphony and the Divertimento for Orchestra were first recorded by the Louisville Orchestra, Peter

Leonard conducting, in 1981. Then, in 1995, the American Composers Orchestra released it—Dennis Russell Davies conducting—along with premiere recordings of the Symphonies Nos 6 and 9. Once again Sessions found comfort in what Dallapiccola wrote referring to the length of time it took to get *Ulisse* performed, "Si sa che la nostra professione è la scuola della patienze." ("One knows that our profession is the school of patience.")[20]

When the Louisville Orchestra first played Sessions Seventh Symphony in 1981, it was called "a work of all but overwhelming neoclassic splendors—logical purposive, and elegant." Comparing the 1967 premiere to the poetry of Robert Frost, the *Chicago Daily News* wrote, "His writing is all bone and muscle, without an ounce of spare flesh, and its meaning is always uncompromisingly evident."[21] (The American Composers Orchestra played the Seventh Symphony, first on November 15, 1982, and then October 31, 1993, in Carnegie Hall, on a program that included Copland's *Grohg*.) Sessions wrote for the Louisville recording liner notes,

> This symphony is somewhat longer than No. 5, finished in the first days of January 1964, and No. 6, finished in July 1966; but it is shorter than my first four, which were written at intervals between 1926 and 1958. The difference in length, however, does not imply a smaller design, but rather a greater concentration of style in my later works. Like all of my other symphonies except No. 3, which consists of four movements—and possibly No. 2, of which the second movement is a very short intermezzo—this one consists of three movements; in this case, however, the final movement, *Allegro misurato*, ends with a short, slow Epilogue.
>
> The term "Symphony" does not imply, for me, adherence to so-called "standard forms," a term with which, for many reasons, I would in any case quarrel, if it is thought to apply to the great classics of the past. The attentive listener to this symphony, as to other works of mine, will certainly be aware of ideas which recur though never in the same context, and never in the quite the same guise. These ideas, in fact all of the ideas in the Symphony, are all derived from a pattern of tones which lies at the basis of the whole piece. Such recurrent elements serve the purpose of large musical design—the larger the design, the plainer the recurrence must be. In my later music—that of the last thirty-five years or so—this element of recurrence almost never takes the form of literal repetition; the recurrent elements, though always recognizable as such, are constantly varied, according to both the immediate context and the musical movement as related to the whole.[22]

The power of the opinion of *The New Yorker*'s critic Andrew Porter among musical and intellectual circles was such that it may have helped inspire the American Composers Orchestra to continue performing all nine of Sessions's symphonies. After their first Sessions foray, the November 1982 performance of the Seventh Symphony, Porter wrote, "The concert going public still wants symphonies, and big ones, too: its appetite for Bruckner and Mahler is apparently endless." He went on:

> Roger Sessions is America's greatest symphonist. None of his nine symphonies is long, but all of them are nourishing. He has written a body of works for large orchestra—it further includes three concertos, the Divertimento, the Rhapsody, the recent Concerto for Orchestra—that should figure as regularly in American orchestral programs as the symphonic works of Elgar and Michael Tippett do

in British programs. But another New York Philharmonic season is passing without even one of Sessions' symphonies billed, or any of the concertos. (The Philharmonic's miserable record during the half century and more since Koussevitzky introduced Sessions' First Symphony, in Boston, shows just three appearances of his symphonies—the Second in 1950, the Eighth in 1968, and the Third in 1976—and one of the Violin Concerto, in 1959). However, the Pittsburgh Symphony, under André Previn, is playing the Second Symphony in Avery Fisher Hall on December 10th, in the month of Sessions's eighty-sixth birthday. . . .

The Seventh is a beautiful work, and perhaps the most Bergian of the series in its romanticism of melodies and textures and its amalgam of rhapsodic feeling and very clear construction.[23]

Of the American Composers Orchestra's second, 1993 performance *The New York Times* wrote: "Roger Sessions Symphony No. 7 is obdurately dense, a rock pile of a piece, its jaw jutting with sincerity and purpose . . . for this is music that cares very little if listeners like it or not."[24]

The Eighth Symphony, commissioned by the New York Philharmonic and under-written by the Gulbenkian Foundation and Francis Goelet, was meant to have been performed April 18, 1968, but had to be postponed until May 2, because of Sessions's lateness in completing it. William Steinberg conducted the premiere. In 1968 Sessions wrote a letter concerning the Eighth Symphony to Frederik Prausnitz, who was prepar-ing a recording. Prausnitz had written about a D flat that appeared only once, when in similar passages the note was D natural. Sessions answered:

The question of the D flat [m. 126 as against m. 17] has intrigued me very much. The D flat is correct (in m. 126, not m. 17); but it took me some effort to be sure of this fact, and even more to discover the reason for it. I looked at the blueprint of the Ms. + there it was, D [natural] in m. 17, D flat in m. 126. Then, as I read the passages through, my ear confirmed it—I still wanted it that way, but couldn't discover the reason why. I started a letter to you last night in that vein. This morning I looked at it again, just to make sure I was not deceiving myself; and the reason jumped out at me. Excuse me if I go into some detail, but it is rather interesting to me, as I hope it may be to you.

First of all, the two passages differ in that the first one goes on for 3 more measures—the phrase ends at m. 20. The next one breaks off abruptly in the next measure (127) + is interrupted by a very sharp contrast. Now—since the 3rd horn, which takes the lowest voice at this point, establishes F–D as a bass over five beats, my ear undoubtedly shied away from the D natural following the F in the previous measure. I admit that it is a minute point, and in a way has more to do [with] the way my mind works (or rather my ear, since it was probably unconscious + simply the result of my "hearing ahead" to the next measure—one never "thinks" such things "out" + I don't see how one could do so)—than with anything at noticeable in performance. But the D flat is correct here, as the D natural is in the earlier passage.[25]

The American Composers Orchestra, under Dennis Russell Davies, performed Sym-phony No. 8, October 23, 1994, in Carnegie Hall. Alex Ross wrote for *The New York Times*:

The Eighth is characteristic of the composer's late style, combining the fearsome rhythmic and harmonic densities of his mature Modernist period with the extended melodic phrases that marked his language from the beginning. The music is tough and desolate, growing from tight, static thematic cells into chaotic masses of sound. The final pages are a luminous Mahlerian vision; long violin phrases and a final chord of A major hang in the air.[26]

Sessions's subsequent Rhapsody for Orchestra (1970) has enjoyed some recent performances, one at the BBC Symphony, January 14, 2006, conducted by David Robertson and broadcast on the BBC Radio 3, January 16.

John Harbison has remarked that composers make their own history. He means that the musical identity of a composer is the sum of that composer's choices, conscious or not, of his own influences. We could say, for instance that Harbison's influences (Schütz, Bach, Verdi, Stravinsky, and Sessions) represent a personal history of compositional style that lead inevitably to Harbison himself. Similar connections have been made by composers such as Boulez, who traces his own stylistic development from Berlioz, Debussy, Webern, and Messiaen. Provided that we restrict our analysis to purely musical criteria, the knowledge of a composer's influences can help focus our attention on the most obvious traits of an artist's personality.

The opening of Sessions's First Piano Sonata, for instance, has often been compared with a Chopin prelude. If we accept this superficial comparison, it actually deflects us from the stylistic elements that make Sessions's piece truly connected to the music of his predecessors. A closer listening to this opening shows Sessions's characteristic use of the Wagnerian "long line." Sessions stated that this piece's sense of line is more like a Bach aria. If we look further, we will find a quite polyphonic texture, spacing not relative to the overtone series, and a wealth of motivic development not characteristic of Chopin's music to the same degree. From the listener's perspective this kind of misunderstanding is quite common in relation to much of the music of the twentieth century, be it progressive or conservative. In the case of the Sessions Sonata the listener who thinks that this piece is like Chopin will be disappointed in its development or feel disoriented by the work's failure to live up to expectations that are, in fact, quite foreign to the work itself.

Sessions's Ninth Symphony presents another case of this kind of misunderstanding. The typical adjectives (knotty, academic, cerebral) were invoked in the usual knee-jerk criticism of music thought incomprehensible. A closer look at this symphony shows what is actually there instead of what we might like to find.

The Ninth Symphony came at the end of a long compositional career. By 1978, when the symphony was completed, Sessions had been writing symphonies for over 60 years. During this long career we can see evidence that Sessions, too, was making his own history. The long, singable melodic lines set in a rich polyphonic texture owe as much to the influence of Bach in Sessions's Ninth Symphony as they did half a century earlier in his First Piano Sonata. In addition, we have an extraordinary richness of harmony, texture, and motivic detail whose natural predecessors are Wagner and Beethoven. Are Bach, Beethoven, and Wagner knotty, academic, and cerebral? If we start by placing Sessions in the right historical context, we have a better chance of understanding the elements of his style and, ultimately, perceiving the emotional impact of his vision.

Regarding the Ninth Symphony Sessions told his intimate circle the work had something to do with William Blake's poem, "Tyger, Tyger burning bright / In the forests of the night / What immortal hand or eye / Could frame thy fearful symmetry?" Perhaps one of the most famous poems in the English language, it asks a profound question: "Did He who made the lamb make thee?" The uncharacteristically abrupt, loud ending of the Symphony is perhaps a musical analog to Blake's question. The two forces, the Tyger and the Lamb, come to an accommodation. Probably Sessions's first encounter with William Blake was at Harvard: the *Harvard Musical Review*'s lead article in December 1913 was "The unwritten music of a great man" by later Blake scholar (and Sessions's predecessor as *Review* editor) S. Foster Damon.[27] Sessions wrote, "I set myself a rather special task in this work and it involves both agony and joy in the making of it. . . . I find it comforting to read the score of my [recently published] 7th symphony and to discover that it did, from my point of view come out right that time!"[28]

The "special task" refers to the portrayal of evil through the use of two themes. The poem opposes the violent tyger to the lamb, representative of a cooperative and peaceful spirit. A conflict arises between brutality and gentleness, especially in the first movement. Sessions said its initial measures represent the tiger lying in wait. The opening fast section contrasts with the quieter, slower, and more lyrical B section, only to return to the (much varied) opening material and end with the question "Did He who made the lamb make thee?" Unlike the quiet "petering out" of the Seventh Symphony and *Lilacs*, this work concludes with a definite cadence, a "sudden bang."

Another connection with "Tyger, tyger" is Sessions's leitmotif-like association of the interval of a major second, most prominent in the first and third movements. Whenever it occurs, it is set in a syncopated, asymmetrical fashion that sounds very much like the words *Tyger, Tyger* being spoken in American English. This technique is so common in advertising jingles, most of us would never think to listen for it in a symphonic context. Nevertheless, once one makes this connection, the piece begins to reveal its deeper significance. Consider how Wagner's Tristan and Isolde sing their own names toward the end of the first act of that opera, thereby creating a powerful emotional connection to the preceding instrumental music that foreshadows this moment.

An additional similarity to the music of Wagner and Bach is Sessions's sense of continuity. An inexorable *Fortspinnung* in Sessions, directly related to Bach and to Wagner's famous "endless melody" (or, more precisely, "endless progression"), is a feature found in all of Session's music, especially the Ninth Symphony. As in Wagner, the listener becomes absorbed in a continuous progression of overlapping phrases and saturated by an ever-evolving series of pyramidal crests of climaxes followed by waves of relaxation.

As in the important works of literature by Virginia Woolf and James Joyce, Sessions seems to take for granted the perspectives of stream of consciousness, relativism, and evolution (in music endless melody or endless progression). Precisely these points of view (espoused by Wagner before Sessions was born) had a profound impact on the music of the first half of the twentieth century. Composers after Wagner either followed his precepts implicitly (as with Schoenberg) or rebelled against him completely (such as Stravinsky).

A problem for Sessions in relation to the concert-going public is that, although he was thoroughly American, his music is highly Germanic in expression and form. His historical connection with Bach and Wagner is as clear as it was for Schoenberg. Unlike all of Sessions's American contemporaries, however, his published music never seemed to go through a "French" period.[29] This is most noticeable in Sessions's Ninth where, as was mentioned earlier, never does a chord or harmony appear for its own coloristic sake, such as one is apt to find in much French music, either Neo-Classic or serial. Listeners hoping to bathe in the perfume of sonority will be disappointed by Sessions's rigorous sense of organic development and polyphony. There are, nevertheless, more than intellectual rewards in Sessions's Ninth.

Sessions was commissioned to write the Ninth Symphony in 1974 when Frederik Prausnitz, the dedicatee, was conductor of the Syracuse Symphony. The New York State Council of the Arts gave the Symphony a grant of $10,000 to commission the work. Syracuse itself brought back many family memories for Sessions of the Bishop, while meanwhile Hannah's sons still lived near the city. The work was finished in 1978, and Christopher Keene, by then the Syracuse Symphony conductor, gave its premiere, January 17, 1980, and shortly afterward in New York.

There is the usual break between the first and second movements. The second begins and ends with a trombone solo whose conclusion overlaps the beginning of the Allegro vivace third movement. The rate of musical information was higher in Sessions's works of the 1960s. But here, a decade after the completion of the short and concise Eighth Symphony, Sessions gives the musical gestures (and us) more time to breathe. The expansive solo passages do not have to compete with such densely contrapuntal accompaniment. The sprawling Adagio movement relaxes more than is usual in Sessions's slow music.

While composing the second movement he wrote to this author, "I'm afraid it will not be easy to play, but it has to be what it has to be!" In the Allegro vivace Sessions uses meter as a method to articulate form. Here the slippery and sliding tempi produce a musical vertigo typical of Sessions's late music. This last movement is the most difficult to grasp formally, the rhythmic and metric dizziness simultaneously produce formal distinctions and blur them.

The American Composers Orchestra performed Symphony No. 9 on May 15, 1994. *The New York Times* reported, "Brusquely ardent, dense with ideas, organized with undeniable craftsmanship and strong in character, this late work from 1980 [*sic*] concedes the listener few ordinary comforts. The Ninth's language is at once expressive and reclusive, with a stony grammar and blunt rhetorical style that demands attention but will not please for it."[30]

One doctoral dissertation discusses the Ninth Symphony at length, an almost a measure-by-measure analysis and a careful view of the two "tone rows" involved.[31] The author provides a formal analysis of the first movement: Exposition, mm. 1–76 (including Prologue, mm. 1–6); first subject, mm. 6–43 (first statement, mm. 6–21; restatement, mm. 22–44); second subject, mm. 44–76 (first statement, mm. 44–66; restatement, mm. 66–67); Development, mm. 77–150; including first part (1st subject, mm. 77–98); second part (first subject, mm. 98–124); third part (2nd subject, mm. 125–50); Recapitulation, mm. 150–211, including first statement (subjects mixed), mm. 150–81; second statement (subjects mixed), mm. 182–211; and finally, Coda, mm. 212–17.[32]

Despite his lengthy examination of the symphony, at the end of the dissertation the writer throws up his hands:

> Without consciousness of narrative sonata form, the various alternations of material, style and pace in the first movement might appear arbitrary. To an even greater extent, the third movement might sound amorphous, lacking direction. . . . The structural analogues to traditional sonata forms observed in the first movement may be nothing more than signifiers of progress. Obviously, such metaphors can be carried only so far: at bottom, sonata form requires tonality (or an audible equivalent) for the logical necessity of its direction, since its basis is a polarity between . . . tonal regions.[33]

The third movement is diffuse. The dissertation writer had not penetrated the devices that keep the symphony moving. If doctoral students find they cannot understand the procedures in Sessions's music, it may be fairly asked, who can? Perhaps we should take Sessions at his word, when he insists that the 12-tone technique may be the least interesting ingredient of the piece.

Unusually, Sessions incorporates two tone rows, or more precisely, two themes, here, although "Nothing is conditioned by the row; the row is conditioned by the piece." He would object to discussion of his symphonies as 12-tone. Mention of the term always engendered a gentle diatribe about the unimportance of such techniques: what was important was the music. "Also I consider the hexachord, in a scale-like formation, a perfectly regular permutation."[34] This last point is crucial in understanding Sessions's use of 12-tone materials: in other words, he uses six-note scales freely.

Robert Morgan described the technique used in all of Sessions's 12-tone music.

> Sessions found it useful simply as a means of more consciously controlling two features that had long marked his style: full chromaticism and motivic-intervallic cohesiveness. Like Copland, however, he employed the method with great freedom, often using pairs of unordered complementary hexachords [six-note scales] to provide "harmonic" definition without determining the note-by-note succession, or using the series primarily for the principal thematic material while allowing the subsidiary parts to be more freely construed.[35]

From the Second Symphony onwards Sessions's music tends to alternate between one of the two forms of the whole-tone scale with added half-step embellishments. This is most clearly seen in the opening of the Fifth Symphony and the most "problematic" movements of the Ninth. The Ninth is only problematic if one uses the analytical tools of 12-tone theory, because the music is not based upon these techniques.

It is true that there is no sense of harmonic modulation in Sessions's music. Instead we see a tendency (as early as the First Sonata) to alternate freely between a scale—major, minor, whole-tone, or octatonic—and its half-step transposition. The "row," if it can be discovered at all, is often a melodically thematic statement that results from the fluctuation of two scales a half-step apart.

While working on the Ninth Symphony, Sessions wrote to Prausnitz,

> I have made many sketches, and like them; and little by little the design of the whole has begun to clarify itself in my mind. *Quite between ourselves*, I haven't yet summoned up the effrontery to call it Symphony No. 9 though I might have to do so eventually. Forgive me for being so vague; but this is the way I work—I keep things "flexible" in my mind for a very long time whenever I am working on a long piece, and I am not yet ready to commit myself to anything more than to say it will definitely be a much bigger work than the Rhapsody and will probably contain more large contrasts ("movements," possibly) than my Eighth symphony. A few things I must still keep under my hat—please forgive me. I *can* tell you however that it will definitely be a *major* work of mine, though not really a long one.[36]

The Boston Symphony Orchestra commissioned and premiered Sessions's last orchestra work; it would have been his Tenth Symphony, but here the composer decided not to tempt fate and called it instead Concerto for Orchestra. That title recalled an earlier BSO commission, Bartók's Concerto for Orchestra. The Sessions work was given, under Seiji Ozawa, on October 23 and 24, 1981; January 22, and 23, 1982; and on April 7, 8, 9, and 12, 1988. The Concerto won for Sessions his first non-honorary Pulitzer Prize, at the age of 85.

Andrew Porter of *The New Yorker* described the Concerto: "One ascends it with animated tread, moves with slow wonder across its central reach, speeds again toward its close, and at the end pauses for a moment, quietly rapt, to consider both the journey made and the realms to which it may lead."[37]

Robert Morgan concludes his assessment as follows,

> Sessions is arguably the finest symphonist yet produced in the United States, whose large-scale orchestral works deserve a place beside those of the twentieth-century composers, such as Sibelius and Shostakovich, who have contributed most to the preservation and continued evolution of this traditional genre. Moreover, his symphonies have defined a unique course of evolution, tracing—perhaps more than those of any other composer of his generation—a direct descent from the German symphonic heritage, from Strauss's tone poems through the orchestral works of Schoenberg. Yet to this tradition Sessions adds his own distinctly American voice, evident above all in the buoyancy and vigor of his rhythmic ideas.[38]

DEATH AND POSTHUMOUS
REPUTATION

After Lisl's death, July 9, 1982, Sessions lived alone at 63 Stanworth Lane in Princeton. A year later he stopped teaching at Juilliard, thus ending his 16-year weekly commute and overnight stay in New York City at the Hotel Empire. A Spanish-speaking housekeeper cooked for him and cleaned everything except his second-floor study. He worked on a violin and cello duo for Giovina and John Sessions, doubtless meant as a conciliatory gesture toward John. The work was not finished; nevertheless Richard Aldag later completed the Duo and premiered it in New York (and recorded it) despite the fact that Sessions did not view it as done and, had he been alive, would not have let it be performed.[1] That the Duo is a wonderful piece complicates the situation.

From the time of *Montezuma*'s 1976 performance in Boston, Sessions and Andrew Porter collaborated on a comic opera. Sessions frequently taught a semester at Juilliard on *Falstaff* and doubtless had noted the coincidence between his own age and that of Verdi (both 80) when the Italian finished his last opera and only successful comedy. The subject of the new opera was to be *The Emperor's New Clothes*. Here, unlike in the fairy tale, the emperor would be in on the joke, and so would his wife—possibly a sop to Lisl. Sessions wants the emperor to show that he was unembarrassed by his new suit.

Over the next several years Porter, who, like Borgese, had never written a libretto, found it difficult to derive a workable libretto from the fairy tale and was proceeding slowly. Sessions, however, had been setting music already and still had "Noten im Kopf [notes in his head]." The subject matter, which Prausnitz viewed as an "almost certainly unconscious irony," this author thinks was chosen with complete "malice aforethought," as Sessions had once observed about his choice of the text *Turn, O Libertad*. Sessions had lived long enough to see the folly of many who were considered important or influential. He had seen the 12-tone method co-opted by his own pupil Babbitt, among others, and made into "nonsense." (He frequently and slyly observed, "You must take what Mr Babbitt says with a large grain of salt.") He had found himself thoroughly misunderstood by the public "as the purveyor of mostly bristling and difficult music. It is not, in [Sessions's] view, a very accurate picture. 'My image as I read it in the newspapers is not what I really am,' he said the other day [in 1981] in his office at The Juilliard School. 'I'm supposed to be a radical 12-tone composer and so forth. Well, that's just not true.' "[2] He had confessed to being "a sinner and a fool." Human folly was a subject dear to him; *Falstaff*'s parting words are "All the world's a joke." Sessions would have loved to have accomplished a similar comic achievement. After Sessions's hard-won maturity, he found himself more capable than ever at sympathizing with the human condition. He never lost his sense of humor, one of the characteristics that had endeared him to so many. *The New York Times* quoted a colleague, "Everyone loves Roger Sessions except the public."[3]

In September 1981 Sessions agreed to perform as the Soldier in Stravinsky's *The Soldier's Tale*, with Aaron Copland speaking the Narrator part and Virgil Thomson the Devil. Perhaps he remembered the excitement of driving with Jean Binet in 1924 past the Swiss town in which the piece was written. The performance by Speculum Musicae at the Whitney Museum was the last time he would see either his old friend Copland or (his unknown nemesis) Thomson. When he was 83 he attended the New Jersey Symphony, Thomas Michalak conducting, performing his Eighth Symphony at Princeton in the McCarter Theater.

At the end of his life he behaved as he had his entire career: he took on more than he could handle and unreasonably thought he could finish an entire opera in the short time he had left. He could not stop himself from broadcasting plans still in the most preliminary stages: Sarah Caldwell had agreed to produce the new opera, he told people. Without Lisl, he reverted to his customary irrationality about money. He felt that he should not have to pay rent; argued with his daughter about financial matters; and uncharacteristically gave a student and a performer funds to help present his Piano Concerto.

This author saw Sessions for the last time in Princeton, October 12, 1984, five months before his death. We had known each other well for 11 years, and he had called me his "confidante." Sessions was alone at Stanworth Lane, the dining room table where we sat piled with unanswered mail. His face looked fallen on the left side, asymmetrical. His memory was poor: despite many arrangements, he did not expect me at the appointed hour. We had not seen each other in over two years (I had been living at the American Academy in Rome), and I was well aware it would be our last visit. His speech was slower than ever, as was his ability to catch the drift of what one was saying, partly because his hearing was also worse. He showed me an old group photograph and asked if it was he and what he was doing in a uniform. The photo looked circa 1940s, and I guessed that it was Sessions and that he may have been uniformed in performing the duties of an air-raid warden or volunteer policeman in Princeton during World War II. I told him my book, the first about him, *Roger Sessions and His Music*, was in production, and he gave me the then-recent premiere recording of Symphony No. 7. Sylvia Babbitt called to check up on him. When I left, I tried to keep the tears back. We shook hands, he a New England gentleman and I a midwesterner, neither given either to emotional outbursts or physical affection. No modern-day casual hugs and kisses; just as dignified behavior as we both could manage.

At the Princeton Medical Center in the last weeks of his life, the hospital's dietitian, Kathy Ercoli, who knew Sessions's music (and was not impressed by it), liked the composer a great deal. She had studied with D. Kern Holoman at the University of California at Davis and remembered he admired Roger Sessions. She sent a Christmas card to a friend and described Sessions as "a patient at the nursing home connected with the medical center . . . before he passed away there. He was a rather funny, charming little man who hid candy bars in his bed clothes. He didn't like the food in the nursing home. Can't say that I blame him." The treats hidden in bed harken back almost 80 years to Cloyne. Sessions gave Kathy an autograph she had requested; she sent the card to her friend Mary (last name not known), with instructions she could keep it or give it to Professor Holoman. Mary gave the signature—probably the last thing Sessions ever wrote—to Holoman.[4]

Milton Babbitt, and even more often, his wife Sylvia, as well as Edward Cone, who all still lived in Princeton, made frequent visits and phone calls to the aging composer. Sessions's daughter Elizabeth and her husband Bob visited from New York, but could not be there all the time. John declined to visit or be reconciled with the composer who

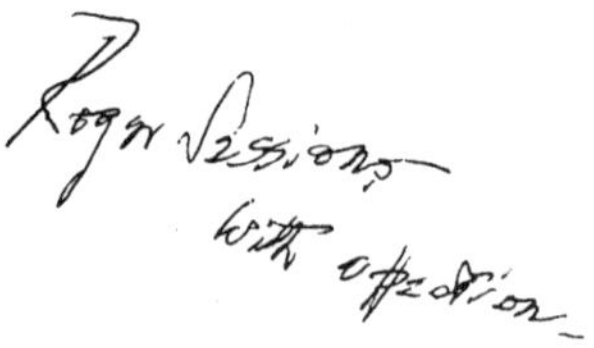

Figure 47 Sessions's last signature.

he apparently thought had not helped him enough in his own career as a cellist and neglected him. Sessions, who once "looked like a man who would be happiest if he could go down in history as a successful father,"[5] would die without seeing his son again, the son for whom he had divorced Barbara, incurred Boulanger's wrath, lost Copland's friendship, and suffered the trauma of the son's premature birth, as well as career blows and personal slights. Father Sill's hopeful prediction about Sessions's own son, who indeed attended Kent, had backfired with usurous interest. Sessions had been in Italy when his own father died in 1927; he never had a chance to say goodbye. In 1959, despite Suzanne Bloch's pleas, Sessions had not gone to see his father figure, Ernest Bloch, before his death; now he would himself suffer a worse fate. No family member was present when he died.

After grappling with death in his symphonic works, now it was Sessions's turn to face death himself. Almost no one had realized that much of his music was about death. Babbitt described the last time he saw Sessions. He visited the 88-year-old in the Princeton Medical Center where he had been recovering from a stroke and had contracted pneumonia; he came on a Tuesday. Babbitt chatted with his former teacher, whom he had been close to for over half a century. Finally, he urged Sessions to get some rest; he was leaving and would return. Sessions responded, "If I go to sleep, I'm afraid I'll never wake up." That was precisely what happened on March 16, 1985, the following Saturday. Prausnitz claimed that Sessions's last words were "What a damned nuisance!," which sounds entirely plausible.[6]

Princeton's newspaper announced that contributions in lieu of flowers could be sent in Sessions's memory to the Friends of Music at Princeton, the Opera Company of Boston, or the League of Composers-ISCM in New York City. Sessions's children inherited little money: scores and specific books, including the first edition of *War and Peace* bought in Rome, were bequeathed to them. He had never owned a house, but BMI continued to pay royalties for his music, all of which was in copyright. John refused all royalty earnings (which go to his daughter). John, originally the executor of the will, then shared that duty with his sister, but declined to perform any duties associated with it and eventually disassociated himself entirely from any legal responsibility. The Edward B. Marks catalog was sold to Hal Leonard. No one at Hal Leonard Music knew Sessions personally, and few did much to promote his music. Theodore Presser still owns some of Sessions's catalog (listed on the Roger Sessions Society website).

Evidently Sessions wanted to be cremated like both his parents; in any case, he was. The time came to arrange the funeral. Neither adult child was up to the task: Elizabeth because she was so upset, John because he wanted nothing to do with his father (he continues to prefer that no one mention his name in his presence). The ashes remained in John's car, according to his cousin Sarah Chapin, for months. Sessions had often told me that he wanted Mozart's C major quintet played at his funeral. No funeral was held and no music was played at his burial.

Sessions's once-close friend Copland suffered a similar fate at 90. He too had pneumonia and a stroke in the weeks preceding his death. He, however, had no daughter to visit him. Copland was also cremated, and his ashes buried in a private ceremony at Tanglewood, some 60 miles from Sessions's grave in Hadley.

Finally, Sessions's daughter-in-law Giovina and niece Jane Ann Byrne took matters into their own hands. A bronze plate was made, and in the summer of 1985 the two of them buried Sessions in his ancestor's graveyard, the Old Hadley Cemetery. The bronze plaque flat on the ground has two mistakes stemming from the two women's lack of knowledge of their composer relative. First, Sessions had long before dropped his middle name (never legally his), Huntington, for at least two reasons. One was that three names had gone out of fashion; the other, that his mother, a Huntington, had died. The grave plaque nevertheless reads "Roger H Sessions."

The second mistake was more serious. Seeking a birth date, Giovina and Jane Ann consulted a highly untrustworthy source: *Sixty-Odd*, Ruth Sessions's autobiography. There, as we have noticed, Ruth gave Sessions's birthdate as December 27, 1896, the fifth anniversary of Mary Huntington Sessions's death. Any number of music encyclopedias would have provided the correct birth date as the following day, but the two relied on Ruth's book. The result was that Ruth's obsession with her dead daughter haunted Sessions even to the grave: his birth date on his gravestone is Mary's death date: December 27 (the year 1896 is correct). The women's last decision seemed entirely appropriate, the addition of the single word "Composer."

His geographical placement is, also accurate, seen chronologically. On the left of his grave is the white marble cross marking Mary's remains with her dates barely legible, and even closer, on the immediate right and in the same-sized bronze plaque, is his younger brother John's grave with his dates (1899–1948). Ruth and Archibald are both buried in the Old Hadley Cemetery near these graves. There are no markers for their graves. Sessions's uncle George, his aunt Arria, his grandparents Frederic Dan and Hannah Dane Huntington are not far away in the same cemetery and clearly marked.

Figure 48 Sessions's grave marker in the Old Hadley Cemetery.

Sessions and Barbara had walked through this cemetery on the day of the Armistice, when he wished the dead could rise again to see that day.

A memorial at The Juilliard School, one in a long tradition of memorials for faculty, was held October 31, 1985, at the Juilliard Theater. The Suite from *The Black Maskers* was conducted by Paul Zukofsky, as well as Stravinsky's Symphonies of Wind Instruments and Schoenberg's Concerto for String Quartet and Orchestra (adapted from Handel, played by the Juilliard String Quartet). Dean Gideon Waldrop, as well as Edward T. Cone and David Diamond, spoke at the beginning of the concert, which was "Dedicated to the Memory of Roger Sessions." President Joseph Polisi, who did not know the composer and had taken over the presidency after Peter Mennin's death in 1983 and Sessions's retirement in 1984, did not attend.

The Fromm Music Foundation presented a concert in Sanders Theater at Harvard in Sessions's memory, November 2, 1985. Robert Helps performed *Pages from a Diary* and the Piano Sonata No. 3, while the Composers String Quartet played the Second Quartet. Despite both the reputation of Harvard as a musicological center and the presence of half-inch black borders on every page of the program, the program notes referred incorrectly to eight symphonies and stated, grotesquely, "Sessions is presently at the Juilliard School of Music [*sic*] in New York."

Other concerts and newspaper articles noted the composer's passing. *The New York Times* announced it with a photograph of the composer on the front page, March 18.[7] The Spring–Summer edition of *Perspectives of New Music* (founded at Princeton during Sessions last years teaching there) devoted the issue to memorial tributes and reminiscences by Milton Babbitt, Arthur Berger, Elliott Carter, Edward T. Cone, Gordon C. Cyr, David Diamond, Joel Feigin, Ross Lee Finney, Vivian Fine, Miriam Gideon, Andrew Imbrie, David Lewin, Frederik Prausnitz, Harold Schiffman, S. Earl Saxton, William O. Smith, and Vincent Persichetti.

Elliott Carter also wrote a commemorative tribute in *Tempo*.[8] Evidently still angry over the negative press about the 1982 Juilliard production of *Montezuma*, Carter complained, "Roger has had hostile reviews in the New York newspapers for many years, to such an extent that even his obituary was used as an opportunity to attack him on the grounds of the very academicism that he inveighed against in his essays."[9]

The Roger Sessions Society, founded by pianist Barry Salwen soon after his death, gave a centennial conference on Sessions's music in 1996 at Elon College in North Carolina. The other newsworthy event of that year was that Sessions would have become a first-time great-grandfather, with the birth of Maxwell Lindsey Peacock, on December 11, Teresa Sessions Peacock's son. The child was born autistic. Julian Peacock was born on July 20, 1998, and Samuel Hunt Peacock on April 2, 2000.

One historian spent ten pages on Sessions in his 1995 book, *The History of American Classical Music*. Of *Montezuma* John Struble wrote, "Sessions clearly showed an affinity for the theatre and for the music as dramatic gesture . . . his rarely staged theatrical works remain among the most effective dramatic music conceived by an American."[10] And "Moreover, *Montezuma*, particularly, forms an important if unintentional bridge from the expressionistic serial atonality of Alban Berg's *Wozzeck* and *Lulu* to the later stage rituals of American composers as diverse as Pauline Oliveros and Philip Glass . . . The framing of violent actions in ritualistic tableaux, characteristic of *Montezuma*'s second act, anticipates similar procedures in Glass's later work, especially *Akhnaten*."[11]

Struble concludes,

Throughout his career Sessions' music, like that of most academic composers, was largely unknown to the American public, and it remains so today. Much of his music is still unpublished (although this is less true of him than of many of his contemporaries), and his influence on the development of American classical music outside of academia has thus far been negligible. However, while Sessions' music rarely inspires affection or enthusiasm among lay listeners, he is held in great respect by most of the musicians who have made any systematic study of his oeuvre, even those few who were not his students or students-of-his-students. . . . His formal designs are deserving of serious study because of their tremendous scope and ingenious structure, and his orchestration, especially after *Montezuma*, is always the work of a master craftsman. While the memorability of his vocal lines is complicated by the serial method, he nevertheless had a strong sense of melody and was capable of extraordinary lyricism within the parameters he imposed on himself. Today serialism is out of fashion and, as a consequence, Sessions' music is likely to languish in oblivion for some time to come. But, once musicians have achieved a more balanced perspective on the historical role played by this unique method of composition, and serial music can be heard in the context of a historical style, there is more than enough substance in Sessions to predict a future revival of interest in his work.[12]

Although, as we have seen, Sessions is not a serialist composer, it is still fair to say that high modernism has fallen on hard times. More recent histories have demoted Sessions. The seventh edition of W. W. Norton's *A History of Western Music* (2005) mentions him only once (under "The University as Patron"), rather than the page devoted to him in the previous editions.[13] Richard Taruskin's six-volume history of music (also 2005) mentions him only a few times.[14] Taruskin is generally unsympathetic to modernism.[15]

At the end Sessions told a friend, "I've had such a wonderful life!"[16] This was due in part, he felt, to his friendships, with Copland, Schoenberg, Stravinsky, Dallapiccola, and many others. He had refused to become a hypocrite and chastise or judge others for sins he himself had committed. He had faced squarely his own failings: "I've been a sinner and a fool." He refrained from speaking negatively about his colleagues' music, considering it unprofessional. He advised students "If you don't stick your neck out, nobody will ever put their arms around it. But if you go out on a limb, all your friends sort of fade away."[17] Like Jean-Christophe Krafft, Sessions outlived his family and many friends. He also outlived composers who were younger than he: Francis Poulenc, Dimitri Shostokovich, Roy Harris, Luigi Dallapiccola, Benjamin Britten, and Samuel Barber. Also like Jean-Christophe, he had reached a plane of detachment in which his ego was not invested in success. His concern for others, kindness, sympathy, and a rock-like hard-won self-realization meant he could both teach and console others. He rose above his own neuroses to be able to help others conquer self-criticism. He clung fast to his upbringing, emphasized by the Episcopalian Huntingtons and by Edward B. Hill, always to remain a "New England gentleman." Roger Sessions may have been one of the last idealistic composers in the twentieth century to subscribe to Romain Rolland's "great composer" theory, as exemplified in *Jean-Christophe*.

NOTES

In citing works in the notes, short titles have generally been used. Books and collections frequently cited are identified by the following abbreviations:

CIM   Cleveland Institute of Music Archives.
COHC   Columbia University Oral History Collection, five interviews with Roger Sessions:
                March 13, 1962 (pp. 1–66); April 12, 1962 (pp. 66–116); April 17, 1962
                (pp. 117–185); May 10, 1962 (pp. 186–338); and October 24, 1962 (pp. 339 to
                the end), conducted by Frank Rounds.
Collected Essays Edward T. Cone, ed. *Roger Sessions; Collected Essays* (Princeton: Princeton
                University Press, 1979).
Conversations Andrea Olmstead, *Conversations with Roger Sessions* (Boston: Northeastern Uni-
                versity Press, 1987. Available at www.AndreaOlmstead.com).
Correspondence Andrea Olmstead, ed. *The Correspondence of Roger Sessions* (Boston: Northeastern
                University Press, 1992. Available at www.AndreaOlmstead.com).
FPRS   Frederik Prausnitz, Roger Sessions, *Roger Sessions: How a "Difficult" Composer got
                that Way* (New York: Oxford University Press, 2002).
HMR   *Harvard Musical Review.*
LCRSC   Library of Congress, Roger Sessions Collection.
RS+HM   Andrea Olmstead, *Roger Sessions and His Music* (Ann Arbor, MI: UMI Research
                Press, 1985. Available at www.AndreaOlmstead.com).
Sixty-Odd   Ruth Sessions, *Sixty-Odd: A Personal History* (Brattleboro, VT: Stephen Daye
                Press, 1936).
The Tin Box Collection Sarah Chapin, ed. *The Tin Box Collection: Letters of Roger Sessions and his
                Family and Friends* (Concord, MA: privately printed, 1992).

INTRODUCTION

1   Stephen Walsh, "The Symphony," *The New Grove Dictionary of Music and Musicians*, rev. edn
    (New York: Oxford University Press, 2001), vol. 24, p. 844.
2   Aaron Copland, "Contemporaries at Oxford, 1931," *Modern Music* 9 (November 1931): 23.
3   Igor Stravinsky, in RS's BMI brochure, 1965.
4   Interview with Leon Kirchner. Arnold Schoenberg to RS, July 17, 1948, in *Correspondence*,
    p. 356.
5   John Harbison and Andrea Olmstead, "RS," *The New Grove Twentieth-Century American Masters*
    (New York: W. W. Norton & Co., 1987), p. 86.
6   Edward T. Cone, "In Defense of Song: The Contribution of RS," *Critical Inquiry* vol. 2 no. 1
    (Autumn 1975): 95. The interior quotation is from RS's *Questions About Music* (New York:
    W. W. Norton & Co., 1970), p. 166.
7   FPRS. The interviews are not dated.
8   RS interview, COHC, p. 188.
9   Andrea Olmstead, "RS: a personal portrait," *Tempo* 127 (December 1978): 13.
10 *Correspondence*, p. xxi.

1 FAMILY HISTORY

Forty Acres and Phelps House

1 The concert program was Lekeu's G major Sonata, (L. Couperin-)Kreisler's violin arrange-ment, Magnard's Movement *lent–calme* (the second US performance), Ravel's *Ondine*, d'Indy's *Laufenburg*, and the Franck A major Sonata.

2 Joint diary/scrapbook of the Red Cross tour kept by Quincy Porter and Bruce Simonds (Simonds writing in the third person), Yale University Music Archives, Porter Papers, mss 15, Series IX, fol. 31, 1, p. 127.

3 Porter diary, p. 127.

4 Porter diary, pp. 127–28.

5 Guestbook, LCRSC, Box 4, fol. 12.

6 RS to George Bartlett, August 12, 1917, *The Tin Box Collection*, p. 150. The Porter–Simonds diary says it was a curtain.

7 Arria S. Huntington, *Under a Colonial Roof-tree: Fireside Chronicles of Early New England* (Boston: Houghton Mifflin, 1891).

8 RS interview, COHC, p. 4.

9 *Conversations*, pp. 155–56. James Lincoln Huntington, *Forty Acres: The Story of the Bishop Huntington House* (New York: Hastings House, 1949).

10 RS to George Bartlett, August 12, 1917, *The Tin Box Collection*, p. 150.

11 Porter, diary, p. 129.

12 *Conversations*, p. 150.

13 RS interview, COHC, p. 8.

14 *Conversations*, pp. 149–50.

15 *Conversations*, pp. 155–56.

16 The eleven children were Charles (1802–1868), Elizabeth (1803–1864), William (1804–1885), Bethia (1805–1879), Edward (1807–1843), John (1809–1832), Theophilus (1811–1862), Theodore (1813–1880?), Mary (1815–1839), Catherine (1817–1830), and Frederic Dan (1819–1904).

17 Hannah Dane Sargent Huntington (1822–1910).

18 Henry Barrett (1875–1965); Constant Davis (1876–1962); Elizabeth (born and died in 1879); James Lincoln (1880–1968); Michael Paul (1882–1967); Charles (born and died in 1885); Catharine Sargent (1897 [born a year and a day after Sessions]–1987); and Frederic Dane (1889–1940).

19 Bishop Huntington's letter to his wife, in *Sixty-Odd*, p. 178.

20 *Conversations*, p. 155.

21 Sarah Chapin, "Introduction," *The Tin Box Collection*, p. 2.

22 *Conversations*, pp. 154–55. Emphasis mine.

23 *Sixty-Odd*, p. 32.

24 *Sixty-Odd*, p. 42.

25 *Sixty-Odd*, p. 43.

26 *Sixty-Odd*, p. 45.

27 *Sixty-Odd*, p. 50.

28 The Forty Acres house now is a museum called the Porter-Phelps-Huntington House. Tours are given daily in the summer, and the furniture is original seventeenth and eighteenth century. Dr James Lincoln Huntington (George's son) had taken care of the home from the 1920s to his death in 1968; a private, non-profit foundation has run it since. Phelps House was run as a farm by Ruth and her son John Sessions from 1929, then by his widow, Dawn, until 1988. She had been an associate curator of Forty Acres since 1968, and from 1977 to 1988 she was the curator of both it and Phelps House. Numerous family papers, diaries, and letters were donated as an extended loan in 1980 to the Amherst College Archives.

29 *Sixty-Odd*, p. 183.

30 *Sixty-Odd*, p. 183.

31 RS interview, COHC, p. 3.

32 John Sessions (October 26, 1820–February 1, 1899) married Elizabeth Phelps Fisher Huntington (March 29, 1825–July 24, 1897) on December 24, 1851.

33 *Sixty-Odd*, p. 336.

34 *Sixty-Odd*, p. 184.
35 John Henry Cardinal Newman (1801–1890) had been an Anglican who published a great deal in that field. He converted to Catholicism and wrote books discussing the philosophy of Catholicism, including *An Essay in Aid of a Grammar of Assent* (1870).
36 *Sixty-Odd*, p. 186.
37 *Sixty-Odd*, p. 188.
38 *Sixty-Odd*, p. 190.
39 *Sixty-Odd*, p. 194.
40 *Sixty-Odd*, p. 195.
41 *Sixty-Odd*, p. 198.
42 Sarah Chapin, "Introduction," p. 2.
43 RS interview, COHC, p. 25.
44 *Sixty-Odd*, p. 247. The incident is elaborated in *RS+HM*, pp. 6–7, and Ruth's letter is given in full in "Suddenly . . . music!" *The Christian Science Monitor* (November 12, 1975). Letter dated Thursday in Holy Week, 1883.
45 *Sixty-Odd*, p. 253.
46 *Sixty-Odd*, p. 255.
47 *Sixty-Odd*, p. 262.
48 *Sixty-Odd*, p. 262.
49 Archibald Sessions to George Huntington, October 1, 1885, Porter-Phelps-Huntington Family Papers, Amherst Archives, Box 127, fol. 3.
50 Archibald Sessions to Ruth Huntington, September 13, 1887, Porter-Phelps-Huntington Family Papers, Amherst Archives, Box 127, fol. 5.
51 *Sixty-Odd*, p. 272.

Archibald Sessions

1 *Conversations*, p. 151. Also RS interview, COHC, p. 28.
2 FPRS, p. 5. As stated in the Introduction, this author is more prepared to rely on statements made earlier than those at the very end of his life.
3 Clara Fisher Sessions married Edwin W. Wheeler (1845–1922) on October 22, 1885. Elizabeth Fisher Wheeler was born September 25, 1886, and Edwin Sessions Wheeler was born July 11, 1891, and died in 1960(?).
4 Edwin Sessions Wheeler, a civil and metallurgical engineer, who worked for International Nickel, married, on December 3, 1929, Mildred Hunting, born June 11, 1895. They had two children: Richard Hunting Wheeler (b. 1931) and Elizabeth Hunting Wheeler (b. 1932). Richard Wheeler married Barbara Hodges. Elizabeth Hunting Wheeler became an ordained Congregationalist minister and later ran the Porter-Phelps-Huntington Foundation. Helen McCoy Wheeler lived to 101: 1894–1995.
5 Grace Sessions married Franklin Hooper (1862–1940) on October 19, 1887.
6 Catherine Hooper was born May 26, 1889; Leverett Hooper was born February 5, 1893. Leverett, Sessions's cousin and classmate at Harvard, became a Wall Street banker and eventually Vice President of the First National Bank. He married Lucia Gates in 1921 and adopted two children, Gerald Huntington (b. 1932) and Gail Hooper (b. 1936).
7 In a coincidence between the author and her subject, this author's wedding reception was held at a friend's loft at 140 Nassau Street, in 1982.
8 *Conversations*, p. 148. This is a somewhat simplistic view of Blaine.
9 RS interview, COHC, p. 8.
10 See Mary Cable, *The Blizzard of '88* (New York: Atheneum, 1998).
11 *Sixty-Odd*, p. 277.
12 *Sixty-Odd*, p. 284.
13 *Sixty-Odd*, pp. 294–95.
14 *Sixty-Odd*, p. 295.
15 *Sixty-Odd*, p. 296.
16 *Sixty-Odd*, p. 296.
17 Quoted in FPRS, p. 5.
18 *Sixty-Odd*, p. 297.
19 Harvard class of 1883 fourth report, 1900.

20 Hooper retired in 1938 and was killed, at age 78. "Franklin H. Hooper is Killed by Truck," *The New York Times* (August 15, 1940): 25.
21 Archibald moved to a job (in "ins[urance?]") at 302 Broadway; he lived in 1901–1902 at 131st Street, James Place, Brooklyn.
22 Quoted in FPRS, p. 7.
23 Chapin, "Introduction," p. ix.

417 Washington Avenue

 1 RS interview, November 13, 1979, NYC.
 2 Quoted in Edwin G. Burrows and Mike Wallace, *Gotham: A History of New York City to 1898* (New York: Oxford University Press, 1999): 1173. Some of this discussion is taken from this source.
 3 Quoted in Burrows and Wallace, *Gotham*, p. 1178.
 4 Years later, when Archibald edited *Ainslee's Magazine*, a man from the deep south submited the same story, thinking he would not be caught plagiarizing.
 5 *Sixty-Odd*, pp. 330–31.
 6 "Consumer's League Meets," *Brooklyn Daily Eagle* (December 4, 1896): 14.
 7 *Sixty-Odd*, p. 326.
 8 RS interview, COHC, p. 10.
 9 Lois Mandel, *New York Herald Tribune* (Sunday, January 30, 1966): sec. 2, p. 3.
10 Richard F. Shepard, "The Brooklyn Crowd on Mount Parnassus," *The New York Times* (February 21, 1971): BQ75, 94.
11 *Conversations*. I visited the house and met its occupant on April 14, 2005. She showed me the two newspaper articles cited here as well as others about Sessions. She asked me to sign *Conversations*.
12 *Sixty-Odd*, p. 328.
13 See *Sixty-Odd*, page 398; "I was proud of my young son's [John's] managerial achievement and now and then indulged a secret hope, developed from my own love of the soil, that I might one day see him squire of Phelps Farm." This was written when John was a Harvard student. Ruth did nevertheless rob John of his future and confine him to Phelps Farm.
14 *Sixty-Odd*, p. 329.
15 *Sixty-Odd*, p. 331.
16 Sessions's baptism was number 2,243 recorded in the Registry (vol. 5) of St Mary's, which had been established in 1836.
17 *Sixty-Odd*, p. 332.
18 *Sixty-Odd*, p. 332.
19 *Sixty-Odd*, p. 345.
20 *Sixty-Odd*, p. 326.
21 *Sixty-Odd*, p. 342.
22 *Sixty-Odd*, p. 343.
23 *Sixty-Odd*, p. 346.
24 *Sixty-Odd*, pp. 348–49.
25 *Conversations*, p. 150.
26 *Sixty-Odd*, p. 349.
27 *Sixty-Odd*, p. 350.
28 "The Brooklyn Crowd," *The New York Times*, p. 94.
29 *Conversations*, p. 150.

109 Elm Street

 1 *Sixty-Odd*, p. 362.
 2 *Sixty-Odd*, p. 368.
 3 Chapin, "Introduction," p. 2.
 4 Chapin, "Introduction," p. 2 note 4.
 5 *Conversations*, p. 155.
 6 *Conversations*, p. 155.
 7 *Sixty-Odd*, p. 375.

8 Quoted in FPRS, p. 295.
9 *Sixty-Odd*, p. 377.
10 Listed in the 1900 Northampton/Easthampton city directory, p. 215.
11 RS interview, COHC, p. 19.
12 RS interview, COHC, pp. 19–20. In fact, his examination scores would not have let him enter at 13; see Harvard section pp. 52–53.
13 *Sixty-Odd*, p. 385.

Cloyne, Kingsley, and Kent

1 *Sixty-Odd*, p. 377.
2 Arthur Leslie Green was born in July 1868 in Illinois. He was listed as single during the 1900 census, but as widowed in the 1920 census. It appears that he died in 1949. Little else has been discovered about him.
3 A sense of the social class that attended Cloyne can be gleaned from a perusal of the names of some of Sessions's classmates of 1906–1907: Van Clef Herrin, Huntington Erhart, Arthur Eaton, Winthrop Brooks, Worthington Davis, Chamberlain Brown, Cleve Cox, Heywood Cutting, and Sloan Walker.
4 *Cloyne Magazine*, no. 1 (October 1900) is the first issue.
5 *Cloyne Magazine*, 15 no. 6 (June 1912): 151.
6 *Cloyne Magazine*, 10 no. 1 (October 1906): 20.
7 *Cloyne Magazine*, 10 no. 1 (October 1906): 24.
8 *Cloyne Magazine*, 10 no. 2 (November 1906): 49.
9 RS interview, COHC, p. 12.
10 RS interview, COHC, pp. 13–14.
11 RS interview, COHC, pp. 15–16.
12 *Cloyne Magazine*, 10 no. 3 (December 1906): 69.
13 *Cloyne Magazine*, 10 no. 3 (December 1906): 80.
14 RS interview, COHC, p. 17.
15 *Cloyne Magazine*, 10 no. 3 (December 1906): 72–73.
16 FPRS, p. 32.
17 *Sixty-Odd*, pp. 377–78.
18 *Cloyne Magazine*, 15 no. 5 (May 1912): 123.
19 RS to Father Frederick Sill, December 1912, *Correspondence*, p. 8.
20 *Conversations*, pp. 151–52.
21 (1858–1924) Harvard Class of 1881, eighth report (1931), p. 187.
22 Campbell to Ruth Sessions, January 9, 1907, LCRSC, Box 2, fol. 2.
23 Quoted in FPRS, p. 33.
24 Quoted in FPRS, p. 33.
25 FPRS, pp. 33–34.
26 RS interview, COHC, p. 18.
27 RS interview, COHC, p. 18.
28 Ruth Sessions to Father Sill, May 15, 1908.
29 Quoted in William H. Armstrong, "The Miracle in Algo's Shadow," *Kent Quarterly* 8, no. 1 (Fall 1988): 28.
30 Anson Gardner, "The Most Unforgettable Character I've Met," *Reader's Digest* (January 1961): 2.
31 Quoted in Gardner, "The Most Unforgettable," p. 3.
32 RS interview, COHC, p. 19.
33 RS to Ruth Sessions, no date, Porter-Phelps-Huntington Papers, Amherst archives, box 127 fol. 20.
34 Archibald Sessions to Father Sill, November 14, 1908.
35 RS to Father Sill, July 31, 1910.
36 Ruth Sessions to Father Sill, December 13, 1908.
37 RS, "The Music of Wagner's 'The Nibelung's Ring'," unpublished manuscript.
38 Ruth Sessions to Father Sill, March 11, 1910.
39 Reproduced as an illustration in *Correspondence*, p. 8.
40 Ruth Sessions to Father Sill, November 10, 1910.

41 Quoted in Judson Scruton, "Roger H. Sessions: 1896–1985," *Kent News* 71, no. 8 (April 20, 1985): 1.

42 Ruth Sessions to Father Sill, January 5, 1911.

43 Ruth Sessions to Father Sill, January 25, 1911.

44 Ruth Sessions to Mr Hobbie (in the absence of Father Sill), January 30, 1911.

45 RS interview, COHC, p. 50.

Harvard

1 Untaped conversation, March 1, 1978, NYC.

2 RS, *Lancelot and Elaine*, Princeton University Department of Rare Books and Special Collections, CO 288 vol. 6.

3 *Conversations*, p. 151.

4 Quoted in FPRS, p. 49.

5 Quoted in Janet Baker-Carr, "A Conversation with Roger Sessions," *Harvard Magazine* (April 1976): 46.

6 Percy Goetschius, *The Larger Forms of Musical Composition* (NY: G. Schirmer, 1915). Goetschius wrote numerous books.

7 See Andrea Olmstead, *Juilliard: A History* (Champaign, Ill.: University of Illinois Press, 1999).

8 Lowell's new entrance requirements were as follows: 1) a candidate must present evidence of an approved school course satisfactorily completed, and 2) must show in four examinations (see text for list) that his scholarship is of a satisfactory quality a) that his course work has extended over four years, b) that his course has been concerned chiefly with languages, science, mathematics and history, no one of which has been omitted, and c) that two of the studies of his school program have been pursued beyond elementary stages, that is, to the stage required by the present advanced examinations of Harvard College or the equivalent examinations. Catalog, Harvard archives, HUC 911. 3.

9 Harvard University, Reports of the President and Treasurer of Harvard College, 1911–12, pp. 77–79.

10 John T. Bethell, *Harvard Observed* (Cambridge, MA: Harvard University Press, 1998), pp. 54–59.

11 Walter Raymond Spalding, *Music at Harvard; A Historical Review of Men and Events* (New York: Coward-McGann, Inc., 1935), p. 159. Spalding, writing in 1935, points to Foote, Paine, Converse, and Carpenter as illustrious graduates, in part by including photographs of them. Although reasonably well known by 1935, Sessions was mentioned only once, as one of four Harvard graduates to receive the Rome Prize (the others were Randall Thompson, Walter Helfer, and Alexander Steinert).

12 At Princeton University's Rare Books and Special Collections is found a box (CO 288, box 21) of "miscellaneous sketches, 1911–1936." In it is a "projected symphony, 1911–12."

13 *Harvard University Gazette* (March 24, 1962), quoted in Elliot Forbes, *A History of Music at Harvard to 1972* (Harvard University: Department of Music, 1988), p. 68.

14 No date, FPRS, p. 43.

15 George Bartlett to RS, October 15, 1915, *The Tin Box Collection*, p. 36.

16 *Sixty-Odd*, p. 384.

17 RS quoted in Baker-Carr, *Harvard Magazine* (April 1976): 44–49.

18 For more on James Loeb and the IMA, see Olmstead, "The toll of idealism: James Loeb—musician, classicist, philanthropist," *Journal of Musicology* 14 (Spring 1996): 233–62. Also Olmstead, *Juilliard: A History*.

19 In 1958 the Opera House was torn down and replaced by a Northeastern University building.

20 Philip Hale, quoted in M. A. DeWolfe Howe, *The Boston Symphony Orchestra; 1881–1931* (Boston: Houghton Mifflin, 1931), p. 131.

21 Untaped conversation, March 14, 1978, NYC.

22 Karl Muck programmed the Sibelius Symphony No. 4 in A minor, op. 63, twice during Sessions's time at Harvard: October 24 and 25, 1912, at the Symphony, and November 13, 1913, at Sanders Theater, as well as November 13 and 14, 1914.

23 RS interview, COHC, pp. 36–37.

24 RS interview, COHC, p. 38.

25 The orchestra would not play the work again until 1958 under Richard Burgin.

26 RS interview, COHC, p. 39.

27 Quoted in Edward T. Cone, "Conversation with Roger Sessions," *Perspectives on American Composers*, eds Edward T. Cone and Benjamin Boretz (New York: W. W. Norton & Co., 1970), p. 91. Originally published in *Perspectives of New Music*, 1966.

28 RS to Ruth Sessions, FPRS, pp. 44–45. Pages 46 and 47 show the original handwritten letter. Prausnitz does not provide dates for many of his cited letters, possibly because they did not appear on the letters themselves. This sounds like an early Harvard letter, if for no other reason than later, Roger addressed Ruth simply as "Dear Mother."

29 Quoted in FPRS, probably late December 1914, pp. 45, 46, and 47.

30 G. B. Weston, 1897, had beat him to it; he wrote a review of *Harmonielehre* in the November 1912 *Harvard Musical Review*, p. 22.

31 Harvard Class of 1915 Freshman Red Book.

32 *Sixty Odd*, p. 406.

33 RS to Father Sill, November 21, 1911.

34 RS interview, COHC, p. 20.

35 RS interview, COHC, p. 21.

36 John T. Bethell, "Prodigies," *Harvard Observed* (Cambridge, MA: Harvard University Press, 1998), p. 49.

37 RS to Father Sill, November 21, 1911.

38 RS interview, COHC, p. 48.

39 RS interview, COHC, p. 49.

40 RS interview, COHC, p. 50.

41 Quoted in FPRS, no date, p. 55.

42 *Conversations*, p. 156.

43 Cone, "Conversation with RS," *Perspectives*, p. 91.

44 Edward B. Hill to Miss MacReady, February 23, 1915, quoted in Paul Anderson, "An analysis of the aesthetic writings of Aaron Copland and Roger Sessions," Ph.D. diss., Brandeis University, 2004, p. 183.

45 RS to Father Sill, spring 1912.

46 Ruth Sessions to Dean Henry A. Yeomans, May 7, 1912, Sessions student file, Harvard archives. UAIII 15.88.10.

47 He probably studied with the BSO's second oboist, C. Lenom; the principal was Georges Longy.

48 One is reproduced in manuscript in FPRS, p. 54.

49 Untaped conversation, March 14, 1978, NYC.

50 Quoted in FPRS, no date, p. 54.

51 RS to Father Sill, before March 1914.

52 Psychology A 2 and Philosophy A, B, or C were regular Freshman courses, would not be counted toward a degree if taken by seniors, and would only count if taken in the same year as each other. When Loewenberg was a professor at the University of California 32 years later, he met Sessions, who said, "You know, you flunked me in philosophy at Harvard." RS interview, COHC, p. 45. Loewenberg expressed astonishment that Sessions could have become a full professor at Berkeley and yet have flunked his Philosophy course.

53 Harvard University Catalogue, 1912, p. 365.

54 Letter from A. H. Herrick to the Dean, February 5, 1914, in E. W. Lombard file at the Harvard archives. UAIII15.88.10

55 His annotated copy of *King Henry IV*, Part I, 1915, is at Yale's Beinecke Library.

56 Sessions class record, Harvard archives. UAIII 15.75.12

57 *Conversations*, p. 157.

58 "Ragnar Brovik" [a pseudonym], "The younger generation," *HMR* 3, no. 4 (January 1915): 17–18; and unsigned (by RS?), "Some facts and opinions about Siegfried," *HMR* 3, no. 8 (May 1915): 19–21.

59 RS to Father Sill, approximately fall 1914.

60 RS to Father Sill, before Thanksgiving 1914.

61 Ruth Sessions to B. S. Hurlbert, January 9, 1914 [*sic*; 1915], Sessions student file, Harvard archives, UAIII 15.88.10.

62 Archibald Sessions to B. S. Hurlbert, January 16, 1915, Sessions student file, Harvard archives, UAIII 15.88.10.

63 B. S. Hurlbert to Archibald Sessions, January 21, 1915, Sessions student file, Harvard archives, UAIII 15.88.10.
64 B. S. Hurlbert to Ruth Sessions, January 15, 1915, Sessions student file, Harvard archives, UAIII 15.88.10.
65 RS to Ruth Sessions, 1915, FPRS, p. 51.
66 *Conversations*, p. 158.
67 *Conversations*, p. 158.
68 Quoted by Bethell, *Harvard Observed*, p. 71.
69 RS to George Bartlett, probably September 28, 1915, *The Tin Box Collection*, p. 28.
70 Ruth Sessions to RS, October 19, 1915, *The Tin Box Collection*, p. 39.
71 RS to Father Sill, fall 1912.
72 RS to Father Sill, November 21, 1911.
73 Gardner's guest book, Fenway Court. Isabella Stewart Gardner Museum archives.
74 Both letters are quoted, with deletions, no dates, FPRS, pp. 52–53.
75 Sessions, "Euripides and Mr. Barker," *The Harvard Monthly* (July 1915): 127, 129, 130.
76 RS to Ruth Sessions, no dates, FPRS, p. 53.

Harvard Musical Review

1 Therefore Sessions's first academic probation would not have affected his ability to write for the magazine; he came off probation October 8, 1912, just as the *Review* had begun publishing.
2 The poet Samuel Foster Damon taught English at Brown and was known for his work on William Blake. For musicians he is most important as the editor of *Old American Songs*, a collection of facsimiles which gave Aaron Copland's two sets of *Old American Songs* both its title and several of the actual songs Copland arranged.
3 Walter Raymond Spalding, *Music at Harvard: A Historical Review of Men and Events* (New York: Coward-McGann, Inc., 1935), p. 250.
4 RS, "Wagner's opinions of other composers," *HMR* 1, no. 8 (May 1913): 17–20.
5 RS interview, COHC, pp. 66–67.
6 RS interview, COHC, p. 68.
7 RS interview, COHC, p. 68.
8 RS, *Reflections on the Music Life in the United States* (New York: Merlin, 1956), pp. 43–44. Lectures translated from the Italian.
9 RS, *Reflections*, p. 126.
10 RS interview, COHC, p. 71.
11 Chapin, editor, *The Tin Box Collection*, p. 4.
12 RS, "Wagner's opinions of other composers," *HMR* 1, no. 8 (May 1913): 17–20.
13 RS, "The case against professional music criticism," *HMR* 2, no. 2 (November 1913): 3–6.
14 RS, "The case against," p. 4.
15 RS to Ruth Sessions, November 1913, FPRS, p. 49.
16 Unsigned editorial, "Musical review criticized," *The Harvard Crimson* (December 2, 1913) (online version, no pagination).
17 FPRS, p. 117.
18 Editorial, *HMR* 2, no. 3 (December 1913): 23–24.
19 RS, "Our attitude towards contemporary musical tendencies," *HMR* 2, no. 4 (January 1914): 3–6, 23.
20 RS to Ruth Sessions, December 1913, FPRS, p. 50.
21 RS, "Our attitude towards contemporary musical tendencies," 5.
22 RS review of "*Symphonies and Their Meaning* by Philip H. Goepp, Philadelphia: Lippincott, 1914," *HMR* 2, no. 5 (February 1914): 22.
23 RS, "New Boston Opera House productions," *HMR* 2, no. 5 (February 1914): 17. *Meistersinger* was given on January 23, 1914.
24 RS, "Parsifaliana," *HMR* 2, no. 6 (March 1914): 13–15.
25 RS, editorial, *HMR* 3, no. 4 (January 1914): 13–14.
26 "Ragnar Brovik," "Communications; the younger generation," *HMR* 3, no. 4 (January 1915): 17–18.
27 Ernest Newman, *Wagner as Man and Artist* (London: 1914, revised 1924 and 1963).
28 RS, "A new Wagner essay," *HMR* 2, no. 3 (November 1914): 3–7.

29 RS, "The psychological basis of modern dissonance," *HMR* 3, no. 3 (December 1914): 3–10.
30 RS, editorial, *HMR*, 3, no. 3 (December 1914): 16.
31 RS, "Fifty years of Richard Strauss—I," *HMR* 2, no. 8 (May 1914): 15.
32 RS interviewed in Cole Gagne and Tracy Caras, *Soundpieces; Interviews with American Composers* (Metuchen, NJ: Scarecrow Press, 1982), p. 361. Interview November 19, 1975, NYC.
33 Frederik van den Arend, "The retort courteous," *HMR* 2, no. 9 (June 1914): 16–18. George Bartlett wrote a hilarious review of "Advice to singers," *HMR* 3, no. 3 (December 1914): 18–19.
34 RS, "Fifty years—I," p. 15.
35 RS, "Fifty years of Richard Strauss—II," *HMR* 2, no. 9 (June 1914): 20.
36 RS, "Fifty years—I," p. 17.
37 RS, "Fifty years of Richard Strauss—III," *HMR* 2, no. 10 (July 1914): 25.
38 RS, "Fifty years—I," p. 17.
39 RS, "Fifty years—I," p. 14.
40 RS, "Fifty years—I," p. 18.
41 RS, "Fifty years of Richard Strauss—III," p. 19.
42 RS, "Richard Strauss as a tone poet," *HMR* 4, no. 1 (October 1915): 4.
43 RS, "Richard Strauss as a tone poet," p. 4.
44 RS, "Richard Strauss as a tone poet—III," *HMR* 4, no. 3 (December 1915): 11.
45 RS, "Richard Strauss as a tone poet," p. 5.
46 RS, "Richard Strauss as a tone poet," p. 6. The Parker quote was taken from *North American Review* (April 1910), according to Sessions's footnote.
47 RS, "Richard Strauss as a tone poet—II," *HMR* 4, no. 2 (November 1915): 15.
48 RS, "Richard Strauss as a tone poet—III," p. 11.
49 *The Harvard Crimson*, unsigned editorial (March 23, 1916) (online version, no pagination).

2 YALE THROUGH THE CLEVELAND INSTITUTE

Yale

1 RS to George Bartlett (GB), probably September 17, 1915, *The Tin Box Collection*, p. 24.
2 Hannah Sessions to RS, September 29, 1915, *The Tin Box Collection*, p. 32.
3 See the Porter–Simonds 1917 diary at Yale's Gilmore Library.
4 RS to GB, July 9, 1915, *Correspondence*, p. 9.
5 Louis Auchincloss, introduction to *Jean-Christophe*, by Romain Rolland (New York: Carroll & Graff Publishers, 1996), pp. vi–vii.
6 David Sices, *Music and the Musician in* Jean-Christophe; *The Harmony of Contrasts* (New Haven: Yale University Press, 1968), p. 50.
7 Paul Anderson, "An analysis of the aesthetic writings of Aaron Copland and Roger Sessions" (Ph.D. diss., Brandeis University, 2004), p. 44.
8 Sices, *Music and the Musician*, pp. 66–67.
9 Romain Rolland, *Jean-Christophe*, "The Dawn" (New York: Carroll & Graff Publishers, 1996), p. 91.
10 Anderson, "An analysis of the aesthetic writings," p. 32.
11 RS to GB, probably March 7, 1916, *The Tin Box Collection*, p. 89.
12 Anderson, "An analysis of the aesthetic writings," pp. 51–52.
13 Sices, *Music and the Musician*, p. 77. Recall the baby Roger's early fear of descending staircases.
14 Sices, *Music and the Musician*, p. 89.
15 See letters exchanged between RS and Mann in *Correspondence*, pp. 359–62.
16 Hillyer won a Pulitzer Prize for poetry in 1934 and taught at Harvard.
17 RS to GB, probably November 1916, *The Tin Box Collection*, p. 122.
18 RS to GB, July 19, 1915, *The Tin Box Collection*, p. 7. More information on this collection appears in the section on George Bartlett.
19 RS to GB, August 12, 1915, Hadley, MA, *The Tin Box Collection*, p. 14.
20 John Burk on GB, Harvard Class of 1918, 25th Anniversary Report, pp. 45–46.
21 Van was born October 5, 1894, and died October 8, 1979, at 85.
22 Frederik Francis van den Arend to RS, probably August 10, 1915, *The Tin Box Collection*, p. 12. He later dropped the Francis from his name.

23 RS to GB, November 2, 1915, *The Tin Box Collection*, p. 56.
24 Ruth Sessions to RS, May 17, 1916, *The Tin Box Collection*, p. 97.
25 RS to GB, probably late December 1916/early January 1917, *The Tin Box Collection*, pp. 125–26.
26 RS to GB, March 3, 1917, *The Tin Box Collection*, p. 131.
27 RS to GB, October 29, 1915, *The Tin Box Collection*, p. 49.
28 RS, *Reflections on the Music Life in the United States* (New York: Merlin, 1956), pp. 142–43. Translated from the Italian (no translator given).
29 Gilbert Chase, *America's Music: From the Pilgrims to the Present*, rev. third edn (Champaign: University of Illinois Press, 1987), p. 380.
30 RS to GB, late October 1915, *Correspondence*, pp. 16–17.
31 Cone, "Conversation with Roger Sessions," *Perspectives*, p. 92.
32 RS interview, COHC, p. 74.
33 RS interview, COHC, pp. 75 and 77.
34 Archibald Sessions to RS, October 22, 1915, *Correspondence*, p. 17.
35 Archibald Sessions to RS, October 7, 1915, *The Tin Box Collection*, p. 33.
36 Archibald Sessions to RS, October 9, 1915, LCRSC, Box 4, fol. 1.
37 Ruth Sessions to RS, October 8, 1915, *The Tin Box Collection*, p. 34.
38 RS to GB, October 29, 1915, *The Tin Box Collection*, p. 48.
39 RS to GB, approximately November, 1915, *The Tin Box Collection*, p. 63.
40 RS to GB, February 2, 1917, *The Tin Box Collection*, p. 129.
41 RS to GB, probably May 17, 1917, *The Tin Box Collection*, p. 144.
42 Archibald Sessions to RS, February 3, 1916, *The Tin Box Collection*, p. 82.
43 Quoted in William F. Kearns, *Horatio Parker, 1863–1919* (Metuchen, NJ: Scarecow Press, Inc., 1990), p. 36.
44 RS to Ruth Sessions, fall 1916, quoted in FPRS, p. 59.
45 RS to Father Sill, November 7, 1915.
46 Archibald Sessions to RS, December 3, 1915, *The Tin Box Collection*, p. 67.
47 GB to RS, December 10, 1915, *The Tin Box Collection*, p. 67.
48 RS to GB, probably late December 1915, *The Tin Box Collection*, p. 73.
49 RS to GB, probably March 7, 1916, *The Tin Box Collection*, p. 87.
50 RS to GB, probably January 3, 1916, *The Tin Box Collection*, p. 77.
51 RS to GB, January 16, 1916, *The Tin Box Collection*, pp. 78–79.
52 RS to Father Sill, January 14, 1917.
53 Ruth Sessions to RS, January 16, 1917, *The Tin Box Collection*, p. 159.
54 *Sixty-Odd*, p. 395.
55 Ruth Sessions to RS, February 9, 1916, *The Tin Box Collection*, p. 82.
56 Ruth Sessions to RS, March 17, 1916, *The Tin Box Collection*, p. 91.
57 Ruth Sessions to RS, no date, *The Tin Box Collection*, p. 170.
58 RS to GB, probably March 26, 1916, *The Tin Box Collection*, p. 93.
59 RS to GB, probably March 26, 1916, *The Tin Box Collection*, p. 93. Perhaps writing the dance movement from *The Black Maskers* fulfilled this desire for Sessions.
60 Archibald Sessions to RS, April 21, 1916, *The Tin Box Collection*, pp. 96–97.
61 Ruth Sessions to RS, May 17, 1916, *The Tin Box Collection*, p. 98.
62 RS, "To the Editor of the Holy Cross Magazine," July 24, 1916.
63 John Burk to RS, probably summer 1916, *The Tin Box Collection*, p. 102.
64 Van to RS, July 14, 1917, *The Tin Box Collection*, p. 180.
65 Van to RS, October 31, 1916, *The Tin Box Collection*, p. 120.
66 RS to GB, September 29–October 2, 1916, *The Tin Box Collection*, p. 112.
67 RS to GB, probably March 1917, *The Tin Box Collection*, p. 137
68 RS to GB, December 14, 1916, *The Tin Box Collection*, p. 124.
69 RS to GB, September 1, 1917, LCRSC, Box 5, fol. 2.
70 GB to RS, July 8, 1919, *The Tin Box Collection*, p. 204.
71 RS to GB, August 25, 1916, *The Tin Box Collection*, p. 106.
72 *Sixty-Odd*, p. 164.
73 Martha Bianchi first published "Selections from the unpublished letters of Emily Dickinson to her brother's family," *Atlantic Monthly* XV (1915): 35–42. She edited *The Life and Letters of Emily Dickinson* (Boston: Houghton Mifflin, 1925), *Poems by Emily Dickinson*, with Alfred L.

Hampson (Boston: Little Brown, 1937), *Emily Dickinson Face to Face: Unpublished Letters with Notes and Reminiscences* (Boston: Houghton Mifflin, 1932), and *Unpublished Poems of Emily Dickinson* (Boston: Little, Brown, 1932).

74 RS to GB, August 12, 1917, *The Tin Box Collection*, p. 148.
75 RS to GB, September 12, 1917, *The Tin Box Collection*, p. 156.
76 Ruth Sessions to RS, October 29, 1916, *The Tin Box Collection*, p. 102.
77 RS to GB, probably November 1916, *The Tin Box Collection*, p. 120.
78 RS to GB, probably November 1916, *The Tin Box Collection*, p. 121.
79 RS to GB, probably November 1916, *The Tin Box Collection*, pp. 121–22.
80 RS to Father Sill, December 13, 1916.
81 RS to GB, January 9, 1917, *The Tin Box Collection*, p. 127.
82 RS to GB, February 2, 1917, *The Tin Box Collection*, p. 129.
83 RS to GB, probably March 1917, *The Tin Box Collection*, p. 137.

World War I

1 RS to Ruth Sessions, quoted in FPRS, p. 61.
2 Van to RS, March 21, 1917, *The Tin Box Collection*, p. 170. Van probably means 1898, the year of the Spanish–American War.
3 *Sixty-Odd*, p. 388.
4 RS to GB, April 9, 1917, *The Tin Box Collection*, p. 139.
5 Ruth Sessions to RS, April 8, 1917, *The Tin Box Collection*, p. 173.
6 Ruth Sessions to RS, April 16, 1917, *The Tin Box Collection*, p. 174.
7 RS to GB, probably May 7, 1917, *The Tin Box Collection*, p. 142.
8 GB to RS, May 11, 1917, *The Tin Box Collection*, p. 176.
9 RS to GB, probably May 17, 1917, *The Tin Box Collection*, p. 143.
10 RS to GB, probably May 21, 1917, *The Tin Box Collection*, p. 145.
11 The other composers were Ruth Caldwell Monson (an Overture, probably conducted by Parker), Douglas Stuart Moore (Fantasie Polonaise, conducted by Moore), Charles Arthur Hackney (Overture, conducted by Hackney), Mildred Sylvester Thomas (Overture, she conducted), Sessions's Symphonic Prelude (conducted by Parker), and Walter Alfred Allen (Overture, conducted by the composer).
12 Ropartz (1864–1955) was a friend of Magnard and pupil of Franck.
13 Philip Greeley Clapp (1888–1954) to RS, June 1, 1917, *The Tin Box Collection*, pp. 187–88.
14 RS to GB, July 11, 1917, *The Tin Box Collection*, p. 146.
15 Van to RS, May 17, 1917, *The Tin Box Collection*, p. 178.
16 RS to GB, after August 14, 1917, *The Tin Box Collection*, p. 149.
17 Van to RS, May 17, 1917, *The Tin Box Collection*, p. 177.
18 Dos Passos published *Streets of Night* in 1923, a novel of his Harvard period.
19 John Dos Passos, *An Informal Memoir: The Best of Times* (New York: The New American Library, 1966), p. 42.
20 Cummings's imprisonment led to his memoir *The Enormous Room*.
21 Van to RS, August 21, 1917, *The Tin Box Collection*, p. 183.
22 Van to RS, August 15, 1917, *The Tin Box Collection*, p. 182.
23 Van to RS, July 14, 1917, *The Tin Box Collection*, p. 178.
24 Dos Passos, undated, to Arthur McComb, cited in Melvin Landsberg, *Dos Passos's Path to U.S.A.* (Boulder: The Colorado Associated University Press, 1972), p. 52. In a second letter to McComb, July 20, 1917, Dos again asked if Sessions was jailed.
25 RS to GB, after August 14, 1917, *The Tin Box Collection*, p. 147.
26 RS to GB, after August 14, 1917, *The Tin Box Collection*, p. 148.
27 RS to GB, after August 14, 1917, *The Tin Box Collection*, p. 148.
28 RS to GB, September 4, 1917, *The Tin Box Collection*, p. 153.
29 RS to GB, September 12, 1917, *The Tin Box Collection*, p. 155.
30 Emile Verhaeren's (1855–1916) *Poems of Emile Verhaeren, Selected and Rendered into English by Alma Strettell* (London: J. Lane, 1915) reproduces a portrait of Verhaeren by John Singer Sargent.
31 RS interview, April 4, 1978, NYC.
32 RS interview, COHC, p. 59.

33 RS, "Russian choral music at Smith," *Smith College Monthly* 26, no. 1 (October 1918): 1–4. Ivan Gorohkov (1879–1949) had been choirmaster at the cathedral in Kursk before coming to New York in 1912 to direct the choir in the Russian Cathedral. He taught at Smith from 1918 to 1945.

34 RS to GB, November 18, 1918, *Correspondence*, p. 20.

35 RS to GB, September 12, 1917, *The Tin Box Collection*, p. 155.

36 RS to GB, January 21, 1919, *The Tin Box Collection*, pp. 234–35.

37 Sleeper was an organist, composer, and ordained minister, who had studied at Harvard and taught at Smith 1899–1924.

38 RS interview, COHC, p. 98.

39 RS interview, April 4, 1978, NYC.

40 RS interview, COHC, p. 96.

41 RS interview, COHC, p. 59.

42 *Sixty-Odd*, p. 389. Sessions began wearing glasses at Harvard.

43 *Sixty-Odd*, p. 393.

44 The Delpit letter, the newspaper clipping, and a draft of Sessions's letter to her are found at the LCRSC, Box 2, fol. 1. Louise Delpit taught French at Smith from 1908–1940.

45 RS to GB, September 29, 1917, *Correspondence*, pp. 24–25.

46 RS to GB, September 29, 1917, *Correspondence*, pp. 25–26.

47 RS to GB, probably January 7, 1918, *The Tin Box Collection*, p. 197.

48 See Barbara Tischler, "One hundred percent Americanism and music in Boston during World War I," *American Music* 4, no. 2 (Summer 1986): 164–76.

49 RS to Father Sill, November 25, 1918. Part of this letter is reprinted in *Kent Quarterly* (Winter 1986): 4.

50 RS to Father Sill, August 4, 1918, *Correspondence*, p. 19.

51 RS, "Artists and this war: a letter to an imaginary colleague," *Modern Music* 20, no. 1, pp. 3–7; repr. in *Collected Essays*, pp. 313–18.

52 RS, "Artists and this war," pp. 313–14.

53 *Conversations*, pp. 158–59.

54 Archibald Sessions to RS, July 14, 1918, LCRSC, Box 4, fol. 4.

55 RS to Father Sill, August 4, 1918.

56 Father Sill to RS, September 9, 1918.

57 RS to Father Sill, September 14, 1918.

58 RS to Father Sill, probably November 1918, *Correspondence*, p. 28. See *Kent Quarterly* (Winter 1986): 4–5, for Sessions's glowing response to the visit and Pater's letter to him.

59 RS to GB, probably May 10, 1918, *The Tin Box Collection*, p. 200.

60 GB to RS, June 10, 1918, *The Tin Box Collection*, p. 200.

61 RS to GB, probably June 21, 1918, *The Tin Box Collection*, p. 202.

62 GB to RS, July 8, 1918, *The Tin Box Collection*, pp. 203–04.

63 GB to RS, July 18, 1918, *The Tin Box Collection*, p. 207.

64 RS to GB, July 29, 1918, *The Tin Box Collection*, p. 208.

65 GB to RS, August 16, 1918, *The Tin Box Collection*, p. 210.

66 RS to GB, August 18, 1918, *The Tin Box Collection*, p. 210.

67 RS to GB, September 24, 1918, *The Tin Box Collection*, p. 214.

68 *Sixty-Odd*, p. 401.

69 GB to RS, Monday morning 6:15 November 11, 1918, *The Tin Box Collection*, p. 221.

70 RS to GB, November 12, 1918, *The Tin Box Collection*, p. 222.

71 John Dos Passos, *Three Soldiers* (New York: George H. Doran Co., 1921, and Modern Library, 1932).

72 Landsberg, *Dos Passos's Path to U.S.A.*, p. 72.

73 Dos Passos, *Three Soldiers* (New York: Penguin Books, 1997), p. 26.

74 Dos Passos, *Three Soldiers*, p. 294.

75 Virginia Spencer Carr, *Dos Passsos: A Life* (Garden City, New York: Doubleday & Co., Inc., 1984), p. 186. Perhaps Carr edited Van's prose, which is suspiciously well spelled here.

76 Dos Passos, *An Informal Memoir*, p. 42.

77 RS to GB, probably October 7, 1918, *The Tin Box Collection*, p. 217.

Barbara Foster

1 Because of a house fire, Barbara's sister Rosamond did not have any photographs or letters. In the late 1980s I sent her two photos. In addition, Barbara was one of only three graduates who declined to have her picture printed in the 1920 Smith yearbook.

2 Chapin, conversation with the author, September 8, 1989.

3 Rosamond Foster, conversation with the author, January 24, 1989.

4 *Sixty-Odd*, p. 411.

5 Suzanne Bloch interview, March 17, 1977, NYC.

6 Frank Foster (September 10, 1869–September 17, 1941); Inez Foster (February 9, 1871–October 10, 1938). They married on January 10, 1895.

7 Eleanor Foster (June 1, 1897–1986).

8 Rosamond (May 27, 1907–December 18, 2001).

9 Quoted in Bertha Emond, "Return of the natives," *Eagle Times*, Claremont, New Hampshire, 1975.

10 Koehler (1884–1959) was German; his younger brother Wolfgang founded the school of gestalt psychology. An eminent art historian, Koehler began work in the Italian Renaissance writing on Michelangelo and the Medici Chapel. His volumes on the School of Tours, published 1930–1933 became a model of art historical scholarship. In 1918, after serving in the war, he was director of the Weimar Art Collections, where he became interested in the Bauhaus. He was close with painters Klee and Feininger. He married in 1920 and had two sons. In 1932 Koehler came to Harvard, teaching medieval art; he also lectured in German culture, modern expressionist painting and German Baroque architecture, as well as in his own field of Carolingian art. He was a connoisseur of music as well. In 1941, Koehler went to Dumbarton Oaks, where he stayed three years. Back at Harvard, his studies expanded to Flemish painting (Rubens and Rembrandt). He worked with Barbara Sessions on a book on manuscript illumination of the Early Middle Ages. Frederick B. Deknatel, "Wilhelm Reinhold Walter Koehler, obituary notice," *The Art Journal* 20, no. 1 (Fall 1960): 26–27.

11 He rededicated his Symphonic Prelude to Barbara, giving this date.

12 Frank Foster to RS, December 21, 1918, *The Tin Box Collection*, pp. 226–27.

13 RS to GB, typed, probably December 27, 1918, *Correspondence*, pp. 29–31.

14 GB to RS, December 30, 1918, *The Tin Box Collection*, pp. 227–28.

15 RS to GB, January 1, 1919, *The Tin Box Collection*, pp. 228–29.

16 Archibald Sessions to RS, January 4, 1919, LCRSC, Box 4, fol. 5.

17 RS to Father Sill, probably January 1919.

18 One of the married John Burk's letters to Roger, during the engagement, detailed birth control information at length.

19 RS to GB, probably May 8, 1919, *The Tin Box Collection*, pp. 237–38.

20 RS to GB, probably June 5, 1919, *The Tin Box Collection*, p. 240. John Burk to RS, June 3, LCRSC Box 3 fol. 1.

21 Frank Foster to RS, June 30, 1919, *The Tin Box Collection*, p. 240.

22 RS to Barbara Foster, summer 1919, *The Tin Box Collection*, p. 246.

23 Quotations from undated letters to Barbara Foster, LCRSC, Box 1.

24 RS to Barbara Foster, July 7, [1923], LCRSC, Box 1.

25 RS to Barbara Sessions, August 16, 1924, LCRSC, Box 1, fol. 7.

26 RS to Barbara Sessions, "Boston, Thursday p.m.—Friday a.m. [1922?], LCRSC, Box 1.

27 RS to Father Sill, August 22, 1919.

28 Father Sill to RS, August 25, 1919, *Correspondence*, p. 32.

29 RS to BF, undated, LCRSC, Box 1.

30 RS to GB, probably July 31, 1919, *The Tin Box Collection*, p. 248.

31 RS to GB, probably July 31, 1919, *The Tin Box Collection*, p. 249.

32 GB to RS, August 6, 1919, *The Tin Box Collection*, p. 249.

33 GB to Father Sill, August 4, 1920, LCRSC, Box 5, fol. 7.

34 RS to GB, August 9, 1919, *The Tin Box Collection*, p. 250.

35 Ruth Sessions to Barbara and Roger, August 19, 1919, *The Tin Box Collection*, p. 251.

36 GB to RS, May 10, 1919, *The Tin Box Collection*, p. 239.

37 GB to RS, May 22, 1920, *The Tin Box Collection*, p. 264.

38 GB to Father Sill, copy typed by RS, August 17, 1920, LCRSC, Box 5, fol. 7.

39 Quoted in David M. G. Huntington, *Hadley Memories* (privately printed, 2002), pp. 39–40.

40 Archibald Sessions to RS, January 14, 1919, *The Tin Box Collection*, p. 233.
41 RS interview, COCH, p. 86.
42 RS to Barbara Foster, summer 1919, *The Tin Box Collection*, p. 243.
43 RS to Barbara Foster, July 1919, *The Tin Box Collection*, p. 244.
44 RS to GB, January 19, 1919, *The Tin Box Collection*, p. 231.
45 Cone, "Conversation with Roger Sessions," *Perspectives*, p. 93.

George Bartlett

1 RS to GB, December 17, 1919, *The Tin Box Collection*, p. 258; *Correspondence*, pp. 35–36.
2 RS to GB, December 17, 1919, *The Tin Box Collection*, p. 259.
3 GB to RS, December 26, 1919, *The Tin Box Collection*, p. 260.
4 GB to RS, December 26, 1919, *The Tin Box Collection*, p. 260.
5 RS to GB, January 18, 1920, *The Tin Box Collection*, p. 261.
6 GB to RS, May 20, 1920, *The Tin Box Collection*, pp. 262–63.
7 Archibald Sessions to RS, October 18, 1920, *The Tin Box Collection*, p. 271.
8 RS to GB, October 31, 1920, *The Tin Box Collection*, pp. 272–73.
9 RS to GB, January 10, 1921, *The Tin Box Collection*, p. 278.
10 RS to GB, January 10, 1921, *The Tin Box Collection*, p. 279.
11 RS to GB, January 10, 1921, *The Tin Box Collection*, p. 280.
12 GB to RS, January 13, 1921, *The Tin Box Collection*, p. 281.
13 GB to RS, January 18, 1921, *The Tin Box Collection*, p. 282.
14 GB to RS, January 18, 1921, *The Tin Box Collection*, p. 281.
15 RS to GB, January 15, 1921, *The Tin Box Collection*, p. 282.
16 RS to GB, February 16–17, 1921, *The Tin Box Collection*, p. 286.
17 Barbara and RS to GB, February 25, 1921, *The Tin Box Collection*, pp. 287–89.
18 Georgia Bartlett to Barbara Sessions, March 14, 1921, *The Tin Box Collection*, p. 293.
19 RS to GB, April 3, 1921, *The Tin Box Collection*, p. 294.
20 RS to GB, April 3, 1921, *The Tin Box Collection*, p. 296.
21 GB to RS, March 24, 1921, *The Tin Box Collection*, p. 293.
22 Barbara Sessions to GB, March 29, 1921, *The Tin Box Collection*, p. 304.
23 RS to GB, April 29, 1921, *Correspondence*, pp. 36–39.
24 Hannah Andrews to RS, May 14, 1921, LCRSC, Box 4, fol. 15.
25 *Correspondence*, p. 33.
26 Editorials, *The Kent Quarterly* XIII, no. 3 (May 1921): 1.
27 Rev. Frederick H. Sill, "George Hodges Bartlett," *Kent Quarterly* (1921): 60–63.
28 Memorial booklet for Bartlett, LCRSC, Box 4, fol. 5.

Ernest Bloch

1 RS interview, COHC, p. 86.
2 See FPRS, p. 58.
3 RS to Ernest Bloch, March 3, 1921, Bloch Collection, Library of Congress, in Michael Nott, "Roger Sessions's fugal studies with Ernest Bloch: a glimpse into the workshop," *American Music* 7, no. 3 (Fall 1989): 258. All six of Sessions's surviving letters to Bloch date from 1921.
4 RS, *Reflections on the Music Life in the United States* (New York: Merlin, 1956), pp. 130–31.
5 The Boston Symphony, which ultimately played considerably more of Bloch's music, also performed Bloch's Concerto Grosso for String Orchestra and Piano Obbligato with Jesús Maria Sanromà on December 24 and 26, 1925 (in Boston) and on January 9, 1926 (in New York).
6 RS interview, COHC, p. 89.
7 Roger Sessions quoted in Janet Baker-Carr, "A conversation with Roger Sessions," *Harvard Magazine* (April 1976): 46.
8 RS interview, COHC, p. 91.
9 RS interview, COHC, p. 91.
10 Cone, "Conversation with Roger Sessions," *Perspectives*, p. 94.
11 RS to Barbara Foster, Day 94 [December 17, 1919], LCRSC, Box 1.
12 Knorr, who sometimes published under the pseudonym I. O. Armand, wrote *P.I. Tchaikowsky* (1900), *Augfaben für den Unterricht in der Harmonielehre* (Leipzig, 1903, 1931), *Lehrbuch der*

Fugenkomposition (Leipzig, 1911), and *Die Fugen des "Wohl-Temperierte Klavier" von J. S. Bach in bildlichen Darstellung.*

13 Nott, "Roger Sessions's fugal studies." See also Nott, "Ernest Bloch's pedagogical writings: an artistic legacy of twentieth-century America" (Ph.D. diss.: University of Rochester, 1986).
14 RS to Father Sill, August 17, 1920.
15 After having asked Pater to lend him all of George's letters to Father Sill, which Sessions then typed up, kept the typescript, and returned the originals.
16 RS to Father Sill, April 18, 1921.
17 RS to Ernest Bloch, March 3, 1921, Bloch collection.
18 RS to Ernest Bloch, June 25, 1921, *Correspondence*, pp. 39–41.
19 RS to Ernest Bloch, July 20, 1921, Bloch collection.
20 RS to Ernest Bloch, August 27, 1921, *Correspondence*, pp. 41–42.

Cleveland Institute of Music

1 RS to Jean and Denise Binet, probably early summer 1922, but possibly 1923, Paul Sacher Stiftung, Basel.
2 RS interview, COHC, p. 120.
3 It would remain at this location until May 1932.
4 Ruth Sessions to "Dearest children," September 20, 1921, *The Tin Box Collection*, p. 312.
5 Ruth Sessions to Barbara Sessions, November 10, 1921, LCRSC, Box 2, fol. 14.
6 Archibald Sessions to "Dear little babes in the woods of the Western Reserve!" November 1, 1921, *The Tin Box Collection*, p. 313.
7 Ruth Sessions to "Dearest Children," p. 315.
8 RS to Ernest Bloch, August 27, 1921, Library of Congress, Bloch collection.
9 Barbara Sessions, possibly to Ruth Sessions, no date, quoted in FPRS, p. 68.
10 Adella Hughes founded the Cleveland Orchestra in 1918 and served as its first general manager from 1918–1933.
11 Suzanne Bloch interview, March 17, 1977, NYC.
12 RS interview, COHC, p. 101.
13 RS, "A teacher views a problem," *The Outpost* 2 (December 2, 1922), CIM Archives.
14 *Chanting Wheels* (1922) and *From Rome to Florence*, both G. P. Putnam and Sons.
15 RS to Jean and Denise Binet, probably summer 1922, Paul Sacher Stiftung.
16 "Music theory classes as conducted at the Cleveland Institute of Music," *Musical Observer* 21 (September 1922), CIM Archives. Two other photos show Bloch teaching his class and Hubbard Hutchinson's beginning theory class (16 students).
17 Suzanne Bloch interview, March 17, 1977, NYC.
18 RS to Ruth Sessions, undated, but probably 1922, FPRS, pp. 67–68.
19 Some are at the Princeton Library in ms form.
20 "RS," *Topics* (December 1, 1923), CIM Archives.
21 RS to Jean and Denise Binet, probably summer 1922, Paul Sacher Stiftung.
22 RS, "The significance of the Wagner performances," *The Outpost* 2, no. 3 (January 5, 1924): 1 and 4. CIM Archives.
23 Suzanne Bloch interview, March 17, 1977, NYC. "When the Cleveland Institute gave all the Beethoven quartets, Roger gave courses. We all went to courses preparing us to hear the Beethoven quartets."
24 RS interview, COHC, pp. 105–06 and 108.
25 RS interview, COHC, pp. 125–26.
26 Suzanne Bloch interview, March 17, 1977, NYC.
27 RS interview, COHC, pp. 114–16.

The Black Maskers

1 Franz Wedekind, *Tragedies of Sex*, trans. by Samuel Eliot, Jr (New York: Boni & Liveright, 1914). Wedekind, *Erdgeist*, trans. by Samuel Eliot, Jr (New York: A. & C. Boni, 1914).
2 *The Yellow Jacket* was written for an all-Asian cast by G. C. Hazelton and J. H. Benrimo, Smith College library. The score was published by C. W. Thompson, 1919. The score of *The Merchant of Venice* was published in Boston by C. W. Thompson, 1920, Library of Congress.

3 S. A. Eliot, Jr. "The Black Maskers," *The Smith Alumnae Quarterly* XV, no. 4 (July 1923): 381.

4 Page Williams, "Why did 1923 choose the Black Maskers?" *The Smith Alumnae Quarterly* XV, no. 4 (July 1923): 381–82.

5 The Czech, Marie Arnsteinovà, wrote in favor, stating that if one understood Russian litera-ture one understood Russia; Elizabeth McFadden (1898) opposed having women play men's parts; and the three anonymous alumnae (1905, 1919, and 1910) felt the seniors should present "something lovely" to entertain their elders. *The Smith Alumnae Quarterly* XV, no. 4 (July 1923): 382–84.

6 "1891," and Maud (Skidmore) Barber, 1906, "What do Alumnae owe the seniors?" and "Just what is entertainment?" *The Smith Alumnae Quarterly* XV, no. 1 (November 1923): 49–51. No mention was made of the music.

7 Samuel A. Eliot, Jr letter to the author, November 17, 1978.

8 Clarence Brown, review of *Visions: Stories and Photographs by Leonid Andreyev*, ed. Olga Andreyev Carlisle, *The New Republic* (February 29, 1988): 41–42.

9 Maksim Gorki, *Reminiscences of Tolstoy, Chekhov and Andreev* (1931), trans. by Katherine Mansfield, S. S. Koteliansky, and Leonard Woolf (London: The Hogarth Press, 1968).

10 RS interview, October 16, 1974, NYC. See Leonid Andreyeff, *Plays*, trans. by Clarence L. and Fred Newton Scott with an introduction by V. V. Brusyanin (New York: Charles Scribner's Sons, 1915), the only English translation and the version Eliot used for his production.

11 RS interview, October 16, 1974, NYC.

12 " 'Black Maskers' interestingly successful production of seniors," *Smith College Weekly* (June 20, 1923): 1, 7. These pages were reprinted from Brusyanin, "The symbolic dramas of Andreyeff," pp. xi–xxvi.

13 Eliot letter, November 17, 1978.

14 *Conversations*, pp. 14–18.

15 Elliott Carter, "Expressionism and American music," *Perspectives on American Composers*, eds Benjamin Boretz and Edward T. Cone (New York: W.W. Norton & Co., 1971), p. 224.

16 In the Orchestral Suite this music occurs at two measures after rehearsal number 68.

17 Mss at Princeton University Library, Library of Congress, NYPL Library of Performing Arts, and City College of the CUNY (Mark Brunswick collection).

18 See *RS+HM*, p. 37, for the music to both endings.

19 The descriptions of the performance of *The Black Maskers* in this paragraph and following are from Sessions's entry (June 19–20, 1923) in James L. Huntington's Forty Acres guest diary. Porter-Phelps-Huntington Papers, Amherst Archives, Box 80B, pp. 16–19.

20 RS to Barbara Sessions, June 3, 1923, *The Tin Box Collection*, p. 328.

21 RS to Barbara Sessions, "Sat 11.20, Batavia NY," 1923, LCRSC, Box 1. This may be Sessions's first mention of Copland in his letters.

22 Eliot letter, November 17, 1978.

23 Katharine Abbot Wilder, "A memorable experience of my college years," typescript, written circa 1974, Smith College Archives.

24 Letter from Caroline (Bedell) Thomas to Kathleen M. and Stephen L. O'Connor, January 16, 1989, Smith College Archives.

25 Eliot letter, November 17, 1978.

26 RS interview, November 15, 1978, NYC. See *RS+HM*, pp. 27–39, for a description of specific lines set to music.

27 Cabin guestbook, June 16, 1923, LCRSC, Box 4, fol. 12.

28 Quoted in FPRS, p. 71.

29 RS to Barbara Sessions, June 24, 1923, *The Tin Box Collection*, p. 330.

30 Quoted in FPRS, no date, p. 70.

31 "Smith senior dramatics," *Boston Evening Transcript* (June 14, 1923).

32 Rosenfeld liked *The Black Maskers*, but did not care for Sessions's First Symphony, then liked the First String Quartet.

33 Paul Rosenfeld, "Roger H. Sessions," *Port of New York* (New York: Harcourt & Brace, 1924), 145–48, 150–52.

34 RS to Barbara Sessions, June 24, 1923, *The Tin Box Collection*, p. 330.

35 RS, *Reflections on the Music Life in the United States*, trans. from Italian to English, no translator given (New York: Merlin, 1956), pp. 130–31.

36 Roy Dickinson Welch, "Professor Welch comments on music of the *Black Maskers*" manu-script, Smith College archives.

37 Ernest Bloch to Romain Rolland, May 18, 1924, *Ernest Bloch-Romain Rolland Lettres (1911–1933)*, ed. by José-Flore Tappy (Lausanne: Collection "Les Musiciens" Edition Payot, 1984), No. 51, p. 141; trans. by Suzanne Bloch in "Ernest Bloch and Roger Sessions at the Cleveland Institute," *Ernest Bloch Society Bulletin* 17 (1985): 4–7.

38 Quoted in RS to Barbara Sessions, [June 1923], LCRSC, Box 1, fol. 6.

39 Suzanne Bloch interview, March 17, 1977, NYC.

40 Ernest Bloch to Romain Rolland, May 18, 1924, *Ernest Bloch-Romain Rolland Lettres (1911–1933)*, No. 51, pp. 141–42; trans. by Elaine Brody, "Romain Rolland and Ernest Bloch," *The Musical Quarterly* LXVIII, no. 1 (1982): 72–73; trans. Andrea Olmstead; trans. Suzanne Bloch in "Ernest Bloch and Roger Sessions," *Bulletin*, p. 7.

41 RS to Barbara Sessions, June 30, 1924, *Correspondence*, p. 46.

42 RS to Barbara Sessions, July 3, 1924, *Correspondence*, p. 47.

43 RS to Barbara Sessions, September 6, 1924, *Correspondence*, pp. 53–54.

44 RS to Aaron Copland, December 25, 1930, *Correspondence*, p. 157.

45 RS interview, October 16, 1974, NYC.

46 "Black Maskers by Roger Sessions is introduced to Philadelphians," *Musical America* (November 10, 1933): 12.

47 "Bacon Suite given," *The New York Times* (May 12, 1946): 42.

48 Howard Taubman, "Music: Monteux conducts," *The New York Times* (July 15, 1955): 16.

Friends

1 RS interview, COHC, p. 154.

2 RS in *Jean Binet–17 Octobre 1893–24 Février 1960* (Nyon, Switzerland: Courrier de la Côte, 1961). This volume includes reminiscences of Binet by Ernest Ansermet, Frank Martin, Nadia Boulanger, Luigi Dallapiccola, and others. In 1947 Jean wrote to Barbara from Zurich—she was living at 28 John Street, Providence, Rhode Island—and she composed a long letter preceded by a postcard. "And how easy it is!—to put a few words, today, on a card, and know that soon all this distance, all this long, heart-breaking, and *stupid* silence will be annihilated. It means *everything* to be talking to you! *Love* Barbara" Barbara Sessions to "My dears," September 2, 1947, Binet Collection, Paul Sacher Stiftung.

3 She donated it to the Library of Congress.

4 Mina Kirstein to RS, no date [possibly summer 1922], *The Tin Box Collection*, p. 316.

5 Mina Curtiss, *Other People's Letters: A Memoir* (Boston: Houghton Mifflin, 1978), p. 14.

6 RS to Barbara Sessions, July 1922, *The Tin Box Collection*, pp. 318–19.

7 Mina Kirstein to RS, August 22, 1922, *The Tin Box Collection*, p. 321.

8 Mina Kirstein to RS, no date, but at least 1922, *The Tin Box Collection*, p. 326.

9 Mina Curtiss, *Bizet and his World* (New York: Knopf, 1958).

10 Mina Curtiss, "Fromental Halévy," *The Musical Quarterly* 39 No. 2 (April 1953): 196–214.

11 See Anthony Tommasini, *Virgil Thomson's Musical Portraits* (New York: Pendragon Press, 1986).

12 RS to Barbara Sessions, June 29, 1923, *The Tin Box Collection*, pp. 330–31.

13 RS to Barbara Sessions, July 4, 1923, *The Tin Box Collection*, p. 332.

14 RS to Barbara Sessions, July 30, 1923, *The Tin Box Collection*, p. 336

15 RS to Barbara Sessions, July 9, 1923, *The Tin Box Collection*, p. 333.

16 Ruth Sessions to "Dearest Children," December 8, 1921, *The Tin Box Collection*, p. 314.

17 Theodore Chanler to RS, January 18, [1923], *The Tin Box Collection*, p. 341.

18 Theodore Chanler to RS, January 17, [1924], *The Tin Box Collection*, p. 342.

19 The incipit of the Nocturne in Sessions's handwriting is in the Amherst Archives, Porter-Phelps-Huntington Papers, Box 127.

20 Theodore Chanler to RS, no date, from Geneseo, New York, *The Tin Box Collection*, p. 344.

21 Theodore Chanler to RS, June 7, *The Tin Box Collection*, p. 347.

22 Archibald Sessions to RS, January 23, 1924, *The Tin Box Collection*, p. 354.

Summer of 1924

1 RS interview, COHC, p. 155.
2 *Topics*, June 1924, CIM archives.
3 Minutes of the Board of the CIM, May 12, 1924, CIM archives.
4 RS to Barbara Foster Sessions (BFS), June 19, 1924, *The Tin Box Collection*, p. 364. Unless otherwise indicated, all letters from RS to Barbara in this section are from this source.
5 RS to BFS, June 18, 1924, p. 363.
6 RS to BFS, June 19, 1924, p. 364.
7 RS to BFS, June 14, 1924, p. 356.
8 RS to BFS, June 16, 1924, p. 359.
9 RS to BFS, June 14, 1924, p. 357.
10 RS to BFS, June 17, 1924, p. 360.
11 RS to BFS, June 21, 1924, p. 365.
12 Harold Clurman, quoted in Copland/Perlis, *Copland 1900 through 1942* (New York: St Martin's/Marek, 1984), p. 60.
13 A letter from John Burk mentions getting a BSO ticket for "Copeland," LCRSC, Box 3, fol. 1.
14 RS interview, COHC, p. 156.
15 RS to BFS, June 25, 1924, p. 373.
16 RS to BFS, June 28, 1924, p. 376.
17 RS to BFS, June 24, 1924, p. 371.
18 RS to BFS, June 25, 1924, p. 372.
19 RS to BFS, June 25, 1924, p. 372.
20 RS to BFS, June 28, 1924, p. 377.
21 RS to BFS, July 21, 1924, p. 401.
22 RS to BFS, August 28, 1924, pp. 432–33.
23 RS to BFS, June 28, 1924, p. 376.
24 RS to BFS, June 30, 1924 *Correspondence*, p. 46.
25 RS to BFS, June 30, 1924, p. 380.
26 RS to BFS, June 30, 1924, p. 377.
27 RS to BFS, July 3, 1924, *Correspondence*, pp. 47–48.
28 RS to BFS, July 4, 1924, p. 383.
29 Her brother Lincoln Kirstein became the founder of the New York City Ballet.
30 RS to BFS, July 12, 1924, p. 388.
31 RS to BFS, 1924, p. 417.
32 RS to BFS, July 14, 1924, p. 390.
33 RS to BFS, July 15, 1924, p. 391.
34 RS to BFS, July 18, 1924, p. 394.
35 RS to BFS, July 21, 1924, p. 400.
36 *Musical Courier*, September 25, 1924, CIM archives. The photograph has seven of the people named; Ribaupierre evidently took it.
37 RS to BFS, July 29, 1924, p. 410.
38 RS to BFS, July 29, 1924, p. 410.
39 RS to BFS, August 1, 1924, p. 411.
40 Cited in Nott, "RS," *American Music* 7, no. 3 (Fall 1989): 258.
41 RS to Jean Binet, August 4, 1924, translated from the French by Paul Suits, Paul Sacher Stiftung.
42 RS to Jean Binet, probably August 6, 1924, in English, Paul Sacher Stiftung.
43 RS to BFS, August 12, 1924, p. 419.
44 RS to BFS, August [no date], 1924, p. 423.
45 RS to BFS, August 22, 1924, p. 424.
46 RS to BFS, August 25, 1924, p. 430.
47 Letters from Hannah Sessions (Andrews) to RS, ca. 1917, LCRSC, Box 4, fols. 15 and 16.
48 RS to BFS, August 21–August 22, 1924, *Correspondence*, pp. 48–52.
49 Claire Reis to RS, May 9, 1924, LCRSC, Box 3, fol. 2.
50 RS to BRS, August 21–August 22, 1924, p. 426.
51 RS to BFS, August 21–August 22, 1924, p. 427.
52 RS to BFS, September 6, 1924, *Correspondence*, pp. 52–59.
53 RS to BFS, September 6, 1924, pp. 437–49.

54 RS interview, November 5, 1975, NYC.
55 RS radio interview WFMT, [1960], Library of Congress.

Stravinsky

1 Cone, "Conversation with Roger Sessions," p. 95.
2 Suzanne Bloch interview, March 17, 1977, NYC.
3 RS interview, COHC, p. 157.
4 RS interview, COHC, p. 158.
5 RS interview, COHC, p. 158.
6 Stravinsky was not performing with the Philadelphia Orchestra that Sunday, but with another orchestra.
7 RS interview, COHC, p. 159. Stravinsky related his own entertaining account of the rehearsal and performance of his Piano Concerto in *An Autobiography* (New York: Simon & Schuster, 1936; repr. New York: Norton, 1962), p. 122.
8 RS interview, COCH, p. 160.
9 RS to Igor Stravinsky, February 1925, translated by the author, *Correspondence*, p. 62.
10 RS interview, COCH, p. 160.
11 Milton Babbitt interviewed by Cole Gagne and Tracy Caras, *Soundpieces: Interviews with American Composers* (Metuchen, NJ: Scarecrow Press, 1982), p. 45.
12 RS interview, COHC, p. 161.
13 RS, "Notes on music; *Œdipus Rex*," *The Hound & Horn* 1, no. 3 (Spring 1928): 246–49. "On *Œdipus Rex*," *Modern Music* 5, no. 3 (March–April 1928): 9–15; repr. *Collected Essays*, pp. 339–46.
14 RS, "Notes on music; *Œdipus Rex*," *The Hound & Horn*, p. 246.
15 RS, "On *Œdipus Rex*," *Collected Essays*, p. 345.
16 RS to John Duke, May 26, 1928, *Correspondence*, p. 115.
17 RS to Nicolas Slonimsky, September 8, 1927, *Correspondence*, p. 85.
18 Aaron Copland to RS [early April 1928], *Correspondence*, p. 101. Evidently Roy Harris did not agree with Sessions's positive view of the Stravinsky work. In a letter to Copland, July 25, 1928, Sessions referred to an argument with Harris on the subject.
19 The Chicago Symphony Orchestra gave *Lilacs* January 29, 30, and 31, 1976. Sarah Beatty, Josephine Veasy, and Dominic Cossa sang the solo parts.

3 THE EUROPEAN PERIOD 1925–1933

Father figures

1 Quoted in CIM scrapbooks, November 8, 1924, CIM archives.
2 "Girls new string quartet adds zest to activities in Cleveland Institute," *Musical America* (November 22, 1924), and "Cleveland Institute feminine string quartet," *Musical Courier* (December 4, 1924). The quotation is from *Musical Courier*. CIM scrapbooks for 1924–1925, CIM archives.
3 RS, "Will tomorrow bring retracing of steps in musical creation?" *Musical America* (February 9, 1924).
4 RS interview, November 5, 1974, NYC. No wonder Sessions was so enamored of Schoenberg's phrase about the Chinese philosopher. See Schoenberg and Dallapiccola section.
5 RS interview, FPRS, p. 76.
6 See Appendix 3 in FPRS, pp. 304–06, which gives excerpts from Bloch's notes now at the Library of Congress.
7 RS interview, COHC, p. 132.
8 RS interview, COHC, p. 189.
9 RS interview, COHC, p. 193.
10 RS to Barbara Foster Sessions (BFS), June 27, 1925, *The Tin Box Collection*, p. 454. All letters to Barbara in this section are from this source.
11 RS to BFS, July 1, 1925, p. 455.
12 RS to BFS, July 4, 1925, p. 456.
13 RS to BFS, June 27, 1925, p. 454.

14 RS to BFS, July 1, 1925, p. 455.
15 RS to BFS, July 5, 1925, pp. 456–57.
16 RS to BFS, July 21, 1925, p. 459.
17 RS to BFS, July 24, 1925, p. 461.
18 RS interview, COHC, p. 123.
19 Suzanne Bloch interview, March 17, 1977, NYC.
20 RS interview, COHC, p. 123.
21 RS interview, COHC, p. 124.
22 RS interview, COHC, p. 126.
23 RS, "Ernest Bloch," *Collected Essays*, p. 331; repr. from *Modern Music* 5, no. 1 (November 1927): 3–11.
24 RS, "Ernest Bloch," *Collected Essays*, pp. 331–32.
25 RS, "Ernest Bloch," *Collected Essays*, pp. 334–35.
26 RS, "Ernest Bloch," *Collected Essays*, p. 337.
27 RS, "Ernest Bloch," *Collected Essays*, pp. 336–37.
28 Milton Babbitt, "I remember Roger," *Perspectives of New Music* (Spring–Summer 1985): 113.
29 RS, "Ernest Bloch," *Collected Essays*, p. 338.
30 RS, "Ernest Bloch," *Collected Essays*, p. 338.
31 RS, "Ernest Bloch: an appreciation," *A Festival of Three Concerts* (New York: Juilliard School of Music, 1947), no pagination.
32 RS interview, COHC, p. 129. This was Sessions's second wife, Lisl, and her mother Ruby Marble Franck.
33 RS interview, COHC, p. 130.
34 Suzanne (August 9, 1907–2002), although she married Paul Smith, went by the name Bloch. Among Lucienne Bloch's (January 1909–March 13, 1999) many famous works is *The Evolution of Music*, a Works Progress Administration (WPA) fresco painted on three walls of the music room of George Washington High School in New York City in 1937 and 1938. Ernest Bloch appears in the fresco. Lucienne worked with Frida Kahlo, and her mentor was Diego Rivera; she worked on the notorious Rockefeller Center murals Rivera painted.
35 Suzanne Bloch interview, March 17, 1977, NYC.
36 Suzanne Bloch interview.
37 Harvard 1883 seventh class report, 1933.
38 O. Henry [William Sydney Porter], *The Voice of the City: Further Stories of the Four Million*, with a note by Archibald Sessions (Garden City, NY: Doubleday, Page & Co., 1925), pp. vii–viii.
39 Porter, *The Voice of the City*, p. x.
40 *Sixty-Odd*, pp. 413–14.
41 Archibald Sessions to RS, October 9, 1924, *The Tin Box Collection*, p. 450.
42 Archibald Sessions to RS, May 9, 1925, *The Tin Box Collection*, p. 451.
43 RS to BFS, June 30, 1925, p. 454.
44 *The John Simon Guggenheim Memorial Foundation; 1925–2000: A Seventy-Fifth Anniversary Record* (New York: John Simon Guggenheim Memorial Foundation, 2001), pp. 34–35.
45 RS interview, COHC, p. 133.
46 Ernest Bloch to RS, June 27, 1926, trans. by Suzanne Bloch, *Correspondence*, pp. 63–64. "De Leone" probably is Bloch's student Robert Mills Delaney. The ellipses are Bloch's own. In the fall of 1927 Bloch had another breakdown.
47 Archibald Sessions to RS, July 22, 1925, *The Tin Box Collection*, p. 460.
48 RS to BFS, July 28, 1925, p. 462.
49 RS, Harvard Class of 1915 Decennial Report, pp. 246–48.

Florence

1 The manuscript of "Inconstant Lovers" and the Suite for two oboes, etc., is in the Princeton Rare Books Library. In 1927 Binet would dedicate a chamber suite to Barbara and Roger.
2 RS interview, COHC, p. 194.
3 RS interview, COHC, p. 197.
4 Prausnitz asserts that Sessions paid a two-week visit to Bernard and Mary Berenson's Villa I Tatti at the end of his 1924 stay in Europe; there is no mention of this in the letters.
5 Suzanne Bloch interview, March 17, 1977, NYC.

6 Quoted in FPRS, p. 81.

7 Ernest Samuels, *Bernard Berenson: The Making of a Connoisseur* (Cambridge, MA: Harvard University Press, 1979), pp. 345, 347. See Count Umberto Morra, *Conversations with Berenson* (Boston: Houghton Mifflin, 1965).

8 Ernest Bloch to RS, June 27, 1926, *Correspondence*, p. 63.

9 RS to Aaron Copland, September 23, [1932], *Correspondence*, p. 185.

10 Barbara Sessions to Nadia Boulanger, August 19, [1926], *Correspondence*, p. 68.

11 RS to Aaron Copland, August 24, 1926, *Correspondence*, p. 67.

12 *John Simon Guggenheim Memorial Foundation: Report of the Educational Advisory Board, 1925–1926* (New York: John Simon Guggenheim Foundation, 1927), p. 41.

13 Ernest Samuels, *Bernard Berenson: The Making of A Legend* (Cambridge, MA: Harvard University Press, 1987), p. 334.

14 RS to Ruth Sessions, February 10, 1927, FPRS, pp. 86–87.

15 Undated, last three pages of a letter from Rome, possibly late 1928 or early 1929, FPRS, p. 106.

16 RS to Ruth Sessions, March 9–11, 1929, FPRS, p. 107.

17 RS to Ruth Sessions, July 27, 1929, FPRS, pp. 109–10.

Symphony No. 1

1 RS lecture for his Juilliard Advanced Composition and Analysis doctoral class, February 13, 1980. Dates from the autograph manuscript at Houghton Library at Harvard University.

2 On Boulanger's death the score was donated to Harvard University.

3 RS to Aaron Copland, February 25, 1927, *Correspondence*, pp. 73 and 75.

4 Aaron Copland to RS, March 18, [1927], *Correspondence*, p. 76.

5 RS to Rev. Frederick Sill, April 6, 1910. Letter reproduced in *Correspondence*, p. 8.

6 RS to Ruth Sessions, February 10, 1927, FPRS, p. 87.

7 Elliott Carter, "Roger Sessions admired," *Perspectives of New Music* (Spring–Summer 1985): 120. Carter attended all three productions of *Montezuma*: Berlin, Boston, and New York.

8 Elliott Carter, "Roger Sessions: a commemorative tribute," *Tempo* 156 (March 1986): 4. This article is a reprint of a tribute read at a meeting of the Academy of Arts in Letters, New York, on December 6, 1985.

9 See RS to Koussevitzky, November 10, [1927], trans. from the French by this author, *Correspondence*, p. 89.

10 From four bars after no. 16 to no. 19.

11 The music originally between nos. 21 and 28.

12 The music originally after rehearsal no. 28.

13 The "popular piece" was Edward B. Claypoole's 1915 hit "Ragging the Scale."

14 RS interview, November 5, 1974, NYC.

15 H. T. Parker, "Composer revealed: the mind and hand of Roger Sessions," *Boston Evening Transcript* (April 23, 1927); H. T. Parker, "Week-end concert: Mr. Sessions again; rare chamber music," *Boston Evening Transcript* (April 25, 1927).

16 Paul Rosenfeld, "New symphony at symphony concert," *Boston Globe* (April 23, 1927).

17 L. A. S. "Sessions symphony produced in Boston," *Christian Science Monitor* (April 23, 1927). Boston Public Library Boston Symphony Orchestra scrapbooks, Brown Collection, vol. 46, 1926–1927.

18 A. H. M. "Music of the time: the first symphony of Roger Sessions," no date, Boston Public Library BSO Scrapbooks. The quotations from Sessions are problematic, since the article's first paragraph contains three biographical misstatements.

19 Philip Hale, "Symphony in 23d Concert," *Boston Herald* (April 23, 1927)

20 "A new symphony," *The New York Times* (May 1, 1927), sec. 10, 7: 2.

21 RS to Ruth Sessions, July 27, 1929, FPRS, p. 114.

22 No author, "Philadelphia boos music; Sessions symphony at premiere arouses hisses of hearers," *The New York Times* (December 21, 1935): 10.

23 A. P., *Journal de Genève* (April 7, 1929), FPRS, p. 114.

24 G. D., *Courier de Genève* (April 7, 1929), FPRS, p. 115.

25 Otto Wend, *Tribune de Genève* (April 9, 1929), FPRS, p. 115.

26 RS to Ruth Sessions, July 13, 1929, FPRS, p. 110.

27 RS interview, November 5, 1974, NYC.
28 Quoted by Felix Lamond, American Academy in Rome *Annual Report* 1931–32, p. 40.
29 RS to Copland, April 29, 1929, Library of Congress Copland collection.
30 C. H. "Juilliard offers work by Sessions," *The New York Times* (November 5, 1949): 10.
31 Shirley Fleming, "Sax appeal's tricky business for American Composers," *New York Post* (January 13, 1998).
32 Paul Griffiths, "Saxophones, for heat and color," *The New York Times* (January 13, 1998): E5.
33 Allan Kozinn, "Americana, unabashedly romantic," *The New York Times* (September 27, 2005): B6.
34 Eric Salzman, "Records: Sessions' first at last," *The New York Times* (June 19, 1960): X16. CRI Recordings issued a performance by the Japan Philharmonic Symphony under Akeo Watanabe, CRI SD 131, re-released on CD.
35 RS interview, November 5, 1974, NYC.
36 Alex Ross, "Native sons: in pursuit of the Great American Symphony," *The New Yorker* (February 17, 1997).
37 David Wright, "Symphonists, native and fervent, American symphonists of the fervent era," *The New York Times* (September 22, 1996): H28.

Boulanger and Copland

1 Copland/Perlis, *Copland: 1900 through 1942* (New York: St Martin's/Marek, 1984), pp. 149–50. Perlis interview with RS, May 4, 1983, NYC.
2 Suzanne Bloch interview, March 17, 1977, NYC.
3 Nadia Boulanger to RS, [December 1932], LCRSC.
4 Leonie Rosenstiel, *Nadia Boulanger, A Life in Music* (New York: W. W. Norton & Co., 1982), p. 412.
5 RS to Copland, June 26, 1928, *Correspondence*, p. 120.
6 The gift of the score of the concerto appears to be a gesture of reconciliation after his remarriage only two months earlier. In addition Sessions wanted to convince the musical world, through her, that the concerto was indeed completed.
7 Burk to RS, no date, LCRSC, box 3, fol. 1.
8 RS to Aaron Copland, November 25, 1929, Copland Collection at the Library of Congress. This paragraph was eliminated in *Correspondence*, pp. 150–52.
9 RS to George Bartlett, September 29–October 2, 1916: "But the most disgusting thing of all is the way the modern dilettantes and snobs have 'taken up' folk music. I can't think of any more nauseating performance than the deliberate exploitations of the finest impulses of the races in this manner. Folk-song as a parlor entertainment! *Shit!*" *The Tin Box Collection*, p. 111.
10 RS to Copland, August 24, 1926, *Correspondence*, p. 65.
11 Copland to RS, May 26, [1927], *Correspondence*, p. 78.
12 Barbara Sessions to Copland [April 25, 1928], Library of Congress, Copland collection.
13 Copland to RS, [1928], LCRSC.
14 RS to Copland, [March 21, 1928], *Correspondence*, p. 95.
15 Copland to RS, [March 26, 1928], *Correspondence*, p. 98.
16 RS to Copland, March 30, 1928, Library of Congress, Copland collection.
17 RS to Copland, [April 12, 1928], *Correspondence*, p. 102.
18 Barbara Sessions to Copland, [April 13, 1928], *Correspondence*, pp. 103–04.
19 Copland to Barbara and RS, [April 15, 1928], *Correspondence*, pp. 104–05.
20 Copland to Barbara and RS, [April 23, 1928], *Correspondence*, p. 106.
21 Copland, "Contemporaries at Oxford, 1931," *Modern Music* 9 (November 1931): 23.
22 Quoted in Copland, *The New Music: 1900–1960*, rev. edn (New York: W. W. Norton & Co., 1968), p. 75.
23 RS in Janet Baker-Carr, "A conversation with Roger Sessions," *Harvard Magazine* (April 1976): 47.
24 Paul Anderson, "An analysis of the aesthetic writings of Aaron Copland and Roger Sessions" (Ph.D. diss., Brandeis University, 2004), p. 62.
25 Anderson, "An analysis of the aesthetic writings," p. 67.
26 Anderson, "An analysis of the aesthetic writings," p. 88. Although remarkably even-handed throughout his discussion, Anderson ultimately blames Sessions: "Nevertheless, the unpleasant

situation of the university composer today is due, in large part, to the pervasiveness of premises representative of Sessions' worldview" (p. 164).

27 Howard Pollack, *Aaron Copland; The Life and Work of an Uncommon Man* (New York: Henry Holt and Co., 1999), page 168. Pollack cites *Correspondence*, pp. 177–82, 190–93, 211–12, 226. Pollack quotes William R. Trotter, in *Priest of Music: The Life of Dimitri Mitropoulos* (Portland, OR: Amadeus Press, 1995), p. 457n8, who quotes David Diamond saying Sessions was "particularly jealous and suspicious of Copland" in the late 1940s. In an interview with Pollack, Diamond changed his story somewhat and now "claimed that Sessions was jealous but not suspicious of Copland," 7 April 1996 (p. 601n30). In the same location Pollack quotes my e-mail defending Sessions: "All I can say is that Sessions never said anything against Copland in my hearing, and he called me his 'confidante.' Jealousy and suspicions were not part of his personality at that stage of his life" (E-mail 1 April 1997).

28 Perlis/Copland, *Copland*, p. 150. Perlis interview with RS, May 4, 1983, NYC.

29 Pollack, *Aaron Copland*, p. 8.

30 RS interview, COHC, pp. 170–71.

31 Adapted from Olmstead, "The Copland-Sessions letters," *Tempo* no. 175 (December 1990): 2–5.

32 Ross Parmenter, "Copland and Sessions 30 years later, *The New York Times* (May 12, 1958): 25.

33 Aaron Copland, *Our New Music* (New York: McGraw-Hill, 1941), pp. 127–31; rev. and enlarged as *The New Music 1900–1960* (1968).

34 Philip Ramey, "Copland at 80," *Chicago* 30, 1 (January 1981), pp. 124, 148.

35 RS, *Reflections on the Music Life in the United* States (New York: Merlin Press, 1956), pp. 146–66.

36 Pollack interview with Milton Babbitt, November 18, 1996, cited in Pollack, *Aaron Copland*, p. 610n32.

37 Copland to RS, April 15, 1974, LCRSC.

American Academy in Rome

1 Mysteriously, these letters are not in the American Academy in Rome (AAR) archives file in NYC.

2 Andrea Olmstead, "The Rome Prize from Leo Sowerby through David Diamond." In *Music and Composition at the American Academy in Rome*, ed. Martin Brody (Rochester: University of Rochester Press, forthcoming [2009]).

3 See Andrea Olmstead, *Juilliard: A History* (Champaign, Ill.: University of Illinois Press, 1999), ch. 3, for how Frederick spent his uncle's money, some of which would eventually go to the Juilliard Graduate School.

4 RS to Copland, October 7, 1928, *Correspondence*, p. 126.

5 RS to Copland, November 8–9, 1928, *Correspondence*, p. 128.

6 James Lincoln Huntington, *Forty Acres: the Story of the Bishop Huntington House*, photographs by Samuel Chamberlain (New York: Hastings House Publishers, 1949).

7 RS to Ruth Sessions, July 13, 1929, FPRS, pp. 111–12. Dohenny Hackett Sessions was born September 11, 1905, and died June 6, 1994. John Sessions married Dawn July 2, 1927. Two children were born to the Sessionses: Jane Ann (Byrne, b. November 12, 1929) and Sarah Fischer (Chapin, b. December 19, 1931).

8 RS to Ruth Sessions, July 13, 1929, FPRS, p. 111.

9 James Huntington, *Forty Acres*, p. 63.

10 The American pianist Frank Mannheimer was six months older than Sessions. After earning a B.M. at the Chicago Academy of Music in 1916 he served in World War I and returned to Berlin to study with Leonard Kreutzer and Artur Schnabel. By the mid-1920s he had gone to London to study with Tobias Matthay and was appointed to the Tobias Matthay Piano School, where he earned a reputation as a teacher.

11 RS to Ruth Sessions, June 13, 1929, FPRS, p. 116.

12 Felix Lamond, Annual Report, 1929–1930, AAR, p. 46.

13 RS to Copland, November 26, 1930, *Correspondence*, p. 153.

14 See their exchange of letters in *Correspondence*.

15 Lamond, *Annual Report* 1930–1931, AAR, p. 39. The book was published.

16 *RH+HM*, p. 53.

17 Lamond, letter to Dr Roscoe Guernsey, Executive Secretary of the Academy, February 5, 1938, AAR archives, NYC.
18 Mario Labroca, "Roger Sessions," *The Christian Science Monitor* (August 8, 1931): 7. "Sessions belongs to the artistic life through an inner necessity; he did not allow his art to become commercialized, and there were no obstacles he did not overcome in order to reach his goal. . . . His art is one which appeals to a public of intelligence, refinement and taste, far removed from catering for easily won applause and material benefits. Its sincerity, loftiness of expression and solidity of structure, are beyond the range of the ordinary musical Philistine."
19 RS interview, COHC, p. 140.

Berlin

1 RS interview, COHC, p. 141.
2 RS interview, COHC, p. 179.
3 FPRS, p. 132.
4 RS interview, COHC, p. 142.
5 RS interview, COHC, p. 143.
6 RS interview, COHC, p. 144.
7 RS interview, COHC, p. 181.
8 RS interview, COHC, pp. 182–83. Saerchinger wrote *Artur Schnabel: A Biography* (New York: Dodd, Mead, 1957) and translated Alfred Einstein's *Greatness in Music* (New York: Oxford University Press, 1941). A short chapter on Schnabel by Sessions appears in Saerchinger's book. Edward R. Murrow replaced Saerchinger at CBS in 1937.
9 RS to Copland, June 12, 1931, *Correspondence*, p. 165.
10 RS interview, COHC, p. 147.
11 RS interview, COHC, p. 152.
12 RS interview, COHC, p. 150.
13 Quoted in FPRS, p. 131.
14 RS to Jean Binet, probably November 1932, translated by Paul Suits, *Correspondence*, pp. 194, 195, 197.
15 RS interview, COHC, p. 201.
16 The correspondence in its entirety was published in *The New York Times* (April 16, 1933): IV, 1–2.
17 RS, "Some notes on Dr. Goebbels' letter to Furtwaengler," *Collected Essays*, pp. 272, 276, 279, 280–81; repr. from *Modern Music* 11, no. 1 (November–December, 1933): 3–12.
18 "Florence Music Convention," *The New York Times* (June 11, 1933): X4, article bylined from Florence, May 19, 1933.
19 RS interview, November 5, 1974, NYC.
20 RS interview, COHC, p. 150.
21 See Olin Downes, "Problem of adjustment," *The New York Times* (January 19, 1941), 9: 7, and Downes, "Refugee problem," the *Times* (January 26, 1941), 9: 7. For a discussion of this issue, see David Josephson, "The exile of European music: documentation of upheaval and immigration in *The New York Times*," in *Driven into Paradise: the Musical Migration from Nazi Germany to the United States*, Brinkmann and Wolff, eds (Berkeley: University of California Press, 1999), pp. 92–154.
22 "Music hurt by Nazis, two composers say," *The New York Times* (June 12, 1933): 20.
23 Quoted in David Leddick, *Intimate Companions: A Triography of George Platt Lynes, Paul Cadmus, Lincoln Kirstein, and their Circle* (New York: St Martins Press, 2000), p. 70.

4 THE DECADE 1936–1946

Marriage and the Violin Concerto

1 Quoted in FPRS, p. 152.
2 RS interview, November 16, 1976, NYC.
3 Hermann Franck (1873–d. January 27, 1941); Ruby Marble Franck (1879–1962).
4 John Sessions to Prausnitz, March 15, 1998, FPRS, p. 201.

5 Cousin James Lincoln Huntington divorced Sarah Pierce in 1944 and married Agnes G. Keefe that year. Sessions's niece Sarah Chapin divorced and remarried.

6 For details on the difficulties with Mrs Coolidge regarding the commission of the First String Quartet, see letters to her in *Correspondence*, pp. 248, 251–52, 252–54, 266–69, 309–10.

7 Hannah Andrews to RS, undated, FPRS, p. 156.

8 Catharine Huntington to RS, September 12, 1936, quotes Barbara, FPRS, p. 157.

9 The letter does not survive (see section "Boulanger and Copland").

10 Hannah Sessions to RS, April 17, 1935, FPRS, p. 155.

11 FPRS, p. 163.

12 RS to Ruth Sessions, September 23, 1936, FPRS, pp. 158–63.

13 John Sessions to Frederik Prausnitz, March 15, 1998, FPRS, p. 203.

14 RS to Ruth Sessions, undated, FPRS, p. 165.

15 "I wish to finish my violin concerto this winter that you suggested to me and that I have already begun." RS to Koussevitzky, November 10, 1927, *Correspondence*, p. 89.

16 Copland to RS, August 18, 1927; RS to Slonimsky, September 8, 1927, in *Correspondence*, pp. 79 and 84.

17 RS to Copland, June 26, 1928, *Correspondence*, p. 120. Of the four pieces mentioned only the concerto was completed. *The Nightingale* was the Boccaccio story Sessions had wanted to set as a ballet; see *Conversations*, p. 224.

18 RS to Copland August 19, 1928, *Correspondence*, p. 123.

19 Bloch won for his work, *America*.

20 The mss are in the Princeton University Rare Books Library. Sessions returned to these sketches in 1948–1949, but he again abandoned them.

21 RS to Binet, June 21, 1931, trans. from French by Paul Suits, *Correspondence*, p. 166.

22 *The New York Times* (September 29, 1932): 17, and "Koussevitzky back in New York," *The New York Times* (October 2, 1932): X6.

23 RS to Koussevitzky, October 15, 1932, trans. from Russian by Theodore Levin, *Correspondence*, p. 189.

24 RS to Klemperer, February 17, 1934, *Correspondence*, p. 220.

25 Klemperer to RS, March 12, 1934, *Correspondence*, p. 221.

26 RS, "Composition and Review," *The New York Times* (March 11, 1934): 10, 6: 7, and letter to *The New York Times* (October 28, 1934): 9, 8: 3.

27 "Composers League's new plans," *The New York Times* (March 18, 1934): X5.

28 "Activities of musicians here and afield," *The New York Times* (October 13, 1935): X7.

29 RS to Copland, spring 1934, *Correspondence*, p. 226.

30 RS to Koussevitzky, November 12, 1934, *Correspondence*, p. 230.

31 RS to Koussevitzky, November 21, 1934, *Correspondence*, p. 232.

32 "Novelties named by Koussevitzky," *The New York Times* (September 30, 1935): 12.

33 Koussevitzky to RS, November 26, 1934, *Correspondence*, p. 233.

34 RS to Spalding, October 15, 1935, *Correspondence*, p. 246.

35 "With the country's orchestras," *The New York Times* (October 11, 1936): X7. The article mentioned "new works will include a Soviet symphony by Shaporin, a violin concerto by Roger Sessions, the piano rhapsody by Rachmaninoff, and Prokofiev's third concerto."

36 "Music: for F.D.R.," *Time* (January 20, 1947): 72.

37 RS to Krasner, October 26, 1937, *Correspondence*, pp. 285–88.

38 RS to Gideon, August 12, 1939, *Correspondence*, pp. 318–19.

39 Benjamin Britten, *Letters*, ed. Donald Mitchell (Berkeley: University of California Press, 1991), p. 761.

40 Tossy Spivakovsky to RS, December 19, 1949, LCRSC.

41 Reviewed by Howard Taubman, "Music: Sessions Concerto," *The New York Times* (February 21, 1959): 24, and by Paul Henry Lang, "Music," *New York Herald Tribune* (February 21, 1959).

42 Elliott Carter, "RS: Violin Concerto," *The Musical Quarterly* (July 1959): 376–77; repr. *Elliott Carter: Collected Essays and Lectures, 1937–1995*, ed. by Jonathan W. Bernard (Rochester: University of Rochester Press, 1997): 175–80. William Empson, *Seven Types of Ambiguity*, 2nd edn (London: Chatto and Windus, 1947).

43 RS, radio interview, WFMT, [1960], Library of Congress.

44 Nan Andrews to Lisl Sessions, March 18, 1937, FPRS, p. 200.

45 Barbara Sessions to RS, December 22, 1937, *Correspondence*, p. 292.
46 Barbara Sessions to James Huntington, June 20, 1936, Porter-Phelps-Huntington Papers, Amherst archives, box 127, fol. 23.
47 Barbara Sessions to James Huntington, August 20, 1941, Porter-Phelps-Huntington Papers, Amherst archives, box 127, fol. 23. She closed "Your always devoted cousin Barbara Sessions."
48 We know nothing about the episode in Providence.
49 Barbara Sessions to James Huntington, September 30, [1952?], Porter-Phelps-Huntington Papers, Amherst archives, box 127, fol. 23.
50 Bertha Emond, "Return of the Natives," *Eagle-Times*, Claremont, New Hampshire, 1975. Smith College archives Foster folder.
51 Published by Edward B. Marks in *American Composers of Today*, 1965.
52 RS interview, October 15, 1975, NYC.
53 Suzanne Bloch interview, March 17, 1977, NYC.
54 The author and Elizabeth were both born on September 5, which we have celebrated for the past 30 years.

David Diamond

1 July 9, 1915–June 13, 2005.
2 David Diamond (DD), "Roger Sessions remembered," *Perspectives of New Music* (Spring–Summer 1985): 139. Diamond delivered this as a talk at Sessions's memorial at The Juilliard School, October 31, 1985.
3 Suzanne Bloch interview, March 17, 1977, NYC.
4 RS to Nadia Boulanger, [Spring 1936], *Correspondence*, p. 249.
5 RS to DD, September 20, 1936, *Correspondence*, p. 255. All letters between RS and DD cited here are from this source.
6 DD, "RS remembered," p. 139.
7 Several letters were burned in a fire and are here reconstructed.
8 RS to DD, June 15, 1937, p. 263.
9 DD to RS, July 12, 1937, p. 265.
10 RS to DD, August 10, 1937, p. 275.
11 DD to RS, August 22, 1937, pp. 276–78.
12 RS to DD, August 20, 1937, pp. 270–75.
13 DD to RS, August 29, 1937, pp. 280–83.
14 RS to DD, September 7, 1937, p. 285.
15 RS to DD, November 17, 1937, p. 289.
16 DD to Charles Naginski, February 14, 1938 In *Letters of Composers: An Anthology, 1603–1945*. Eds Gertrude Norman and Miriam Lubell Shrifte (New York: Knopf, 1946), p. 414.
17 RS to DD, [March 1939], p. 313.
18 RS to DD, March 19, 1939, p. 313.
19 RS to DD, April 5, 1939, p. 315.
20 RS to DD, February 25, 1941, pp. 326–27.
21 RS to DD, April 18, 1941, p. 328.
22 RS telegram to DD, [early May] 1941, *Correspondence*, p. 328.
23 DD, "RS: Symphony No. 2," *Notes* 7 (June 1950): 438–39.
24 RS to DD, August 10, 1968, p. 467.
25 DD, "RS remembered," p. 139.
26 George Tsontakis, "Primary sources," *The Musical Quarterly* 77, No. 4 (Winter 1993): 769–80.
27 DD, "RS remembered," p. 139.

Princeton

1 Cole Gagne and Tracy Caras, *Soundpieces: Interviews with American Composers* (Metuchen, NJ: Scarecrow Press, 1982), p. 357. Their RS interview, November 19, 1975, NYC.
2 RS interview, COHC, p. 202. Founded by director and cellist Joseph Malkin and his brother, dean and pianist Manfred, the Malkin Conservatory, at 299 Beacon Street, ran from 1933 to 1943 and boasted singer Eva Gauthier and Dalcroze specialist Renée Longy among its faculty. A third brother, Cecil Carol Malkin, was also a musician.

3 RS interview, October 15, 1975, NYC.
4 See a reproduction in *Conversations*, p. 175.
5 RS interview, COHC, pp. 202–03. No records of Sessions teaching exist at Boston University.
6 Sessions's résumé, Berkeley music department archives. The following year, 1934–1935, Sessions continued at the New Music School, now as co-director and teacher of composition, as well as at the Dalcroze Institute, in New York, earning him about $1,500. Israel Citkowitz was Sessions's assistant at the New School, which Babbitt believed cheated Sessions of some of the money due him. In addition, Sessions continued as lecturer at Boston University, for about $800. During the summer of 1935, his first in California, he earned $650. Beginning in the fall of 1935 he taught as lecturer at Princeton University (paid privately in the fall and then $110 a month for five months, January–May 1936, by Princeton), at the New Jersey College for Women ($1,000), and again in 1936 at the University of California summer school ($650). In 1936–1937 he was an instructor half time for $1,250. Finally, in the fall of 1937, he moved to Princeton, where his home was shared by two cats named after Italian saints: Francis and Dominic. The Princeton car was named Agatha and cost $100. Sessions continued to commute to New York until 1945.
   From 1936–1937 Sessions taught again at the New Jersey College for Women ($1,000). By 1937 his salary at Princeton was raised to $3,000, while he still earned $1,000 at the College for Women. In 1939 he was made lecturer with the rank of assistant professor at Princeton, only after he threatened not to come back, and received $3,000 plus $600 (the $600 for taking Professor Hufstader's work during the first term). The summer of 1940 he taught at the Columbia University summer school for $1,000. In 1939–1940, when Sessions was receiving $4,000 at Princeton, the sudden retirement of a colleague meant that he earned an additional $1,200. Welch had tried for four years to get Sessions the position of associate professor. Finally, in April 1942 Sessions became associate professor for $4,500 and continued to earn the extra amount of $1,500 during those years. (Information from Sessions's faculty file at the Princeton University Archives.) Between 1935 and 1945 Sessions taught privately in New York, earning yearly between $600 and $1,000. He also was receiving yearly royalties for his compositions from 1933 on, amounting to between about $100 and, as of 1945, $1,050.
7 RS, "The American composer and the music schools," *New York Herald Tribune* (November 5, 1933).
8 Letter from RS responding to "F.D.P.," *New York Herald Tribune* (October 22, 1933).
9 "School for composers," *The New York Times* (January 14, 1934): X6. The school opened on February 5.
10 "Sessions gives address," *The New York Times* (January 30, 1934): 16.
11 Suzanne Bloch interview, March 17, 1977, NYC.
12 From Florence, delivered in Italian and summarized by the reporter, "American opera's evolution," *The New York Times* (June 23, 1933): X4. "Composition and review," *The New York Times* (March 11, 1934): X6, repr. in *Collected Essays* as "Composer and critic," pp. 120–22.
13 Milton Babbitt, "I remember Roger," *Perspectives of New Music* (Spring–Summer 1985): 112.
14 Arthur Berger, "Roger Sessions: a reminiscence," *Perspectives of New Music* (Spring–Summer 1985): 117.
15 RS interview, December 11, 1974, NYC.
16 Miriam Gideon quoted in Deena and Bernard Rosenberg, *The Music Makers* (Berkeley: University of California Press, 1979), p. 63.
17 Guild Recordings, set no. RSSI (78 r.p.m.)
18 Virginia Spencer Carr, *Paul Bowles; A Life* (New York: Scribner, 2004), p. 100.
19 FPRS, p. 148, quotes a letter from Dick to Sessions September 8, 1935.
20 Miriam Gideon, [RS,] *Perpsectives of New Music* (Spring–Summer 1985): 147.
21 RS interview, COHC, pp. 204–05.
22 RS interview, COHC, p. 205.
23 "Composer to join women's college," *The New York Times* (September 14, 1935): N5.
24 Welch (January 19, 1885–January 8, 1951).
25 RS interview, COHC, pp. 205–06.
26 Babbitt, "I remember Roger," p. 116.
27 Welch biographical file, Princeton University Seeley G. Mudd Manuscript Library.
28 Welch letter in Sessions's faculty file at Princeton, May 8, 1945.

29 G.G., "Composers forum heard at library," *The New York Times* (November 30, 1939): 18.
30 It appears that by now he had discarded his 1935 songs "Nightpiece" by Joyce, and "The Last Invocation" by Whitman.
31 "Composers' contest," *The New York Times* (November 7, 1937): 189.
32 "Protest on embargo," *The New York Times* (January 25, 1939): 2. Copland was not on the list.
33 Sayre had received a B.S. from MIT in 1924, earned a pilot's license, and participated in the establishment of the first commercial US airline, between Boston and New York. He had taught at MIT from 1927 to 1933, edited *Aviation Magazine*, and worked for the government in Washington. At Princeton he struggled through a five-year illness and died October 13, 1956. Rosamond would remarry—Roy Sheldon, a furniture designer who lived in Paris much of his life.
34 Wallace Stevens to Henry Church, January 28, 1942, *Letters of Wallace Stevens* (New York: Alfred Knopf, 1977), pp. 400–01.
35 Henry Church to Wallace Stevens, February 11, 1942, quoted in Peter Brazeau, *Parts of a World, Wallace Stevens Remembered: An Oral Biography* (New York: Random House, 1977), note p. 87.
36 Andrew Imbrie, "Remembering Roger," *Perspectives of New Music* (Spring–Summer 1985): 149.
37 Imbrie, "Remembering Roger," p. 148.
38 RS, "Why I oppose a change in administration," *The Princeton Herald* (September 29, 1944): 1, 5, and 10.
39 The following discussion is taken from three sources: Martin Duberman, *Black Mountain: An Exploration in Community* (New York: Dutton, 1972); Mary Emma Harris, *The Arts at Black Mountain College* (Cambridge: MIT Press, 1987; repr. 2002); and Martin Brody, "The scheme of the whole: Black Mountain and the course of American music," *Black Mountain College: Experiment in Art*, ed. by Vincent Katz (Cambridge: MIT Press, 2002), pp. 237–68.
40 John Evarts quoted in Brody, "The scheme of the whole," p. 240.
41 Mary Emma Harris, *The Arts at Black Mountain College*, p. 35. The establishment Guggenheim Foundation had a harder time seeing through Fiorillo's con than did the spunky Black Mountain College. Moe granted Fiorillo an unparalleled four consecutive Guggenheim Fellowships. Fiorillo disappeared from the music scene in 1950 leaving behind a huge list of compositions, but only a few manuscripts in his own hand.
42 Brody, "The scheme of the whole," p. 246.
43 Duberman, *Black Mountain College*, p. 172.
44 Brody, "The scheme of the whole," p. 248.
45 RS, "Report on Black Mountain," *The New York Times* (September 24, 1944): 2, 4: 5. Quoted in Brody, "The scheme of the whole," p. 248.
46 RS, "Schoenberg in the United States," Black Mountain College, 1944, printed, with numerous footnotes added in 1972, in *Collected Essays*, pp. 353–69. Reprinted from *Tempo*, no. 103 (1972): 8–17. RS to Schoenberg, October 30, 1944, *Correspondence*, pp. 336–37.
47 Schoenberg to RS, December 3–8, 1944, *Correspondence*, pp. 337–38.
48 Babbitt, "I remember Roger," p. 116.

Symphony No. 2

1 RS interview, COHC, p. 244.
2 RS interview, COHC, p. 240. Eleanor Roosevelt, *Book of Common Sense Etiquette* (New York: Macmillan, 1962).
3 RS interview, COHC, p. 245.
4 RS interview, COHC, p. 246.
5 RS interview, COHC, p. 247.
6 Philharmoic Symphonic Orchestra of New York with Dimitri Mitropoulos, 78 r.p.m. set no. MM920; re-released on CRI CD 593.
7 The San Francisco Symphony also performed the work October 2–5, 1985, in the 1990 season, and again in May 1993. They recorded the work that year under Herbert Blomstedt, London CD 443-376-2 (see Discography online at www.AndreaOlmstead.com).
8 Andrew Imbrie, "Remembering Roger," *Perspectives of New Music* (Spring–Summer 1985): 151.
9 Marjory M. Fisher, "Sessions symphony has premiere," *Musical America* (January 25, 1957).

10 Michael Mann to RS, January 12, 1947, LCRSC.
11 Quoted in Michael Steinberg, program notes for the San Francisco Symphony, repr. *The Symphony: A Listener's Guide* (New York: Oxford University Press, 1995), p. 532.
12 RS, *The New York Times* (January 8, 1950): 89; repr. *Collected Essays*, pp. 169–71.
13 "The idiom is advanced," *Time* (January 16, 1950).
14 Olin Downes, "Corigliano soloist for Philharmonic," *The New York Times* (January 13, 1950): 19.
15 Howard Taubman, "Records: Sessions," *The New York Times* (July 2, 1950): X6.
16 Sessions wrote a thank-you letter: RS to Mitropoulos, February 1, 1950, *Correspondence*, p. 372.
17 Steinberg, *The Symphony*, p. 531.
18 Greg Sandow, "Musical postcards from the edge," *The Wall Street Journal* (January 21, 1997).
19 Paul Griffiths, "Rock, war and death: call it a reality check," *The New York Times* (January 14, 1997): C12.
20 Jeremy Eichler, "Fanfare for Copland, who wasn't always a common man," *The New York Times* (August 24, 2005): online.
21 Karen Horney, M.D., *Neurosis and Human Growth: The Struggle Toward Self-Realization* (New York: W.W. Norton & Co., 1950).
22 *Conversations*, p. 240.
23 See *Conversations*, p. 244.
24 Sessions was not consistently able to obey his own dictates. While frequently maintaining musical criticism as totally meaningless and "gossip," he nevertheless was glad to get a good review.
25 FPRS, p. 214.

5 *THE TRIAL OF LUCULLUS* THROUGH *MONTEZUMA*

Berkeley

1 *Harmonic Practice* (New York: Harcourt Brace, 1951) was known in his household as "That God-damned book," as opposed to the published Juilliard lectures (*The Musical Experience*), called, after a review, "The fascinating little book."
2 RS interview, COHC, p. 208.
3 These articles appear in *Collected Essays*.
4 The manuscript is in the Bancroft Library at Berkeley; the work was published by Casa Rustica Publications in 2006 and given its world premiere by Larry Bell, October 15, 2006, in Boston.
5 RS interview, COHC, p. 250. Perhaps the piece was the unfinished 1938 Symphony in A minor.
6 RS interview, November 27, 1974, NYC.
7 Gordon C. Cyr, "Roger Sessions at Berkeley: a personal reminiscence," *Perspectives of New Music* (Spring–Summer 1985): 132.
8 Cyr, "Roger Sessions at Berkeley," p. 132.
9 Cyr, "Roger Sessions at Berkeley," pp. 134–35.
10 RS interview, COHC, pp. 250–51.
11 Jonathan Elkus e-mail to the author, March 30, 2006. He thought the original teller of the story was likely Alan Rich.
12 "Institute splits on Thomas attack," *The New York Times* (February 14, 1948): 18. 129 members of the Institute signed the letter, while 29 members wrote Congress a letter disassociating themselves from it.
13 Olin Downes, "Eisler selections played in tribute," *The New York Times* (February 29, 1948): 64. The other organizing composers were Bernstein, Diamond, Copland, Harris, Piston, and Randall Thompson.
14 RS to the Progressive Citizens of America, January 5, 1948, LCRSC.
15 RS to the Honorable Henry A. Wallace, January 5, 1948, LCRSC.
16 Henry A. Wallace to RS, January 15, 1948, LCRSC.
17 "An appeal to members of the academic profession to support Adlai Stevenson for president," LCRSC.
18 "The University Loyalty Oath; a 50th anniversary retrospective," symposium and websource,

part of the University of California History Project: *http://sunsite.berkeley.edu/uchistory/archives _exhibits/loyaltyoath/*. See George R. Stewart, *The Year of the Oath* (New York: Doubleday & Co., Inc, 1950).

19 *Correspondence*, p. 383.

20 FPRS mistakenly gives the dates of this espisode because he thought Sesssions went to Florence during the 1950–1951 year, p. 230.

21 Aaron Copland to the Board of Directors of the League-ISCM, February 9, 1953, in *The Selected Correspondence of Aaron Copland*, eds Elizabeth B. Crist and Wayne Shirley (New Haven: Yale University Press, 2006), pp. 208–09.

22 Aaron Copland and Vivian Perlis, *Copland Since 1943* (New York: St Martin's Press, 1989), p. 186.

23 Frederick Kuh, "Top American composers' works barred at U.S. libraries abroad," *Chicago Sun-Times* (April 26, 1953), Copland Collection, Library of Congress, cited in Howard Pollack, *Aaron Copland*, 454.

24 *Conversations*, pp. 169–70.

25 *Conversations*, p. 170.

26 RS interview, COHC, p. 211.

27 Sessions's salary history for the next ten years, before he was forced to retire when he became 68, is as follows: July 1, 1955, $1,000 increase to $12,500; February 24, 1956, $500 grant from research committee; April 27, 1956, $600 research grant; November 26, 1956, $600 research grant; July 1, 1957, salary increased to $13,500; July 1, 1958, increased to $14,500; 1958–1959, as well as 1960–1961 and 1963–1964, three second terms leaves of absence at full salary; February 1, 1959, salary increase to $15,500; July 1, 1959, increase to $16,000; August 17–September 5, 1959, Princeton Seminar for Advanced Musical Studies, $1,000; July 15–August 31, 1960, $2,500 specially determined honorarium for the Seminar for Advanced Musical Studies; February 1, 1961, salary increased to $16,500; July 1, 1961, increased to $17,000; July 1, 1962 increased to $18,000; July 1, 1964 increased to $18,500. Sessions and the University were also contributing to TIAA.

28 Milton Babbitt, "I remember Roger," *Perspectives of New Music* (Spring–Summer 1985): 116.

29 RS interview, COHC, pp. 264–65.

30 RS interview, COHC, p. 269.

31 RS interview, COHC, p. 274.

32 RS to Sir William Glock, May 24, 1958, FPRS, p. 276.

33 RS interview, COHC, pp. 308–09.

The Trial of Lucullus

1 Ralph Manheim and John Willett, eds Introduction, "The crisis years 1938–39 and their aftermath," *Bertolt Brecht: Collected Plays*, 9 vols, *Lucullus* trans. by Frank Jones (New York: Pantheon Books, 1972), vol. 5, p. x.

2 John Willett and Tom Kuhn, eds Editorial notes, *Bertolt Brecht: Collected Plays*, 8 vols, *Lucullus* trans. by H. R. Hays (London: Methuen, 2003), vol. 4, p. 382. This is the first published version of the Hays translation of the 1940 version in over 60 years.

3 Manheim and Willett, Introduction, vol. 5, pp. x–xi.

4 Repr. in Willett and Kuhn, vol. 4, pp. 373–81.

5 This play began life as *99%* (referring to the popular support of Hitler). It was set to music by Paul Dessau, the composer's first work on a Brecht text, and performed in May 1938. The score has not survived. A version of *Private Life*, from May 1942 and retitled *Fear and Misery of the Third Reich*, was translated by Eric Bentley and is regularly performed now under that title. Hofmann Hays had been commissioned to make a translation of *Private Life*, but, since Brecht simultaneously allowed Bentley to translate it, Hays retreated. Although Brecht licensed the first performance of the new version to Schnitzler at Berkeley, he had also arranged a New York premiere under the *Private Life* title (its three parts and 17 scenes reordered). That performance was not a success.

6 RS to Bertolt Brecht, September 15, 1946, listed in Thorsten Preuss, *Brechts "Lukullus" und seine Vertonungen durch Paul Dessau und Roger Sessions. Werk und Ideologie* (Würzburg: Ergon, 2007), p. 287. The letter is No. 1762/24 in the Bertolt Brecht Archiv in Berlin. Schnitzler's letter (No. 1762/25), dated September 26, 1946, followed Sessions's. Preuss's book gives an

analysis of the opera, with numerous music examples, pp. 215–96. *Der Jasager* (*He Says Yes*) was set by Kurt Weill in 1930.

7 Manheim and Willett, vol. 5, pp. 316–17.

8 Lecture on *Montezuma*, LCRSC.

9 Marchbanks Press of New York, and New Directions, Norfolk, Conn., 1943.

10 Princeton students gave the work April 1955, Northwestern University performed it in January 1961, and in May 1966 the Juilliard School of Music presented it during RS's first year teaching there.

11 RS program notes for the 1966 Juilliard production.

12 RS interview, April 25, 1979, NYC.

13 The Hays–Sessions libretto used by Juilliard appends the second scene to the end of the first, thus renumbering the remainder of the scenes, and it also shows a division between scenes 13 and 14. The scene numbers here will use the score's numbering.

14 The libretto and ms score read "tilt the bier," however in the Juilliard performance these words (and several others) were changed, here to "set it down."

15 This scene was eliminated in the Juilliard production.

16 David Drew, "Out of Limbo," *New Statesman* (June 24, 1966): 937.

17 The original cast is given in Sessions's hand in the manuscript score.

18 Cyr, "Roger Sessions at Berkeley," p. 133.

19 S. Earl Saxton, "S. Earl Saxton," *Perspectives of New Music* (Spring–Summer 1985): 160–61. The cartoon appears there and in *RS+HM*, pp. 86–87.

20 RS interview, COHC, p. 218.

21 Alfred Frankenstein, "U.C. theater's music-dramas reflect attitudes after two wars," *San Francisco Chronicle*, April 26, 1947, Berkeley archives.

22 Clifford Gessler, "Impressive 'experiments' heard," *Oakland Tribune* (April 19, 1947), Berkeley archives.

23 Ross Parmenter, "Mozart and Sessions of [*sic*] operas may be done at Tanglewood during festival," *The New York Times* (May 25, 1947): X7.

24 Maxfield committed suicide in 1969.

25 Milton Babbitt, "My Vienna triangle at Washington Square revisited and dilated," *Driven into Paradise: The Musical Migration from Nazi Germany to the United States*, eds Reinhold Brinkmann and Christoph Wolff (Berkeley: University of California Press, 1999), pp. 51–52.

26 Quoted in Manheim and Willett, vol. 5, p. xiii.

27 Willett and Kuhn, Introduction, vol. 4, quoting Brecht diary dated November 6, 1944, p. xxv.

28 Von Einem had achieved international recognition with his first opera, *Dantons Tod*, after Büchner, performed in Salzburg in 1947.

29 Willett and Kuhn, Introduction, vol. 4, p. xxiii.

30 Joy Calico, "The trial, the condemnation, the cover-up; behind the scenes of Brecht/Dessau's *Lucullus* opera(s)," *Cambridge Opera Journal* 3 (November 2002), 14: 313–42. Calico states the two 1951 versions are virtually identical. Preuss documents changes made between March 24 and May 5, 1951. See Preuss, pp. 73–74, 383–89, 467–82. He also argues in Ch. 8 that the important changes Brecht and Dessau made had nothing to do with the political pressure in the GDR.

31 Eric Bentley, "*Mahagonny*: Notes in the Margin," Lincoln Center Metropolitan Opera program notes, 1979, p. 18.

32 Scherchen conducted the March 17, 1951, Deutsche Staatsoper production in East Berlin.

33 Willett and Kuhn, Introduction, vol. 4, pp. xxviii–xxix.

34 Published in East Berlin by Aufbau-Verlag. The 1951 version of the play, *Das Verhör des Lukullus*, was published by Suhrkamp Verlag, Frankfurt am Main in 1951. The new passages are given in Willett and Kuhn, vol. 4, pp. 383–90.

35 Reviewed by Howard Taubman, "Opera 'Trial of Lucullus'," *The New York Times* (May 2, 1955): 17.

36 RS quoted in *The Princeton Review*, April 29, 1955. Princeton University Archives. Reviews of the performance appeared in *Time* magazine (May 9, 1955, unsigned) and the *New York Herald Tribune* by Jay S. Harrison.

37 Some are quoted in *RS+HM*, pp. 87–90.

Schoenberg and Dallapiccola

1 RS, "Thoughts on Stravinsky," *Collected Essays*, pp. 377–78.
2 RS interview, January 29, 1975, NYC.
3 RS, "Exposition by Krenek," *Modern Music* 15, no. 2 (1938): 123–28; repr. *Collected Essays*.
4 RS interview, COHC, pp. 168–69.
5 *Tempo* 9 (Old Style, December 1944); rev. in *Tempo* 103 (December 1972): 8–17; repr. in *Collected Essays*, 353–69.
6 RS interview, January 29, 1975, NYC.
7 All the letters are published in Olmstead, "The correspondence between Arnold Schoenberg and Roger Sessions," *Journal of the Arnold Schoenberg Institute* 13, no. 1 (June 1990): 47–62. Some letters are in *Correspondence*.
8 Arnold Schoenberg to RS, December 3–8, 1944, *Arnold Schoenberg Letters*, ed. Erwin Stein (London: Faber & Faber, 1964), no. 196, pp. 222–23; and *Correspondence*, pp. 337–38.
9 RS interview, COHC, p. 258.
10 RS interview, COHC, p. 259.
11 RS, "Schoenberg in the United States," *Collected Essays*, pp. 366–67.
12 Leon Kirchner interview by the author.
13 RS to Schoenberg, Summer 1948, "The correspondence between," *Journal*, p. 52.
14 Schoenberg to RS, July 17, 1948, *Correspondence*, p. 356.
15 RS to Schoenberg, July 22, 1948, "The correspondence between," *Journal*, p. 53.
16 Quoted in Donal Henahan, "Victories and vicissitudes of Roger Sessions," *The New York Times* (April 14, 1968): 23.
17 Quoted in Henahan, "Victories and vicissitudes of Roger Sessions," p. 23.
18 The Six Pieces were reviewed in Donal Henahan, "Sessions, 71-plus, feted in concert," *The New York Times* (April 1, 1968): 56.
19 Thomas Mann, *Doctor Faustus: The Life of the German Composer Adrian Leverkühn as told by a Friend*, trans. by H. T. Lowe-Porter (New York: Alfred A. Knopf, Inc., 1948), originally published in German by Bermann-Fischer Verlag in 1947. Mann to RS, December 31, 1948, trans. by Gerhard and Annette Koeppel and Juliane Brand, *Correspondence*, pp. 361–62.
20 See Giovanni de Stefano, " 'Italienische Optik, furios behauptet.' Giuseppe Antonio Borgese– der Schwierige Schwiegersohn," *Thomas Mann Jahrbuch* 8 (1995): 239–65.
21 *Conversations*, pp. 171–72.
22 Schoenberg to RS, November 7, 1949, *Correspondence*, pp. 367–68.
23 RS, repr. in *Collected Essays*, "Heinrich Schenker's contribution" (1935): 231–40; "Escape by theory" (1938): 256–62; and "The function of theory" (1938): 263–68.
24 Schoenberg to RS, November 7, 1949, *Correspondence*, pp. 367–68.
25 Violin (1879–1956) taught piano at the Akademie in Vienna 1909–1912, during which time he knew and supported Schoenberg. After emigrating to the US in 1939, he settled in San Francisco. He was never able to resume a full-time professional career as a musician.
26 RS to Schoenberg, December 23, 1949, "The correspondence between," *Journal*, p. 58.
27 Arnold Schoenberg, *Style and Idea*, ed. and trans. Dika Newlin (New York: Philosophical Library, 1950).
28 RS to Schoenberg, probably June 1951, *Correspondence*, p. 375.
29 RS, "Some notes on Schoenberg," *Collected Essays*, p. 370. Schoenberg to RS, December 3, 1944. He also concluded his *Reflections* essays with this quotation, quoted it elsewhere, and repeated it often.
30 RS, "Some notes on Schoenberg," *Collected Essays*, pp. 371, 375.
31 RS interview, COHC, p. 299.
32 RS interview, COHC, pp. 162–63.
33 RS interview, COHC, p. 163. The friend may have been Schoenberg's son-in-law Felix Greissle.
34 RS interview, COHC, pp. 164–65. The Schoenberg scores are Three Satires, op. 28, SATB chorus, November–December, 1925: "Am Scheideweg," "Vielseitigkeit," and "Der neue Klassizismus" with viola, cello, and piano.
35 RS, *Reflections* (New York: Merlin, 1956).
36 RS, *In recordo di Luigi Dallapiccola* (Milan: Suvini Zerboni, 1975), 44.
37 RS to Harold Schiffman, December 8, 1951, *Correspondence*, p. 378.
38 Dallapiccola, *Parole e musica* (Milan, 1980), first published as *Appunti, incontri e meditazione* (Milan: Suvini Zerboni, 1970).

39 See Luigi Dallapiccola, "The genesis of the 'Canti di Prigionia' and 'Il Prigioniero'," *The Musical Quarterly* (July 1953) 39: 355–72, and his liner notes for the Antal Dorati recording, London OSA-1166. RS was not at the performance.

40 RS to Dallapiccola, September 26, 1952, trans. by Pina Pasquantonio, *Correspondence*, p. 384. The reference is to a character in *Don Giovanni*.

41 Scarpini (1911–1997) had studied with Casella and earned a doctorate in musicology.

42 See *Correspondence*, pp. 408–9, and 414.

43 RS to Dallapiccola, January 24, 1956, trans. by Pina Pasquantonio, *Correpondence*, p. 412.

44 The author and her husband, composer Larry Bell, another student of Sessions, also met Laura Dallapiccola in Florence.

45 Premiered January 15, 1956, by the Louisville Orchestra, Robert Whitney conducting. RS to Dallapiccola, January 24, 1956, trans. by Pina Pasquantonio, *Correspondence*, pp. 411–13.

46 *Theocritus* was also performed by the Princeton Symphony Orchestra, April 11, 1960, with Sessions conducting. Long had sung in the premiere of *Lucullus*.

47 RS to Dallapiccola, October 6, 1960, trans. by Pina Pasquantonio, *Correspondence*, p. 427.

48 Dallapiccola to RS, June 16, 1960, trans. by Valeria Secchi Short, *Correspondence*, p. 426.

49 RS, *Conversations*, p. 200.

50 "Problems of modern music: the Princeton seminar in advanced musical studied," *The Musical Quarterly* 46, no. 2 (April 1960). RS wrote "Problems and issues facing the composer today," repr. in *Collected Essays*.

51 RS to Dallapiccola, December 1, 1960, trans. by Pina Pasquantonio, *Correspondence*, pp. 430–31.

52 Both quoted in Edward T. Cone, "A tribute to Roger Sessions," *Kent Quarterly* (Winter 1986): 31.

53 Dallapiccola to RS, September 16, 1963, trans. Valeria Secchi Short, *Correspondence*, p. 440.

54 RS to Dallapiccola, April 23, 1964, trans. by Pina Pasquantonio, *Correspondence*, p. 448.

55 RS to Dallapiccola, September 6, 1964, trans. by Pina Pasquantonio, *Correspondence*, pp. 454–55.

56 RS to Dallapiccola, October 27, 1964, trans. by Pina Pasquantonio, *Correspondence*, p. 443.

57 RS to Dallapiccola, September 26, 1967, trans. by Pina Pasquantonio, *Correspondence*, p. 461.

58 Ross Lee Finney, [memories of Sessions], *Perspectives of New Music* (Spring–Summer 1985): 142.

59 RS to Dallapiccola, March 31–April 1, 1968, trans. by Pina Pasquantonio, *Correspondence*, pp. 464–65.

60 Dallapiccola to RS, October 3, 1968, trans. by Valeria Secchi Short, *Correspondence*, p. 468.

61 RS to Dallapiccola, October 19, 1968, trans. by Pina Pasquantonio, *Correspondence*, p. 470.

62 Dallapiccola to RS, November 13, 1968, trans. by Valeria Secchi Short, *Correspondence*, pp. 471–72.

63 RS to Dallapiccola, December 8, 1974, trans. by Pina Pasquantonio, *Correspondence*, pp. 486–87.

64 Lisl Sessions to Laura Dallapiccola, February 24, 1975, *Correspondence*, p. 483.

65 RS to Laura Dallapiccola, March 14, 1975, *Correspondence*, pp. 488–89.

66 RS, *Conversations*, pp. 97–98.

67 RS, *Conversations*, p. 128.

Symphonies Nos 3 and 4

1 RS quoted in "Sessions première planned," *The Christian Science Monitor* (December 4, 1957). All articles about the premiere of the Third Symphony cited here are from the Boston Symphony Archives Press 56, vol. 95, pp. 97–110.

2 RS interview, COHC, p. 284.

3 RS to Aaron Copland, August 22, 1955, *Correspondence*, p. 404.

4 RS interviewed in "Munch to conduct premiere of Sessions' Third Symphony," *Boston Sunday Globe* (December 1, 1957).

5 RS interview, November 12, 1975, NYC.

6 Edward Downes, "Sessions' Third," *The New York Times* (December 8, 1957): D13.

7 RS interview, COHC, p. 316.

8 RS interview, November 12, 1975, NYC.

9 RS, program notes for the BSO, 1957–1958, repr. (having been excised from the BSO

published notes) in the program book for the Celebration of Contemporary Music with the New York Philharmonic and The Juilliard School, 1976.

10 John Harbison and Andrea Olmstead, "Roger Sessions," *The New Grove Dictionary of American Music*, 4 vols ed. H. Wiley Hitchcock, vol. 4: 194. Repr. in *New Grove Twentieth-Century American Masters* (New York: W. W. Norton & Co., 1986), pp. 81–97.

11 Tse-Ying Koh, "The twelve-tone method and the classical tradition in Roger Sessions' *Symphony No. 3*," M.M. thesis: Rice University, 1995, p. 2. Some of the discussion of this work's form is taken from Koh's thesis for which this author was consulted.

12 RS interview, November 12, 1975. The last four bars are reproduced in *RS+HM*, p. 113.

13 Koh, "The twelve-tone method," p. 18.

14 RS, "Symphony No. 3," BSO program notes, December 6, 1957, 465–66.

15 For a thorough analysis of the Third Symphony, see Koh, "The twelve-tone method," 1995.

16 Harold Rogers, "Première of Sessions symphony," *Christian Science Monitor* (December 7, 1957).

17 Cyrus Durgin, "Boston Symphony Orchestra; Sessions' new Third Symphony," *The Boston Globe* (December 7, 1957).

18 Harriet Johnson, "Words and music; Bostonians play Sessions' 'Third'," *The New York Post* (December 12, 1957).

19 Paul Henry Lang, "Music," *New York Herald Tribune* (December 12, 1957).

20 Louis Biancolli, "Symphony in debut at Carnegie," *New York World Telegram and Sun* (December 12, 1957).

21 Howard Taubman, "Music: Sessions' Third Symphony," *The New York Times* (December 12, 1957): 34.

22 A.M.K., "Boston Symphony Orchestra," *Musical Courier* (December 11, 1957).

23 Irving Kolodin, "Music to my ears," *Saturday Review* (December 28, 1957). It was not an upbeat sixty-first birthday message.

24 Joseph Kerman, "Modern music is best served by the orchestra," *San Francisco Chronicle* (January 12, 1958).

25 Andrew Porter, "Musical events; music to attending ears," *The New Yorker* (March 29, 1976): 96–101.

26 Robert Kimball, "Boulez leads Sessions," *The New York Post* (March 5, 1976).

27 Harold C. Schonberg, "Music: impressive score by Sessions," *The New York Times* (March 5, 1976): 19.

28 Allan Kozinn, "Eerie Clangor in a Parade of High-Tech Ghosts," *The New York Times* (April 6, 2000): E10.

29 Howard Taubman wrote, "Mr Sessions, who has a reputation for writing in austere styles, has contributed a symphony that seems to make an effort at immediate communication. But he has not turned out the equivalent of light summer reading. This is not his manner. Nevertheless, his idiom steadily grows less thorny. If he does not watch out, he may yet produce a work that is popular on first acquaintance." "Music: two new American works," *The New York Times* (February 15, 1960): 22.

30 RS interview, COHC, p. 302.

31 RS interview, COHC, pp. 286–88.

32 RS interview, COHC, p. 301.

33 RS interview, November 26, 1975, NYC.

34 Howard Stern, "Techniques of formal articulation and association in the *Pastorale* of Roger Sessions' Symphony No. 4." Ph.D. diss.: Brandeis University, 2001, p. 10.

35 Reviewed by Don Henahan, " 'A willing ear' for Sessions," *The New York Herald Tribune* (February 5, 1961). "Sessions seldom writes anything that might even remotely be called lovable. . . . [He] was greeted on each appearance not only with respect, but also with a degree of warmth and affection that could not have been anticipated. . . . It was impossible, for instance, not to be struck by the preponderance of slow, elegiac movements in Sessions' scores; it might almost be taken as a trademark."

36 Hannah Sessions Andrews is buried in Oakwood Cemetery in Syracuse.

37 FPRS, p. 281.

38 Bernard Holland, "Music: American composers concert," *The New York Times* (October 22, 1985).

39 Michael Steinberg, program notes, Minnesota Symphony Orchestra, *Showcase* (January 1990): 26.
40 Sessions, who had been lured from ASCAP to BMI by Haverlin, was grateful enough to dedicate his Divertimento for Orchestra (1960) to Haverlin.
41 "U.S. selects group for visit to Soviet," *The New York Times* (June 10, 1958): 21. The next year, in 1960, Aaron Copland and Lukas Foss traveled to the USSR to make up the final two of the six composers exchanged, in order to secure an even number on each side of the political divide.
42 Harold C. Schonberg, "Exchange composers," *The New York Times* (September 21, 1958): X11.
43 *Conversations*, p. 238.
44 "4 Composers tell of trip to Russia," *The New York Times* (November 13, 1958): 38.
45 Donald W. Kramer, "Sessions warns 'get serious' or fall behind Soviet culture," *The Daily Princetonian* (October 27, 1958), and Kramer, "Sessions: no 'crash program' for culture," *The Daily Princetonian* (October 30, 1958).
46 Kramer, "Sessions," *Princetonian* (October 30, 1958).
47 Howard Taubman, "Music: U.S. and Soviet composers reach summit," *The New York Times* (November 7, 1959): 28.
48 *Conversations*, pp. 238–39.
49 Howard Taubman, "Exchange in depth," *The New York Times* (November 22, 1959): X9.
50 "Soviet composers describe U.S. trip," *The New York Times* (December 18, 1959): 35.

Montezuma

1 RS interview, COHC, pp. 229–30.
2 RS interview, COHC, p. 231.
3 See Andrea Olmstead, "The Plum'd Serpent: Antonio Borgese and Roger Sessions's 'Montezuma'," *Tempo* no. 152 (March 1985): 11–22.
4 Heinrich Schenker, *Harmony*, ed. and annotated by Oswald Jonas, trans. by Elizabeth Mann Borgese (Chicago: University of Chicago Press, 1980).
5 RS interview, COHC, pp. 237–338.
6 They lived at Kastanienalle, 34, 1 Berlin, 19. Princeton had granted Sessions a second-semester leave of absence in 1960 that was to have been used to attend the rehearsals and premiere of *Montezuma*.
7 The collaboration between Sessions and Borgese is detailed in letters in *Correspondence*.
8 In 1933, Borgese was William Allan Neilson Professor of Italian Literature at Smith College. He lived near Forty Acres where he and Sessions met. After Borgese's 1935 trip to Mexico, he had the idea for an opera.
9 Lecture at the LCRSC.
10 FPRS, p. 283.
11 See *RS+HM*, pp. 133–36.
12 Reviewed by John Rockwell, "Sessions 'Montezuma' comes to U.S.," *The New York Times* (April 1, 1976): 19. This review concluded, "the evening was not a triumphant success. It was eminent, respectable, but that couldn't compensate for the boredom." Ten days later Harold Schonberg, who had not seen *Montezuma*, included it in a long essay entitled "Strike three for modern opera," *The New York Times* (April 11, 1976): 57.
13 RS to Peter Mennin, February 26, 1982.

6 THE LAST TWO DECADES

California and Juilliard

1 Private papers, Christopher Wagstaff.
2 FPRS, p. 284.
3 Ross Lee Finney, "Ross Lee Finney," *Perspectives of New Music* (Spring–Summer 1985): 143.
4 Michael Steinberg, "RS," *Choral Masterworks: A Listener's Guide* (New York: Oxford University Press, 2005), repr. of program notes for the BSO.
5 Michael Steinberg, "A century set to music," San Francisco Symphony program notes (December 1999), p. 39.

6 The Double Concerto, for violin and cello, may have begun life as a cello concerto (possibly meant for John, who did premiere the Double Concerto) commissioned by BMI around 1965 and never finished.

Religious music

1 Dated "Florence, August 19, 1924 and Cleveland, Ohio, April 10–14, 1925," LCRSC.
2 Victoria Sirota, "The keyboard works of Roger Sessions," *Kent Quarterly* (Winter 1986): 23.
3 RS interview, October 23, 1974, NYC.
4 RS interview, December 11, 1974, NYC.
5 Sirota, "The keyboard works," p. 25.
6 *Conversations*, pp. 168–69.
7 RS interview, December 11, 1974, NYC.
8 Reviewed by Ross Parmenter, "Showcase fetes Roger Sessions," *The New York Times* (October 27, 1961): 26.
9 RS interview, November 5, 1975, NYC. In September of 1975 Sessions saw the headmaster again, by accident, in Rome.
10 RS interview, November 5, 1975, NYC.
11 RS interview, December 3, 1975, NYC.
12 RS, Boston Symphony Programs, February 11–12, 1966, pp. 984–85.
13 Harold Rogers, "Sessions' Psalm 140," *The Christian Science Monitor* (February 12, 1966): 7.
14 RS in "The genesis of a commission: Roger Sessions, Three Choruses on Biblical Texts," published by the Friends of Amherst College Music on the Occasion of the Amherst College Sesquicentennial Celebration," pp. 6–7.
15 RS interview, January 18, 1977, NYC.
16 RS interview, January 18, 1977, NYC.
17 RS interview, January 18, 1977, NYC.
18 RS interview, January 18, 1977, NYC.
19 "The genesis of a commission," p. 7.
20 "The genesis of a commission," p. 11.
21 "Sessions concert scores a success," *The Amherst Student* (February 10, 1975), no author given.
22 Richard Dyer, "John Oliver Chorale delivers in adventurous programs," *The Boston Globe* (October 30, 1989).

The symphonies

1 Elliott Carter, "Roger Sessions: a commemorative tribute," *Tempo* 156 (March 1986): 6.
2 Michael Steinberg, "Roger Sessions," *The Symphony: A Listener's Guide* (New York: Oxford University Press, 1995), pp. 524–25. Only one conductor has pulled off the feat of performing all nine Sessions's symphonies, Dennis Russell Davies of the American Composers Orchestra. In New York he performed No.1 January 11, 1998; No. 2 January 12, 1997; No. 3 April 2, 2000; No. 4 October 20, 1985; No. 5 February 25, 1996; No. 6 June 16, 1993; No. 7 November 15, 1982, and October 31, 1993; No. 8 October 23, 1994; and No. 9 May 15, 1994.
3 Steinberg, "RS," pp. 525–26.
4 Steinberg, "RS," p. 526.
5 Steinberg, "RS," p. 528.
6 RS, *Questions about Music* (New York: W. W. Norton & Co., 1971), pp. 43, 45.
7 Andrew Porter, "Musical events," *The New Yorker* (November 29, 1982): 166.
8 The Second Quartet opens with a double fugue, but here I am discussing the symphonies.
9 Alex Ross, "Modernist works, with illustrations," *The New York Times* (December 24, 1992): C11.
10 RS interview, April 6, 1977, NYC
11 Harrison A. Williams, Jr to RS, March 12, 1971, LCRSC.
12 RS interview, March 22, 1977, NYC.
13 Quoted in Oliver Daniel, "RS," *Ovation* (March 1984): 14.
14 Charles Michener, "Journeys on the open-ended trails of American music," *The New York Observer* (June 28, 1993).

15 Bernard Holland, "American composers orchestra," *The New York Times* (June 22, 1993): C16.

16 Quoted in "The ACO performs Sessions' Symphony #7," *The Roger Sessions Society Newlestter*, twelfth issue (July 1994): 4.

17 For a review quoting Sessions, see Kenneth Sanson, "Roger Sessions fits the cliche on greatness," ["The greater the man the bigger the person"] *Chicago's American* (October 8, 1967), Princeton archives.

18 RS interview, February 25, 1976, NYC.

19 RS interview, April 6, 1977, NYC.

20 Luigi Dallapiccola to RS, October 3, 1968, *Correspondence*, p. 468.

21 Both William Mootz and Bernard Jacobson quoted in the liner notes by Marshall A. Portnoy, Louisville recording LS776 stereo, 1981.

22 RS, liner notes, Symphony No. 7, Louisville LS776 stereo, 1981.

23 Andrew Porter, "Musical events," *The New Yorker* (November 29, 1982): 166.

24 Bernard Holland, "Two ways for composers to sound new," *The New York Times* (November 3, 1993): C23.

25 RS to Prausnitz, August 1, 1968, FPRS, p. 270.

26 Alex Ross, "Selecting composers from 4 different Worlds," *The New York Times* (October 25, 1994): C15.

27 S. Foster Damon, "The unwritten music of a great man," *Harvard Musical Review* 1, no. 3 (December 1913): 1ff.

28 RS to Andrea Olmstead, July 26, 1977, *Correspondence*, pp. 495–96.

29 The Symphonic Prelude of 1917 is indebted to Franck, among others.

30 Bernard Holland, "A forgotten U.S. composer [Collins] is resurrected," *The New York Times* (May 19, 1994): C16.

31 Jerome Hoberman, "Idea and style in two late works of Roger Sessions [Five Pieces for Piano and the Ninth Symphony]," D.M.A. dissertation, Peabody Conservatory of Music, 1999. See pp. 81–207. He worked with Prausnitz.

32 Hoberman, "Idea and style," p. 82.

33 Hoberman, "Idea and style," pp. 205–06.

34 RS interview, COHC, p. 224.

35 Robert P. Morgan, *Twentieth-Century Music* (New York: W. W. Norton & Co., 1991), pp. 294–95.

36 RS to Prausnitz, September 23, 1974, FPRS, p. 189.

37 Andrew Porter, "Musical events," *The New Yorker* (November 9, 1981).

38 Morgan, *Twentieth-Century Music*, p. 295.

Death and posthumous reputation

1 Premiered in January 1989 by ACCESS in Merkin Hall, NYC, Curtis Macomber, violin, Theodore Mook, cello. The work is recorded on a Koch CD 7153 by Macomber and Joel Krosnick.

2 John Rockwell, "Roger Sessions, nearing 85, is still a maverick composer," *The New York Times* (March 22, 1981): D17.

3 Donal Henahan, "Roger Sessions, a composer and professor, is dead at 88," *The New York Times* (March 18, 1985): A1.

4 Holoman showed it to Jerome Rosen, who sent me a copy.

5 Donal Henahan, "Victories and vicissitudes of Roger Sessions," *The New York Times* (April 14, 1968): D17, 23. The remark is made at the end of a multi-column article about Sessions.

6 Babbitt personal communication with the author. FPRS, p. 294.

7 Henahan, "Roger Sessions," obituary.

8 Elliott Carter, "RS: a commemorative tribute," *Tempo* no. 156 (March 1986): 4ff. This paper was first read at a meeting of the Academy of Arts and Letters in New York on December 6, 1985.

9 Elliott Carter, "RS: a commemorative tribute," p. 6.

10 John Warthen Struble, *The History of American Classical Music: MacDowell Through Minimalism* (New York: Facts On File, Inc., 1995).

11 Struble, *The History*, p. 160.

12 Struble, *The History*, pp. 161–62.

13 Donald J. Grout, Claude V. Palisca, and Peter Burkholder, *A History of Western Music*, 7th edn (New York: W.W. Norton & Co., 2005).

14 Richard Taruskin, *The Oxford History of Western Music* (Berkeley: University of California Press, 2005). Taruskin does not mention David Diamond at all, gives only the briefest mention of Dallapiccola, and refers to Ellen Zwilich once.

15 Three other recent histories mention Sessions only a few times: *The Cambridge History of Twentieth-Century Music*, eds Nicholas Cook and Anthony Pople (New York: Cambridge University Press, 2004); Richard Crawford, *An Introduction to America's Music* (New York: W. W. Norton & Co., 2001); and Joseph Horowitz, *Classical Music in America: A History of Its Rise and Fall* (New York: W. W. Norton & Co., 2005).

16 Quoted in Prausnitz, "Roger Sessions remembered," *Perspectives of New Music* (Spring–Summer 1985): 158.

17 RS interview, May 7, 1975, NYC.

BIBLIOGRAPHY

Primary sources

Letters by Roger Sessions, Ruth Sessions, Archibald Sessions, George Bartlett, Frederik van den Arend, Theodore Chanler, and Mina Kirstein to Sessions, among others, are at the Library of Congress in the Sessions Collection. The Library of Congress contains numerous manuscripts of later Sessions's works, versions of *Montezuma*'s libretto and music, and lectures. All of the large collection was donated by Elizabeth Sessions Pease. The Ernest Bloch, David Diamond, and the Aaron Copland archives are also at the Library.

Columbia University's Oral History Collection contains five interviews with Roger Sessions by Frank Rounds and Edward T. Cone from 1962.

The Cleveland Institute of Music Archives contains catalogs, scrapbooks, board minutes, concert programs, and other materials relating to Ernest Bloch and Roger Sessions's sojourn there.

Smith College Archives contains records of Roger Sessions as faculty, as well as Barbara Foster as a student, Mina Kirstein Curtiss, Roy Dickinson Welch, Samuel Eliot, Jr as a faculty members, and records of the premiere of *The Black Maskers*.

Princeton University Archives contains numerous early manuscripts of Sessions's music in the Rare Books Room. See *RS+HM* for list. Sessions himself donated this collection. Sessions's faculty file is in the Seeley Mudd Library.

Harvard University Archives holds records of Frederic Dan Huntington, George and James Huntington, Archibald Sessions, Roger Sessions, John Sessions, George Bartlett, and Frederik van den Arend as students at Harvard. In addition are records of the Pierian Sodality. The *Harvard Musical Review* is in Harvard's Eda Kuhn Loeb Music Library. Nadia Boulanger's scores of Sessions's music were donated to the Houghton and Loeb libraries.

The Irving S. Gilmore Music Library at Yale contains concert programs, the Quincy Porter collection including his and Bruce Simonds's diary, and other items. Yale's Beinecke Library has Sessions's Harvard Shakespeare course notes.

Yale's Oral History Collection of American Music has the author's tape-recorded interviews and transcripts of interviews with Roger Sessions held between October 1974 and December 1980. Transcripts are also in the author's private collection.

This author's transcripts of interviews with Sessions's students and friends include Suzanne Bloch, Milton Babbitt and others. I have the letter solicited from Samuel Eliot, Jr. I also have copies of letters from the numerous correspondents found in *The Correspondence of Roger Sessions*. Sessions's letters to the author are in the author's private collection.

The Juilliard School's Lila Acheson Wallace Library contains faculty records of Sessions's tenure on the faculty. In addition are scores, recordings, and programs of performances, including Juilliard's productions of *The Trial of Lucullus* and *Montezuma*.

The University of California at Berkeley Hargrove Music Library has programs, reviews, and an LP recording of the first production of *The Trial of Lucullus*, as well as numerous files on Sessions and Elkus as faculty members.

Archives with letters from Sessions include the Paul Sacher Stiftung, in Basel, Switzerland; the

Bibliotèque Nationale in Paris; the Archivio Contemporaneo "A. Bonsanti" in Florence; the Arnold Schoenberg Institute in Vienna, as well as the Nadia et Lili Boulanger Fondation, and collections of private individuals.

Amherst Library's Special Collections houses the numerous Porter-Phelps-Huntington Foundation letters and papers. Forty Acres, run by the Foundation, is open to the public.

The Boston Symphony Orchestra archives have records of all BSO performances and reviews of Sessions's works played there.

Selected secondary sources

Aldag, Richard. "Roger Sessions's duo for Violin and Violoncello: an edition and an examination of the compositional process." Ph.D. diss., City University of New York, 1991.

Anderson, Paul. "An analysis of the aesthetic writings of Aaron Coland and Roger Sessions." Ph.D. diss., Brandeis University, 2004.

Andreyeff, Leonid. *Plays*. Trans. Clarence L. and Fred Newton Scott with an introduction by V. V. Brusyanin. New York: Charles Scribner's Sons, 1915.

Armstrong, William H. "The miracle in Algo's shadow," *Kent Quarterly* 8, 1 (Fall 1988): 26–33.

Babbitt, Milton. "I remember Roger," *Perspectives of New Music* (Spring–Summer 1985): 113.

Baker-Carr, Janet. "A conversation with Roger Sessions," *Harvard Magazine* (April 1976): 44–9.

Bethell, John T. *Harvard Observed*. Cambridge, MA: Harvard University Press, 1998.

Ernest Bloch–Romain Rolland Lettres (1911–1933). Ed. José-Flore Tappy. Lausanne: Collection "Les Musiciens" Edition Payot, 1984.

Brazeau, Peter. *Parts of a World Wallace Stevens Remembered: An Oral Biography*. New York: Random House, 1977.

Brecht, Bertolt. *Bertolt Brecht: Collected Plays*. Ralph Manheim and John Willett, eds. 9 vols. *Lucullus* trans. by Frank Jones. New York: Pantheon Books, 1972, vol. 5.

—— *Bertolt Brecht: Collected Plays*. John Willett and Tom Kuhn, eds. 8 vols. *Lucullus* trans. by H. R. Hays. London: Methuen, 2003, vol. 4.

Brody, Elaine, "Romain Rolland and Ernest Bloch," *The Musical Quarterly* 68, no. 1 (January 1982): 60–79.

Brody, Martin. "The scheme of the whole; Black Mountain and the course of American Music." In *Black Mountain College: Experiment in Art*. Ed. Vincent Katz. Cambridge: MIT Press, 2002.

Calico, Joy. "The trial, the condemnation, the cover-up: behind the scenes of Brecht/Dessau's *Lucullus* opera(s)," *Cambridge Opera Journal* 3, 14 (November 2002): 313–42.

Caras, Tracy and Cole Gagne. "Roger Sessions," *Soundpieces: Interviews with American Composers*. Metuchen, NJ: Scarecrow Press, 1982.

Carr, Virginia Spencer. *Dos Passsos: A Life*. Garden City, New York: Doubleday & Co., 1984.

Carter, Elliott. "Roger Sessions: Violin Concerto," *The Musical Quarterly* (July 1959): 376–77.

—— "Expressionism and American music." In *Perspectives on American Composers*. Eds Benjamin Boretz and Edward T. Cone. New York: W. W. Norton & Co., 1971.

—— "Roger Sessions admired," *Perspectives of New Music* (Spring–Summer 1985): 120.

—— "Roger Sessions: a commemorative tribute," *Tempo* 156 (March 1986): 4.

—— *Elliott Carter: Collected Essays and Lectures 1937–1995*. Ed. Jonathan W. Bernard. Rochester: University of Rochester Press, 1997.

Chapin, Sarah, ed. *The Tin Box Collection: Letters of Roger Sessions and His Family and Friends*. Concord, MA: privately printed, 1992.

Chase, Gilbert. *America's Music: From the Pilgrims to the Present*, rev. third edn. Champaign: University of Illinois Press, 1987.

Cone, Edward T. "Conversation with Roger Sessions." In *Perspectives on American Composers*. Eds Benjamin Boretz and Edward T. Cone. New York: W. W. Norton & Co., 1971.

—— "In defense of song: the contribution of Roger Sessions," *Critical Inquiry* 2, 1 (Autumn 1975): 93–112.

—— "A tribute to Roger Sessions," *Kent Quarterly* (Winter 1986): 31.

Copland, Aaron. *The Selected Correspondence of Aaron Copland*. Eds Elizabeth B. Crist and Wayne Shirley. New Haven: Yale University Press, 2006.

Copland, Aaron and Vivian Perlis. *Copland 1900 through 1942*. New York: St Martin's/Marek, 1984.

—— *Copland Since 1943*. New York: St Martin's Press, 1989.

Curtiss, Mina. *Other People's Letters; A Memoir*. Boston: Houghton Mifflin, 1978.

Cyr, Gordon C. "Roger Sessions at Berkeley: a personal reminiscence," *Perspectives of New Music* (Spring–Summer 1985): 132.

Diamond, David. "Roger Sessions remembered," *Perspectives of New Music* (Spring–Summer 1985): 139.

Dos Passos, John. *Three Soldiers*. New York: Penguin Books, 1997.

Duberman, Martin. *Black Mountain: An Exploration in Community*. New York: Dutton, 1972.

Eliot, Jr, S. A. "The Black Maskers," *The Smith Alumnae Quarterly* XV, 4 (July 1923): 381.

Finney, Ross Lee. [memories of Sessions], *Perspectives of New Music* (Spring–Summer 1985): 142.

Forbes, Elliot. *A History of Music at Harvard to 1972*. Harvard University: Department of Music, 1988.

Gardner, Anson. "The most unforgettable character [Father Sill] I've met," *Reader's Digest* (January 1961): 1–6.

Gideon, Miriam. *Perspectives of New Music* (Spring–Summer 1985): 147.

Gorki, Maksim. *Reminiscences of Tolstoy, Chekhov and Andreev* (1931). Trans. Katherine Mansfield, S. S. Koteliansky, and Leonard Woolf. London: The Hogarth Press, 1968.

Harbison, John and Andrea Olmstead. "Roger Sessions." *The New Grove Dictionary of American Music*, 4 vols. Ed. H. Wiley Hitchcock, vol. 4: 194. Repr. in *New Grove Twentieth-Century American Masters*. New York: W. W. Norton & Co., 1986.

Harris, Mary Emma. *The Arts at Black Mountain College*. Cambridge: MIT Press, 1987; repr. 2002.

Hoberman, Jerome. "Idea and style in two late works of Roger Sessions." D.M.A. diss.: Peabody Conservatory of Music, 1999. [Five Pieces for Piano and Symphony No. 9]

Horney, Karen, M.D. *Neurosis and Human Growth: The Struggle toward Self-Realization*. New York: W. W. Norton & Co., 1950.

DeWolfe Howe, M. A. *The Boston Symphony Orchestra: 1881–1931*. Boston: Houghton Mifflin, 1931.

Huntington, Arria S. *Under a Colonial Roof-tree: Fireside Chronicles of Early New England*. Boston: Houghton Mifflin, 1891.

Huntington, David M. G. *Hadley Memories*. Privately printed, 2002.

Huntington, James Lincoln. *Forty Acres: The Story of the Bishop Huntington House*. New York: Hastings House, 1949.

Imbrie, Andrew. "Remembering Roger," *Perspectives of New Music* (Spring–Summer 1985): 149.

Kearns, William F. *Horatio Parker, 1863–1919*. Metuchen, NJ: Scarecow Press, Inc., 1990.

Koh, Tse-Ying, "The twelve-tone method and the classical tradition in Roger Sessions' *Symphony No. 3*." M.M. thesis: Rice University, 1995.

Kozinn, Allan. "Seeking a broader audience for Roger Sessions," *The New York Times* (November 13, 1988): 25.

Kushner, David A. *The Ernest Bloch Companion*. Westport, Conn.: Greenwood Press, 2002.

Landsberg, Melvin. *Dos Passos's Path to U.S.A.* Boulder: The Colorado Associated University Press, 1972.

Leddick, David. *Intimate Companions: A Triography of George Platt Lynes, Paul Cadmus, Lincoln Kirstein, and their Circle*. New York: St Martins Press, 2000.

Lucchesi, Joachim. "From trial to condemnation: the debate over Brecht/Dessau's 1951 opera *Lucullus*," *Contemporary Theater Review*, 4, 2 (1995): 13–23.

Mason, Charles Norman. "A comprehensive analysis of Roger Sessions' opera *Montezuma*." D.M.A. diss., University of Illinois, 1982.

Morgan, Robert, P. *Twentieth-Century Music*. New York: W. W. Norton & Co., 1991.

Newsletters of the Roger Sessions Society, 1989–2001.

Nott, Michael. "Roger Sessions's fugal studies with Ernest Bloch: a glimpse into the workshop," *American Music* 7, 3 (1989): 245–59.

Olmstead, Andrea. *Roger Sessions and His Music*. Ann Arbor, MI: UMI Research Press, 1985. (online at *www.AndreaOlmstead.com*)

—— ed. *Conversations with Roger Sessions*. Boston: MA: Northeastern University Press, 1987. (online at *www.AndreaOlmstead.com*)

—— "The correspondence between Arnold Schoenberg and Roger Sessions," *Journal of the Arnold Schoenberg Institute* 13, 1 (June 1990): 47–62.

—— "The Copland-Sessions letters," *Tempo* 175 (December 1990): 2–5.

—— ed. *The Correspondence of Roger Sessions*. Boston, MA: Northeastern University Press, 1992. (online at *www.AndreaOlmstead.com*)

—— *Juilliard: A History*. Champaign, Ill.: University of Illinois Press, 1999.

—— "'Like One of the Trees:' Roger Sessions and Hadley." In *Changing Winds: Essays in the History of Hadley, Massachusetts*. Ed. Marla R. Miller. Amherst: University of Massachusetts Press, 2009. [forthcoming]

—— "The Rome Prize from Leo Sowerby through David Diamond." In *Music and Composition at the American Academy in Rome*. Ed. Martin Brody. Rochester: University of Rochester Press, 2009. [forthcoming]

—— "The Plum'd Serpent: Antonio Borgese and Roger Sessions's 'Montezuma'," *Tempo* 152 (March 1985): 11–22.

Pollack, Howard. *Aaron Copland: The Life and Work of an Uncommon Man*. New York: Henry Holt and Co., 1999.

Prausnitz, Frederik. *Roger Sessions: How a "Difficult" Composer Gets that Way*. New York: Oxford University Press, 2003.

—— "Roger Sessions remembered," *Perspectives of New Music* (Spring–Summer 1985): 158.

Preuss, Thorsten. *Brechts "Lukullus" und seine Vertonungen durch Paul Dessau und Roger Sessions. Werk und Ideologie*. Würzburg: Ergon, 2007.

Rolland, Romain. *Jean-Christophe*. New York: Carroll & Graff Publishers, 1996.

Rosenfeld, Paul. "Roger H. Sessions." In *Port of New York*. New York: Harcourt & Brace, 1924.

Rosenstiel, Leonie. *Nadia Boulanger, A Life in Music*. New York: W. W. Norton & Co., 1982.

Samuels, Ernest. *Bernard Berenson: The Making of a Connoisseur*. Cambridge, Mass.: Harvard University Press, 1979.

—— *Bernard Berenson: The Making of A Legend*. Cambridge, Mass.: Harvard University Press, 1987.

Schnabel, Artur. *Reflections on Music*. Trans. César Saerchinger. New York: Simon and Schuster, 1934.

Schoenberg, Arnold. *Arnold Schoenberg Letters*. Ed. Erwin Stein. London: Faber & Faber, 1964.

Sices, David. *Music and the Musician in* Jean-Christophe: *The Harmony of Contrasts*. New Haven: Yale University Press, 1968.

Sessions, Roger. "Euripides and Mr Barker," *The Harvard Monthly* LX, 5 (July 1915): 127–31.

—— "An American evening abroad," *Modern Music*, 4, 1 (November–December 1926): 33–36.

—— "Notes on music; *Œdipus Rex*," *The Hound & Horn: A Harvard Miscellany* 1, 3 (Spring 1928): 246–49.

—— "Ernest Bloch: an appreciation." In *A Festival of Three Concerts*. New York: Juilliard School of Music, 1947.

—— *The Musical Experience of Composer, Performer, Listener*. Princeton, NJ: Princeton University Press, 1950; repr. New York: Antheneum, 1962.

—— *Harmonic Practice*. New York: Harcourt, Brace & World, Inc., 1951.

—— *Reflections on the Music Life in the United States*. [no translator given] New York: Merlin Press, 1956.

—— "Schnabel's Symphonies." In *Artur Schnabel: A Biography* by César Saerchinger. New York: Dood, Mead & Co., 1959.

—— *Questions About Music*. Cambridge, Mass.: Harvard University Press, 1970; repr. New York: W. W. Norton & Co., 1971.

—— *Roger Sessions on Music: Collected Essays*. Ed. Edward T. Cone. Princeton: Princeton University Press, 1979.

Sessions, Ruth Huntington. *Sixty-Odd: A Personal History*. Brattleboro, Vt.: Stephen Daye Publishers, 1936.

Sill, Rev. Frederick H. "George Hodges Bartlett," *Kent Quarterly* XIII, 3 (May 1921): 60–63.

Sirota, Victoria, "The keyboard works of Roger Sessions," *Kent Quarterly* (Winter 1986): 21–28.

Slonimsky, Nicolas. "Roger Sessions." In *Writings on Music. Volume Three: Music of the Modern Era*. Ed. Electra Slonimsky Yourke. New York: Routledge, 2005.

Spalding, Walter Raymond. *Music at Harvard: A Historical Review of Men and Events*. New York: Coward-McGann, Inc., 1935.

Stefano, Giovanni de. " 'Italienische Optik, furios behauptet.' Giuseppe Antonio Borgese–der Schwierige Schwiegersohn," *Thomas Mann Jahrbuch* 8 (1995): 239–65.

Steinberg, Michael. "Roger Sessions." In *The Symphony: A Listener's Guide*. New York: Oxford University Press, 1995.

—— "Roger Sessions." In *Choral Masterworks: A Listener's Guide*. New York: Oxford University Press, 2005.

Stern, Howard. "Techniques of formal articulation and association in the *Pastorale* of Roger Sessions' Symphony No. 4." Ph.D. diss., Brandeis University, 2001.

Stevens, Wallace. *Letters of Wallace Stevens, Selected and Edited by Holly Stevens*. New York: Alfred Knopf, Inc., 1977.

Stewart, George R. *The Year of the Oath*. New York: Doubleday & Co., Inc., 1950.

Struble, John Warthen. *The History of American Classical Music: MacDowell Through Minimalism*. New York: Facts On File, Inc., 1995.

Tsontakis, George. "Primary sources," *Musical Quarterly* 77, 4 (Winter 1993): 769–80.

DISCOGRAPHY AND WORKS LIST

A Works List with Discography, arranged chronologically by creative periods in Sessions's life, appears online at www.AndreaOlmstead.com.

INDEX

Abbott, Herbert 200, 201
Abramowitsch, Bernhard 273, 285, 304
Academy of Music (Northhampton) 156
Accademia Nazionale Luigi Cherubini 307, 308
Adagio (Prelude) for Organ (RS) 162
Addison, Adele 346
Adelphi Academy 13
Adler, Guido 270
Aeschylus 62
Afternoon of a Faun (Debussy) 97, 105
Ahknaten (Glass) 372
Aid to Spain 250
Aïda (Verdi) 57
Ainslee's Magazine 23, 36, 68, 144, 196, 377n4
Alceste (Gluck) 15
Alcott, Bronson 10
Alcott, Louisa May 10
Aldag, Richard 368
Alexander Hall 266
Alfaro, Franco 206
Alice M. Ditson Fund 274
All Round 196
Allen, Mildred 186
Allen, Walter Alfred 384n11
Alpers, Josef 269
Alphin, Albert 263
Alpine Symphony (Strauss) 76, 233
Alps 83
Also Sprach Zarathustra (Strauss) 72, 76
America (Bloch) 398n19
American Academy in Rome 84, 205, 214, 215,
    220, 226–33, 247, 346, 369; *see also* Rome Prize
American Academy of Arts and Letters xv, 313
American Composers Orchestra 213, 214, 276,
    322, 324, 359, 361, 362, 365
American Concert Choir 186
American Federation of Musicians 325
American Friends Service Committee 252
American Musicological Society 285
American Recording Society 163
American Symphony Orchestra 213, 276, 357
Amherst Archives 229
Amherst College 3, 6, 351, 412
Amirov, Fikret 326

Amore dei Tre Re, L' (Montemezzi) 57
Analysis of the Sexual Impulse (Ellis) 193
Anderson, Frederick (Fritz) 88, 108
Anderson, Paul 83, 222
Anderson, Sherwood 167
Andover Historical Society 253
Andrews, Hannah Sessions (Nan, sister) (photo 38)
    3, 5, 8, 21, 37, 120, 244, 254, 364; and Ruth
    37, 81, 179, 245, 251, 277; college 39, 50, 109,
    133, 134; death 324; *see also* Hannah Sessions
Andrews, Judge 9
Andrews, Mary Raymond Shipman 174
Andrews, Nigel Lyon (nephew) 133
Andrews, Paul Shipman (brother-in-law) 9, 91,
    107, 109, 198, 205, 244, 251, 324
Andrews, William 9
Andreyeff, Alexandra Mikhailovna 154
Andreyeff, Leonid 153, 154, 293
Anglican Mass 349
An Mathilde (Dallapiccola) 310
Anna Karenina (Tolstoy) 85
d'Aprile, Giovina (daughter-in-law) 254; *see also*
    Giovina Sessions
Ansermet, Ernest 175, 212, 213, 235, 390n2
Antheil, George 198, 220
Anthony, Susan B. 58
anti-Semitism 130
Archivio Contemporaneo "A. Bonsanti" (Florence)
    413
Arend, Frederik van den (photo 87) 48, 55, 61, 74,
    85, 90, 94, 99, 101, 102, 106, 120, 128, 139,
    316, 382n21n22, 412; Bartlett 96, 100–01,
    102–03, 135, 136; *Harvard Musical Review* 72, 76;
    Kent 122; lends RS money 121; pacifism 86;
    Red Cross 100, 102; returned from war 111,
    113, 114; *Three Soldiers* 115
Ariadne auf Naxos (Strauss) 76
Ariane et Barbe-Bleue (Maeterlinck) 92
Aristophanes 62
Armstrong, Mr 101, 124
Arnsteinovà, Marie 389n5
ASCAP 325, 408n40
Aspen Music Festival 307, 313, 347
Auchincloss, Louis 8

Augusteo Orchestra 206, 231, 233
Auric, Georges 173, 203
Aus Italien (Strauss) 76
Austin, J. D. 69
Avery Fisher Hall 362
Aviation Magazine 401n33

Babbitt (Lewis) 165
Babbitt, Milton xv, xvii, 185, 195, 224, 225, 264,
  265, 268, 273, 290, 305, 311, 368, 369, 370,
  372, 400n6, 412
Babbitt, Sylvia 369
Bach, J. S. 15, 65, 72, 86, 107–8, 140, 148, 156,
  173, 182, 200, 214, 239, 268, 342, 348, 349,
  354, 363, 364
Bagatelle (RS) 148, 162, 203
Bagatelles op. 126 (Beethoven) 268
Baily, Louis 130
Baker, Alan 344
Balakirev, Mily 97
Balch, Ellen Mary 40
Ballantine, Edward 53, 56
Ballata (RS, incomplete) 231
Ballet Russe 97, 173, 203
Barati, George 268
Barber of Seville (Rossini) 15
Barber, Samuel (photo 186) 185, 213, 214, 227,
  326, 327, 373
Bard College 276
Barlow, Samuel 267
Barnard College 254
Bartlett, George (photos 86, 100) 3, 5, 54, 55, 65,
  69, 85–87, 94, 95–96, 100, 101, 102, 103–04,
  118–19, 123, 124, 128–36, 156, 176, 180, 182,
  278, 316, 317, 319, 349, 412; and RS 95–96,
  122; death 134, 140, 141, 218, 255, 346;
  Harvard Musical Review 72, 76; homosexuality
  119; lending RS money 90, 121, 131; letters 81,
  85, 87, 91, 93, 111–12, 113, 118, 230;
  performing with RS 98; playing *Sacre* 130, 184;
  religion 105; Rev Huntington 131; review
  382n33; teaching at Kent 112, 125, 317;
  teaching music 106; Van 96, 100–01, 102–03, 135
Bartlett, Georgia 85, 112, 132, 176
Bartlett, Paulding 85, 176
Bartlett, Samuel 91, 129–30, 176
Bartók, Béla 185, 208, 234, 239, 250, 285, 320,
  326, 367
Barzin, Leon 163, 274
Basset, John Spencer 104
Bauer, Harold 56, 101, 132, 148, 284
Bauhaus 269
Baumgartner, Hope LeRoy 156
Bayreuth 49, 55, 346
BBC 328, 344
BBC Symphony 363
Beatles, The 357
Beatty, Sarah 392n19

Beauchamp's Career (Meredith) 85
Beecher, Catherine 10
Beethoven, Ludwig van 9, 15, 18, 69, 73, 62, 82,
  93, 97, 105, 132, 135, 139, 148, 151, 210, 234,
  236, 238, 247, 264, 268, 302, 305, 328, 349,
  351, 353, 354, 355, 357, 358, 363, 388n23
Beinecke Library (Yale) 412
Bekker, Paul 267
Belasco, David 92, 144, 168, 183, 197
Bell, Clive 175
Bell, Larry xv, 402n4, 406n44
Bellinger, Father W. W. 29
Benrimo, J. H. 388n2
Bentley, Eric 300, 403n5
Berenson, Bernard 66, 104, 200–01, 202, 203–04,
  208, 233, 239, 252, 253
Berenson, Bessie 104, 200
Berenson, Mary 201
Berenson, Senda (Abbott) 104, 200, 201
Berezowski, Nicolai 249
Berg, Alban (photo 240) 153, 234, 235, 239, 250,
  270, 275, 276, 296, 306, 308, 320, 341, 362, 372
Berger, Arthur 265, 372
Bergman, Sybil 94
Berio, Luciano 293, 307
Berkeley, Lennox 216
Berle, Adolph 59
Berlin Philharmonic Orchestra 234, 235
Berlin Symphony Orchestra 235
Berlin, Irving 211
Berlioz, Hector 105, 121, 125, 363
Bernard, Annabelle 314, 329
Bernstein, Leonard 289, 402n13
Bianchi, Martha 3, 5, 96, 383n73
Biancolli, Louis 321
Bible *see* King James Bible
Bibliotèque Nationale (Paris) 413
Biches, Les (Poulenc) 173
Binet, Denise 156, 158, 160, 175, 180, 183, 203
Binet, Jean (photo 157) xvi, 143, 146, 148, 156,
  157, 158, 160, 164, 166, 167, 174, 175, 176,
  177, 178, 180, 200, 203, 230, 237–38, 238,
  247, 264, 346, 369, 393n1
Bird House (drawing 27) 27, 28, 33; *see also* Four
  seventeen Washington Avenue
bird songs 34
birth control 386n18
Birth of a Nation, The 85
Birthday canons (Schoenberg) 303
Bishop Berkeley, Lord Bishop of Cloyne 40
Bizet, Georges 14, 57, 165
Blacher, Boris 292, 311
Black Maskers, The (RS) (photo 157) 43, 58, 143,
  148, 153–63, 164, 167, 168, 173, 174, 175,
  177, 182–83, 193, 198, 199, 203, 211, 208,
  216, 218, 325, 326; Suite 160, 162, 247, 248,
  265, 267, 293, 295, 301, 303, 311, 316, 324,
  331, 356, 372, 383n59, 408n40, 409n6, 412

Black Mountain College 269
Black Mountain Summer Music Institute (photo 271) 269
Blackstone Theater 250
Blaine, James G. 20
Blake, William 75, 363, 364, 381n2
Bliss, Arthur 284
Bliss, Mr and Mrs Robert Woods 252
Blitzstein, Marc 220
Bloch lectureship 293
Bloch, Ernest (photos 138, 147) xvi, 59, 73, 83, 116, 126, 128, 130, 132, 133, 137–42, 145, 147, 148, 149, 151, 160, 165, 167, 168, 172, 182, 192, 193, 194, 195, 198, 202, 208, 211, 226, 233, 239, 243, 278, 283, 284, 302, 387n5, 398n19; and *Black Maskers* 158, 160, 161, 173, 175, 177, 184, 191–96; compared with Boulanger 168; death 196, 370, 393n46, 412; on RS 178; RS's farewell to 192–93
Bloch, Ivan 178, 196
Bloch, Lucienne 177, 182, 196, 201, 393n34
Bloch, Marguerite (Schneider) 116, 150, 196
Bloch, Suzanne xvii, 116, 146–47, 160–61, 177, 184, 193, 194, 196, 215, 253, 256, 264, 370, 390n37, 393n34, 412
Blomstedt, Herbert 275, 401n7
Bloomsbury group 164, 175
Boccaccio 193, 232, 398n17
Bodanzky, Artur 130, 137
Bodenhorn, Aaron (photo 147) 147
Boepple, Paul 256, 264
Boeuf sur le Toit, Le (Milhaud) 167
Boissier, Alfred 175
Bolivar (Milhaud) 328
Bonaparte, Princess Marie 234
Borgese, Elizabeth (Mann) 328, 330, 408n4
Borgese, Giuseppe Antonio xvi, 283, 305, 307, 328, 329, 331, 338, 368
Borodin, Alexander 97
Boston Conservatory of Music 263
Boston Evening Transcript 158, 210
Boston Globe, The 211, 320
Boston Herald, The 55, 211
Boston Opera Company 55, 57, 72
Boston Symphony Orchestra xiv, 9, 55, 56, 57, 69, 101, 109, 128, 137, 145, 163, 186, 203, 208, 210, 211, 213, 219, 231, 238, 247, 249, 275–76, 316, 324, 350, 366, 387n5
Boston University 263, 264, 344, 347, 350, 400n5n6, 413
Botstein, Leon 213, 276, 357
Boulanger, Nadia xv, xvi, 145, 161, 167, 172–73, 174, 175, 180, 183, 184–85, 193, 203, 215–24, 218, 223, 224, 226, 235, 237, 244, 245, 256, 257, 258, 259, 268, 270, 277, 348, 390n2, 412; and Symphony No. 1 207, 208
Boulez, Pierre 321, 363
Bowdoin College 48, 252

Bowles, Paul 265
Brahms, Johannes xiv, 62, 69, 70, 73, 74, 76, 84, 90, 103, 105, 304, 322, 356
Brahms-Wagner controversy 70, 72
Brandeis Creative Arts Award xv
Brandeis University 254
Brandes, George 112
Brattle Hall 58
Breaking Point (Artzibasheff) 85, 103
Brecht, Bertolt 294–301
Brewbaker, Daniel 310
Bridgman, Sidney 35
Brieux, Eugene 153
Britten, Benjamin 250, 373
Broadcast Music, Inc (BMI) 309, 312, 370, 409n6
Brooklyn Daily Eagle, The 26
Brooklyn Philharmonic Society 18
Brooklyn Symphony 267
Brothers Karamazov, The (Dostoyevsky) 166
Brown University 381n2
Brown, Lois 191
Brown, Mary 36
Bruckner, Anton 53, 55, 72, 105, 361
Brunswick, Mark (photo 271) 173, 174, 175, 270, 389n17
Bryn-Julson, Phyllis 329
Buchman, Carl 156
Büchner, Georg 404n28
Buhlig, Richard 167, 302–03
Building the Union 183, 197
Bukofzer, Manfred 284, 285, 294
Burgin, Richard 238, 247, 248, 249, 380n25
Burgoyne, John (Gentleman Johnny) 35
Bürgschaft, Die (Weill) 235
Burk, Alberta 112, 121, 123
Burk, John 68, 69, 74, 76, 85, 93, 94, 96, 112, 120, 121, 123, 128, 136, 316, 391n13
Burton, Pres Marion LeRoy 107
Busch, Adolf 238
Busch, Fritz 234
Byrne, Jane Anne (Sessions) (niece) 371, 396n7

Cabot, Nora 15
Cady, Mrs 54
Caesar (Brecht) 294
Cage, John 224, 269, 272, 299
Caldwell, Sarah 327, 330, 338, 369
California Quartet 285
Calvary Church (Syracuse) 10
Calvinism 5
Camp Devens 107, 110, 112
Canons (RS) 347
Canti di Liberazione (Dallapiccola) 310
Carmen (Bizet) 14, 57
Carnegie grant 233, 234, 259
Carnegie Hall 213, 275, 276, 316, 322, 324, 346, 359, 361, 362
Carpathia 172

Carpenter, John Alden 53, 227, 249, 379n11
Cartan, Jean 216
Carter, Elliott (photo 292) xiv, 155, 208, 214, 224, 251, 311, 313, 348, 354, 357, 372, 394n7
Casella, Alfredo 206, 233, 239, 307, 406n41
Catholicism xv, 26, 117, 167, 216, 223, 254, 334, 348, 350
Caverno, Julia 34
CBS 233, 397n8
Cecelia Music School 267
Cello Concerto (Shostakovich) 326
Cello Sonata op. 102 (Beethoven) 268
Cézanne, Paul 103
Chadwick, George Whitefield 53, 72, 88, 211
Chamajians, Alan (Hovhaness) 224, 263
Chamber Symphony No. 2 (Schoenberg) 303
Chanler, Margaret 167, 168
Chanler, Theodore 52, 146, 148, 167–68, 172, 173, 183, 224, 412
Channing, William Ellery 5
Chant du Rossignol (Stravinsky) 184, 185
Chapin, Sarah Fischer (Sessions) (niece) 7, 14, 36–37, 69, 116, 136, 178, 229, 370, 396n2, 398n5
Chase, Gilbert 89
Chase, Mr 38
Chatham Square Music School 267
Chausson, Ernest 98, 101, 105
Chávez, Carlos 224
Chestnut Hill Academy 48
Chicago Academy of Music 396n10
Chicago Daily News 361
Chicago Symphony Orchestra 18, 313, 344, 360, 392n19
Chickering Hall 9
Chickering pianos 7
Children 166, 243, 244, 251, 283, 348
Chisholm Residence (photo 144) 388n3
Chopin, Frédéric 101, 132, 363
Chorale Preludes for Organ (RS) 182, 253, 267, 303, 324, 350
Chotzinoff, Samuel 267
Christian Democrats 205
Christian Science Monitor, The 211, 233, 320, 351, 352
Christian Socialists 205
Christian Workers Party 205
Christoph Colomb (Milhaud) 328
Church Association for the Advancement of the Interests of Labor (CAIL) 25
Church of the Redeemer (Brooklyn) 47
Church, Henry 268
Churchill, Alfred V. 104
Churchill, Mary 219
Churchill, Winston 314
Cincinnati Conservatory of Music 52
Cincinnati Symphony 162, 193
Cinque canti (Dallapiccola) 309, 310

Citkowitz, Israel 264, 400n6
City College of New York 270
Civic Opera (Berlin) 234, 238
Civil War 9, 35, 65, 109
Clapp, Philip Greeley 53, 56, 101, 138
Clark, Kenneth 201
Claypoole, Edward B. 394n13
Cleveland Institute of Music (photo 144) 52, 132, 141, 143–52, 158, 164, 166, 167, 170, 172, 177, 184, 191, 192, 195, 256, 266, 278, 293, 412
Cleveland Playhouse 191
Cleveland Symphony Orchestra 143, 145, 149, 184, 265, 344
Cleveland, Pres Grover 20, 44
Cliburn, Van 326
Clifton, Chalmers 53, 267
Clio Hall 290
Cloyne Alumni Association 43
Cloyne House School 40–44, 45, 123, 276, 284, 369
Cloyne Magazine 41, 42, 43
Clurman, Harold 172
Coccius, Herr 15
Cocteau, Jean 174, 203
Code, Marion 158
Cohen, Frederic (photo 271) 270, 271–72
Cohu, Jan Merry *see* Jan Merry
Cold War 300, 325, 338
Cologne Opera 270
Columbia Percussion Ensemble 185
Columbia University 46, 134, 164, 265, 274, 400n6
Columbia University Oral History Collection 412
Combattimento de Trancredi e Clorinda (Monteverdi) 301
communists 237, 287, 288
Compassionate Arts of the Fellowship of Reconciliation 346
Complete Story 196
Composers Forum and Workshop 285
Composers Showcase 224, 349
Composers String Quartet 372
Composers Union 325, 327
Concertgebouw Orchestra 275
Concertino for Chamber Orchestra (RS) 315, 351
Concerto for Orchestra (Bartók) 367
Concerto for Orchestra (RS) xiv, 324, 351, 354, 357, 366–67
Concerto for piano in G minor (Mendelssohn) 15
Concerto for String Quartet and Orchestra (Handel-Schoenberg) 372
Concerto Grosso (Bloch) 387n5
Concord Summer Music Institute 269
Cone, Edward T. xv, 134, 268, 273, 290, 291, 311, 316, 322, 369, 372, 412
Connolly, Cyril 201
conscription 99, 102

conservatism 71
Consumers' League 25, 29
Conversations with Roger Sessions (Olmstead) xvi
Converse, Frederick S. 53, 56, 379n11
Cooke, Dr Josiah P. 40
Cooke, Mary Huntington 40
Cooley, Carton 170
Coolidge Prize 267
Coolidge String Quartet 267
Coolidge, Elizabeth Sprague 138, 244, 245, 398n6
Copland, Aaron (photos 186, 292) xiv, xvi, 18, 134,
    168, 172, 173, 176, 185, 187, 198, 203, 207,
    208, 211, 212, 213, 214, 215–25, 227, 230,
    232, 233, 234, 235, 236, 244, 246, 247, 257,
    265, 268, 276, 285, 288, 289, 292, 310, 311,
    317, 318, 327, 348, 355, 356, 357, 366, 369,
    370, 373, 381n2, 389n21, 391n13, 392n18,
    401n32, 402n13, 408n41, 412; and *Black
    Maskers* 156, 162
Copland, Harris 28, 361
Copland-Sessions Concerts 162, 219, 220, 224,
    226, 232, 233
Correspondence of Roger Sessions, The (Olmstead) xvi,
    262
Corriere della Sera 330
Cos Cob Press 208, 209, 265
Così fan Tutte (Mozart) 296
Cossa, Dominic 392n19
Coster, Henry 204
Council of the Humanities 289
Counterpoint (Cherubini) 126
Courier de Genève 212
Cours de Composition (d'Indy) 126
Cowell, Henry 214, 220, 326
Cowin, Margaret T. 265
Cox, James 130
Craft, Robert 311
Crawford, Ruth 219
Création du Monde, La (Milhaud) 210
Creation, The (Haydn) 10
Cristo s'è fermato a Eboli (Levi) 315
Croce, Benedetto 204
Cui, César 97
Cummings, E. E. 59, 66, 102, 384n20
Cummings, W. H. 91
Cunningham, Merce 269
Curtiss, Henry Tomlinson 165
Curtiss, Mina *see* Mina Kirstein
Cuyler, Richard (Buzz) 88, 130, 171
Cyr, Gordon D. 285, 298, 372

Dalcroze Eurhythmics 143, 148, 164, 399n2
Dalcroze School 259, 264, 265, 400n6
Dalcroze, Jaques 164, 175, 180
Dallapiccola, Annalibera 314
Dallapiccola, Laura Coen (Luzzatto) 307, 308, 310,
    315, 406n44
Dallapiccola, Luigi (photo 309) xvi, 51, 73, 202,

296, 299, 307–15, 341, 361, 373, 390n2,
    411n14
Damon, S. Foster 68, 85, 364, 381n2
Damrosch Fellowship 227
Damrosch, Frank 13, 52
Damrosch, Leopold 13
Damrosch, Walter 13, 108, 226, 227, 238
Dankevich, Konstatin 326
Danson, Ted 47
Dante (Alighieri) 178
Dantons Tod (Büchner) 404n28
Daphnis et Chloe (Ravel) 97
Dartmouth College 101, 307, 313
Davies Symphony Hall 275
Davies, Dennis Russell 213, 214, 276, 322, 324,
    361, 362
Davies, Peter Maxwell xv
Davison, Archibald 53, 54
Dean, Winton 341
Debs, Eugene V. 130
Debussy, Claude 38, 57, 62, 68, 69, 72, 97,
    98, 105, 130, 139, 150, 268, 286, 296, 322,
    363
De Kooning, Willem 269
De Kooning, Elaine 269
Del Tredici, David xv, 285
Delaney, Robert Mills 198, 219, 227, 393n46
Delius, Frederick 73
Dello Joio, Norman 325, 327
Delpit, Mlle Louise 107, 385n44
Democratic party 21, 287, 288, 355
Denny, William 268
Dent, Edward 239
Deo Cassius 294
Depression, the 233, 243
De Profundis (di Lasso) 195
Der Rosenkavalier (Strauss) 69, 71
Dessau, Paul 234, 295, 296, 299, 403n5
Dessoff, Margarthe 264
Deutsch, Monroe 284, 289
Deutsche Oper 314
Deutsche Staatsoper 404n32
DeVeau, Fritz J. 69
DeVoto, Mark xv
Dewey, Admiral 30, 33
Diaghilev, Serge 203
Dial, The 137, 158, 216
Diamond, David xv, xvi, 223, 246, 249, 251,
    256–62, 265, 275, 288, 307, 372, 396n27,
    402n13, 411n14, 412
Dick, Marcel (photo 271) 265
Dickens, Charles 343
Dickinson, Austin 3, 96
Dickinson, Emily 3, 96
Dickinson, Lavinia 10, 96
Diderot, Denis 103
Dietsch, James 329
Dietz, Frederick 113

dissonance 73

Divertimento for Orchestra (RS) 360, 408n40

Doctor Faustus (Mann) 84, 304

Dodds, Harold Willis 266, 290

Dolmetsch, Arnold 52

Dominican College 305

Don Giovanni (Mozart) 56, 296, 406n40

Don Juan (Strauss) 74

Don Pasquale (Donizetti) 57

Don Quixote (Strauss) 72, 76

Dorati, Antal 322, 406n39

Dos Passos, John 59, 100, 102, 103, 114, 167, 384n18; Paris 172, 174;*Three Soldiers* 114–15; Van 115

Dostoyevsky, Fydor 166, 171

Double Concerto (Berg) 235

Double Concerto (RS) 304, 347, 351, 360, 361, 409n6

Douglass College 265

Downes, Olin 70

Downes, Ralph 266

Drain, Gertrude 86

Draper, Ruth 201

Dream of Gerontius, The (Elgar) 87

Drei Klavierstücke (Schoenberg) 73

Drew, David 298

Driscoll, Loren 186, 314, 329

Drury, Irene 94

Duberman, Martin 270

Duel, The (Kuprin) 103

Duke, John 186, 221, 267,

Dukelsky, Vladimir (Vernon Duke) 167, 173, 220

Dumbarton Oaks 244, 253

Duo Concertant (Stravinsky) 235

Duo for Violin and Cello (RS) 368

Duo for Violin and Piano (RS) 283, 285

Durey, Louis 203

Dushkin, Samuel 235

Dvořák, Antonín 137

Eagle-Times (Claremont) 252

Eastman School 148

Eastman, Max 86

Eaton, John xv

Ebert, Carl 238

Eda Kuhn Loeb Music Library (Harvard) 412

Edgar Stillman-Kelly Society 265

Edlin, Louis 143

Edwards, Jonathan 156, 344

Edwards, Mr 38

Edwards, Ruth 143, 148, 170, 177

Eels, Harriet 267

Egoist, The (Meredith) 85

Ehring, Sixten 310

Ein Heldenleben (Strauss) 105, 233

Einstein, Albert 179, 237

Einstein, Alfred 239, 397n8

Eisenhower, Dwight 288

Eisler, Hanns 286, 294, 295, 299

El Salon Mexico (Copland) 214

Elegy (of Symphony No. 4, RS) 323

Elektra (Strauss) 57, 66, 75, 76, 346

Elfrida Whiteman Scholarship 256

Elgar, Anne 350

Elgar, Edward 72, 87, 361

Elijah (Mendelssohn) 10

Eliot, Jr, Samuel A. 58, 153, 155, 157, 158, 160, 162, 299, 412

Elizabethan Club 88

Elkus, Albert Israel 243, 284–85, 286, 288, 289, 294

Elliot, Mike 88, 108, 193

Elliott, Jr, Gilbert 68

Ellis, Brent 329

Ellis, Havelock 193

Elon College 372

Elwell, Herbert 146, 172, 174, 175, 227

Emerson, Ellen 107

Emerson, Dr L. E. 120

Emmanuel Church (Boston) 6, 7

Emperor's New Clothes, The (RS) 368

Empson, William 251

Encyclopedia Britannica 23, 31

Engel, Carl 202, 303

Engel, Lehman 265

Episcopal Theological Seminary 124

Episcopalianism 5, 6, 13, 25, 26, 45, 117, 254, 349, 353, 373

Erb, Herr Doktor 15

Ercoli, Kathy 369

Erdgeist (Wedekind) 153

Espionage Act 108

Evan Harrington (Meredith) 85

Evangeline (Longfellow) 43

Evans, Joey 329

Evarts, John 269

expressionism 154, 155, 183, 218, 320

FAAR degree 231, 232

Fâcheux, Les (Auric) 173

Fairbanks, Frank P. 230

Fairleigh-Dickinson University 295

Fairyland (Parker) 88

Fall of the House of Usher, The (Poe-RS, incomplete) 162, 193, 203, 246, 331

False Gods (Brieux) 153

Falstaff (Verdi) 296, 368

Fanciulla del West, La (Puccini) 51

"Fanfare for the Common Man" (Copland) 355, 357

Farnam, Lynnwood 349

Fascism 203, 204, 205, 240, 287, 313, 333

Fauré, Gabriel 62, 69, 168, 185

Fay, Sidney B. 104

Fêtes (Debussy) 268

Fear and Misery of the Third Reich (Brecht) 403n5

Feen, die (Wagner) 93
Feigen, Joel xv, 372
Feininger, Lyonel 386n10
Fergusson, Francis 330
Feuersnot (Strauss) 74
Fidelio (Beethoven) 15
Fiedler, Max 56
Fine, Vivian xv, 265, 372
Finney, Ross Lee 265, 313, 344, 372
Fiorillo, Dante 270, 401n41
Firebird (Stravinsky) 184, 185
Fireworks (Stravinsky) 184, 185
Firkusny, Rudolf 293
Fish, Hamilton 21
Fisher, Dr Caroline 302
"Fishwife's Song" (RS) 346, 347, 350
Fitelberg, Jerzy 267
Fitzgerald, F. Scott 114, 167
Five Pieces for Orchestra (Schoenberg) 56, 57, 69, 73
Five Pieces for Piano (RS) 315, 360
Flagler, Harry Harkness 226
Fleg, Edmond 150
Fliegende Höllander, Der (Wagner) 235, 308
Flonzaley Quartet 137
Foldes, Andor 273–74
folk music 395n9
Foote, Arthur 56, 68, 76, 379n11
Forbes, George Shannon 62
Ford Foundation 328
Forêt Bleue, Le (Aubert) 57
formalism 300
Fort Devens *see* Camp Devens
Fort Oglethorpe 109
Fortunato, D'Anna 344
Forty Acres (drawing 11) 3–17, 28, 31, 34, 35, 63, 96, 100, 142, 156, 157, 158, 176, 228, 351, 375n28, 408n8, 413; *see also* Porter-Phelps-Huntington Foundation
Foss, Lukas (photo 186) 185, 324, 408n41
Foster, Barbara (wife) (photos 117, 125, 147) 85, 113, 116–27, 412; *see also* Barbara Sessions
Foster, Eleanor Stewart (sister-in-law) 116, 119, 124, 148, 157, 160, 203, 208, 252
Foster, Frank H. (father-in-law) 166, 120, 123, 160, 386n6
Foster, Inez E. Fairbanks (mother-in-law) 116, 118, 120, 123, 130, 160, 386n6
Foster, Rosamond (sister-in-law) 116, 124, 208, 221, 233, 401n33; *see also* Rosamond Sayre
Four Saints in Three Acts (Thomson) 168
Four seventeen Washington Avenue (drawing 27) 25–33; *see also* Bird House
Fox Film Corporation 198
Fox, Bill 197
Français, Jean 216
Francesca da Rimini (Zandonai) 72
Francis Boott Prize 59

Franck, César 62, 74, 86, 90, 92, 97, 101, 132, 139, 195
Franck, Hermann (father-in-law) 243, 246
Franck, Rhoda 243
Franck, Robert E. (brother-in-law) 243
Franck, Ruby Marble (mother-in-law) 243, 246, 284, 338
Franck, Sarah Elizabeth (Lisl, wife) 223, 243, 245, 249, 256; *see also* Elizabeth Franck Sessions
Franck, Tom 243
Frank, Anita (photo 147) 146, 150, 151
Frankenstein, Alfred 299
Frankenthaler, Helen 269
Frazelle, Kenneth xv
Free German Youth 300
Freelands, The (Galsworthy) 85
Freer, Charles L. 200
French Academy in Rome 227
French, Daniel Chester 226
Freshman Red Book 57
Freud, Sigmund 85, 102, 122
Freudian Wish, The (Holt) 85
Frick, Henry 200
Friedman, Stephanie 344
Friends of Music (NYC) 132, 137, 161
Friends Relief Committee 252
Frijsh, Povla 137
Fromm Music Foundation 324, 372
Fromm, Paul 163, 311, 322
Frost, Robert 361
Fryer, Nathan 143
Fulbright Fellowship 261, 289, 290, 299, 307, 308, 310, 328
Furtwängler, Wilhelm 234, 235, 236, 238, 239

Galileo Galilei (Brecht) 295
Galimir Quartet 265, 267
Ganz, Rudolf 56
Garden of Paradise (Sheldon) 153
Gardner, Anson 46
Gardner, Isabella Stewart 66, 200
Garnett, David 165, 175
Gasparri, Pietro Cardinal 206
Gates, Lucia 376n6
Gauthier, Eva 399n2
Gay, Robert 301
Gebhardt, Heinrich 148
General Theological Seminary 46
generazione dell'ottanta 206, 307
Genius, The (Dreiser) 85
George Washington High School 393n34
George, Henry 25, 30, 53
Gerhard, Roberto 139
Gershwin, George 75, 172, 173, 211, 220, 227, 289
Gewandhaus (Leipzig) 28
Gewandhaus orchestra 15
Giannini, Vittorio 293
Gideon, Miriam xv, 249, 250, 265, 267, 372

Gieseking, Walter 221
Gilman, Lawrence 70
Ginastera, Alberto 292, 311
Girls String Quartet 191
Glass, Philip 372
Gluck, Christoph Willibald 15, 69
Godowsky, Leopold 240
Goebbels, Dr Joseph 238, 239
Goelet, Francis 362
Goepp, Philip H. 72
Goethe, Johann Wolfgang von 62, 72, 85
Goetschius, Percy 52, 167
Goldmark, Rubin 216
Goldwater, Sen Barry 312, 313, 350
Gomez, Victor de 143, 170
Goode, Blanche 104, 126, 141
Goossens, Eugene 168, 175
Gordon, Jacques 249, 267
Gore Hall 55
Gorki, Maksim 154
Gorohkov, Ivan 105, 126, 385n33
Götterdämmerung, Die (Wagner) 18, 56, 149
Gottschalk, Stephen 341
Gouk, Yuri 325,
Graff, Curt 301
Graff, Grace 301
Graitzer, Murray 285
Gramm, Donald 329
Granberry Piano School 264
Grant, Ulysses S. 65
Graudan, Johanna (photo 271)
Graudan, Nikolai (photo 271)
Graun, Carl Heinrich 328
Grayson, Robert 329
Green, Arthur Leslie 40, 41, 42, 43, 84, 378n2
Greene, William 85
Greissle, Felix 71, 311, 405n33
Grogh (Copland) 218, 361
Gross, Robert 250
Groton School 40
Gruenberg, Louis 247
Guernsey, Rosco 397n17
Guggenheim Foundation 198, 202, 203, 219, 226, 259, 266, 270, 401n41
Gulbenkian Foundation 362
Guntram (Strauss) 76
Gypsy Life (Schumann) 18

Hackney, Charles Arthur 384n11
Hadley Farm Museum 228
Hadley, Arthur 87
Hadley, Henry 72
Haesche, William 87, 88
Hal Leonard publishers 370
Hale, Edward Everett 18
Hale, Philip 55, 70, 211
Halévy, Fromental 165
Haley, Eben R. 46, 48, 49

Hall, Leland 156
Handel & Haydn Society 9
Handel, George F. 10, 82, 101, 187
Hanfstängl, "Putzi" 237
Hanscom, Elizabeth 34
Hanson, Howard 213, 214, 226, 227, 325
Hapgood, Hutching 201
Harbison, John xv, 289, 310, 318, 324, 363
Harcourt Brace 286
Harding, Warren G. 21, 130
Hargrove Music Library (Berkeley) 412
Harmonic Practice (RS) xv, 283, 286, 289, 305
Harmonie (Schenker) 328
Harmonielehre (Schoenberg) 57, 73, 305
Harmonium (Stevens-Persichetti) 268
Harris, Roy 163, 214, 220, 247, 268, 289, 293, 317, 325, 327, 355, 373, 392n18, 402n13
Harrison, Benjamin 20
Harrison, Lou 269
Harry Hall organ 135, 349
Harsanyi, Janice 301, 350
Harsanyi, Nicholas 301
Harvard Club (New York) 112
Harvard College/University xv, 5, 6, 10, 40, 48, 51–68, 88, 158, 201, 202, 204, 216, 233, 237, 253, 265, 277, 317, 344, 372, 293, 394n2, 412
Harvard Crimson 68, 70, 76–77
Harvard Divinity School 6
Harvard entrance requirements 379n8
Harvard Glee Club 186
Harvard Lampoon 68
Harvard Law Review 77
Harvard Monthly, The 59, 68, 200
Harvard music building 55, 74
Harvard Musical Review 54, 55, 57, 60, 61, 66, 68–77, 85, 93, 104, 149, 364, 412; finances 69, 106
Harvard-Radcliffe Orchestra 58
Hatch, Azel (Junior) 48, 91, 111
Hauptmann, Elisabeth 301
Haverlin, Carl 324, 325, 408n40
Haydn, Franz Joseph 239, 328
Hays, Hofmann Reynolds 294, 295, 296, 403n5
Hazelton, G. C. 388n2
He Says Yes (Brecht) 294
Hee, Park Chung 313
Heilman, Mr 62
Heilner, Irwin 265
Held, Ernest 9
Heldenleben, Ein (Strauss) 76
Helfer, Walter 227, 379n11
Helmholtz, Hermann 73
Helps, Robert 372
Henderson, William J. 52, 70, 74
Henshaw, Judge Samuel 34–35
Herald Tribune 264, 289, 404n36
Herrick, A. H. 62

Hertz Hall 284
Herz, Das (Pfitzner) 235
Hexachords 306
Hickox, Mrs Charles G. 177
Higginson, Henry 109
Hill, David B. 20
Hill, Edward Burlingame 53–54, 60, 62, 66, 69, 184, 227, 249, 373
Hill, Henry 53
Hill, Thomas 53
Hillis, Margaret 186
Hillyer, Robert 48, 59, 61, 85, 102, 103, 106, 114, 115, 382n16
Hindemith, Paul xv, 234, 235, 236, 251, 283, 326, 346
Hinrichs, Frederick 20
Histoire du Soldat, L' (Stravinsky) 175, 209, 225, 294, 299, 369
History of American Classical Music, The (Struble) 372
Hitchel, Maria 10
Hitler, Adolf 237, 238, 287, 294, 303
Hiver-Printemps (Bloch) 137
Hobbie, Mr 46
Hochschule für Musik 234
Hodges, Barbara 376n4
Hoffmann, Lydia 264
Hofmann, Josef 56
Hogland, Diana 344
Holbrooke, Joseph 72
Hollreiser, Heinrich 329
Hollywood Bowl 220
Holmes, Rebecca Wilder 104, 126
Holsapple, Lloyd B. 46
Holtcamp organ 349
Holy Cross Magazine 94
Holy Trinity (Middletown, CT) 47
Homeric 165
Homo Sapiens (Przybyczewski) 85
homosexuality 232, 259–60; *see also* George Bartlett
Honegger, Arthur 203
Hong, Hei-Kyung 329
Hooper, Catherine (cousin) 20, 376n6
Hooper, Edwin 199
Hooper, Franklin (uncle) 18, 20, 23, 376n5, 377n20
Hooper, Gail 376n6
Hooper, Leverett (cousin) 20, 376n5
Hoover, Herbert 205
Hora Novissima (Parker) 88
Horney, Karen 276, 279
Hotel Empire 368
Hotel Statler 143, 148
Hotel Sylvania 185
Houghton, Cedric 59
Hound & Horn 187
Hour with American Music, An (Rosenfeld) 158

House Committee on Un-American Activities 286, 295
Houseman, John 164
Hovhaness, Alan 224, 263
Howe, Julia Ward 10
Howells, William Dean 23
Huberman, Bronislaw 248
Hufstader, Robert 350, 400n6
Hughes, Adella Prentiss 145, 388n10
Huguenots 12
Humperdinck, Engelbert 51
Humphrey, Hubert 313, 314
Hun School 290
Hunt, Captain Jonathan 35
Hunt, Lucy 35
Hunter Dunn estate 40
Hunting, Mildred 20, 376n4
Huntington, Arria Sargent (aunt) (photo 38) 3, 6, 10, 20, 39, 58, 141; breakdown 92; death 133, 371; RS's baptism 29
Huntington, Barrett (cousin) 102, 228
Huntington, Bethia 10
Huntington, Bishop Frederick Dan (grandfather) (photos 6, 38) 5, 6, 7, 9, 10, 16, 22, 32, 45, 52, 55, 66, 104, 114, 172, 228, 349, 365, 412; death of 37, 84, 371
Huntington, Catharine Sargent (cousin) (photos 38, 125) 116, 158, 228, 246, 375n18
Huntington, Charles Edward (uncle) 6
Huntington, Constant (cousin) (photo 38) 175
Huntington, Dan (great-grandfather) 5, 12
Huntington, Elizabeth Phelps (great-grandmother) 5
Huntington, Elizabeth Phelps Fisher (grandmother) 375n32
Huntington, Eluard Vermilye 54
Huntington, George Putnam (uncle) (photo 38) 6, 9, 10, 11, 16, 17, 25, 37–38, 114, 228, 229, 371, 412
Huntington, Gerald 376n6
Huntington, Gladys 175
Huntington, Hannah (grandmother) (photos 6, 38) 5, 6, 7, 114; death 39, 84, 371; *see also* Hannah Sargent
Huntington, Henry Barrett (cousin) (photo 38) 29
Huntington, Dr James Lincoln (cousin) (photo 38) 6, 228, 229, 252, 375n28, 389n19, 398n5
Huntington, Lilly St Agnan (aunt) (photo 38) 7, 228
Huntington, Mary Lincoln (Molly, aunt) (photo 38) 3, 7, 11, 16, 20, 22, 39, 92, 118, 141, 144, 245
Huntington, Michael Paul St Agnan (cousin) (photo 38) 7, 124, 375n18
Huntington, Oliver Mayhew Whipple 40, 41, 42, 44
Huntington, Ralph 55
Huntington, Rev George 123

Huntington, Rev James Otis Sargent (uncle) (photo 38) 6, 10, 11, 17, 25, 37, 39, 46, 63, 83, 121, 412; Kent School 45, 131
Huntington, Ruth (mother) (photos 8, 32, 38, 125) 6, 7, 344; *see also* Ruth Sessions
Huntington, Samuel 7
Huntington, William (uncle) 6
Hurlbert, Bryon Satterlee 64
Hutchinson, Hubbard (photo 147) 388n16 146, 147
Hymn and Fuguing Tune No. 3 (Cowell) 326

iconoclastism 71
Ideale, Die (Liszt) 72
Idyll of Theocritus (RS) 202, 291, 301, 309, 310, 311, 315, 328, 331, 344, 350, 406n46
Idylls of the King (Tennyson) 51
Illinois Symphony 250
Imbrie, Andrew xv, 268, 274, 285, 298, 372
Inch, Herbert 227
Inconstant Lovers (Binet) 200
Indianapolis Symphony 163
d'Indy, Vincent 62, 92, 97, 98, 101, 106, 128, 139, 195
influenza epidemic 113, 115, 119
Inscriptions (Whitman-Kay) 358
Institute for Advanced Study 313
Institute of Musical Art 52, 167
International Educational Exchange Service 325
International Society for Contemporary Music (ISCM) 212, 215, 228, 233, 235, 260, 275, 299, 307, 310
Internationale Literatur 296, 301
internationalism 108
Iphigenia in Tauris (Euripides) 68
Iron Horse, The (A. Sessions) 197
Irving S. Gilmore Music Library (Yale) 412
Israel 353
Israel Symphony (Bloch) 133, 137, 141, 194
Istar (d'Indy) 97
I Tatti 200, 202, 203, 204, 239, 393n4
Ives, Charles 88, 214

Jackson, Prof 62
Jacobson, Bernard 410n21
Jagemann, Prof Hans Carl Gunther von 62
Jakobsleiter, Die (Schoenberg) 271, 303
Jalowetz, Heinrich (photo 271) 270
Jalowetz, Johanna 270
James, Henry 68, 85, 165
Janáček, Leoš 234
Janssen, Werner 227, 231
Japan Philharmonic Society 394n34
Järvi, Neeme 213
jazz 210, 218, 238, 357
Jean-Christophe (Rolland) 75, 81–85, 96, 138, 142, 176, 178, 217, 277, 303, 357, 373
"Jesu, meine freude" (Bach) 182

"Jesu, meine freude" (RS) 348
Jewels of the Madonna (Wolf-Ferrari) 57
Job (Dallapiccola) 308
John Oliver Chorale 353
Johns Hopkins University 48
Johnson, Dr Ben 202
Johnson, Clifton 228
Johnson, Pres Lyndon 313, 314
Johnson, Thor 301
Jones, Edgar 298
Jones, Ernest 175
Jones, Frank 295
Jones, Mrs 158
Jooling, R. M. 69
Jordan Hall 55
Jordan, Jr, Eben D. 55
Jordan, Mary August 34
Joseph, Helene 344
Josephslegende, Das (Strauss) 76
Journal de Genève 212
Joyce Book, The 232
Joyce, James 165, 174, 179, 232, 364, 401n30
Juilliard Graduate School 396n3
Juilliard lectures 288, 402n1
Juilliard Orchestra 347, 359
Juilliard School, The xv, xvi, 52, 195, 196, 213, 250, 262, 278, 279, 290, 293, 301, 309, 310, 321, 325, 338, 341–47, 351, 360, 368, 372, 399n2, 404n10, 407n9, 412
Juilliard String Quartet 372
Juilliard, Augustus D. 226, 396n3
Juilliard, Frederick 226, 396n3
Juilliard: A History (Olmstead) xvi

Kabalevsky, Dimitri 325, 326
Kahl, Elsa (photo 271)
Kahlo, Frida 393n34
Kaiser Wilhelm II 87, 109
Karl V (Krenek) 328
Katz, Heidi 267
Kay, Ulysses 163, 293, 325, 327, 358
Keefe, Agnes G. 398n5
Keefe, Robert 329
Keene, Christopher 365
Kendall, Raymond 285
Kenin, Herman D. 325
Kennedy, Pres John F. 291, 311
Kennedy, Robert F. 314, 344
Kent Quarterly 48, 135
Kent School 45–50, 61, 91, 97, 106, 119, 122, 125, 130, 135, 140, 194, 254, 317, 349
Kenyon College 272, 273
Kerman, Joseph 285, 321, 341
Kerner, Leighton xiv, 359
Khatchaturian, Aram 325, 326
Khuner, Felix 285
Kidder, Miss 156

Kim, Earl 279, 285, 298
Kimball, Everett 104
King Henry IV (Shakespeare) 380n55
King James Bible 344, 347, 348, 350, 351, 352
King Lear (Shakespeare) 326
King, Jr, Rev Martin Luther 314, 344, 350
Kingsley School (photo 44) 44–45, 54
Kirchner, Leon xiv, xv, 285, 298, 304, 344
Kirkpatrick, John 267
Kirkpatrick, Ralph 341
Kirstein, George 164, 175
Kirstein, Lincoln 164, 175, 240, 391n29, 397n23
Kirstein, Mina 133, 134, 164, 168, 170, 171, 175, 240, 412
Klee, Paul 386n10
Klemperer, Otto 163, 212, 230, 232, 233, 234, 235, 238, 239, 247, 249, 265
Klieber, Erich 234
Kline, Franz 269
Kneisel Quartet 52
Knights of Labor 25
Knoch, Ernest 149
Knorr, Iwan 140, 387n12
Kodály, Zoltan 239
Koehler, Wilhelm 117, 252, 253, 386n10
Koenigskinder (Humperdinck) 51
Koh, Tse-Ying 319
Kolisch, Lorna Freedman (photo 271) 306
Kolisch, Rudolf (photo 271) 235, 265, 270, 285, 289, 306
Kolodin, Irving 321
Korean War 288
Kotlarsky, Serge 249
Koussevitzky Foundation 261
Koussevitzky, Natalie 317
Koussevitzky, Olga 317
Koussevitzky, Serge xvi, 163, 186, 202, 207, 208, 210, 213, 215, 219, 226, 227, 246, 247, 248, 249, 251, 316, 318; death 316, 317, 319, 362
Kraft, Edwin Arthur 143
Kraft, Victor 218
Krasner, Louis 250
Krehbiel, Henry E. 52
Krenek, Ernst (photo 271) 236, 239, 250, 265, 270, 283, 299, 302, 311, 328
Krennikov, Tikhon N. 325, 326
Krensky, Alexander 126
Kreutzer, Leonard 396n10
Kroll Opera 234
Krosnick, Joel 410n1
Krukowski, Ernst 314
Kucenic, Pamela 329

Labroca, Mario 206, 233, 239, 261, 307, 397n18
Lakmé (Delibes) 57
Lameer, Harriet 161
Lamond, Felix 226, 227, 228, 231, 232, 233
L'Amore dei Tre Re (Montemezzi) 72

Lancelot and Elaine (RS) 49, 51–52, 331
Landau, Dore 183
Landesman, Else 177
Lang, Paul Henry 285, 311, 320–21
La Scala 233, 312
Lasso, Orlando di 140, 195
Last Invocation, The (Whitman, RS discarded) 401n30
Lateran Treaty 205
Laufenburg (d'Indy) 375n1
Laughton, Charles 295
Laurence, Bishop 66
Lawrence, D. H. 360
League of Composers 179, 221, 247, 267, 288
Leaves of Grass (Whitman) 134, 346
Lederman, Minna 219
Lee, Gerald Stanley 34
Lee, Jenette 34
Lee, Ming Cho 301
Legg, Lodema 267
"Leggenda" (Steinert) 231
Leginska, Ethel 167
Leichtenstein 83
Leinsdorf, Erich 350
Leipzig Conservatory 14
L'Elisir d'Amore (Donizetti) 57
Lemon, C. 380n47
Lenin Cantata (Brecht) 294
Lennon, John 278
Lenox Art Gallery 267
Lenox Quartet 148, 311
Lento moderato (RS) 148
Leonard, Lotte (photo 271) 270
Leonard, Peter 360–61
Lermontoff, Mikhail 96
Les Adieux (Beethoven) 15
Leschetizky, Theodor 143
Letz Quartet 141
Levi, Carlo 315
Levine, James xiv
Levy, H. M. 69
Levy, Kenneth 291
Lewin, David 372
Lewis, Richard 329
Lhevinne, Joseph 284
Liberal Weekly 164
Library of Congress 179, 266, 374
Liebestod (Wagner) 135
Liebesverbot, Das (Wagner) 235
Lieder, Paul Robert 104
Life of Galileo (Brecht) 294
Life of Man (Andreyeff) 153
Life of Tolstoy (Rolland) 85
Life's Little Ironies (Hardy) 103
Lila Acheson Wallace Library (Juilliard) 412
Lincoln Center 344
Lincoln Portrait (Copland) 288
Lincoln, Pres Abraham 9, 344, 346

Linscott, Hubert 177
Lippman, Walter 6, 201
Lipps, Theodore 73
Liszt, Franz 69, 101
"Little Piece (for John)" (RS) 253
Little Review 85
Livermore, Mary A. 10
Lloyd-George, David 87
Locke, Arthur Ware 104, 105, 111
Lockwood, Lewis xv, 291
Lockwood, Norman 231
Lodge, Henry Cabot 65
Loeb, James 18, 52, 54, 55, 379n18
Loeb, Morris 18
Loeffler, Charles Martin 69, 72, 145, 202
Loewenberg, Prof Jacob 62, 380n52
Lohengrin (Wagner) 56
London Morning Post 236
Long, Martha 298, 310
Longy School 148
Longy, Georges 56, 380n47
Longy, Renée 399n2
Lopatikoff, Nicolai 220
Lord Ormont (Meredith) 85
Los Angeles Philharmonic 163, 247, 274
Loudon, Charlton 101
Louis, Rudolf 140
Louise (Charpentier) 57
Louisville Orchestra 360, 361
Love and Pain (Ellis) 193
Love One's Neighbor (Andreyeff) 153
Lowell, Pres Abbott Lawrence 52, 53, 58, 65, 66
Lowinsky, Edward (photo 271) 269, 285
loyalty oath 284, 341
Lucullus in Court (Brecht) 294
Lulu (Berg) 153, 276, 372
Lusitania 99
Lutheranism 15

Maazel, Lorin 314
Macbeth (Bloch) 150, 158, 194
Macbeth (Strauss) 76
MacBride, Mrs Malcolm 170, 198, 202
McCarter Theater 301, 369
McCarthy, Eugene 314
McCarthyism 287, 288, 289
McCormick Hall 266
McCoy, Helen 20
MacDowell Colony 220
MacDowell Medal xv
MacDowell, Edward 72, 175, 265
McFadden, Elizabeth 389n5
Machover, Tod xv, 310
MacKaye, Percy 153
McKinley, Pres William 30
MacLeish, Ada 264
MacLeish, Archibald 264
Macomber, Curtis 410n1

McPhee, Colin 220
MacVeigh, Mr 168
Macy's department store 26
Madonna House Settlement 267
Magic Flute, The (Mozart) 15, 172, 175, 296
Magnard, Albéric 98
Mahagonny (Weill) 235
Mahler, Gustav 52, 69, 72, 73, 75, 101, 124, 137, 268, 270, 286, 355, 359, 361
Majestic 171, 180
Malipiero, Gian Francesco (photo 240) 131, 132, 206, 239, 307
Malkin Conservatory 238, 263, 264, 399n2
Mamlock, Ursula xv
Man in the Zoo, The (Garnett) 175
Man who ate the Popermack, The (Turner) 192
Manhattan School of Music 254, 261
Mann, Elizabeth 305
Mann, Michael 275, 304
Mann, Thomas xvi, 84, 237, 275, 304, 305, 328
Mannes College 137, 139
Mannes, Leopold Damrosch 202
Mannheimer, Frank 396n10
Manziarly, Marcelle de 215
Markevitch, Igor 216
Marks, Edward B. 250, 296, 322, 360, 370
Marshall Plan 287
Martha's Vineyard 158, 166, 170, 176
Martin, Frank 390n2
Martin, Marie 191
Martino, Donald xv, 310
Martinon, Jean 275, 313, 360
Martirano, Salvatore 310
Marxism 99, 205
masks 42
Mason, Daniel Gregory 53
Mason, Lowell 9
Masonic Auditorium 145, 149
Masque of the Red Death, The (Poe) 154
Mass (RS) 285, 301, 315, 317, 324, 349
Mass in B Minor (Bach) 72, 349
Masselos, William 224
Masses, The 85, 86, 90, 105, 108
Massine, Léonide 256
Masters of Modern Art (Pach) 193
Masterworks of French Music 252
Matthay, Tobias 396n10
Mattise, Henri 203
Mauretainia 199
Maxfield, Richard 299, 404n24
Mechert, Helmut 329
Medici Chapel 386n10
Medici, Giuliano de 180
Medici, Lorenzo de 180
Meiklejohn, Alexander 96
Meistersinger von Nürnberg, Die (Wagner) 18, 52, 56, 72
Melcher, Herbert 314

Men's League for Women's Suffrage 58
Mendel, Arthur 267, 291, 354
Mendelssohn, Felix 10, 69, 101
Mengelberg, Willem 132
Mennin, Peter 163, 293, 325, 327, 338, 355, 356,
    359, 372
Menotti, Gian Carlo 327
Merchant of Venice, The (Shakespeare) 153, 388n2
Mercker, Karl Ernst 314
Mercury Theater of the Air 164
Meredith, George 85, 96
Merry (Cohu), Jan 116, 203, 208, 252
Messiaen, Olivier 363
Messiah (Handel) 10
Mester, Jorge 301
Metropolitan Opera xiv, 31, 51, 56, 88, 108, 346
Michalak, Thomas 369
Michelangelo Buonarroti 178, 180, 274, 386n10
Mighty Five 97, 130
Milhaud, Darius 167, 173, 203, 210, 220, 239,
    283, 285, 307, 310, 312, 315, 328, 344
Mills College 283, 285
Milyukoff, Pavel 126
Minneapolis Symphony 322
Minnesota Symphony Orchestra 275, 324
Mishkin, Henry G. 352
Miss Elizabeth Clarke's School 39
Miss Julie (Strindberg) 85
Missa Solemnis (Beethoven) 105, 349, 353
MIT 401n33
Mitropoulos, Dimitri 250, 261, 275, 307, 322
Modern Music 186, 187, 219, 222, 238
Moe, Henry Allen 202, 270, 401n41
Moerike, Eduard 149
Molinari, Bernadino 206
Mona (Parker) 88
Monet, Claude 104
Monna Vanna (Fevier) 57, 72
Monroe, Arthur E. 48
Monson, Ruth Caldwell 384n11
Montaigne, Michel de 103
Monteux, Pierre 128, 137, 163, 233, 274, 316
Monteverdi, Claudio 73, 301
Montezuma (RS) 293, 296, 305, 306, 310, 311, 312,
    313, 314, 328–38, 347, 257, 368, 372, 373,
    394n7, 412
Moog, Wilson 104, 126
Mook, Theodore 410n1
Moor, Weyert 143
Moore, Crucita 156
Moore, Douglas (photo 292) 88, 182, 274, 384n11
Moore, Emily 182
Mootz, William 410n21
Moravia, Alberto 201
Morel, Jean 213
Morgan, Robert 366, 367
Morra, Umberto 201
Moses und Aron (Schoenberg) 296, 341

Mosher, Dr Eliza 22, 29
Moszkowski, Moritz 15
Mother Courage (Brecht) 294, 299
Motherwell, Robert 269
Motte, Mlle Gabrielle de la 9
Moulson, John 329
Mount Everest 291
Mount Holyoke College 229
Movement for violin and piano (Magnard) 375n1
Mozart, W. A. 15, 56, 105, 151, 172, 173, 175,
    234, 236, 239, 296, 332, 343, 344, 370, 406n40
Mr. Britling Sees it Through (Wells) 85
Mrs Piatt's Seminary 17
Mrs Porter's School 17
M. Steinert & Sons 227
Muck, Karl 14, 55, 56, 108, 316, 379n22
Munch, Charles 316
Munsey's Magazine 26
Münsterberg, Prof Hugo 62
Murray, Gilbert 68
Murray-Dodge 266
Murrow, Edward R. 397n8
Museum of Modern Art 273
Music Critics Circle of New York 261, 274
Music for Double String Orchestra (Diamond) 261
Music for the Theater (Copland) 162, 219
Music Hall (Smith) 126
Musical America 162, 191, 275
Musical Chronicle 137, 158
Musical Courier 177, 191, 321
Musical Experience of Composer, Performer, Listener, The
    (RS) xv
Musical Portraits (Rosenfeld) 158
Musical Quarterly, The 121, 262, 311
Musicians' Committee to Aid Spanish Democracy
    268
Mussolini, Benito 203, 204–05, 206
Mussorgsky, Modest 97, 327
Mychetsky, Princess Raissa 215

Nadia et Lili Boulanger Fondation 413
Naginski, Charles 259, 268
Nancarrow, Conlon xv
National Academy of Arts and Letters 261
National Committee for Refugee Musicians 270
National Institute of Arts and Letters 296
National Symphony Orchestra 132
National Woodrow Wilson Fellowship Program 289
National Youth Orchestra 250
nationalism 86, 222, 355, 357
Naumburg Musical Foundation 274
Nazis 237, 238, 239, 294, 297, 300
NBC 233
NBC Symphony 163, 274
Neilson, Pres William Allan 54, 104, 106, 107,
    126, 160, 408n8
Neo-Classicism xiv, 183, 186, 210, 307, 348, 355,
    364

Neugeboren, Heinrich 215
Neurosis and Human Growth (Horney) 276
Newark Academy 48
Newberlin Academy 47
New England Conservatory of Music 52, 324
New Haven Symphony 88, 92, 227
"New Horizons" Overture (Kay) 325
New Jersey College for Women 266, 400n6
New Jersey Symphony 369
Newlin, Dika xv, 304
Newman, Ernest 70, 72–73
Newman, John Henry Cardinal 13, 376n35
New Music School and Dalcroze Institute 256, 264, 266, 400n6
New Music, The (Copland) 222
New Republic, The 85, 287
New School for Social Research 263, 267
Newton, Elmer 85
Newton, J. Earl 266
New York Chorus Society 18
New York City Ballet 391n29
New Yorker, The 214, 322, 361, 367
New York Herald 226
New York Observer, The 359
New York Philharmonic Orchestra 18, 74, 124, 137, 138, 247, 250, 275, 321, 362
New York Post 214, 320, 322
New York Public Library 243, 267, 285
New York State Council on the Arts 365
New York Times, The 28, 33, 146, 163, 212, 213, 214, 247, 270, 275, 276, 289, 299, 317, 321, 322, 324, 325, 326, 327, 359, 362, 365, 368, 369, 372
New York World Telegram and Sun 321
Newport Performing Arts Center 196
Neylan, John Francis 288
Nielsen, Carl 275
Nietzsche, Friedrich 75, 192
Nightingale, The (RS, incomplete) 246
Nightpiece (Joyce, RS discarded) 401n30
Nijinski, Vaslav 97
Nin, Anaïs 289
Nin-Culmell, Joaquín 287, 289
99% (Brecht) 299, 403n5
Nixon, Richard 314, 315
Nixon, Roger 304
Nobel Prize 81, 84
Noces, Les (Stravinsky) 173, 174, 185, 187, 302
Nocturne for Orchestra (RS) 162, 168
Nollner, Walter 291, 304
North Carolina School of the Arts 293
Northeastern University 379n19
Northwestern University 163, 301, 347, 349, 404n10
Noyes, Alfred 65
Nozze di Figaro, Le (Mozart) 296
Nuages (Debussy) 268

Oakwood Cemetery 407n36

Oates, Whitney J. (Mike) 289, 290
Oberlin Conservatory of Music 52
Oboe 61, 128
Octet (Stravinsky) 187
"Ode for St. Cecilia's Day" (Dryden) 59
Œdipus Rex (Stravinsky) 186, 187, 226, 302
Office of War Information 164
O. Henry 196
Old Hadley Cemetery 371
Olive, Cypress and Palm 165
Oliver, Robert 186
Oliveros, Pauline 372
Olmstead, Andrea (photo 345) 134
Olschki, Leonardo 308
Ondine (Ravel) 375n1
"On the Beach at Fontana" (RS) 232, 267
Opera Company of Boston 329, 338, 370
Opéra-Comique 150
Oral History Colletcion of American Music (Columbia) 412
Orchestre Romande 213
Order of the Holy Cross 10, 45
O'Reilly, Leonora 26
Organ 61, 348
Orgelbüchlein (Bach) 349
Ormandy, Eugene 249, 267, 326
Ornstein, Leo 52, 167
Orpheus (Liszt) 72
Otello (Verdi) 5, 296
Other People's Letters (Curtiss) 165
Our New Music (Copland) 225
Outpost, The 146, 149
Oxford University 167
Ozawa, Seiji 276, 347, 367

Pach, Walter 193
pacifism 85, 94, 99, 103, 107–08, 109, 110, 300
Paderewski, Ignacy 227
Pagan Poem, A (Loeffler) 202
Pages From a Diary (RS) 224, 267, 268, 372
Paine Hall 55
Paine, John Knowles 53, 56, 265, 322, 379n11
Palazzo Vecchio 200
Palestrina, Giovanni Pierluigi da 93
Pandora's Box (Wedekind) 153
Pankurst, Mrs Emmeline 58
Parade (Satie) 173
Paris Opéra 172, 264, 328
Parish, Maxfield 174
Parker Fellowship 227
Parker, H. T. 70, 75, 210, 212, 322
Parker, Horatio 69, 87, 88–89, 91, 93, 98, 101, 137, 138, 265, 277
Parsifal (Wagner) 55, 56, 72, 91, 92
Parsons, Marjory 128, 129
Partita for Orchestra (Dallapiccola) 307
Pasternak, Boris 326
Pastorale for flute (RS) 208

Patterson, Rev John Oliver 349
Paul Sacher Stiftung 412
Peabody Conservatory 52
Peabody, Dr 40
Peacock, Julian (great-grandson) 372
Peacock, Maxwell Lindsey (great-grandson) 372
Peacock, Robert 255
Peacock, Samuel Huntington (great-grandson) 372
Peacock, Teresa Sessions (granddaughter) 372; *see also* Teresa Sessions
Pease, Elizabeth Phelps Sessions (daughter) (photos 254, 358) 251, 279, 315, 369, 370, 412; *see also* Elizabeth Sessions
Pease, Robert (son-in-law) 254, 369
Pease, Roger (grandson) (photo 358) 255
Pelléas et Mélisande (Debussy) 57, 130, 296
Penitential Psalms (di Lasso) 133
People's Favorites 196
People's Symphony Orchestra of Boston 163, 248
Perry, R. D. 49
Persichetti, Vincent 268, 326, 355, 356, 360, 372
Perspectives of New Music 372
pessimism 71
Petrassi, Goffredo 307, 310
Petrouchka (Stravinsky) 52, 97, 173, 184, 214
Peyrot, Fernande 175
Pfitzner, Hans 235
Phaedo (Plato) 103
Phelps Farm 4, 22–23, 100, 102, 122, 157, 323
Phelps House (photo 12) 3–17, 34, 133, 156, 178, 228, 229, 230, 265, 351
Phelps, Charles 10
Phelps, Charles Porter 10
Phelps, Charlotte 10
Phelps, Elizabeth 30
Phelps, Sarah Parsons 10
Phelps, Theophilus 10
Phelps, William 11
Phi Beta Kappa 124
Philadelphia Academy of Music 327
Philadelphia Orchestra 137, 162, 184, 193, 212, 247, 392n6
Philharmonic Society of Brooklyn 18
Philharmonisches Konzert (Hindemith) 236
Philip II of Spain 311
Piano Concerto (Copland) 211, 220
Piano Concerto (Diamond) 251
Piano Concerto (Schoenberg) 303
Piano Concerto (RS) xiv, 261, 324, 347, 361, 369
Piano Concerto (Stravinsky) 185, 187
Piano Concerto No. 5 (Prokofiev) 235
Piano Fantasy (Copland) 224
Piano Rag Music (Stravinsky) 210
Piano Sonata (Chávez) 221
Piano Sonata (Stravinsky) 302
Piano Sonata No. 1 (RS) xiv, 214, 216, 220–22,

226, 231, 232, 233, 246, 264, 265, 267, 268, 348, 363, 364
Piano Sonata No. 2 (RS) xiv, 273, 275, 283, 285, 347, 353
Piano Sonata No. 3 (RS) 372
Piano Sonata op. 2 no. 1 (Beethoven) 139
Piano Sonata op. 101 (Beethoven) 264
Piano Sonata op. 109 (Beethoven) 264
Piano Variations (Copland) 215, 224
Piatagorsky, Gregor 227
Picasso, Pablo 174, 179, 203
Piccoli, Rafaello 104
Pierce, Sarah 398n5
Pierian Sodality 55, 56, 58, 61, 63, 412
Piston, Walter (photo 292) 247, 327, 402n13
Pitti gallery 180
Pittsburgh Symphony 275, 298, 362
Pizzetti, Ildebrando 206, 239
Placci, Carlo 201
Plato 85, 103
Plato and Platonism (Pater) 85
Plutarch 294
Pochon, Alfred 137
Poe, Edgar Allan 154, 193
Poet in the Desert, The (Wood) 85
Polisi, Joseph 372
politics 104, 109; *see also* Roger Sessions; politics
Pollack, Howard 222–23
Pollikoff, Max 224
Pollin, Harvey 264
Pope Benedict XV 205
Pope John XXIII 350, 351
Pope Pius XI 205
Porgy and Bess (Gershwin) 227
Porter, Andrew xiv, 322, 355, 361, 367, 368
Porter, Cole 227
Porter, Eleazar 3
Porter, Elizabeth Pitkin 29
Porter, Hezekiah 3
Porter, Moses 5
Porter, Quincy (photo 147) 3, 81, 88, 103, 141, 146, 148, 156, 158, 160, 192, 219, 226, 412
Porter-Phelps-Huntington Foundation 229, 376n4, 413; *see also* Forty Acres
Portnoy, Marshall A. 410n21
Port of New York (Rosenfeld) 158
Possessed, The (Dostoyevsky) 171
Post, Chandler R. 66
Potter, Bishop 25
Poulenc, Francis 168, 173, 373
Pradella, Massimo 163
Pratt, Joel 46
Pratt, Waldo S. 88
Prausnitz, Frederik xvii, 43, 45, 71, 116, 134, 137, 234, 245, 293, 324, 329, 362, 365, 366, 368, 370, 372, 393n4, 410n31
Pravda 326, 327
Prelude for Organ (RS) 348

Prelude, Chorale and Fugue (Franck) 132
Presbyterianism 350
Presser, Theodore 250, 360, 370
Preuss, Thorsten 300
Previn, André 275, 362
Price, Dorothy 170, 177
Prigioniero, Il (Dallapiccola) 296, 309, 311
Prince Igor (Borodin) 91, 97
Princeton Herald, The 269
Princeton High School 349
Princeton Public Library 290
Princeton Review, The 404n36
Princeton Seminar for Advanced Musical Studies
    311, 403n27
Princeton Symphony Orchestra 406n46
Princeton Theological Seminary 350
Princeton University xv, 48, 52, 88, 254, 263–72,
    289, 293, 299, 236, 370, 372, 404n10, 408n6,
    412
Private Life of the Master Race, The (Brecht) 297
Proctor, Adelaide 148
program music 73
Progressive Citizens of America 286
Prokofiev, Sergei 235, 251, 275, 398n35
Proust, Marcel 165, 179
Prunières, Henry 173, 239
Psalm 140 (RS) 182, 301, 315, 350, 351
Psalms (Bloch) *Psalm 137* 128, 138; *Psalm 114* 137;
    Psalm 22 138, 194
Psalms, Book of 348
psychoanalysis 235, 252
Publishers Weekly 262
Puccini, Giacomo 51
Pulcinella (Stravinsky) 173
Pulitzer prize xv, 354, 367
Puritanism 5, 12
Pushkin, Alexander 96

Quartet (Bloch) 137, 138, 141, 195
Quartet (Copland) 224
Quartet in D minor (Schoenberg) 97
Quartet No. 1 (RS) 140, 265, 267, 273, 283,
    389n32
Quartet No. 2 (RS) 285, 286, 289, 310, 317, 322,
    341, 343, 347, 372, 409n8
Quartet No. 3 (Diamond) 261
Quartet No. 4 (Schoenberg) 285, 303
Quartet No. 9 (Diamond) 251, 261
Quartet op. 7 (Schoenberg) 56, 69
Quartet op. 59 no. 1 (Beethoven) 264, 268
Quartet op. 131 (Beethoven) 264
Quartet op. 132 (Beethoven) 268
Queens College 307, 311
Questions About Music (RS) xv, 253,
Quetzalcoatl (drawing 335) 334
Quintet (Bloch) 148, 195, 226
Quintet (Franck) 97, 195
Quintet (RS) 196, 284, 306

Rachmaninoff, Sergei 398n35
Radcliffe College 39, 50, 164
radicalism 71
Radiodiffusion Nationale 213
"Ragging the Scale" 394n13
Ragtime (Stravinsky) 210
ragtime 71
Rahm, Barbara 285
RAI Orchestra of Rome 163
Rands, Bernard 307
Rathaus, Karol 265
Rauschenberg, Robert 269, 357
Ravel, Maurice 60, 69, 73–74, 87, 97, 150, 185, 203,
    210, 224, 227
RCA Victor Prize 246
Reagan, Ronald 341
realism 71
Red Cross 5, 100, 102, 103, 107, 115, 179
Redemption, The (Gounod) 18
Redon, Odlion 193
Reed, John 58
Reese, Gustav 285
Reflections on the Music Life in the United States (RS)
    xv, 224
Reger, Max 140
Reichstag 240, 294
Reid, Christopher C. 286
Reid, James 286
Reiner, Fritz 162
Reinhardt, Max 238
Reis, Claire 179, 221
Rembrandt van Rijn 386n10
Renan, Ernest 82
Renard (Stravinsky) 175
Republic (Plato) 103
Republican party 21, 287, 288, 289
Requiem (Lockwood) 346
Requiem (Mozart) 105, 173
Research Magnificent, The (Wells) 85
Respighi, Ottorino 206, 239
Revolutionary War 7, 35
Rezke, Jean de 66
Rhapsody for Orchestra (RS) 347, 360, 361, 363,
    366
Rhoda Fleming (Meredith) 85
Ribaupierre, André de 143, 147, 148, 170, 177,
    191, 391n36
Rice, John Andrew 269
Rich, Alan 402n11
Richard Feveral (Meredith) 85
Richmond, Grace Angela 65, 91, 95
Richmond, William 65, 91
Riegger, Wallingford (photo 292) 52
Rienzi (Wagner) 92, 235, 299
Rimsky-Korsakoff, Nikolai 97
Ring cycle (Wagner) 49, 85, 149
Rivera, Diego 393n34
Robertson, David 363,

Rockefeller, Nelson 313
Rodgers, Richard 52
Roger Sessions and His Music (Olmstead) xvi, 369
Roger Sessions on Music: Collected Essays (RS) xv
Roger Sessions Society 370, 372
Rogers, Bernard 146, 148, 198
Rogers, Francis 76
Rogers, Lillian 148, 151
Rogers, Merrill 108
Rolland, Romain 75, 82, 84, 85, 92, 95, 108,
    160, 178, 195, 215, 278, 303, 308, 338, 348;
    and Bloch 138, 160; *see also Jean-Christophe*
Rome Opera 233
Rome Prize 174, 220, 259, 261, 267, 310, 379n11;
    see also American Academy in Rome
Romeo and Juliet (Berlioz) 105
Romeo and Juliet (Cocteau) 174
"Romualdo's Song" (RS) 155, 267, 347
Roosevelt, Eleanor 273
Roosevelt, Pres Franklin D. 268, 269, 273, 274,
    287, 346, 356
Roosevelt, Pres Theodore 20, 30, 87
Ropartz, Joseph Guy 101, 384n12
Rosen, Charles 328
Rosen, Jerome 410n4
Rosenberg, Hilding 294
Rosenfeld, Paul 137, 158–59, 161, 167, 202,
    211, 216
Rosenkavalier, Der (Strauss) 76
Ross, Alex 214, 362
Ross, Hugh 162
Rostrapovich, Mstislav 326
Rothschild, Baron Edmond de 200
Rounds (Diamond) 261
Rounds, Frank 374
Roussel, Albert 185, 203
Royal Opera House (Berlin) 109
Royce, Dr Josiah 62
Rubens, Peter Paul 386n10
Rubenstein, Anton 15
Rubin, Nathan 285
Rubinstein, Beryl 143, 148, 170, 172, 173, 192
Rudhyar, Dane 220
Russell, Alys 200
Russell, Bertrand 92, 96, 200
Russell, John 197, 198
Russian language 85
Russian revolution 99
Rzewski, Frederic xv, 310

Saastemoinin, Ione 191
Sabine, Wallace 55
Sacchini, Antonio 328
Sacre du Printemps, Le (Stravinsky) 130, 131, 155,
    173, 174, 184, 187, 209
Saerchinger, Cesar 135, 191, 233, 235, 236, 387n8
Sagrestia Nuova 180
St Andrews Church (Kent) 46

St Andrews Theological Seminary 10
St Anne's fugue (Bach) 122
St Chrysostom's Chapel 46
St George's School 40
Saint Joan (Shaw) 175)
Saint Joan of the Stockyard (Brecht) 299
St Luke's (Baltimore) 47
St Matthew Passion (Bach) 72, 107–8
St Paul's Church (Baltimore) 47
St Paul's Club 66
St Paul's School 66
St Stephen's College 47
Sallust 294
Salome (Strauss) 56, 66, 70, 76, 151
Salvemini, Gaetano 204
Salwen, Barry 372
Salzman, Eric xv, 213
Sandburg, Carl 167
Sanders Theater 55, 372
Sanders, Martha (Mrs Franklyn B.) 145, 147, 148,
    160, 170, 185, 192, 215, 266, 277
Sanders, Robert 227
Sandra Belloni (Meredith) 85
San Francisco Chronicle 299, 321
San Francisco Conservatory of Music 284
San Francisco Opera House 274
San Francisco Philharmonic (Symphony Orchestra)
    145, 274, 275, 284–85, 304, 344, 401n7
Sanine (Artzibasheff) 85
Sanromà, Jesús Maria 387n5
Santa Maria del Fiore 180
Santayana, George 85, 92
Sappho and Phaon (MacKaye) 153
Sarafaty, Regina 186
Sarasate, Pablo 15
Sargent, Epes 7
Sargent, Hannah Dane (grandmother) *see* Hannah
    Huntington
Sargent, John Singer 384n30
Sargent, Kate (great-aunt) 9, 13
Sassetta 201
Saxe-Meinigen Orchestra 15
Saxon, David 288
Saxton, S. Earl 298, 372
Sayre, Daniel Clemens 268, 401n33
Sayre, Rosamond (Foster) 268; *see also* Rosamond
    Foster
Scarpini, Pietro 310, 406n41
Scenes from Goethe's "Faust" (Schumann) 18
Scharwenka, Xaver 15
Schelomo (Bloch) 132, 137, 194
Schenker, Heinrich 264, 283, 305, 328
Scherchen, Herman 300
Schiedt, Horace E. 48
Schiffman, Harold 308, 372
Schiller, Heinrich 62
Schirmer music publisher 138, 161, 250
Schmidt, Ernst 109

Schmied von Gent, Der (Schreker) 235

Schmitt, Florent 185

Schnabel Society 235

Schnabel, Artur 235–36, 238, 239, 265, 297, 396n10

Schnitzler, Arthur 294

Schnitzler, Henry 295, 297, 299, 403n5

Schoenberg, Arnold xiv, xvi, 56, 57, 69, 73, 83, 93, 97, 137, 160, 194, 208, 234, 238, 239, 250, 263, 265, 268, 270, 271, 283, 285, 294, 296, 302–07, 328, 341, 355, 357, 364, 367, 372, 373, 392n4, 405n34, 413

Schoenberg, Ronald 304

Schoenemann, Dr Friedrich 62

Schonberg, Harold 322

Schotts Söhne publishers 230, 265

Schreker, Franz 235

Schroeder, Alwin 56

Schubart, Mark 265, 290

Schubert, Franz 15, 148, 236, 239

Schulé 215

Schuller, Gunther 251, 329

Schuman, William (photo 292) 214, 250, 327, 356

Schumann, Clara 15

Schumann, Robert xiv, 15, 18, 69, 101, 132, 250, 304, 355

Schumann-Heink, Ernestine 346

Schütz, Heinrich 363

Schwartz, Charles 224

Schweitzer, Albert 193

Scola Cantorum 172

Scriabine, Alexander 193

Sea Stories 196

Second Viennese School 206, 234, 239, 270, 302, 308; *see also* Arnold Schoenberg, Alban Berg

Seeley Mudd Library (Princeton) 412

Seelye, Pres Laurenus Clark 32, 34

Senturia, Michael 344

Serebrier, José 359

"Sessions ending" 323, 356, 357, 360

Sessions House (photo 35) 34, 39, 115, 128, 133, 228

Sessions, Adeline (aunt) 12, 18, 44, 101, 170, 199, 244, 245

Sessions, Archibald Lowery (father) (photos 19, 38) 5, 12, 13, 14, 15, 18–24, 25, 38, 44, 50, 51, 64, 90, 91, 101, 103, 109, 116, 119, 120, 124, 130, 136, 144, 157, 160, 179, 194, 196, 198, 276, 277, 278, 338, 412; death 207, 208, 371; editor of *Ainslee's* 68; finances 27, 92, 93–94, 121, 122, 131, 168, 199; creative work 89–90, 93; politics 27, 236; religion 16, 17, 22, 26; RS view of 43; *The Iron Horse* 92, 183; and Ruth 17, 23, 110, 179

Sessions, Barbara (wife) (photos 117, 125, 147) 129, 131, 145, 148, 151, 158, 164, 165, 166, 168, 180, 191, 193, 194, 197, 201, 215, 217, 219, 224, 227, 228, 233, 234, 237, 239, 240,

244, 245, 249, 251, 278, 350; divorce 223, 243, 244, 245, 263, 370, 386n10, 390n2; health 170, 203, 208, 229, 230, 252, 253; letters 174, 176, 178, 221, 230, 251–52; *see also* Barbara Foster

Sessions, Clara Fisher (Wheeler) (aunt) 12, 18, 22, 229, 376n3

Sessions, Dohenny (Dawn, sister-in-law) 228, 229, 245, 375n28, 396n7

Sessions, Elizabeth Franck (Lisl, wife) (photos 244, 255) 244, 246, 251, 253, 261, 283, 284, 285, 322, 323, 328, 338, 344, 347, 369; death 368; *see also* Sarah Elizabeth Franck

Sessions, Elizabeth Huntington (aunt) 12

Sessions, Elizabeth Phelps (daughter) (photos 254, 358) 251, 254, 284; *see also* Elizabeth Pease

Sessions, Elizabeth Phelps Fisher Huntington (grandmother) 11–12, 30

Sessions, Giovina (daughter-in-law) 368, 371; *see also* Giovina d'Aprile

Sessions, Grace Martin (Hooper) (aunt) 12, 20, 44, 376n5

Sessions, Hannah (Nan, sister) 29, 54, 85, 92; and Ruth 37, 81, 179, 245, 251, 277; marriage 107; on women's suffrage 58; religion 26; *see also* Hannah Andrews

Sessions, John (brother) (photos 32, 38) 4, 8, 26, 29, 31, 36, 39, 49, 66, 109, 136, 216, 228, 229, 230, 236, 245, 254, 256, 323, 375n28, 377n13; Harvard 90, 133

Sessions, John (grandfather) 12, 20, 30, 104

Sessions, John (uncle) 13

Sessions, John Porter (son) (photo 254) 244, 246, 253, 254, 277, 278–79, 284, 304, 338, 347, 350, 368, 369, 370, 409n6, 412

Sessions, Mary Huntington (sister) 22, 28, 29, 114, 135, 371

Sessions, Roger (photos 32, 36, 38, 39, 47, 62, 125, 147, 173, 186, 209, 231, 240, 255, 271, 292, 245, 359); Bartlett 95–96, 101, 112, 119, 122, 128–36 (*see also* George Bartlett); birth 23, 170; Bloch 128, 137, 150, 151, 164, 194, 387n3; as character in *Three Soldiers* 114–15; and death 134–35; divorce 257; finances and debts 85, 90, 93–94, 111, 120, 121, 131, 135, 140, 144, 149, 166, 167, 168, 170, 180, 194, 198, 199, 215, 219, 226, 230, 233, 245, 246, 251, 259, 263, 264, 265, 283–84; health 48, 50; incomplete symphonies 53, 90, 230, 246, 267, 402 (*see also* Symphonic Prelude); memorial concerts 262, 372; music criticism 69, 159, 264, 343, 402n24; nervousness xvii, 120–21, 168, 174, 193, 210, 217; on modern music 148; politics 204, 205, 208, 238, 268, 269, 278, 286, 296, 311, 312, 313, 314, 348, 354, 356, 360; Ruth 8, 37, 120–21; on teaching 97, 106, 146, 182, 236, 263, 264, 267, 269, 290, 293; on World War I 99, 107, 112, 114; piano lessons 41, 90; rebelliousness 26; religion 45–46, 63, 65, 68,

86, 87, 93, 94, 105, 111, 167, 182, 205, 216, 253, 350; religious music 348–53; retirement 293; salaries 141, 143, 144, 145, 149, 158, 170, 193, 226, 283–84, 286, 288, 289, 341, 400n6, 403n17; self-evaluation 181–82, 193; sexuality 217, 360; symphonies 354–67

Sessions, Ruth (mother) (photos 8, 32, 38, 125) 4, 32, 93, 116, 118, 120, 122, 123, 139, 144, 145, 160, 167, 197, 203, 207, 226, 228, 229, 251, 276, 277, 278, 353, 371, 412; and Hannah 37, 81, 179, 245, 251, 277; and John 323; as piano teacher 38, 216; death 217, 274, 316; finances 17, 90, 92, 117; health 92–93, 102, 144; letters 85, 136, 147, 204, 208, 230; nerves 21; on RS as student 61, 64; on RS's finances 110, 122; on war 99, 100, 103, 107; on women's suffrage 58; pacifism 109–10; piano lessons 28; RS view of 43; *Sixty-Odd* 371; social causes 25; view of RS 48, 51, 91; *see also* Ruth Huntington

Sessions, Samuel 12

Sessions, Teresa Alba (granddaughter) 255; *see also* Teresa Peacock

Sette Canzoni (Malipiero) 131

Severance Hall 145

Sevitzky, Fabien 163, 248

Shahn, Ben 269

Shakespeare, William 62, 64, 72, 112, 150, 153, 200, 326, 380n55, 388n2, 412

Shapey, Ralph 224

Shapiro (Bamberger), Jeanne 304, 305

Shaporin, Yuri 325, 398n35

Shaw, George Bernard 70, 175

Shearer, Allen 344

Sheherazade (ballet) 97

Sheldon, Edward 153

Sheldon, Roy 401n33

Shostakovich, Dmitri 276, 325, 327, 355–56, 367, 373

Shubert Theater 329

Shuler, Craig 310

Sibelius, Jean 56, 69, 101, 367, 379n22

Sidis, William James 58

Siegfried (Wagner) 49, 132, 149, 227

Sigmeister, Elie 327

Sill, Father Frederick (Pater) 43, 45, 46, 47, 61, 91, 92, 94, 96, 105, 111, 113, 114, 118, 121, 125, 129, 130, 135, 194, 217, 254, 370; Bartlett 134, 135; letters from RS 119, 140

Silverstein, Joseph 224

Simonds, Bruce 3, 88, 103, 412

Since Cezanne (Bell) 175

Sinfonia Domestica (Strauss) 56, 76, 84

Sirota, Victoria 348, 349

Sister Beatrice (Maeterlinck) 92

Six Pieces for Violoncello (RS) 304, 314

Six, Les 175

Sixty-Odd (Ruth Sessions) 8, 229, 245, 246, 371

Slavic Language Club 59

Sleeper, Henry Dike 104, 106, 124, 126, 139, 385n37

Slonimsky, Nicolas xvi, 187, 227, 263, 285, 327

Sly, Alan 270

Smallens, Alexander 212,

Smith Alumnae Quarterly 153

Smith College 10, 32, 34, 39, 52, 65, 104, 106, 107, 109, 111, 115, 116, 117, 131, 137, 140, 153, 164, 165, 199, 200, 220, 226, 228, 243, 253, 254, 255, 260, 266, 277, 278, 293, 301, 408n8, 412

Smith College Monthly 105

Smith College Weekly 154

Smith, Leland 285

Smith, Ormand Gerald 23

Smith, Paul 393n34

Smith, Sophia 10

Smith, William O. 285, 372

Social Reform Club 25, 29

Social Register 25

socialism 26, 66, 88, 108

Socialism Club (Yale) 88

Socialist Club (Harvard) 66

Socialist Realism 300, 325

Society for Music in Liberal Arts Colleges 285

Sokoloff, Nikolai 145, 148, 174, 177, 184

Solesmes monks 350

Solfège 192

Solomon, Izler 250

Solti, Georg 187

Sonata for Solo Violin (RS) 306

Sonata in A major (Franck) 375n1

Sonatina canonica (Dallapiccola) 310

Songs without Words (Mendelssohn) 10

Sons and Lovers (Lawence) 102, 168

Sophocles 62

Sorbonne 82, 202

South Kent School 129–30, 136

Souvenirs (d'Indy) 97

Soviet Union *see* USSR

Sowerby, Leo 226, 227

Spalding, Albert 191, 248, 249, 250

Spalding, Walter 54, 61, 62, 68, 89, 379n11

Spanish-American War 44, 384n2

Speculum Musicae 369

Spivakovsky, Tossy 250

Spontini, Gaspare 328

Spoon River Anthology (Masters) 85

Sports Stories 196

Spratlan, Lewis 351

Sproul, Pres Robert Gordon 287, 288, 290

Staatsoper 234

Stalin, Joseph 325

Stanford University 299

Stanton, Elizabeth Cady 10

Star-Spangled Banner 107, 108

Stassevich, Paul 267

State Department 325

State University of New York (New Paltz) 254
Steffin, Margaret 294
Steiglitz, Alfred 132
Stein, Gertrude 203
Steinberg, Michael xiv, 275, 324, 344, 347, 354, 362
Steinert Prize 101, 104, 227
Steinert, Alexander 227, 231, 379n11
Steinert, Sylvia 227
Steinway piano 28, 66
Stern, Howard 323
Steuermann, Edward (photo 271) 235, 265, 270, 311
Stevens, Gorham 228
Stevens, Wallace 268
Stevenson, Adlai 287, 311
Stevenson, Miriam 156
Stewart, D. McC. 69
Stiedry, Fritz 234, 238, 265
Stokowski, Leopold 145, 161, 162, 174, 193, 199, 247, 250
Story of O, The (Declos) 360
Stowe, Harriet Beecher 10
Stransky, Josef 74, 101, 108, 124, 125, 126, 138, 149
Strasfogel, Ian 301
Straus, Trudi (photo 271)
Strauss, Richard 38, 56, 57, 66, 69, 70, 71, 72, 74, 75, 76, 84, 101, 105, 139, 151, 211, 233, 239, 286, 346, 367
Stravinsky, Igor (photos 186, 209) xiv, xvi, 52, 69, 97, 130, 131, 137, 145, 150, 152, 155, 160, 162, 173, 174, 175, 179, 184–87, 193, 208, 209, 210, 211, 214, 225, 226, 234, 235, 251, 283, 285, 294, 299, 302, 306–07, 311, 312, 355, 356, 363, 364, 369, 372, 373
Street & Smith 23
Strindberg, Johan August 153
String Trio (Schoenberg) 303
Strong, George Templeton 175
Strophe (RS) 232
Strub, Max 232, 234, 235, 247, 249
Strube, Gustav 72
Struble, John 372
Strum, George 310
Strunk, Oliver 266–67, 272, 285
Stuckenschmidt, H. H. 212, 238
Studio Bern 294
Stumpf, Carl 73
Style and Idea (Schoenberg) 306
Suetonius 294
Suhrkamp Verlag 301
Suite for Piano op. 35 (Schoenberg) 302
Sullivan, Cornelius 329
Superfluous Husband (A. Sessions) 94
Surette, Thomas Whitney 269, 270
Swift, Isabel (photo 147) 146, 157, 158
Sylphides, Les (Chopin-Fokine-Glazunov) 97

Symphonic Prelude (RS, incomplete) (music ex. 318) 91, 95, 97, 98, 101, 103, 104, 106, 126, 137, 207, 233; abandoned 128, 129, 138, 139, 317; dedications 124; Smith 111
Symphonie Funebre et Triomphale (Berlioz) 125
Symphonies of Wind Instruments (Stravinsky) 372
Symphony Hall (Boston) 249, 263
Symphony in B-flat major (d'Indy) 98
Symphony in C-sharp minor (Bloch) 137
Symphony in F minor (Strauss) 74
Symphony in G minor (Mozart) 344
Symphony in Three Movements (Stravinsky) 285
Symphony No. 1 (Organ) (Copland) 219, 235
Symphony No. 1 (Brahms) 105
Symphony No. 1 (Carter) 208
Symphony No. 1 (RS) 140, 203, 207–14, 215, 216, 219, 228, 235, 246, 248, 265, 285, 317, 356, 362, 389n32
Symphony No. 1 (Sibelius) 101
Symphony No. 2 (Beethoven) 135
Symphony No. 2 (Bruckner) 72
Symphony No. 2 (Diamond) 261
Symphony No. 2 (Krennikov) 326
Symphony No. 2 (Schuman) 250
Symphony No. 2 (RS) 250, 273–79, 283, 284, 289, 299, 304, 317, 318, 322, 356, 361, 362, 366
Symphony No. 3 (Beethoven) 56, 76, 234
Symphony No. 3 (Copland) 276, 317, 355
Symphony No. 3 (Harris) 317, 355
Symphony No. 3 (Schuman) 355
Symphony No. 3 (RS) (music ex. 318) 211, 291, 311, 316–27, 356, 357, 361, 362
Symphony No. 4 (Brahms) 73
Symphony No. 4 (Bruckner) 72
Symphony No. 4 (Diamond) 261
Symphony No. 4 (RS) 285, 309, 310, 314, 356
Symphony No. 4 (Sibelius) 56, 69, 379n22
Symphony No. 5 (Beethoven) 234, 247
Symphony No. 5 (Bruckner) 72
Symphony No. 5 (Harris) 325
Symphony No. 5 (Mahler) 72
Symphony No. 5 (RS) 322, 357, 361, 366
Symphony No. 6 (Mennin) 325
Symphony No. 6 (RS) 322, 347, 357, 358, 359, 360, 361
Symphony No. 6 (Tchaikovsky) 184
Symphony No. 7 (Beethoven) 234
Symphony No. 7 (Bruckner) 72, 105
Symphony No. 7 (RS) 313, 322, 356, 357, 358, 359, 360, 361, 364, 369
Symphony No. 7 (Shostakovich) 356
Symphony No. 8 (Bruckner) 72
Symphony No. 8 (Mahler) 268
Symphony No. 8 (RS) 315, 357, 358, 362, 365, 366, 369
Symphony No. 9 (Beethoven) 18, 97, 105, 114, 234, 305

Symphony No. 9 (RS) 322, 360, 363, 364, 365, 366
Symposium (Plato) 103
Syracuse Symphony 365
Szigeti, Joseph 248

Tailleferre, Germaine 203
Tambour provençal 299, 319
"Tam O'Shanter" (Chadwick) 211
Tanglewood Music Festival 163, 224, 292, 299, 307, 316, 317, 344, 358, 371
Tanner, Mary Creusa 104
Tannhäuser (Wagner) 15, 18, 56, 92, 149; Pilgrim's Chorus 31, 51
Taruskin, Richard 373
Tchaikovsky, Peter 62, 73, 74, 184, 356
Temple Emanu-El 267, 348
TH Ranch 245
Thamar (Balakirev) 97
Theocritus 202
Theodore Thomas Chorus 52
Theodore Thomas Orchestra 10
Thibaud, Jacques 101
Thomas à Kempis 13
Thomas, Caroline (Bedell) 156, 389n24
Thomas, Mildred Sylvester 384n11
Thomas, Theodore 13, 18, 59, 74, 101
Thompson, Randall 214, 226, 247, 284, 379n11, 402n13
Thomson, Virgil 165, 168, 220, 225, 289, 369
Thorpe, Margaret (Ferrand) 104
Three Chorale Preludes (RS) 182, 216
Three Choruses on Biblical Texts (RS) 315, 350, 351, 360
Three Jewish Poems (Bloch) 128, 137, 167, 194
Three Musketeers, The (Dumas) 28
Three Piano Pieces op. 11 (Schoenberg) 56
Three Satires op. 28 (Schoenberg) 405n34
Three Soldiers (dos Passos) 114–15
Thuclydides 62
Thuille, Ludwig 140
Til Eulenspiegel (Strauss) 75, 76
Time magazine 250, 275, 404n36
tin box collection 85, 136, 229
Tippett, Michael 361
Titanic 56, 65, 172
Tod und Verklärung (Strauss) 74, 76, 105
Tolles Home 253
Tolstoy, Leo 83, 85, 96, 227
Tom (Diamond) 256
Topics 148
Toscanini, Arturo 57, 227, 234
Tovey, Donald Francis 342
Town Hall 185, 267, 286
Train Bleau, Le (Milhaud) 173
Travers, Patricia 250
Trevelyan, Robert 201, 202
Trevor, Denny 298

Trial of Lucullus, The (RS) 283, 284, 285, 286, 294–301, 324, 328, 331, 341, 346, 348, 349, 350, 352, 404n13n14n15, 406n46, 412
Tribune de Genève 212
Trio (RS, abandoned) 97
Tristan und Isolde (Wagner) 15, 49, 56, 72, 132, 149, 268, 317, 364
Trojan Women, The (Euripides) 68, 82
Truman, Pres Harry 287
Tsontakis, George xv, 262
Tudor, David 269
Tukey, John 311
Turandot (Gozzi-Vollmüller-RS) 162, 191, 194, 203
Turn, O Libertad (Whitman-RS) 285, 315, 348, 368
Turner, F. J. 191
twelve-tone system 218, 271, 273, 289, 291, 303, 305, 306, 308, 309, 319, 327, 328, 355, 366, 369
Twombly, Cy 269

Über neue Musik (Krenek) 302
Uccello, Paolo 202
Uffizi gallery 180
Ulisse (Dallapiccola) 296, 310, 312, 313, 314, 341, 361
Ulysses (Joyce) 165, 174
Unaufhöhliche, Das (Hindemith) 235
Union of Soviet Composers *see* Composers Union
Unitarianism 5
United Nations 269, 283, 325
universalism 222
University of California at Berkeley 52, 243, 261, 265, 272, 283–93, 302, 303, 307, 309, 349, 351, 400n6, 412
University of California at Davis 369
University of California at Los Angeles 283, 288, 341, 344
University of Michigan 313, 359–60
University of Oregon 250
University of Southern California 283
University of Washington 290
Ussachevsky, Vladimir 311
USSR 163, 293, 296, 322, 325, 327, 408n40

Valéry, Paul 312
Valses Nobles et Sentimentales (Ravel) 69
Vance, Cyrus 47
Varèse, Edgard 137, 267, 311
Variations (Dallapiccola) 313
Vatican 233
Vatican II 350
Veasy, Josephine 392n19
Veblen, Thorstein 108
Verdi, Giuseppe 57, 296, 332, 363, 368
Verhaeren, Emile 92, 104
Verklärte Nacht (Schoenberg) 238
Victoria Hall 212, 228
Vieh, George C. 53, 140

Vietnam war 313, 314, 352, 353, 357, 358
Villa Chiaraviglio 230
Villa I Tatti *see* I Tatti
Villa Sforza 233
Villino Corbignano at I Tatti (photo 201) 201
Viola Sonata (RS, incomplete) 265
Viola Suite (Bloch) 130, 138, 148, 165, 172, 195
Violin Concerto (Bartók) 250
Violin Concerto (Berg) 250, 275
Violin Concerto (Brahms) 73
Violin Concerto (Schoenberg) 250, 303
Violin Concerto (RS) 216, 232, 235, 246–51, 253, 261, 265, 278, 298, 309, 316, 361, 395n6
Violin Concerto (Stravinsky) 235
Violin Concerto No. 2 (Bartók) 285
Violin Sonata (Bloch) 132, 151, 195
Violin Sonata (RS) 224, 285, 291, 310, 343
Violin Sonata (RS, withdrawn) 93, 94, 97
Violin, Moritz 305, 405n25
Viotti, Giovanni Battista 101
Virgil 202
Vittoria (Meredith) 85
Vivaldi, Antonio 328
Voice of the City, The (O. Henry) 196
Volo di notte (Dallapiccola) 296, 308
Von Bülow, Hans 15
Von Einem, Gottfried 299, 404n28
Vulcania 240

Waart, Edo de 324
Wagenaar, Bernard 220, 268
Wagner, Minna 73
Wagner, Richard xiv, 15, 18, 31, 49, 51, 52, 55, 56, 68, 69, 72, 84, 85, 91, 92, 93, 132, 135, 139, 140, 149, 151, 160, 167, 194, 227, 235, 237, 238, 239, 268, 299, 308, 317, 332, 346, 355, 363, 364; endless melody 214; long line 363; RS's essays on 48, 49
Wagner, Siegfried 145
Wagner, Winifred 145
Wagnerian Opera Company 149
Wagstaff, Christopher 341
Waldheim-Eberle Verlag 162
Waldrop, Gideon 372
Waldstein Sonata (Beethoven) 132
Walküre, Die (Wagner) 15, 132, 149, 167
Wallace, Henry A. 286, 287
Wallenstein, Alfred 268, 274
Wall Street Journal 276
Walter, Bruno 234, 238
Walters, Henry 200
War and Peace (Tolstoy) 227
war hysteria 109–110
War of 1812 65
Warren, Earl 287
Washington Post 289
Washington Square Players 153
Washington, George 7

Wassermann, Jacob 132
Watanabe, Akeo 395n34
Watergate 315, 352, 353
Watts, Wintter 227, 232
Weber, Carl Maria von 69
Webern 239, 270, 308, 363
Wedekind, Franz 153
Weill, Kurt 235, 299, 404n6
Weimar Republic 203, 234
Weinberg, Henry 310, 314
Weiner, Norbert 59
Weingartner, Felix 14, 57
Weisgall, Hugo xv, 265
Weiss, Adolph 219
Weisse, Hans 265
Welch, Roy Dickinson 66, 104, 123, 126, 133, 139, 159–60, 202, 226, 266–67, 274, 285, 290, 291, 400n6, 412
Welch, Sylvia 123, 254, 301
Welles, Orson 164
Wellesz, Egon (photo 240) 239, 355
Well-Tempered Clavier (Bach) 140, 268, 342
Wertheim, Alma 265
Westergaard, Peter 291
Weston, G. B. 380n30
Wharton, Edith 204
"What is Art?" (Tolstoy) 83, 85
Wheeler Auditorium 297
Wheeler, Edwin Sessions (cousin) 19, 376n3, 376n4
Wheeler, Edwin W. (uncle) 18, 229, 376n4
Wheeler, Elizabeth Fisher (cousin) 19, 229, 376n3
Wheeler, Helen McCoy 376n4
Wheeler, Richard Hunting 376n4
When Lilacs Last in the Dooryard Bloom'd (Hindemith) 346
When Lilacs Last in the Dooryard Bloom'd (RS) xvi, 34, 187, 225, 298, 314, 315, 341, 344, 347, 351, 356, 357, 360, 364
White List 25–26, 29
White, Misses 157
Whiting, Arthur 69
Whitman, Walt 134, 196, 231, 344, 347, 348, 358
Whitney, Robert 406n45
Whittingham, William H. 47
Why Men Fight (Russell) 92
Widener Library (Harvard) 54, 65
Widor, Charles-Marie 53
Wilder, Katherine Abbot 156
Wilhelm Meister (Goethe) 85
William Shubael Conant Professorhip 267
William Wilson (Poe) 154
Williams College 146
Williams, Jr, Harrison A. 358
Willian, Ruth (photo 147) 143, 147
Williard, Edna 143
Wilmerding, Mrs Charles Henry 59
Wilson, Edmund 167

Wilson, Pres Woodrow 99, 107, 108, 109, 112, 114
Winds of Doctrine (Santayana) 92
Wings of the Dove, The (James) 165
Winter's Tale, A (Shakespeare) 153
Wister, Owen 68, 72, 76
Wolf, Hugo 56, 65, 103
Wolpe, Stefan 224, 270
Women's Club 29
Women's Congress of 1875 10
Women's suffrage 53
Wood, Irving 34
Woodrow, Mrs Wilson 197, 198
Woolf, Virginia 364
Woolworth Center 290
World War I xvi, 3, 5, 44, 85, 98, 99–115, 135, 149, 194, 226, 233, 319, 396n10; *Three Soldiers* 115
World War II 109, 200, 236, 266, 273, 276, 283, 299, 333, 353, 369
World's Illusion, The (Wasserman) 132
Wozzeck (Berg) 234, 235, 296, 306, 341, 372
WPA Composers Forum-Laboratory 267
Wright, Cuthbert 48, 96, 106, 114

Wyner, Yehudi 224

Yaddo conference 264
Yale Artillery School 109
Yale University 75, 81–98, 216, 265, 274, 277, 412
"Yankee Doodle" 319, 356
Yarustovsky, Boris 326
Yellow Jacket, The 153, 388n2
Young Composers Group 265
Young Ladies' Seminary 16
Yun, Isang 313

Zakrzewska, Dr Marie 13–14, 15, 16
Zandonai, Riccardo 206
Zarathustra (Nietzsche) 75
Zeit, Die 313
Zemlinsky, Alexander von 234
Ziel, Das (Klemperer) 234
Zimbalist, Epfrem 56, 248
Zingarelli, Nicola Antonio 328
Zukofsky, Paul 251, 347, 372
Zwilich, Ellen Taaffe (photo 345) xv, 411n14